The Complete Guide to Option Strategies

Founded in 1807, John Wiley & Sons is the oldest independent publishing company in the United States. With offices in North America, Europe, Australia, and Asia, Wiley is globally committed to developing and marketing print and electronic products and services for our customers' professional and personal knowledge and understanding.

The Wiley Trading series features books by traders who have survived the market's ever-changing temperament and have prospered—some by reinventing systems, others by getting back to basics. Whether a novice trader, professional, or somewhere in between, these books will provide the advice and strategies needed to prosper today and well into the future.

For a list of available titles, please visit our web site, www.WileyFinance.com.

The Complete Guide to Option Strategies

Advanced and Basic Strategies on Stocks,
ETFs, Indexes, and Stock Index Futures

MICHAEL D. MULLANEY

WILEY

John Wiley & Sons, Inc.

Published by John Wiley & Sons, Inc., Hoboken, New Jersey.
Published simultaneously in Canada.

Limit of Liability/Disclaimer of Warranty: While the publisher and author have used their best efforts in preparing this book, they make no representations or warranties with respect to the accuracy or completeness of the contents of this book and specifically disclaim any implied warranties of merchantability or fitness for a particular purpose. No warranty may be created or extended by sales representatives or written sales materials. The advice and strategies contained herein may not be suitable for your situation. You should consult with a professional where appropriate. Neither the publisher nor author shall be liable for any loss of profit or any other commercial damages, including but not limited to special, incidental, consequential, or other damages.

Before trading options, you should read the Options Clearing Corporation *Characteristics and Risks of Standardized Options*. It states, in part, that trading in futures and options is subject to a complete loss of capital (and, in some situations, more than the amount initially invested) and is only appropriate for persons who can bear that risk. Futures and options trading is speculative and subject to a high degree of risk; option sellers are subject to margin calls and exposed to virtually unlimited risk, and you should carefully consider whether such trading is suitable for you in light of your financial condition. The high degree of leverage that is often obtainable in futures and options trading can work against you as well as for you, and the use of leverage can lead to large losses as well as gains. Past performance is not necessarily indicative of future results.

For general information on our other products and services or for technical support, please contact our Customer Care Department within the United States at (800) 762-2974, outside the United States at (317) 572-3993 or fax (317) 572-4002.

Wiley also publishes its books in a variety of electronic formats. Some content that appears in print may not be available in electronic books. For more information about Wiley products, visit our web site at www.wiley.com.

Library of Congress Cataloging-in-Publication Data:

Mullaney, Michael D.
  The complete guide to option strategies : advanced and basic strategies on stocks, ETFs, indexes, and stock index futures / Michael D. Mullaney.
        p. cm. – (Wiley trading series)
    Includes index.
    ISBN 978-0-470-24375-6 (cloth)
  1. Options (Finance)   2. Stock options.   3. Exchange traded funds.   I. Title.
    HG6024.A3M848 2009
    332.63'2283–dc22

                                                                2008026324

Printed in the United States of America.

10   9   8   7   6   5   4   3   2   1

*To my wife, Sue, for her support, encouragement,
and guidance along the way.*

*To my daughter, Melissa, who has always made me proud and
continues to do so as she pursues her dream of becoming a
physician at Florida State University's medical school.*

*To my daughter, Michele, who is attending Emory University
and who always amazes me with her passion and
determination to excel.*

Contents

Preface

W hy should you read a book on options? Rapid and severe declines in the stock market demonstrate that the buy and hold method of investing has a lot of risk and that traders need a different vehicle to control risk. Individuals who recognize and embrace the shift to a trader's market have the best chance to prosper, and the best trading vehicle available is options. Options can help you in volatile and unpredictable markets by enabling you to profit in numerous ways.

Options are probably the most versatile trading tool today. No other investment vehicle seems to have such a unique set of characteristics and flexibility. Options have become a popular tool for individuals and, fortunately, you do not have to work on the floor of an exchange to understand options. Trading options can empower an individual trader to move quickly in comparison to institutions, which must stay invested at all times with large and diversified portfolios.

Your chances of success increase if you have a game plan, establish goals, and understand how options move. Focusing on becoming a better trader to make money should be the main purpose of reading a book on options. I realize that a book on options can also be read for the enjoyment of learning the theory, mathematical applications, and technical jargon. (Who would not enjoy learning about the assumptions underlying options?) There is nothing wrong with tackling the intellectual challenges associated with learning, but our time is valuable, and it is more important to stay focused on how to become a better trader.

The Complete Guide to Option Strategies is intended to describe option principles in an understandable manner by starting with the basics, then moving up the educational ladder to the intermediate level, and finally to an advanced level. This book provides the tools that will allow you to prosper in many market conditions and enable you to trade options not only on stocks but also on exchange-traded funds (ETFs), stock indexes, and stock index futures. The content of these pages describes the option buying and selling strategies that you should know and would most likely be interested in using.

This book addresses simple and complex strategies by using hundreds of examples, tables, and graphs. Some option strategies are known to be difficult, but the examples, tables, and graphs add great clarity; as they say, a picture is worth a thousand words. The presentation means you have a comprehensive and step-by-step analysis of each strategy. The consistency of the examples is designed to make it easy for you to compare one strategy with another. I even decided to include a chapter on option terminology to provide a framework with which you can view options so you can quickly analyze any option position at a glance.

A separate chapter is devoted to every main strategy. This book avoids shortcuts when describing strategies so it gives you full and complete understanding. As much as possible, each chapter stands on its own. Occasionally, of course, you may want to flip back and forth between chapters. This approach is intended to help you gain a thorough understanding of option strategies and make the book easier to follow. As a result of this approach, you will notice some repetition; however, this is intentional because it should help reinforce your knowledge of strategies and principles. The book uses similar language to describe variations of the same strategy, again, to make it easier to follow. The overall approach is to first show how a strategy can be executed from the approach of buying calls, then buying puts, followed by selling calls, and then selling puts. The typical strategy, therefore, approaches the strategy from four different perspectives.

Each strategy chapter (Chapters 7 to 22) is organized in a similar manner to make the chapters easier to read and to ease comparisons of one strategy with another. Chapters typically include opening remarks, an overview, a description of each variation of the strategy, and a comprehensive example of each strategy. After strategy examples, each chapter includes a section called "Beyond the Basics" and concludes with a section called "Final Thoughts."

HOW TO USE THIS BOOK

The Complete Guide to Option Strategies is intended to be a reference book, although it also can be read from cover to cover. If you are very familiar with basic concepts, you can simply skip chapters and go directly to the discussion that you are looking for.

The book begins with the basics and, in the process, describes hundreds of options terms, most accompanied by an example. It then covers more fundamentals, such as option pricing, the Greeks, buying versus selling, and terminology.

It takes the approach that basic option strategies can be broken down into buying a call, buying a put, selling a call, and selling a put. Once you understand this framework, you should be able to comprehend any option strategy at a glance. A separate chapter is devoted to each of the four basic option strategies before moving forward to more complex strategies in later chapters. Each basic strategy is analyzed from different perspectives; for example, the chapter on a call option provides a description of the strategy and comprehensive examples at strike prices of 90, 95, 100, 105, and 110. Likewise, the chapter on a put option provides a description of the strategy and comprehensive examples at the same strike prices. Spread strategies are covered in later chapters. After considering the different variations in strategies, this book covers hundreds of option strategies.

After the strategy chapters, a comparison of options on stocks, ETFs, stock indexes, and stock index futures is presented. The final part of the book covers advanced topics, such as volatility, exercise and assignment, risk management, margin, and taxes. *The Complete Guide to Option Strategies* is divided into the following five parts:

Part One: Learning the Fundamentals
Chapters 1 to 6 describe option basics in depth. Part One includes Chapter 1, "Getting Ready to Trade"; Chapter 2, "Option Fundamentals"; Chapter 3, "What Determines an Option's Price?"; Chapter 4, "Tools of the Trade—Greeks"; Chapter 5, "Buying versus Selling"; and Chapter 6, "Understanding Spread Terminology."

Part Two: The Four Basic Option Strategies
Chapters 7 to 10 cover the four basic strategies. Part Two includes Chapter 7, "Long Call"; Chapter 8, "Long Put"; Chapter 9, "Short Call"; and Chapter 10, "Short Put."

Part Three: Spread Strategies
Chapters 11 to 22 cover spread strategies. Part Three includes Chapter 11, "Vertical Spread"; Chapter 12, "Iron Condor"; Chapter 13, "Unbalanced Spreads"; Chapter 14, "Straddle and Strangle"; Chapter 15, "Butterfly Spread"; Chapter 16, "Condor Spread"; Chapter 17, "Calendar Spread"; Chapter 18, "Diagonal Spread"; Chapter 19, "Covered Call"; Chapter 20, "Combination"; Chapter 21, "Collar"; and Chapter 22, "Covered Combination."

Part Four: Comparing Underlying Instruments
Chapters 23 to 26 examine the differences in trading options on different underlying instruments. Part Four includes Chapter 23, "Comparing Stocks, ETFs, Indexes, and Stock Index Futures"; Chapter 24, "ETF Options"; Chapter 25, "Stock Index Options"; and Chapter 26, "Stock Index Futures Options."

Part Five: Advanced Topics
The final part of this book (Chapters 27 to 32) covers advanced topics. Part Five includes Chapter 27, "Assessing Volatility"; Chapter 28, "Exercise and Assignment"; Chapter 29, "Risk Management"; Chapter 30, "Margin"; Chapter 31, "Placing an Order"; and Chapter 32, "Taxation of Options."

Appendixes A, B, and C
Appendix A covers ETF option strategies, Appendix B covers index option strategies, and Appendix C covers stock index futures option strategies. At a glance, the strategies included in the appendixes illustrate many of the strategies covered throughout this book.

A glossary with approximately 200 definitions is included as a reference tool that can be used before, during, and after your reading of the book. A comprehensive index is provided to assist you in finding key topics and definitions.

From what I can tell, the Greeks seem to scare new (and some experienced) traders. The Greeks are tools that tell you how option values are expected to change based on certain assumptions. The Greeks are addressed step-by-step throughout this book, in case you are interested in advanced principles. However, you do not need to be an expert in the Greeks to trade many option strategies. You should not let specialized options terminology scare or intimidate you from becoming an outstanding option trader.

This book explains the option terms you need to know because the option industry has its own language. For simplicity, most of the discussions and examples in this book refer to options on stocks, but the principles and strategies can be applied equally to ETFs, indexes, and stock index futures. For the most part, I use the word *stock* to mean any underlying instrument, such as a stock, ETF, index, or stock index futures. Continually using the phrase *underlying instrument* can be cumbersome and confusing because most traders do not use the phrase very often. The word *stock* is simple and to the point. I contemplated using the word *security*, but it seems legalistic. So, let us just call it "stock," among friends. I realize that there are important differences in underlying instruments (primarily relating to the size of contracts, exercise, margin), and that is why an entire part of this book is devoted to explaining how each works.

Examples Are Consistent

To make it easy to compare one strategy with another, examples are presented in a consistent format from chapter to chapter. Each example assumes that XYZ stock (a hypothetical stock) is initially trading at $100 a share and then shows the gain or loss from each strategy, at the expiration date of the option, assuming that the stock is at $75 to $125, in five-point increments.

Before engaging in any option transaction, you should determine your maximum gain, maximum loss, break-even point, and probabilities of success. It is useful to back test option strategies, like you would other strategies. With options, however, you should learn how to forward test strategies by making assumptions about a range of possible outcomes in the future. In this book, the comprehensive examples show a wide range of possible outcomes. A table and chart both show the gain or loss. After you examine the table, you get a chance to graphically see the gain and loss pattern on a chart. It does not get any better than this.

Examples assume an initial XYZ stock price of $100 a share, consistent option pricing for both puts and calls, rounded option prices, the same entry date for the trade, and the same expiration date so that you can focus on the principles that need to be understood without having to deal with the confusion associated with changing facts. The use of $100 a share and the same entry date of the trade should make it easier to see how options move.

The prices on the profit and loss graphs are consistent from example to example and from chapter to chapter to make them easier to follow. After the graph, each example includes hypothetical Greeks, the effects of later expiration, and exercise and assignment. The consistency of the examples is designed to make things easy for you to compare one strategy with another.

Putting It All Together

You do not need to become an expert on each strategy, but learning multiple strategies will enable you to choose which strategy or strategies are best for you. You should refer to Appendixes A, B, and C and examine the strategies at a glance because they illustrate many of the strategies covered throughout this book and are presented according to whether they are primarily bullish, bearish, profit inside a trading range, or profit outside a trading range.

There are risks associated with buying and selling options because there is no free lunch (or any other free meal, for that matter). Personally, I prefer to sell options instead of buying them. In some respects, selling options is like eating chocolates: Once you get a taste of it, you will want more. In fact, I have gained a few pounds since I began selling options.

New Option Traders

The book provides all of the definitions and fundamentals of options that you need. However, it is helpful to actually trade options to more easily understand the principles.

Some individuals to whom I have talked are afraid to try trading options because they are confused or intimidated by the complexity of strategies and option terminology, especially the Greeks. A great way to overcome such concerns is to open an account at a brokerage firm and trade in a practice account (also called paper trading or simulated trading). This way, you can practice buying and selling options without the fear of losing money. If simulated trading is not available at your broker, you can trade one option at a time, making sure that the amount of money you are paying is small and that you have limited risk. It is certainly understandable how difficult option strategies can appear without actually having the benefit and experience of executing some trades.

PREPARATION IS THE KEY

In some cases, traders do not fully understand the risks of trading and the probabilities of success and are forced to spend a great deal of time and effort (and money) cleaning up the mess. They seem to be relying on the Will Rogers risk management strategy: "If stupidity got us into this mess, then why can't it get us out?" No investment strategy is risk-free, but the risk–reward profile of options can be attractive if you understand what you are doing. Risk management strategies are described throughout this book, and an entire chapter is devoted to this important topic.

As you can tell, I am very excited about the opportunities in option trading. My intention is to provide a great tool to help you elevate your trading to the next level and, therefore, help you trade options with confidence. This book is written from the perspective of how an individual trader can make money by trading options. After reading this book, you should have an understanding of the power of options. Let us get started.

MICHAEL D. MULLANEY

Acknowledgments

I am grateful to all the individuals who have contributed to this book. I express my appreciation to Dr. W. Edward Olmstead, professor at Northwestern University, for his technical review; David Johnson, for all his time and contributions (looks like your MBA degree from the Kellogg School of Northwestern University has paid off); Tony Golden, of Managed Capital Advisory Group, for his comments and suggestions; and Julie Humpress, Matt Kush, and the editors at John Wiley, including Emilie Herman and Kevin Commins. Also, thanks for contributions go to the Chicago Board Options Exchange, Chicago Mercantile Exchange, New York Mercantile Exchange, Options Industry Council, thinkorswim, and Fidelity Investments. Special thanks go to my wife, Sue, for providing many valuable suggestions.

M. D. M.

Learning the Fundamentals

Part One provides the fundamentals necessary to build a solid foundation before you begin trading options. It includes how to get ready to trade, the all-important basics of options, factors that affect an option's price, the *Greeks*, the advantages and disadvantages of buying versus selling options, spread terminology, and more. After learning the fundamentals, you should be ready to move on to other parts of this book and learn the four basic option strategies, advanced spread strategies, how to apply what you have learned to different underlying instruments, and advanced concepts.

CHAPTER 1

Getting Ready to Trade

T he good news is that there are many different ways to make money by trading options. You may be attracted to buying call or put options because you want large gains for a relatively small price, or you may be attracted to selling options because you want consistent returns and the odds on your side. Option buying and selling is sometimes described in a manner that makes you think option trading is simple. The reality is that making money in the financial markets on a consistent basis over a long period of time is not easy. However, it can be accomplished with proper preparation. Probably the best way to maximize your chances of success in the financial markets is to become as knowledgeable as possible so you can make educated decisions.

To get the most out of this book, you should read the Preface to understand how the book is organized. This chapter will cover the reasons why you should trade options, the importance of developing a game plan, risk management, option basics, and key definitions.

WHY TRADE OPTIONS?

Options can be used to manage risk, generate income, take advantage of leverage, and potentially profit under almost any market condition. Options can enable you to *speculate* on whether a stock, *exchange-traded fund* (*ETF*), *stock index*, or *futures* will rise, decline, or move sideways within your selected time frame. With options, you can engage in a high- or low-probability trade or a trade with limited or unlimited risk. With options, you have the ability to take advantage of a price decline in a stock (or other instrument) just as easily as a price increase, and even potentially profit from sideways movement. The versatility of options, in combination with leverage, is what distinguishes options from other trading vehicles.

With options, you can generate income from the up, down, and sideways movements of a stock, ETF, index, or futures. The key is to first determine your view of a stock (or market) and time frame and then determine the option strategy that can meet that perspective.

Sometimes the markets go through periods in a trading range that can last for weeks, months, or years. In these periods of consolidation, markets seem to fluctuate sideways and back and forth. Traditional stock and mutual-fund investing is typically not profitable in such an environment and can cost you the opportunity of earning interest on the money (or investing elsewhere) while you are waiting for the markets to move higher. Using options, you can speculate that a stock (or futures) will be stuck in neutral and you can design option strategies to profit from the lack of movement. For example, the S&P 500 index reached the 1,500 level in 2000, declined to below 800, and did not reach 1,500 again until 2007, only to substantially decline again. Even worse, the NASDAQ Composite reached the 5,000 level in 2000, plunged all the way down to nearly the 1,000 level, and has had great difficulty getting back to its old highs. The emerging markets have produced outstanding returns in some years, but they are inconsistent, and there are significant risks involved.

To understand options, you need to think a little outside the box because an option is unlike other investments. Trading options can be a way to diversify your income in a manner that is uncorrelated to other investments. Option strategies come in all shapes and sizes. Option strategies can be used to generate income, manage risk, *speculate*, and *hedge* in rising, declining, and sideways markets. Buying an option can be an attractive strategy because you can have limited risk with high profit potential, whereas *selling* (*writing*) an option can be attractive because you may have the odds on your side. Many traders are familiar with buying, in which the object is to buy low and sell high. Option selling works contrary to how trading is viewed by many people. The goal of option selling is the same as that of traditional trading but in reverse order: When selling an option, the goal is to sell high and buy low. If you are a novice trader, at first you may be confused about what it means to write (sell) an option because it involves selling first and buying later. Because markets can trend sideways for many years, selling options can provide a unique tool to potentially profit in sideways markets. The fact that option selling can work is demonstrated by the large number of institutional investors and professionals who sell options to enhance returns.

DEVELOPING A GAME PLAN

You may be under the impression that buying an option is the best strategy because you have a defined risk and can quickly make a lot of money; or you may have heard that selling an option is best because you have the odds on your side. So which is it? The answer is that sometimes buying an option is best and, at other times, selling is best, depending on what you are trying to accomplish and your views of the underlying stock and market.

Many option traders may be attracted to buying options because they are familiar with buying stocks (or other assets, such as a home), and they are attracted to limited risk and the possibility of large profits. Buying a call can be a good place to start when learning how to trade options. However, remember that consistent profits are possible by selling options, without having to pick the home run along the way. One advantage of selling an option is that close is sometimes good enough—in comparison to buying, where you need to be more precise in timing and direction. Ideally, you should develop strategies for both buying and selling options.

Selecting the best underlying instrument is one of the most important trading decisions you will make. In general, I have found that a broad-based index, such as the S&P 500 index, can be a good candidate for option selling: An option sale is a bet against volatility, and an index is typically less volatile than an individual stock. On the other hand, I find that stocks can be a good candidate for buying options because stocks can be very volatile.

Treat Option Trading Like a Business

If you were running a business, you would put together a business plan that encompasses trading strategies and details of how to operate the business and control expenses. The same perspective and focus should be developed when trading options. Developing a plan and working hard are essential to your success. Remember that the definition of luck is "preparation meets opportunity." The more knowledge you have, the greater your chances of success.

You cannot always play the offensive if you want to win. Playing the defense is important if you want to trade successfully over the long run. As a result, before trading options, you should have an understanding of risks. You should have a thorough understanding of risk management strategies, have access to specialized option software and trading platforms (free or low-cost software are accessible), learn strategies that maximize your probabilities of success and can limit losses, and appreciate the importance of education. You should keep expenses low; maximum interest income credited to your account; and open accounts to trade options on stocks, ETFs, indexes, and futures. You should try to utilize their strengths when trading options. It is important to protect your investment capital. Manage risk by observing the following tips:

- If selling options, establish positions with probabilities of success of at least 75 percent.
- Trade limited-risk strategies.
- Have an exit strategy with defined profit and loss objectives.
- Have the courage to exit a position at a loss to protect capital.
- Use stop losses to automatically exit positions.

- Do not overtrade or feel compelled to be in the market at all times.
- Use *technical analysis* to time when and where to establish positions.
- Trade liquid options.
- Control expenses.
- Keep your losses small.
- Have a plan.
- Do not get greedy.

Create a Plan

Before engaging in any option transaction, you should determine your maximum profit, maximum loss, break-even point, and probabilities of success. You should develop a clear view of the direction, timing, and magnitude of the underlying stock and have strategies readily available to place yourself in a position to maximize your return and limit your losses. Unfortunately, some option positions are doomed from the start because they are poor trades from a risk–reward perspective and have little chance of success.

Before you get started, you should open brokerage accounts to take advantage of margin, and you should understand how option trading can be affected, depending on whether an account is a taxable account versus an individual retirement account (IRA) or a futures account. You should also understand how to maximize interest income and minimize commissions and taxes. You should practice option strategies using a practice (simulated) account until you become proficient at what you plan to trade.

Discipline and decisiveness are factors critical to your success, and you should not allow your emotions to control your investment decisions. To trade successfully, it is important that you develop guidelines on when to buy and when to sell. Buying and selling options, like other investments, can be an emotional roller coaster, if you let it become one. You should trade when you are levelheaded and calm, using a systematic approach determined beforehand.

Establish Goals

Which option strategies are best for you depends in part on the amount of your capital; your risk tolerance; and your confidence in determining the direction, timing, and magnitude of various moves in the marketplace. For example, if you are confident in your ability to predict direction, timing, and magnitude, then you may want to buy a call or put, depending on the direction. If you are uncomfortable with being so precise, you may want to sell options.

An option can, in some cases, be sold for what can appear to be a small premium, but when returns are calculated on an annualized basis, the returns can be outstanding. The object is to repeat the selling cycle monthly or quarterly to enhance returns throughout the year. Because you have the short-term odds on your side, you may be tempted to generate large profits by selling a large number of options; however, you should resist the urge because it usually means excessive risk. Remember the Wall Street adage: Bulls make money, bears make money, and pigs get slaughtered.

Ideally, you should exit a position with predetermined profit or loss objectives; for instance, if you buy an option, a rule of thumb may be to exit a position if a loss reaches 50 percent of the amount paid to establish a trade. If you sell an option, a guideline may be to close out a position if you have a profit of 70 percent of the maximum possible profit in a position.

One of the main risks that many option buyers and sellers encounter is that they trade too many contracts: thus, when things go wrong, the leverage of options works against them. If, in addition, they engage in low-probability trades, they are setting the stage for financial failure. Overtrading and establishing excessive positions should be avoided. Risk increases where too many options are bought (or sold), as leverage cuts both ways. In the world of options, each option you add affects the mathematical probabilities of the others you already own or have sold to establish a position.

Develop an Edge

The average investor finds it difficult to compete with big mutual funds that spend millions of dollars on research. However, the small investor can have an edge over big funds because he can enter and exit the market as opportunities develop and not be hindered by requirements to be invested at all times. Confidence and discipline are key components of developing your edge, and it is important to remember that always following the crowd can be hazardous to your wealth.

Protect Capital

It is important to protect your investment capital. A popular risk and money management strategy is to let profits run and keep losses small. You simply cannot let your losses run too high. As the old saying goes: An ounce of prevention is worth a pound of cure. If you lose a certain level of capital, it becomes more difficult to ever get back to where you began; for example, if you have $100,000 in an account and lose $50,000, you must earn 100 percent to get back to even. As you can see, once you lose a substantial amount of your capital, it will limit how much you can invest going forward, and it may take you completely out of the investment picture if you are not careful. If you do not have the emotional or psychological ability to cut your losses, then you should not trade options.

Probably one of the most difficult aspects of successful trading is deciding when to exit a position. Most of the damage that was done after the stock market bubble burst in 2000 and 2008 was the result of investors who were frozen like a deer in headlights. More important, when wrong, know when to get out and act accordingly. It is best to take proactive action for risk management purposes. In such times, capital preservation should be your main priority.

Use Limited Risk Strategies and Stop Losses

There are numerous option strategy techniques that can reduce the net cost of options purchased and limit the exposure for options written (sold). A *stop loss order* is an order placed with a broker to sell an option when it reaches a certain price. It is designed to limit an investor's loss on an option position. For example, if you purchase an option for $5, you can have a plan to close the position at a loss if it reaches $2.50. You should use discipline in adhering to protective stop losses. Your goal in some market conditions is simply to preserve capital.

Utilize a Practice Account

New option traders are understandably nervous about trading options because options are more complicated than stocks. But, the good news is that some firms have developed practice accounts (also called "paper trading" or "simulated trading") so you can buy and sell options without the fear of losing money. In a practice account, some brokerage firms have developed trading platforms that parallel their live trading platforms but with simulated trading, which does not use real money. Therefore, simulated trading enables you to practice trading, as well as track gains and losses, without the risk of loss by using the trading platform of your broker. It can be an effective way to learn the unique features and capabilities of your broker's software (trading platform) so you can efficiently enter and exit option trades. Simulated trading can help you become familiar with the types of option orders that can be entered; using a practice account prior to executing any real trades can help you gain confidence. If simulated trading is not available at your broker, you can trade one option at a time, making sure that the risk is small.

WHAT IS AN OPTION?

There are two types of options: *calls* and *puts*. A call option is a contract that provides the *buyer* (purchaser) the right, but not the obligation, to buy an asset (100 shares, if a stock) at a particular price (called the *strike price* or *exercise price*) within a defined time frame. A put option is a contract that provides the buyer the right, but not the obligation, to sell an asset (100 shares, if a stock) at the strike price within a defined time frame. You can buy or sell a call or put option. A call *seller* is obligated to sell at the strike price within a defined time frame, and a put seller is obligated to buy at the strike price within a defined time frame.

Buy Call: Right to buy 100 shares at strike price

Buy Put: Right to sell 100 shares at strike price

Sell Call: Obligation to sell 100 shares at strike price

Sell Put: Obligation to buy 100 shares at strike price

In general, if you expect an increase in the value of a stock, you buy a call, but if you expect a decrease in a stock, you buy a put. How to profit from option selling will be covered later in this book.

Describing an Option

An option is typically described with the underlying stock (or other instrument) name, followed by the expiration month, strike price, and type of option. A call and a put option are described in the following sections.

Call Option   A call option on XYZ stock (a hypothetical stock) expiring in February, with a strike price of 100, is described as the "XYZ February 100 call." A call option *premium* (what you pay for the option) is priced on a per-share basis, and each option corresponds to 100 shares. As a result, one call option provides the option owner (*holder*) the right to buy 100 shares of a stock. The call option in this example gives the buyer (owner or holder) the right to purchase 100 shares of XYZ stock at $100 a share (strike price) on or before the *expiration date* (the third Friday in the February expiration month). If the XYZ February 100 call option is priced at $5, the total premium would be $500, calculated as $5 times 100 (shares controlled by one option contract). You would buy a call, in this example, if you believe that the price of the XYZ stock will rise because you have a right to purchase 100 shares at $100 a share, no matter how high the stock value climbs.

As you can imagine, the value of the option will change in response to the change in stock price. If the XYZ stock price rises, then the call price will also rise, and if the XYZ stock price declines, then the call price will also decline. The value of the call option, however, will not change in lockstep, dollar for dollar with the XYZ stock. As a result, if the XYZ stock immediately rises to $102, the February 100 call option may rise to approximately $6, and if the XYZ stock immediately declines to $98, the February 100 call option may decline to approximately $4. I will cover these concepts in greater detail throughout this book.

Put Option   An XYZ put option expiring in February with a strike price of 100 is described as the "XYZ February 100 put." Like a call option, a put option premium is priced on a per share basis, and each option on a stock corresponds to 100 shares. One put option provides the owner the right to sell 100 shares of a stock. The put option in this example provides the option buyer the right to sell 100 shares of XYZ stock at $100 a share (strike price) on or before the third Friday in February, the expiration date. If the XYZ February 100 put option is priced at $5, the total premium would be $500, calculated at $5 times 100. You would buy a put, in this example, if you believe that the price of the XYZ stock will decline because you have a right to sell 100 shares at $100 a share, no matter how low the XYZ stock value declines. If the stock price declines, then the put price will rise, and if the stock price rises, then the put price will decline.

The value of the put option will not change dollar for dollar with the stock. If the XYZ stock immediately declines to $98, the February 100 put option may rise to approximately $6, and if the XYZ stock immediately rises to $102, the February 100 put option may decline to approximately $4.

Example Using Real Estate

You may be able to understand better how a call option works from the perspective of an option on real estate. Assume that you are paying rent on a house that is selling for $100,000, and you want the right (an option) to buy the house at $100,000 (strike price) within the next six months (expiration date). Instead of buying the house directly for $100,000, you instead pay $2,000 (premium) for the right to buy (call option) the house at any time during the lease term of six months. Under this arrangement, you have the right to purchase the house at $100,000, even if the house value rises substantially. If the house price declines to $95,000, for instance, you are under no obligation to purchase the house. Assume further that you have the right to sell the option to a third party, who can step into your shoes in the $100,000 purchase price transaction. If the price of the house rises, you may be able to sell your right (option) for more than $2,000 or, alternatively, exercise your right to buy the house at the agreed price of $100,000. For example, if the house price rises to $110,000 in three months, you may be able to sell the option (to purchase the house) to a third party for $10,000 (or more), enabling you to gain $8,000 (or more), and you do not actually have to buy the house. It only makes sense that the longer the time frame of the option, the more expensive the option, ignoring all other factors, because it provides additional time for the option owner to make a decision and for the value to rise. As a result, a 3-month option may have a premium of $1,000, a 6-month option a premium of $2,000, a 9-month option a premium of $3,000, and a 12-month option a premium of $4,000. If the buyer was able to purchase the house at a price of $105,000, instead of $100,000, then he may be willing to pay only $500 for the option instead of $2,000.

The current owner of the house is like a call seller because he collects the $2,000 (premium) on the contract and is obligated to sell the house at the $100,000 agreed price within the next six months, should the owner of the (call) option exercise his right to buy the house at the agreed price of $100,000. If the house price declines to $95,000, the option buyer should not exercise his right to purchase the house at the option price of $100,000 because he can purchase the house at the then-current market price of $95,000. In this case, the seller profits by the $2,000 he collected. The $2,000 collected represents the maximum profit to the seller. All of this is going on, and the house owner (option seller) may not even know the identity of any third party buying the option. Keep in mind that in this example, the original seller of the option owns the underlying asset (house), but in the options trading world, the option seller commonly does not own the underlying asset (stock). These concepts, and option selling, are covered extensively throughout this book.

Similarity to Equity Options   Options on equities work with the same principles; however, in the world of stock options, there is a centralized marketplace for trading options, where intermediaries act as the clearing agents (buyers do not actually meet or know the identity of sellers, and vice versa), with standardized terms and conditions, such as predetermined strike price intervals, at which the underlying asset can be bought or sold and the time frame (expiration dates) at which the options expire. The centralized marketplace for options usually provides sufficient volume so that orders can be filled according to the supply and demand of the market. In the world of options, a seller may not actually own the underlying asset (stock), and buyers and sellers can select the strike price and expiration date that are available to meet their own risk–reward profile, according to standardized option contracts and terms.

The Power of Leverage   In our real estate example, notice the leverage that buying the real estate (call) option provides. A $2,000 payment enables the trader to control a $100,000 asset and produce an $8,000 gain if the price of the house increases to $110,000. The underlying asset rose 10 percent (from $100,000 to $110,000), but the option value rose 400 percent (from $2,000 to $10,000). It would take $100,000 of capital (ignoring any loan) to profit from the house appreciation, but it only took $2,000 to potentially profit using an option. That is the power of leverage and is why options are attractive to many traders. There is no free lunch, however; the option buyer also risks losing the entire $2,000 paid because the power of leverage cuts both ways.

With a call option, you have the potential to profit, based on the number of points a stock increases in value instead of the percentage increase in the stock price. For example, if you purchase 100 shares of stock, trading at $100 a share, for $10,000, the stock price would have to double by rising 100 points for you to make a profit of $10,000. With 10 call options, however, you can achieve nearly a $10,000 profit if the stock rises only 10 percent, from $100 to $110 (ignoring the premium paid). Likewise, a put option can provide leverage from the decline in the value of a stock. With 10 put options, you can achieve nearly a $10,000 profit if a stock trading at $100 declines only 10 percent, from $100 to $90 (ignoring the premium paid). Such examples illustrate why options can attract a lot of attention from traders and investors.

An Option Is Like an Insurance Contract

A put option can be compared to insurance, where the difference between the strike price and stock price is like the deductible, the option expiration period is like the insurance coverage period, and the option premium is similar to the premium paid for rights under the insurance contract. For example, if XYZ stock is trading at $100, the purchase of the XYZ February 95 put for $2 ($200) protects you against loss for a decline in the value of the stock below the strike price of 95. The difference between 100 and 95 is like the deductible, the time until the February expiration date is like the insurance coverage period, and the $2 ($200) option premium is similar to the insurance premium. If risk is perceived to be high, a high insurance (and option) premium will be charged; if risk is low, a low insurance (and option) premium will be charged. Insurance companies charge a greater premium for longer-term coverage and a lower deductible (option premiums are similar in that respect). With options, when there is a greater chance of the underlying stock's advancing or declining through the exercise price, risk is perceived to be greater, and the premium is increased.

Like put options, calls can also be compared to insurance, except that movement is in the opposite direction. For example, if XYZ stock is trading at $100, the price of the XYZ February 105 call may be $2 ($200) because you can profit from a rise in the value of the stock above the strike price of 105 (ignoring the premium). The difference between 100 and 105 is like the deductible, the time until the February expiration date is like the insurance coverage period, and the $2 ($200) option premium is similar to the insurance premium.

What makes option trading attractive is that you can sell options just as easily as you can buy them. In this analogy, an option seller can take the place of the insurance company.

DEFINING KEY TERMS

Now it is time to understand definitions that will lay the groundwork for trading options. Key terms include *option buyer*, *option seller*, *long*, *short*, *debit*, *credit*, *intrinsic value*, *extrinsic value*, *exercise*, *assignment*, and *break-even point*, among others.

In the previous example regarding real estate, the terms and conditions were entirely negotiated between the buyer and seller, and money was paid by the buyer directly to the seller. However, in the listed equity and futures options markets, contract terms are standardized, the buyer and seller never meet, and payments are made to or received from a third-party intermediary (centralized clearinghouse). The buyer and seller of an option on a listed stock or futures option can choose among available standardized contracts. Orders are handled by option exchanges, which clear the trades and establish the fixed strike prices, expiration dates, and other terms.

Exchange-traded (listed) equity options are standardized contracts that have predetermined terms and conditions, such as standard strike prices, expiration dates, and number of shares controlled. The *premium* is the price at which an option is bought (or sold). The *option buyer* is the person who pays the premium, and the option seller (*writer* or *grantor*) collects the premium.

When you buy an option, you are *long* the option and profit if the option increases in value. When you sell (write) an option, you are *short* the option and profit if the option declines in value. In a long option, the buyer cannot lose more than the premium paid (in addition to commission and other transaction costs, of course). In a short option, the seller (writer) cannot gain more than the premium collected (minus commission and other transaction costs). A person who has bought an option contract is considered to

TABLE 1.1 Rights and Obligations

Option	Right or Obligation
Long call	Right to buy 100 shares at strike price
Long put	Right to sell 100 shares at strike price
Short call	Obligation to sell 100 shares at strike price
Short put	Obligation to buy 100 shares at strike price

be long the option contract. A person who has sold an option contract (that is still open) is considered to be short the option contract.

An option is a *derivative* financial instrument. This means that the price of the option is directly dependent on (i.e., derived from) the value of a stock (or other underlying instrument, e.g., an ETF, index, or stock index futures), in combination with other factors. An option involves the trading of rights or obligations but does not directly transfer property. Derivatives include futures and options.

A long call provides the right to buy and a short call provides the obligation to sell. This may be easier to remember once you realize that a buy of a call provides a right to buy and a sell of a call provides an obligation to sell. However, a put works in the opposite way: A buy of a put provides the right to sell, and a sell of a put provides the obligation to buy. The rights and obligations of long and short calls and puts are summarized in Table 1.1.

Table 1.2 shows how option values change based on movement in the underlying stock.

A premium paid by the buyer is reflected as a *debit* in his account because it results in a subtraction (expense) in the account. A premium collected by the seller is reflected as a *credit* in his account because it results in an addition to the account.

As previously noted, an option is a derivative instrument whose value is linked to (i.e., derived from) an underlying instrument. The *underlying instrument* is the asset from which the option bases its value. An option value can be based on an underlying instrument, such as a stock, index, ETF, or futures. The futures options covered in this book are based on stock indexes and are called *stock index futures*. Throughout this book, the underlying instrument is usually described as *stock*, for simplicity, but the principles are intended to apply equally to an index, ETF, and stock index futures. For ease of discussion, I will use the word *stock* to mean any underlying instrument, such as a stock, index, ETF, or stock index futures.

TABLE 1.2 How Stock Change Affects Option Value

Stock	Call Typically	Put Typically
Rises	Rises	Declines
Declines	Declines	Rises

The *exercise price*, commonly referred to as the *strike price*, is the price at which the stock (underlying instrument) can be bought (in the case of a call) or sold (in the case of a put) by the holder (buyer) of the option. Strike prices are standardized at set intervals, depending on the price of the stock; for example, stocks priced under $25 per share usually have strike price intervals in increments of 2.50; stocks priced between $25 and $200 per share typically have strike price intervals in increments of 5; and stocks trading above $200 per share typically have strike price intervals in increments of 10. To further illustrate, a stock trading at $100 a share may have strike prices ranging from 60 to 140 at intervals of 5, so its strike prices are at 60, 65, 70, . . ., 130, 135, 140. For example, if XYZ stock is trading at $100, you may select from a host of strike prices to purchase a call, such as the May 95 call, May 100 call, or May 105 call.

Many ETF option strike price intervals are, in contrast, at a minimum of one-point interval increments. For example, an ETF trading at $100 a share may have strike prices ranging from 50 to 150 at intervals of 1, so strike prices are at 50, 51, 52, . . ., 148, 149, 150; and, as another instance, if an ETF is trading at $100, you may select from a number of strike prices to purchase a call, such as the May 99 call, May 100 call, or May 101 call.

The *expiration date* is the date at which the option terminates. The expiration date for stock options is usually the Saturday immediately after the third Friday of the expiration month. To a trader, however, the significant date is the third Friday of each month. It is on this Friday that equity options last trade and an option may be exercised by its owner. Saturday is reserved at brokerage firms to confirm their customers' option positions and for related paperwork involved with expiration and exercise procedures. For simplicity, in this book, I will refer to the Friday date as the expiration date. If XYZ stock is trading at $100 in January, for example, you may select from a number of expiration dates to purchase a call such as the January 100 call, February 100 call, or March 100 call. The expiration date of an option can be short term, such as one week, or longer term, such as more than one year. This book usually covers options with an expiration date from 30 to 90 days because they are the most commonly traded.

Option expiration dates are on standardized cycles. An *option cycle* (or expiration cycle) provides the months in which options expire. Equity options generally expire in the current month and immediate subsequent month, in addition to being on an option cycle. The three most common option cycles follow:

- January, April, July, October (January cycle).
- February, May, August, November (February cycle).
- March, June, September, December (March cycle).

For example, assume it is February and a stock is on the January cycle: Options would be open for February, March, April, July, and October, in addition to January of the following year. An option cycle can vary, depending on the type of underlying instrument, so that an equity option may have a different cycle than that of an option on an index or stock index futures.

Options have option cycles that typically extend to nine months, but the option cycle may also include longer-term options, known as *long-term equity anticipation securities (LEAPS)*. LEAPS are longer-dated options that typically have an expiration date of January of each year. LEAPS have all of the rights and obligations of a traditional option but are longer dated, typically up to three years, giving you an extended period of time in which to invest.

Intrinsic and Extrinsic Value

The *intrinsic value* of an option is the amount at which the current price for the underlying stock is above the strike price of a call option or below the strike price of a put option. The remainder of the option premium is *extrinsic value*. For example, assume that a stock is selling at $100 and that a call option with a strike price of 95 is selling for $6. The intrinsic value is $5, and the extrinsic value is $1. Intrinsic value can be viewed as the minimum price inherent in the value of the option relative to the stock value. Extrinsic value is commonly called *time value*.

In-the-Money   *In-the-money* describes an option contract that has intrinsic value. For example, if XYZ stock is trading at $100, the May 95 call is $5 in-the-money and the May 105 put is $5 in-the-money. An option contract, as a general rule, that is in-the-money by at least two strike prices and consists almost entirely of intrinsic value is referred to as *deep-in-the-money*.

The concept of *parity* applies if an option is trading in-the-money. An option is at parity if the option price is equal to the intrinsic value (in-the-money amount). If the option is trading for more than intrinsic value, it is trading above parity; if it is trading at the same amount as intrinsic value, it is selling at parity; and if it is trading at less than intrinsic value, it is trading below parity. For example, assume that XYZ stock is trading at $100 a share: If the XYZ February 95 call is more than $5, it is trading above parity; if it is at $5, it is trading at parity; and, if it is less than $5, it is trading below parity. Most options trade above parity.

At-the-Money   *At-the-money* means that an option's strike price is the same as, or closest to, the current trading price of the underlying stock. For example, if XYZ stock is trading at $100 per share, the May 100 call and May 100 put are at-the-money. If XYZ stock is trading at $99 per share, the May 100 call and May 100 put options are still considered at-the-money.

Out-of-the-Money   *Out-of-the-money* describes an option that has no intrinsic value and, instead, consists entirely of extrinsic value. For example, if XYZ stock is trading at $100 per share, the May 105 call and May 95 put are out-of-the-money. In general, an option contract is *far-out-of-the-money* if the strike price is at a level where it is highly unlikely to ever become in-the-money. If a call is in-the-money, a put with the same strike price must be out-of-the-money. Conversely, if the put is in-the-money, a call at the same strike price must be out-of-the-money.

At-the-money options tend to have the highest liquidity, with the greatest *open interest*. Open interest is the total number of options and/or futures contracts that are not closed or delivered on a particular day. An option has sufficient liquidity if there are sufficient buyers and sellers (volume) to execute an orderly market, without a disruption in price. Open interest is the total number of option contracts that are outstanding and are still open (have not been exercised, closed out, or allowed to expire). A *liquid market* is a market in which selling and buying can be accomplished with minimal effect on price.

Exercise and Assignment

If you are long a call and choose to *exercise*, you buy stock at the strike price; if you are long a put and choose to exercise, you sell stock at the strike price. If the buyer decides to exercise his right under the option contract, the option seller (writer) is *assigned*, requiring him to sell (in the case of a call) or buy (in the case of a put) the underlying stock at the strike price.

An *American-style option* can be exercised by the option holder (buyer) at any time up until the expiration date, whereas a *European-style option* can be exercised only at expiration. Equity options, including ETFs, are generally American-style expirations.

When an option is exercised by the owner, the seller of the option is assigned. An *exercise notice* is a notification by a broker of assignment. *Assignment* is a designation by which the option writer is required (forced) to sell a stock at the specified exercise price if it is a call and buy a stock at the specified exercise price if it is a put. You should keep in mind that most options are not exercised and instead are either offset in the marketplace or expire worthless. Chapter 28 is entirely devoted to covering exercise and assignment.

If you are long a call, you can have the stock *called* away from the call seller. If you are long a put, you can *put* the stock to the put seller by forcing him to buy it. Although anything is possible, it is rare that a stock with extrinsic value is exercised because the holder is better off selling the option rather than exercising it. As an example, assume that XYZ stock is trading at $100 and you own (are long) a May 95 call valued at $7: If you exercise the call option, it gives you the right to purchase the stock at $95, which is $5 below the stock's current value; however, you can recognize a $7 value simply by selling the option.

Break-Even Point

When buying or selling an option, a trader should determine in advance the point (or points) where the underlying stock must rise or fall for an option position to *break even*. Assuming you do not have a position in the underlying stock, when buying (or selling) a call, the break-even point is typically where the underlying stock, at the expiration date, equals the strike price plus the premium paid for the option contract. When buying (or selling) a put, the break-even point is typically where the underlying stock, at the expiration date, equals the strike price minus the premium paid. For example, assume that XYZ stock is trading at $100 and the price of the XYZ February 105 call is $2. The buyer or seller, at the expiration date of the call option, has a break-even point at a stock price of $107 (105 strike price plus $2 premium paid). If you assume that the XYZ February 95 put is at $2, the buyer or seller, at the expiration date of the put option, has a break-even point at a stock price of $93 (95 strike price minus $2 premium paid).

FINAL THOUGHTS

Probably the greatest advantage of trading options is leverage. Probably the greatest disadvantage of trading options is leverage. The true nature of option trading is the ability to control large sums of assets with small amounts of capital. Leverage is a double-edged sword and could lead to losses as well as gains. Knowledge is the key. Of course, some luck along the way will not hurt either.

We all come to the markets with our own strengths. Some traders are naturally bearish (and that can be an advantage in some cases), whereas others are naturally bullish; some are confident in the long term, whereas others believe in trading short term; some do not like the stress of trading, whereas others seem to thrive on it; some like to follow the markets closely, whereas others do not look at their investments more than once a month (or longer). The key seems to be to find trading strategies that fit your strengths. Each trader has his own unique risk tolerance, personality, and investing style, and you should therefore try to match your risk tolerance and investing style with how you trade options. The good news is that options provide many potential ways to profit.

There is probably an option strategy that can fit your risk profile and help you gain an edge. Which option strategies are best for you depends in part on the amount of capital you have, your risk tolerance, and your confidence level. When trading, you should not trade to the point where you cannot sleep at night. Most of the time you are trading options, you should be trading conservatively, but there are other times when you need to know when to put on a full-court press. This does not mean that you should take excessive risk, but there are times when you should be more heavily invested than others. Of course, there are also times when you should be out of the market entirely. You should never feel compelled to be in the market. Technical analysis can be a valuable tool in determining trends and can place you on a more level playing field with professional traders.

It is best to have a well-diversified portfolio. Trading in your brokerage account should be coordinated with your overall financial situation and should be part of a diversified portfolio; for example, your portfolio of investments should include domestic and international mutual funds, stocks, bonds, and homeownership. After you have determined your portfolio investments and weighed them against your debts, you are in a position to determine how much money you can risk on trading options. Most of all, do not get greedy.

Traditional buy and hold strategies only profit if the investment moves in one direction: higher. Although this works in many instances, many investors and traders are looking to increase their returns and manage risk. Using options wisely can be a way to do just that. As you gain experience in trading options, you should identify strategies that you like best, in view of your risk profile and profit objectives. Not only that, but some strategies may fit your lifestyle better than others, depending on whether you want to trade every day, once a week, or only once in a while. In Chapter 2, I describe key option fundamentals.

Option Fundamentals

B efore you begin to trade, you should understand how options work. Once you have mastered the fundamentals, you can begin to trade with confidence. This chapter covers opening and closing an option position; the fundamentals of option buying versus selling; and an introduction to margin, option spreads, the bid/ask spread, and option chain.

OVERVIEW

Some option strategies are best in bull markets, some are best in bear markets, and others are best in sideways markets. Many novice option traders may be attracted to buying options because they are familiar with buying stocks (or other assets such as a home), and they are attracted to the possibility of large and unlimited profits. Buying calls can be a good place to start to learn how to trade options. You should understand the fundamentals of opening and closing an option position, the fundamentals of option buying versus selling, and other basics. We will progress in later chapters to option pricing and strategies.

OPENING AND CLOSING POSITIONS

When it comes to options, the terms *buy* and *sell* can be confusing at first. You can establish (*open*) a position by buying an option; you can subsequently *close* (*offset*) it by selling it in the marketplace. You can establish (open) a position by selling an option; you can subsequently close (offset) it by buying it in the marketplace. Throughout this book, the terms buy and sell refer to opening/establishing positions unless otherwise indicated.

At first, the idea that an open option position is offset can be a little confusing. When you purchase a stock, for instance, you sell the same shares that you bought in the marketplace; you do not offset it. But, in the unique options world, you are not dealing with ownership interests; rather, you are dealing with contracts representing rights and obligations. When you close an option position, you are taking the opposite side of the established position. The term "offset" simply means to eliminate a long or short option position that was previously established. In the options world, many option contracts are initially sold, so the term "offset" is useful to indicate that something is being closed.

When you establish a position, you enter an order to buy (long position) or an order to sell (short position) to open, and when you close a position, you enter an order to sell or an order to buy to close. When closing an option position you previously purchased, you would enter a *sell to close* order, in which you offset the original position. When you sell (write) an option, you are opening a short option position, and you can subsequently close (offset) it by buying it in the marketplace. When closing such an option position, you would enter a *buy to close* order, in which you offset the original position. Both an option buyer and an option writer can close the option position by closing out (offsetting) the original position prior to the expiration date. To do so, you place an order to buy or sell the same number of contracts with the same terms. Chapter 31 covers what you need to know when placing an order to buy or sell, including the types of orders that can be used to open or close an option position.

OPTION BUYING

Now that we have covered some basic definitions, let us examine why you would want to purchase an option and the alternatives you have for exiting a long position. Buying an option is covered first because most investors are familiar with buying. Let us start by taking a look at purchasing equity options. We will cover ETFs, indexes, and stock index futures in later chapters.

In general, you would typically buy a call if you believe the underlying stock is going to move higher and you want limited risk. You would typically buy a put if you believe the underlying stock is going to move lower and you want limited risk. One of the main attractions of a long option is limited risk.

Exiting a Long Option Position

When you enter into a long option position (call or put), you are not required to hold the position until the expiration date. Instead, you can exit the position in a number of different ways. To become a skilled trader, you should thoroughly understand how to exit an option position. For an option buyer, there are three methods to exit a position:

1. Close the position.
2. Let the option expire worthless.
3. Exercise the option.

Assume that XYZ stock is trading at $100 per share in January, and you buy to open one XYZ February 100 call option at $5, paying $500 (remember that each option controls 100 shares). Following is a description of how to exit the long call position. The same exit strategies are available for a long put.

Close the Position   You can offset an option position in a closing transaction at any time before expiration. In fact, most options are offset prior to expiration. To do so, you place an order to sell the same number of contracts with the same terms; for example, if the stock rises to $108 two weeks prior to expiration, the call option might trade at $10, so you can sell it in a closing transaction at that time and not wait until the expiration date. Notice in this example that the stock price rose 8 percent (increased from $100 to $108), but the option trade produced a return of 100 percent (increased from $5 to $10). That is the power of leverage.

If the stock instead declines to $98 two weeks prior to expiration, the call option might trade at $1, so you can sell it (to avoid further loss) in a closing transaction at that time. Notice in this example that the stock price declined 2 percent, but the option trade produced a loss of 80 percent (declined from $5 to $1). It goes to show that the power of leverage cuts both ways.

Let the Option Expire Worthless   You can let the option expire worthless on the expiration date if it settles out-of-the-money, thus realizing a loss equal to the premium paid for the option. For example, if the stock declines to $94 on the expiration date, the call option would be worthless. In this example, the stock price declined 6 percent, but the option trade lost 100 percent. Of course, if you owned 100 shares of stock, you would have lost $600, but you lost only $500 on the option. In this example, your loss on the option is greater on a percentage basis but less in dollar terms, relative to owning the stock.

Exercise the Option   By exercising a call option, you are choosing to buy the underlying stock at the strike price. Of course, you would only exercise an option if it is advantageous to do so. If XYZ stock is trading at $108, you can exercise your right to purchase the stock at a price of $100, even though the stock is selling for $108 a share. In this example, the total you effectively paid is $105 (the 100 strike price plus the $5 premium). As a result, the gain at the time of exercise is $300, calculated as the difference between the $108 stock price and the deemed $105 purchase price (stock value of $108 minus $105 purchase price). If XYZ stock is trading below the 100 strike price, it would not be to your advantage to exercise the option.

As a reminder, the same exit strategies are available for a long put. By exercising a put option, you are choosing to sell the underlying stock at the strike price.

Limited Risk/Unlimited Reward

An option buyer is commonly described as having unlimited reward potential with limited risk, and an option seller is commonly described as having limited reward potential with unlimited risk. A long option is a *limited-risk* strategy because an option buyer cannot lose more than the premium paid (in addition to commission and other transaction costs, of course). A call option buyer is commonly described as having unlimited reward potential based on the theory that there is no limit to how high numbers can go.

A long put is described as an *unlimited* reward strategy, although, mathematically speaking, a long put profit is limited to the difference between the exercise price and zero times the number of options (at $100 per contract). Some commentators may use the words *limited* and *unlimited* in their descriptions of risks and rewards for options because options are leveraged instruments, and these terms provide a quick and convenient way to describe option risks and rewards.

OPTION SELLING

The goal of option selling is the same as in traditional trading but in reverse order. In traditional trading, the goal is to buy low and sell high, whereas in option selling, the goal is to sell high and buy low. An option buyer makes a profit when he buys an option and later sells it at a price above the level at which it was purchased. An option writer (seller) makes a profit when the option that was sold is later purchased at a price below the level at which it was written or when it expires worthless. Remember that you are an option writer if you sell an option to open a position.

A call obligates the writer (seller) to sell the underlying stock on or before an expiration date at the strike price. Typically, you would write a call if you believe that the underlying stock is going to move lower or sideways. A put, on the other hand, obligates the writer to buy the underlying stock on or before an expiration date at the strike price. You would typically write a put if you believe the underlying stock is going to move higher or sideways.

Writing an option involves selling first and buying later and is a strategy used to take advantage of an anticipated decline in the price of the option. When writing an option, you are considered short the option. An option writer profits if he can later buy (offset) that option at a lower price and loses if he later buys (offsets) at a higher price.

Principles of Short Selling

At first, you may be confused regarding what it means to write an option because it involves selling first and buying later. This strategy is contrary to the way most people think about profiting from a trade; for instance, when you invest in real estate, you first purchase the property and sell it later. Also, typically, when you engage in a stock transaction, you purchase the stock with the expectation that the price will rise so that you can sell it later at a higher price; for example, you might purchase a stock currently trading at $100 a share, anticipating that it will rise to $105 a share, so that you can sell it at a $5 profit.

It is useful to examine how *selling short* a stock works to illustrate how you can profit from a short sale. A popular technique to profit from a decline in a stock is to sell it short. Many individuals are confused, at first, by short selling because it first involves selling the stock and then later buying the stock. In a short sale of stock, a trader borrows stock to sell. A gain results if he subsequently buys that stock at a lower price, and a loss results if he buys at a higher price. Depending on the rules in effect, the shorting of a stock may be subject to the uptick rule, which does not permit the shorting of a stock unless the last trade was higher than the previous trade (an uptick). Thus, buying a put can be an effective way to avoid the uptick rule if it is in effect.

For example, a trader may anticipate a decline in the price of XYZ shares, so on January 5, he sells short 100 XYZ shares when the stock is trading at $100, for $10,000. If XYZ drops to $85 on February 3, the trader can buy the shares for $8,500, thus covering the short sale and profiting by $1,500. If XYZ rises to $115, the trader can buy the shares for $11,500, thus covering the short sale at a loss of $1,500 (see Table 2.1).

Likewise, a trader may anticipate a decline in the price of a call option, so on January 5, he sells (writes) one XYZ February 100 call option at $5 (for a $500 credit). The trader, by the expiration date, must offset (buy) the contract in the marketplace or meet his obligation under the contract to sell 100 shares of XYZ stock (if assigned). If the option price drops to $3 on January 15, the trader can buy the call option in the marketplace for $300, thus closing the position and profiting by $200. Alternatively, if the option expires worthless at expiration, the option obligation to sell shares is canceled and, in effect, the option is deemed purchased at zero and the entire $500 credit collected is a gain. If the option rises to $8, the trader can buy the call option in the marketplace for $800, thus canceling the obligation at a loss of $300 (see Table 2.2).

TABLE 2.1 Short Sale Followed by Purchase

Description	Gain ($)	Loss ($)
Short stock sale	10,000	10,000
Subsequent stock purchase	(8,500)	(11,500)
Gain (loss)	1,500	(1,500)

TABLE 2.2 Sale of Option Followed by Offset or Expiration

Description	Offset at Gain ($)	Expires at Gain ($)	Offset at Loss ($)
Option sale price	500	500	500
Option purchase price	(300)	0	(800)
Gain (loss)	200	500	(300)

Exiting a Short Option Position

Playing defense is especially important when selling options. When you enter into a short option position, you are not required to continue the position until the expiration date, and you can exit the position in a number of different ways. For an option seller (writer), three methods can be used to exit a position:

1. Close the position.
2. Let the option expire worthless.
3. Assignment of option.

Assume that XYZ stock is trading at $100 per share in January, and you sell one XYZ February 100 call option at $5, collecting $500. Following is a description of how to exit the short call position. The same exit strategies are available for a short put.

Close the Position   You can close the position at any time before expiration; for example, if the stock rises to $108 two weeks prior to expiration, the call option might trade at $10, so you can buy (offset) it in a closing transaction at that time. Notice in this example that the stock price rose 8 percent (increased from $100 to $108), but the option trade produced a loss of 100 percent (increased from $5 to $10). Remember that the goal of option selling is the same as in traditional trading but in reverse order.

If the stock instead declines to $98 two weeks prior to expiration, the call option might trade at $1, so you can buy it in a closing transaction at that time. Notice in this example that the stock price declined 2 percent, but the option trade produced a gain of 80 percent (declined from $5 to $1).

Let the Option Expire Worthless   You can let the option expire worthless on the expiration date, thus realizing a gain equal to the premium collected; for example, if the stock is at $94 on the expiration date, the call option would be worthless. In this example, the stock price declined 6 percent, but the option trade gained 100 percent. If you sell an option to open, then you want it to expire worthless because you get to keep the entire credit you received from the option premium.

Assignment of Option   If the option buyer exercises an option, it is assigned to the seller (writer). Under an assignment, a call option writer is required to sell (or buy, in the case of a put) the underlying stock at the strike price. If XYZ stock is trading at $108 and you are assigned on a short 100 call, you are obligated to sell the stock at a price of $100, even though the stock is trading at $108 a share at that time. In this example, at the time of assignment, the call seller lost $300 (60 percent), calculated as the difference between the $108 stock price and the deemed $105 sale price ($100 strike price plus $5 premium). If the stock is below $100 a share, the short call should not be assigned.

Unlimited Risk/Limited Reward

A *naked option* is a short call or put option without the holding of an opposite position to limit your potential loss. It can be called an *uncovered option, naked call,* or *naked put.* It makes sense that it is called "naked" because the seller (writer) is fully exposed to risk. For a naked option call writer, the risk is unlimited because there is no mathematical limitation to how high an underlying stock can rise. A naked put seller is often described as having unlimited risk when, mathematically, in fact, his risk is limited to the underlying stock declining to zero. A naked option writer can lose more of the premium collected and is typically described as someone who has unlimited risk.

For example, assume that XYZ stock is trading at $100 per share in January, and you sell one XYZ February 100 call option at $5, collecting $500. If the stock immediately rises to $110, the call option might trade at $10 (or above); if the stock rises to $115, the call option might trade at $15 (or above); if the stock rises to $120, the call option might trade at $20 (or above), and so on. The position would not be considered naked if, instead, you owned 100 shares of XYZ or purchased a call option at a higher price in a spread transaction (discussed in Chapter 6).

Mathematically, a call seller has unlimited risk based on the fact that there is no limit to how high a number can go. The risk of selling one at-the-money call contract is the same as shorting 100 shares of stock (less the premium collected). The risk of selling one at-the-money put contract is the same as owning 100 shares of stock (less the premium collected). Mathematically speaking, the risk of a put is limited to the difference between the exercise price and zero (because a stock cannot decline below zero) times the number of options (at $100 per contract) less the premium collected.

Margin

Chapter 30 is devoted to explaining *margin* on stocks, ETFs, indexes, and stock index futures, but some basic concepts on stocks are worth mentioning at this point. Briefly, margin on equities is typically determined under 20 percent standard margin or portfolio margin, and margin on futures is typically determined under the Standard Portfolio Analysis of Risk (SPAN) margining system. Margin rules are also covered in Chapter 5.

Margin is the mechanism by which options gain leverage. A margin requirement for options is the amount of cash (or other assets) an option seller is required to deposit and maintain to cover a position as collateral. It is the amount of assets (e.g., cash, treasury bills) that must be deposited by an option seller to ensure performance of the seller's obligations under an option contract. *Initial margin* is the amount of margin required when a position is opened. *Maintenance margin* is the amount that must be maintained on deposit after a position is open. A *margin call* is a request from a brokerage firm to a customer to bring margin deposits up to initial levels after a position is open.

When you buy an option, the entire cost of a long option position is typically required to be paid at the time an option order is executed; for example, if you enter into a long call, 100 percent of the cost of the position must be paid up front (your broker may allow you to add money to your account to cover the purchase). Option margin rules, conversely, are concerned with short option positions.

The minimum initial margin requirement for an equity uncovered option varies from broker to broker but is typically set at the option premium credited plus 20 or 25 percent (15 percent for a *broad-based index*) of the underlying security or index minus the amount the option is out-of-the-money, subject to a minimum. I will refer to this as the *20 percent margin requirement*; for example, if XYZ stock is trading at $100, a put option seller may have a required margin of only $200, even though the maximum risk is $1,000 (ignoring the premium collected).

SPREADS

The same principles covered in this chapter apply to *spreads*. A spread can be broadly defined as two or more options working together to form a position. A spread typically involves the purchase of one option contract (e.g., an XYZ February 100 call) and the sale of another option contract (e.g., an XYZ February 105 call) on the same underlying stock. Likewise, a spread can consist of the simultaneous sale of one option (e.g., an XYZ February 100 call) and the purchase of another option (e.g., an XYZ February 105 call) on the same underlying stock. A spread can include options that expire in the same month or in different months and with the same strike prices or different strike prices. If a spread includes options with different expiration dates, the *near-term* (*front month*) is the expiration month closest to the present date, and the *longer-term* option (*back month, far month, distant month*, or *deferred month*) is the month after the near-term month. For example, for an option spread with expiration dates of February and March, the near-term month is February and the longer-term month is March. A spread can consist of all calls or all puts or a combination of calls and puts.

When you enter into a spread position, you can offset the position, let the options expire worthless, exercise any long option, or wait for assignment on any short option. Spreads are covered in later chapters.

BID/ASK SPREAD

The *bid* price represents the price you will likely receive if you place a market order to sell (for a specific quantity). The *ask* price (offer price) is the price you will likely pay if you place a market order to buy (for a specific quantity). The difference between the two prices is the *bid/ask spread*. In other words, the bid represents the highest price a prospective buyer is willing to pay you at a particular time for an option. The ask price represents the lowest price a prospective seller is willing to receive from you at a particular time for an option.

When trading equity options, you should be able to see the bid/ask spreads in your trading platform. Some options trade in nickel increments; others trade in pennies. In addition, bid/ask spreads tend to be less onerous when they are at-the-money because they tend to be the most liquid options. Bid/ask spreads tend to narrow for options with high trading volumes, especially on large capitalization stocks. Before trading any option, you should determine the size of the bid/ask spread. Bid/ask spreads vary, depending on the volume and volatility in the underlying stock.

For simplicity, throughout this book, the examples presented assume that an option can be bought or sold at the same price. In reality, options are typically purchased at the midpoint or at or near the ask price and sold at the midpoint or at or near the bid price. For example, the XYZ February 100 call option in this chapter has been assumed to be trading at $5, but a typical bid/ask might be $4.80 and $5.20, respectively. Such a bid/ask spread would be shown in this book as 4.80/5.20. Examples showing purchases at the ask and sales at the bid may be confusing and become a distraction from the main point of each example. As a result, the examples presented assume that the bid and ask prices are the same. The bid/ask spread is covered in later chapters.

OPTION CHAIN

A good place to find option prices is an *option chain*. An option chain is a list of option prices at a specific point in time and is similar to a stock screen, except that it has information on option prices. An option chain shows prices at various strike prices, with the lowest strike price typically shown at the top and higher strike prices shown as you move down the page. You should notice that call prices decline and put prices rise as you move to higher strike prices.

An option chain is included for each expiration month. New option strike prices are added when the underlying shares trade near the highest or lowest strike prices available or when options expire and new expiration months are added. Strike prices are listed above and below the current price of the underlying stock. Some option chains show calls for one month on one page and puts separately on another page; other option chains show calls on the left-hand side of the chain and puts on the right-hand side of the chain because they share common strike prices. An option chain will usually show near-term options at the top of the screen and later-term options as you move down the option chain page.

Table 2.3 shows a representative sample of options that expire on the third Friday in May, and Table 2.4 shows corresponding amounts for an expiration in June. The bid/ask

TABLE 2.3 XYZ February Option Chain (40 Days to Expiration)

Call Bid	Call Ask	Strike Price	Put Bid	Put Ask
25.50	25.70	75	0.00	0.05
20.80	21.50	80	0.25	0.35
16.20	16.80	85	0.55	0.70
11.90	12.10	90	1.15	1.30
7.90	8.30	95	2.20	2.35
4.90	5.10	100	4.00	4.30
2.60	2.75	105	6.70	7.00
1.25	1.45	110	10.30	10.70
0.55	0.65	115	14.80	15.10
0.20	0.30	120	19.50	19.90
0.10	0.20	125	24.40	24.90

TABLE 2.4 XYZ March Option Chain (68 Days to Expiration)

Call Bid	Call Ask	Strike Price	Put Bid	Put Ask
30.90	31.60	70	0.20	0.30
26.20	26.90	75	0.40	0.50
21.60	22.20	80	0.70	0.85
17.20	17.70	85	1.25	1.35
13.10	13.50	90	2.05	2.25
9.40	9.90	95	3.30	3.50
6.40	6.80	100	5.30	5.50
4.10	4.40	105	7.90	8.20
2.50	2.70	110	11.20	11.60
1.40	1.60	115	15.20	15.70
0.80	0.90	120	19.80	20.10
0.40	0.50	125	24.40	24.90

prices are actually taken from options on a stock, with the stock trading at $100.25. In this example, February is 40 days until expiration and March is 68 days until expiration. Bid/ask prices for calls are shown on the left side and bid/ask prices for puts are shown on the right side. Strike prices are listed in the middle column.

Option chains can be viewed in the trading platform supplied by your broker or on various web sites. Your trading platform should provide real-time bid/ask prices, whereas some web sites may have a delay in pricing.

FINAL THOUGHTS

You should use a trading platform that specializes in option trading that can automatically open or close option orders at the click of a mouse; for example, your option trading platform should automatically present an opening or offsetting order so that you only have to review it and make changes before transmitting the order. There are more than a dozen order types you can place for stocks, such as market and limit orders, and you can generally enter the same types of orders for options. Likewise, the mechanics of placing an equity option order are similar to entering an order for stocks. You execute a trade by calling your broker or entering an order online. You should have a trading platform that enables you to open or close a simple or complex equity option order in the same order. Chapter 31 discusses how to place an option order. Now it is time to address option pricing. In Chapter 3, we will take a look at what goes into determining an option price and what affects its value.

CHAPTER 3

What Determines an Option's Price?

When you buy a stock, pricing is relatively straightforward because the value of your investment is directly attributable to the price of the stock itself. An option, conversely, is a derivative instrument whose value is, in part, based on the price of an underlying stock and, in part, on other factors. Analyzing option pricing can be a challenge because sometimes it is like trying to hit a moving target.

This chapter discusses option pricing from the perspective of establishing a position and changes in the option price after the position has been established. It covers the five factors that affect an option's price and the basics of how to forecast a change in price. Chapter 4, "Tools of the Trade—Greeks," provides further option pricing analysis.

OVERVIEW

Before you establish an option position, you should understand what causes one option to be priced higher or lower than the other. An option, in general, commands a higher premium under the following conditions:

- The lower the strike price of a call,
- The higher the strike price of a put,
- More time remaining until expiration,
- Greater *implied volatility*,
- Increase in the assumed interest rate for a call,
- Decrease in the assumed interest rate for a put,
- Decrease in the assumed dividend for a call,
- Increase in the assumed dividend for a put.

An option, in general, commands a lower premium under the following conditions:

- The higher the strike price of a call,
- The lower the strike price of a put,
- Less time remaining until expiration,
- Lower implied volatility,
- Decrease in the assumed interest rate for a call,
- Increase in the assumed interest rate for a put,
- Increase in the assumed dividend for a call,
- Decrease in the assumed dividend for a put.

Everything else being equal, a higher-priced stock will have higher-priced option premiums in absolute dollar terms; for example, a stock trading at $100 a share will, in general, have options priced higher than a stock trading at $40 a share.

Pricing Based on Changing Conditions

We will now turn our attention to how an option price (premium) changes based on changing conditions. Once an option position is established, the strike price is fixed and never changes. When the stock price moves up or down, the stock is either closer to or further from the strike price, thus affecting the option premium value. If you examine an option chain, you should notice that call prices decline (and puts rise) as you move to higher strike prices. Some general rules follow:

- For a fixed strike price, a higher stock price results in a higher call option premium (and a lower put option premium).
- For a fixed strike price, a lower stock price results in a lower call option premium (and a higher put option premium).
- As time passes (it only moves in one direction), call and put prices decline.
- As implied volatility declines, call and put prices decline.
- As implied volatility rises, call and put prices rise.

Said another way, the following are general rules that can be used to determine whether an option value will likely increase or decrease:

- A call increases in value when the underlying stock rises, volatility rises, or there is a later expiration.
- A call declines in value when the underlying stock declines, volatility contracts, or time passes.
- A put increases in value when the underlying stock declines, volatility rises, or there is a later expiration.
- A put declines in value when the underlying stock rises, volatility contracts, or time passes.

One variable (e.g., volatility, time) can have a greater or smaller effect than another variable, and not all of them always work in the same direction for instance, a call option

TABLE 3.1 How a Change in Factors Affects an Option's Value

Factor	Call Typically	Put Typically
Underlying stock rises	Rises	Declines
Underlying stock declines	Declines	Rises
Volatility rises	Rises	Rises
Volatility declines	Declines	Declines
Time passes	Declines	Declines
More time remaining	Greater premium	Greater premium
Less time remaining	Declines	Declines

may be inclined to rise in value because the underlying stock price rises, but that effect may be partially or totally negated by the passage of time or volatility contraction. The effect of changing market conditions on an option's value is summarized in Table 3.1.

If you own a call option and the value of the underlying stock rises, the value of your option will likely rise as well because the option value is partially determined by the value of the stock. However, the rise in the value of the option may not be dollar for dollar because there are other factors from which an option derives its value. In effect, a stock price is one-dimensional because the stock price is the only thing that matters, but options are multidimensional. For example, if you own 100 shares of a stock and the stock price increases by one point, the value of your holding increases by $100. If you own one call option and the stock price increases by one point, the value of your holding may increase by $50, depending on a number of factors. You can think of options as being three-dimensional because they are easy to understand that way, with the three most important dimensions being strike price versus stock price, time to expiration, and volatility. The remainder of this chapter will discuss the factors affecting an option's price and how to predict a change in price based on various assumptions.

FACTORS AFFECTING OPTION PRICING

One option can be priced higher or lower than another based on the following variables:

- Strike price versus stock price (the lower the strike price, the higher the price of a call; the higher the strike price, the higher the price of a put),
- Time (the more time remaining until expiration, the higher the premium),
- Volatility (the higher the implied volatility built into an option price, the higher the premium),
- Interest rate (the higher the assumed interest rate, the higher the call premium but the lower the put premium),
- Dividend (the higher the dividend on the underlying stock, the lower the call premium but the higher the put premium).

The first three variables have the greatest effect on an option's price, so that is where you should focus your attention. The last two variables, interest and dividends, have an effect on an option's value, but to a much lesser degree, and rarely affect your decisions when trading options. Each of these variables is discussed in this chapter.

Strike Price versus Stock Price

After your strike price selection has been made, the option value will change when the stock price changes. The change in price of a stock has the opposite effect on calls and puts; for instance, as the value of a stock rises, a call will generally increase in value and a put will generally decrease in value. As the price of a stock declines, call prices generally decline in value and put prices generally increase in value.

Table 2.3 shows a representative option chain for calls and puts. Option prices decline for calls if you start deep-in-the-money and move to higher strike prices. Option prices decline for puts if you start deep-in-the-money and move to lower strike prices. You can use an option chain to estimate the effect on the price of an option based on a change in stock price by taking the difference between an option price at different strike prices. For example, if a 95 strike call is priced at $7.90 and a 100 strike call is priced at $4.90, then a five-point increase in the stock price would theoretically increase the 100 strike price call option value by $3, assuming that all other factors remain constant.

Time to Expiration

In general, an option commands a higher premium where there is more time remaining until expiration and a lower premium where there is less time remaining; for instance, if XYZ is selling at $100 a share in early January, the at-the-money April 100 call may trade at $10, the March 100 call at $7, and the February 100 call at $5.

Options are commonly known as a wasting asset as the extrinsic value decays over time. If you assume that XYZ stock is trading at $100 and a February 95 call option can be purchased at $7, the call would consist of $5 intrinsic value and $2 extrinsic value. The $2 extrinsic value is subject to the forces of *time decay*. Assuming the stock remains unchanged until the expiration date, the extrinsic value will decay (i.e., decline or depreciate) and will be zero on the expiration date. The same time-decay concept applies to a put; for example, if you assume that XYZ stock is trading at $100 and a February 105 put option can be purchased at $7, the put would consist of $5 intrinsic value and $2 extrinsic value. The $2 extrinsic value is subject to time decay.

Time decay can be compared to the depreciation or amortization of an asset; for example, if an asset costs $10,000 and is depreciated over a five-year period, then on a straight-line basis, the depreciation would be $2,000 per year. Although time decay is similar to depreciation, the decay is usually over a shorter period of time and is not in a straight line. The strategies illustrated in this book typically anticipate an initial period to expiration of 30 to 90 days.

An option decays over time, but the rate of decay depends on a number of factors, including time to expiration and whether the option is in-the-money, at-the-money, or out-of-the-money, and depending on the type of underlying instrument such as a stock, stock index, ETF, or futures. The rate of time decay can also differ to some degree depending on whether the option is a call versus a put. A way to look at time decay is that an option's extrinsic value will depreciate from the time the option position is established until the expiration date. The rate of decay, however, is not on a straight-line basis and can be projected with the assistance of an option calculator or the analysis page of your trading platform.

If you were to list intrinsic and extrinsic values beside each strike price on an option chain (your trading platform should show this), you would see that extrinsic value reaches its peak when the strike price is at-the-money and then declines as you go further out-of-the-money. In other words, if you start deep-in-the-money and move along the option chain, you will see that extrinsic value gets larger and reaches its peak when the strike price is at-the-money and then declines as you move further out-of-the-money. Table 3.2 shows intrinsic and extrinsic values for strike prices from 75 to 125, taken from a representative stock trading near $100 a share.

Table 3.2 shows that the extrinsic value reaches its peak when the strike price is at-the-money and declines as you go further out-of-the-money. Figure 3.1 graphically illustrates this principle. You can conclude from this analysis that at-the-money options, as a general rule, have the greatest amount of premium subject to time decay.

It is sometimes taught that the further out in time you go, the smaller the time decay. Although this may be true on a percentage basis, you should examine each option on a facts-and-circumstances basis to determine if that same theory holds true on a dollar basis. For example, an option with 10 days remaining until the expiration date may have projected average time decay equal to $0.10, but a 30-day option may have time decay equal to $0.50. The 30-day option decay may be smaller on a percentage basis but larger in dollar terms. To illustrate the effect of time decay, I have assumed that XYZ stock is

TABLE 3.2 Pattern of Extrinsic Value

Call Option Strike Price	Call Value ($)	Intrinsic Value ($)	Extrinsic Value ($)
75	25.50	25.00	0.50
80	20.80	20.00	0.80
85	16.20	15.00	1.20
90	11.90	10.00	1.90
95	7.90	5.00	2.90
100	4.90	0	4.90
105	2.60	0	2.60
110	1.25	0	1.25
115	0.55	0	0.55
120	0.20	0	0.20
125	0.10	0	0.10

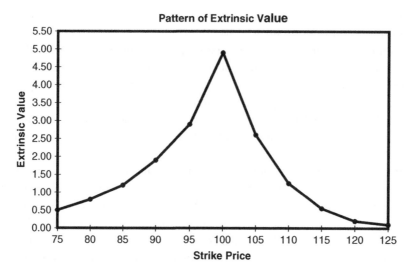

FIGURE 3.1 Pattern of Extrinsic Value

trading at $100 a share and an at-the-money call option with 10 weeks remaining until expiration is trading at $11. By using an option calculator, you can isolate time decay on a daily or weekly basis to demonstrate the amount of decay on dollar and percentage bases. Table 3.3 shows the projected time decay pattern at a particular point in time for each week using the theoretical price feature of the thinkorswim (a brokerage firm specializing in options) trading platform on an actual stock (Research in Motion).

Table 3.3 demonstrates that time decay accelerates the closer you get to expiration in dollar terms as well as on a percentage basis. The average weekly decay column is based on the remaining weeks to expiration at a particular point in time. Figure 3.2 is a

TABLE 3.3 Time Decay: At-the-Money Call

Weeks to Expiration (Beginning of Week)	Call Value ($)	Weekly Decay ($)	Percentage Decay	Average Weekly Decay To Expiration ($)
10	11.00	0.55	5.00	1.10
9	10.45	0.61	5.84	1.16
8	9.84	0.65	6.61	1.23
7	9.19	0.69	7.51	1.31
6	8.50	0.76	8.94	1.42
5	7.74	0.83	10.72	1.55
4	6.91	0.94	13.60	1.73
3	5.97	1.11	18.59	1.99
2	4.86	1.46	30.04	2.43
1	3.40	3.40	100.00	3.40

Call value data from thinkorswim platform.

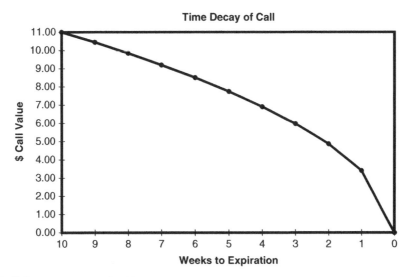

FIGURE 3.2 Time Decay of Call

graph of the dollar value of the call from week 10 to expiration. As can be seen in Figure 3.2, the dollar amount of the decay is fairly constant and accelerates in the last three or four weeks. This is one reason why many option buyers prefer to purchase options with at least 60 to 90 days remaining until expiration; many option sellers, however, prefer to write options with 45 days or less to expiration.

Figure 3.3 shows the percentage changes in the call value from week 10 to expiration. As can be seen in Figure 3.3, the percentage decay accelerates as you approach expiration.

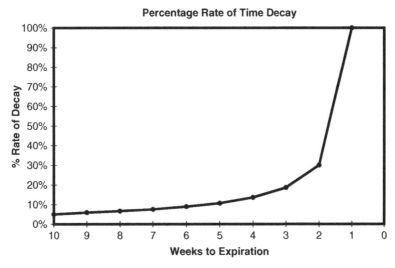

FIGURE 3.3 Percentage Rate of Time Decay

You should be aware that the projected time-decay profile can vary depending on whether an option is in-the-money, at-the-money, or out-of-the-money and can vary depending on whether it is a put or a call and on the type of instrument (stock, ETF, stock index, or stock index futures) you are trading.

Volatility

Volatility is one of the most important variables affecting an option's price, but it is the most complex component and probably the most misunderstood. Chapter 27 is devoted to analyzing volatility and its role in determining an option's price, but for now, let us cover the basics.

As previously noted, there are five variables that affect an option's price. Four of these components are known. The only missing link (i.e., input into an option pricing model) is implied volatility. The implied volatility is the number that must be imported into a theoretical option pricing model to produce the price of the option in the marketplace. You can think of implied volatility as the plug figure that is backed into an option pricing model to make it work because it is the only missing link. Implied volatility is built into an option's price by the marketplace and it is available using a computer model available at most brokerage firms. The implied volatility of an option should be available in your trading platform.

A basic principle of economics is that assets are priced according to the laws of supply and demand. Option pricing is no exception to this rule because implied volatility can be viewed as a gauge that isolates and quantifies the demand component for an option at a particular moment in time. If all other factors are held constant, when demand is high, an option price is high; when demand is low, an option price is low. In that respect, the price of an option is determined by the same economic forces as other assets. With an option price, you have a quantifiable mechanism to capture the demand component: implied volatility.

Volatility is a statistical measurement of risk or uncertainty. As a general rule of thumb, when the market declines quickly, the implied volatility for an option increases because of the increase in uncertainty and fear. Likewise, if the market rises or moves sideways, implied volatility declines because of a reduction of fear and uncertainty. Another factor affecting implied volatility that is rarely discussed is its correlation to volume. As a general rule, I have observed anecdotally that as volume of the underlying stock increases, implied volatility tends to increase. Likewise, as volume declines, implied volatility, everything else being equal, tends to decline. I imagine that the reason for this is that an increase in the volume of stocks tends to signal an increase in the level of uncertainty, whereas a decline in volume may be associated with complacency.

Implied volatility can be viewed as a gauge of fear and uncertainty; for example, when fear or uncertainty is high, the price of an option rises and implied volatility is high. When fear or uncertainty is low, the price of an option declines, and implied volatility is said to be low. The *Chicago Board Options Exchange (CBOE) Volatility index (VIX)* measures implied volatility of options on the S&P 500 index and is often referred to as the fear gauge of the overall market (the VIX is discussed in Chapter 27). Similarly, implied volatility can be viewed as the fear gauge of an individual option. When Shakespeare said, "There is something in the wind," I do not believe he was referring to implied volatility, but it sure seems to apply.

There can be wide variation in the implied volatility of options. Implied volatility differs for each individual option and can differ dramatically from stock to stock, from futures contract to futures contract, and from strike price to strike price, and for puts versus calls. For instance, assume that XYZ stock is trading at $100 a share and the at-the-money February 100 call is $5. Another stock, such as ABC, trading at the same $100 stock price would likely have a February at-the-money option trading at an amount more than or less than $5, depending on its own level of implied volatility.

Assume that in January, IBM and Research in Motion stocks are both selling at $100 a share, but IBM has an implied volatility reading of 30 and Research in Motion has an implied volatility reading of 60. The February 100 call option may be $5 for IBM and $9 for Research in Motion. In this example, both options have the same strike price, time to expiration, dividend, and interest rate. The only difference is implied volatility, which in this case results in almost double the value for the Research in Motion option versus the comparable IBM option.

Implied volatility is the percentage you can see on your trading platform or option calculator for a particular option. It is not a measure of the actual volatility of the stock. Implied volatility is expressed in percentage terms because it measures annual *standard deviation*. As a result, a higher implied volatility percentage prices in (signals) a likely wider variation in the stock price and a lower percentage prices in a likely narrower variation in the stock price, at least according to how the option is priced at a particular point in time. A higher percentage implies greater volatility; a lower percentage implies lower volatility. For a stock, my general rule of thumb is that implied volatility of less than 30 percent is considered relatively low and implied volatility of greater than 70 percent is considered relatively high. By comparing the implied volatilities of various options across a number of different stocks and indexes, you can begin to develop a feel for what is considered below average, average, or above average implied volatility.

If you show implied volatility beside each strike price on an option chain, you will see that there is a different implied volatility at each strike price, even though it is the same underlying stock. Your trading platform should provide the implied volatility of an option.

Time and volatility are closely interconnected. More time to expiration means that there is more time for volatility to occur, whereas less time to expiration may mean that any change in volatility will have less of a dollar effect on an option value. Therefore, everything else being equal, a longer-term option is more sensitive in dollar terms to a change in volatility. For example, if XYZ is selling at $100 a share in January, the at-the-money March 100 call will, in general, be more sensitive in dollar terms to a change in volatility than the February 100 call.

TABLE 3.4 Interest Rate Effect

Factor	Call Typically	Put Typically
Interest rate rises	Rises	Declines
Interest rate declines	Declines	Rises

Interest Rate

A portion of the extrinsic value decay is attributable to the interest component of an option's value. Interest reflects the cost of carry of alternative investments such as a U.S. Treasury bill. As shown in Table 3.4, a higher interest rate results in call values rising and put values declining. A lower interest rate results in call values declining and put values rising. Option models include an interest rate assumption, typically using a risk-free interest rate such as a short-term U.S. Treasury rate.

If the interest rate is high, the amount of foregone interest (carrying costs) is high. If an interest rate is low, the amount of foregone interest is low. Because buying a call requires less of a cash outlay than buying the stock, a call buyer should be willing to pay more for the call option because he can invest the difference. Interest rates have an opposite effect on puts.

Initially, you may expect the price of a call to be equal to the price of a put if both have the same expiration date and the strike prices are equidistant from the underlying stock; for example, you may expect a February 105 call to be trading at the same price as a February 95 put if the underlying stock is trading at $100 a share. The interest rate factor can be one of the reasons why call prices do not have premiums that are symmetrical with put premiums. For simplicity, throughout this book, examples are presented in which it is assumed that call premiums are symmetrical with put premiums, where the strike price is equidistant from the price of the underlying stock price. In reality, call prices on stocks are typically higher in comparison to put prices, where the call and put are at an equal distance from the price of the underlying instrument. For example, if it is January and XYZ stock is trading at $100, the February 105 call could be trading at $2.50, whereas the February 95 put could be at $2.00.

There are a number of factors that can create this asymmetrical environment. In general, option pricing models have a tendency to value calls more than comparable puts because of interest rate assumptions and because of the fact that a stock can theoretically increase in value to infinity, but a stock can only decline in value to zero. It is interesting that, conversely, on broad-based indexes, the call/put pricing relationship is reversed. An out-of-the-money call on an underlying broad-based index typically has a lower value relative to a put. Apparently, there is a greater demand for buying puts relative to calls on broad-based indexes such as the *S&P 500 index*, creating higher put prices relative to calls for out-of-the-money options. Options on broad-based indexes are discussed in Part Four.

TABLE 3.5 Dividend Effect

Factor	Call Typically	Put Typically
Dividend paid or anticipated	Declines	Rises

Dividend

When a dividend is paid, the owner of the stock receives the dividend, but no dividend is received by an option holder, nor is a dividend paid by an option writer. However, the stock price is adjusted downward (on the ex-dividend date) by the amount of the dividend, which can have an effect on the price of an option. As a result, a cash dividend can result in a lower call premium and a higher put premium when the stock opens trading at the lower price (see Table 3.5).

Assume that XYZ stock is trading at $100 per share, and you buy to open one XYZ 100 strike price call option at $5. If XYZ stock goes ex-dividend by $1 the next morning, the stock will open the next day at $99 because of the dividend (assuming that no other factors influence the stock at the opening of trading), thus reducing the call value, unless the effect was already anticipated in the option price. Similarly, if you had purchased a 100 strike price put at $5, the put would rise in value because of the stock price decline, unless the effect was already anticipated in the option price.

An option price typically anticipates a dividend and takes into account the payment in advance of the ex-dividend date. Special dividends may come as a surprise and may not be reflected initially in the option price. The dividend effect on an option can be especially pronounced if a large dividend, such as an annual dividend distribution, is paid. An extraordinary dividend above a certain threshold may result in a strike price adjustment.

Dividends and the risk-free interest rate have an effect on option premiums, but this effect is small in most cases and does not enter into most trading decisions.

FORECASTING OPTION PRICES

I like to use three estimation methods to stress test (forward test) an option's value:

1. Examine an option chain to compare option values at various strike prices within the same month and compare option values at the same strike prices from month to month. The usefulness of an option chain is covered later in this chapter.

2. Use an option calculator to estimate option values at future points in time based on changes in assumptions for the strike versus stock volatility, interest, and/or dividends. If you want to run numerous scenarios with your own assumptions, you can run an almost unlimited number of scenarios with an option calculator.

3. Utilize the Greeks (discussed in Chapter 4). Keep in mind that the Greeks only estimate the change in an option value for a small change in the underlying stock price, time, or implied volatility. Each call and put option has its own Greeks, which change throughout the trading day. The Greeks essentially show a host of what-if scenarios at a particular point in time and are concerned with what will happen to an option value in the future if certain assumptions are made. Your trading platform should show the Greeks.

Examine an Option Chain

An option chain includes a wealth of information. You can use an option chain to estimate time decay from month to month or forecast the change in an option's value based on a change in the stock price.

By taking the difference between an option premium that expires in two months and subtracting the near-term month premium at the same strike price, you can estimate the amount of time decay that will be applicable to the first four-week (or five-week) period if you were to buy or sell the longer-term-month contract. For example, assume that in January, the XYZ March at-the-money call option premium is $7 and the February premium at the same strike price is $5. With this information, you can assume that there is $2 time decay ($7 March minus $5 February) over the next four weeks for the March option because the March premium will look like the February premium at that time (assuming that there is no change in the underlying stock price or in volatility).

Option Calculator

You can use an option calculator to determine estimated option values (theoretical values) based on assumptions you choose. With an option calculator, you can customize input parameters such as option type, price of the underlying stock, strike price, time remaining to expiration, implied volatility, interest rate, and dividends. An option calculator can be downloaded, presently free of charge, from the CBOE web site (www.cboe.com). Your trading platform should also have this capability.

As an example, assume that XYZ stock is trading at $100 a share, the XYZ February 100 call option is at $5, there are 30 days to expiration, and that particular option has implied volatility (seen on an option calculator or trading platform) of 40 percent. You can use an option calculator (or trading platform) to change the assumptions, for example, to where XYZ stock is trading at $105 a share, with 25 days to expiration, and with an implied volatility of 39 percent. In this example, you can forecast time decay and the estimated value of your option assuming your view of the stock under whatever assumptions you choose. You can, for instance, estimate a future option value assuming the stock rises by 5 points, declines by 10 points, or moves sideways. It is common to focus on what happens at the expiration date, but the real action, in many cases, is prior to expiration.

FINAL THOUGHTS

When you purchase a stock, you profit when the stock price rises and you lose when the stock price declines; that is straightforward. But, an option is a different animal because its value is affected by several factors. Understanding strike price versus stock price, volatility, and how an option value erodes over time is important if you want to become a successful option trader; for example, time decay is one reason why option selling can be a higher-probability strategy in comparison to option buying. The option buyer is racing against the clock, whereas the option seller has time on his side. We will cover this extensively in later chapters.

To forward test an option price, various other tools are at your disposal, such as option calculators and analytical tools available through your broker. Forward testing utilizing an option chain, option calculator, trading platform, or the Greeks has certain inherent limitations, but I guess it is always difficult to predict the future. Now let us move on to discuss the Greeks in Chapter 4, a popular subject among option traders.

Tools of the Trade—Greeks

W hen trading options, you need to understand what causes option values to change. If you had a crystal ball to determine this, you would be able to manage and predict your positions. The *Greeks* are essentially the crystal ball for option trading because they provide information about option values based on certain assumptions.

The Greeks are a tool that can enable you to estimate future option values based on a small change in the stock price, time, volatility, and other factors. This chapter covers the Greeks. While learning the Greeks, you will also be learning the specialized option terminology of option traders and be introduced to the way traders think about option strategies. Although the Greeks will not answer all of your questions, they can be a great starting point for learning terminology and how to assess simple and complex option positions at any point in time.

OVERVIEW: GREEK BASICS

How an option price will change in the future can be difficult to predict because there are several factors that can be changing at the same time. Fortunately, option-pricing software is available to isolate and measure the effect of these variables on the future price of an option. Five letters from the Greek alphabet are used (actually, vega is not Greek, but please play along here) to measure each of these factors and are collectively called the "Greeks."

The Greeks enable you to use computer software to help estimate future values and manage your position. It can be useful to have information on your computer screen showing how much money you will theoretically gain or lose based on a one-point increase in your stock, a one-day passage of time, or a one-percentage-point increase in volatility. The Greeks essentially show you at a glance what your future position will be based on these assumptions.

The Greeks measure the sensitivity of your option position (gain or loss) from a small change in price in the underlying stock, time, volatility, and interest rate. The four main Greeks follow:

1. *Delta* measures the change in the price of an option in response to a one-point increase in the underlying stock.

2. *Gamma* measures the change in the delta of an option resulting from a one-point increase in the underlying stock.

3. *Theta* measures the change in the price of an option from the passage of one day in time (time value).

4. *Vega* measures the change in the price of an option from a one-point increase in implied volatility.

Another Greek, *rho*, measures the sensitivity of an option value from a one-point increase in the assumed interest rate. Each individual option has its own delta, gamma, theta, vega, and rho. If you have difficulty remembering theta and vega, remember that the first letter, *T*, in *theta* equates to time, and the first letter, *V*, in *vega* equates to volatility.

Greek Software

The Greeks are included in *option pricing models* provided by specialized option-trading software such as thinkorswim (www.thinkorswim.com), TradeStation (www.tradestation.com), and OptionsXpress (www.optionsxpress.com). The Greeks can also be derived by option calculators, which can be found on various web sites such as that of the Chicago Board Options Exchange (www.cboe.com). It is not necessary for you to understand the model's mathematical details to trade options, but it is helpful to understand the model's assumptions and limitations. The software at your broker's office can calculate Greeks for individual options as well as for your entire option portfolio.

The best-known option pricing model is *Black-Scholes*, developed by Fischer Black and Myron Scholes. Other option pricing models are Cox-Ross and Bi Nomal. Some advanced traders and firms create their own pricing models. The Greeks generated by an option pricing model can help save time by enabling you to view your individual and total positions at a glance. An option pricing model is especially valuable if you have multiple positions or complex positions; for instance, you may be long calls in one position and short puts and/or short calls in another position. Keep in mind that option pricing models showing Greeks are only estimates.

Greek Assumptions

Remember that any number derived from a model is just an estimate based on underlying assumptions. With that in mind, the Greeks are simply theoretical values, meaning they are projections based on the mathematical formulas of the option pricing model. Assumptions of the Black-Scholes model include the following:

- There is a one-unit change.
- One Greek changes, while the other Greeks do not change.
- In determining whether a sign is positive or negative, the Greeks assume that there is an increase in the underlying stock, an increase in delta, an increase in time, an increase in volatility, or an increase in interest rates.

Delta provides an indication of how your option value will change as a result of a small movement in the underlying stock price, assuming all other variables remain constant. Theta provides an indication of one-day time decay, assuming all other variables remain the same. Vega provides an indication of how much your option value will change for each point increase in implied volatility, all other variables remaining the same. These assumptions are useful as a starting point to handle the various moving parts involved in the projection of option values. Rarely do stocks change exactly one point, and never do the other factors affecting option prices remain constant. Therefore, you should approach the Greeks with an open mind, understanding that they can provide valuable information but do not provide all the information you need to quantify your risks and potential rewards with respect to an option position. Keep in mind that a one-point move in a stock trading, for instance, at $100 a share may be more meaningful than a one-point move in a stock trading at $500 or a one-point move in a stock index at 1,500.

It is not necessary for you to understand all the assumptions inherent in option pricing models to become a great trader. Some other option-pricing-model assumptions include the following: no dividend is paid, European exercise, volatility is constant, interest rates remain constant, no commission is charged, and returns are lognormally distributed (I think this is a fancy way of saying that call and put prices are not symmetrical, even though they may be equidistant from the underlying stock price).

Positive or Negative Sign

A plus or minus sign for a Greek is based on the assumption that the underlying stock rises, time is moving forward, volatility is increasing, and the interest rate is rising. A Greek can be a positive or a negative number, depending on whether you are long or short the option and whether it is a call or a put. A summary follows:

- If delta is positive, you profit if the underlying stock rises. If delta is negative, you lose if the underlying stock rises. As a result, a long call and short put would have positive signs, whereas a short call and long put would have negative signs.
- If theta is positive, you profit with the passage of time. If theta is negative, you lose with the passage of time. As a result, a short call and short put would have positive signs, whereas a long call and long put would have negative signs.

TABLE 4.1 Positive versus Negative Greek Signs

Option	Delta	Gamma	Theta	Vega
Long call	+	+	−	+
Long put	−	+	−	+
Short call	−	−	+	−
Short put	+	−	+	−

- If vega is positive, you profit if volatility rises. If vega is negative, you lose if volatility rises. As a result, a long call and long put would have positive signs, whereas a short call and short put would have negative signs.
- Unlike the other Greeks, gamma does not indicate whether you have a profit or loss. Instead, gamma measures the effect on delta based on certain assumptions. Gamma is positive if you are long an option and is negative if you are short an option.
- If rho is positive, you profit if the assumed interest rate rises. If rho is negative, you lose if the assumed interest rate rises. As a result, a long call and short put would have positive signs, whereas a short call and long put would have negative signs.

As result, except for gamma, if your position reflects a gain from an increase in what it measures, then it will show a positive sign. If your position reflects a loss from an increase in what it measures, then it will show a negative sign. An illustration of positive and negative signs is shown in Table 4.1, assuming an at-the-money long call, long put, short call, and short put.

Whether a Greek is positive or negative can be confusing, and I view this as a weakness of the Greeks. Greeks can be expressed as a fraction (or percentage) or converted to dollars to reflect an actual position.

Delta (Fractional Response to Stock)

Delta is a measure of the fractional (percentage) change in an option value in response to a one-point increase in the price of the underlying stock at any given moment. Delta, and the other Greeks, can be expressed as a decimal or percentage and can be converted to dollars. A delta expressed as a decimal can easily be expressed as a percentage; for example, an option with a delta of 0.50 means 50 percent and can be converted to $50. Delta is measured from zero (0 percent) to 1.0 (100 percent) and can be a positive or negative number.

In general, an at-the-money option typically has a delta of approximately 0.50 (50 percent). It is common to refer to such a delta as 50 because it is understood to mean a percentage. I will express the Greeks in decimals, but you should get the idea. This means that a one-point increase in a typical stock results in an increase in the price of a call of $50 (each option represents 100 shares). In this case, the option price changes at a rate of 50 percent relative to the change in the stock price (e.g., if the stock price

TABLE 4.2 Delta Range

Option	Long Call	Long Put	Short Call	Short Put
Delta	0 to 1.00	0 to −1.00	0 to −1.00	0 to 1.00

rises by $1, the option price rises by 50 percent of the $1). As an aside, the delta is typically around 0.55 for calls and 0.45 for puts if they are at-the-money, but it is assumed for simplicity in this book that all at-the-money options have a delta of 0.50. The delta for an in-the-money option is usually greater than 0.50 and increases the further the underlying stock moves in-the-money; for example, an in-the-money call with a delta of 0.70 means that a one-point increase in the stock results in a change in the call of $70 (in other words, a fractional rate of 70 percent relative to the stock). The delta for an out-of-the-money option is usually less than 0.50 and declines the further the underlying stock moves out-of-the-money; for example, an out-of-the-money call with a delta of 0.35 means that a one-point increase in the stock results in a change in the call of $35 (in other words, a fractional rate of 35 percent relative to the stock). The problem with delta is that it only calculates what occurs if there is a one-point increase in the stock and does not calculate the value if there is a one-point decline in the stock, although you can reasonably conclude that it would approximate the change from an increase but in the opposite direction.

A long stock has a delta of positive 1.0 (100 percent), whereas a short stock has a delta of negative 1.0 (100 percent). A long call has a delta ranging from zero (far-out-of-the-money call) to 1.00 (deep-in-the-money call). A short call has a delta ranging from zero (far-out-of-the-money call) to −1.00 (deep-in-the-money call). A long put has a delta ranging from zero (far-out-of-the-money put) to −1.00 (deep-in-the-money put). A short put has a delta ranging from zero (far-out-of-the-money put) to 1.00 (deep-in-the-money put) (see Table 4.2).

Keep in mind that the delta of an option changes throughout the trading day as there are changes in the price of the underlying stock, time, and volatility.

Position Delta   Delta can be expressed as a fraction (or percentage), such as 0.50, or converted to dollars to reflect an actual position, such as $50. Accordingly, delta (and other Greeks) can be converted from a fraction derived from the option pricing model to how it affects your position, stated in dollars; for instance, if a call has a delta of 0.75, it would translate to a *position delta* of $75 (0.75 times $100 per option point). If you own 10 May 100 call options with a delta of 0.75, they translate to a position delta of $750. This means that if the stock rises one point, you will gain approximately $750, and if the stock declines by one point, you will lose approximately $750. The delta is indicating that, at that moment in time, it is as if you own 750 shares of stock. Keep in mind that in the real world, if the stock price rises or declines by one point, the change in the value of your account will likely be different than $750 because of time decay, changes in volatility, and the fact that the delta is an estimate based on statistics.

TABLE 4.3 Example of Position Delta (Converted to Dollars)

Option	Long Call	Long Put	Short Call	Short Put
Delta	$50	−$50	−$50	$50

Your trading platform should help you determine your position delta for long and short option positions. Your position can also be converted to dollars to create a position gamma, position theta, and position vega so you can see the dollar effect of your actual positions held. Your trading platform should be able to convert your position so you can see the dollar impact. At the end of the day, you want to know your total exposure by converting your positions to dollars. To normalize the Greeks to dollars, you typically multiply the number of contracts times the Greek percentages times 100 (if a stock).

Assume that it is January and XYZ stock is trading at $100 per share, and the XYZ long February 100 call has a delta of 0.50. In that case, a $1 change in the price of the stock would result in a 0.50 increase in the option price. Translated to dollars, if the call is originally at $5 and the stock rises one point, the call rises to $5.50. Table 4.3 shows an illustration of the position delta for this example.

Delta as Probability Gauge   The great thing about delta (if you can get excited about these things) is that it can be used to measure the probability of an option finishing in-the-money on the expiration date. If we ignore the sign of the delta, the delta is approximately equal to the probability, according to pricing in the marketplace, that the option will finish in-the-money. For example, an option with a delta of 0.25 (call or put) has an approximate 25 percent chance of finishing in-the-money by at least $0.01 at the expiration date. Likewise, an option with a delta of 0.75 (call or put) has an approximate 75 percent chance of finishing in-the-money (by at least $0.01) at the expiration date. As delta moves closer to 1.00, the option becomes more and more likely to finish in-the-money. As delta moves closer to zero, the option becomes less and less likely to finish in-the-money.

You may be able to see why at-the-money options have deltas close to 0.50. For an at-the-money call option, if it is assumed that price changes of the underlying stock are random, there is a 50 percent chance that the stock will rise (the option goes in-the-money) and a 50 percent chance that the stock will fall (the option goes out-of-the-money). Option software, provided by various brokers, has the capability of showing strike prices and their probability of expiring in-the-money on the expiration date. Option software is typically agnostic with respect to whether a stock will rise or fall because it does not predict the likely direction. If you compare the probability of expiring in-the-money to the delta, you will see that the two percentages are relatively close. Your option software may also provide, for each option, the probability of the underlying stock ever touching the strike price on or before the expiration date.

Gamma (Change in Delta)

Gamma measures the change in the delta of an option as a result of a one-point increase in the stock. The delta of an option is not a stagnant number and instead expands and contracts in response to changing conditions. Delta moves closer to 1.0 as a stock moves deeper in-the-money and moves closer to zero as a stock moves further out-of-the-money. This concept is important from a trader's perspective; for example, assume that in January, XYZ stock is trading at $100 a share, and you own one at-the-money call option. If the stock continues to rise, the call moves from at-the-money to in-the-money. As a result, the delta will accelerate from approximately 0.50 to near 1.0. With a delta of 0.50, your potential gain from a one-point move in the stock is $50; however, with a delta of 0.60 your potential gain is $60; with a delta of 0.70; it is $70, and so on. This is especially useful information if you are short the option because it tells you how much your risk is growing.

If you are long a call option, for instance, as delta increases, it is like owning additional shares of stock, and as delta declines, it is like owning fewer shares of stock. For instance, assume that XYZ stock is trading at $100 a share, and you purchase 10 at-the-money call options at $5 each, for a total cost of $5,000. In this example, you would control 1,000 shares because you purchased 10 call options, but this is considered the equivalent of 500 shares if delta is 0.50. As the delta changes, the equivalent number of shares changes accordingly, so if delta rises to 0.60, it is like owning 600 shares, and if delta declines to 0.40, it is like owning 400 shares at that moment in time. Remember that gamma measures this change in delta as a result of a one-unit change in the underlying stock.

Gamma is sometimes referred to as the curvature of an option because it is the rate at which an option delta changes as the price of the underlying stock changes. For example, assume that it is January and XYZ stock is trading at $100 per share, and you buy one XYZ February 100 call at $5 (position value is $500). Also assume the XYZ long February 100 call has a delta of 0.50 ($50) and a gamma of 0.023 ($2.30). In that case, a $1 increase in the price of the stock would result in a 0.50 ($50) increase in the option price and a $0.023 ($2.30) change in delta. If the call is originally at $5 ($500) and the stock rises one point, the call rises to $5.50 ($550, $5 plus a delta of $0.50), but on the subsequent (second) point rise in the stock, the call rises to $6.23 ($623, $5.50 plus a new delta of $0.523). The 100 shares in this example are multiplied by the new delta of 0.523 to arrive at a new position delta of $52.30 for this particular option. Table 4.4 shows an illustration of gamma and the new delta converted to dollars (position gamma and delta) at various strike prices.

Table 4.4 shows the new position delta of $52.30 for the February 100 call, assuming the stock is at $101 a share (a one-point increase in the stock price). The bottom line is that, in this example, when the stock immediately rises from $100 to $101, you gain $50; when the stock immediately rises from $101 to $102, you gain $52.30; and when the stock immediately rises from $102 to $103, you gain some greater amount. If you were short the call option, gamma would be an indication of your growing exposure. Gamma

TABLE 4.4   Example of Gamma and Its Effect on Delta

Option	Current Delta	Gamma	New Delta if Subsequent Increase
February 90 call	$75	$1.50	$76.50
February 95 call	$65	$2.00	$67.00
February 100 call	$50	$2.30	$52.30
February 105 call	$42	$2.00	$44.00
February 110 call	$23	$1.75	$24.75

TABLE 4.5   Example of Position Gamma (Converted to Dollars)

Option	Long Call	Long Put	Short Call	Short Put
Gamma	$2.30	$2.30	−$2.30	−$2.30

can be viewed as the gift that keeps on giving because it tells you how your position will accelerate (or decelerate). In effect, it can be viewed as the hidden leverage buried in the option.

Gamma reaches its peak when an option is close to at-the-money and declines gradually the further it moves out-of-the-money or in-the-money. A long call and long put have positive gamma and a short call and short put have negative gamma; for example, suppose that an at-the-money long call and long put both have a gamma of 0.023. If the underlying contract rises one point, you add the 0.023 to the 0.50 call delta to get the new delta of 0.523. When you add the gamma of 0.023 to the −0.50 put delta, you get the new delta of −0.477. Positive and negative gammas under various scenarios are summarized in Table 4.5.

Gamma is positive for a long call because the positive delta increases as the underlying stock moves higher. Gamma is positive for a long put because the negative delta contracts as the underlying stock moves higher. Gamma is negative for a short call because the negative delta increases as the underlying stock moves higher. Gamma is negative for a short put because the positive delta contracts as the underlying stock moves higher. I know this is confusing, but just remember for now that delta expands and contracts, and the change in delta from a change in the stock price is measured by gamma.

Theta (Time Decay)

Theta is the sensitivity of an option value in response to a change in time when all other factors remain the same. A long option position has a negative theta, and a short option position has a positive theta. A positive theta represents a potential gain with respect to the passage of time, and a negative theta represents a risk with respect to the passage of time. For example, assume that one XYZ long February 100 call is trading at $5 (position value is $500) and has a theta of −0.15 (−$15). If one day passes in time, assuming

TABLE 4.6 Example of Position Theta (Converted to Dollars)

Option	Long Call	Long Put	Short Call	Short Put
Theta	−$15	−$15	$15	$15

no other changes, you would incur a loss of $15, where the option value would be revised to $485. Positive and negative thetas under various scenarios are summarized in Table 4.6.

Conversely, assume that one XYZ short February 100 call is trading at $5 (position value is $500) and has a $15 theta. If one day passes in time, assuming no other changes, you would have a gain of $15, where the option value would be revised to $485. If you are long a call, the increase of the underlying stock helps to increase the value of the option, but the passage of time hurts the value of the option. Said another way, if price movement in the underlying stock helps you (positive gamma), the passage of time hurts you (negative theta). As a general principle, an option position will have a gamma and a theta of opposite signs. Theta reaches its peak when an option is close to at-the-money and declines gradually the further it moves out-of-the-money or in-the-money. Time decay was covered in Chapter 3. Do not forget to refer to Chapters 7 to 10 for additional analysis of the Greeks.

Vega (Volatility)

Vega measures the change in the theoretical option value for a one-percentage-point increase in implied volatility. Because an option gains value with rising volatility, the vega for both long calls and long puts is positive. Because an option loses value with declining volatility, the vega for both a short call and a short put is negative. A position with a positive vega gains from an increase in implied volatility, whereas a position with a negative vega gains from a decline in implied volatility. If an option has a position vega of 0.12 ($12), with a one-percentage-point increase in volatility, the option will gain 0.12 ($12). For example, assume that one XYZ long February 100 call is trading at $5 (position value is $500) and has a vega of 0.12 ($12), and implied volatility is at 30 percent. If implied volatility is increased to 31 percent, assuming no other changes, you would have a gain by the 0.12 ($12) vega, where the option value would be revised to $512. Positive and negative vegas under various scenarios are summarized in Table 4.7.

TABLE 4.7 Example of Position Vega (Converted to Dollars)

Option	Long Call	Long Put	Short Call	Short Put
Vega	$12	$12	−$12	−$12

Conversely, assume that one XYZ short May 100 call is trading at $5 (position value is $500) and has a −$12 vega, and implied volatility is at 30 percent. If implied volatility is increased to 31 percent, assuming no other changes, you would incur a loss by the $12 vega, where the option value would be revised to $512 (remember that you have a loss on a short option when it increases in value). Vega, like gamma and theta, reaches its peak when an option is close to at-the-money and declines gradually the further it moves out-of-the-money or in-the-money. You should refer to Chapters 7 to 10 for additional analysis of the Greeks, and Chapter 27 for assessing volatility.

Rho (Sensitivity to Interest Rate Change)

Rho measures the absolute change in an option value for a one-percentage-point change in the assumed interest rate. A position with a positive rho rises in value from an increase in the assumed interest rate, whereas a position with a negative rho declines in value from an increase in the assumed interest rate. If an option has a position rho of 0.03 ($3), a one-percentage-point increase in the assumed interest rate increases the option value by 0.03 ($3). For example, assume that an XYZ long February 100 call is trading at $5 (position value is $500) and has a 0.03 ($3) rho, and the assumed interest rate is 2 percent. If the assumed interest rate is increased to 3 percent, assuming no other changes, you would have a gain of $3, where the option value would be revised to $503. Positive and negative rhos under various scenarios are summarized in Table 4.8.

Conversely, assume that an XYZ long February 100 put is trading at $5 (position value is $500) and has a rho of −0.03 (−$3), and the assumed interest rate is 2 percent. If the assumed interest rate is increased to 3 percent, assuming no other changes, you would incur a loss of $3, where the option value would be revised to $497. The interest rate is usually the least important of the inputs into a theoretical pricing model. Rho reaches its peak for a call the further an option is in-the-money. It declines gradually as the option is at-the-money and declines further as it moves out-of-the-money.

POSITION GREEKS

Understanding the technical aspects of the Greeks is good, but at the end of the day, it is more important to understand how much money you would gain or lose on a current or proposed option position. Your trading platform should include option software that shows your position Greeks so that you can see how the profitability of the strategy is

TABLE 4.8 Example of Position Rho (Converted to Dollars)

Option	Long Call	Long Put	Short Call	Short Put
Rho	$3	−$3	$3	−$3

TABLE 4.9 Example of Position Greeks (Converted to Dollars)

Symbol	Delta	Gamma	Theta	Vega
Long 10 ABC calls	$784.38	$42.55	−$46.40	$89.57
Long 10 XYZ puts	−$304.50	$16.09	−$139.37	$134.34
Position Greeks	$479.88		−$185.77	$223.91

affected by changes in stock price, time to expiration, volatility, and so on; for example, Table 4.9 shows sample position Greeks assuming that you are long 10 in-the-money ABC calls and long 10 out-of-the-money XYZ puts.

The Greeks for this position are described as follows:

- Delta is $479.88. A $1 increase in the price of both stocks results in a $479.88 gain.
- Assuming both stocks rise by $1, a subsequent $1 increase in the price of the stocks results in delta rising.
- Theta is −$185.77. A one-day lapse in time results in a $185.77 loss.
- Vega is $223.91. A one-percentage-point rise in volatility results in a $223.91 gain.

The Greeks can be a valuable tool in determining in advance how a change in assumptions can affect your overall position, including spreads (covered in later chapters).

CONVERTING AN OPTION CHAIN TO GREEKS

An option chain does not explicitly provide the Greeks, but it can be used to determine the equivalent of delta, gamma, and theta if you know how to interpret the chain.

Delta and Gamma

There is nothing magical about only using a one-unit point change to calculate the Greeks, so if you want to use another unit of measure (e.g., a five-point change in the underlying stock or a one-month period), that is your prerogative, especially if you think it can help you make money. Assuming that an option chain shows strike prices in five-point increments, you can move up and down the chain to the next strike price to determine what would occur if there was a five-point move in the underlying stock. For example, for an out-of-the-money call option, to estimate the option price from a five-point rise in the stock, move to the strike price five points lower (because that strike price is already five points closer to the underlying stock price); to estimate the option price from a 10-point rise in the stock, move to the strike price 10 points lower; to estimate the option price from a five-point decline in the stock, move to the strike price five points higher; to estimate the option price from a 10-point decline in the stock, move to the strike price 10 points higher. To further illustrate, assume that a call strike price of 100 is at \$5, a call strike price of 105 is at \$2, and a call strike price of 110 is at \$1:

- If the stock rises five points, you could assume that the 110 call would be equal to the 105 strike price of \$2 and the 105 strike price would be equal to the 100 strike price of \$5.
- Likewise, if the stock declines five points, you could assume that the 100 call would be equal to the 105 strike price of \$2 and the 105 strike price would be equal to the 110 strike price of \$1.
- You can continue moving up and down the chain to other strike prices to determine how a 10-point stock change would affect option prices and other factors.
- To estimate gamma, you can move up and down the chain to compare how a 5-point stock change would affect the option price versus a 10-point change, and so on.

This analysis is easy to perform and can give you a reasonable estimate and feel for how option pricing may change. Keep in mind that this technique is only an estimate and does not take into account the effect of changes in volatility and time decay. It should be kept in mind that the delta of an option, calculated by option pricing models, assumes a one-point change, so it is not a perfect tool either. Although knowing the delta of a one-point change may be useful to some degree, adding an analysis of what a five-point change looks like may also be helpful.

Theta

You can use an option chain to estimate time decay (theta) from month to month. For instance, by taking the difference between an option premium that expires in two months and subtracting the option premium from the near-term month, you can determine an estimate of time decay for the first four weeks of the longer-dated-month contract. For example, assume the February at-the-money call option is \$5 and the March premium at the same strike price is \$7. With this information, you could assume that there is a \$2 time decay (\$7 March minus \$5 February) over the first four weeks in the March option because the March premium will look like the February premium at that time (assuming that there is no change in the underlying stock price or in volatility).

MORE ON DELTA

Probably one of the most valuable pieces of information you can derive from the Greeks is delta. Delta not only indicates the likely magnitude of a change in an option value from a small change in the underlying stock, but it is also a probability gauge and can help determine the number of positions needed to hedge a position. Remember that the Greeks produced by typical option pricing models do not address large movements in the underlying stock, volatility, or time. The use of delta as a probability indicator can be a valuable tool in assessing probabilities to establish positions and manage risk.

Delta Rules of Thumb

Understanding the Greeks, or any option strategy, for that matter, can be difficult if you do not have a framework. Option strategies can be broken down into whether they are in-the-money, at-the-money, or out-of-the-money. A more thorough understanding can be obtained if option strategies are broken down even further. General rules of thumb for purposes of this book, assuming that a typical stock is trading at $100 a share, follow:

- A deep-in-the-money option has a strike price 10 or more points in-the-money and typically has a delta of 0.75 to 1.0 (positive or negative). This would be a call strike at 90 and a put strike at 110.
- A slightly-in-the-money option has a strike price five points in-the-money and typically has a delta of 0.55 to 0.75 (positive or negative). This would be a call strike at 95 and a put strike at 105.
- An at-the-money option typically has a delta of 0.45 to 0.55 (positive or negative). This would be a call and put with the strike price of 100.
- A slightly-out-of-the-money option has a strike price five points out-of-the-money and typically has a delta of 0.25 to 0.45 (positive or negative). This would be a call strike at 105 and a put strike at 95.
- A far-out-of-the-money option has a strike price 10 or more points out-of-the-money and typically has a delta of zero to 0.25 (positive or negative). This would be a call strike at 110 and a put strike at 90.

We will use these general rules to analyze the Greeks and option strategies from different angles. An option that is deep-in-the-money is intended to represent an option that consists almost entirely of intrinsic value and has a nominal extrinsic value. A slightly-in-the-money option is intended to represent an option that consists mostly of intrinsic value but has a relatively small extrinsic value. An at-the-money option is intended to represent an option with a strike price the same as, or closest to, the current trading price of the stock. A slightly-out-of-the-money option is intended to represent an option that is fairly close to the at-the-money strike price, and a far-out-of-the-money option is intended to represent an option that is relatively low priced and unlikely ever to become in-the-money. Option strategies will be analyzed in later chapters using these categories for the four basic option strategies of a long call, long put, short call, and short put. Table 4.10 shows general guidelines for each category of option.

Delta and Strike Prices

It is interesting to observe how delta varies based on the strike price versus the stock price. The deeper in-the-money an option, the more the option moves like the underlying

TABLE 4.10 Delta Range Rules of Thumb

Option	Delta Range
Deep-in-the-money	0.75–1.00
Slightly-in-the-money	0.55–0.75
At-the-money	0.45–0.55
Slightly-out-of-the-money	0.25–0.45
Far-out-of-the-money	0–0.25

stock and has a delta closer to 1.0. In this case, it changes at a rate almost point for point equal to that of the underlying stock. If the underlying stock price rises one point, a call will rise by approximately one point. Likewise, if the underlying stock price declines one point, the call will decline by approximately one point.

When an option is far-out-of-the-money, its value may change only a small fraction relative to the stock value but may move a high percentage relative to itself (the option value); for instance, assume XYZ stock is trading at $100 a share and the far-out-of-the-money February 110 call is trading at $1. An immediate two-point increase in the stock might result in a $0.50 increase in the option. In this example, the stock increased 2 percent (from $100 to $102), but the option value increased 50 percent (from $1 to $1.50). Far-out-of-the-money options are the most leveraged.

Assume that XYZ stock is trading at $100 per share. Table 4.11 shows sample call and put deltas at various strike prices for options that expire on the third Friday in February. This is only an illustration because delta can vary for a variety of factors. The numbers were derived from an actual stock (IBM), with the stock trading near $100 a share.

Figure 4.1 is a graph of a call delta, and Figure 4.2 is a graph of a put delta, where the negative sign of the put is ignored (for ease of illustration).

TABLE 4.11 Example of Call versus Put Delta

XYZ Stock Price ($)	Call Delta	Put Delta	Combined
75	$0.95	$0.05	$1.00
80	$0.92	$0.08	$1.00
85	$0.88	$0.12	$1.00
90	$0.81	$0.19	$1.00
95	$0.70	$0.30	$1.00
100	$0.54	$0.46	$1.00
105	$0.37	$0.63	$1.00
110	$0.22	$0.78	$1.00
115	$0.12	$0.88	$1.00
120	$0.06	$0.94	$1.00
125	$0.03	$0.97	$1.00

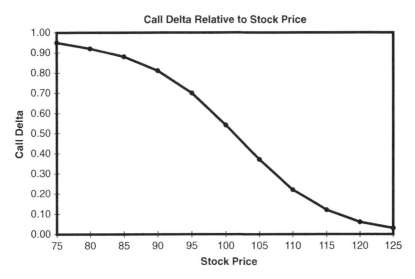

FIGURE 4.1 Call Delta Relative to Stock Price

This example shows the typical pattern of delta. The delta is greatest when the option is deep-in-the-money, approaches 50 percent when the option is at-the-money, and approaches zero as it goes far-out-of-the-money. The delta of the call plus the delta of the put (ignoring the negative sign) is equal to 1. In your trading platform, there may be rounding so that the delta of the call and the absolute value of the put are not exactly equal to 1, but you should get the idea.

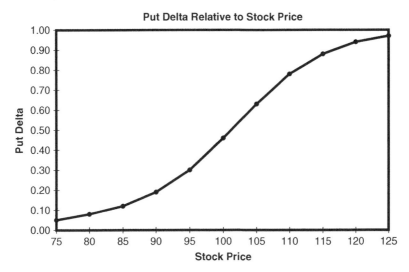

FIGURE 4.2 Put Delta Relative to Stock Price

TABLE 4.12 Example of Call Delta Based on Days to Expiration

XYZ Stock Price ($)	5 Days to Expiration ($)	40 Days to Expiration ($)	68 Days to Expiration ($)	159 Days to Expiration ($)	432 Days to Expiration ($)
75	0.97	0.95	0.91	0.89	0.84
80	0.97	0.92	0.88	0.86	0.80
85	0.96	0.88	0.84	0.80	0.76
90	0.93	0.81	0.77	0.74	0.71
95	0.82	0.70	0.67	0.66	0.65
100	0.53	0.54	0.55	0.57	0.60
105	0.23	0.37	0.42	0.47	0.54
110	0.08	0.22	0.30	0.38	0.48
115	0.03	0.12	0.20	0.29	0.42
120	0.01	0.06	0.13	0.22	0.37
125	0.01	0.03	0.07	0.16	0.32

Delta and Time Remaining to Expiration

It is interesting to observe how delta varies based on time remaining to expiration. As options near expiration, far-out-of-the-money contracts approach a delta of zero and deep-in-the-money contracts approach a delta of 1.00. Assume that it is January and that XYZ stock is trading at $100 per share. Table 4.12 shows the delta for a range of stock prices, where time to expiration is short term (5 days) to longer term (more than 400 days). Table 4.12 was derived from an actual stock (IBM), with the stock trading near $100 a share.

Table 4.12 illustrates that the further in time from the expiration date, delta for an in-the-money option declines, delta for an at-the-money option increases, and delta for an out-of-the-money option increases. Said another way, delta for an in-the-money option rises as the option expiration date approaches (read the table starting with 432 days to expiration and move to shorter time frames), delta for an at-the-money option declines as the expiration date approaches, and delta for an out-of-the-money option declines at a more rapid rate than the at-the-money option.

Figure 4.3 shows that, in this example, the at-the-money call delta has a slight upward bias as a result of an increase in time remaining to expiration.

Figure 4.4 shows that, in this example, the in-the-money call delta declines as a result of an increase in time remaining to expiration.

Figure 4.5 shows that, in this example, the out-of-the-money call delta rises as a result of an increase in time remaining to expiration.

Delta and Volatility

As a general rule, a rise in volatility moves options toward a 0.50 delta. As a result, if volatility rises, the in-the-money option delta declines because it is above 0.50 and the out-of-the-money delta rises because it is below 0.50. For instance, assume that XYZ

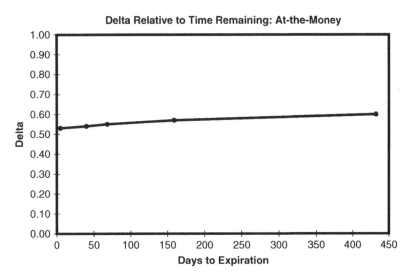

FIGURE 4.3　Delta Relative to Time Remaining: At-the-Money

stock is trading at $100 a share, the February 95 call has a delta of 0.65, and the February 105 call has a delta of 0.42. A rise in volatility, assuming no other changes, will, in general, cause the delta of the February 95 call to decline and the delta of the February 105 call to rise.

Likewise, as a general rule, a decline in volatility moves options away from a 0.50 delta. As a result, if volatility declines, the in-the-money option delta rises and the out-of-the-money delta declines. For instance, assume that XYZ stock is trading at $100 a share,

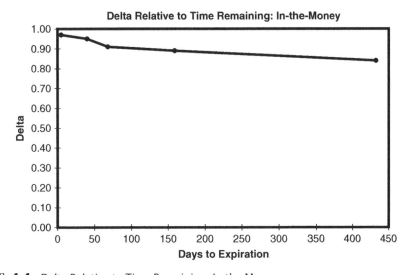

FIGURE 4.4　Delta Relative to Time Remaining: In-the-Money

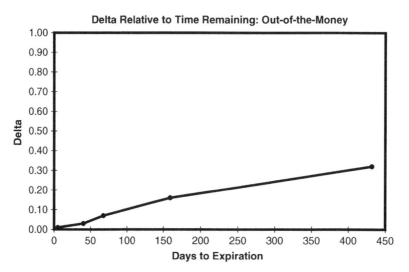

FIGURE 4.5 Delta Relative to Time Remaining: Out-of-the-Money

the February 95 call has a delta of 0.65, and the February 105 call has a delta of 0.42. A decline in volatility, assuming no other changes, will cause the delta of the February 95 call to rise and the delta of the February 105 call to decline.

Delta as Hedge Ratio

Option strategies that attempt to profit from a trading range (as opposed to *directional* strategies) strategy are, in many cases, called *delta-neutral* because a loss on one side of the position is approximately offset by another side. For example, if you own 100 shares of stock and you want to shift to a delta-neutral position, you would sell two at-the-money call options with a delta of −0.50, so that a change in the underlying stock is offset by a change in the option value. A *hedge ratio* can be determined by dividing 1.00 by an option delta. For example, because an at-the-money option typically has a delta of approximately 0.50, the proper hedge ratio is 1.00 divided by 0.50, or two option contracts. Conversely, if you have an existing option position, you may look to hedge that position by buying or selling the underlying stock; for example, for every two call options you are short (and that have a delta of −0.50), you would buy 100 shares.

FINAL THOUGHTS

The Greeks are widely used by option traders because they essentially show you at a glance what your future position will be based on various assumptions and can help manage simple and complex positions. The Greeks can be used as money and risk management tools; for example, if your Greeks indicate that you may lose $300 on a one-point increase in the underlying stock (delta) but gain $500 a day in time decay (theta), you may find the risk–reward profile attractive because you are being well compensated for taking risk. The Greeks can be especially useful in evaluating potential trades and monitoring multiple positions. The Greeks are addressed throughout the remainder of this book. Numerous examples will provide an opportunity to analyze the Greeks from many different perspectives.

CHAPTER 5

Buying versus Selling

C hapter 2 described the fundamentals of buying and selling options, but this chapter goes further, as it compares buying versus selling options, addresses probabilities, describes attributes of buying and selling an option, compares bullish versus bearish strategies, and shows how to roll from one position to another. This chapter discusses outright (single) option positions. Spreads are discussed in Chapter 6 and spread strategies are covered in Chapters 11 to 22.

OVERVIEW

Before entering into an option transaction, you should determine whether the underlying stock is likely to move higher, lower, or sideways and then select an option strategy that best matches that prediction. Because an option has a fixed expiration date, you should determine the time horizon of the move in the underlying stock as well as how far and how fast (velocity) the underlying stock will move. As a result, the best option strategy should involve a determination regarding the direction, timing, and velocity of a move in the underlying stock. In general, you would want to buy an option if you were expecting a large movement in an underlying stock or an increase in volatility, and you would want to sell an option if you were expecting movement in the stock within a range or a decline in volatility, or if you wanted to take advantage of time decay. Remember that options are commonly known as wasting assets because their extrinsic value decays over time.

A way to look at the difference between buying versus selling is that when you buy, your position can be profitable, at expiration, under one scenario, but if you sell, your position can be profitable under three scenarios. For example, assume that in January, XYZ stock is trading at $100, and you are interested in buying or selling a February 105 call. If you purchase the call, it will be profitable (ignoring the premium), at expiration, only if the stock rises above the 105 strike price; however, if you sell the call, it is profitable (ignoring the premium), at expiration, if the stock declines below $100, moves sideways near $100, or rises, as long as it does not rise above the 105 strike price. Likewise, if you purchase a 95 strike price put, it will be profitable if the stock declines below the 95 strike price. If you sell the put, it is profitable if the stock rises, moves sideways, or declines to the 95 strike price.

COMPARING LONG AND SHORT OPTIONS

You should consider buying (going long) an option if you have confidence that you can predict the direction and magnitude of a stock move. You should consider selling (going short) an option if you are comfortable estimating a trading range and you want short-term statistical probabilities on your side. There are advantages and disadvantages associated with buying and selling options. Table 5.1 shows a side-by-side comparison of long versus short option characteristics.

When you buy or sell an option, a key factor that will determine whether or not you profit from the trade is the strike price you choose. A short option, for example, achieves its maximum profit, at expiration, if the underlying stock finishes at or below the strike price of a call or at or above the strike price of a put. When writing an option, if you select a strike price that is at-the-money, then you do not leave yourself a lot of room for error; however, if you choose a strike price far-out-of-the-money, the stock can move against you to the level of the strike price, and you can still achieve a maximum profit. Of course, you will collect less premium for the out-of-the-money option, but it may be worth the trade-off. A short option can be structured so that it has a higher probability of success, but the downside is a lower relative premium collected, and you can lose more money than the premium collected.

Delta can be used as a general guideline to determine what options are best to buy and sell. If you want to see a breakdown, Chapter 4 provides a sample of call and put deltas for strike prices from 75 to 125, assuming that a stock is trading at $100. Table 5.2 shows general guidelines, using delta, regarding the probability of an option expiring in-the-money based on whether the option is deep-in-the-money, slightly-in-the-money, at-the-money, out-of-the-money, slightly-out-of-the-money, or far-out-of-the-money. As a reminder, delta can be used to approximate the statistical probability of an option finishing in-the-money on the expiration date.

Based on Table 5.2, for example, if you are bullish and want to buy an option, then purchasing a slightly-in-the-money option (call at 95 strike price) may provide a reasonable risk–reward trade because it offers a statistical probability of between a 55 and a 75 percent chance of expiring in-the-money. Conversely, if you are bullish and want to sell an option, then a far-out-of-the-money put option (put at 90 strike price) may be a reasonable choice because it offers a statistical advantage. If you are bearish and want to buy an option, then purchasing a slightly-in-the-money option (put at 105 strike price) may

TABLE 5.1 Long versus Short Options

Characteristic	Long Call or Put	Short Call or Put
Direction	Bullish if a call, bearish if a put	Bearish if a call, bullish if a put; at expiration, want stock price below call strike, above put strike
Debit or credit	Debit	Credit
Profit potential	Unlimited	Limited to premium collected
Risk	Limited to premium paid	Unlimited
Time decay	Negative	Positive
Volatility	Increase is positive, decrease is negative	Increase is negative, decrease is positive
Delta	Positive if a call, negative if a put	Negative if a call, positive if a put
Gamma	Positive	Negative
Theta	Negative	Positive
Vega	Positive	Negative
Breakeven	Stock at strike price plus premium paid if a call, minus premium if a put	Stock at strike price plus premium collected if a call, minus premium if a put
Margin	Premium paid at time of purchase	Required
How to exit	Offset in closing transaction, exercise, or expire worthless	Offset in closing transaction, assignment, or expire worthless
IRA	Permitted	Call not permitted unless own stock (covered), put permitted if fully funded
Main advantages	Unlimited profit potential; risk is limited; leverage	Time decay; probabilities on your side
Main disadvantages	Can cost more than you are willing to pay; time decay; can lose entire premium	Limited profit potential; risk unlimited
Skill required	Correct on direction, timing, and magnitude of stock	Predicting a trading range
Profitable	Narrow set of circumstances	Number of circumstances

provide a reasonable risk–reward trade. If you are bearish and want to sell an option, then a far-out-of-the-money call option (call at 110 strike price) may be a reasonable choice because it offers a statistical advantage.

Probabilities Favor the Seller

Keep in mind that the statistical percentages are based on representative delta amounts and that delta can be viewed as a measurement of the likelihood that an option will finish (by $0.01) in-the-money. If you look closer at the delta numbers, you will realize that the

TABLE 5.2 Probability Rules of Thumb

Option	Sample Call Strike Price	Sample Put Strike Price	Probability of Expiring In-the-Money (%)
Deep-in-the-money	90 and lower	110 and higher	75–100
Slightly-in-the-money	95	105	55–75
At-the-money	100	100	45–55
Slightly-out-of-the-money	105	95	25–45
Far-out-of-the-money	110 and higher	90 and lower	0–25

statistical probabilities are naturally slanted in favor of the option seller. For example, if an at-the-money has a 0.50 delta, it may initially appear that the option buyer has a 50 percent chance of making money and the option seller has a 50 percent chance of making money—but this is not the case. A 0.50 delta means that there is a 50 percent chance that the option will expire in-the-money. As a result, an at-the-money option that costs $5 ($500) and has a delta of 0.50 does not mean that there is a 50 percent chance that the buyer will be able to sell the option for at least $5 ($500) if he waits until option expiration.

Assume that in January, you purchase a February 100 at-the-money call option for $5 ($500) and that you are trying to determine the statistical probability that you will break even and recoup the $5 ($500) premium. At first glance, you may think there is 50 percent probability because the option is at-the-money and has a delta of 0.50 (remember that delta is a probability gauge, as well). However, remember that delta is only a rough measurement of whether the option will expire by $0.01 in-the-money, not $5 in-the-money. You would therefore need to determine the probability of the option expiring $0.01 above the 105 strike price (100 strike price plus the $5 premium paid). Therefore, you would need to determine the delta of the February 105 strike price, instead of the February 100 strike price. If you assume the February 105 option has a delta of 0.40, this tells you that there is approximately a 40 percent chance that the underlying stock will expire above the 105 exercise price, your break-even point. This tells you that, in this example, an option buyer has a 40 percent chance of breaking even, but a seller has a 60 percent chance.

In baseball, a tie goes to the runner; in options, it seems that a tie goes to the option seller because the option seller profits if the underlying stock does not move sufficiently. If the underlying stock moves sideways, the at-the-money or out-of-the-money option seller is allowed to earn the entire premium, and the buyer loses the entire premium. Therefore, delta does not equate to the probability of profiting, but instead is the probability of finishing in-the-money, which is nice to know but does not put food on the table.

OPTION BUYING

In general, buying an in-the-money option can enable you to benefit from a rise in a stock almost dollar for dollar, with a built-in limited risk feature and the ability to take advantage of leverage. Buying an at-the-money or out-of-the-money option has the benefit of lower cost, but if the underlying stock does not move far and fast enough, an option buyer may lose money because of time decay. Examples throughout this book illustrate these principles. Remember that extrinsic value is not the friend of the option buyer because it represents the premium subject to time decay.

The option buyer should have the mind-set that he may hold an option until expiration, but the more likely scenario is that the buyer will offset the position prior to expiration when he determines that his price target is met, facts have changed, or he is unwilling to take further risk in the position. For instance, you may be bullish on a stock that is going to report earnings in three days, and you anticipate that the stock will rise in value ahead of the earnings release. You can buy a call, in this example, three days ahead of earnings and sell (offset) the call prior to the release of earnings. You can even offset your position the same day it is bought.

Buying an option can make a lot of sense because the purchase of a deep-in-the-money call can serve as a proxy for owning stock, and a put can serve as a proxy for shorting stock. Buying a deep-in-the-money option can be a cost-effective, limited-risk strategy preferable to trading the underlying stock itself. For example, if you believe a stock will increase in value, you can buy a deep-in-the-money call that will enable you to pay less than the full value of the stock but enable you to benefit almost dollar for dollar with the rise in the value of the stock. If you believe a stock will decline in value, you can buy a deep-in-the-money put that will enable you to profit from a decline in the stock without having to short stock. As mentioned in Chapter 2, depending on the rules in effect, the shorting of a stock may be subject to the uptick rule. The uptick rule does not permit the shorting of a stock unless the last trade was higher than the previous trade (an uptick). Buying a put can be an effective way to avoid the uptick rule if it is in effect.

Momentum Trading by Buying Options

During the roaring Internet bull market of the 1990s, some traders would buy a large number of far-out-of-the-money call options for cents on the dollar on high-flying technology stocks that were going through stock splits. When a stock goes through a two-for-one stock split, the share price, strike prices, and option prices are cut in half, whereas the number of shares and options double. Similarly, a three-for-one stock split would cut the prices to one third and would triple the number of shares and options. Traders would prepare a calendar of stocks planning to split, indicating whether they were going through a two-for-one or three-for-one split. Traders observed that stocks would rise after the announcement of the split and leading up to the split date and, in many cases, after the split date. I understand that there are studies that indicate that, in the long run, companies that split their stock do not have a higher return than those that do not; however, the 1990s were a rare time. In many cases, companies that announced a stock split were doing so because they were optimistic about their results and prospects for the future (not to mention that it juiced their stock price during a bubble period). Identifying stocks that were going through splits was an effective way to find out which companies were bullish on themselves.

Some traders observed that a stock that would rise five points a day prior to a split would often rise by five points immediately after the split, and that was the equivalent of a 10-point move on a stock splitting two for one. As a result, a stock going through a two-for-one stock split would have twice the volatility immediately after the split, whereas a stock going through a three-for-one stock split would have three times the volatility. Some traders bought a large number of far-out-of-the-money options on high-flying stocks such as Dell, Intel, Microsoft, and other software and technology stocks. If you look at more recent charts of these stocks, they are as flat as the plains of Kansas or slant in a downward direction like a ski slope. But they were not flat or downward during those days. Instead, there was a frenzy to buy high-flying technology stocks involved in the computer industry, software, and the Internet. Of course, when the Internet bubble burst in 2000 and a bear market began, buying far-out-of-the-money call options was no longer a viable strategy. But, not to worry: You could buy far-out-of-the-money put options if you believed a stock (or the market) would decline dramatically. You just had to know in which type of market you were.

OPTION SELLING

The object of selling an out-of-the-money option can be to make a limited but consistent profit, by stacking the statistical probability on your side. When you write an option, the option premium is your maximum profit (ignoring your ability to offset it and establish a new position) and is set at the time of sale. Option writing, as a result, offers the unique opportunity to know in advance the target profit from the transaction. As a result, you can establish a goal to earn a certain amount each month or quarter from the sale of options.

When selling an out-of-the-money option, you should first determine where the underlying stock will not go; for instance, when you sell a far-out-of-the-money option, you are concerned about where stock prices will not be headed, which can be an easier task than determining where a stock is headed, when, and to what magnitude. When selling an option, you can still make money, even though your market prediction was incorrect, as long as there is not drastic movement in the stock in the wrong direction. For example, you may believe that the market is ready to surge higher, so you sell out-of-the-money puts; if the market moves sideways or lower by a small amount (to the strike price), you can still make a profit. As long as the underlying stock does not make a move through the strike price, the option seller should be able to profit if the position is held to the expiration date.

Writing a far-out-of-the-money option can provide you with a statistical edge, where you can take advantage of time decay, while not having to worry about minor movements in the underlying stock. Selling an out-of-the-money option can be an appropriate strategy investment for a trader who is not comfortable predicting precisely the direction of an underlying stock, index, ETF, or futures.

A far-out-of-the-money option is considered the most leveraged, and some traders find the risk–reward trade-off to be worthwhile. A far-out-of-the-money call option can usually be written at a fairly inexpensive price, which is why some option sellers initially shy away from them, but to an informed option trader, it can offer a leveraged way to make a higher-probability trade and possibly consistent profit. Keep in mind that greater risk accompanies the potential for greater profit. Although the markets can have a tendency to move in a range or to trend, which creates an environment that can be attractive to option selling, the market can break out of its range or trend and create havoc (that is a euphemism for losing money) for option sellers. On occasion, when selling naked options, the ups and downs (volatility) are so severe that it seems you should wear a seat belt and helmet.

Many publications emphasize the difference between option buyers and sellers by contrasting the rights of option buyers and the obligations of option sellers. This can imply that the terms of option contracts give all the rights to buyers and no rights to sellers. It should be noted, however, that option sellers have a number of choices they can make; for instance, an option seller, like an option buyer, can offset his position in the marketplace at any time during regular trading hours. Also, an option seller can manage overall risk by buying and selling the underlying stock to hedge his current position or adding other options to limit risk. Remember that if you write an option, you do not have to stay short until expiration; instead, you can offset it at any time (the market is open).

The Option Seller Has a Margin Requirement

When you buy an option, the entire cost of the long option position is typically required to be paid at the time an option order is executed. For example, if you enter into a long call, 100 percent of the cost of the position must be paid up front (your broker may allow you to add money to your account to cover the purchase).

Option margin rules are concerned with short option positions. In general, when a trader enters into a short option position, he is required to post (have on deposit by the date set by the broker) an initial margin of an amount specified by the broker, exchange, or clearing organization. Thereafter, the position is monitored daily. If the amount of money in the margin account falls below the specified maintenance margin, the trader is required to take appropriate action to bring the account up to the initial margin level. A margin requirement for options is the amount an option seller is required to deposit and maintain to cover a position as collateral. It is the amount of money or other assets that must be deposited by an option seller to ensure performance of the seller's obligations under an option contract.

Margin rules are covered in Chapter 30. Briefly, margin on equities is typically determined under the 20 percent standard margin or portfolio margin, and margin on futures is typically determined under the Standard Portfolio Analysis of Risk Assessment (SPAN) margining system.

In general, under traditional margining rules, the minimum initial margin requirement for uncovered options is set at the option premium credited plus 20 or 25 percent (15 percent for a broad-based index) of the underlying security or index minus the amount the option is out-of-the-money, subject to a minimum. I refer to this as the *20 percent standard margin*. The 20 percent standard margin requirement is a strategy-based methodology that primarily uses the price of the underlying stock or index as a starting point. For example, if XYZ stock is trading at $100 a share and you sell a call with a strike price of $100, the 20 percent standard margin requirement is $2,000 (ignoring the premium collected). If you sell a 100 strike price put, the standard margin requirement would also be $2,000 (ignoring the premium collected). If you sell a 105 strike price call, the out-of-the-money amount is considered to be $500 (five points times $100) and would reduce the margin requirement.

In contrast, *portfolio margining* is a method for computing margin option positions based on the risk profile of the account, rather than on fixed percentages, for qualified customers. The portfolio margining method uses a risk-based scheme, instead of a strategy-based scheme, by using theoretical pricing models to calculate the loss of a position at different price points above and below the current stock or index price. Portfolio margining will essentially stress test a position, assuming that the underlying instrument rises and falls by a certain percentage such as up or down 5 or 8 percent.

Futures margins are typically determined by the SPAN margining system, which takes into account all positions in a customer's account and, in general, usually produces a lower margin requirement than the 20 percent standard margin methodology. Portfolio margining may bring equity margin rules more in line with futures margin requirements under various circumstances. SPAN margining, like portfolio margining, essentially stress tests a position.

For options, the margin is essentially a bookkeeping entry and does not represent the actual use of money. As a result, interest can be earned in an account for the full amount; for example, if you have $100,000 in a brokerage account and you have a margin requirement of $60,000 from option sales, you still earn interest on the entire $100,000 plus the additional premium collected.

Leverage and margin are interrelated because the margin requirement affects the amount of leverage allowed by a seller of an option. The Federal Reserve Board and the option exchange where an option trades establish minimum margin requirements for short options. A broker or exchange may impose more stringent margin requirements. You should contact your own brokerage regarding its minimum margin requirements because the requirements can vary from firm to firm.

BULLISH VERSUS BEARISH

Buying an option does not automatically mean that you are bullish, and selling an option does not necessarily mean that you are bearish. Instead, if you are bullish, you can buy a call or sell a put, and if you are bearish, you can buy a put or sell a call. In general, if you buy an option, you want unlimited profit potential with limited risk, and if you sell an option, you want a high probability of success in exchange for limited profit potential (with unlimited risk). Following is a comparison of buying versus selling options by bullish versus bearish strategies.

Bullish: Long Call versus Short Put

Although a long call and a short put are bullish strategies, the similarities, risks, and rewards seem to end there; for example, buying a call is a limited-risk strategy, and selling a put is an unlimited-risk strategy. Which strategy is better in your particular circumstance depends on your risk profile, time frame, and anticipated magnitude of the move. If you are bullish in the short run, then the purchase of a call may be appropriate; however, if you are bullish but believe that the underlying stock can fluctuate to a lower level and that it will take time for the bullish move to occur, then selling an out-of-the-money put may be appropriate. Table 5.3 compares the characteristics of a long call to the characteristics of a short put.

Bearish: Long Put versus Short Call

A long put and a short call are bearish strategies but have opposite risks and rewards. For example, buying a put is a limited-risk strategy, and selling a call is an unlimited-risk strategy. Which strategy is better in your particular circumstance depends on your risk profile, time frame, and anticipated magnitude of the move. If you are bearish in the short run, then the purchase of a put may be appropriate; however, if you are bearish but believe that the underlying stock can fluctuate to a higher level and that it will take time for the bearish move to occur, then selling an out-of-the-money call may be appropriate. Table 5.4 compares the characteristics of a long put versus the characteristics of a short call.

LEARNING HOW TO ROLL

You should be familiar with *rolling* options. When you roll an option position, you offset your current position and reestablish a new position on the same underlying stock. In some cases, you may offset your current position because there are only a few days left in an option's expiration cycle and you are interested in reestablishing a new position in

TABLE 5.3 Long Call versus Short Put

Characteristic	Long Call	Short Put
Direction	Bullish	Bullish; at expiration, want stock price at or above put strike (range)
Debit or credit	Debit	Credit
Profit potential	Unlimited	Limited to premium collected
Risk	Limited to premium paid	Unlimited
Time decay	Negative	Positive
Volatility	Increase is positive, decrease is negative	Increase is negative, decrease is positive
Delta	Positive	Positive
Gamma	Positive	Negative
Theta	Negative	Positive
Vega	Positive	Negative
Breakeven	Stock at strike price plus premium paid	Stock at strike price minus premium collected
Margin	Premium paid at time of purchase	Required
How to exit	Offset in closing transaction, exercise, or expire worthless	Offset in closing transaction, assignment, or let expire worthless
IRA	Permitted	Permitted if covered or fully funded
Main advantages	Unlimited profit potential; risk is limited; leverage	Time decay; probabilities on your side
Main disadvantages	Can cost more than you are willing to pay; time decay; can lose entire premium	Limited profit potential; risk unlimited
Skill required	Correct on direction, timing, and magnitude of stock	Predicting a trading range
Profitable	Narrow set of circumstances	Number of circumstances

the subsequent expiration month. In other cases, you may roll options to minimize risk, cut losses, and/or take into account your new view of the market. For example, when you first established your option positions, you may have been bearish and now you have changed to bullish. When rolling, you can establish the new position with the same or a different number of options and with the same or a different strike price and expiration date. You are readjusting your option positions to take advantage of opportunities, play defense, or take into account new market conditions.

Rolling up occurs when one position is closed out at a lower strike price and another position is opened at a higher strike price (offset long February 100 call and buy February 110 call). *Rolling down* means closing out one option at one strike price and simultaneously opening another option at a lower strike price (offset long February 100 put and buy February 95 put). *Rolling out* means one option position is closed at a near-term

TABLE 5.4 Long Put versus Short Call

Characteristic	Long Put	Short Call
Direction	Bearish	Bearish; at expiration want stock price at or below call strike (range)
Debit or credit	Debit	Credit
Profit potential	Unlimited	Limited to premium collected
Risk	Limited to premium paid	Unlimited
Time decay	Negative	Positive
Volatility	Increase is positive, decrease is negative	Increase is negative, decrease is positive
Delta	Negative	Negative
Gamma	Positive	Negative
Theta	Negative	Positive
Vega	Positive	Negative
Breakeven	Stock at strike price minus premium	Stock at strike price plus premium collected
Margin	None; premium paid at time of purchase	Required
How to exit	Offset in closing transaction, exercise, or let expire worthless	Offset in closing transaction, assignment, or expire worthless
IRA	Permitted	Not permitted unless own stock (covered)
Main advantages	Unlimited profit potential; risk is limited; leverage	Time decay; probabilities on your side
Main disadvantages	Can cost more than you are willing to pay; time decay; can lose entire premium	Limited profit potential; risk unlimited
Skill required	Correct on direction, timing, and magnitude of stock	Predicting a trading range
Profitable	Narrow set of circumstances	Number of circumstances

expiration date and another position is opened at the same strike but at a longer-term expiration date (offset long February 100 call and buy March 100 call). *Rolling up and out* occurs by closing out one option at one strike price and simultaneously opening another option at a higher strike price and a later expiration date (offset long February 100 call and buy March 105 call). *Rolling down and out* occurs by closing out one option at one strike price and simultaneously opening another option at a lower strike price and a later expiration date (offset long February 100 put and buy March 95 put). *Rolling back* is when an investor replaces an old option position with a new one having an earlier expiration date and the same strike price (offset long March 100 call and buy February 100 call). This is sometimes referred to as a roll backward. Flipping (I made up this term) occurs by closing out a call option and simultaneously opening a put option to change directions (offset short February 105 call and sell February 95 put) or by closing out a put option and simultaneously opening a call option to change directions (offset short February 95 put and sell February 105 call).

FINAL THOUGHTS

Consistent profits are possible by selling options, without having to pick the home run along the way. One advantage of selling an option is that close is sometimes good enough, in comparison to the situation of the option buyer, who needs to be more precise in his timing and predictions. When you buy an option, in effect, you are playing on the home turf of the option seller to the extent of the extrinsic value, and we all know that playing on the home field can offer a distinct advantage. You should develop strategies for both buying and selling options. Buying calls can be a good place to start to learn how to trade options.

A reasonable approach, in general, can be to buy an option on some underlying instrument and sell an option on another; for example, buying an option on a stock can make sense because a long option is typically a bet that volatility will increase (or the stock will move in a particular direction). Conversely, selling an option on an index, ETF, or stock index futures can make sense because a short option takes advantage of time decay.

CHAPTER 6

Understanding Spread Terminology

W hat is in a name? If the question relates to options, the answer is—a lot. You should understand option terminology so you can effectively use your option trading platform (supplied by your broker) to become a better trader. Your trading platform should enable you to enter and exit simple and complex positions, such as spreads, with the click of a mouse. This chapter defines a *spread* from the perspective of buying versus selling, debit versus credit, and bull versus bear and provides examples of spreads. Spread strategies are covered extensively throughout this book.

WHAT IS A SPREAD?

A spread trade is the standard bread-and-butter type of trade of many professionals. In the business world, a spread can have a variety of meanings but generally refers to the difference between two (or more) prices from different *sides*, or *legs*, of a trade. For example, outside the world of options, a spread trade may involve buying the S&P 500 index and selling (shorting) the Russell 2000 index in an attempt to profit from large capitalization stocks outperforming small capitalization stocks. A spread trade may involve, for example, buying the 30-year bond and selling the 2-year note. Another type of spread is the *bid/ask spread*, which represents the difference in the price at which an instrument can be purchased versus bought, as determined by the marketplace.

An option *spread* is the purchase (or sale) of one option contract against the sale (or purchase) of another option contract on the same underlying stock; for example, you can buy one XYZ April 100 call and sell one XYZ April 110 call. An option spread can be executed with all calls or puts, or with a combination of calls and puts, and can be executed for a debit, credit, or zero cost.

When describing an option spread, it is assumed that all options are based on the same underlying instrument (stock) and are of the same type (all calls or all puts), unless otherwise noted. For example, a common type of spread would be to sell simultaneously one call option at one strike price and buy one call option at a higher strike price on the same underlying stock, where the call purchased serves to limit the risk of the call sold. A spread typically consists of a long market position and a short market position, but this is not always the case.

A spread trade consists of option positions, referred to as legs (in the previous example, the XYZ April 100 call is one leg and the XYZ April 110 call is a second leg). In a two-legged spread, a trader buys one leg and sells the other. The two legs typically profit from opposing directional price movements. Spreads are typically executed in your trading platform in one order, even though there are multiple legs.

Reasons for Spreading

Instead of either buying or selling an option *outright* (no spread is involved), a spread can enable you to fine-tune the amount of premium paid or collected, limit potential losses, minimize fluctuations in your account, and reduce margin. If you are buying an option, a spread can enable you to collect premium to finance, in effect, a portion of the purchased leg or side. If you are writing an option, a spread can enable you to convert an unlimited risk position into a defined risk position. A spread can provide traders more ways to profit; for example, a spread trader can be expressing an opinion about whether the spread will widen or narrow and not necessarily whether the underlying stock will rise or fall in price. A short spread position is typically recognized as a lower-risk trade than an uncovered short option. As a result, margin requirements can be substantially reduced. Spread trading is popular among professional traders. In addition, a broker may not permit uncovered short options in an IRA but may permit defined-risk spread trades.

Depending on your trading platform and broker, you can generally enter the same types of orders for outright (single position) and spread orders as you can for stocks. Your trading platform should permit you to enter and exit spreads as one order rather than entering separate orders. As a result of entering an order in this manner, you will not be executed on only one side of a transaction, unless the entire transaction is executed. The types of option orders are covered in Chapter 31.

SPREAD BUYING VERSUS SELLING

What constitutes buying an option versus selling an option may seem obvious at first, but in the world of options, it is not that simple; for example, buying may involve purchasing a call or a put outright to open a position. However, when trading options, it is common to sell one option and buy another option as part of the same transaction in a spread. If an option is bought for an amount greater than that for which the option is sold, it is for a debit and can be viewed, in general, as a purchase, even though the transaction as a whole involves buying and selling. If the option is sold for an amount greater than that

TABLE 6.1 Spread: General Rules

Spread Strategy	Debit/Credit	Risk-Reward General Rule
Buy	Debit	Limited loss, limited profit
Sell	Credit	Limited loss, limited profit

for which the option is purchased, it is for a credit and can be viewed, in general, as a sale. Table 6.1 shows that a spread typically has limited risk and limited reward.

For example, assume that in January, XYZ stock is trading at $100. If you purchase a February 100 call at $5 and sell a February 110 call at $1, you have executed a call debit spread for $4, and this would be considered a purchase. If you sell a February 100 call at $5 and buy a February 110 call at $1, you have executed a call credit spread for $4, and this would be considered a sale. The maximum potential profit of the call debit spread is $600 (difference in the strike prices times 100 shares minus the $400 premium paid) and the maximum loss is the $400 premium paid. The maximum potential loss of the call credit spread is $600 (difference in the strike prices times 100 shares minus the $400 premium collected) and the maximum gain is the $400 premium collected.

Debit versus Credit Spread

Option positions are commonly classified according to whether they produce a debit (*debit spreads*), in which the amount paid is greater than the amount collected, or a credit (*credit spreads*), in which the amount collected is greater than the amount paid. *Debit spreads*, in general, attempt to profit by directional bets as a net buyer. *Credit spreads*, in general, attempt to take advantage of time decay as a net seller:

- A *net debit* transaction typically means that you are long a position and want the underlying stock to move in a certain direction, by a certain amount, and within a certain time frame.
- A *net credit* typically implies that you are short the option position and benefit from a trading range, the passage of time, and declining volatility.

A debit–spread strategy attempts to profit from the widening of the spread between the various options. A credit–spread strategy attempts to profit from the narrowing of the spread between the various options. Table 6.2 provides a general definition of a credit versus a debit spread.

An option executed as a debit is typically considered a long position, whereas an option position executed for a credit is typically considered a short position. A debit position usually means that the position will lose money because of time decay, unless there is sufficient price movement in the underlying stock. A credit position typically means that the position will lose money if there is sufficient price movement in the wrong direction:

TABLE 6.2 Credit versus Debit Spread

Spread Type	Example
Debit spread	Buy in, at, or out-of-the-money and sell farther out-of-the-money; profit from widening of spread
Credit spread	Sell at-the-money or out-of-the-money and buy farther out-of-the-money; profit from narrowing of spread

- A call debit spread typically wants the underlying stock to increase in price.
- A put debit spread typically wants the underlying stock to decline in price.
- A call credit spread typically wants the underlying stock to decline in price and move sideways and time to pass.
- A put credit spread typically wants the underlying stock to rise in price and move sideways and time to pass.

Stated another way, in general, a debit position needs movement to occur, whereas a credit position profits when movement does not occur (in a particular direction). Following are examples of debit and credit spreads that will be discussed more thoroughly in later chapters. Each example assumes that in January, XYZ stock is trading at $100.

Call debit spread: Buy XYZ February 100 call for $5 and sell February 105 call for $2, for a debit of $3.

Put debit spread: Buy XYZ February 100 put for $5 and sell February 95 put for $2, for a debit of $3.

Call credit spread: Sell XYZ February 100 call for $5 and buy February 105 call for $2, for a credit of $3.

Put credit spread: Sell XYZ February 100 put for $5 and buy February 95 put for $2, for a credit of $3.

Table 6.3 summarizes call and put debit and credit spreads.

TABLE 6.3 Call/Put Debit versus Credit Spreads

Spread Strategy	Strike Prices	Risk–Reward	Profitable
Call debit spread (also called bull call spread)	Buy lower strike call, sell higher strike call	Limited loss, limited profit	Bullish
Put debit spread (also called bear put spread)	Buy higher strike put, sell lower strike put	Limited loss, limited profit	Bearish
Call credit spread (also called bear call spread)	Sell lower strike call, buy higher strike call	Limited loss, limited profit	Bearish and neutral
Put credit spread (also called bull put spread)	Sell higher strike put, buy lower strike put	Limited loss, limited profit	Bullish and neutral

Bull versus Bear Spread

An option strategy is often described from the perspective of how the strategy is profitable, primarily based on whether it profits when the underlying stock rises (bullish), declines (bearish), or moves within a range (neutral or sideways). Keep in mind that some option strategies can be profitable in more than one market environment; for example, if you sell an out-of-the-money call option, it can be profitable if the stock declines, moves sideways, or rises to the strike price (ignoring the premium). This profit profile is difficult to describe quickly, so it is simply described as bearish because that is the primary direction in which the stock needs to move so a profit is generated most easily. Similarly, if you sell an out-of-the-money put option, it can be profitable if the stock rises, moves sideways, or declines to the strike price (ignoring the premium). This profit profile is described as bullish because that is the primary direction in which a profit is generated.

There are a host of option strategies that are nondirectional and do not attempt to profit when the underlying stock moves in one direction or the other. Instead, such strategies profit when the underlying stock moves within a selected trading range. Other terms used to describe a trading range are *neutral*, sideways, and sluggish. The word *neutral* means that the option strategy will profit if the underlying stock moves sideways, but it can also be profitable if it moves in a particular direction, as long as it does not pierce the strike price at expiration (ignoring the premium). Table 6.4 summarizes the definitions of a bull, bear, and neutral spread for long and short positions.

Strategies that attempt to profit from a trading range (nondirectional) strategy, in many cases, are called delta-neutral because a loss on one side, or leg, of a position is approximately offset by another side or leg, as long as the underlying stock stays within a trading range; for example, a loss on the call side of a spread may be offset by a gain on the put side.

A spread strategy can be viewed from the perspective of whether it primarily profits from a bullish or bearish move in the underlying stock. Following are examples of bear and bull spread strategies. Each example assumes that the underlying stock is selling at $100 a share in January.

TABLE 6.4 Long Call versus Short Put

Term	Long Option Definition	Short Option Definition
Bull spread	Profit if underlying stock rises	Profit if underlying stock rises, but also if underlying stock moves sideways or moderately lower
Bear spread	Profit if underlying stock declines	Profit if underlying instrument stock declines, but also if underlying stock moves sideways or moderately higher
Neutral spread	Profit if underlying stock moves within a range	Profit if underlying stock moves within a range

Bull call spread (same as call debit spread): Buy XYZ February 100 call for $5 and sell February 105 call for $2, for a debit of $3.

Bear put spread (same as put debit spread): Buy XYZ February 100 put for $5 and sell February 95 put for $2, for a debit of $3.

Bear call spread (same as call credit spread): Sell XYZ February 100 call for $5 and buy February 105 call for $2, for a credit of $3.

Bull put spread (same as put credit spread): Sell XYZ February 100 put for $5 and buy February 95 put for $2, for a credit of $3.

A bull call spread and bull put spread are profitable primarily if the underlying stock moves higher, and a bear call spread and bear put spread are profitable primarily if the underlying stock declines.

Vertical, Ratio, and Calendar Spreads

A spread is not always described as debit versus credit or bull versus bear. Instead, a spread can also be described based on whether the options expire in the same month but have different strike prices (*vertical*), different numbers of options that are long versus short (*ratio spread* or *backspread*), and different expiration dates (*calendar spread*).

A *vertical spread* involves the simultaneous purchase and sale of options with the same expiration date but different strike prices. *Vertical* in this context means having the same expiration date. A vertical debit spread is an option position with different strike prices and the same expiration date, and that is established for a debit (an option bought at a higher price than the option sold); for example, you can buy one XYZ February 100 call and sell one XYZ February 110 call or buy one XYZ February 100 put and sell one XYZ February 90 put. For instance, if you purchase a February 100 call at $5 and sell a February 110 call at $1, you have executed a vertical call debit spread for $4. The maximum potential profit of this vertical debit spread is $600 (difference in the strike prices times 100 shares minus the $400 premium paid) and the maximum loss is the $400 premium paid.

A vertical credit spread is an option position with different strike prices and the same expiration date, and that is established for a credit (an option sold at a higher price than the option bought); for example, you can sell one XYZ February 100 call and buy one XYZ February 110 call or sell one XYZ February 100 put and buy one XYZ February 90 put. For instance, if you sell a February 100 call at $5 and buy a February 110 call at $1, you have executed a vertical call credit spread for $4. The maximum potential loss of the call credit spread is $600 (difference in the strike prices times 100 shares minus the $400 premium collected) and the maximum gain is the $400 premium collected.

The profit potential of a vertical debit spread is typically limited to the difference in the strike prices times 100 shares per contract minus the premium paid. The loss in a vertical credit spread is typically limited to the difference in the strike prices times 100 shares minus the premium collected. For ease of presentation, in this book, a vertical spread is assumed to have an equal number of short and long options, unless otherwise noted.

A ratio spread can be loosely defined as any spread in which the numbers of long market contracts and short market contracts are unequal. A ratio strategy can be constructed with either calls or puts. In this book, a *front spread* (a type of ratio spread) is defined as a strategy in which you buy one (or more) options and sell a larger number of further out-of-the-money options. For example, a front spread can consist of buying one close-to-the-money call and selling two calls at a higher strike price, or buying one close-to-the-money put and selling two puts at a lower strike price. To confuse matters, a ratio spread is also called a ratio vertical spread, a front spread, or a short ratio spread. A backspread (a type of ratio spread) is defined as a strategy in which you sell one (or more) options and buy a larger number of further out-of-the-money options. It is probably more common to refer to a front spread as a ratio spread.

A calendar spread (also called a *time spread*) involves the purchase of an option and the simultaneous sale of the same type of option (call or put) with the same strike price but a different expiration date. A summary of spread strategies follows.

SPREAD STRATEGY SUMMARY

Following are descriptions and examples of common spread strategies. Each example illustrates strategies using calls, assuming that XYZ stock is selling at $100 a share in January. Only one example is provided because each strategy will be covered in depth in later chapters.

Vertical spread: Purchase and sale of options at different strike prices, with the same expiration date; for example, sell one February 100 call and buy one XYZ February 110 call.

Iron condor: Combination of vertical call and vertical put spreads; for example, sell a February 105/110 call spread (sell one February 105 call and buy one February 110 call) and sell a February 90/95 put spread (sell one February 95 put and buy one February 90 put).

Ratio (front) spread: Purchase and sale of options at different strike prices, where the number of options sold exceeds the number purchased; for example, buy one XYZ February 100 call and sell two February 110 calls.

Backspread: Purchase and sale of options at different strike prices, where the number options purchased exceeds the number sold; for example, sell one February 100 call and buy 2 February 110 calls.

Straddle: Sell (or buy) call and put options at the same strike price and maturity date; for example, sell one February 100 call and sell one February 100 put.

Strangle: Sell (or buy) call and put options with the same maturity date but different strike prices; for example, sell one February 105 call and sell one February 95 put.

Butterfly spread: Options at three equally spaced exercise prices, where all options expire at the same time. In a long butterfly, the same number of outside exercise prices are purchased and twice the number of the inside exercise prices are sold; for example, buy one February 95 call, buy two February 100 calls, and sell one February 105 call.

Condor: A four-legged option spread in which each leg has the same expiration date but different strike prices. In a long condor, two outside exercise prices are purchased and two inside exercise prices are sold (four total contracts); for example, buy one February 95 call, sell one February 100 call, sell one February 105 call, and buy one February 110 call.

Calendar spread: Purchase of a put or call option and the simultaneous sale of the same type of option (call or put) with the same strike price but different expiration date; for example, sell one February 100 call and buy one March 100 call.

Diagonal spread: Buy and sell options with different strike prices and different expiration dates; for example, sell one February 100 call and buy one March 105 call.

Double diagonal spread: Combination of vertical and calendar spreads, where you buy and sell options where there is a difference of at least two strike prices and two expiration dates; for example, sell one February 100 call and buy one XYZ April 110 call.

Combination: Any option strategy utilizing both call and put options; for example, if XYZ stock is trading at $100 a share, a 95/105 long combination involves buying a 105 strike price call and selling a 95 strike price put. A straddle and strangle can be considered a type of combination.

A spread can be executed from the call side or from the put side, or involve both calls and puts, and can be executed for a credit, debit, or zero cost. Each of the credit spread trades illustrated previously can be converted to a debit spread by changing the buys to sells and the sells to buys. Each spread strategy can be broken down into the perspective of long calls, long puts, short calls, and short puts.

The Wall Street Dictionary

Throughout this book, I provide serious definitions of option terminology. I think it can be interesting, not to mention entertaining, to decipher the humorous side of Wall Street terminology from the perspective of traders so that you can understand what is really being said.

Some traders (not me, of course) believe that if a portfolio manager is on business news television and says he expects the market to rise, he is usually fully invested and will make a profit from such an advance. If he says the economy looks like it is headed for recession, he is lobbying for a Federal Reserve rate cut. Some would go so far as to say that if a portfolio manager says that he expects a correction in the near term, it is likely that he is underinvested, missed the latest advance, wants to get back in, and is underperforming his peers. The only way he can get a top bonus is for the market to go down, with your help. The portfolio manager is basically asking you to help save his job.

Wall Street seems to love touting so-called dollar cost averaging, saying that when markets are down, you get to purchase more shares. They argue that when the markets go up, that is good because investors are making money, and when markets go down, that is good because you can buy more shares. There seems to be something wrong with that picture. The dollar-cost-averaging crowd makes it seem so easy.

It is fairly common for Wall Street commentators to make statements like "we are in the fifth inning" of a cycle, so therefore you have plenty of time to invest and make a lot of money. Some traders may think, rumor has it, that what they really mean is that they need the market to move higher so that they can dump their stocks before the market declines.

Traders may think that in Wall Street parlance, when a pundit says that he is bullish on the market, he wants you to buy because his firm is probably long calls; if a pundit says that he sees a correction in the market, he wants you to sell because his firm is probably long puts; when the same person says that the market is due for a consolidation, he wants you to stay neutral because his firm is probably short calls and puts. I know it is hard to believe, but when there is a bull market, some traders may think that if the portfolio manager sees a bear market, he will not be allowed to be on business news television very often.

Volatility in options is defined, in general, as the amount an instrument is expected to fluctuate within a given time. On Wall Street, however, when they say you can expect "volatility," what they really mean is that the market is going lower. It seems that in Wall Street lingo, volatility is a polite way of saying that you are going to lose money, but it will be a good thing in the long run.

Some traders may think that if you are urged by a Wall Street pundit to invest for the long term and to ride out various fluctuations in the market, what this really means is that the pundit is an asset manager, paid on a percentage of assets under management and not on performance. Telling an investor to invest for the long run can be a great way to put lipstick on this pig by convincing the investor that he should not fire the advisor if he has a large loss because short-term losses are healthy (remember that according to these pundits, dips in the market are always buying opportunities). The great thing about emphasizing the long run is that no one is responsible for the short run, and when the long run arrives, the advisor can claim that that decision was made years ago and that a lot has changed since then. Besides, the advisor may not be around then. Go figure.

Covered versus Uncovered

An option position is typically considered covered if there is an offsetting opposite market position; for example, a short call is considered covered if you are also long a call at the same or lower strike price on the same stock. However, the word *covered* is also used to indicate whether underlying stock is owned; for example, a short call is considered covered if you also long the stock, called a *covered call* strategy. An option strategy where stock is owned can be called covered and an option strategy where stock is not owned can be called uncovered. This can lead to confusion because, for example, the name "covered strangle" is a misnomer because the position is not covered in the usual sense, because the call portion of the trade is covered by the long stock, but the put is actually uncovered.

The name "covered" in this context means an underlying stock is owned and is used to differentiate it from an uncovered position where stock is not owned. Such terminology may have some traders shaking their heads, but please do not let the terminology get in the way of your trading. Any type of option sale can be covered (long or short stock) or uncovered (no underlying stock). The covered option sale strategy is similar to a covered call writing strategy. The uncovered option sale can be attractive to a trader interested in selling time premium. The examples in Chapters 7 to 18 assume that the strategy is uncovered, while the examples in Chapters 19, 21, and 22 assume that the strategy is covered. Practically any strategy can be modified to add a long or short stock position.

FINAL THOUGHTS

I have decided to include a chapter on option terminology to provide a framework with which you can view options so that you can quickly analyze any option position at a glance. At a minimum, you will be able to impress your friends at your next neighborhood gathering. All you have to do is mention a vertical spread or a bull spread, and they will automatically assume that you know what you are talking about. Spread strategies are described throughout the remainder of this book.

PART TWO

The Four Basic Option Strategies

Basic option strategies can be broken down into long call, long put, short call, and short put. Once you understand this framework, you should be able to comprehend any option strategy at a glance, whether it is an outright (single leg) position or a multileg spread. A separate chapter is devoted to each one of these four basic option strategies before we move forward in later chapters to cover more complex strategies.

To make it easy to compare one strategy to another, examples in Part Two, Chapters 7 to 10, are presented in a consistent format. Each example includes the following:

- Strategy summary,
- Table showing values at expiration date,
- Chart showing values at expiration date,
- Illustrative Greeks for a near-term expiration month,
- Illustrative Greeks for a longer-term expiration month,
- Ramifications of exercise and assignment.

Each example assumes that XYZ stock is initially trading at $100 a share. To gain an understanding under various scenarios, each strategy is analyzed from the perspective that an option is established in the following ways:

- Deep-in-the-money at $11,
- Slightly-in-the-money at $7,
- At-the-money at $5,

- Slightly-out-of-the-money at $2,
- Far-out-of-the-money at $1.

Each example shows a wide range of potential option values at the expiration date (expiration analysis). This expiration analysis shows the gain or loss from each strategy, assuming that the underlying stock closes from $75 to $125 at the expiration date. Option values are rounded to make it easier to focus on option principles. For the purposes of this book, remember the following:

- A deep-in-the-money option has a strike price approximately 10 or more points in-the-money.
- A slightly-in-the-money option has a strike price approximately 5 points in-the-money.
- An at-the-money option has a strike price closest to the underlying stock price.
- A slightly-out-of-the-money option has a strike price approximately 5 points out-of-the-money.
- A far-out-of-the-money option has a strike price approximately 10 points out-of-the-money.

These definitions assume that a typical representative stock (XYZ) is trading at $100 a share.

Each example includes sample Greeks, assuming an expiration in a near-term month (February) and a longer-term expiration month (March), so that you can compare the effects an expiration month can have on an option position. The Greeks are converted to dollars in the examples to demonstrate how they can help you, as a trader, manage your position. After the examples, a section titled "Beyond the Basics" further analyzes issues. As a reminder, the Greeks reflect estimated values for a one-point increase in the price of the underlying stock, a one-day lapse of time, and an increase of one percentage point in implied volatility.

Keep in mind that you can close out an option position by offsetting it in the marketplace at any time prior to expiration, and you should use your trading platform software, option calculator, and option chain to estimate option values. Your trading platform should provide the bid/ask spread, intrinsic versus extrinsic values, and Greeks.

For ease of comparison, examples from chapter to chapter assume that call premiums are symmetrical (equal) with put premiums where the strike price is equidistant from the price of the underlying stock price. For example, it is assumed that a February 105 call is priced the same as a February 95 put (at $5). In reality, call prices for stocks are typically higher than relative put prices.

Examples throughout this book assume that the prices to buy and sell do not differ as a result of the bid/ask spread. In addition, the effects of commissions and taxes are not shown. In many cases, the same or similar wording is used to describe various strategies to make them easier to understand.

In case you are curious, XYZ options and Greeks are based on values derived from options on IBM at a particular point in time when the stock was trading near $100 a share.

The examples in Chapters 7 to 18 assume that the strategy is uncovered (no underlying stock is owned or is shorted), whereas Chapters 19, 21, and 22 assume that the strategy is covered.

As a reminder, the examples in Part Two illustrate an option on a stock (XYZ), but the strategies and principles can be equally applied to ETFs, indexes, and futures. It can be to your advantage to learn how to trade options on multiple underlying instruments because opportunities in each tend to present themselves at different times and under different market conditions. The strategies at a glance included in the appendixes summarize many of the strategies covered throughout this book. Prior to engaging in any option strategy, you should develop a view of the market or underlying instrument. Whatever your market prediction, there is likely an option strategy that can be used to profit from that view.

CHAPTER 7

Long Call

This chapter covers buying call options and will set the stage in later chapters for buying put options, selling options, and more advanced strategies. Buying a call is probably the most basic option strategy and the easiest to learn for a beginner because most individuals are familiar with buying an asset and profiting from its increase in value. A beginning option trader may want to start out by buying a call and then moving to other strategies. Buying versus selling options were covered in Chapter 5, so you may want to review that chapter for additional insights. This chapter will provide an overview of a long call, present numerous comprehensive examples, and then move to beyond the basics, including a discussion of the Greeks and rolling.

OVERVIEW

The beauty of the long-call strategy is its simplicity, as sometimes KISS is the best strategy: "Keep it simple, stupid." A long call involves the purchase of a call option and is a bullish strategy. An advantage of a long call is that if the stock rises, you have unlimited profit potential with limited risk. A long call typically increases in value from a rise in the underlying stock and volatility expansion and declines in value from a decline in the underlying stock, time decay, and volatility contraction. Following is a summary profile of a long call:

Direction: Bullish.
Profit potential: Unlimited.
Risk: Limited to premium paid.
Time decay: Negative (theta).

Volatility: Increase is positive (positive theta), decrease is negative.
Delta: Positive.
Gamma: Positive.
Theta (time): Negative.
Vega (volatility): Positive.
Breakeven: Stock at strike price plus premium paid.
Margin: None; premium paid in full at time of purchase.
Exercise and assignment: Can exercise if in-the-money.
How to exit: Sell in closing transaction, exercise, or let expire worthless.
IRA: Permitted.
Main advantages: Unlimited profit potential; risk is limited; requires less capital in comparison to long stock.
Main disadvantages: Can cost more than you are willing to pay; time decay; can lose entire premium.

A risk of a long call is that the underlying stock will decline, or not rise far or fast enough, forcing the extrinsic value to decline in value. If implied volatility (a measurement of the volatility component built into your trading platform model) increases, assuming that all other factors remain constant, a call option will increase in value. If implied volatility declines, assuming that all other factors remain constant, a call option will decline in value; for example, assume that a stock is trading at $100 and you purchase a call option with a strike price of $100 and pay $5 ($500) for the option. If implied volatility rises, the call premium could rise from $5 ($500) to something like $6 ($600). If implied volatility declines, the call premium could decline from $5 ($500) to something like $4 ($400). A change in volatility is a two-edged sword because a spike in volatility helps an existing long option holder but hurts a short option position.

If you are long a call and choose to exercise, you buy the underlying stock at the exercise price. An American-style option can be exercised by the option holder (buyer) at any time up until the expiration date, whereas a European-style option can be exercised only at expiration. Equity options are American-style expirations.

Fraction and Probability Gauge

The fractional (percentage) movement of a long call relative to the movement in a stock price (delta) varies based on the strike price versus the stock price; for example, the deeper in-the-money an option, the more the option moves like the underlying stock and the closer delta is to 1.0. (A delta of 1.0 means 100 percent, so when the stock moves one point, the option moves one point.) In this case, when an option is deep-in-the-money, it changes at a rate almost point for point equal to that of the underlying stock. If the underlying stock price rises one point, such a call rises by approximately one point; likewise, if the underlying stock price declines one point, such a call declines by approximately one point. When an option is at-the-money, its value typically changes at

TABLE 7.1 Long Call Rules of Thumb

Option	Sample Call Strike Price	Delta Range (Fractions and Probabilities, %)
Deep-in-the-money	90 and lower	75–100
Slightly-in-the-money	95	55–75
At-the-money	100	45–55
Slightly-out-of-the-money	105	25–45
Far-out-of-the-money	110 and higher	0–25

approximately 50 percent relative to the underlying stock. When an option is far-out-of-the-money, its value may change only a small fraction relative to a change in the underlying stock.

Also, the higher the strike price, the lower the probability that a call option will end up in-the-money at the expiration date. Table 7.1 shows general rules of thumb based on the strike price versus the stock price. The stock is assumed to be trading at $100 a share.

STRATEGY EXAMPLES

Following are descriptions and examples of long-call strategies. As a reminder, you can close out an option position by offsetting it in the marketplace any time prior to expiration, and the principles that are demonstrated for a stock can be applied to options on an ETF, index, and stock index futures. Appendixes A, B, and C illustrate many of the strategies covered throughout this book.

Deep-in-the-Money

A long deep-in-the-money call option typically has a strike price 10 points or more below the stock price and a delta of 0.75 to 1.0 (75 to 100 percent). If you believe a stock is ready to increase in value, you can buy a deep-in-the-money call option, which will enable you to pay less than the full value of the stock yet benefit almost dollar for dollar on the rise in the value of the stock. If a stock is trading at $100, for instance, you may be able to purchase a call option at a strike price of 90 and pay $11 ($1,100) for the option, which has only $1 ($100) extrinsic value. That purchase will enable you to participate in the movement of that stock as though you fully owned the shares, except for the $1 ($100) premium you paid above the intrinsic value for this right. At the same time, you have a built-in risk management feature because you cannot lose more than the premium paid. An example follows.

Example: Deep-in-the-Money Long Call

Assumptions: XYZ stock is trading at $100 a share in January; buy one February 90
  call at $11.
Strategy direction: Bullish.
Debit or credit: $1,100 debit.
Maximum profit: Unlimited.
Maximum loss: $1,100 (premium paid).
Exercise and assignment: Can exercise if in-the-money.
Break-even stock price: $101 (strike price plus premium paid).
Maximum profit achieved: Unlimited above break-even stock price.

TABLE 7.2 Deep-in-the-Money Long Call

XYZ Stock Price ($)	Long Call Value	Cost of Call	Call Profit (Loss)	Call Profit (Loss) Percentage
75	0	1,100	(1,100)	(100)
80	0	1,100	(1,100)	(100)
85	0	1,100	(1,100)	(100)
90	0	1,100	(1,100)	(100)
95	500	1,100	(600)	(54)
100	1,000	1,100	(100)	(9)
105	1,500	1,100	400	36
110	2,000	1,100	900	81
115	2,500	1,100	1,400	127
120	3,000	1,100	1,900	172
125	3,500	1,100	2,400	218

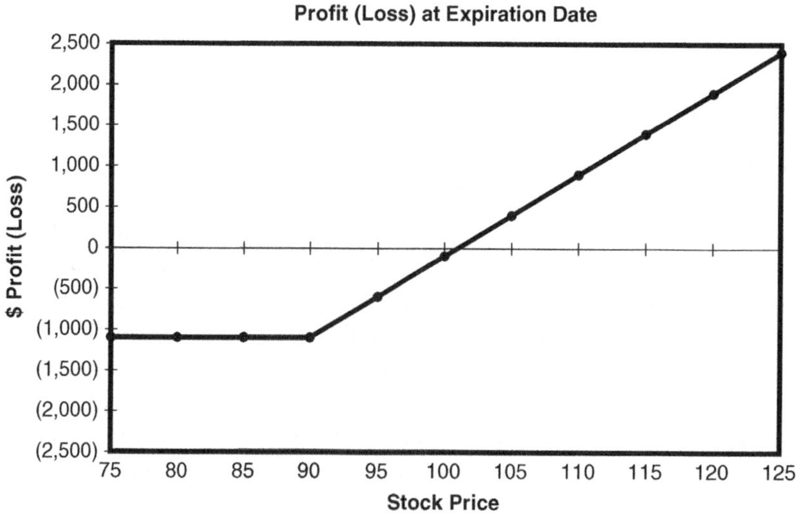

FIGURE 7.1 Deep-in-the-Money Long Call

TABLE 7.3 Summary of Greeks: February Expiration

Option	Delta	Gamma	Theta	Vega
1 February 90 call	$80	$1.50	−$13	$9

TABLE 7.4 Summary of Greeks: March Expiration

Option	Delta	Gamma	Theta	Vega
1 March 90 call	$75	$1.10	−$10	$15

Maximum loss achieved: Stock price at or below strike price.

Profit (loss) if stock unchanged: $100 loss (extrinsic value).

Greeks: Table 7.3 shows sample Greeks converted to dollars at the time the position is established.

Position would reflect a gain from stock rise (delta) and a gain from volatility (vega) expansion. Position would reflect a loss from stock decline (delta), time decay (theta), and volatility (vega) contraction. Gain is $80 from XYZ stock rising to $101; loss is $13 from one day of time decay.

Later expiration: The price and Greeks will differ if expiration is at a later date; for example, if the call option expires in March, instead of February, the price of the call may be valued, for example, at $15 (value of $1,500), with representative Greeks as given in Table 7.4.

Gain is $75 from XYZ stock rising to $101; loss is $10 from one day of time decay.

Exercise and assignment: If you were to exercise the long call, you would buy the stock at $90 per share.

The attraction of buying a deep-in-the-money call is that it can serve as a proxy for long stock, is straightforward, and can mimic the stock to the extent of intrinsic value. Buying a deep-in-the-money option removes some of the uncertainty associated with time decay because there is little extrinsic value. If you can buy a call option as a proxy for stock and are paying a small extrinsic value, it may make sense to purchase a call option in lieu of paying the full price for the stock.

Slightly-in-the-Money

A long slightly-in-the-money call option typically has a strike price five points below the stock price and a delta of 0.60 to 0.75 (60 to 75 percent). A slightly-in-the-money call option can, in some circumstances, track almost dollar for dollar a rise in a stock's price and, at the same time, limit risk. If a stock is trading for $100, for instance, you may be able to purchase a call option with a strike price of 95 and pay $7 ($700) for the option, which is only $2 ($200) above the intrinsic value. That purchase will enable you to participate in the rise in the stock as though you fully owned the shares, except that you had to pay a $2 ($200) premium above the intrinsic value for this right. At the same time, you have a built-in risk management feature because you cannot lose more than the $700. An example follows.

Example: Slightly-in-the-Money Long Call

Assumptions: XYZ stock is trading at $100 a share in January; buy one February 95 call at $7.

Strategy direction: Bullish.

TABLE 7.5 Slightly-in-the-Money Long Call

XYZ Stock Price ($)	Long Call Value	Cost of Call	Call Profit (Loss)	Call Profit (Loss) Percentage
75	0	700	(700)	(100)
80	0	700	(700)	(100)
85	0	700	(700)	(100)
90	0	700	(700)	(100)
95	0	700	(700)	(100)
100	500	700	(200)	(28)
105	1,000	700	300	43
110	1,500	700	800	114
115	2,000	700	1,300	185
120	2,500	700	1,800	257
125	3,000	700	2,300	328

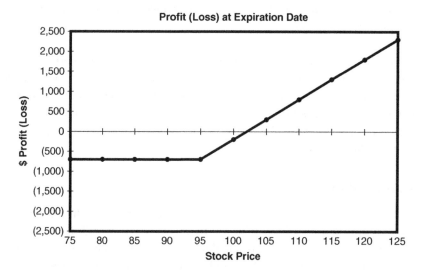

FIGURE 7.2 Slightly-in-the-Money Long Call

TABLE 7.6 Summary of Greeks: February Expiration

Option	Delta	Gamma	Theta	Vega
1 February 95 call	$65	$2.0	−$14	$11

TABLE 7.7 Summary of Greeks: March Expiration

Option	Delta	Gamma	Theta	Vega
1 March 95 call	$63	$1.20	−$11	$16

Debit or credit: $700 debit.

Maximum profit: Unlimited.

Maximum loss: $700 (premium paid).

Exercise and assignment: Can exercise if in-the-money.

Break-even stock price: $102 (strike price plus premium paid).

Maximum profit achieved: Unlimited above break-even stock price.

Maximum loss achieved: Stock price at or below strike price.

Profit (loss) if stock unchanged: $200 loss (extrinsic value).

Greeks: Table 7.6 contains sample Greeks converted to dollars at the time the position is established.

Position would reflect a gain from stock rise (delta) and a gain from volatility (vega) expansion. Position would reflect a loss from stock decline (delta), time decay (theta), and volatility (vega) contraction. Gain is $65 from XYZ stock rising to $101; loss is $14 from one day of time decay.

Later expiration: The price and Greeks will differ if expiration is at a later date; for example, if the call option expires in March, instead of February, the price of the call may be valued, for example, at $12 (value of $1,200), with representative Greeks as given in Table 7.7.

Gain is $63 from XYZ stock rising to $101; loss is $11 from one day of time decay.

Exercise and assignment: If you were to exercise the long call, you would buy the stock at $95 per share.

A slightly-in-the-money option can be an attractive strategy because it can provide a reasonably attractive (high) delta with relatively low extrinsic value. As time approaches the expiration date, especially during the last week of option expiration, some stocks may have little extrinsic value and can be bought relatively cheaply. Buying such a call option near parity can be an attractive strategy, especially if volatility is expected to increase from an event such as an earnings report. For example, assume that on Wednesday, a stock is trading at $98 (during option expiration week) and the company will release earnings the following day, on Thursday. If a call option with a strike price of 95 is priced at $3.25 ($325), you could purchase that option at $3.25 ($325) and only pay $0.25 ($25) above parity (extrinsic value). If the stock rises in value, you are entitled to the full move minus the $0.25 ($25). If the stock should decline, your losses are limited to $3.25 ($325). In effect, you get full upside potential but have a built-in insurance component because you do not have exposure if the stock drops below the strike price of 95.

At-the-Money

A long at-the-money call option has a strike price nearest the stock price and a delta of 0.45 to 0.55 (45 to 55 percent). With an at-the-money call option, there is no intrinsic value, and the option consists entirely of extrinsic value. If a stock is trading at $100, for instance, you may be able to purchase a call option with a strike price of $100 and pay $5 ($500) for the option. You have a built-in risk management feature because you cannot lose more than the $500. An example follows.

Example: At-the-Money Long Call

Assumptions: XYZ stock is trading at $100 a share in January; buy one February 100 call at $5.
Strategy direction: Bullish.
Debit or credit: $500 debit.
Maximum profit: Unlimited.
Maximum loss: $500 (premium paid).
Exercise and assignment: Can exercise if in-the-money.
Break-even stock price: $105 (strike price plus premium paid).
Maximum profit achieved: Unlimited above break-even stock price.
Maximum loss achieved: Stock price at or below strike price.

TABLE 7.8   At-the-Money Long Call

XYZ Stock Price ($)	Long Call Value	Cost of Call	Call Profit (Loss)	Call Profit (Loss) Percentage
75	0	500	(500)	(100)
80	0	500	(500)	(100)
85	0	500	(500)	(100)
90	0	500	(500)	(100)
95	0	500	(500)	(100)
100	0	500	(500)	(100)
105	500	500	0	0
110	1,000	500	500	100
115	1,500	500	1,000	200
120	2,000	500	1,500	300
125	2,500	500	2,000	400

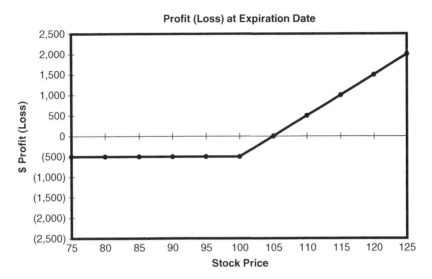

FIGURE 7.3 At-the-Money Long Call

Profit (loss) if stock unchanged: $500 loss (extrinsic value).

Greeks: Table 7.9 contains sample Greeks converted to dollars at the time the position is established.

Position would reflect a gain from stock rise (delta) and a gain from volatility (vega) expansion. Position would reflect a loss from stock decline (delta), time decay (theta), and volatility (vega) contraction. Gain is $53 from XYZ stock rising to $101; loss is $15 from one day of time decay.

Later expiration: The price and Greeks will differ if expiration is at a later date; for example, if the call option expires in March, instead of February, the price of the call may be valued, for example, at $8 (value of $800), with representative Greeks as given in Table 7.10.

TABLE 7.9 Summary of Greeks: February Expiration

Option	Delta	Gamma	Theta	Vega
1 February 100 call	$53	$2.30	−$15	$12

TABLE 7.10 Summary of Greeks: March Expiration

Option	Delta	Gamma	Theta	Vega
1 March 100 call	$52	$1.30	−$12	$17

Gain is $52 from XYZ stock rising to $101; loss is $12 from one day of time decay.

Exercise and assignment: If you were to exercise the long call, you would buy the stock at $100 per share.

Slightly-Out-of-the-Money

A long slightly-out-of-the-money call option typically has a strike price five points above the stock price and a delta of 0.25 to 0.45 (25 to 45 percent). With a slightly-out-of-the-money call option, there is no intrinsic value, and the option consists entirely of extrinsic value. If a stock is trading for $100, for instance, you may be able to purchase a call option with a strike price of 105 and pay $2 ($200) for the option. You have a built-in risk management feature because you cannot lose more than the $200. An example follows.

Example: Slightly-Out-of-the-Money Long Call

Assumptions: XYZ stock is trading at $100 a share in January; buy one February 105 call at $2.

Strategy direction: Bullish.

Debit or credit: $200 debit.

Maximum profit: Unlimited.

Maximum loss: $200 (premium paid).

Exercise and assignment: Can exercise if in-the-money.

Break-even stock price: $107 (strike price plus premium paid).

Maximum profit achieved: Unlimited above break-even stock price.

Maximum loss achieved: Stock price at or below strike price.

Profit (loss) if stock unchanged: $200 loss (extrinsic value).

TABLE 7.11 Slightly-Out-of-the-Money Long Call

XYZ Stock Price ($)	Long Call Value	Cost of Call	Call Profit (Loss)	Call Profit (Loss) Percentage
75	0	200	(200)	(100)
80	0	200	(200)	(100)
85	0	200	(200)	(100)
90	0	200	(200)	(100)
95	0	200	(200)	(100)
100	0	200	(200)	(100)
105	0	200	(200)	(100)
110	500	200	300	150
115	1,000	200	800	400
120	1,500	200	1,300	650
125	2,000	200	1,800	900

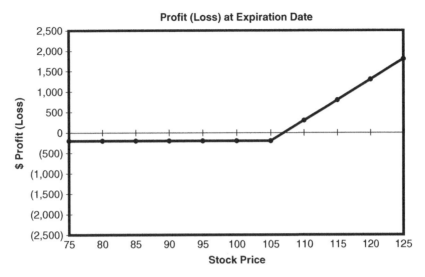

FIGURE 7.4 Slightly Out-of-the-Money Long Call

Greeks: Table 7.12 contains sample Greeks converted to dollars at the time the position is established.

Position would reflect a gain from stock rise (delta) and a gain from volatility (vega) expansion. Position would reflect a loss from stock decline (delta), time decay (theta), and volatility (vega) contraction. Gain is $42 from XYZ stock rising to $101; loss is $14 from one day of time decay.

Later expiration: The price and Greeks will differ if expiration is at a later date; for example, if the call option expires in March, instead of February, the price of the call may be valued, for example, at $3 (value of $300), with representative Greeks as given in Table 7.13.

Gain is $40 from XYZ stock rising to $101; loss is $10 from one day of time decay.

Exercise and assignment: If you were to exercise the long call, you would buy the stock at $105 per share.

TABLE 7.12 Summary of Greeks: February Expiration

Option	Delta	Gamma	Theta	Vega
1 February 105 call	$42	$2.00	−$14	$11

TABLE 7.13 Summary of Greeks: March Expiration

Option	Delta	Gamma	Theta	Vega
1 March 105 call	$40	$1.20	−$10	$15

Far-Out-of-the-Money

A long far-out-of-the-money call option typically has a strike price 10 points or more above the stock price and a delta of zero to 0.25 (0 to 25 percent). A far-out-of-the-money call option consists entirely of extrinsic value and is the most leveraged strategy. This can be a low-probability strategy because the further you move away from the price of the underlying stock, the lower the probability will be that the stock or futures will end up in-the-money. Although it has a low probability of success in many cases, it can be an effective strategy for a stock making a big move to the upside; for example, if a stock is trading at $100, you may be able to purchase a call option with a strike price of 110 and pay $1 ($100) for the option. You have a built-in risk management feature because you cannot lose more than the $100. An example follows.

Example: Far-Out-of-the-Money Long Call

Assumptions: XYZ stock is trading at $100 a share in January; buy one February 110 call at $1.
Strategy direction: Bullish.
Debit or credit: $100 debit.
Maximum profit: Unlimited.
Maximum loss: $100 (premium paid).
Exercise and assignment: Can exercise if in-the-money.
Break-even stock price: $111 (strike price plus premium paid).
Maximum profit achieved: Unlimited above break-even stock price.
Maximum loss achieved: Stock price at or below strike price.
Profit (loss) if stock unchanged: $100 loss (extrinsic value).

TABLE 7.14 Far-Out-of-the-Money Long Call

XYZ Stock Price ($)	Long Call Value	Cost of Call	Call Profit (Loss)	Call Profit (Loss) Percentage
75	0	100	(100)	(100)
80	0	100	(100)	(100)
85	0	100	(100)	(100)
90	0	100	(100)	(100)
95	0	100	(100)	(100)
100	0	100	(100)	(100)
105	0	100	(100)	(100)
110	0	100	(100)	(100)
115	500	100	400	400
120	1,000	100	900	900
125	1,500	100	1,400	1,400

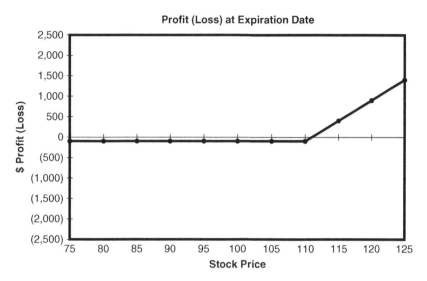

FIGURE 7.5 Far-Out-of-the-Money Long Call

Greeks: Table 7.15 shows sample Greeks converted to dollars at the time the position is established.

Position would reflect a gain from stock rise (delta) and a gain from volatility (vega) expansion. Position would reflect a loss from stock decline (delta), time decay (theta), and volatility (vega) contraction. Gain is $23 from XYZ stock rising to $101; loss is $12 from one day of time decay.

Later expiration: The price and Greeks will differ if expiration is at a later date; for example, if the call option expires in March, instead of February, the price of the call may be valued, for example, at $2 (value of $200), with representative Greeks as shown in Table 7.16.

Gain is $20 from XYZ stock rising to $101; loss is $7 from one day of time decay.

Exercise and assignment: If you were to exercise the long call, you would buy the stock at $110 per share.

TABLE 7.15 Summary of Greeks: February Expiration

Option	Delta	Gamma	Theta	Vega
1 February 110 call	$23	$1.75	−$12	$8

TABLE 7.16 Summary of Greeks: March Expiration

Option	Delta	Gamma	Theta	Vega
1 March 110 call	$20	$1.00	−$7	$10

BEYOND THE BASICS

Playing Defense

A trader should consider rolling an in-the-money option if the value of a long call has increased dramatically. Under this strategy, the trader should offset an existing position and reestablish it at a higher strike price, where there is lower intrinsic value and minimal extrinsic value. In this way, the trader has locked in profits for the difference between the original strike price and the newly established strike price; for example, assume XYZ stock is trading at $100 a share, you are long one 95 XYZ call option, and the stock surges to $110. You could offset the 95 strike price call option (at a profit) and purchase a new call option at a strike price of 105. Later, if the stock surges to $120 a share, you can sell the 105 strike price call (at a profit) and purchase a call option at a strike price of 115, and so on. An experienced option trader might exit only part of the position or roll the option position to a different strike price or expiration month as the underlying stock fluctuates, potentially locking in profits along the way. Rolling is covered in Chapter 29.

More on the Greeks

Strike versus Stock Price By analyzing the Greeks included in this chapter, you can develop general rules of thumb to help you determine the characteristics of various options. Table 7.17 summarizes the Greeks for the February call options based on differences in strike price. Each Greek has been converted to dollars.

On the basis of these examples, patterns emerge when comparing call options with different strike prices:

- A deep-in-the-money call moves almost dollar for dollar (delta), reaches near 0.50 at-the-money, and approaches zero the further it is out-of-the-money.
- Theta, vega, and gamma reach their peaks near at-the-money and decline the further the option moves in-the-money or out-of-the-money.

TABLE 7.17 Near-Month (February) Greek Summary: Strike Price

Option	Delta	Gamma	Theta	Vega
1 February 90 call	$80	$1.50	−$13	$9
1 February 95 call	$65	$2.00	−$14	$11
1 February 100 call	$53	$2.30	−$15	$12
1 February 105 call	$42	$2.00	−$14	$11
1 February 110 call	$23	$1.75	−$12	$8

TABLE 7.18 Later Month (March) Greek Summary

Option	Delta	Gamma	Theta	Vega
1 March 90 call	$75	$1.10	−$10	$15
1 March 95 call	$63	$1.20	−$11	$16
1 March 100 call	$52	$1.30	−$12	$17
1 March 105 call	$40	$1.20	−$10	$15
1 March 110 call	$20	$1.00	−$7	$10

Like theta and vega, extrinsic value is also at its peak when the strike price is at-the-money and declines the further the option moves in-the-money or out-of-the-money.

Table 7.18 summarizes the Greeks for the March call options based on differences in strike price. Each Greek has been converted to dollars.

On the basis of these examples, the March options have patterns similar to the February options.

Shorter versus Longer-Dated Options Table 7.19 summarizes the Greeks comparing February versus March options based on differences in expiration date.

Patterns emerge when comparing shorter-dated options versus longer-dated options. The shorter-dated February options, regardless of strike price, in these examples have a higher delta, higher gamma, greater time decay (theta), and lower sensitivity to volatility (vega).

An increase in volatility, by itself, has the effect of increasing an option's price, but the passage of time works in the opposite direction (time only moves in one direction). Shorter-dated options, in general, are more sensitive to time decay than longer-dated options. Keep in mind that the closer to expiration the option is, the smaller the premium will be, and the longer to expiration, the higher the premium.

TABLE 7.19 Greek Summary: February versus March Expiration

Option	Delta	Gamma	Theta	Vega
1 February 90 call	$80	$1.50	−$13	$9
1 March 90 call	$75	$1.10	−$10	$15
1 February 95 call	$65	$2.00	−$14	$11
1 March 95 call	$63	$1.20	−$11	$16
1 February 100 call	$53	$2.30	−$15	$12
1 March 100 call	$52	$1.30	−$12	$17
1 February 105 call	$42	$2.00	−$14	$11
1 March 105 call	$40	$1.20	−$10	$15
1 February 110 call	$23	$1.75	−$12	$8
1 March 110 call	$20	$1.00	−$7	$10

Playing Defense: A Case Study

Joe (not his real name) was bullish on Google when Google was trading at $100 a share, and he decided to buy 10 May 100 call options at $8 each ($8,000 total). The stock rose to $130 a share, and Joe was thrilled as his options rose to $32 ($32,000 total). But when the stock began to plunge, Joe had visions of losing all of his investment in the options, so he sold when the calls plunged to $7 ($7,000 total). Joe, however, felt comforted by the fact that he had only lost $1 per contract ($1,000 total). Joe was still very bullish on the stock but he was afraid that the stock would reverse quickly again and he would lose money, so he decided not to get back in and buy any calls. As the weeks went by, Google surged to $500 a share (his options would have been worth $400,000, for a profit of $392,000, based on his original purchase price). Joe was devastated, so he entered into a 12-step recovery program to deal with the thought that he had sacrificed so much money because he was worried about protecting a relatively small amount. The mistake he made on the Google trade, he thought, was that he did not hold on to his call option long enough.

Joe thought he had learned his lesson, so when the next high-flier stock came along, he decided he would not sell his options so quickly. Joe purchased 10 July 50 calls of XYZ Corporation at $3 ($3,000 total) when the stock was trading at $50 a share. Joe watched CNBC every day and heard about XYZ's great prospects. Sure enough, the stock began to rise, and when it hit $60 a share, Joe decided that he should make up for his Google mistake by purchasing 20 more July 50 calls at $13 each ($26,000). Joe was determined to get back the money that he thought the market owed him from the Google debacle and felt comforted by the fact that the pundits on CNBC were optimistic about the stock. As the stock hit $90 a share and his profits grew to more than $100,000, Joe was calling his friends and relatives (and the buddies he had made at his 12-step recovery program) to let them know how easy it was to trade the financial markets if you were talented and smart. When the stock hit $100 a share, it began to reverse and lower, but the CNBC pundits proclaimed it just another buying opportunity. He began to listen to more pundits on television and joined the crowd, thinking that when stocks go higher, it is good because people make money, and when stocks go lower, it is good because it is a buying opportunity. What a great country. As the stock plunged to $65 a share, Joe felt that this could be another buying opportunity and bought more options, feeling even more optimistic because the company was to report earnings the following week. Joe felt especially optimistic because so many people were saying good things about the company's prospects. He felt that although the Google trade was devastating, he was smarter than most people and felt confident about his investing abilities, so he was looking forward to hearing about XYZ Corporation's earnings and decided to hold all his options. However, when XYZ Corporation's earnings were released, the stock plunged and fell to $30 a share, and Joe lost all of his option premium.

Joe was again devastated, so he decided to learn more about options because it was obvious to him that simply buying options and holding them does not always work. Joe learned about a strategy called "rolling." Under this strategy, when a call option has a large increase in intrinsic value and a corresponding contraction in extrinsic value, it can be a great risk management strategy to sell (offset) the call options and reestablish call options at a higher strike price, where the extrinsic value is minimized and there is a relatively small amount of intrinsic value. Using this rolling strategy, a trader can continue to have the full upside potential of a stock, while limiting the risk to the amount paid for the reestablished option. For example, in retrospect, Joe could have sold his long call options in Google and XYZ Corporation every time the stocks rose by 10 or 20 points and, at the same time, reestablish a new call position at a higher strike price, thus locking in the gains of the original options and limiting the risk on the newer options. For example, if Joe owned Google call options with a strike price of 100 and the stock surged, he could have sold Google the call options at a profit and purchased new call options at a strike price of 120. Later, if the stock continued to surge, he could have sold the Google 120 strike call options at a profit and purchased new call options at a strike price of 140, and so on. Joe learned not to always follow the crowd and get overly optimistic but, more important, he learned that education in options and how they work is critical to making and keeping a profit. Once Joe learned about the rolling strategy, he began to trade happily ever after. Joe still attends the 12-step program and is now able to counsel others. As you can imagine, the person depicted in this example is fictitious.

FINAL THOUGHTS

A key ingredient to becoming a successful option trader is to select the best strike price and time frame to match your risk profile and goals. Some traders buy a small number of in-the-money options, looking for singles, whereas others buy a large number of out-of-the-money options, looking for the home run. Selecting the best strike price is somewhat of a trade-off between paying as little as possible but trying to gain as much upside potential as possible. Your goal should be to choose a strike price and expiration date that provide sufficient profit potential at a reasonable cost. You should review an option chain to see the options available.

A call option can be purchased at a strike price below, at, or above the actual price of the underlying stock, and you should pick the strike price and time frame that best fit your forecast. The higher the strike price of a call, the lower the option price, the lower the delta, and the greater the leverage. The attraction of buying a deep-in-the-money call option is that it is straightforward and can mimic the stock to the extent of intrinsic value. The built-in insurance is an attractive feature of long options. Keep in mind that buying out-of-the-money call options can provide great leverage with which to capture a big move. At-the-money and out-of-the-money options seem to attract the attention of option buyers. The problem with out-of-the-money option purchases is that they may not provide you with an edge and can be a low-probability strategy.

You have probably heard the saying "money cannot buy happiness." I have a hunch that the person who made up that saying did not have a great year trading. If money cannot buy happiness, how come it makes me feel great when I make money trading options? Just kidding, of course. As a reminder, the principles and examples in this chapter illustrate an option on a stock (XYZ), but the strategies and principles can be equally applied to ETFs, indexes, and futures. We now move on to Chapter 8, to analyze a long put, before we move on to short-option strategies.

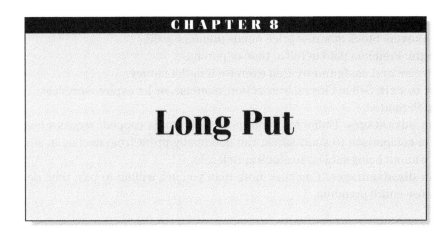

Long Put

I n Chapter 7, we discussed that buying a call is probably the most basic option strategy and the easiest to learn for a beginner. Buying a put option has many of the same characteristics as buying a call option, except a put option profits in the opposite direction. Most individuals are familiar with buying and profiting from an increase in the value of an underlying stock, but a put option makes it equally as easy to profit from a decline in a stock. This chapter provides an overview of a long put, presents numerous comprehensive examples, and then moves to beyond the basics, including a discussion of rolling, protective and married puts, and equivalent positions.

OVERVIEW

A long put involves the purchase of a put option and is a bearish strategy. An advantage of a long put is that if the stock declines, you have unlimited potential with limited risk. A long put typically increases in value from a decline in the underlying stock or volatility expansion and declines in value from a rise in the underlying stock, time decay, or volatility contraction. Following is a summary profile of a long call:

Direction: Bearish.
Profit potential: Unlimited. (Technically, strike price minus premium paid.)
Risk: Limited to premium paid.
Time decay: Negative (theta).
Volatility: Increase is positive (positive theta), decrease is negative.
Delta: Negative.
Gamma: Positive.
Theta (time): Negative.

Vega (volatility): Positive.

Breakeven: Stock at strike price minus premium paid.

Margin: Premium paid in full at time of purchase.

Exercise and assignment: Can exercise if in-the-money.

How to exit: Sell in closing transaction, exercise, or let expire worthless.

IRA: Permitted.

Main advantages: Unlimited profit potential; risk is capped; requires less capital in comparison to short stock; can potentially profit from decline in stock price without being subject to stock uptick rule.

Main disadvantages: Can cost more than you are willing to pay; time decay; can lose entire premium.

A risk for a long put is that the underlying stock will rise or not decline far or fast enough, forcing the put to decline in value. If implied volatility increases, assuming that all other factors remain constant, a put option will increase in value. If implied volatility declines, assuming that all other factors remain constant, a put option will decline in value; for example, assume that a stock is trading at $100 and you purchase a put option with a strike price of 100 and pay $5 ($500) for the option. If implied volatility rises, the put premium could rise from $5 ($500) to something like $6 ($600). If implied volatility declines, the put premium could decline from $5 ($500) to something like $4 ($400). A change in volatility is a two-edged sword because a spike in volatility helps an existing long option holder but hurts a short option position.

If you are long a put and choose to exercise, you sell the underlying stock at the exercise price. An American-style option can be exercised by the option holder (buyer) at any time up until the expiration date, whereas a European-style option can be exercised only at expiration. Equity options are American-style expirations.

Fraction and Probability Gauge

The fractional (percentage) movement of a long put relative to the movement in a stock price (delta) varies based on the strike price versus the stock price; for example, the deeper in-the-money an option, the more the option moves like the underlying stock and the closer its delta is to -1.0. (A delta of -1.0 means 100 percent, so when the stock moves one point, the option moves one point.) In this case, when an option is deep-in-the-money, it changes at a rate almost point for point equal to that of the underlying stock. If the underlying stock price declines one point, such a put will rise by approximately one point; likewise, if the underlying stock price rises one point, such a put will decline by approximately one point. When an option is at-the-money, its value typically changes at approximately 50 percent relative to the underlying stock. When an option is far-out-of-the-money, its value may change only a small fraction relative to a change in the underlying stock.

TABLE 8.1 Long Put Rules of Thumb

Option	Sample Put Strike Price	Delta Range (Fractions and Probabilities, %)
Deep-in-the-money	110 and higher	75–100
Slightly-in-the-money	105	55–75
At-the-money	100	45–55
Slightly-out-of-the-money	95	25–45
Far-out-of-the-money	90 and lower	0–25

Also, the lower the strike price, the lower the probability that a put option will end up in-the-money at the expiration date. Table 8.1 contains general rules of thumb based on the strike price versus the stock price. The stock is assumed to be trading at $100 a share.

STRATEGY EXAMPLES

The following examples analyze long-put strategies. Do not forget that you can close out an option position by offsetting it in the marketplace any time prior to expiration, and it can be to your advantage to learn how to trade options on multiple underlying instruments such as stocks, ETFs, indexes, and stock index futures. Appendixes A, B, and C illustrate many of the strategies covered throughout this book.

Deep-in-the-Money

A long deep-in-the-money put option typically has a strike price 10 points or more above the stock price and a delta of -0.75 to -1.0 (75 to 100 percent). If you believe a stock is ready to decline in value, you can buy a deep-in-the-money put option, which will enable you to pay less than the full value of the stock yet benefit almost dollar for dollar on the decline in the value of the stock. If a stock is trading at $100, for instance, you may be able to purchase a put option at a strike price of 110 and pay $11 ($1,100) for the option, which has only $1 ($100) extrinsic value. That purchase will enable you to participate in the movement of that stock as though you shorted the shares, except for the $1 ($100) premium you paid above the intrinsic value for this right. At the same time, you have a built-in risk management feature because you cannot lose more than the premium paid. An example follows.

Example: Deep-in-the-Money Long Put

Assumptions: XYZ stock is trading at $100 a share in January; buy one February 110 put at $11.

Strategy direction: Bearish.

Debit or credit: $1,100 debit.

Maximum profit: $9,900 (strike price minus premium paid).

Maximum loss: $1,100 (premium paid).

Exercise and assignment: Can exercise if in-the-money.

Break-even stock price: $99 (strike price minus premium paid).

Maximum profit achieved: Below break-even stock price.

Maximum loss achieved: Stock price at or above strike price.

Profit (loss) if stock unchanged: $100 loss (extrinsic value).

TABLE 8.2 Deep-in-the-Money Long Put

XYZ Stock Price ($)	Long Put Value	Cost of Put	Put Profit (Loss)	Put Profit (Loss) Percentage
75	3,500	1,100	2,400	218
80	3,000	1,100	1,900	172
85	2,500	1,100	1,400	127
90	2,000	1,100	900	81
95	1,500	1,100	400	36
100	1,000	1,100	(100)	(9)
105	500	1,100	(600)	(54)
110	0	1,100	(1,100)	(100)
115	0	1,100	(1,100)	(100)
120	0	1,100	(1,100)	(100)
125	0	1,100	(1,100)	(100)

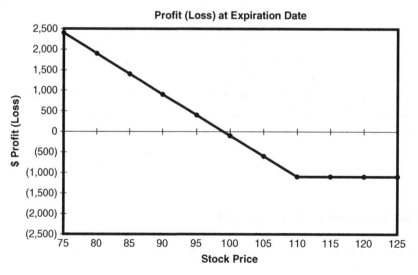

FIGURE 8.1 Deep-in-the-Money Long Put

TABLE 8.3 Summary of Greeks: February Expiration

Option	Delta	Gamma	Theta	Vega
1 February 110 put	−$80	$1.50	−$13	$9

TABLE 8.4 Summary of Greeks: March Expiration

Option	Delta	Gamma	Theta	Vega
1 March 110 put	−$75	$1.10	−$10	$15

Greeks: Table 8.3 shows sample Greeks converted to dollars at the time the position is established.

Position would reflect a gain from stock decline (delta) and a gain from volatility (vega) expansion. Position would reflect a loss from stock rise (delta), time decay (theta), and volatility (vega) contraction. Loss is $80 from XYZ stock rising to $101; loss is $13 from one day of time decay.

Later expiration: The price and Greeks will differ if expiration is at a later date; for example, if the put option expires in March, instead of February, the price of the put may be valued, for example, at $15 (value of $1,500), with representative Greeks as shown in Table 8.4.

Loss is $75 from XYZ stock rising to $101; loss is $10 from one day of time decay.

Exercise and assignment: If you were to exercise the long put, you would sell the stock at $110 per share.

The attraction of buying a deep-in-the-money put is that it can serve as a proxy for short stock, is straightforward, and can mimic the stock to the extent of intrinsic value. Buying a deep-in-the-money option removes some of the uncertainty associated with time decay because there is little extrinsic value. If you can buy a put option as a proxy for short stock and are paying a small extrinsic value, it may make sense to purchase a put option in lieu of shorting the stock.

Slightly-in-the-Money

A long slightly-in-the-money put option typically has a strike price five points above the stock price and a delta of −0.60 to −0.75 (60 to 75 percent). A slightly-in-the-money put option can, in some circumstances, track almost dollar for dollar a decline in a stock's price and, at the same time, limit risk. If a stock is trading for $100, for instance, you may be able to purchase a put option with a strike price of 105 and pay $7 ($700) for the option, which is only $2 ($200) above its intrinsic value. That purchase will enable you to participate in the decline in the stock as though you were short the shares, except that you had to pay a $2 ($200) premium above the intrinsic value for this right. At the same time, you have a built-in risk management feature because you cannot lose more than the $700. An example follows.

Example: Slightly-in-the-Money Long Put

Assumptions: XYZ stock is trading at $100 a share in January; buy one February 105 put at $7.

Strategy direction: Bearish.

TABLE 8.5 Slightly-in-the-Money Long Put

XYZ Stock Price ($)	Long Put Value	Cost of Put	Put Profit (Loss)	Put Profit (Loss) Percentage
75	3,000	700	2,300	328
80	2,500	700	1,800	257
85	2,000	700	1,300	185
90	1,500	700	800	114
95	1,000	700	300	43
100	500	700	(200)	(28)
105	0	700	(700)	(100)
110	0	700	(700)	(100)
115	0	700	(700)	(100)
120	0	700	(700)	(100)
125	0	700	(700)	(100)

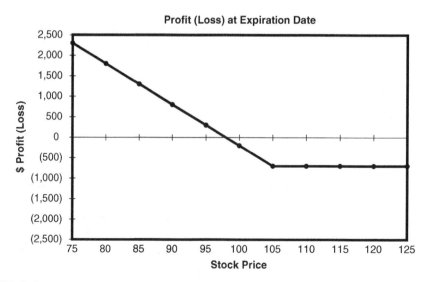

FIGURE 8.2 Slightly-in-the-Money Long Put

TABLE 8.6 Summary of Greeks: February Expiration

Option	Delta	Gamma	Theta	Vega
1 February 105 put	−$65	$2.00	−$14	$11

TABLE 8.7 Summary of Greeks: March Expiration

Option	Delta	Gamma	Theta	Vega
1 March 105 put	−$63	$1.20	−$11	$16

Debit or credit: $700 debit.

Maximum profit: $9,800 (strike price minus premium paid).

Maximum loss: $700 (premium paid).

Exercise and assignment: Can exercise if in-the-money.

Break-even stock price: $98 (strike price minus premium paid).

Maximum profit achieved: Below break-even stock price.

Maximum loss achieved: Stock price at or above strike price.

Profit (loss) if stock unchanged: $200 loss (extrinsic value).

Greeks: Table 8.6 contains sample Greeks converted to dollars at the time the position is established.

Position would reflect a gain from stock decline (delta) and a gain from volatility (vega) expansion. Position would reflect a loss from stock rise (delta), time decay (theta), and volatility (vega) contraction. Loss is $65 from XYZ stock rising to $101; loss is $14 from one day of time decay.

Later expiration: The price and Greeks will differ if expiration is at a later date; for example, if the put option expires in March, instead of February, the price of the put may be valued, for example, at $12 (value of $1,200), with representative Greeks as given in Table 8.7.

Loss is $63 from XYZ stock rising to $101; loss is $11 from one day of time decay.

Exercise and assignment: If you were to exercise the long put, you would sell the stock at $105 per share.

As time approaches the expiration date, especially during the last week of option expiration, some stocks may have little extrinsic value and can be bought relatively cheaply. Buying such a put option near parity can be an attractive strategy, especially if volatility is expected to increase from an event such as the release of an earnings report. For example, assume that on Wednesday, a stock is trading at $102 (during option expiration week) and the company will release earnings the following day, on Thursday. If a put option with a strike price of 105 is priced at $3.25 ($325), you could purchase that option at $3.25 ($325) and only pay $0.25 ($25) above parity (extrinsic value). If the stock declines in value, you are entitled to the full move minus the $0.25 ($25). If the stock should rise, your losses are limited to $3.25 ($325). In effect, you get full upside potential but have a built-in insurance component because you do not have exposure if the stock rises above the strike price of 105.

At-the-Money

A long at-the-money put option has a strike price nearest the stock price and a delta of -0.45 to -0.55 (45 to 55 percent). With an at-the-money put option, there is no intrinsic value, and the option consists entirely of extrinsic value. If a stock is trading at $100, for instance, you may be able to purchase a put option with a strike price of 100 and pay $5 ($500) for the option. You have a built-in risk management feature because you cannot lose more than the $500. An example follows.

Example: At-the-Money Long Put

> **Assumptions**: XYZ stock is trading at $100 a share in January; buy one February 100 put at $5.
> **Strategy direction:** Bearish.
> **Debit or credit:** $500 debit.
> **Maximum profit**: $9,500 (strike price minus premium paid).
> **Maximum loss:** $500 (premium paid).
> **Exercise and assignment**: Can exercise if in-the-money.
> **Break-even stock price**: $95 (strike price minus premium paid).
> **Maximum profit achieved**: Below break-even stock price.
> **Maximum loss achieved**: Stock price at or above strike price.
> **Profit (loss) if stock unchanged:** $500 loss (extrinsic value).

TABLE 8.8   At-the-Money Long Put

XYZ Stock Price ($)	Long Put Value	Cost of Put	Put Profit (Loss)	Put Profit (Loss) Percentage
75	2,500	500	2,000	400
80	2,000	500	1,500	300
85	1,500	500	1,000	200
90	1,000	500	500	100
95	500	500	0	0
100	0	500	(500)	(100)
105	0	500	(500)	(100)
110	0	500	(500)	(100)
115	0	500	(500)	(100)
120	0	500	(500)	(100)
125	0	500	(500)	(100)

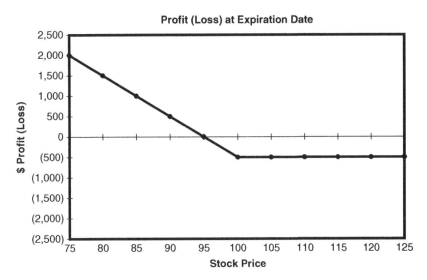

FIGURE 8.3 At-the-Money Long Put

Greeks: Table 8.9 contains sample Greeks converted to dollars at the time the position is established.

Position would reflect a gain from stock decline (delta) and a gain from volatility (vega) expansion. Position would reflect a loss from stock rise (delta), time decay (theta), and volatility (vega) contraction. Loss is $53 from XYZ stock rising to $101; loss is $15 from one day of time decay.

Later expiration: The price and Greeks will differ if expiration is at a later date; for example, if the put option expires in March, instead of February, the price of the put may be valued, for example, at $8 (value of $800), with representative Greeks as given in Table 8.10.

Loss is $52 from XYZ stock rising to $101; loss is $12 from one day of time decay.

Exercise and assignment: If you were to exercise the long put, you would sell the stock at $100 per share.

TABLE 8.9 Summary of Greeks: February Expiration

Option	Delta	Gamma	Theta	Vega
1 February 100 put	−$53	$2.30	−$15	$12

TABLE 8.10 Summary of Greeks: March Expiration

Option	Delta	Gamma	Theta	Vega
1 March 100 put	−$52	$1.30	−$12	$17

Slightly-Out-of-the-Money

A long slightly-out-of-the-money put option typically has a strike price five points below the stock price and a delta of −0.25 to −0.45 (25 to 45 percent). With a slightly-out-of-the-money put option, there is no intrinsic value, and the option consists entirely of extrinsic value. If a stock is trading for $100, for instance, you may be able to purchase a put option with a strike price of 95 and pay $2 ($200) for the option. You have a built-in risk management feature because you cannot lose more than the $200. An example follows.

Example: Slightly-Out-of-the-Money Long Put

Assumptions: XYZ stock is trading at $100 a share in January; buy one February 95 put at $2.

Strategy direction: Bearish.

Debit or credit: $200 debit.

Maximum profit: $9,300 (strike price minus premium paid).

Maximum loss: $200 (premium paid).

Exercise and assignment: Can exercise if in-the-money.

Break-even stock price: $93 (strike price minus premium paid).

Maximum profit achieved: Below break-even stock price.

Maximum loss achieved: Stock price at or above strike price.

Profit (loss) if stock unchanged: $200 loss (extrinsic value).

Greeks: Table 8.12 contains sample Greeks converted to dollars at the time the position is established.

Position would reflect a gain from stock decline (delta) and a gain from volatility (vega) expansion. Position would reflect a loss from stock rise (delta),

TABLE 8.11   Slightly-Out-of-the-Money Long Put

XYZ Stock Price ($)	Long Put Value	Cost of Put	Put Profit (Loss)	Put Profit (Loss) Percentage
75	2,000	200	1,800	900
80	1,500	200	1,300	650
85	1,000	200	800	400
90	500	200	300	150
95	0	200	(200)	(100)
100	0	200	(200)	(100)
105	0	200	(200)	(100)
110	0	200	(200)	(100)
115	0	200	(200)	(100)
120	0	200	(200)	(100)
125	0	200	(200)	(100)

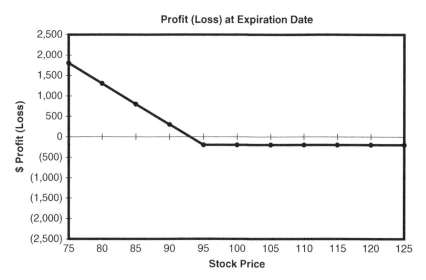

FIGURE 8.4 Slightly-Out-of-the-Money Long Put

time decay (theta), and volatility (vega) contraction. Loss is $42 from XYZ stock rising to $101; loss is $14 from one day of time decay.

Later expiration: The price and Greeks will differ if expiration is at a later date; for example, if the put option expires in March, instead of February, the price of the put may be valued, for example, at $3 (value of $300), with representative Greeks as shown in Table 8.13.

Loss is $40 from XYZ stock rising to $101; loss is $10 from one day of time decay.

Exercise and assignment: If you were to exercise the long put, you would sell the stock at $95 per share.

TABLE 8.12 Summary of Greeks: February Expiration

Option	Delta	Gamma	Theta	Vega
1 February 95 put	−$42	$2.00	−$14	$11

TABLE 8.13 Summary of Greeks: March Expiration

Option	Delta	Gamma	Theta	Vega
1 March 95 put	−$40	$1.20	−$10	$15

Far-Out-of-the-Money

A long far-out-of-the-money put option typically has a strike price 10 points or more below the stock price and a delta of zero to −0.25 (0 to 25 percent). A far-out-of-the-money put option consists entirely of extrinsic value and is the most leveraged strategy. This can be a low-probability strategy because the further you move away from the price of the underlying stock, the lower the probability will be that the stock will end up in-the-money. Although the strategy has a low probability of success in many cases, it can be an effective strategy for a stock making a big move to the downside; for example, if a stock is trading at $100, you may be able to purchase a put option with a strike price of 90 and pay $1 ($100) for the option. You have a built-in risk management feature because you cannot lose more than the $100. An example follows.

Example: Far-Out-of-the-Money Long Put

Assumptions: XYZ stock is trading at $100 a share in January; buy one February 90 put at $1.

Strategy direction: Bearish.

Debit or credit: $100 debit.

Maximum profit: $8,900 (strike price minus premium paid).

Maximum loss: $100 (premium paid).

Exercise and assignment: Can exercise if in-the-money.

Break-even stock price: $89 (strike price minus premium paid).

Maximum profit achieved: Below break-even stock price.

Maximum loss achieved: Stock price at or above strike price.

Profit (loss) if stock unchanged: $100 loss (extrinsic value).

Greeks: Table 8.15 contains sample Greeks converted to dollars at the time the position is established.

TABLE 8.14 Far-Out-of-the-Money Long Put

XYZ Stock Price ($)	Long Put Value	Cost of Put	Put Profit (Loss)	Put Profit (Loss) Percentage
75	1,500	100	1,400	1,400
80	1,000	100	900	900
85	500	100	400	400
90	0	100	(100)	(100)
95	0	100	(100)	(100)
100	0	100	(100)	(100)
105	0	100	(100)	(100)
110	0	100	(100)	(100)
115	0	100	(100)	(100)
120	0	100	(100)	(100)
125	0	100	(100)	(100)

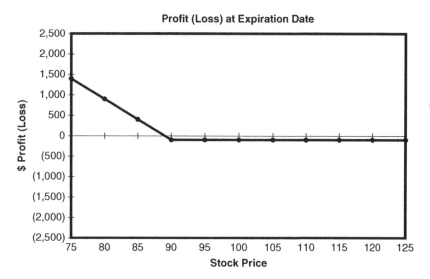

FIGURE 8.5 Far-Out-of-the-Money Long Put

Position would reflect a gain from stock decline (delta) and a gain from volatility (vega) expansion. Position would reflect a loss from stock rise (delta), time decay (theta), and volatility (vega) contraction. Loss is $23 from XYZ stock rising to $101; loss is $12 from one day of time decay.

Later expiration: The price and Greeks will differ if expiration is at a later date; for example, if the put option expires in March, instead of February, the price of the put may be valued, for example, at $2 (value of $200), with representative Greeks as shown in Table 8.16.

Loss is $20 from XYZ stock rising to $101; loss is $7 from one day of time decay.

Exercise and assignment: If you were to exercise the long put, you would sell the stock at $90 per share.

TABLE 8.15 Summary of Greeks: February Expiration

Option	Delta	Gamma	Theta	Vega
1 February 90 put	−$23	$1.75	−$12	$8

TABLE 8.16 Summary of Greeks: March Expiration

Option	Delta	Gamma	Theta	Vega
1 March 90 put	−$20	$1.00	−$7	$10

BEYOND THE BASICS

Playing Defense

A trader should consider rolling an in-the-money option if the value of a long put has increased dramatically. Under this strategy, the trader should offset an existing position and reestablish it at a lower strike price, where there is lower intrinsic value and minimal extrinsic value. In this way, the trader has locked in profits for the difference between the original strike price and the newly established strike price; for example, assume XYZ stock is trading at $100 a share, you are long one 105 XYZ put option, and the stock plunges to 90. You could offset the 105 strike price call option (at a profit) and purchase a new put option at a strike price of 95. Later, if the stock plunges to $80 a share, you can sell the 95 strike price put (at a profit) and purchase a put option at a strike price of 85, and so on. An experienced option trader might exit only part of the position or roll the option position to a different strike price or expiration month as the underlying stock fluctuates, potentially locking in profits along the way. Rolling is covered in Chapter 29.

Protective and Married Puts

Buying a put can be an effective strategy to protect the value of an existing stock position. A *protective put* provides the holder with the right to sell the underlying stock at a strike price, creating a dynamic in which your total stock/option position loss is limited at the strike price minus the premium paid. If you own stock and you want to protect it against a decline, you can buy a put on the stock, allowing you, in effect, to lock in a selling price; for example, if you own 1,000 shares of XYZ stock, you can buy 10 put contracts (one put contract for every 100 shares of stock). If the stock price falls below your strike price, you can sell the puts in the marketplace at a profit or exercise them (sell the shares at that strike price). This type of put protection is similar to an insurance policy, where the cost of insurance is similar to the premium paid, the deductible is similar to the difference between the strike price and stock price, and the term of the policy is similar to the length of the put option. An advantage of the strategy is that if the stock rises, you have unlimited potential minus the premium you paid for the options, while risks are limited.

For example, assume that you have a large unrealized gain on 1,000 shares of XYZ stock, which is trading at $100 a share. You want to protect those paper profits, so you purchase 10 put options at a strike price of 100, paying $5 a contract, or $5,000. If the stock price falls below $100 (the strike price), the put options are in-the-money. You can hold the puts until expiration or sell them in the marketplace. If the stock plunges to $85 and the puts can be sold at $15, your profit on the puts would cushion (except for the premium paid) the decline in the stock. If the stock is below $100 at expiration, you can exercise the put options and use your existing XYZ shares to sell at $100. If the stock price is above $100 at expiration, your puts are out-of-the-money and will expire worthless.

If you own the stock and establish a long put as a protective strategy, you are entitled to the benefits of stock ownership, such as voting rights and dividend distributions, while at the same time limiting the capital that you can lose if the stock price declines. Selecting the best strike price is somewhat of a trade-off between paying as little as possible but trying to gain as much protection as possible. You should review an option chain to see the options available.

Married Put   The simultaneous purchase of stock and a protective put is called a *married put*. In a married put, you buy a stock and a protective put at the same time; for example, you can place one order to purchase 1,000 shares of stock and 10 at-the-money puts. If the stock is trading at $100 and the option is trading at $5, then you can place a single order to pay $105. In the event the stock declines to $90 a share, your loss is capped at $95 ($100 minus $5 paid) a share. It is as though you can sell the shares at $95 a share. A married put can be an effective hedge when adding a new position to your portfolio.

The married put strategy can place you in a position to receive dividends and, at the same time, own the stock with limited downside risk (you also get voting rights, but do not get excited because your interests are probably too small to make a difference). This strategy can be viewed as a way to hedge your investment portfolio by entering into a transaction for the right to sell your shares at a preset exercise price and can be an alternative strategy in lieu of a stop loss on a stock.

The strategy of buying a put to offset a decline in a stock does not have to be executed at the same time as the stock is purchased. Instead, you may want to purchase a put on your existing stocks because you believe they are extended in price. By buying a put option on stocks extended in price, you are, in effect, taking money off the table in the event that a decline occurs, while allowing yourself to fully benefit from the upside potential.

Comparison to Stop Loss Limit Order   The protective (and married) put strategy has advantages over a stop loss order because it enables you to continue to hold on to your underlying stock position, even if the stock moves to what would have been your stop loss price. In a stop loss order, you would automatically trigger a sale order if the stock trades at your stop price, but no such order is triggered if a protective put is used. If you place a stop loss order, the stock can decline to the level of the stop loss, so you are executed on the sale, but then you may watch the stock immediately rise, so you lose on the decline but do not profit on the subsequent stock rise. The stop loss, in effect, took you out of the game. Selling a put against a stock position, however, can provide control over the timing of a sale and, at the same time, provide a guaranteed selling price. It can provide greater staying power than a stop loss because the stock can plunge, and as long as you continue to hold your positions, the stock can rebound, and you are in position to still make a profit.

Puts on Broad-Based Index   Another strategy is to buy a put option against a broad-based index, such as the S&P 500 index, to protect your diversified holdings. This may be an effective way to gain immediate protection, without having to buy put options for each individual stock. Broad-based indexes, stock futures, and ETFs are covered in Part Four.

Equivalent Position

A protective or married put is essentially the same position (called an *equivalent position*) as a long call because the combined stock/put position has many of the risk–reward characteristics of a long call. In a protective or married put, like a long call, you profit fully in the upside of the underlying stock minus the cost of the option, with limited risk. If you are long a call, your loss is limited to the amount paid for the call; likewise, if you enter into an at-the-money married put, your loss is limited to the amount paid for the put; for example, assume that you own 1,000 shares of stock at $100 a share and you buy an at-the-money put for $5. In the event that the stock declines to $90 a share, your loss is capped at $5 (sale price is $100 strike minus $5 paid). The $5 loss is the same as if you had purchased an at-the-money call for $5.

FINAL THOUGHTS

Like buying a call option, selecting the best strike price is somewhat of a trade-off between paying as little as possible but trying to gain as much profit potential as possible. A key ingredient to becoming a successful option trader is to select the best strike price and time frame to fit your risk profile and goals. In some cases, you may want to purchase a small number of in-the-money put options, whereas at other times, you may want to purchase a greater number of at-the-money or out-of-the-money put options. Your goal should be to choose a strike price and expiration date that provides sufficient profit potential at a reasonable cost. You should review an option chain to see the options available.

   Understanding how buying options can be profitable can help you become more effective in understanding the other side of the trade, which is selling, and vice versa. If there is a high-probability strategy for buying an option, then it is likely that there is a low-probability strategy for selling an option; if there is a low-probability strategy for buying an option, there may be high probability in selling an option. Option selling is covered next. As a reminder, the principles that are demonstrated on a stock can be applied to options on an ETF, index, and futures.

CHAPTER 9

Short Call

Now that you understand how buying options can be profitable, you are in a position to learn how to profit from the other side of the trade, which is writing an option. In Chapter 7, we discussed a long call. Many of those principles are also helpful in learning a short call because a short-call option profits in an opposite manner. This chapter will provide an overview of a short call, present numerous comprehensive examples, and then move to beyond the basics, including a discussion of rolling and margin.

OVERVIEW

A short call involves the sale of a call option and is a bearish and neutral strategy. A short call has limited reward potential and unlimited risk. A short call typically increases in value from a rise in the underlying stock or volatility expansion and declines in value from a decline in the underlying stock, time decay, or volatility contraction. Following is a summary profile of a short call.

Direction: Bearish/neutral.
Profit potential: Limited to premium collected.
Risk: Unlimited.
Time decay: Positive (theta).
Volatility: Increase is negative (negative theta), decrease is positive.
Delta: Negative.
Gamma: Negative.
Theta (time): Positive.
Vega (volatility): Negative.
Breakeven: Stock at strike price plus premium collected.

Margin: Generally, 20 percent standard margin, or portfolio margin for equities.
Exercise and assignment: Can be assigned if in-the-money.
How to exit: Offset in closing transaction, assignment, or let expire worthless.
IRA: Not permitted, unless covered.
Main advantages: Time decay; requires less capital in comparison to short stock.
Main disadvantages: Risk is uncapped; can lose more than premium collected.

An option seller profits when the value of an option that was written (sold) is later offset at a price below the level it was written or when it expires worthless. An option seller has a loss when the value of an option that was written is later offset at a price above the level it was written. An attraction of selling a call is that you can profit under three scenarios: the underlying stock can decline, move sideways, or rise by a relatively small amount (up to the strike price if out-of-the-money). An advantage of selling a naked call is that it can be structured to have a higher probability of success than trading the underlying stock or buying a call. A disadvantage to selling any option is that you can lose more than the premium you collect.

Selling a call is typically considered a bearish strategy because you primarily profit if the underlying stock declines. Selling an option, in effect, does not require you to be as precise in comparison to buying, in exchange for limited upside potential but unlimited risk. The maximum gain occurs when the underlying stock is at or below the strike price at expiration.

The initial margin requirement for an uncovered equity option is commonly the premium collected plus 20 percent (or 25 percent) of the underlying stock minus the amount that the option is out-of-the-money, subject to a minimum. Alternatively, for qualified customers, the portfolio margining method typically results in lower margin. Margin is covered in Chapter 30 as well as other chapters.

If implied volatility increases, assuming that all other factors remain constant, a call option will increase in value. If implied volatility declines, assuming that all other factors remain constant, a call option will decline in value; for example, assume that a stock is trading at $100 and you sell a call option with a strike price of $100 and collect $5 ($500) for the option. If implied volatility declines, the call premium could decline from $5 ($500) to something like $4 ($400). If implied volatility rises, the call premium could rise from $5 ($500) to something like $6 ($600).

If you are short a call and are assigned, you are forced to sell the underlying stock at the exercise price. An American-style option can be exercised by the option holder (buyer) at any time up until the expiration date, whereas a European-style option can be exercised only at expiration. Equity options are American-style expirations.

Fraction and Probability Gauge

The fractional (percentage) movement of a short call relative to the movement in a stock price (delta) varies based on the strike price versus the stock price; for example, the deeper in-the-money an option, the more the option moves like the underlying stock, and

TABLE 9.1 Short Call Rules of Thumb

Option	Sample Call Strike Price	Delta Range (Fractions and Probabilities, %)
Deep-in-the-money	90 and lower	75–100
Slightly-in-the-money	95	55–75
At-the-money	100	45–55
Slightly-out-of-the-money	105	25–45
Far-out-of-the-money	110 and higher	0–25

the closer its delta is to -1.0. (A delta of -1.0 means 100 percent, so when the stock moves one point, the option moves one point.) In this case, when an option is deep-in-the-money, it changes at a rate almost point for point equal to that of the underlying stock. If the underlying stock price rises one point, such a call will rise by approximately one point; likewise, if the underlying stock price declines one point, such a call will decline by approximately one point. When an option is at-the-money, its value typically changes at approximately 50 percent relative to the underlying stock. When an option is far-out-of-the-money, its value may change only a small fraction relative to a change in the underlying stock.

Also, the higher the strike price, the lower the probability that a call option will end up in-the-money at the expiration date. Table 9.1 contains general rules of thumb based on the strike price versus the stock price. The stock is assumed to be trading at $100 a share.

STRATEGY EXAMPLES

Following are descriptions and examples of short-call strategies. As a reminder, you can close out an option position by offsetting it in the marketplace any time prior to expiration, and the principles that are demonstrated for a stock can be applied to options on an ETF, index, and stock index futures. Appendixes A, B, and C illustrate many of the strategies covered throughout this book.

To be consistent with Chapters 7 and 8, this chapter will present strategies in the same order of deep-in-the-money, slightly-in-the-money, at-the-money, slightly-out-of-the-money, and far-out-of-the-money, where XYZ stock is initially trading at $100 a share. However, you should keep in mind that the most common option-writing strategies occur with a strike price at-the-money, slightly-out-of-the-money, and far-out-of-the-money. Strategies for writing deep-in-the-money and slightly-in-the-money options are presented to show how options work.

Deep-in-the-Money

A short deep-in-the-money call option typically has a strike price 10 points or more below the stock price and has a delta of -0.75 to -1.0 (75 to 100 percent). If you believe that a stock is ready to decline in value, you can sell a deep-in-the-money call option, which will enable you to benefit almost dollar for dollar on the decline in the value of the stock. If a stock is trading at $100, for instance, you may be able to sell a call option at a strike price of 90 and collect $11 ($1,100) for the option, which has only $1 ($100) extrinsic value. You cannot gain more than the premium collected. That sale will result in a loss from a rise of that stock as though you shorted the shares, except for the $1 ($100) premium you collected above the intrinsic value. You can lose more than the premium collected because you do not have a built-in risk management feature with this strategy. An example follows.

Example: Deep-in-the-Money Short Call

Assumptions: XYZ stock is trading at $100 a share in January; sell one February 90 call at $11.

Strategy direction: Bearish.

Debit or credit: $1,100 credit.

Maximum profit: $1,100 (premium collected).

Maximum loss: Unlimited.

Exercise and assignment: May be assigned if in-the-money.

Break-even stock price: $101 (strike price plus premium collected).

Maximum profit achieved: Stock price at or below strike price.

Maximum loss achieved: Unlimited above break-even stock price.

Profit (loss) if stock unchanged: $100 gain (extrinsic value).

Greeks: Table 9.3 contains sample Greeks converted to dollars at the time the position is established.

Position would reflect a gain from stock decline (delta), time decay (theta), and volatility (vega) contraction. Position would reflect a loss from stock rise (delta) and volatility (vega) expansion. Loss is $80 from XYZ stock rising to $101; gain is $13 from one day of time decay.

TABLE 9.2 Deep-in-the-Money Short Call

XYZ Stock Price ($)	Short Call Value	Premium Collected	Call Profit (Loss)	Call Profit (Loss) Percentage
75	0	1,100	1,100	100
80	0	1,100	1,100	100
85	0	1,100	1,100	100
90	0	1,100	1,100	100
95	500	1,100	600	54
100	1,000	1,100	100	9
105	1,500	1,100	(400)	(36)
110	2,000	1,100	(900)	(81)
115	2,500	1,100	(1,400)	(127)
120	3,000	1,100	(1,900)	(172)
125	3,500	1,100	(2,400)	(218)

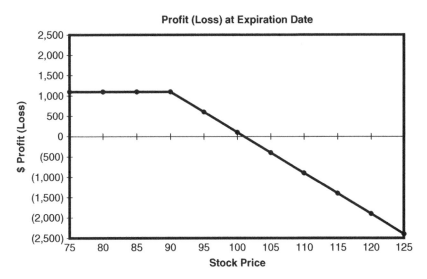

FIGURE 9.1 Deep-in-the-Money Short Call

Later expiration: The price and Greeks will differ if expiration is at a later date; for example, if the call option expires in March, instead of February, the price of the call may be valued at $15 (value of $1,500), with representative Greeks as given in Table 9.4.

Loss is $75 from XYZ stock rising to $101; gain is $10 from one day of time decay.

Exercise and assignment: If you were assigned, you would sell the stock at $90 per share.

If you are selling an option as a proxy for short stock and are collecting a small extrinsic value, selling an option does not usually make a lot of sense. Understanding how selling options can be profitable can help you become more effective in understanding the other side of the trade, which is buying, and vice versa. If there is a high-probability

TABLE 9.3 Summary of Greeks: February Expiration

Option	Delta	Gamma	Theta	Vega
1 February 90 call	−$80	−$1.50	$13	−$9

TABLE 9.4 Summary of Greeks: March Expiration

Option	Delta	Gamma	Theta	Vega
1 March 90 call	−$75	−$1.10	$10	−$15

strategy for selling a call, then it is likely that there is a low-probability strategy for buying a call; if there is a low-probability strategy for selling a call, there may be high probability in buying a call.

Slightly-in-the-Money

A short slightly-in-the-money call option typically has a strike price five points below the stock price and has a delta of −0.60 to −0.75 (60 to 75 percent). If a stock is trading for $100, for instance, you may be able to sell a call option with a strike price of 95 and collect $7 ($700) for the option, which has only $2 ($200) extrinsic value. You cannot gain more than the premium collected. The option sale will result in a loss if the stock rises, as though you fully shorted the shares, except for the $2 ($200) premium you collected above the intrinsic value. You can lose more than the premium collected because you do not have a built-in risk management feature with this strategy. An example follows.

Example: Slightly-in-the-Money Short Call

Assumptions: XYZ stock is trading at $100 a share in January; sell one February 95 call at $7.
Strategy direction: Bearish.
Debit or credit: $700 credit.
Maximum profit: $700 (premium collected).
Maximum loss: Unlimited.
Exercise and assignment: May be assigned if in-the-money.
Break-even stock price: $102 (strike price plus premium collected).
Maximum profit achieved: Stock price at or below strike price.
Maximum loss achieved: Unlimited above break-even stock price.
Profit (loss) if stock unchanged: $200 gain (extrinsic value).

TABLE 9.5   Slightly-in-the-Money Short Call

XYZ Stock Price ($)	Short Call Value	Premium Collected	Call Profit (Loss)	Call Profit (Loss) Percentage
75	0	700	700	100
80	0	700	700	100
85	0	700	700	100
90	0	700	700	100
95	0	700	700	100
100	500	700	200	28
105	1,000	700	(300)	(43)
110	1,500	700	(800)	(114)
115	2,000	700	(1,300)	(185)
120	2,500	700	(1,800)	(257)
125	3,000	700	(2,300)	(328)

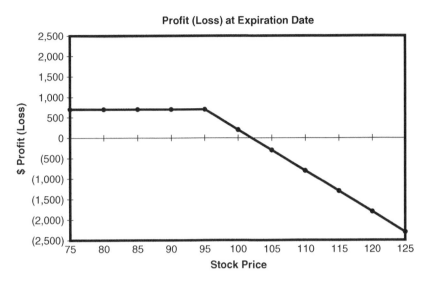

FIGURE 9.2 Slightly-in-the-Money Short Call

Greeks: Table 9.6 contains sample Greeks converted to dollars at the time that the position is established.

Position would reflect a gain from stock decline (delta), time decay (theta), and volatility (vega) contraction. Position would reflect a loss from stock rise (delta) and volatility (vega) expansion. Loss is $65 from XYZ stock rising to $101; gain is $14 from one day of time decay.

Later expiration: The price and Greeks will differ if expiration is at a later date; for example, if the call option expires in March, instead of February, the price of the call may be valued at $12 (value of $1,200), with representative Greeks as given in Table 9.7.

Loss is $63 from XYZ stock rising to $101; gain is $11 from one day of time decay.

Exercise and assignment: If you were assigned, you would sell the stock at $95 per share.

TABLE 9.6 Summary of Greeks: February Expiration

Option	Delta	Gamma	Theta	Vega
1 February 95 call	−$65	−$2.00	$14	−$11

TABLE 9.7 Summary of Greeks: March Expiration

Option	Delta	Gamma	Theta	Vega
1 March 95 call	−$63	−$1.20	$11	−$16

Like the deep-in-the-money options discussed previously, this strategy is being presented to show how options work. It is not as popular as at-the-money or out-of-the-money option-selling strategies.

At-the-Money

A short at-the-money call option has a strike price nearest the stock price and has a delta of -0.45 to -0.55 (45 to 55 percent). With an at-the-money call option, there is no intrinsic value and the option consists entirely of extrinsic value. If a stock is trading at $100, for instance, you may be able to sell a call option with a strike price of 100 and collect $5 ($500) for the option. If the option value declines, you can offset it or let it expire worthless for a profit. If the stock surges, the value of the option will also rise and will generate a loss. You can lose more than the premium collected because you do not have a built-in risk management feature with this strategy. An example follows.

Example: At-the-Money Short Call

> **Assumptions**: XYZ stock is trading at $100 a share in January; sell one February 100 call at $5.
> **Strategy direction**: Bearish.
> **Debit or credit**: $500 credit.
> **Maximum profit**: $500 (premium collected).
> **Maximum loss**: Unlimited.
> **Exercise and assignment**: May be assigned if in-the-money.
> **Break-even stock price**: $105 (strike price plus premium collected).
> **Maximum profit achieved**: Stock price at or below strike price.
> **Maximum loss achieved**: Unlimited above break-even stock price.
> **Profit (loss) if stock unchanged**: $500 gain (extrinsic value).

TABLE 9.8 At-the-Money Short Call

XYZ Stock Price ($)	Short Call Value	Premium Collected	Call Profit (Loss)	Call Profit (Loss) Percentage
75	0	500	500	100
80	0	500	500	100
85	0	500	500	100
90	0	500	500	100
95	0	500	500	100
100	0	500	500	100
105	500	500	0	0
110	1,000	500	(500)	(100)
115	1,500	500	(1,000)	(200)
120	2,000	500	(1,500)	(300)
125	2,500	500	(2,000)	(400)

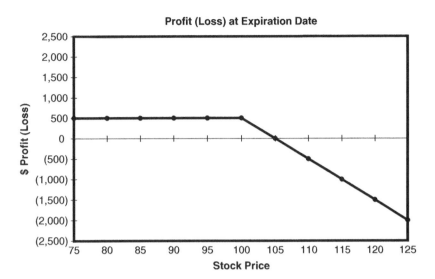

FIGURE 9.3 At-the-Money Short Call

Figure 9.3 is a chart showing the profit (loss) at expiration under the various scenarios.

Greeks: Table 9.9 contains sample Greeks converted to dollars at the time that the position is established.

Position would reflect a gain from stock decline (delta), time decay (theta), and volatility (vega) contraction. Position would reflect a loss from stock rise (delta) and volatility (vega) expansion. Loss is $53 from XYZ stock rising to $101; gain is $15 from one day of time decay.

Later expiration: The price and Greeks will differ if expiration is at a later date; for example, if the call option expires in March, instead of February, the price of the call may be valued at $8 (value of $800), with representative Greeks as given in Table 9.10.

Loss is $52 from XYZ stock rising to $101; gain is $12 from one day of time decay.

Exercise and assignment: If you were assigned, you would sell the stock at $100 per share.

TABLE 9.9 Summary of Greeks: February Expiration

Option	Delta	Gamma	Theta	Vega
1 February 100 call	−$53	−$2.30	$15	−$12

TABLE 9.10 Summary of Greeks: March Expiration

Option	Delta	Gamma	Theta	Vega
1 March 100 call	−$52	−$1.30	$12	−$17

Selling an at-the-money option can enable you to take advantage of a slight statistical probability edge. At-the-money options are, in many cases, the most liquid and the most heavily traded and seem to attract a lot of attention from option traders. Remember that an at-the-money call option consists entirely of extrinsic value and, as a result, you are subject to benefits from time decay and volatility contraction, but you can lose more than the premium collected.

Slightly-Out-of-the-Money

A short slightly-out-of-the-money call option typically has a strike price five points above the stock price and has a delta of −0.25 to −0.45 (25 to 45 percent). With a slightly-out-of-the-money call option, there is no intrinsic value, and the option consists entirely of extrinsic value. If a stock is trading at $100, for instance, you may be able to sell a call option with a strike price of 105 and collect $2 ($200) for the option. If the option value declines, you can offset it or let it expire worthless for a profit. If the stock surges, the value of the option will also rise and will generate a loss. You can lose more than the premium collected because you do not have a built-in risk management feature with this strategy. An example follows.

Example: Slightly-Out-of-the-Money Short Call

Assumptions: XYZ stock is trading at $100 a share in January; sell one February 105 call at $2.

Strategy direction: Bearish/neutral.

Debit or credit: $200 credit.

Maximum profit: $200 (premium collected).

Maximum loss: Unlimited.

Exercise and assignment: May be assigned if in-the-money.

Break-even stock price: $107 (strike price plus premium collected).

Maximum profit achieved: Stock price at or below strike price.

Maximum loss achieved: Unlimited above break-even stock price.

Profit (loss) if stock unchanged: $200 gain (extrinsic value).

Greeks: Table 9.12 contains sample Greeks converted to dollars at the time the position is established.

Position would reflect a gain from stock decline (delta), time decay (theta), and volatility (vega) contraction. Position would reflect a loss from stock rise (delta) and volatility (vega) expansion. Loss is $42 from XYZ stock rising to $101; gain is $14 from one day of time decay.

TABLE 9.11 Slightly-Out-of-the-Money Short Call

XYZ Stock Price ($)	Short Call Value	Premium Collected	Call Profit (Loss)	Call Profit (Loss) Percentage
75	0	200	200	100
80	0	200	200	100
85	0	200	200	100
90	0	200	200	100
95	0	200	200	100
100	0	200	200	100
105	0	200	200	100
110	500	200	(300)	(150)
115	1,000	200	(800)	(400)
120	1,500	200	(1,300)	(650)
125	2,000	200	(1,800)	(900)

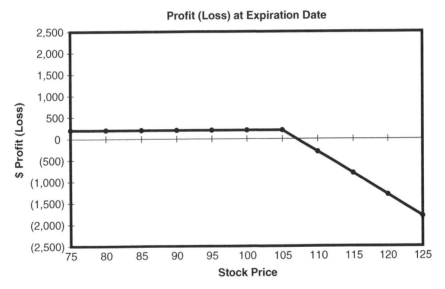

FIGURE 9.4 Slightly-Out-of-the-Money Short Call

Later expiration: The price and Greeks will differ if expiration is at a later date; for example, if the call option expires in March, instead of February, the price of the call may be valued at $3 (value of $300), with representative Greeks as shown in Table 9.13.

Loss is $40 from XYZ stock rising to $101; gain is $10 from one day of time decay.

Exercise and assignment: If you were assigned, you would sell the stock at $105 per share.

TABLE 9.12   Summary of Greeks: February Expiration

Option	Delta	Gamma	Theta	Vega
1 February 105 call	−$42	−$2.00	$14	−$11

TABLE 9.13   Summary of Greeks: March Expiration

Option	Delta	Gamma	Theta	Vega
1 March 105 call	−$40	−$1.20	$10	−$15

Selling slightly-out-of-the-money options can provide a statistical edge. Because a slightly-out-of-the-money call option consists entirely of extrinsic value, you are subject to benefits from time decay and volatility contraction. Unfortunately, you do not have a built-in risk management feature with this strategy, and you can lose more than the premium collected.

As time approaches the expiration date, especially during the last week of option expiration, some stocks may have very little extrinsic value. Selling a call option near parity is usually not an attractive strategy, especially if volatility is expected to increase from an event such as the release of an earnings report. For example, assume that on Wednesday, a stock is trading at $108 (during option expiration week), and the company will release earnings the following day, on Thursday. If a call option with a strike price of 105 is priced at $3.25 ($325), you could sell that option at $3.25 ($325) and only collect $0.25 ($25) above parity (extrinsic value). If the stock rises in value, you are at risk for the full move minus the $0.25 ($25). If the stock should decline, your profit is limited to $3.25 ($325). In effect, you have full upside risk and no built-in insurance component. In general, you should avoid selling naked options close to expiration. The rewards may look attractive because time decay may result in a quick profit, but there is no limit to the losses you could sustain. In some cases, the move may be so swift that you will not be able to exit your position before a large loss occurs. Selling a close-to-the-money call option with minimal extrinsic value is more like gambling and is usually not a wise choice because it is a low-probability trade with unlimited risk and limited profit potential.

Far-Out-of-the-Money

A short far-out-of-the-money call option typically has a strike price 10 points or more above the stock price and has a delta of zero to −0.25 (0 to 25 percent). A far-out-of-the-money call option consists entirely of extrinsic value and is the most leveraged strategy. This can be a high-probability strategy because the further you move away from the price of the underlying stock price, the lower is the probability that the stock will end up in-the-money. It can be an effective strategy to attempt to earn consistent income; for example, if a stock is trading at $100, you may be able to sell a call option with a strike price of 110 and collect $1 ($100) for the option. If the option value declines, you can offset it or let it expire worthless for a profit. If the stock surges, the value of the option will also rise and will generate a loss. You can lose more than the premium collected because you do not have a built-in risk management feature with this strategy. An example follows.

Example: Far-Out-of-the-Money Short Call

Assumptions: XYZ stock is trading at $100 a share in January; sell one February 110 call at $1.

Strategy direction: Bearish/neutral.

Debit or credit: $100 credit.

Maximum profit: $100 (premium collected).

Maximum loss: Unlimited.

Exercise and assignment: May be assigned if in-the-money.

Break-even stock price: $111 (strike price plus premium collected).

Maximum profit achieved: Stock price at or below strike price.

Maximum loss achieved: Unlimited above break-even stock price.

Profit (loss) if stock unchanged: $100 gain (extrinsic value).

Greeks: Table 9.15 contains sample Greeks converted to dollars at the time the position is established.

Position would reflect a gain from stock decline (delta), time decay (theta), and volatility (vega) contraction. Position would reflect a loss from stock rise (delta) and volatility (vega) expansion. Loss is $23 from XYZ stock rising to $101; gain is $12 from one day of time decay.

Later expiration: The price and Greeks will differ if expiration is at a later date; for example, if the call option expires in March, instead of February, the price of the

TABLE 9.14 Far-Out-of-the-Money Short Call

XYZ Stock Price ($)	Short Call Value	Premium Collected	Call Profit (Loss)	Call Profit (Loss) Percentage
75	0	100	100	100
80	0	100	100	100
85	0	100	100	100
90	0	100	100	100
95	0	100	100	100
100	0	100	100	100
105	0	100	100	100
110	0	100	100	100
115	500	100	(400)	(400)
120	1,000	100	(900)	(900)
125	1,500	100	(1,400)	(1,400)

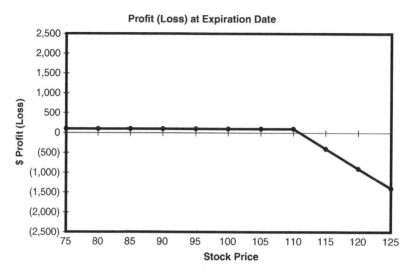

FIGURE 9.5   Far-Out-of-the-Money Short Call

call may be valued at $2 (value of $200), with representative Greeks as given in Table 9.16.

Loss is $20 from XYZ stock rising to $101; gain is $7 from one day of time decay.

Exercise and assignment: If you were assigned, you would sell the stock at $110 per share.

Some traders find the risk-reward trade-off of selling far-out-of-the-money options to be worthwhile. A far-out-of-the-money call option is usually sold at a relatively low price, which is why some option sellers shy away from them initially; but, to some option sellers, they present an opportunity for consistent income. Keep in mind that along with the potential for profit is also greater risk. Selling far-out-of-the-money options can enable a trader to take advantage of a statistical probability edge. Unfortunately, you can lose more than the premium collected.

TABLE 9.15   Summary of Greeks: February Expiration

Option	Delta	Gamma	Theta	Vega
1 February 110 call	−$23	−$1.75	$12	−$8

TABLE 9.16   Summary of Greeks: March Expiration

Option	Delta	Gamma	Theta	Vega
1 March 110 call	−$20	−$1.00	$7	−$10

BEYOND THE BASICS

Playing Defense

As an alternative to offsetting a short call position at a loss, a trader can consider rolling a call option position. Under this strategy, the trader can offset the current position and reestablish it at a higher strike price; for example, assume XYZ is trading at $100 and you are short one February XYZ 105 call. If the stock rises to 104 before expiration, you may consider offsetting the short 105 call (at a loss) and writing a new February call option at a strike price of 110. The idea is that, for example, if you have a loss of $2 ($200) on a short call position, you can offset the current position and sell one further out-of-the-money call at a higher strike price for $2 ($200), in an attempt to earn the amount of the loss. Alternatively, you can sell two call options at $1 ($100) each at a higher strike price or establish a position in a later expiration month at a higher strike price. In this example, you could offset the February 105 strike-price call option (at a loss) and sell two new February call options at a strike price of 115. Alternatively, you could offset the February 105 strike-price call option (at a loss) and sell one new March call option for $2 at a strike price of 110. In this way, you have attempted to earn the amount of your loss in the future. An experienced option trader might exit only part of the position or roll the option position to a different strike price or expiration month as the underlying stock fluctuates, potentially locking in profits along the way. Rolling is covered in Chapter 29.

Margin

A short option position may be subject to a margin requirement. In general, when a trader enters into a short option position, he is required to post (i.e., have on deposit by the date set by the broker) initial margin. When writing an uncovered equity option, the minimum initial margin requirement is, in general, 20 percent (or 25 percent) of the underlying stock minus the amount that the option is out-of-the-money, if any, plus the premium collected, but not less than 10 percent of the stock value. The out-of-the-money amount is the difference between the strike price and stock price times the number of contracts times the unit of measure ($100 for stocks). As mentioned in Chapter 5, for example, if XYZ stock is trading at $100 a share and you sell a call with a strike price of $100, the 20 percent standard margin requirement is $2,000 (ignoring the premium collected). If you sell a 105 strike-price call, the out-of-the-money amount is considered to be $500 (five points times $100) and would reduce the margin requirement.

Portfolio margining is a newer method available for computing equity margin for certain qualified customers based on the risk of the position, rather than on fixed percentages, and the result is often lower margin requirements than would be calculated from the traditional method described previously. A futures option margin is calculated differently than margin on stock options. A broker may, and often does, impose more stringent margin requirements. Margin rules are covered in Chapter 30.

FINAL THOUGHTS

When selling an at-the-money or out-of-the-money call option, you can profit if the underlying stock moves lower, sideways, or even higher up to the strike price at expiration. The advantage of selling options that are slightly-in-the-money, at-the-money, or out-of-the-money is that they provide the advantage of time decay and you can stack the statistical probabilities on your side. An option seller has time on his side and does not need to be precise in his choice of the direction, timing, and magnitude of the move. Another attractive feature of selling a call option is that it does not require a capital outlay, so you can earn interest while you trade. Remember that if there is a high-probability strategy for buying a call, then it is likely that there is a low-probability strategy for selling a call; if there is a low-probability strategy for buying a call, there may be high probability in selling a call. We now move to Chapter 10, which covers a short put.

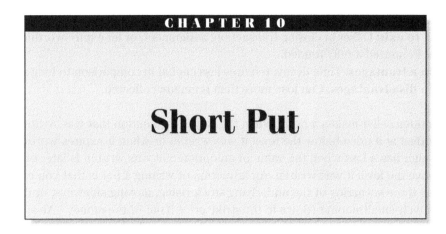

Short Put

In Chapter 9, we discussed a short call. Writing a put option has many of the same characteristics as a short call option, except a put option profits in the opposite direction. This chapter provides an overview of a short put, presents numerous examples, and then moves to beyond the basics, including a discussion of rolling, a cash-secured put, selling puts for income, and margin.

OVERVIEW

A short put involves the sale of a put option and is a bullish and neutral strategy. A short put has limited reward potential and unlimited risk. A put typically increases in value from a decline in the underlying stock or volatility expansion and declines in value from a decline in the underlying stock, time decay, or volatility contraction. Following is a summary profile of a short put:

Direction: Bullish/neutral.
Profit potential: Limited to premium collected.
Risk: Unlimited. (Technically, strike price minus premium collected.)
Time decay: Positive (theta).
Volatility: Increase is negative (negative theta), decrease is positive.
Delta: Positive.
Gamma: Negative.
Theta (time): Positive.
Vega (volatility): Negative.
Breakeven: Stock at strike price minus premium collected.
Margin: Generally, 20 percent standard margin, or portfolio margin for equities.

Exercise and assignment: Can be assigned if in-the-money.
How to exit: Offset in closing transaction, assignment, or let expire worthless.
IRA: Permitted if fully funded.
Main advantages: Time decay; requires less capital in comparison to long stock.
Main disadvantages: Can lose more than premium collected.

An option seller makes a profit when the value of an option that was written (sold) is later offset at a price below the level it was written or when it expires worthless. An option seller has a loss when the value of an option that was written is later offset at a price above the level it was written. An attraction of writing a put is that you can profit under the three scenarios of the underlying stock rising, moving sideways, or declining by a relatively small amount (down to the strike price if out-of-the-money). An advantage of writing a naked put is that it can be structured to have a higher probability of success than trading the underlying stock or buying a put. A disadvantage to writing any option is that you can lose more than the premium you collect. Writing a put is typically considered a bullish strategy because you primarily profit if the underlying stock rises. Writing an option, in effect, does not require you to be as precise, in exchange for limited upside potential but unlimited risk. The maximum gain occurs when the underlying stock is at or above the strike price at expiration.

The initial margin requirement for an uncovered equity option is commonly the premium collected plus 20 percent (or 25 percent) of the underlying stock minus the amount that the option is out-of-the-money, subject to a minimum. Alternatively, for qualified customers, the portfolio margining method typically results in a lower margin. Margin is covered in Chapter 30.

If implied volatility increases, assuming that all other factors remain constant, a put option will increase in value. If implied volatility declines, assuming that all other factors remain constant, a put option will decline in value; for example, assume that a stock is trading at $100 and you sell a put option with a strike price of 100 and collect $5 ($500) for the option. If implied volatility declines, the put premium could decline from $5 ($500) to something like $4 ($400). If implied volatility rises, the put premium could rise from $5 ($500) to something like $6 ($600).

If you are short a put and are assigned, you are forced to buy the underlying stock at the exercise price. An American-style option can be exercised by the option holder (buyer) at any time up until the expiration date, whereas a European-style option can be exercised only at expiration. Equity options are American-style expirations.

Fraction and Probability Gauge

The fractional (percentage) movement of a short put relative to the movement in a stock price (delta) varies based on the strike price versus the stock price; for example, the deeper in-the-money an option, the more the option moves like the underlying stock and the closer its delta to 1.0. (A delta of 1.0 means 100 percent, so when the stock moves one point, the option moves one point.) In this case, when an option is deep-in-the-money,

TABLE 10.1 Short Put Rules of Thumb

Option	Sample Put Strike Price	Delta Range (Fractions and Probabilities, %)
Deep-in-the-money	110 and higher	75–100
Slightly-in-the-money	105	55–75
At-the-money	100	45–55
Slightly-out-of-the-money	95	25–45
Far-out-of-the-money	90 and lower	0–25

it changes at a rate almost point for point equal to that of the underlying stock. If the underlying stock price declines one point, such a put will rise by approximately one point; likewise, if the underlying stock price rises one point, such a put will decline by approximately one point. When an option is at-the-money, its value typically changes at approximately 50 percent relative to the underlying stock. When an option is far-out-of-the-money, its value may change only a small fraction relative to a change in the underlying stock.

Also, the lower the strike price, the lower the probability that a put option will end up in-the-money at the expiration date. Table 10.1 contains general rules of thumb based on the strike price versus the stock price. The stock is assumed to be trading at $100 a share.

STRATEGY EXAMPLES

Following are descriptions and examples of short-put strategies. As a reminder, you can close out an option position by offsetting it in the marketplace any time prior to expiration, and the principles that are demonstrated for a stock can be applied to options on an ETF, index, and stock index futures. Appendixes A, B, and C illustrate many of the strategies covered throughout this book.

To be consistent with the rest of the chapters in Part Two, this chapter will present strategies in the same order of deep-in-the-money, slightly-in-the-money, at-the-money, slightly-out-of-the-money, and far-out-of-the-money, where XYZ stock is initially trading at $100 a share. However, you should keep in mind that the most common option-writing strategies occur with a strike price at-the-money, slightly-out-of-the-money, and far-out-of-the-money. Strategies for writing deep-in-the-money and slightly-in-the-money options are presented to show how options work.

Deep-in-the-Money

A short deep-in-the-money put option typically has a strike price 10 points or more above the stock price and has a delta of 0.75 to 1.0 (75 to 100 percent). If you believe that a stock is ready to rise in value, you can sell a deep-in-the-money put option, which will enable you to benefit almost dollar for dollar on the rise in the value of the stock. If a stock is trading at $100, for instance, you may be able to sell a put option at a strike price of 110 and collect $11 ($1,100) for the option, which has only $1 ($100) extrinsic value. You cannot gain more than the premium collected. The sale will result in a loss from a decline of that stock as though you were long the shares, except for the $1 ($100) premium you collected above the intrinsic value. You can lose more than the premium collected because you do not have a built-in risk management feature with this strategy. An example follows.

Example: Deep-in-the-Money Short Put

Assumptions: XYZ stock is trading at $100 a share in January; sell one February 110 put at $11.

Strategy direction: Bullish.

Debit or credit: $1,100 credit.

Maximum profit: $1,100 (premium collected).

Maximum loss: $9,900 (strike price minus premium paid).

Exercise and assignment: May be assigned if in-the-money.

Break-even stock price: $99 (strike price minus premium collected).

Maximum profit achieved: Stock price at or above strike price.

Maximum loss achieved: Unlimited below break-even stock price.

Profit (loss) if stock unchanged: $100 gain (extrinsic value).

Greeks: Table 10.3 contains sample Greeks converted to dollars at the time the position is established.

Position would reflect a gain from stock rise (delta), time decay (theta), and volatility (vega) contraction. Position would reflect a loss from stock decline (delta) and volatility (vega) expansion. Gain is $80 from XYZ stock rising to $101; gain is $13 from one day of time decay.

TABLE 10.2   Deep-in-the-Money Short Put

XYZ Stock Price ($)	Short Put Value	Cost of Put	Put Profit (Loss)	Put Profit (Loss) Percentage
75	3,500	1,100	(2,400)	(218)
80	3,000	1,100	(1,900)	(172)
85	2,500	1,100	(1,400)	(127)
90	2,000	1,100	(900)	(81)
95	1,500	1,100	(400)	(36)
100	1,000	1,100	100	9
105	500	1,100	600	54
110	0	1,100	1,100	100
115	0	1,100	1,100	100
120	0	1,100	1,100	100
125	0	1,100	1,100	100

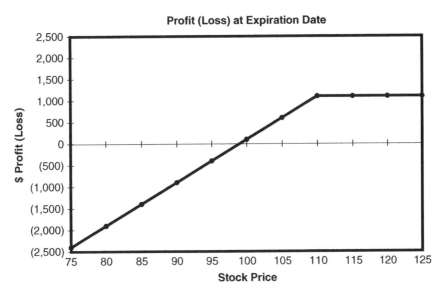

FIGURE 10.1 Deep-in-the-Money Short Put

Later expiration: The price and Greeks will differ if expiration is at a later date; for example, if the put option expires in March, instead of February, the price of the put may be valued at $15 (value of $1,500), with representative Greeks as shown in Table 10.4.

Gain is $75 from XYZ stock rising to $101; gain is $10 from one day of time decay.

Exercise and assignment: If you were assigned, you would sell the stock at $110 per share.

If you are selling an option as a proxy for long stock and are collecting a small extrinsic value, selling an option does not usually make a lot of sense. Understanding how selling options can be profitable can help you become more effective in understanding the other side of the trade, which is buying, and vice versa. If there is a high-probability

TABLE 10.3 Summary of Greeks: February Expiration

Option	Delta	Gamma	Theta	Vega
1 February 110 put	$80	−$1.50	$13	−$9

TABLE 10.4 Summary of Greeks: March Expiration

Option	Delta	Gamma	Theta	Vega
1 March 110 put	$75	−$1.10	$10	−$15

strategy for selling a put, then it is likely that there is a low-probability strategy for buying a put; if there is a low-probability strategy for selling a put, there may be a high probability in buying a put.

Slightly-in-the-Money

A short slightly-in-the-money put option typically has a strike price five points above the stock price and has a delta of 0.60 to 0.75 (60 to 75 percent). If a stock is trading for $100, for instance, you may be able to sell a put option with a strike price of 105 and collect $7 ($700) for the option, which has only $2 ($200) extrinsic value. You cannot gain more than the premium collected. The option sale will result in a loss if the stock declines as though you fully owned the shares, except for the $2 ($200) premium you collected above the intrinsic value. You can lose more than the premium collected because you do not have a built-in risk management feature with this strategy. An example follows.

Example: Slightly-in-the-Money Short Put

Assumptions: XYZ stock is trading at $100 a share in January; sell one February 105 put at $7.
Strategy direction: Bullish.
Debit or credit: $700 credit.
Maximum profit: $700 (premium collected).
Maximum loss: $9,800 (strike price minus premium paid).
Exercise and assignment: May be assigned if in-the-money.
Break-even stock price: $98 (strike price minus premium collected).
Maximum profit achieved: Stock price at or above strike price.

TABLE 10.5 Slightly-in-the-Money Short Put

XYZ Stock Price ($)	Short Put Value	Cost of Put	Put Profit (Loss)	Put Profit (Loss) Percentage
75	3,000	700	(2,300)	(328)
80	2,500	700	(1,800)	(257)
85	2,000	700	(1,300)	(185)
90	1,500	700	(800)	(114)
95	1,000	700	(300)	(43)
100	500	700	200	28
105	0	700	700	100
110	0	700	700	100
115	0	700	700	100
120	0	700	700	100
125	0	700	700	100

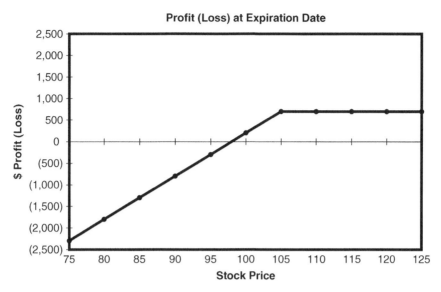

FIGURE 10.2 Slightly-in-the-Money Short Put

Maximum loss achieved: Unlimited below break-even stock price.

Profit (loss) if stock unchanged: $200 gain (extrinsic value).

Greeks: Table 10.6 contains sample Greeks converted to dollars at the time the position is established.

Position would reflect a gain from stock rise (delta), time decay (theta), and volatility (vega) contraction. Position would reflect a loss from stock decline (delta) and volatility (vega) expansion. Gain is $65 from XYZ stock rising to $101; gain is $14 from one day of time decay.

Later expiration: The price and Greeks will differ if expiration is at a later date; for example, if the put option expires in March, instead of February, the price of the put may be valued at $12 (value of $1,200), with representative Greeks as given in Table 10.7.

Gain is $63 from XYZ stock rising to $101; gain is $11 from one day of time decay.

Exercise and assignment: If you were assigned, you would sell the stock at $105 per share.

TABLE 10.6 Summary of Greeks: February Expiration

Option	Delta	Gamma	Theta	Vega
1 February 105 put	$65	−$2.00	$14	−$11

TABLE 10.7 Summary of Greeks: March Expiration

Option	Delta	Gamma	Theta	Vega
1 March 105 put	$63	−$1.20	$11	−$16

Like the deep-in-the-money options discussed previously, this strategy is being presented to show how options work. It is not as popular as at-the-money or out-of-the-money option-selling strategies.

At-the-Money

A short at-the-money put option has a strike price nearest the stock price and has a delta of 0.45 to 0.55 (45 to 55 percent). With an at-the-money put option, there is no intrinsic value, and the option consists entirely of extrinsic value. If a stock is trading at $100, for instance, you may be able to sell a put option with a strike price of 100 and collect $5 ($500) for the option. If the option value declines, you can offset it or let it expire worthless for a profit. If the stock plunges, the value of the option will rise and will generate a loss. You can lose more than the premium collected because you do not have a built-in risk management feature with this strategy. An example follows.

Example: At-the-Money Short Put

> **Assumptions**: XYZ stock is trading at $100 a share in January; sell one February 100 put at $5.
> **Strategy direction**: Bullish.
> **Debit or credit**: $500 credit.
> **Maximum profit**: $500 (premium collected).
> **Maximum loss**: $9,500 (strike price minus premium paid).

TABLE 10.8 At-the-Money Short Put

XYZ Stock Price ($)	Short Put Value	Cost of Put	Put Profit (Loss)	Put Profit (Loss) Percentage
75	2,500	500	(2,000)	(400)
80	2,000	500	(1,500)	(300)
85	1,500	500	(1,000)	(200)
90	1,000	500	(500)	(100)
95	500	500	0	0
100	0	500	500	100
105	0	500	500	100
110	0	500	500	100
115	0	500	500	100
120	0	500	500	100
125	0	500	500	100

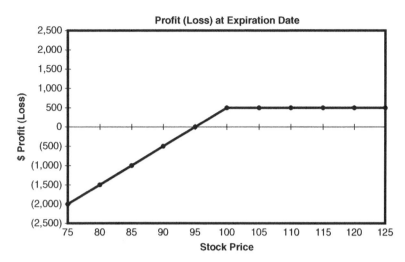

FIGURE 10.3 At-the-Money Short Put

Exercise and assignment: May be assigned if in-the-money.

Break-even stock price: $95 (strike price minus premium collected).

Maximum profit achieved: Stock price at or above strike price.

Maximum loss achieved: Unlimited below break-even stock price.

Profit (loss) if stock unchanged: $500 gain (extrinsic value).

Greeks: Table 10.9 contains sample Greeks converted to dollars at the time the position is established.

    Position would reflect a gain from stock rise (delta), time decay (theta), and volatility (vega) contraction. Position would reflect a loss from stock decline (delta) and volatility (vega) expansion. Gain is $53 from XYZ stock rising to $101; gain is $15 from one day of time decay.

Later expiration: The price and Greeks will differ if expiration is at a later date; for example, if the put option expires in March, instead of February, the price of the put may be valued at $8 (value of $800), with representative Greeks as given in Table 10.10.

    Gain is $52 from XYZ stock rising to $101; gain is $12 from one day of time decay.

Exercise and assignment: If you were assigned, you would sell the stock at $100 per share.

TABLE 10.9 Summary of Greeks: February Expiration

Option	Delta	Gamma	Theta	Vega
1 February 100 put	$53	−$2.30	$15	−$12

TABLE 10.10 Summary of Greeks: March Expiration

Option	Delta	Gamma	Theta	Vega
1 March 100 put	$52	−$1.30	$12	−$17

Selling an at-the-money option can enable you to take advantage of a slight statistical probability edge. At-the-money options are, in many cases, the most liquid and the most heavily traded and seem to attract the attention of option traders. Remember that an at-the-money call option consists entirely of extrinsic value and, as a result, you are subject to benefits from time decay and volatility contraction, but you can lose more than the premium collected.

Slightly-Out-of-the-Money

A short slightly-out-of-the-money put option typically has a strike price five points below the stock price and has a delta of 0.25 to 0.45 (25 to 45 percent). With a slightly-out-of-the-money put option, there is no intrinsic value and the option consists entirely of extrinsic value. If a stock is trading at $100, for instance, you may be able to sell a put option with a strike price of 95 and collect $2 ($200) for the option. If the option value declines, you can offset it or let it expire worthless for a profit. If the stock plunges, the value of the option will rise and generate a loss. You can lose more than the premium collected because you do not have a built-in risk management feature with this strategy. An example follows.

Example: Slightly-Out-of-the-Money Short Put

Assumptions: XYZ stock is trading at $100 a share in January; sell one February 95 put at $2.

TABLE 10.11 Slightly-Out-of-the-Money Short Put

XYZ Stock Price ($)	Short Put Value	Cost of Put	Put Profit (Loss)	Put Profit (Loss) Percentage
75	2,000	200	(1,800)	(900)
80	1,500	200	(1,300)	(650)
85	1,000	200	(800)	(400)
90	500	200	(300)	(150)
95	0	200	200	100
100	0	200	200	100
105	0	200	200	100
110	0	200	200	100
115	0	200	200	100
120	0	200	200	100
125	0	200	200	100

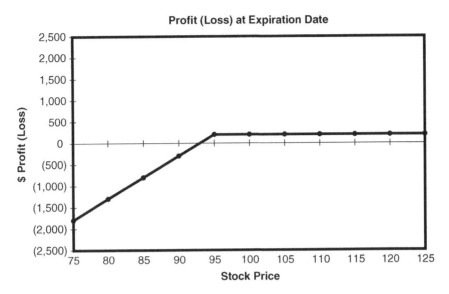

FIGURE 10.4 Slightly-Out-of-the-Money Short Put

Strategy direction: Bullish/neutral.

Debit or credit: $200 credit.

Maximum profit: $200 (premium collected).

Maximum loss: $9,300 (strike price minus premium paid).

Exercise and assignment: May be assigned if in-the-money.

Break-even stock price: $93 (strike price minus premium collected).

Maximum profit achieved: Stock price at or above strike price.

Maximum loss achieved: Unlimited below break-even stock price.

Profit (loss) if stock unchanged: $200 gain (extrinsic value).

Greeks: Table 10.12 contains sample Greeks converted to dollars at the time the position is established.

Position would reflect a gain from stock rise (delta), time decay (theta), and volatility (vega) contraction. Position would reflect a loss from stock decline (delta) and volatility (vega) expansion. Gain is $42 from XYZ stock rising to $101; gain is $14 from one day of time decay.

Later expiration: The price and Greeks will differ if expiration is at a later date; for example, if the put option expires in March, instead of February, the price of the

TABLE 10.12 Summary of Greeks: February Expiration

Option	Delta	Gamma	Theta	Vega
1 February 95 put	$42	−$2.00	$14	−$11

TABLE 10.13 Summary of Greeks: March Expiration

Option	Delta	Gamma	Theta	Vega
1 March 95 put	$40	−$1.20	$10	−$15

put may be valued at $3 (value of $300), with representative Greeks as given in Table 10.13.

Gain is $40 from XYZ stock rising to $101; gain is $10 from one day of time decay.

Exercise and assignment: If you were assigned, you would sell the stock at $95 per share.

Selling slightly-out-of-the-money options can provide a statistical probability edge. A slightly-out-of-the-money call option consists entirely of extrinsic value. As a result, you are subject to benefits from time decay and volatility contraction. Unfortunately, you do not have a built-in risk management feature with this strategy, and you can lose more than the premium collected.

As time approaches the expiration date, especially during the last week of option expiration, some stocks may have very little extrinsic value. Selling a put option near parity is not usually an attractive strategy unless your intent is to own the stock through assignment, especially if volatility is expected to increase from an event such as the release of an earnings report. For example, assume that on Wednesday, a stock is trading at $97 (during option expiration week) and the company will release earnings the following day, on Thursday. If a put option with a strike price of 100 is priced at $3.25 ($325), you could sell that option at $3.25 ($325) and only collect $0.25 ($25) above parity (extrinsic value). If the stock declines in value, you are at risk for the full move minus the $0.25 ($25). If the stock should rise, your profit is limited to $3.25 ($325). In effect, you get full upside risk and no built-in insurance component.

Far-Out-of-the-Money

A short far-out-of-the-money put option typically has a strike price 10 points or more above the stock price and has a delta of zero to 0.25 (0 to 25 percent). A far-out-of-the-money put option consists entirely of extrinsic value and is the most leveraged strategy. This can be a high-probability strategy because the further you move away from the price of the underlying stock, the lower the probability that the stock will end up in-the-money. It can be an effective strategy to attempt to earn consistent income; for example, if a stock is trading at $100, you may be able to sell a put option with a strike price of 90 and collect $1 ($100) for the option. If the option value declines, you can offset it or let it expire worthless for a profit. If the stock plunges, the value of the option will rise and may generate a loss. You can lose more than the premium collected because you do not have a built-in risk management feature with this strategy. An example follows.

Example: Far-Out-of-the-Money Short Put

Assumptions: XYZ stock is trading at $100 a share in January; sell one February 90 put at $1.

Strategy direction: Bullish/neutral.

Debit or credit: $100 credit.

Maximum profit: $100 (premium collected).

Maximum loss: $8,900 (strike price minus premium paid).

Exercise and assignment: May be assigned if in-the-money.

Break-even stock price: $89 (strike price minus premium collected).

TABLE 10.14 Far-Out-of-the-Money Short Put

XYZ Stock Price ($)	Short Put Value	Cost of Put	Put Profit (Loss)	Put Profit (Loss) Percentage
75	1,500	100	(1,400)	(1,400)
80	1,000	100	(900)	(900)
85	500	100	(400)	(400)
90	0	100	100	100
95	0	100	100	100
100	0	100	100	100
105	0	100	100	100
110	0	100	100	100
115	0	100	100	100
120	0	100	100	100
125	0	100	100	100

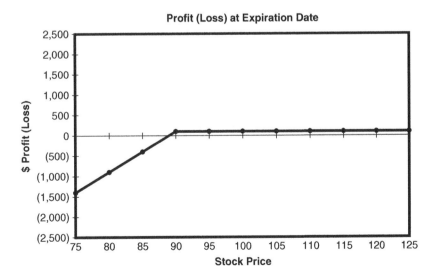

FIGURE 10.5 Far-Out-of-the-Money Short Put

TABLE 10.15 Summary of Greeks: February Expiration

Option	Delta	Gamma	Theta	Vega
1 February 90 put	$23	−$1.75	$12	−$8

TABLE 10.16 Summary of Greeks: March Expiration

Option	Delta	Gamma	Theta	Vega
1 March 90 put	$20	−$1.00	$7	−$10

Maximum profit achieved: Stock price at or above strike price.

Maximum loss achieved: Unlimited below break-even stock price.

Profit (loss) if stock unchanged: $100 gain (extrinsic value).

Greeks: Table 10.15 contains sample Greeks converted to dollars at the time the position is established.

   Position would reflect a gain from stock rise (delta), time decay (theta), and volatility (vega) contraction. Position would reflect a loss from stock decline (delta) and volatility (vega) expansion. Gain is $23 from XYZ stock rising to $101; gain is $12 from one day of time decay.

Later expiration: The price and Greeks will differ if expiration is at a later date; for example, if the put option expires in March, instead of February, the price of the put may be valued at $2 (value of $200), with representative Greeks as given in Table 10.16.

   Gain is $20 from XYZ stock rising to $101; gain is $7 from one day of time decay.

Exercise and assignment: If you were assigned, you would sell the stock at $90 per share.

   Some traders find the risk–reward trade-off of selling far-out-of-the-money options to be worthwhile. A far-out-of-the-money put option is usually sold at a relatively low price, which is why some option sellers shy away from them initially; however, to some option sellers, they present an opportunity for consistent income. Keep in mind that along with the potential for profit is also greater risk. Selling far-out-of-the-money options can enable a trader to take advantage of a statistical probability edge. Unfortunately, you can lose more than the premium collected.

BEYOND THE BASICS

Playing Defense

As an alternative to offsetting a short put position at a loss, a trader can consider rolling a put option position. Under this strategy, the trader can offset the current position and reestablish it at a lower strike price; for example, assume XYZ is trading at $100 and you are short one February XYZ 95 put. If the stock declines to $96 before expiration, you may consider offsetting the short 95 put (at a loss) and writing a new February put option at a strike price of 90. The idea is that, for example, if you have a loss of $2 ($200) on a short put position, you can offset the current position and sell one further out-of-the-money put at a lower strike price for $2 ($200), in an attempt to earn the amount of the loss. Alternatively, you can sell two put options at $1 ($100) each at a lower strike price or establish a position in a later expiration month at a lower strike price.

In this example, you could offset the February 95 strike price put option (at a loss) and sell two new February put options at a strike price of 85. Alternatively, you could offset the February 95 strike price put option (at a loss) and sell one new March put option for $2 at a strike price of 90. In this way, you have attempted to earn the amount of your loss in the future. An experienced option trader might exit only part of the position or roll the option position to a different strike price or expiration month as the underlying stock fluctuates, potentially locking in profits along the way. Rolling is covered in Chapter 29.

Cash-Secured Put

When you sell a put and have the money available in the brokerage account to buy the stock, it is called a cash-secured put. Selling a put option can be used as a strategy to earn premium income if the underlying stock should rise, but buy the stock at a lower price if the stock declines below the strike price. For example, if a stock is at $100 a share and you are only willing to purchase the stock at $95, you can sell a put option with a strike price of 100 and collect an option premium of $5. By doing so, ignoring the fact that you can sell the option in the market at any time, you are obligated to purchase the stock at $100 (your real purchase price is $100 less $5 collected). Under this scenario, if the stock simply continues to rise, you earn the option premium. Should the stock decline to below $95, it has met your targeted purchase price. The maximum risk of a cash-secured put is similar to owning the stock itself (ignoring the premium collected).

Selling a cash-secured put is the sale of a naked option, so it has risk. One risk of selling a naked option is that the stock price could gap below the strike price so that you end up paying substantially more than the new market value of the stock. In the preceding example, if your strike price is 100 and the stock gaps from $100 to $80 a share, your purchase price is $100 because that is the strike price you chose. In any event, if the stock plunged to $80 a share, you could offset the naked put option in the marketplace by buying it back or you could wait for assignment, in which case you will be obligated to purchase the shares at $100 a share.

Selling a cash-secured put can be at an attractive strategy because it can be used to help buy stock at the purchase price you desire. Keep in mind that this may be little consolation if you have a loss in your brokerage account for the difference between the strike price and the stock price. An alternative to the cash-secured put strategy is simply to wait until the stock drops to your targeted purchase price. In that case, however, you do not collect a premium and the stock could simply continue to rise. With a cash-secured put, you are being compensated to wait.

Sell Puts for Income

Another strategy is to sell far-out-of-the-money puts so that they have a low delta and are highly unlikely to be assigned. In this way, your primary focus is on earning premium income and avoiding assignment. As you add more short puts, you are increasing your risks because the market can gap down and the power of leverage can work against you.

In general, I have found that a broad-based index, such as the S&P 500, can be a good candidate for selling far-out-of-the-money options (puts and/or calls). Chapters 23 to 26 cover indexes, ETFs, and stock index futures. For example, assume that it is January, the S&P 500 futures is at 1,500, and you sell four February S&P 500 futures puts at a strike price of 1,350 at $1 a contract (10 percent below the market). The premium collected is $1,000 (four contracts at $250 a point). Assume that you are not interested in purchasing any underlying futures contracts but are solely focused on trading the options. This type of option selling has its own unique risks and rewards. This strategy shows a profit if the S&P 500 futures rises, moves sideways, or moves down by less than 150 points. Its greatest risk is a gap down by a large amount. The strategy tries to take advantage of being able to profit under many market conditions. However, it can be a risky strategy in that the market can gap lower with greater volatility so that the option value can explode, leading to magnified losses because of the leverage of options.

Margin

Although margin is not permitted in an IRA, some brokerage firms allow the shorting of a naked put because the risk is mathematically limited to the difference between the strike price and zero (ignoring the premium). Like a call, when writing an equity option, the minimum margin requirement for uncovered options is 20 percent (or 25 percent) of the underlying stock minus the amount the option is out-of-the-money, if any, plus the premium collected, but not less than 10 percent of the stock value. The out-of-the-money amount is the difference between the strike price and stock price times the number of contracts times the unit of measure ($100 for stocks). As mentioned in Chapter 5, for example, if XYZ stock is trading at $100 a share and you sell a put with a strike price of 100, the 20 percent standard margin requirement is $2,000 (ignoring the premium collected). If you sell a 95 strike-price call, the out-of-the-money amount is considered to be $500 (five points times $100) and would reduce the margin requirement.

Portfolio margining is a newer method available for computing equity margins for qualified customers based on the risk of the position, rather than on fixed percentages, and the result is often lower margin requirements than would be calculated from the traditional method described previously. A futures options margin is calculated differently than margin on stock options. A broker may, and often does, impose more stringent margin requirements. Margin rules are covered in Chapter 30.

FINAL THOUGHTS

An option seller can sell a put, for instance, because he is interested in earning premium income, knowing that the downside risk is that he may be obligated to purchase the underlying stock that he is interested in buying at a lower price. In this case, the seller is not willing to purchase the stock at its current price because he believes that it is overvalued. Alternatively, an option seller may sell put premium to earn income without ever having the intention to own the underlying stock.

When selling an at-the-money or out-of-the-money put option, you can profit if the underlying stock moves higher, sideways, or even lower (down to the strike price if out-of-the-money). The advantage of selling an out-of-the-money put option is that you can shift the statistical probabilities on your side. Unfortunately, leverage cuts both ways and losses can accumulate quickly, and an option may have a wide bid/ask spread. An option seller has time on his side and does not need to be as precise in his choice of the direction, timing, and magnitude of the move. Keep in mind that leverage is greatest the further a put option is out-of-the-money. The next part of this book covers spread strategies, which can be an effective tool to manage and limit risk.

PART THREE

Spread Strategies

S o far, this book has provided a solid foundation in option fundamentals and has described the four basic option strategies of a long call, a long put, a short call, and a short put. Now it is time to apply what you have learned to more advanced strategies. Part Three includes Chapters 11 to 22 and covers spread strategies. This is an important part of your option knowledge development because this part can help you progress to the next level of trading knowledge and proficiency. Chapter 11 describes a vertical spread, a common and basic spread strategy, and subsequent chapters describe more complex spread strategies. Included in Part Three is a vertical spread, iron condor, ratio (front) spread, backspread, straddle, strangle, butterfly, condor, calendar spread, diagonal spread, covered call, combination, collar, and covered combination, and other strategies. Each example is given in a similar format to make it easier for you to compare one strategy to another. A separate chapter is devoted to the most important spread strategies so that you can fully understand them before you move forward in later chapters to strategies on ETFs, indexes, and stock index futures.

The assumptions in Part Two also apply to Part Three. As in Part Two, to make it easy to compare one strategy to another, examples in Part Three, Chapters 11 to 22, are presented in a consistent format. Each example is comprehensive and typically includes a strategy summary, a table showing values at expiration date, a chart showing values at expiration date, illustrative Greeks for near-term and longer-term expiration months, and ramifications of exercise and assignment.

Consistent with Part Two, each example assumes that XYZ stock is initially trading at $100 a share. Each example includes an expiration analysis, showing a range of option values, assuming that the stock closes from $75 to $125 at expiration. Option values are rounded to make it easier to focus on option principles. Examples assume that a representative stock (XYZ) is trading at $100 a share.

Each example includes sample Greeks, assuming an expiration in a near month (February) and a later expiration month (March), so that you can compare the effect an expiration's month can have on an option position. The Greeks are typically converted to dollars in the examples. After the examples, a section called "Beyond the Basics" further analyzes other issues. For ease of comparison, option prices within the same example, and from chapter to chapter, assume that a call premium is symmetrical (equal) with a put premium, where the strike price is equidistant from the price of the underlying stock price; for example, it is assumed that a February 105 call is priced the same as a February 95 put (at $5). In reality, a call price for a stock is typically higher than a relative put price.

Examples assume that the prices to buy and sell do not differ as a result of the bid/ask spread. In addition, the effects of commissions and taxes are not shown. In many cases, the same or similar wording is used to describe various strategies to make them easier to understand.

Each option spread strategy has its own unique risks, rewards, margin requirement, time frames, probabilities of success, and volatility characteristics. As a result, you should be able to tailor your spread strategy to your specific risk–reward profile and view of the markets; for example, you may not want to assume the unlimited risk of a naked option, so there are strategies that offer limited risk. You may not want to pay the full price for an option if it is expensive, so there are strategies that enable you to collect a premium to partially defray a portion of the cost. You may not want to have wide fluctuations in your account's value, so there are strategies that can curtail the day-to-day ups and downs so that you can sleep better at night.

CHAPTER 11

Vertical Spread

A vertical spread can be considered the bread-and-butter strategy of many experienced traders because it limits risk and is relatively straightforward. A vertical spread consists of the simultaneous purchase and sale of options with the same expiration date but different strike prices. Unless otherwise stated, this book assumes that, in a vertical spread, the number of options bought is equal to the number of options sold and that all options have the same expiration month. A vertical spread consists of all calls or all puts. One advantage of a vertical spread is its relative simplicity. A vertical spread is probably the most basic spread strategy and forms the foundation for learning other spread strategies.

In this chapter, we will describe a vertical spread from the perspective of buying versus selling, bullish versus bearish strategies, margin, pricing, and risk. In later chapters, we will explore more complex spreads, such as option strategies in which the legs of the spread expire at different times, strike prices are different, and/or the number of options sold differs from the number of options bought.

OVERVIEW

Instead of purchasing or selling an option outright, many traders prefer to limit risk by establishing a vertical spread. A vertical spread consists of options with the same expiration date but different strike prices. Each option is assumed to be in the same class (same expiration date, same underlying stock, and same type, meaning all calls or all puts). The term *vertical*, in this context, means the same expiration date (but different strike prices). "Vertical" in this sense is comparable to looking at an option chain in a newspaper and moving up and down (vertically) on the same page to select the options in the spread. Table 11.1 is a summary of different vertical-spread strategies.

TABLE 11.1 Vertical Spread Strategies

Spread Strategy	Also Called	Strategy Description	Risk–Reward	Profitable	Margin	Breakeven
Vertical call debit spread	Bull call spread; call debit spread	Buy lower strike, sell higher strike, same expiration date	Limited risk, limited profit	Bullish	Full payment	Lower strike price plus debit
Vertical put debit spread	Bear put spread; put debit spread	Buy higher strike, sell lower strike, same expiration date	Limited risk, limited profit	Bearish	Full payment	Higher strike price minus debit
Vertical call credit spread	Bear call spread; call credit spread	Sell lower strike, buy higher strike, same expiration date	Limited risk, limited profit	Bearish/ neutral	Typically, difference in strike prices minus premium	Lower strike price plus credit
Vertical put credit spread	Bull put spread; put credit spread	Sell higher strike, buy lower strike, same expiration date	Limited risk, limited profit	Bullish/ neutral	Typically, difference in strike prices minus premium	Higher strike price minus credit

A vertical spread is a strategy to trade options with defined and/or reduced risk. When the option purchased is more expensive than the option sold, a net debit results and is a *vertical debit spread*. When the option sold is at a price greater than the option purchased, a net credit results and is a *vertical credit spread*. To exit the spread, you can offset it in a closing transaction, exercise the long option if it is in-the-money, wait for assignment of the short option if it is in-the-money, let both legs expire worthless (if both are out-of-the-money at expiration), or offset one leg at a time.

In a spread, you are, in effect, combining the characteristics of each option (delta, gamma, vega, and theta) into one trade. When you combine these characteristics and convert them to dollars, you have position Greeks; for example, when you combine the two opposing deltas of a vertical spread, you have a net delta (which can be stated in dollars). In a spread, every individual option has its own unique delta, gamma, and theta. In a vertical spread, you are long an option and short an option, and your overall position Greek is the net of both. In a vertical spread, the Greeks for the long leg are offset, in part, by the Greeks from the short leg.

STRATEGY EXAMPLES

Following are descriptions and examples of vertical-spread strategies. As a reminder, you can close out an option position by offsetting it in the marketplace any time prior to expiration. The principles that are demonstrated for a stock can be applied to options on an ETF, index, and stock index futures. Appendixes A, B, and C illustrate many of the strategies covered throughout this book.

Call Debit Spread (Bullish)

A vertical call debit spread consists of buying a call and selling a higher-strike call with the same expiration date. The purpose of such a spread is to profit from a bullish move at a reasonable cost. To execute a call debit spread, you can, for example, buy an at-the-money call option and sell an out-of-the-money call option. Alternatively, you can buy an out-of-the-money call option at one strike price and sell a further out-of-the-money call option at a higher strike price. In effect, in a call debit spread, you are subject to the risks and rewards of a long call, but you have limited profit potential from selling a call. A call debit spread can be considered a type of hedge but, in this case, you are hedging the high cost of the long option by offsetting a portion of its cost with the sale of another option. The maximum profit potential of a vertical debit spread, such as a call debit spread, is limited to the difference in the strike prices times the unit of measure (100 shares per contract for a stock) minus the premium paid.

A call debit spread is bullish, has limited profit potential, has maximum profit occurring when the underlying stock expires at or above the higher exercise price at expiration, and has limited risk equal to the premium paid. The time decay of the long option typically exceeds the time decay of the short option, an increase in volatility typically increases the value of the long option more than the short option, and a decrease in volatility typically decreases the value of the long option more than the short option. The break-even point at expiration is where the underlying stock equals the lower strike price plus net debit. The full net premium must be paid at the time of purchase, and a debit is charged to your account. A call debit spread may be permitted in an IRA.

Example: Call Debit Spread

> **Assumptions**: XYZ stock is trading at $100 a share in January; buy one February 100/105 call debit spread at $3 (buy one February 100 call at $5 and sell one February 105 call at $2).
> **Strategy direction**: Bullish.
> **Debit or credit**: $300 debit.
> **Maximum profit**: $200.
> **Maximum loss**: $300 (premium paid).

Exercise and assignment: Can exercise long option if in-the-money; may be assigned on short option if in-the-money.

Break-even stock price: $103 (strike price plus premium paid).

Maximum profit achieved: Stock at or above strike price of 105.

Maximum loss achieved: Stock at or below strike price of 100.

Profit (loss) if stock unchanged: $300 loss (debit).

Greeks: Table 11.3 contains sample Greeks converted to dollars at the time the position is established.

Position would reflect a gain from stock rise (delta) and from volatility (vega) expansion. Position would reflect a loss from stock decline (delta), time

TABLE 11.2 Call Debit Spread

XYZ Stock Price ($)	Long Call Value	Short Call Value	Spread	Cost of Spread	Spread Profit (Loss)	Profit (Loss) Percentage
75	0	0	0	300	(300)	(100)
80	0	0	0	300	(300)	(100)
85	0	0	0	300	(300)	(100)
90	0	0	0	300	(300)	(100)
95	0	0	0	300	(300)	(100)
100	0	0	0	300	(300)	(100)
105	500	0	500	300	200	67
110	1,000	500	500	300	200	67
115	1,500	1,000	500	300	200	67
120	2,000	1,500	500	300	200	67
125	2,500	2,000	500	300	200	67

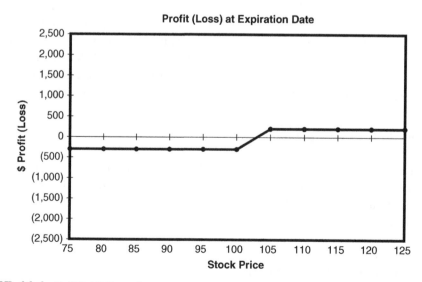

FIGURE 11.1 Call Debit Spread

TABLE 11.3 Summary of Greeks: February Expiration

Option	Delta	Gamma	Theta	Vega
1 February 100 call	$53	$2.30	−$15	$12
1 February 105 call	−$42	−$2.00	$14	−$11
Position	$11		−$1	$1

TABLE 11.4 Summary of Greeks: March Expiration

Option	Delta	Gamma	Theta	Vega
1 March 100 call	$52	$1.30	−$12	$17
1 March 105 call	−$40	−$1.20	$10	−$15
Position	$12		−$2	$2

decay (theta), and volatility (vega) contraction. Gain is $11 from XYZ stock rising to $101; loss is $1 from one day of time decay.

Later expiration: The price and Greeks will differ if expiration is at a later date; for example, if the options expire in March, instead of February, the price of the March 100 call could be $7 (instead of $5) and the 105 call could be $5 (instead of $2), for a net debit of $2, with example Greeks as given in Table 11.4.

Gain is $12 from XYZ stock rising to $101; loss is $2 from one day of time decay.

Exercise and assignment: For the February 100/105 call debit spread, if both strike prices are in-the-money, then you may be assigned on your short call and will be required to sell the XYZ stock at $105 per share. By exercising your long call, you can buy shares at $100 per share. If the stock price closes between the strike prices of the two option positions at expiration, your long call will be in-the-money and your short call will be out-of-the-money. Because the long call is in the money, you can offset it and let the short call expire worthless. If you offset the long leg of the spread, keep in mind that you are then carrying a naked short position, so you need to check with your brokerage firm to determine margin requirements. If the short option expires in-the-money, it may be assigned, but you are protected by the long call.

Put Debit Spread (Bearish)

A vertical put debit spread consists of buying a higher-strike put and selling a lower-strike put with the same expiration date. The purpose of such a spread is to profit from a bearish move at a reasonable cost. To execute a put debit spread, you can, for example, buy an at-the-money put option and sell an out-of-the-money put option. Alternatively, you can buy an out-of-the-money put option at one strike price and sell a further out-of-the-money put option at a lower strike price. In effect, in a put debit spread, you are subject to the risks and rewards of a long put, but you have limited profit potential by selling the put. A put debit spread can be considered a type of hedge but, in this case, you are hedging the high cost of the long option by offsetting a portion of its cost with the sale of another option. The maximum profit potential of a vertical debit spread, such as a put debit spread, is limited to the difference in the strike prices times the unit of measure (100 shares per contract for a stock) minus the premium paid.

A put debit spread is bearish, has limited profit potential, has maximum profit occurring when the underlying stock expires at or below the lower exercise price at expiration, and has limited risk equal to the premium paid. The time decay of the option purchased typically exceeds the time decay of the option sold, an increase in volatility typically increases the value of the option purchased more than the option sold, and a decrease in volatility typically decreases the value of the option purchased more than the option sold. The break-even point is where the underlying stock equals the higher strike price minus the net premium paid. The full net premium must be paid at the time of purchase and a debit is charged to your account. A put debit spread may be permitted in an IRA.

Example: Put Debit Spread

Assumptions: XYZ stock is trading at $100 a share in January; buy one February 95/100 put debit spread at $3 (buy one February 100 put at $5 and sell one February 95 put at $2).

Strategy direction: Bearish.

Debit or credit: $300 debit.

Maximum profit: $200.

Maximum loss: $300 (premium paid).

Exercise and assignment: Can exercise long option if in-the-money; may be assigned on short option if in-the-money.

TABLE 11.5 Put Debit Spread

XYZ Stock Price ($)	Long Put Value	Short Put Value	Spread	Cost of Spread	Spread Profit (Loss)	Profit (Loss) Percentage
75	2,500	2,000	500	300	200	67
80	2,000	1,500	500	300	200	67
85	1,500	1,000	500	300	200	67
90	1,000	500	500	300	200	67
95	500	0	500	300	200	67
100	0	0	0	300	(300)	(100)
105	0	0	0	300	(300)	(100)
110	0	0	0	300	(300)	(100)
115	0	0	0	300	(300)	(100)
120	0	0	0	300	(300)	(100)
125	0	0	0	300	(300)	(100)

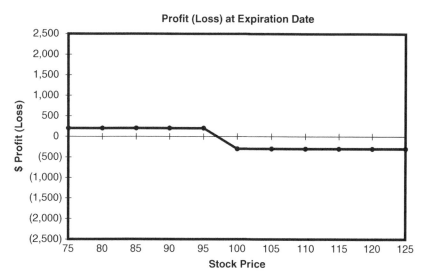

FIGURE 11.2 Put Debit Spread

Break-even stock price: $97 (strike price minus premium paid).
Maximum profit achieved: Stock at or below strike price of 95.
Maximum loss achieved: Stock at or above strike price of 100.
Profit (loss) if stock unchanged: $300 loss (debit).
Greeks: Table 11.6 contains sample Greeks converted to dollars at the time the position is established.

> Position would reflect a gain from stock decline (delta) and volatility (vega) expansion. Position would reflect a loss from stock rise (delta), time decay (theta), and volatility (vega) contraction. Loss is $11 from XYZ stock rising to $101; loss is $1 from one day of time decay.

Later expiration: The price and Greeks will differ if expiration is at a later date; for example, if the options expire in March, instead of February, the price of the March 100 put could be $7 (instead of $5) and the 95 put could be $5 (instead of $2), for a net debit of $2, with example Greeks as given in Table 11.7.

> Loss is $12 from XYZ stock rising to $101; loss is $2 from one day of time decay.

TABLE 11.6 Summary of Greeks: February Expiration

Option	Delta	Gamma	Theta	Vega
1 February 100 put	−$53	$2.30	−$15	$12
1 February 95 put	$42	−$2.00	$14	−$11
Position	−$11		−$1	$1

TABLE 11.7 Summary of Greeks: March Expiration

Option	Delta	Gamma	Theta	Vega
1 March 100 put	−$52	$1.30	−$12	$17
1 March 95 put	$40	−$1.20	$10	−$15
Position	−$12		−$2	$2

Exercise and assignment: For the February 95/100 put debit spread, if both strike prices are in-the-money, then you may be assigned on your short put and will be required to buy stock at $95 per share. By exercising your long put, you can sell those shares at $100 per share. If the stock price closes between the strike prices of the two option positions at expiration, your long put will be in-the-money and your short put will be out-of-the-money. Because the long put is in-the-money, you can sell it and let the short put expire worthless. If you offset the long leg of the spread, keep in mind that you are then carrying a naked short position, so you need to check with your brokerage firm to determine if that is allowable in your account. If the short option expires in-the-money, it may be assigned, but you are protected by the long put.

Call Credit Spread (Bearish)

A vertical call credit spread consists of selling a call and buying a higher-strike call with the same expiration date. Instead of selling an uncovered call, you can limit risk by also purchasing a higher-strike call. The purpose of such a spread is to profit from a neutral to bearish bias, limit risk, and lower volatility. In effect, in a call credit spread, you are subject to the risks and rewards of a short call, but you have limited risk by paying the premium for the long call. To execute a call credit spread, you can, for example, sell an at-the-money call option and buy an out-of-the-money call option. Alternatively, you can sell an out-of-the-money call option at one strike price and buy a further out-of-the-money call option at a higher strike price. The higher-strike call should be close enough to limit losses based on your risk tolerance. In this spread, you, in effect, collect less for the call sold because it is offset by the premium on the call purchased. The maximum loss in a vertical credit spread, such as a call credit spread, is limited to the difference in the strike prices times the unit of measure (100 shares per contract for a stock) minus the premium collected.

A call credit spread is bearish to neutral, has limited profit potential equal to net credit, has maximum profit occurring when the underlying stock expires at or below the lower exercise price at expiration, has limited risk for the difference between the two strike prices times $100 (assuming it is a stock) minus the net credit, and has maximum loss occurring when the underlying stock is at or above the higher exercise price at expiration. The time decay of the option sold typically exceeds the time decay of the option purchased, an increase in volatility typically increases the value of the option sold more than the option bought, and a decrease in volatility typically decreases the value of the option sold more than the option bought. The break-even point is where the underlying stock equals the lower strike price plus the net credit. A credit is reflected in your account. A call credit spread may be permitted in an IRA.

Example: Call Credit Spread

Assumptions: XYZ stock is trading at $100 a share in January; sell one February 100/105 call credit spread at $3 (sell one February 100 call at $5 and buy one February 105 call at $2).

TABLE 11.8 Call Credit Spread

XYZ Stock Price ($)	Long Call Value	Short Call Value	Spread	Premium Collected	Spread Profit (Loss)	Profit (Loss) Percentage
75	0	0	0	300	300	100
80	0	0	0	300	300	100
85	0	0	0	300	300	100
90	0	0	0	300	300	100
95	0	0	0	300	300	100
100	0	0	0	300	300	100
105	0	500	(500)	300	(200)	(67)
110	500	1,000	(500)	300	(200)	(67)
115	1,000	1,500	(500)	300	(200)	(67)
120	1,500	2,000	(500)	300	(200)	(67)
125	2,000	2,500	(500)	300	(200)	(67)

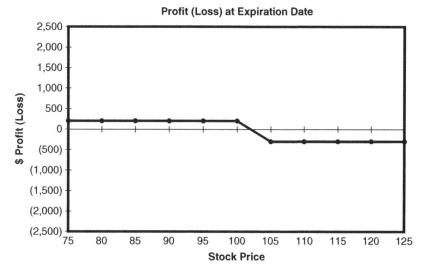

FIGURE 11.3 Call Credit Spread

Strategy direction: Bearish/neutral.

Debit or credit: $300 credit.

Maximum profit: $300 (premium collected).

Maximum loss: $200.

Exercise and assignment: Can exercise long option if in-the-money; may be assigned on short option if in-the-money.

Break-even stock price: $103 (strike price plus premium collected).

Maximum profit achieved: Stock at or below strike price of 100.

Maximum loss achieved: Stock at or above strike price of 105.

Profit (loss) if stock unchanged: $300 gain (credit).

Greeks: Table 11.9 contains sample Greeks converted to dollars at the time the position is established.

Position would reflect a gain from stock decline (delta), time decay (theta), and volatility (vega) contraction. Position would reflect a loss from stock rise (delta) and volatility (vega) expansion. Loss is $11 from XYZ stock rising to $101; gain is $1 from one day of time decay.

Later expiration: The price and Greeks will differ if expiration is at a later date; for example, if the options expire in March, instead of February, the price of the March 100 call could be $7 (instead of $5) and the 105 call could be $5 (instead of $2), for a net credit of $2, with example Greeks as given in Table 11.10.

Loss is $12 from XYZ stock rising to $101; gain is $2 from one day of time decay.

Exercise and assignment: For the February 100/105 call credit spread, if both strike prices are in-the-money, then you may be assigned on your short call and will be required to sell the stock at $100 per share. By exercising your long call, you can sell those shares at $105 per share. If the stock price closes between

TABLE 11.9 Summary of Greeks: February Expiration

Option	Delta	Gamma	Theta	Vega
1 February 100 call	−$53	−$2.30	$15	−$12
1 February 105 call	$42	$2.00	−$14	$11
Position	−$11		$1	−$1

TABLE 11.10 Summary of Greeks: March Expiration

Option	Delta	Gamma	Theta	Vega
1 March 100 call	−$52	−$1.30	$12	−$17
1 March 105 call	$40	$1.20	−$10	$15
Position	−$12		$2	−$2

the strike prices of the two option positions at expiration, your short call will be in-the-money and your long call will be out-of-the-money. Because the short call is in-the-money, you may be assigned, but the loss is limited by the long call.

Put Credit Spread (Bullish)

A vertical put credit spread consists of selling a put and buying a lower-strike put with the same expiration date. Instead of selling an uncovered put, you can limit risk by also purchasing a lower-strike put. The purpose of such a spread is to profit from a neutral to bullish bias, limit risk, and lower volatility. In effect, in a put credit spread, you are subject to the risks and rewards of a short put, but you have limited risk by paying the premium for the long put. To execute a put credit spread, you can, for example, sell an at-the-money put option and buy an out-of-the-money put option. Alternatively, you can sell an out-of-the-money put option at one strike price and buy a further out-of-the-money put option at a lower strike price. The lower-strike put should be close enough to limit losses based on your risk tolerance. In this spread, you, in effect, collect less for the put sold because it is offset by the premium on the put purchased. The maximum loss in a vertical credit spread, such as a put credit spread, is limited to the difference in the strike prices times the unit of measure (100 shares per contract for a stock) minus the premium collected.

A put credit spread is bullish to neutral, has limited profit potential equal to net credit, has maximum profit occurring when the underlying stock expires at or above the higher exercise price at expiration, has limited risk for the difference between the two strike prices times $100 (assuming it is a stock) minus the net credit, and has maximum loss occurring when the underlying stock is at or below the lower exercise price at expiration. The time decay of the option sold typically exceeds the time decay of the option purchased, an increase in volatility typically increases the value of the option sold more than the option bought, and a decrease in volatility typically decreases the value of the option sold more than the option bought. The break-even point is where the underlying stock equals the higher strike price minus the net credit. A credit is reflected in your account. A put credit spread may be permitted in an IRA.

Example: Put Credit Spread

Assumptions: XYZ stock is trading at $100 a share in January; sell one February 95/100 put credit spread at $3 (sell one February 100 put at $5 and buy one February 95 put at $2).
Strategy direction: Bullish/neutral.
Debit or credit: $300 credit.
Maximum profit: $300 (premium collected).
Maximum loss: $200.

Exercise and assignment: Can exercise long option if in-the-money; may be assigned on short option if in-the-money.

Break-even stock price: $97 (strike price minus premium collected).

Maximum profit achieved: Stock at or above strike price of 100.

Maximum loss achieved: Stock at or below strike price of 95.

Profit (loss) if stock unchanged: $300 gain (credit).

Greeks: Table 11.12 contains sample Greeks converted to dollars at the time the position is established.

TABLE 11.11   Put Credit Spread

XYZ Stock Price ($)	Long Put Value	Short Put Value	Spread	Premium Collected	Spread Profit (Loss)	Profit (Loss) Percentage
75	2,000	2,500	(500)	300	(200)	(67)
80	1,500	2,000	(500)	300	(200)	(67)
85	1,000	1,500	(500)	300	(200)	(67)
90	500	1,000	(500)	300	(200)	(67)
95	0	500	(500)	300	(200)	(67)
100	0	0	0	300	300	100
105	0	0	0	300	300	100
110	0	0	0	300	300	100
115	0	0	0	300	300	100
120	0	0	0	300	300	100
125	0	0	0	300	300	100

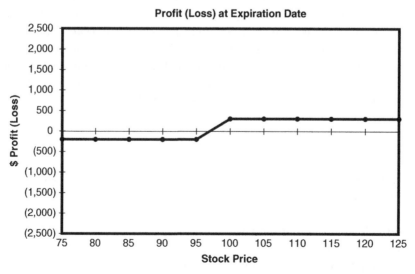

FIGURE 11.4   Put Credit Spread

TABLE 11.12 Summary of Greeks: February Expiration

Option	Delta	Gamma	Theta	Vega
1 February 100 put	$53	−$2.30	$15	−$12
1 February 95 put	−$42	$2.00	−$14	$11
Position	$11		$1	−$1

TABLE 11.13 Summary of Greeks: March Expiration

Option	Delta	Gamma	Theta	Vega
1 March 100 put	$52	−$1.30	$12	−$17
1 March 95 put	−$40	$1.20	−$10	$15
Position	$12		$2	−$2

Position would reflect a gain from stock rise (delta), time decay (theta), and volatility (vega) contraction. Position would reflect a loss from stock decline (delta) and volatility (vega) expansion. Gain is $11 from XYZ stock rising to $101; gain is $1 from one day of time decay.

Later expiration: The price and Greeks will differ if expiration is at a later date; for example, if the options expire in March, instead of February, the price of the March 100 put could be $7 (instead of $5) and the 95 put could be $5 (instead of $2), for a net credit of $2, with example Greeks as given in Table 11.13.

Gain is $12 from XYZ stock rising to $101; gain is $2 from one day of time decay.

Exercise and assignment: For the February 95/100 put credit spread, if both strike prices are in-the-money, then you may be assigned on your short put and will be required to buy the stock at $100 per share. By exercising your long put, you can sell those shares at $95 per share. If the stock price closes between the strike prices of the two option positions at expiration, your short put will be in-the-money and your long put will be out-of-the-money. Because the short put is in-the-money, you may be assigned, but the loss is limited by the long put.

BEYOND THE BASICS

Margin

In general, margin on a vertical credit spread is generally calculated as the lesser of the short option margin or the difference between the strike prices minus the premium collected. For example, if XYZ stock is trading at $100 and you sell a February 100/110 call vertical credit spread for $400, your margin is the lesser of $2,000 under the 20 percent traditional margin requirement (ignoring the premium) and $600 (the difference in strike prices minus premium collected). Likewise, if you sell a February 90/100 put vertical spread for $400, your margin is $600. This result may differ if a trader qualifies for portfolio margining. A long option position is not subject to a margin requirement and, instead, must be paid in full. As a result, for example, full payment is required for a vertical debit spread. Margin rules are covered in Chapter 30.

Bullish versus Bearish

If you are bullish, you can buy a call debit spread or sell a put credit spread, and if you are bearish, you can buy a put debit spread or sell a call credit spread. The next section is a comparison of bullish versus bearish strategies. Chapter 5 provides additional comparisons of bullish versus bearish strategies.

Bullish: Call Debit Spread versus Put Credit Spread   A call debit spread and put credit spread are both bullish, but both have their own unique risk–reward characteristics. Both strategies are bullish, but there are more scenarios in which a put credit spread can be profitable. A call debit spread is profitable if the stock rises but a put credit spread can profit if the stock rises, moves sideways, or moves lower, as long as it stays at or above the strike price of the option sold. In other words, when you write a put credit spread, the odds are more on your side, but you take on more risk in the process in comparison to a call debit spread.

To determine which vertical spread strategy is best, you should project how far the stock will move and how quickly. If you believe that the stock is going to move quickly, you are probably better off buying a call debit spread, but if you believe that it will take time for the stock to move, then a put credit spread may be more appropriate. If you are the type of trader who is only comfortable sleeping at night if the potential loss is relatively small, you may feel more comfortable with a call debit spread and not the higher-dollar risk strategy of the put credit spread. Conversely, you may prefer the higher probabilities of the put credit spread. Table 11.14 highlights the differences between two bullish vertical spreads: the call debit spread and put credit spread.

Bearish: Put Debit Spread versus Call Credit Spread   A put debit spread and call credit spread are both bearish, but both have their own unique risk–reward characteristics. Both strategies are bearish, but there are more scenarios in which a call credit

TABLE 11.14   Bullish Vertical Spread Comparison

Call Debit Spread	Put Credit Spread
Risk limited to premium	Risk limited to width of strike prices minus premium
Profitable when stock price rises above break-even point	Maximum profit when stock price above strike price of option sold at expiration (ignoring premium)

TABLE 11.15 Bearish Vertical Spread Comparison

Put Debit Spread	Call Credit Spread
Risk limited to premium	Risk limited to width of strike prices minus premium
Profitable when stock price declines below break-even point	Maximum profit when stock price below strike price of option sold at expiration (ignoring premium)

spread can be profitable. A put debit spread is profitable if the stock declines, but a call credit spread can profit if the stock declines, moves sideways, or moves higher, as long as it stays at or below the strike price of the option sold. In other words, when you write a call credit spread, the odds are more on your side, but you take on more risk in the process.

To determine which vertical spread strategy is best, you should project how far the stock will move and how quickly. If you believe that the stock is going to move a lot and/or very quickly, you are better off buying a put debit spread, but if you believe that it will take time for the stock to move, then a call credit spread may be more appropriate. If you are the type of trader who is only comfortable sleeping at night if the potential loss is relatively small, you may feel more comfortable with a put debit spread and not the higher-dollar risk strategy of the call credit spread. Conversely, you may prefer the higher probabilities of the call credit spread. Table 11.15 highlights the differences between two bearish vertical spreads: the put debit spread and call credit spread.

Spread Pricing and Risk

A vertical spread at expiration will have a value between zero and the width between exercise prices. As a result, you can expect the price of the spread to be within this range; for example, a 100/105 call vertical spread will trade between zero and five points, a 100/110 call vertical spread will trade between zero and 10 points, and so on. If XYZ stock is currently at $100, the price of the 120/130 call vertical will be close to zero points, whereas the price of the 120/130 put vertical will be close to 10 points. Likewise, if XYZ stock is currently at $100, the price of the 70/80 call vertical will be close to 10 points, whereas the price of the 70/80 put vertical will be close to zero points.

In a spread, you have partially offsetting deltas and other Greeks. You can choose the strike price differential (width) and whether the option purchased is in-the-money, at-the-money, or out-of-the-money. In this manner, you can establish position Greeks that fit your risk–reward profile; for example, the position delta of a vertical call debit spread (bull call spread) is increased if you purchase an option at a lower strike price.

The lower the call strike price of the option purchased, the higher the sensitivity (higher delta) of the call to a change in the underlying stock. The higher the call strike price, the lower the sensitivity (lower delta) to a change in the underlying stock. You can fine-tune the delta and other Greeks based on the width in the strike prices; for instance, if you want to establish a higher delta position, you can purchase a call with a lower strike price and sell a call with a higher strike price. You can increase the delta of a call debit spread by buying an in-the-money call option instead of buying an out-of-the-money call option. For example, assume that in January, XYZ stock is selling at $100 a share, and you buy a February 90/110 call debit spread (buy 10 February 90 calls at $11 and sell 10 February 110 calls at $1). The position delta of this bull call spread would be greater than, for example, a February 100/105 call spread.

You can modify any one or more of these variables to attain the risk–reward profile that you are attempting to achieve. As with other spread strategies, you can pick and choose the strike prices to refine maximum profit, maximum risk, and at what point you make a profit or lose. How you trade will likely be determined by your risk–reward profile; for example, a trader may be comfortable in a credit spread in which the short options have a 60 percent chance of success (0.60 delta), whereas another trader may not be able to sleep well at night unless he has at least an 80 percent chance. Which strategy is right for you, in many cases, comes down to your risk–reward profile. By increasing the probabilities from 60 to 80 percent, you forego a certain amount of premium income. However, if that is what it takes to sleep at night, maybe that is the best choice. Keep in mind that with any strategy, you can lose money, and it is always a wise idea to have predetermined exit points in case the strategy moves against you.

Rule of Thumb: Spread Probabilities

Delta, as mentioned in Chapter 4, can be used as a measure of the probability of an option finishing in-the-money on the expiration date. If we ignore the sign of the delta, the delta is approximately equal to the probability that the option will finish in-the-money (according to option pricing models). A 0.50 delta means that, according to the option price, there is a 50 percent chance that the option will expire in-the-money for any amount ($0.01). As a result, an at-the-money 100 strike-price call option written for $5 with a delta of 0.50 means that there is a 50 percent chance that the seller will earn the entire $5 premium if he waits until option expiration because the stock closing at-the-money (ignoring the $0.01) means that the option seller profits fully.

However, what happens if the writer decides to sell a spread by also buying a 110 call for $1 to limit his loss? In this case, you can also estimate the probability of profiting from the position in addition to the probability of expiring in-the-money. As a rule of thumb, you can estimate the probability of profiting from a spread by taking the difference between the width of the strike prices and the net premium collected and dividing that by the width in strike prices. The resulting percentage can represent the approximate probability of profiting on the spread position; for example, assume you sell one February 100 call at $5 and buy one February 110 call at $1, so you collect a net premium of $4. The strike price width is 10 and the difference in the strike-price width and the premium collected is 6. As a result, you have a 60 percent (6 divided by 10) probability of profiting on the trade, based on the option pricing. Thus, in this example, the probability of profiting by the entire premium is 50 percent (measured by February 100 call delta) and the probability of making any profit is 60 percent.

Outright Position versus Spread Risk

In general, at first, a spread may appear less risky than an outright uncovered option, but things are not always as they appear. In some cases, traders inadvertently convert a lower-risk spread trade into a higher-risk trade; for example, if XYZ stock is trading at $100 and you want to sell one out-of-the-money call outright for $1, you may be able to sell at a strike price of 110. If you instead decide to sell a call spread and want to collect a $1 credit, you may sell a call at a strike price of 105 and buy a call at a strike price of 110. In this case, even though the long 110 call provides some risk management protection, the fact that you are selling a call closer to the underlying stock means that you have greater risk in some respects. Thus, a February 105/110 call debit spread is more risky, in some respects, than an uncovered February 110 call option unless a major move occurs in the underlying stock. In this case, the risk profile of the spread is simply different than the risk profile of the uncovered option, but that does not mean you are assuming less real risk (even though your maximum risk is defined in the spread). Also, traders may be tempted to sell a greater number of spreads versus uncovered options because a spread generates less premium. Selling additional contracts can diminish or eliminate the spread risk advantage.

FINAL THOUGHTS

The width (distance) in exercise prices affects the risk–reward characteristics of a vertical spread; for example, the greater the distance between exercise prices, the greater the net delta; a 100/115 call credit spread has a greater delta (ignoring the positive or negative sign) than a 100/105 call credit spread. Remember that two options with different exercise prices cannot have identical deltas, or other Greeks, for that matter.

In a debit spread, the distance (width) between the strike prices defines the maximum gain, so it is important to balance the benefits of paying less net premium (from narrow strike prices) against the benefits associated with greater profit potential (from wider strike prices). You should always examine this trade-off in any spread position as well as how much capital you are willing to risk in any one trade. It becomes a trade-off between the net premium paid versus less profit potential by having more narrow strikes. In a credit spread, the distance between the strike prices defines the maximum risk, so it is important to balance the benefits associated with greater profit potential with the collection of less net premium. The further the distance between the two strike prices, the greater the potential loss and the less net credit received.

Remember that a debit spread needs to expand for you to profit, whereas a credit spread needs to contract. Expansion of a spread can occur by movement in the underlying stock or a volatility increase. Contraction of a spread can occur by movement in the underlying stock, a volatility decrease, and/or time passing. You may want to consider a vertical spread as one of your main option strategies. As a matter of fact, many experienced traders avoid naked options and trade primarily spreads. Selecting strategies with appropriate risk–reward parameters is important to being successful in trading spreads. In Chapter 12, we will address a more advanced spread strategy: the iron condor.

Iron Condor

We covered many option principles in previous chapters, so describing an *iron condor* is a good opportunity to put a lot of those principles to work. In an iron condor, you simultaneously establish a call vertical spread and a put vertical spread. The iron condor can be executed from the long side to profit from an increase in volatility or the short side to profit from a trading range. If the call and put spreads are purchased, the trader is long the iron condor; if both spreads are sold, the trader is short the iron condor.

Combining call and put spreads together can create a unique risk–reward environment. The idea is to establish positions on both sides of the market from which you can take advantage of volatility expansion (long iron condor) or contraction (short iron condor); for example, if you like the theoretical edge provided by a credit spread, an iron condor can enable you to have a positive theoretical edge on both sides of the spread at the same time.

This chapter covers iron condors where the number of options sold equals the number purchased and options expire in the same month. In later chapters, we will explore option strategies in which the number of options sold differs from the number bought and the sides, or legs, of the spread expire at different times and have different strike prices.

OVERVIEW

A long iron condor is a strategy in which you simultaneously buy a call debit spread and a put debit spread to profit from volatility in either direction. Another way to view a long iron condor is the purchase of an out-of-the-money call and put and the sale of *wings* (outside strike prices in a spread).

TABLE 12.1 Summary: Long and Short Iron Condor

Strategy	Strategy Description	Risk–Reward	Profitable	Debit or Credit	Break-Even Prices	Margin
Long iron condor	Buy call debit spread, buy put debit spread	Limited risk, limited profit	Underlying stock trades outside a range	Debit	Lower strike call plus debit, higher strike put minus debit	Full payment
Short iron condor	Sell call credit spread, sell put credit spread	Limited risk, limited profit	Underlying stock trades within a range	Credit	Lower strike call plus credit, higher strike put minus credit	Call or put side, whichever is greater, plus premium from other side

A short iron condor is a strategy in which you simultaneously sell a call credit spread and a put credit spread to profit from a trading range or volatility contraction, or to take advantage of time decay. Another way to view a short iron condor is the sale of an out-of-the-money call and put and the purchase of wings. Table 12.1 is a summary of a long and short iron condor.

To exit a position, you can offset it in a closing transaction, exercise the long option if it is in-the-money, wait for assignment of the short option if it is in-the-money, let both legs expire worthless (if both are out-of-the-money at expiration), or offset one leg at a time.

In an iron-condor spread, you are, in effect, combining the characteristics of each option (delta, gamma, vega, and theta) into one trade. When you combine these characteristics and convert them to dollars, you have position Greeks; for example, when you combine the four deltas of an iron condor, you have a net delta (which can be stated in dollars). In an iron condor, you are long two options and short two options, and your overall position Greeks will be the net of all four. In an iron condor, the delta (and other Greeks) of the call spread may equal or approximate the corresponding (offsetting) delta of the put spread. In an iron condor, the strike prices do not have to be spaced equally apart because you can tailor the positions to your view of the market and risk–reward parameters. Remember that the greater the width between exercise prices, the greater the net delta of each side of a spread.

STRATEGY EXAMPLES

Following are descriptions and examples of long and short iron–condor spread strategies. As a reminder, you can close out an option position by offsetting it in the marketplace any time prior to expiration. The principles that are demonstrated for a stock can be applied to options on an ETF, index, and stock index futures. Appendixes A, B, and C illustrate many of the strategies covered throughout this book.

Long Iron Condor

A long iron condor consists of a call debit spread and a put debit spread. As covered in Chapter 11, in a call debit spread, you buy a call at one strike price and sell a call at a higher strike price with the same expiration date. In a put debit spread, you buy a put at one strike price and sell a put at a lower strike price with the same expiration date. The purpose of a long iron condor is to be able to profit in either direction, where you do not have to choose that direction. The only thing that matters, at expiration, is whether the stock has made a substantial move.

To execute a long iron condor, you buy out-of-the-money call and put options and sell further out-of-the-money call and put options. This strategy can be weighted more heavily toward puts versus calls, and vice versa, depending on your market outlook and how options are priced, and the strike prices do not have to be spaced equally apart.

A long iron condor is a limited-reward and limited-risk strategy. The maximum gain potential is determined by the difference between the two strike prices of the calls and the two strike prices of the puts minus the premium paid. The maximum loss is limited to the net debit paid and occurs when the underlying stock is at or between the long option strike prices at expiration (when all options are out-of-the-money). For a long iron condor, you pay double (or nearly double) the amount of premium in comparison to trading one side of the market, and the risk is that the underlying stock will fluctuate back and forth in a range, forcing both the call and put debit spreads to decay in value.

In an iron condor, there are two break-even points. The break-even points are the strike price of the long call plus the debit and the strike price of the long put minus the debit. A profit is achieved when the underlying stock advances or declines substantially, thus increasing the value of one side.

In a long iron condor, the time decay of long options typically exceeds the time decay of short options, an increase in volatility typically increases the value of long options more than short options, and a decrease in volatility typically decreases the value of long options more than short options. A profit is made in this strategy, at expiration, as the underlying stock moves beyond one of the break-even points in either direction. A debit is charged to your account and it must be paid in full. A long iron condor may be permitted in an IRA.

Example: Long Iron Condor

> **Assumptions**: XYZ stock is trading at $100 a share in January; buy one iron condor at $2, as follows: Buy one February 105/110 call debit spread (buy one February 105 call at $2 and sell one February 110 call at $1) and buy one February 90/95 put debit spread (buy one February 95 put at $2 and sell one February 90 put at $1).
> **Strategy direction**: Volatility in either direction.

Debit or credit: $200 debit.

Maximum profit: $300.

Maximum loss: $200 debit.

Exercise and assignment: Can exercise long option if in-the-money; may be assigned on short option if in-the-money.

Break-even stock price: $107 and $93 (lower call strike price plus credit; higher put strike price minus credit).

Maximum profit achieved: Stock at or above higher strike price of calls or at or below lower strike price of puts.

Maximum loss achieved: Stock expires at or between the long options at expiration.

Profit (loss) if stock unchanged: $200 loss (debit).

TABLE 12.2 Long Call Spread

XYZ Stock Price ($)	Long Call Value	Short Call Value	Spread	Original Debit Spread	Spread Profit (Loss)
75	0	0	0	100	(100)
80	0	0	0	100	(100)
85	0	0	0	100	(100)
90	0	0	0	100	(100)
95	0	0	0	100	(100)
100	0	0	0	100	(100)
105	0	0	0	100	(100)
110	500	0	500	100	400
115	1,000	500	500	100	400
120	1,500	1,000	500	100	400
125	2,000	1,500	500	100	400

TABLE 12.3 Long Put Spread

XYZ Stock Price ($)	Long Put Value	Short Put Value	Spread	Original Debit Spread	Spread Profit (Loss)
75	2,000	1,500	500	100	400
80	1,500	1,000	500	100	400
85	1,000	500	500	100	400
90	500	0	500	100	400
95	0	0	0	100	(100)
100	0	0	0	100	(100)
105	0	0	0	100	(100)
110	0	0	0	100	(100)
115	0	0	0	100	(100)
120	0	0	0	100	(100)
125	0	0	0	100	(100)

Greeks: Table 12.5 contains sample Greeks converted to dollars at the time the position is established.

Position would reflect no gain from a small stock rise (delta) but a gain from volatility (vega) expansion. Position would reflect no loss from a small stock decline (delta) but a loss from time decay (theta) and volatility (vega) contraction. Gain is zero from XYZ stock rising to $101; loss is $4 from one day of time decay.

Later expiration: The price and Greeks will differ when the position is established if expiration is at a later date; for example, if the options expire in March, instead of February, the price of the March iron condor could be $3 (instead of $2), with example Greeks as given in Table 12.6.

TABLE 12.4   Long Iron Condor

XYZ Stock Price ($)	Long Call/Put Value	Short Call/Put Value	Spread	Original Debit Spread	Spread Profit (Loss)
75	2,000	1,500	500	200	300
80	1,500	1,000	500	200	300
85	1,000	500	500	200	300
90	500	0	500	200	300
95	0	0	0	200	(200)
100	0	0	0	200	(200)
105	0	0	0	200	(200)
110	500	0	500	200	300
115	1,000	500	500	200	300
120	1,500	1,000	500	200	300
125	2,000	1,500	500	200	300

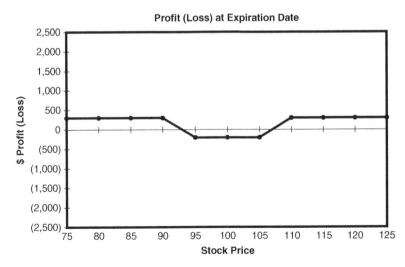

FIGURE 12.1   Long Iron Condor

TABLE 12.5 Summary of Greeks: February Expiration

Option	Delta	Gamma	Theta	Vega
1 February 105 call	$42	$2.00	−$14	$11
1 February 110 call	−$23	−$1.75	$12	−$8
1 February 95 put	−$42	$2.00	−$14	$11
1 February 90 put	$23	−$1.75	$12	−$8
Position	$0		−$4	$6

TABLE 12.6 Summary of Greeks: March Expiration

Option	Delta	Gamma	Theta	Vega
1 March 105 call	$40	$1.20	−$10	$15
1 March 110 call	−$20	−$1.00	$7	−$10
1 March 95 put	−$40	$1.20	−$10	$15
1 March 90 put	$20	−$1.00	$7	−$10
Position	$0		−$6	$10

Gain is zero from XYZ stock rising to $101; loss is $6 from one day of time decay.

Exercise and assignment: For the February 105/110 call side, if both strike prices are in-the-money, then you may be assigned on your short call and will be required to sell the XYZ stock at $110 per share. By exercising your long call, you can buy shares at $105 per share. If the stock price closes between the strike prices of the two option positions at expiration, your long call will be in-the-money and your short call will be out-of-the-money. For the February 95/100 put side, if both strike prices are in-the-money, then you may be assigned on your short put and will be required to buy stock at $95 per share. By exercising your long put, you can sell those shares at $100 per share. If the stock price closes between the strike prices of the two option positions at expiration, your long put will be in-the-money and your short put will be out-of-the-money.

You can, for example, purchase an iron condor before earnings reports or product announcements because the actual direction the stock takes does not matter; the only thing that matters is whether the stock makes a substantial move. To realize a profit from a long iron condor, you do not have to pinpoint where the underlying stock is going at a specific time (the expiration date).

Short Iron Condor

In a short iron condor, you simultaneously sell a call credit spread and a put credit spread. As covered in Chapter 11, a call credit spread is a spread in which you sell a call at one strike price and simultaneously buy a call at a higher strike price with the same expiration date. A put credit spread is a spread in which you sell a put at one strike price and simultaneously buy a put at a lower strike price with the same expiration date. The idea is to establish limited-risk positions on both sides of the stock, where an increase in the value of the call side is offset partially or totally by a decline in the value of the put side, and vice versa. The purpose of such a spread is to profit from a trading range, time decay, and/or volatility contraction, with limited risk.

To execute a short iron condor, you sell out-of-the-money call and put options and buy further out-of-the-money call and put options. This strategy does not need to be executed in a perfect delta-neutral position because it can be weighted more heavily toward puts versus calls, and vice versa, depending on your market outlook and how options are priced, and the strike prices do not have to be equally spaced apart.

A short iron condor is a limited-reward and limited-risk strategy. The maximum profit occurs when the underlying stock is at or between the short option strike prices at expiration (when all options are out-of-the-money). A profit is made in this strategy as the underlying stock fluctuates back and forth in a range allowing both the call and put credit spreads to decay in value over time. This is a strategy that is used to try to double (or nearly double) the amount of premium collected in comparison to what could be obtained by only trading one side of the market. This strategy can make sense because it is based on the fact that the underlying stock cannot be in two places at one time. An advantage of a short iron condor can be its relatively low volatility because of the calls offsetting the puts, and vice versa.

The maximum loss potential is determined by the difference between the two strike prices of the calls and the two strike prices of the puts, minus the premium collected. With a short iron condor, you have risk in both directions. The risk is that the underlying stock will advance or decline dramatically, substantially increasing the value of the put or call side, which would only be partially offset by the other side of the trade.

In an iron condor, there are two break-even points. The break-even points are the strike price of the short call plus the net credit and the strike price of the short put minus the net credit. The margin requirement is the greater of the call side margin or the put side margin, but not both.

In a short iron condor, the time decay of the short options typically exceeds the time decay of the long options, an increase in volatility typically increases the value of short options more than long options, and a decrease in volatility typically decreases the value of short options more than long options. A short iron condor may be permitted in an IRA but requires sufficient buying power.

Example: Short Iron Condor

Assumptions: XYZ stock is trading at $100 a share in January; sell one iron condor at $2, as follows: Sell one February 105/110 call credit spread (sell one February 105 call at $2 and buy one February 110 call at $1) and sell one February 90/95 put credit spread (sell one February 95 put at $2 and buy one February 90 put at $1).

Strategy direction: Neutral.

Debit or credit: $200 credit.

Maximum profit: $200.

Maximum loss: $300 debit.

Exercise and assignment: Can exercise long option if in-the-money; may be assigned on short option if in-the-money.

Break-even stock price: $107 and $93 (lower short call strike price plus credit; higher short put strike price minus credit).

Maximum loss achieved: Underlying stock at or below lower strike price of calls or at or above higher strike price of puts.

Maximum profit achieved: Underlying stock expires at or between the short options at expiration.

Profit (loss) if stock unchanged: $400 gain (credit).

TABLE 12.7 Short Call Spread

XYZ Stock Price ($)	Long Call Value	Short Call Value	Spread	Original Credit Spread	Spread Profit (Loss)
75	0	0	0	100	100
80	0	0	0	100	100
85	0	0	0	100	100
90	0	0	0	100	100
95	0	0	0	100	100
100	0	0	0	100	100
105	0	0	0	100	100
110	0	500	500	100	(400)
115	500	1,000	500	100	(400)
120	1,000	1,500	500	100	(400)
125	1,500	2,000	500	100	(400)

TABLE 12.8 Short Put Spread

XYZ Stock Price ($)	Long Put Value	Short Put Value	Spread	Original Credit Spread	Spread Profit (Loss)
75	1,500	2,000	500	100	(400)
80	1,000	1,500	500	100	(400)
85	500	1,000	500	100	(400)
90	0	500	500	100	(400)
95	0	0	0	100	100
100	0	0	0	100	100
105	0	0	0	100	100
110	0	0	0	100	100
115	0	0	0	100	100
120	0	0	0	100	100
125	0	0	0	100	100

Greeks: Table 12.10 contains sample Greeks converted to dollars at the time the position is established.

Position would reflect no gain from a small stock decline (delta) but a gain from time decay (theta) and a gain from volatility (vega) contraction. Position would reflect no loss from a small stock rise (delta) but a loss on volatility (vega) expansion. Gain is zero from XYZ stock rising to $101; gain is $4 from one day of time decay.

Later expiration: The price and Greeks will differ when the position is established if expiration is at a later date; for example, if the options expire in March, instead

TABLE 12.9 Short Iron Condor (Combined)

XYZ Stock Price ($)	Long Call/Put Value	Short Call/Put Value	Spread	Original Credit Spread	Spread Profit (Loss)
75	1,500	2,000	500	200	(300)
80	1,000	1,500	500	200	(300)
85	500	1,000	500	200	(300)
90	0	500	500	200	(300)
95	0	0	0	200	200
100	0	0	0	200	200
105	0	0	0	200	200
110	0	500	500	200	(300)
115	500	1,000	500	200	(300)
120	1,000	1,500	500	200	(300)
125	2,000	2,500	500	200	(300)

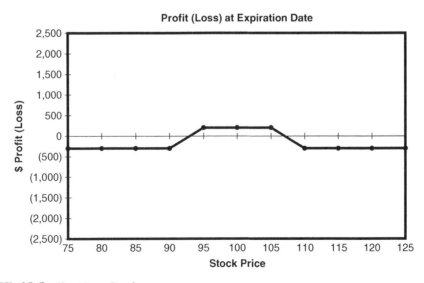

FIGURE 12.2 Short Iron Condor

TABLE 12.10 Summary of Greeks: February Expiration

Option	Delta	Gamma	Theta	Vega
1 February 105 call	−$42	−2.00	$14	−$11
1 February 110 call	$23	$1.75	−$12	$8
1 February 95 put	$42	−$2.00	$14	−$11
1 February 90 put	−$23	$1.75	−$12	$8
Position	$0		$4	−$6

TABLE 12.11 Summary of Greeks: March Expiration

Option	Delta	Gamma	Theta	Vega
1 March 105 call	−$40	−$1.20	$10	−$15
1 March 110 call	$20	$1.00	−$7	$10
1 March 95 put	$40	−$1.20	$10	−$15
1 March 90 put	−$20	$1.00	−$7	$10
Position	$0		$6	−$10

of February, the price of the March iron condor could be $3 (instead of $2), with example Greeks as given in Table 12.11.

Gain is zero from XYZ stock rising to $101; gain is $6 from one day of time decay.

Exercise and assignment: For the February 105/110 call credit spread, if both strike prices are in-the-money, then you may be assigned on your short call and will be required to sell stock at $105 per share. By exercising your long call, you can sell those shares at $110 per share. If the stock price closes between the strike prices of the two option positions at expiration, your short call will be in-the-money and your long call will be out-of-the-money. Because the short call is in-the-money, you may be assigned. For the February 90/95 put credit spread, if both strike prices are in-the-money, then you may be assigned on your short put and will be required to buy stock at $95 per share. By exercising your long put, you can buy those shares at $90 per share. If the stock price closes between the strike prices of the two option positions at expiration, your short put will be in-the-money and your long put will be out-of-the-money. Because the short put is in-the-money, you may be assigned.

BEYOND THE BASICS

Margin

In a short iron condor, initial margin is the call or put side margin, whichever is greater, plus the premium from the other side. Said another way, the short iron-condor margin requirement is the greater of the call side or put side but not the total of both sides. A trader can view this as favorable margin because both sides do not need to be added together.

Margin on each vertical credit spread of the iron condor is generally calculated as the lesser of the short option margin or the difference between the strike prices minus the premium collected; for example, if XYZ stock is trading at $100, and you sell a February 105/110 call vertical credit spread for $100, your call side margin is $400 (the difference in strike prices minus premium collected). If you sell a February 90/100 put vertical spread for $400, your put side margin is $600. As a result, this iron condor would have a margin requirement of $600: the greater of the call side and put side but not the total of both sides ($1,000).

Keep in mind that, in general, margin on a vertical credit spread is generally calculated as the lesser of the short option margin or the difference between the strike prices minus the premium collected. This result may differ if a trader qualifies for portfolio margining. A long option position is not subject to a margin requirement and, instead, must be paid in full. As a result, for example, full payment is required for a long iron condor. Margin rules are covered in Chapter 30.

FINAL THOUGHTS

Most spread strategies are executed with all calls or all puts, but the iron condor simultaneously uses call and put spreads and can be executed from the long side to profit from an increase in volatility or the short side to profit from a trading range. An iron condor combines two vertical spreads and is a good strategy to have in your arsenal of trading strategies. The long iron condor has the benefit of taking advantage of volatility, not having to choose the direction, and lowering cost by selling out-of-the-money options. The short iron condor combines the benefits of collecting double premium, double time decay, having probabilities on your side, defined risk, and margin benefits (because margin is the greater of the call side and put side but not both). The iron condor can be a popular strategy for index, ETF, and stock index futures trading. The ability to trade both sides of the option market at the same time in a limited-risk strategy may present interesting opportunities to the alert option trader. Index, ETF, and stock index futures option strategies are covered in Chapters 23 to 26.

In an iron condor, the strike prices do not have to be spaced equally apart because you can tailor the positions to your view of the market and risk–reward parameters. The principles in this chapter should help set the stage for other strategies; for example, Chapter 16 covers the condor spread, which is similar to an iron condor except that all strike prices are equally spaced. This chapter covered iron condors, in which the number of options sold equals the number purchased, and options expire in the same month. In the next chapter, Chapter 13, we explore spread-option strategies, in which the number of options sold differs from the number bought. In a later chapter, we will examine spread strategies in which options expire at different times.

Unbalanced Spreads

Many spread strategies assume that the number of options sold equals the number of options purchased. However, in the real world, there is no requirement that an equal number of options be bought as sold. When the number of options bought in a spread differs from the number of options sold, it is called a *ratio spread*. A ratio spread can be viewed as a variation of an existing option strategy, where additional options in one leg are bought or sold to create an *unbalanced spread*. In essence, an unbalanced-spread strategy is simply a spread in which there is a difference between the number of options in one leg (or side) versus the number in another leg (or side).

There can be a large number of variations in unbalanced spreads, so each should be analyzed separately to determine the risks and rewards associated with each unique spread. This chapter addresses spreads in which the number of long options differs from the number of short options, assuming that all options expire on the same date. An unbalanced position can be taken on any spread strategy; however, this chapter illustrates these ratio principles using a vertical spread. The first part of this chapter addresses where more options are sold, and the second part addresses where more options are bought.

OVERVIEW

An unbalanced (ratio) spread is defined broadly as any option strategy in which the number of options bought is different than the number sold (see Table 13.1). The trader, for example, can use an unbalanced ratio of two-for-one, three-for-one, three-for-two, and so on. In this chapter, a ratio of two-for-one is assumed, but there is no set rule.

To execute a 100/105 call debit spread, you can buy one 100 call and sell one 105 call. But, if you believe that the net debit is too high, you can sell an additional 105 call

TABLE 13.1 Definitions: Unbalanced Spreads

Spread Type	Strategy
Ratio spread (unbalanced)	Number of short options differs from number of long options
Ratio (front) spread	Number of short options is greater than number of long options
Backspread	Number of long options is greater than number of short options

to reduce the net debit and convert it to a net credit or to zero cost (buy one 100 call and sell two 105 calls). An unbalanced-spread strategy in which more options are sold than bought is commonly called a *ratio spread*, or *front spread*.

Likewise, to execute a 100/105 call credit spread, you can sell one 100 call and buy one 105 call. In this example, you can buy an additional 105 call (or calls). An unbalanced spread strategy in which more options are bought than sold is called a *backspread* (sell one 100 call and buy two 105 calls). In a backspread, the short options are farther out-of-the-money.

Some literature automatically assumes that a front spread is the same thing as a ratio spread, but this can be confusing because, technically, both a front and a backspread can be a ratio spread. As a result, in this book, I will refer to a spread with a greater number of short options as a ratio spread or as a front spread. For this chapter, just remember that in a ratio spread (front spread), the option closest to the stock price is typically bought, and in a backspread, the option furthest from the stock price is typically bought (see Table 13.1).

An unbalanced spread strategy (front spread or backspread) can be constructed with either all calls or all puts, or a combination of both; for example, an unbalanced call spread can consist of buying one close-to-the-money call and selling two calls at a higher strike price, or selling one close-to-the-money call and buying two calls at a higher strike price. An unbalanced put spread can consist of buying one close-to-the-money put and selling two puts at a lower strike price, or selling one close-to-the-money put and buying two puts at a lower strike price.

Table 13.2 is a summary of unbalanced strategies, assuming that a vertical spread is used as a starting point.

It is not uncommon to establish an unequal number of long positions versus short positions because it enables you to tailor your account to your unique prediction of the market. Remember that in a spread, you are, in effect, combining the delta, gamma, vega, and theta of each option into one trade.

STRATEGY EXAMPLES

Following are descriptions and examples of unbalanced spread strategies. As a reminder, you can close out an option position by offsetting it in the marketplace any time prior to expiration, and the principles that are demonstrated on a stock can be applied to options

TABLE 13.2 Summary: Ratio Spread and Backspread

Spread Strategy	Strategy Description	Risk–Reward	Profitable	Initial Margin
Call ratio spread	Long lower call strike, short greater number at higher strike	Limited profit, unlimited risk	Moderately bullish	On short options in excess of long options
Put ratio spread	Long higher put strike, short greater number at lower strike	Limited profit, unlimited risk	Moderately bearish	On short options in excess of long options
Call backspread	Sell lower call strike, buy greater number at higher strike	Unlimited profit, limited risk	Bullish	On short vertical portion of spread
Put backspread	Sell higher put strike, buy greater number at lower strike	Unlimited profit, limited risk	Bearish	On short vertical portion of spread

on an ETF, index, or stock index futures. Appendixes A, B, and C illustrate many of the strategies covered throughout this book.

Ratio (Front) Spread

A ratio spread (front spread) can, for instructional purposes, be viewed as two option transactions. The first part is a vertical debit spread, in which one option is purchased at one strike price and another option is sold further out-of-the-money (with the same expiration date), creating a net debit. The second part of the transaction is the sale of an additional naked short option at the same strike price (and expiration date) as the other short option. Another way to view a ratio spread is that you buy one option and finance the purchase (in whole or in part) by selling two or more further out-of-the money options. The sale of options, in effect, can reduce the cost of the long option and can convert the transaction from a debit to a credit or zero cost. To execute a ratio spread, you can, for example, purchase an at-the-money option and sell two out-of-the-money options. Alternatively, you can buy an out-of-the-money option at one strike price and sell two further out-of-the-money options.

If a call ratio spread is executed for a debit, you will lose the entire amount of the debit if the price of the stock closes at or below the strike price of the long call at expiration. If a call ratio spread is executed for a credit, you will gain the entire amount of the credit if the price of the stock closes at or below the strike price of the long call at expiration.

The maximum profit potential of such a call ratio spread, at expiration, is the difference between the two strike prices times $100 (assuming it is a stock) times the number of long contracts minus any net debit paid (or plus any credit) and is realized when the price of the stock closes at the strike price of the short calls. At the short option strike price, you profit as much as you can from the long option before the negative effects of the short options kick in. The ratio spreader has unlimited risk on the upside in the case of a call ratio spread and unlimited risk on the downside in the case of a put ratio spread because of the excess short options. Losses for a ratio spreader continue to rise, at expiration, the more the short options finish in-the-money.

A ratio spread has two break-even points, and the level of these points is a little more complicated than usual because a different number of long versus short options is involved. One break-even point, at expiration, is where the underlying stock equals the long call option strike price plus the net debit, and the second break-even point is where the excess short option value equals the profit achieved at the short strike price. In other words, assuming a two-for-one ratio, if the profit is $400 at the short option strike price, the break-even point occurs where the value of the excess short option (one short option in this example) equals $400.

For an unbalanced spread, it is difficult to generalize about time decay and volatility because they are affected by the ratio chosen, strike prices, and other factors. If the ratio spread is executed for a debit, the full net premium must be paid at the time of purchase. A ratio spread requires margin in a taxable account. A ratio call spread may not be permitted in an IRA because it involves short naked call options. An example of a ratio spread follows, using a call debit spread as a starting point. A ratio put spread works the same way but in the opposite direction.

Example: Call Ratio Spread

> **Assumptions**: XYZ stock is trading at $100 a share in January; execute a two-for-one February 100/105 call ratio spread at a $1 debit, as follows: Buy one February 100 call at $5 and sell two February 105 calls at $2 each.

TABLE 13.3 Call Front Spread

XYZ Stock Price ($)	Long Call Value	Short Call Value	Spread	Cost of Spread	Spread Profit (Loss)	Profit (Loss) Percentage
75	0	0	0	100	(100)	(100)
80	0	0	0	100	(100)	(100)
85	0	0	0	100	(100)	(100)
90	0	0	0	100	(100)	(100)
95	0	0	0	100	(100)	(100)
100	0	0	0	100	(100)	(100)
105	500	0	500	100	400	400
110	1,000	1,000	0	100	(100)	(100)
115	1,500	2,000	500	100	(600)	(600)
120	2,000	3,000	1,000	100	(1,100)	(1,100)
125	2,500	4,000	1,500	100	(1,600)	(1,600)

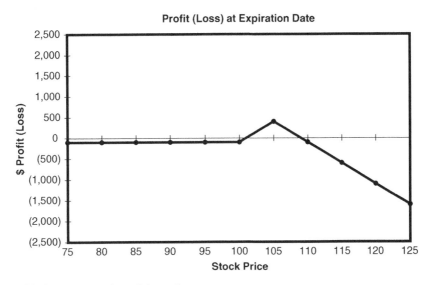

FIGURE 13.1 Call Ratio (Front) Spread

Strategy direction: Moderately bullish.

Debit or credit: $100 debit.

Maximum profit: $400.

Maximum loss: Unlimited.

Exercise and assignment: Can exercise long option if in-the-money; may be assigned on short options if in-the-money.

Break-even stock prices: $101 and $109 (strike price of long option plus debit, and strike price of short options plus where excess short options value equals the profit achieved at short strike price).

Maximum profit achieved: Underlying stock at higher strike price of 105.

Maximum loss achieved: Stock above break-even price of 109.

Profit (loss) if stock unchanged: $100 loss (debit).

Greeks: Table 13.4 contains sample Greeks converted to dollars at the time the position is established.

Option values in this example are rounded to make it easier to focus on option principles. Thus, this example assumes the spread is executed at a debit, while it may be executed at a credit if it were not for the rounding assumption.

TABLE 13.4 Summary of Greeks: February Expiration

Option	Delta	Gamma	Theta	Vega
Long 1 February 100 call	$53	$2.30	−$15	$12
Short 2 February 105 calls	−$84	$4.00	$28	−$22
Position	−$31		$13	−$10

TABLE 13.5 Summary of Greeks: March Expiration

Option	Delta	Gamma	Theta	Vega
Long 1 March 100 call	$52	$1.30	−$12	$17
Short 2 March 105 calls	−$80	−$2.40	$20	−$30
Position	−$28		$8	−$13

As a result, the Greeks are consistent with a credit position, instead of a debit position. The example that follows, assuming March expiration, assumes a debit. On the basis of these February Greeks, the position would reflect a gain from stock decline (delta), time decay (theta), and volatility (vega) contraction. Position would reflect a loss from stock rise (delta) and volatility (vega) expansion. Loss is $31 from XYZ stock rising to $101; gain is $13 from one day of time decay.

Later expiration: The price and Greeks will differ if expiration is at a later date; for example, if the 100 call is $7 (instead of $5) and the 105 call is $5 (instead of $3), a two-for-one ratio spread would be executed for a $3 credit. Example Greeks are given in Table 13.5.

Loss is $28 from XYZ stock rising to $101; gain is $8 from one day of time decay.

Exercise and assignment: For the February 100/105 call ratio spread, if both strike prices are in-the-money, then you may be assigned on your short calls and will be required to sell the XYZ stock at $105 per share. By exercising your long call, you can buy shares at $100 per share. If the stock price closes between the strike prices of the two option positions at expiration, your long call will be in-the-money and your short calls will be out-of-the-money. If the short options expire in-the-money, they may be assigned, but you are not fully protected by the long call.

A call ratio spread may be an appropriate strategy if you forecast that an underlying stock will rise but not beyond the short strike price. If the underlying stock surges, a call ratio spread has unlimited risk potential because there are more short contracts. If the stock plunges, all options expire worthless, and you profit if the position was executed for a credit but lose if it was executed for a debit. A typical call ratio spread is moderately bullish and has limited profit potential and unlimited risk.

Example: Put Ratio Spread A put ratio spread (front spread) is similar to a call ratio spread, except that it is executed with puts. If the underlying stock plunges, a ratio spread has unlimited risk because there are more short contracts. If the stock surges, all options expire worthless, and you profit if the position was executed for a credit but lose if it was executed for a debit. For example, assume that XYZ stock is trading at $100 a share in January, and you execute a two-for-one February 95/100 put spread at a $1

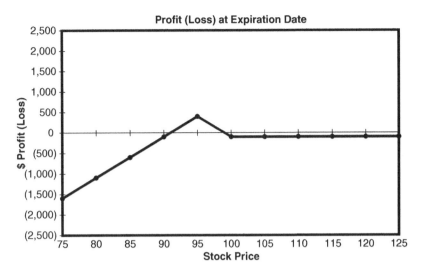

FIGURE 13.2 Put Ratio (Front) Spread

debit, as follows: Buy one February 100 put at $5 and sell two February 95 puts at $2 each. Figure 13.2 is an illustration of such a put ratio (front) spread.

Backspread

For instructional purposes, a backspread can be viewed as two option transactions. The first part is a vertical credit spread, in which one option is sold at one strike price and another option is purchased further out-of-the-money (with the same expiration date), creating a net credit. The second part of the transaction is the purchase of an additional long option at the same strike price (and expiration date) as the other long option. The purchase of options, in effect, reduces the net credit and can even convert the transaction from a credit to a debit or zero cost. To execute a backspread, for example, you can sell an at-the-money call option and buy two out-of-the-money options. Alternatively, you can sell an out-of-the-money option at one strike price and buy two further out-of-the-money options.

If a call backspread is executed for a credit, you will gain the entire amount of the credit if the price of the stock closes at or below the strike price of the short call at expiration. If a call backspread is executed for a debit, you will lose the entire amount of the debit if the price of the stock closes at or below the strike price of the short call at expiration.

A backspread assumes the opposite risk of a ratio spread. As a result, a backspread has unlimited profit potential on the upside in the case of a call and unlimited profit potential on the downside in the case of a put because of the excess long options. Gains for a backspread continue to rise, at expiration, the more the long options finish in-the-money.

The maximum loss of such a call backspread, at expiration, is the difference between the two strike prices times $100 (assuming it is a stock) times the number of short contracts minus any net credit (or plus any debit) and is realized when the price of the stock closes at the strike price of the long calls. At the long option strike price, you lose as much as you can from the short option before the positive effects of the long options kick in.

A backspread has two break-even points. One break-even point, at expiration, is when the underlying stock equals the short option strike price plus the net credit (or minus the net debit), and the second break-even point is when the excess long option value equals the loss achieved at the long strike price. In other words, assuming a two-for-one ratio, if the loss is $400 at the long option strike price, the break-even point occurs where the value of the excess long option (one long option, in this example) equals $400.

For an unbalanced spread, it is difficult to generalize about time decay and volatility because they are affected by the ratio chosen, strike prices, and other factors. If the backspread is executed for a debit, the full net premium must be paid at the time of purchase. A backspread requires margin in a taxable account for the net short position. A backspread may be permitted in an IRA because there are no naked options. The example that follows shows a backspread using a call credit spread as a starting point. A put backspread works the same way but in the opposite direction.

Example: Call Backspread

> **Assumptions**: XYZ stock is trading at $100 a share in January; execute a two-for-one February 100/105 call backspread and collect a $1 credit, as follows: Sell one February 100 call at $5 and buy two February 105 calls at $2 each.
> **Strategy direction**: Bullish.

TABLE 13.6 Call Backspread

XYZ Stock Price ($)	Long Call Value	Short Call Value	Spread	Original Spread Credit	Spread Profit (Loss)	Profit (Loss) Percentage
75	0	0	0	100	100	100
80	0	0	0	100	100	100
85	0	0	0	100	100	100
90	0	0	0	100	100	100
95	0	0	0	100	100	100
100	0	0	0	100	100	100
105	0	500	500	100	(400)	(400)
110	1,000	1,000	0	100	100	100
115	2,000	1,500	500	100	600	600
120	3,000	2,000	1,000	100	1,100	1,100
125	4,000	2,500	1,500	100	1,600	1,600

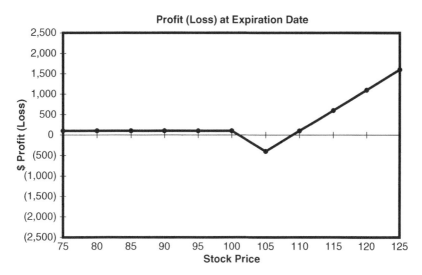

FIGURE 13.3 Call Backspread

Debit or credit: $100 credit.

Maximum profit: Unlimited.

Maximum loss: $400.

Exercise and assignment: Can exercise long options if in-the-money; may be assigned on short option if in-the-money.

Break-even stock price: $101 and $109 (strike price of short option plus credit and strike price of long options plus where excess long option value equals the profit achieved at long strike price).

Maximum profit achieved: Stock above break-even price of 109.

Maximum loss achieved: Underlying stock at higher strike price of 105.

Profit (loss) if stock unchanged: $100 gain (credit).

Greeks: Table 13.7 contains sample Greeks converted to dollars at the time the position is established.

　　Option values in this example are rounded to make it easier to focus on option principles. Thus, this example assumes the spread is executed at a credit, while it may be executed at a debit if it were not for the rounding assumption. As a result, the Greeks are consistent with a debit position, instead of a

TABLE 13.7 Summary of Greeks: February Expiration

Option	Delta	Gamma	Theta	Vega
Short 1 February 100 call	−$53	−$2.30	$15	−$12
Long 2 February 105 calls	$84	$4.00	−$28	$22
Position	$31		−$13	$10

TABLE 13.8 Summary of Greeks: March Expiration

Option	Delta	Gamma	Theta	Vega
Short 1 March 100 call	−$52	−$1.30	$12	−$17
Long 2 March 105 calls	$80	$2.40	−$20	$30
Position	$28		−$8	$13

credit position. The example that follows, assuming March expiration, assumes a debit. On the basis of these February Greeks, the position would reflect a gain from stock rise (delta) and volatility (vega) expansion. Position would reflect a loss from stock decline (delta), time decay (theta), and volatility (vega) contraction. Gain is $31 from XYZ stock rising to $101; loss is $13 from one day of time decay.

Later expiration: The price and Greeks will differ if expiration is at a later date; for example, if the 100 call is $7 (instead of $5) and the 105 call is $5 (instead of $3), a two-for-one backspread would be executed for a $3 debit. Example Greeks are given in Table 13.8.

Gain is $28 from XYZ stock rising to $101; loss is $8 from one day of time decay.

Exercise and assignment: For the February 100/105 call backspread, if both strike prices are in-the-money, then you may be assigned on your short call and will be required to sell the XYZ stock at $100 per share. By exercising your long calls, you can buy shares at $105 per share. If the stock price closes between the strike prices of the two option positions at expiration, your short call will be in-the-money and your long calls will be out-of-the-money.

A call backspread may be an appropriate strategy if you forecast that an underlying stock will rise beyond the long strike price. If the underlying stock surges, a call backspread has unlimited risk potential because there are more long contracts. If the stock plunges, all options expire worthless, and you profit if the position was executed for a credit but lose if it was executed for a debit.

Example: Put Backspread   A put backspread is similar to a call backspread, except it is executed with puts. If the underlying stock plunges, a backspread has unlimited reward potential because there are more long contracts. If the stock surges, all options expire worthless, and you profit if the position was executed for a credit but lose if it was executed for a debit. For example, assume that XYZ stock is trading at $100 a share in January. Execute a two-for-one February 95/100 put backspread at a $1 credit, as follows: Sell one February 100 put at $5 and buy two February 95 puts at $2 each. Figure 13.4 is an illustration of such a put backspread.

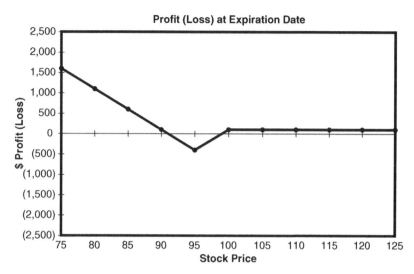

FIGURE 13.4   Put Backspread

BEYOND THE BASICS

Margin

In a call or put ratio (front) spread, margin is generally required on the short options if uncovered; for example, if you buy one February 100 call and sell two February 105 calls, an initial margin is required on one short 105 call. In a call or put backspread, margin is generally required for the short vertical portion of the spread; for example, if you sell one February 100 call and buy two February 105 calls, margin is required on one 100/105 vertical credit spread. Margin on a vertical credit spread is generally calculated as the lesser of the short option margin or the difference between the strike prices minus the premium collected. For example, if XYZ stock is trading at $100 and you sell a February 100/110 call vertical credit spread for $400, your margin is $600 (the difference in strike prices minus premium collected). Likewise, if you sell a February 90/100 put vertical spread for $400, your margin is $600. Margin rules are covered in Chapter 30.

Debit versus Credit

An unbalanced strategy can encompass a broad range of spread strategies, so it can be difficult to generalize how each spread will react. For example, in a vertical spread, a ratio spread or backspread can be executed for a debit or a credit, depending on the number of options bought versus sold and the relative values of options bought versus sold. Such relative values are affected by the width of strike prices and time remaining to expiration.

As mentioned earlier, an unbalanced strategy can encompass a broad range of spread strategies, so it can be difficult to generalize. However, there are some general rules of thumb I like to use. As a general rule, a ratio (front) spread with a low ratio, wider strike prices, and shorter time to expiration will more likely be executed at a debit. A ratio (front) spread with a high ratio, narrower strike prices, and longer time to expiration will more likely be executed at a credit. Likewise, as a general rule, a backspread with a high ratio, narrower strike prices, and longer time to expiration will more likely be executed at a debit. A backspread with a low ratio, wider strike prices, and shorter time to expiration will more likely be executed at a credit.

For example, assume that XYZ stock is trading at $100 a share and you are contemplating a ratio (front) spread, in which you want to buy one at-the-money call and sell two or more 105 strike price calls. This spread could be executed for a credit or a debit, depending on a number of factors. As a general rule of thumb, if there are 30 days or fewer remaining to expiration, a 105 strike option will typically be less than one half the 100 strike option (e.g., $2 for the 105 call versus $5 for the 100 call). Of course, this is only a general rule because options with lower volatility would likely be less than half, but options with higher volatility may be more than half. As a result, if you execute a two-for-one ratio (front) spread in this example, it will be executed at a debit of $1. However, if there are 60 days or more remaining to expiration, for example, then the 105 strike call is typically more than one half the value of the 100 strike price call (e.g., $4 for the 105 call and $7 for the 100 call). As a result, you would execute a two-for-one ratio (front) spread at a credit of $1.

FINAL THOUGHTS

An unbalanced spread is a strategy within a strategy. An unbalanced strategy can be applied to any spread strategy, so you can fine-tune your risk–reward parameters. It is common to vary the number of long options versus short options. Buying and selling options in unequal numbers should be a nice addition to your list of strategies. Keep in mind that you have unlimited profit potential if the number of long options is greater and unlimited risk if the number of short options is greater.

The terminology in the options industry regarding unbalanced spreads can sometimes be confusing: Option strategies come in all different sizes and shapes, and an unbalanced spread can be viewed as a strategy that captures many strategies that would not be defined otherwise. You should learn the terminology used by your trading platform so that you can trade effectively.

A ratio (front) spread can be considered a type of hedge but, in this case, you are hedging the high cost of the long option by offsetting all or a portion of its cost with the sale of other options. In an unbalanced spread, you have offsetting deltas and other Greeks, and you get to choose the distance between strike prices, the number of options bought versus sold, whether the transaction is for a debit or a credit, how far options are out-of-the-money, and the time to expiration. You should, hopefully, be able to create a position that fits your risk–reward profile.

Typically, a spread is executed with all calls or all puts and not a combination of both. However, in the next chapter, Chapter 14, which covers straddles and strangles, we explore option strategies in which calls and puts are used in the same position. In a later chapter, we will explore spread strategies where the options expire at different times.

Straddle and Strangle

nlike a spread strategy, which consists of all calls or all puts, a *straddle* or a *strangle* each consists of a long call and long put or a short call and a short put. If the call and put are purchased, the trader is long the straddle or strangle; if both options are sold, the trader is short the straddle or strangle. The idea is to establish a position on both sides of the market, where you can take advantage of volatility expansion and trading outside a range (long straddle and strangle) or volatility contraction, time decay, and trading within a range (short straddle and strangle).

This chapter covers both a straddle and a strangle in which the number of options sold equals the number purchased and for which options expire in the same month. Other chapters explore option strategies in which the number of options sold differs from the number bought and in which the sides, or legs, of the spread expire at different times. A straddle and a strangle are both addressed in this chapter because they have similar characteristics. The first part of this chapter addresses a straddle, and the second part addresses a strangle.

OVERVIEW

A straddle consists of a call and a put with the same terms (strike price, expiration date, and underlying stock). A long straddle consists of a long call and a long put with the same strike price and expiration date and is used to profit from volatility; for example, buy one February 100 call and buy one February 100 put. A short straddle consists of a short call and put with the same strike price and expiration date and is used to profit from a trading range or volatility contraction; for example, sell one February 100 call and sell one February 100 put.

TABLE 14.1   Summary: Long and Short Straddle and Strangle

Spread Strategy	Strategy Description	Risk–Reward	Profitable	Debit or Credit	Breakeven	Initial Margin
Long straddle	Buy call and put at same strike price	Unlimited profit, limited risk	Trade outside range	Debit	Strike price plus and minus debit	Full payment
Short straddle	Sell call and put at same strike price	Limited profit, unlimited risk	Trade within range	Credit	Strike price plus and minus credit	Call or put margin, whichever is greater, plus the premium of the other side
Long strangle	Buy call and put at different strike prices	Unlimited profit, limited risk	Trade outside range	Debit	Call strike price plus debit, put strike price minus debit	Full payment
Short strangle	Buy call and put at different strike prices	Limited profit, unlimited risk	Trade within range	Credit	Strike price plus credit, put strike price minus credit	Call or put margin, whichever is greater, plus the premium of the other side

A strangle is similar to a straddle except that a strangle involves two different strike prices. A long strangle consists of a long call and long put with different strike prices and the same expiration date; for example, buy one February 105 call and buy one February 95 put. A short strangle consists of a short call and put with different strike prices and the same expiration date; for example, sell one February 105 call and sell one February 95 put.

Table 14.1 is a summary of a long and short straddle and strangle.

To exit a position, you can offset it in a closing transaction, exercise a long option if it is in-the-money, wait for assignment of a short option if it is in-the-money, or let both legs expire worthless (if both are at or out-of-the-money at expiration).

In a straddle or a strangle, you are, in effect, combining the characteristics of each option (delta, gamma, vega, and theta) into one trade. When you convert these characteristics to dollars, you have position Greeks. In a straddle or a strangle, you are long or short opposing options, and your overall position will be the net of the two. In a straddle or a strangle, the Greeks for one side of the trade offset, in part, the Greeks in the other side. A straddle and a strangle are both good examples of where delta does not measure the true risk and reward of the strategy. As previously mentioned, delta only measures a one-point change in the underlying stock. However, if you execute a straddle or a strangle, you are betting for or against a large move in the underlying stock and, by definition, delta will not necessarily give you the information you need. In essence, delta is a measurement of a small move; but, with a straddle or a strangle, you need to know what happens in a big move. Instead, it is sometimes best to examine an option chain or option calculator to project values under various scenarios.

STRATEGY EXAMPLES

Following are descriptions of a long and short straddle. As a reminder, you can close out an option position by offsetting it in the marketplace any time prior to expiration, and the principles that are demonstrated for a stock can be applied to options on an ETF, index, and stock index futures. Appendixes A, B, and C illustrate many of the strategies covered throughout this book.

Long Straddle (Want Volatility)

A long straddle consists of a long call and long put with the same strike price and expiration date. A long straddle has unlimited profit potential in both directions, and a profit is made in this strategy as the underlying stock moves beyond a break-even point in either direction. It is a strategy that has unlimited profit potential on both sides of the trade and is used to take advantage of extreme volatility, without having to determine direction. To be profitable at expiration, the call or put side must exceed the total premium collected (on both sides). Prior to expiration, for a long straddle to be profitable, a rise on the call side must exceed the corresponding decline on the put side, or a rise on the put side must exceed the corresponding decline on the call side. A long straddle can be executed at any strike price but is commonly established at-the-money.

The maximum loss is limited to the debit paid and occurs when the underlying stock is at the strike price at expiration (where all options expire worthless). For a long straddle, you pay double (or nearly double) the amount of premium in comparison to trading one side of the market. The risk is that the underlying stock will fluctuate back and forth within a range, forcing both the call and the put to decay in value over time.

In a straddle, there are two break-even points. The break-even points are the strike price plus the debit and the strike price minus the debit. A profit is achieved when the underlying stock advances or declines dramatically, substantially increasing the value of the put or call side, which is partially offset by the other side of the trade.

A long straddle is subject to the effects of time decay. Prior to expiration, an increase in volatility typically increases a straddle value, and a decrease in volatility typically decreases a straddle value. For a long straddle, a debit is charged to your account and must be paid in full. A long straddle may be permitted in an IRA.

Example: Long Straddle

Assumptions: XYZ stock is trading at $100 a share in January; buy one February 100 straddle for $10, as follows: Buy one February 100 call at $5 and buy one February 100 put at $5.

Strategy direction: Volatility in either direction.

Debit or credit: $1,000 debit.

Maximum profit: Unlimited in both directions.

Maximum loss: $1,000 debit ($500 debit call side plus $500 put side).

Exercise and assignment: Can exercise either long option if in-the-money.

TABLE 14.2 Long Straddle Values

XYZ Stock Price ($)	Long Call Value	Long Put Value	Spread	Original Spread Debit	Spread Profit (Loss)
75	0	2,500	2,500	1,000	1,500
80	0	2,000	2,000	1,000	1,000
85	0	1,500	1,500	1,000	500
90	0	1,000	1,000	1,000	0
95	0	500	500	1,000	(500)
100	0	0	0	1,000	(1,000)
105	500	0	500	1,000	(500)
110	1,000	0	1,000	1,000	0
115	1,500	0	1,500	1,000	500
120	2,000	0	2,000	1,000	1,000
125	2,500	0	2,500	1,000	1,500

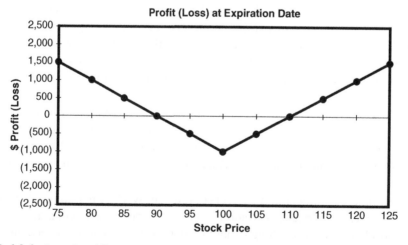

FIGURE 14.1 Long Straddle

TABLE 14.3 Summary of Greeks: February Expiration

Option	Delta	Gamma	Theta	Vega
Long 1 February 100 call	$53	$2.30	−$15	$12
Long 1 February 100 put	−$53	$2.30	−$15	$12
Position	$0		−$30	$24

TABLE 14.4 Summary of Greeks: March Expiration

Option	Delta	Gamma	Theta	Vega
Long 1 March 100 call	$52	$1.30	−$12	$17
Long 1 March 100 put	−$52	$1.30	−$12	$17
Position	$0		−$24	$34

Break-even stock price: $110 or $90 (strike price plus debit; strike price minus debit).

Maximum profit achieved: Underlying stock beyond break-even point in either direction.

Maximum loss achieved: Underlying stock at strike price at expiration.

Profit (loss) if stock unchanged: $1,000 loss (equal to debit).

Greeks: Table 14.3 contains sample Greeks converted to dollars at the time the position is established.

Position would reflect no gain from a small stock rise (delta) but would have a gain from volatility (vega) expansion. Position would reflect no loss from stock decline (delta) but would have a loss from time decay (theta) and volatility (vega) contraction. Gain is zero from XYZ stock rising to $101; loss is $30 from one day of time decay.

Later expiration: The price and Greeks will differ when the position is established if expiration is at a later date. For example, if the options expire in March, instead of February, the price of the March straddle could be $16 (instead of $10), with example Greeks as given in Table 14.4.

Gain is zero from XYZ stock rising to $101; loss is $24 from one day of time decay.

Exercise and assignment: By exercising your long call, you can buy shares at $100 per share or, by exercising your long put, you can sell shares at $100.

Short Straddle (Want Trading Range)

In a short straddle, you simultaneously sell a call and put at the same strike price and with the same expiration date. An advantage is that you collect double the premium and can benefit from double time decay and volatility contraction. In a short straddle, you want the underlying stock to fluctuate back and forth within a range, forcing both the call and the put sides to decay in value over time. Prior to expiration, a short straddle will show a loss if a rise on the call side exceeds the corresponding decline on the put side or a rise on the put side exceeds the corresponding decline on the call side. The purpose of such a spread is to profit from time decay and/or volatility contraction, ideally on both sides. A short straddle can be executed at any strike price but is commonly established at-the-money.

The maximum profit occurs when the underlying stock is at the strike price at expiration (when all options are worthless). A profit is made in this strategy as the underlying stock fluctuates back and forth in a range, allowing both the call and put sides to decay in value over time. This is a strategy that is used to try to double (or nearly double) the amount of premium collected in comparison to what could be obtained by only trading one side of the market. This strategy makes sense because it is based on the fact that the underlying stock cannot be in two places at one time.

The maximum loss potential is unlimited in both directions. The risk is that the underlying stock will advance or decline dramatically, substantially increasing the value of the put or call side, which would only be partially offset by the other side of the trade. The risk of writing a straddle is that the loss is theoretically unlimited; you have upside risk because of your uncovered short calls and downside risk because of your uncovered short puts.

In a straddle, there are two break-even points. The break-even points are the strike price plus the premium credit collected and the strike price minus the premium collected.

A short straddle benefits from the effects of time decay. Prior to expiration, an increase in volatility typically increases a straddle value, and a decrease in volatility typically decreases a straddle value. For a short straddle, a credit is reflected in your account and margin is the greater of the call side margin or the put side margin, but not both. A short straddle is not permitted in an IRA because of the margin requirement.

Example: Short Straddle

>   **Assumptions**: XYZ stock is trading at $100 a share in January; sell one February 100 straddle for $10, as follows: Sell one February 100 call at $5 and sell one February 100 put at $5.
>   **Strategy direction**: Neutral (trading range).
>   **Debit or credit**: $1,000 credit.
>   **Maximum profit**: $1,000 credit ($500 call side and $500 put side).
>   **Maximum loss**: Unlimited in both directions.
>   **Exercise and assignment**: Subject to assignment if call or put is in-the-money.
>   **Break-even stock price**: $110 or $90 (strike price plus credit; strike price minus credit).
>   **Maximum profit achieved**: Underlying stock at strike price at expiration.

Maximum loss achieved: Underlying stock beyond the break-even point in either direction.

Profit (loss) if stock unchanged: $1,000 gain (equal to credit).

Greeks: Table 14.6 contains sample Greeks converted to dollars at the time the position is established.

Position would reflect no gain from a small stock decline (delta) but would show a gain from time decay (theta) and volatility (vega) contraction. Position would reflect no loss from stock rise (delta) but would show a loss from volatility (vega) expansion. Gain is zero from XYZ stock rising to $101; gain is $30 from one day of time decay.

TABLE 14.5 Short Straddle

XYZ Stock Price ($)	Short Call Value	Short Put Value	Spread	Original Spread Credit	Spread Profit (Loss)
75	0	2,500	2,500	1,000	(1,500)
80	0	2,000	2,000	1,000	(1,000)
85	0	1,500	1,500	1,000	(500)
90	0	1,000	1,000	1,000	0
95	0	500	500	1,000	500
100	0	0	0	1,000	1,000
105	500	0	500	1,000	500
110	1,000	0	1,000	1,000	0
115	1,500	0	1,500	1,000	(500)
120	2,000	0	2,000	1,000	(1,000)
125	2,500	0	2,500	1,000	(1,500)

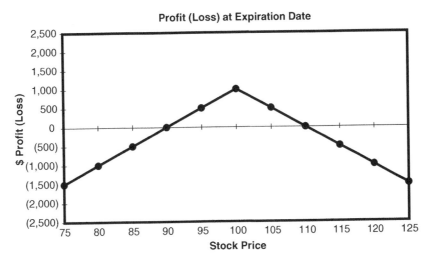

FIGURE 14.2 Short Straddle

TABLE 14.6 Summary of Greeks: February Expiration

Option	Delta	Gamma	Theta	Vega
Short 1 February 100 call	−$53	−$2.30	$15	−$12
Short 1 February 100 put	$53	−$2.30	$15	−$12
Position	$0		$30	−$24

TABLE 14.7 Summary of Greeks: March Expiration

Option	Delta	Gamma	Theta	Vega
Short 1 March 100 call	−$52	−$1.30	$12	−$17
Short 1 March 100 put	$52	−$1.30	$12	−$17
Position	$0		$24	−$34

Later expiration: The price and Greeks will differ when the position is established if expiration is at a later date; for example, if the options expire in March, instead of February, the price of the March straddle could be $16 (instead of $10), with example Greeks as given in Table 14.7.

Gain is zero from XYZ stock rising to $101; gain is $24 from one day of time decay.

Exercise and assignment: For the short straddle, you may be assigned on your short call or put, but both options cannot be in-the-money at the same time because they share the same strike price.

This is a strategy that is used to nearly double the amount of premium collected in comparison to what could be obtained by only trading one side of the market based on the fact that the underlying stock cannot be in two places at one time. Realizing the theoretical maximum profit from a short straddle requires great pinpoint precision because the underlying stock must close at a specific price, the strike price, at a specific point in time (the expiration date). However, you do not have to earn the entire premium to show a healthy profit.

Long Strangle (Want Volatility)

A strangle is similar to a straddle. A long strangle consists of a long call and long put with different strike prices but the same expiration date. A long strangle has unlimited profit potential in both directions, and a profit is made in this strategy as the underlying stock moves beyond a break-even point in either direction. It is a strategy that has unlimited profit potential on both sides of the trade and is used to take advantage of extreme volatility, without having to determine direction. To be profitable at expiration, the call or put side must exceed the total premium collected (on both sides), which occurs when the underlying stock moves beyond the break-even point in either direction. Prior to expiration, for a long strangle to be profitable, a rise on the call side must exceed the corresponding decline on the put side or a rise on the put side must exceed the corresponding decline on the call side. A long strangle can be executed with a combination of any two strike prices but is commonly established with the midpoint of the strike prices near at-the-money.

The maximum loss is limited to the debit paid and occurs when the underlying stock is at or between the strike prices at expiration (where all options expire worthless). For a long strangle, you pay double (or nearly double) the amount of premium in comparison to trading one side of the market, and the risk is that the underlying stock will fluctuate back and forth within a range, forcing both the call and put sides to decay in value over time.

In a strangle, there are two break-even points. One break-even point is the call strike price plus the debit, and the other is the put strike price minus the debit. A profit is achieved when the underlying stock advances or declines dramatically, substantially increasing the value of the put or call side, which is partially offset by the other side of the trade.

A long strangle is subject to the effects of time decay. Prior to expiration, an increase in volatility typically increases a strangle value and a decrease in volatility typically decreases a strangle value. For a long strangle, a debit is charged to your account and must be paid in full. A long strangle may be permitted in an IRA.

Example: Long Strangle

> **Assumptions**: XYZ stock is trading at $100 a share in January; buy one February 95/105 strangle for $4, as follows: Buy one February 105 call at $2 and buy one February 95 put at $2.
> **Strategy direction**: Volatility in either direction.
> **Debit or credit**: $400 debit.

TABLE 14.8 Long Strangle

XYZ Stock Price ($)	Long Call Value	Long Put Value	Spread	Original Spread Debit	Spread Profit (Loss)
75	0	2,000	2,000	400	1,600
80	0	1,500	1,500	400	1,100
85	0	1,000	1,000	400	600
90	0	500	500	400	100
95	0	0	0	400	(400)
100	0	0	0	400	(400)
105	0	0	0	400	(400)
110	500	0	500	400	100
115	1,000	0	1,000	400	600
120	1,500	0	1,500	400	1,100
125	2,000	0	2,000	400	1,600

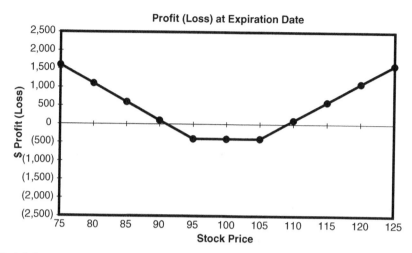

FIGURE 14.3 Long Strangle

Maximum profit: Unlimited in both directions.

Maximum loss: $400 debit ($200 debit call side and $200 put side).

Exercise and assignment: Can exercise either long option if in-the-money.

Break-even stock price: $109 or $91 (call strike price plus debit; put strike price minus debit).

Maximum profit achieved: Underlying stock beyond the break-even point in either direction.

Maximum loss achieved: Underlying stock at or between call and put strike price at expiration.

Profit (loss) if stock unchanged: $400 loss (equal to debit).

Greeks: Table 14.9 contains sample Greeks converted to dollars at the time the position is established.

Position would reflect no gain from a small stock rise (delta) but would show a gain from volatility (vega) expansion. Position would reflect no loss from stock decline (delta) but would have a loss from time decay (theta) and volatility (vega) contraction. Gain is zero from XYZ stock rising to $101; loss is $28 from one day of time decay.

Later expiration: The price and Greeks will differ when the position is established if expiration is at a later date; for example, if the options expire in March, instead

TABLE 14.9 Summary of Greeks: February Expiration

Option	Delta	Gamma	Theta	Vega
Long 1 February 105 call	$42	$2.00	−$14	$11
Long 1 February 95 put	−$42	$2.00	−$14	$11
Position	$0		−$28	$22

TABLE 14.10 Summary of Greeks: March Expiration

Option	Delta	Gamma	Theta	Vega
Long 1 March 105 call	$40	$1.20	−$10	$15
Long 1 March 95 put	−$40	$1.20	−$10	$15
Position	$0		−$20	$30

of February, the price of the March strangle could be $7 (instead of $4), with example Greeks as given in Table 14.10.

Gain is zero from XYZ stock rising to $101; loss is $20 from one day of time decay.

Exercise and assignment: By exercising your long call, you can buy shares at $105 per share or, by exercising your long put, you can sell shares at $95.

Short Strangle (Want Trading Range)

In a short strangle, you simultaneously sell a call and put at different strike prices but with the same expiration date. An advantage is that you collect double the premium and can benefit from double time decay and volatility contraction. In a short strangle, you want the underlying stock to fluctuate back and forth within a range, forcing both the call and the put sides to decay in value over time. Prior to expiration, a short strangle will show a loss if a rise on the call side exceeds the corresponding decline on the put side or a rise on the put side exceeds the corresponding decline on the call side. The purpose of such a spread is to profit from time decay and/or volatility contraction, ideally on both sides. A short strangle can be executed with a combination of any two strike prices but is commonly established with the midpoint of the strike prices near at-the-money.

The maximum profit occurs when the underlying stock is at or between the option strike prices at expiration (when all options are at-the-money or out-of-the-money). A profit is made in this strategy as the underlying stock fluctuates back and forth within a range (defined by the strike prices), allowing both the call and put sides to decay in value over time. This is a strategy that is used to try to double (or nearly double) the amount of premium collected in comparison to what could be obtained by only trading one side of the market. This strategy makes sense because it is based on the fact that the underlying stock cannot be in two places at one time.

The maximum loss potential is unlimited in both directions. The risk is that the underlying stock will advance or decline dramatically, substantially increasing the value of the put or call side, which would only be partially offset by the other side of the trade. The risk of writing a strangle is that the loss is theoretically unlimited; you have upside risk because of your uncovered short calls and downside risk because of your uncovered short puts.

In a short strangle, there are two break-even points. The break-even points are the strike price of the short call plus the premium credit collected and the strike price of the short put minus the premium collected.

A short strangle benefits from the effects of time decay. Prior to expiration, an increase in volatility typically increases a strangle value and a decrease in volatility typically decreases a strangle value. For a short strangle, a credit is reflected in your account and margin is the greater of the call side margin or the put side margin, but not both. A short strangle is not permitted in an IRA because of the margin requirement.

Example: Short Strangle

Assumptions: XYZ stock is trading at $100 a share in January; sell one February 100 strangle for $4, as follows: Sell one February 105 call at $2 and sell one February 95 put at $2.

Strategy direction: Neutral (trading range).

Debit or credit: $400 credit.

Maximum profit: $400 credit ($200 call side and $200 put side).

Maximum loss: Unlimited in both directions.

Exercise and assignment: Subject to assignment if call or put is in-the-money.

Break-even stock price: $109 or $91 (call strike price plus credit; put strike price minus credit).

Maximum profit achieved: Underlying stock between strike prices at expiration.

Maximum loss achieved: Underlying stock beyond the break-even point in either direction.

Profit (loss) if stock unchanged: $400 gain (equal to credit).

TABLE 14.11 Short Strangle

XYZ Stock Price ($)	Short Call Value	Short Put Value	Spread	Original Spread Credit	Spread Profit (Loss)
75	0	2,000	2,000	400	(1,600)
80	0	1,500	1,500	400	(1,100)
85	0	1,000	1,000	400	(600)
90	0	500	500	400	(100)
95	0	0	0	400	400
100	0	0	0	400	400
105	0	0	0	400	400
110	500	0	500	400	(100)
115	1,000	0	1,000	400	(600)
120	1,500	0	1,500	400	(1,100)
125	2,000	0	2,000	400	(1,600)

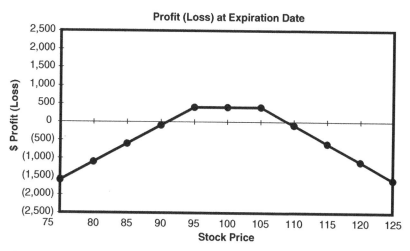

FIGURE 14.4 Short Strangle

Figure 14.4 shows the profit (loss) at expiration under the various scenarios.

Greeks: Table 14.12 contains sample Greeks converted to dollars at the time the position is established.

Position would reflect no gain from a small stock decline (delta) but would show a gain from time decay (theta) and volatility (vega) contraction. Position would reflect no loss from stock rise (delta) but would show a loss from volatility (vega) expansion. Gain is zero from XYZ stock rising to $101; gain is $28 from one day of time decay.

Later expiration: The price and Greeks will differ when the position is established if expiration is at a later date. For example, if the options expire in March, instead of February, the price of the March straddle could be $7 (instead of $4), with example Greeks as given in Table 14.13.

Gain is zero from XYZ stock rising to $101; gain is $20 from one day of time decay.

Exercise and assignment: For the short strangle, you may be assigned on your short call or put, but both options cannot be in-the-money at the same time.

TABLE 14.12 Summary of Greeks: February Expiration

Option	Delta	Gamma	Theta	Vega
Short 1 February 105 call	−$42	−$2.00	$14	−$11
Short 1 February 95 put	$42	−$2.00	$14	−$11
Position	$0		$28	−$22

TABLE 14.13 Summary of Greeks: March Expiration

Option	Delta	Gamma	Theta	Vega
Short 1 March 105 call	−$40	−$1.20	$10	−$15
Short 1 March 95 put	$40	−$1.20	$10	−$15
Position	$0		$20	−$30

This is a strategy that is used to try to nearly double the amount of premium collected in comparison to what could be obtained by only trading one side of the market. This is based on the fact that the underlying stock cannot be in two places at one time.

BEYOND THE BASICS

Margin

The initial margin for a short straddle or strangle is the greater of the call side or put side, whichever is greater, but not the total of both (ignoring the premium). This margin formula requirement is based on the fact that the underlying stock cannot be in two places at one time. When writing an uncovered equity option, the traditional minimum margin requirement is, in general, 20 percent of the underlying stock minus the amount the option is out-of-the-money, if any, plus the premium collected, but not less than 10 percent of the stock value. Portfolio margining is a method available for computing equity margins for certain qualified customers based on the risk of the position, rather than on fixed percentages, and the result is often lower margin requirements than would be calculated from the traditional method. Futures options margin is calculated differently than margin on stock options. A broker may, and often does, impose more stringent margin requirements. Full payment is required if the straddle or strangle is a long position. A long straddle or strangle must be paid in full. Margin rules are covered in Chapter 30.

Selecting the Best Strategy

A straddle is typically executed at-the-money, but it can be established at any strike price. If you are neutral about direction, you can establish an at-the-money long straddle; if you are bullish, you can establish a long straddle with a strike price below the level of the stock price (the call delta will exceed the put delta); and if you are bearish, you can establish a long straddle with a strike price above the level of the stock price (the put delta will exceed the call delta). For example, if XYZ stock is trading at $100 a share, you can establish a long straddle at a strike price of 100 if you are neutral, of 95 if you are bullish, or of 105 if you are bearish.

Remember that a short straddle profit is maximized if the underlying stock is at the strike price at expiration. If you are neutral about direction, you can establish an at-the-money short straddle; if you are bullish, you can establish a short straddle with a strike price above the level of the stock price; and if you are bearish, you can establish a short straddle with a strike price below the level of the stock price. For example, if XYZ stock is trading at $100 a share, you can establish a short straddle at a strike price of 100 if you are neutral, of 105 if you are bullish, or of 95 if you are bearish.

A strangle can be executed when the call and put strike prices are equidistant from the underlying stock price, but it can be established with any two out-of-the-money strike prices. If you are neutral on the market, you can establish a long strangle in which the strike prices are equidistant from the underlying stock price (or based on having equal deltas); if you are bullish, you can establish a long strangle with a call strike price closer to the stock price (or based on the call having a higher delta); and if you are bearish, you can establish a long strangle with a put strike price closer to the stock price (or based on the put having a higher delta). For example, if XYZ stock is trading at $100 a share, you can establish a long 95/105 (long 95 put, long 105 call) strangle if you are neutral, a long 90/105 (long 90 put, long 105 call) strangle if you are bullish, or a long 95/110 (long 95 put, long 110 call) strangle if you are bearish.

Likewise, if you are neutral, you can sell a strangle with strike prices equidistant from the stock price (or based on having equal deltas); if you are bullish, you can establish a short strangle with a put strike price closer to the stock price (or based on the call having a lower delta); if you are bearish, you can establish a short strangle with a call strike price closer to the stock price (or based on the put having a lower delta). For example, if XYZ stock is trading at $100 a share, you can establish a short 95/105 strangle if you are neutral, a short 95/110 strangle if you are bullish, or a short 90/105 strangle if you are bearish.

The maximum profit from a short strangle is achieved if the underlying stock closes at or between the two strike prices so that both options expire worthless. Therefore, you can attempt to stack the odds more in your favor by selling a strangle with increased odds of success by widening the strike prices until you have the probability for which you are looking.

Managing the Position

Keep in mind that you can close out an option position by offsetting it in the marketplace at any time prior to expiration, and you should use your trading platform software, option calculator, or option chain to estimate option values based on your own assumptions. It is best to examine your trading platform prior to buying or selling an option because it should provide the bid/ask spread, intrinsic versus extrinsic value, and the Greeks.

You can roll a straddle or strangle by offsetting your current position and reestablishing a new position. You may offset your current position because there are only a few days left in the option expiration cycle and you are interested in reestablishing a new position in a subsequent expiration month. In other cases, you may roll options to minimize risk, cut losses, and/or take into account your new view of the market. For example, assume that XYZ stock was trading at $100 a share and you were neutral, so you established a short 90/110 strangle. With four days remaining to expiration, XYZ stock is now trading at $104 and you have turned slightly bullish. As a result, you can offset the existing strangle and establish a 90/115 strangle expiring in the next month. When rolling, you can establish the new position with the same or a different number of options, strike prices, and expiration dates. You are readjusting your option positions to take advantage of opportunities, play defense, or take into account new market conditions. Remember that, in addition, you can vary the number of call versus put options and select different months to expiration according to your market view. Keep in mind that the closer an option is to expiration, all other factors being equal, the smaller the premium, and the longer to expiration, the higher the premium.

Mind the Gap

Selling a straddle or strangle involves naked options. Although the premium received by a seller is fixed, the seller may sustain a loss well in excess of that amount. A seller of an option who is in-the-money is subject to the risk of loss for the difference between the stock price and strike price at the expiration date multiplied by $100 (if a stock) minus the premium received. Although it may be your intention to exit an option position quickly should it reach a predetermined price, you may not be given that opportunity if the price of the underlying stock gaps.

A gap in an underlying stock is a quick jump higher or lower from one price to another, in which you may not have enough time to react. Gaps mostly occur at the opening of a trading session but can occur throughout the trading day, including during the overnight session. When a gap occurs at the opening, the opening price of a stock differs greatly from the close of the previous session. In such a case, you would not be able to offset your current option position until the market opens, and the prices of your options may be very unfavorable. A risk of selling a naked call (or put) option is that the stock price could gap higher (or lower) so that the price of an option rises dramatically; for example, a stock closing at $100 on one day may open the next day at $120 or at $80. The short straddle and strangle strategies are a bet against major volatility. The biggest risk to the short straddle and strangle strategies is a major gap in the market, either up or down, accompanied by increased volatility.

The price of a call or put can inflate dramatically well before the underlying stock reaches the strike price. It may seem at first that an option seller will have great staying power with the intention of simply waiting out the volatility as the stock moves toward the strike price; but, while he waits, the value of the trader's option may be exploding. As a result, out-of-the-money option sellers should be concerned with major fluctuations of the underlying stock prior to it reaching the strike price.

Risk Management

When selling a straddle or strangle, it is important that you establish the call and put sufficiently far enough away from the underlying stock price so that the net delta remains relatively low. Your option calculator and trading platform should show the probability of an underlying stock expiring above a call strike price or below a put strike price. Your trading platform may also be able to show the probability of an underlying stock touching a particular strike price prior to the expiration date. My general rules of thumb are that you should not establish a short option position unless the probability of success is at least 75 percent; conversely, on the flip side, I like to have at least a 60 percent chance of success with a long option. Under these guidelines, you would sell far-out-of-the-money options and would, in general, avoid buying far-out-of-the-money options. One of the biggest mistakes that a trader can make, in my opinion, is selling options with strike prices too close to the underlying stock. In such a case, you do not have the probabilities on your side, and you do not need to trade so close to the underlying stock to make a reasonable profit.

Should the underlying stock move dramatically toward either strike price, you may need to take defensive action to avoid large losses. There are a number of risk management strategies that you should learn to help mitigate such losses and reposition the straddle or strangle to potentially turn it into a profit. Risk management strategies are covered in Chapter 29.

Unbalanced Straddle or Strangle

A strangle, like a straddle, can be executed with a one-for-one ratio (one call for each put). However, a trader may want to establish a position with some other ratio. It is not uncommon to establish an unequal number of calls versus puts because it enables you to tailor that position to your unique prediction of the market. Simply because the numbers of calls and puts are equal does not mean that the total call and put value is equal or that the delta of the calls equals the delta of the puts. If a call, for example, has a delta of 0.20 and the put has a delta of 0.10 (ignoring the sign), and a trader wants to be delta-neutral, he can trade twice as many puts versus calls. It should be noted that the delta of calls is likely different than the delta of puts, even if the calls and puts expire in the same month and are sold for the same dollar amount. For instance, if calls are more sensitive to price movement, you would sell fewer calls than puts. If a call, for example, has a delta of 0.10 and the put has a delta of 0.20 (ignoring the sign), and a trader wants to be delta-neutral, he can trade twice as many calls versus puts.

A straddle or strangle trader may want to establish a position with one side expiring in one month and the other side expiring in a later month. It is not uncommon to establish a straddle or strangle with differing expiration months because it can enable you to tailor the position to your unique prediction of the market. For example, a February 100/April 100 straddle or a February 90/March 110 strangle can be established, where the numbers of calls versus puts are equal or different. Spread strategies where expiration months differ are covered in Chapter 17.

FINAL THOUGHTS

A long straddle or strangle is typically a bet on volatility expansion and a short straddle or strangle is typically a bet on volatility contraction. Earnings reports, product announcements, and economic reports can have a tendency to move stock prices violently either up or down. Some traders purchase a straddle or strangle in a period of low volatility before such an announcement and then sell it immediately after the announcement.

A straddle or strangle does not need to be executed in a perfect delta-neutral position because it can be weighted more heavily toward puts or calls, depending on your market outlook and how the options are priced. Remember that you can execute practically any option strategy in which the number of options sold differs from the number bought and/or the sides of the spread expire at different times. Many traders prefer a short strangle instead of a short straddle because it provides an opportunity to select strike prices within a range.

When selling naked options, you should not sell both puts and calls if your market forecast does not justify it; for instance, if you are wildly bullish, you would sell puts but no calls (or a limited number of calls). If you are bearish, you would sell calls but no puts (or a limited number of puts). I like to use technical analysis to determine areas of support and resistance.

Although this chapter provides examples of a straddle and a strangle using a stock as the underlying instrument, it may be worthwhile to consider using an underlying broadbased index, such as the S&P 500 index or S&P 500 futures. Chapter 26 includes an example of a short strangle using S&P 500 futures.

In the next chapter, Chapter 15, "Butterfly Spread," we explore another spread option strategy in which the number of options sold is the same as the number bought. In a later chapter, we will explore spread strategies in which the options expire at different times.

Butterfly Spread

A long call *butterfly* consists of purchasing one call at a lower strike, selling two calls at a middle strike, and purchasing one call at a higher strike. The outside strikes are referred to as the wings, whereas the two short options located at the middle strike are referred to as the body. A butterfly is a limited-risk/limited-reward strategy with which you can take advantage of a range-bound market (long butterfly) or of an increase in volatility (short butterfly) with a relatively low margin requirement. A butterfly gets its name from the shape of its profit and loss graph at expiration. This chapter will cover a long butterfly and then a short butterfly. It will describe a butterfly from the perspective of a long call, long put, short call, and short put and then address how to analyze a butterfly.

OVERVIEW

A long *butterfly spread* is a strategy designed to profit from a trading range, with limited risk. A short butterfly spread is a strategy designed to profit from volatility, with limited risk. You might establish a long butterfly if you believe that the stock will trade within a trading range and a short butterfly if you believe that the stock will trade outside a range. A butterfly is executed with all calls or all puts.

A long butterfly spread consists of three equally spaced exercise prices, in which the same number of options are purchased at the outside exercise prices and twice the number of options are sold at the inside exercise price (four total contracts). A long butterfly spread might consist of one long call at a 95 strike price, two short calls at a 100 strike price, and one long call at a 105 strike price. When you buy a butterfly, you typically (but not always) pay a net debit; for example, if you predict that XYZ stock will be trading at $100 a share at a particular expiration date, you can buy a call butterfly centered on a 100 strike with strike price increments of $5. You can, for instance, buy one XYZ 95 call at $7, write two XYZ 100 calls at $4 ($2 each), and buy one XYZ 105 call at $2. In this position, you are long the 95/100/105 call butterfly, and you pay $1 ($100) for it.

A short butterfly spread consists of three equally spaced exercise prices, in which the same number of options are sold at the outside exercise prices and twice the number of options are purchased at the inside exercise price (four total contracts). A short butterfly spread might consist of one short call at a 95 strike price, two long calls at a 100 strike price, and one short call at a 105 strike price. When you sell a butterfly, you typically (but not always) collect a credit.

A long butterfly is considered a long position because the lowest strike price (assuming calls are used) is long. A short butterfly is considered a short position because the lowest strike price (assuming calls are used) is short. The lowest and highest strike prices in a long butterfly are long legs, whereas the lowest and highest strike prices in a short butterfly are short legs. A long and a short butterfly are defined as follows:

- **Long butterfly**: Three equally spaced exercise prices; all options expire at the same time, the same number of options at outside exercise prices are purchased, and twice the number of options at inside exercise price are sold.
- **Short butterfly**: Three equally spaced exercise prices; all options expire at the same time, the same number of options at outside exercise prices are sold, and twice the number of options at inside exercise price are purchased.

If you assume that a long butterfly is established for $1 ($100) with a five-point width in strike prices, you would have a maximum profit of $4 ($400) ($5 strike width less $1 debit) and a maximum risk of $1 ($100). If you were to collect $1 ($100) in a short butterfly with the same strikes, you would have a maximum risk of $4 ($400) ($5 strike width less $1 credit) and a maximum gain of $1 ($100).

In a short butterfly, margin is generally required for the short vertical portion of the spread. Assume a short butterfly spread consists of one short call at a 95 strike price, two long calls at a 100 strike price, and one short call at a 105 strike price. In this case, margin would be required on the 95/100 strike price vertical credit spread portion of the position. Full payment is required if the spread is a long butterfly. You can execute a long or short butterfly with all calls or all puts, as shown in Table 15.1.

An advantage of a long or short butterfly is its limited risk and the low volatility of the position (because the option positions trend to offset one another). A butterfly (at expiration) will have a value (ignoring the premium paid or collected) somewhere between zero and the width between exercise prices ($5, in this example). A call butterfly, at expiration, has a value of zero when the stock is at or below the lowest strike price (95, for example), achieves its maximum value when the stock is at the middle strike price (100, for example), and declines to zero when the stock is at or above the highest strike price (105, for example). As a result, the butterfly will have some value, provided it stays within the 95 to 105 10-point strike price range, and will have values of 1, 2, 3, 4, 5, 4, 3, 2, or 1 for each point interval above 95 and below 105, respectively.

TABLE 15.1 Summary: Long and Short Butterfly

Spread Strategy	Strategy Description	Risk–Reward	Profitable	Debit or Credit	Two Breakevens	Greatest Profit at Expiration Date
Long call butterfly	Buy one call at lower strike, sell two calls at middle strike, buy one call at higher strike	Limited profit, unlimited risk	Trade within range	Typically debit	Lowest strike plus debit; highest strike minus debit	At middle strike
Long put butterfly	Buy one put at higher strike, sell two puts at middle strike, buy one put at lower strike	Limited profit, limited risk	Trade within range	Typically debit	Lowest strike plus debit; highest strike minus debit	At middle strike
Short call butterfly	Sell one call at lower strike, buy two calls at middle strike, sell one call at higher strike	Limited profit, limited risk	Trade outside range	Typically credit	Lowest strike plus credit; highest strike minus credit	Above highest or below lowest strike
Short put butterfly	Sell one put at higher strike, buy two puts at middle strike, sell one put at lower strike	Limited profit, limited risk	Trade outside range	Typically credit	Lowest strike plus credit; highest strike minus credit	Above highest or below lowest strike

In a long butterfly, you typically pay a debit and profit if the underlying instrument trades within a range. This is contrary to the general rule for a vertical spread, for example, that a debit strategy typically attempts to profit as an underlying stock moves by a large amount in one direction. Likewise, a credit in a short butterfly profits if the underlying stock trades outside a range, contrary to the general rule for a vertical spread, for example, that a credit strategy typically profits because an underlying stock trades sideways or in one direction. Whether a butterfly is executed for a debit or a credit depends, in part, on the width of strike prices, time remaining to expiration, the relative value of the options that are bought and sold, and the bid/ask spread. As a general rule, wider strike prices mean a larger debit (if long) or credit (if short), whereas a wider bid/ask spread increases a debit and decreases a credit. Keep in mind that although this chapter presents examples with a five-point strike spread width, you can vary the width of the strike prices to fine-tune to the risk profile for which you are looking.

An attraction of a butterfly is that it has low volatility because there are two long options and two short options that tend to offset one another. In a butterfly, time decay of short options typically approximates time decay of long options, and a volatility increase or decrease affects the value of short options by approximately the same amount as long options. Keep in mind that the value of a butterfly declines as the underlying stock moves farther away from the middle strike price. In a butterfly, you combine the delta, gamma, theta, and vega of each option to establish your overall position.

STRATEGY EXAMPLES

Following are descriptions of a long and a short butterfly from the perspective of a call and put. As a reminder, you can close out an option position by offsetting it in the marketplace any time prior to expiration, and the principles that are demonstrated for a stock can be applied to options on an ETF, index, and stock index futures. Appendixes A, B, and C illustrate many of the strategies covered throughout this book. Option values and Greeks for these examples have been slightly changed because of rounding to make it easier to focus on option principles.

Long Call Butterfly

Before establishing a long call butterfly spread, you should first determine at what price you believe the underlying stock will be trading at the expiration date. That price is the strike price for two options that you will sell for a long butterfly and is the middle strike price. At the same time, you will buy an option with a lower strike price and buy an option with a higher strike price, where the distance between strike prices is equal. A long butterfly is a strategy that has limited profit potential, limited risk, and is profitable if the underlying stock trades within the range of strike prices.

A long butterfly maximum profit occurs when the stock is at the middle strike price at expiration, and its maximum loss occurs (at expiration) if the stock closes at or below the lowest strike price or at or above the highest strike price. It is worth zero if the underlying stock is at or below the lowest exercise price or at or above the highest exercise price. A long butterfly is considered a limited-reward strategy because it cannot be worth more than the difference between the strikes; for example, a 95/100/105 long call butterfly cannot be worth (ignoring the premium) more than the strike price differential of $5. As a result, if you paid $1 ($100), your profit is a maximum of $4 ($400). A long butterfly is considered a limited-risk strategy because you cannot lose more than the debit paid.

In a butterfly, there are two break-even points. The break-even points in a long butterfly occur when the stock (at expiration) is at the lowest strike price plus the debit or at the highest strike price minus the debit.

In a long butterfly, the time decay of the short options typically approximates the time decay of the long options, and a volatility increase or decrease affects the value of short options by approximately the same amount as long options. For a long butterfly, a debit charged to your account must be paid in full. A long butterfly may be permitted in an IRA.

You might consider employing a long call butterfly if you believe that the stock will trade within a range. A long call butterfly can be viewed as a combination of a bull call spread (the lower two strikes) and a bear call spread (the upper two strikes); for example, if you predict that XYZ stock will be trading at $100 a share at a particular expiration date, you can buy a call butterfly centered on a 100 strike, with strike price increments of $5. You can buy one XYZ 95 call at $7 ($700), write two XYZ 100 calls at $4 ($400), and buy one XYZ 105 call at $2 ($200). In this position, you are long the 95/100/105 call butterfly, and you pay $1 ($100) for it. In a perfect world, you want the stock to trade at 100 at the expiration date so that the two short 100 calls are worthless and the 95 call is in-the-money. Your maximum profit is achieved when the stock closes exactly at the short strike price of 100 at expiration. If this occurs, the long 95 call expires in-the-money and has an intrinsic value of $5, the short 100 calls expire exactly at-the-money and are worthless, and the long 105 call expires out-of-the-money and is worthless. Your maximum gain would be $400 ($500 for the 95 call minus $100 debit paid to enter the butterfly). Your break-even point is when the stock (at expiration) is at 96 or 104 (ignoring commissions).

Example: Long Call Butterfly

Assumptions: XYZ stock is trading at $100 a share in January; buy a February 95/100/105 long call butterfly at $1, as follows: Buy one February 95 call at $7, sell two February 100 calls at $4 each, and buy one February 105 call at $2.

Strategy direction: Neutral (trading range).

Debit or credit: $100 debit.

Maximum profit: $400 ($500 for five-point difference in strike prices less $100 debit).

Maximum loss: $100 (premium paid).

Exercise and assignment: Can exercise long options if in-the-money; may be assigned on short options if in-the-money.

Break-even stock price: $96 and $104 (lowest strike price plus debit, highest strike price minus debit).

Maximum profit achieved: Stock at middle strike price of 100.

Maximum loss achieved: Stock at or below $95 or at or above $105.

Profit (loss) if stock unchanged: $400 profit (stock at middle strike price of 100).

The maximum payoff is achieved when XYZ stock finishes at $100 and loses value as the stock price moves from 100 in either direction. When the price reaches 95 or 105, the trade leads to the maximum loss of $100. The worst that can happen is that the trader loses $100, no matter how high or low the stock price goes. If XYZ stock is below 95 at expiration, the spread is worthless because all options are out-of-the-money. If the stock is at 100, the spread is worth $500 because the February 95 call is worth five points more than the February 100 calls. If the stock is above $105, the short 100 calls are offset dollar for dollar by the long calls.

Greeks: Table 15.3 contains sample Greeks converted to dollars at the time the position is established.

Position would reflect no gain or loss from stock rise (delta), time decay (theta), and volatility (vega) expansion. Gain or loss is zero from XYZ stock rising to $101; gain or loss is zero from one day of time decay.

Later expiration: The price and Greeks will differ at the purchase date if expiration is at a later date. For example, if the options expire in March, instead of February, the price of the March 95 call could be $9, the March 100 calls could

TABLE 15.2 Long Call Butterfly

XYZ Stock Price ($)	Long Call (Lowest Strike)	Short Calls (Middle Strike)	Long Call (Highest Strike)	Spread	Cost of Spread	Spread Profit (Loss)	Profit (Loss) Percentage
75	0	0	0	0	100	(100)	(100)
80	0	0	0	0	100	(100)	(100)
85	0	0	0	0	100	(100)	(100)
90	0	0	0	0	100	(100)	(100)
95	0	0	0	0	100	(100)	(100)
100	500	0	0	500	100	400	400
105	1,000	(1,000)	0	0	100	(100)	(100)
110	1,500	(2,000)	500	0	100	(100)	(100)
115	2,000	(3,000)	1,000	0	100	(100)	(100)
120	2,500	(4,000)	1,500	0	100	(100)	(100)
125	3,000	(5,000)	2,000	0	100	(100)	(100)

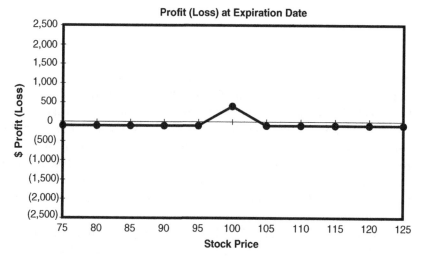

FIGURE 15.1 Long Call Butterfly

TABLE 15.3 Summary of Greeks: February Expiration

Option	Delta	Gamma	Theta	Vega
Long 1 February 95 call	$64	$2.00	−$16	$13
Short 2 February 100 calls	−$106	−$4.60	$30	−$24
Long 1 February 105 call	$42	$2.00	−$14	$11
Position	$0		$0	$0

TABLE 15.4 Summary of Greeks: March Expiration

Option	Delta	Gamma	Theta	Vega
Long 1 March 95 call	$64	$1.20	−$14	$19
Short 2 March 100 calls	−$104	−$2.60	$24	−$34
Long 1 March 105 call	$40	$1.20	−$10	$15
Position	$0		$0	$0

be $6 (instead of $5), and the March 105 call could be $4, for a net debit of $1. Example Greeks are given in Table 15.4.

Gain or loss is zero from XYZ stock rising to $101; gain or loss is zero from one day of time decay.

Exercise and assignment: If XYZ stock closes above the highest strike price of 105 at expiration (each call expires in-the-money) and you allow the exercise and assignment process to run its course to generate the maximum loss, you would (1) exercise the long 95 call and buy 100 shares at $95, (2) exercise the long 105 call and buy 100 shares at $105, and (3) be assigned on the two short 100 calls and sell 200 shares at $100. The net of all these transactions would be to lose the $1 debit ($100) you initially paid for the butterfly spread. You would, however, pay plenty of commissions along the way.

Long Put Butterfly

The characteristics of a long put butterfly are the same as those of a long call butterfly. You should first determine at what price you believe the underlying stock will be trading at the expiration date. That price is the strike price for two options that you will sell and is the middle strike price. At the same time, you will buy an option with a lower strike price and buy an option with a higher strike price, for which the distance between strike prices is equal. A long butterfly is a strategy that has limited profit potential, limited risk, and is profitable if the underlying stock trades within the range of strike prices.

A long butterfly maximum profit occurs when the stock is at the middle strike price at expiration, and its maximum loss occurs (at expiration) if the stock closes at or below the lowest strike price or at or above the highest strike price. At expiration, a long butterfly is worth its maximum if the underlying stock is at the inside exercise price and is worth zero if the underlying stock is at or below the lowest exercise price or at or above the highest exercise price. A long put butterfly, like a long call butterfly, is considered a limited-reward strategy because it cannot be worth more than the difference between the strikes. For example, a 95/100/105 long put butterfly cannot be worth (ignoring the premium paid) more than the strike price differential of $5. As a result, if you paid $1 ($100), your profit is a maximum of $4 ($400). A long butterfly is considered a limited-risk strategy because you cannot lose more than the debit paid.

In a butterfly, there are two break-even points. The break-even points in a long butterfly occur when the stock (at expiration) is at the lowest strike price plus the debit or at the highest strike price minus the debit.

In a long butterfly, the time decay of the short options typically approximates the time decay of the long options, and a volatility increase or decrease affects the value of short options by approximately the same amount as long options. For a long butterfly, a debit charged to your account must be paid in full. A long butterfly may be permitted in an IRA.

Example: Long Put Butterfly

Assumptions: XYZ stock is trading at $100 a share in January; buy a February 95/100/105 long put butterfly and pay a net debit of $1, as follows: Buy one February 105 put at $7, sell two February 100 puts at $4 each, and buy one February 95 put at $2.

Strategy direction: Neutral (trading range).

Debit or credit: $100 debit.

TABLE 15.5 Long Put Butterfly

XYZ Stock Price ($)	Long Put (Highest Strike)	Short Put (Middle Strike)	Long Put (Lowest Strike)	Spread	Cost of Spread	Spread Profit (Loss)	Profit (Loss) Percentage
75	3,000	(5,000)	2,000	0	100	(100)	(100)
80	2,500	(4,000)	1,500	0	100	(100)	(100)
85	2,000	(3,000)	1,000	0	100	(100)	(100)
90	1,500	(2,000)	500	0	100	(100)	(100)
95	1,000	(1,000)	0	0	100	(100)	(100)
100	500	0	0	500	100	400	400
105	0	0	0	0	100	(100)	(100)
110	0	0	0	0	100	(100)	(100)
115	0	0	0	0	100	(100)	(100)
120	0	0	0	0	100	(100)	(100)
125	0	0	0	0	100	(100)	(100)

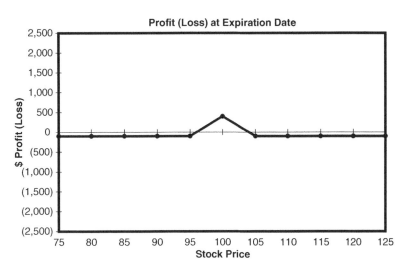

FIGURE 15.2 Long Put Butterfly

Maximum profit: $400 ($500 for five-point difference in strike prices less $100 debit).

Maximum loss: $100 (premium paid).

Exercise and assignment: Can exercise long options if in-the-money; may be assigned on short options if in-the-money.

Break-even stock price: $96 and $104 (lowest strike price plus debit, highest strike price minus debit).

Maximum profit achieved: Stock at short strike price of 100.

Maximum loss achieved: Stock at or below 95 or at or above 105.

Profit (loss) if stock unchanged: $400 profit (stock at middle strike price of 100).

The maximum payoff is achieved when XYZ stock finishes at $100, and the trade loses value as the stock price moves from $100 in either direction. When the stock price reaches $95 or $105, the trade leads to the maximum loss of $100. The worst that can happen is that the trader loses $100, no matter how high or low the stock price goes. If XYZ stock is above $105 at expiration, the spread is worthless because all options are out-of-the-money. If the stock is at $100, the spread is worth $500 because the February 105 put is worth five points more than the February 100 puts. If the stock is below 95, the short 100 puts are offset dollar for dollar by the long puts.

Greeks: Table 15.6 contains sample Greeks converted to dollars at the time the position is established.

Position would reflect no gain or loss from stock rise (delta), time decay (theta), and volatility (vega) expansion. Gain or loss is zero from XYZ stock rising to $101; gain or loss is zero from one day of time decay.

Later expiration: The price and Greeks will differ at the purchase date if expiration is at a later date. For example, if the options expire in March, instead of February,

TABLE 15.6 Summary of Greeks: February Expiration

Option	Delta	Gamma	Theta	Vega
Long 1 February 105 put	−$64	$2.00	−$16	$13
Short 2 February 100 puts	$106	−$4.60	$30	−$24
Long 1 February 95 put	−$42	$2.00	−$14	$11
Position	$0		$0	$0

TABLE 15.7 Summary of Greeks: March Expiration

Option	Delta	Gamma	Theta	Vega
Long 1 March 105 put	−$64	$1.20	−$14	$19
Short 2 March 100 puts	$104	−$2.60	$24	−$34
Long 1 March 95 put	−$40	$1.20	−$10	$15
Position	$0		$0	$0

the price of the March 105 put could be $9, the March 100 puts could be $6 (instead of $5), and the March 95 put could be $4, for a net debit of $1. Example Greeks are given in Table 15.7.

Gain or loss is zero from XYZ stock rising to $101; gain or loss is zero from one day of time decay.

Exercise and assignment: If XYZ stock closes above the lowest strike price of 95 at expiration (each put expires in-the-money) and you allow the exercise and assignment process to run its course, to generate the maximum loss you would (1) exercise the long 105 put and sell 100 shares at $105, (2) exercise the long 95 put and sell 100 shares at $95, and (3) be assigned on the two short 100 puts and buy 200 shares at $100. The net of all these transactions would be to lose the $1 debit ($100) you initially paid for the butterfly spread. You would, however, pay plenty of commissions along the way.

Short Call Butterfly

Before establishing a short call butterfly spread, you should first determine at what price you believe the underlying stock will most likely not be trading at the expiration date. That price is the strike price for two options that you will buy and is the middle strike price. At the same time, you will sell an option with a lower strike price and sell an option with a higher strike price, where the distance between strike prices is equal. A short butterfly (at expiration) will have a value somewhere between the amount between the exercise prices and zero. A short butterfly is a strategy that has limited profit potential and limited risk, and its maximum profit is achieved if the underlying stock trades outside the range of strike prices.

A short butterfly maximum gain occurs (at expiration) if the stock closes at or below the lowest strike price or at or about the highest strike price. The maximum gain is the credit collected (less commissions). Its maximum loss occurs when the stock is at the middle strike price at expiration. At expiration, a butterfly is worth its maximum if the underlying stock is at the inside exercise price and is worth zero if the underlying stock is at or below the lowest exercise price or at or above the highest exercise price. A short butterfly is considered a limited-risk strategy because it cannot be worth more than the difference between the strikes; for example, a 95/100/105 short call butterfly cannot be worth (ignoring the premium collected) more than the strike price differential of $5 ($500). As a result, if you collected $1 ($100), your loss is a maximum of $4 ($400).

In a butterfly, there are two break-even points. The break-even points in a short butterfly occur when the stock (at expiration) is at the lowest strike price plus the credit or at the highest strike price minus the credit.

In a short butterfly, the time decay of the short options typically approximates the time decay of the long options, and a volatility increase or decrease affects the value of short options by approximately the same amount as long options. In a short butterfly, is generally required for the short vertical portion of the spread. A short butterfly may be permitted in an IRA.

Example: Short Call Butterfly

Assumptions: XYZ stock is trading at $100 a share in January; sell a February 95/100/105 short call butterfly and collect a net credit of $1, as follows: Sell one February 95 call at $7, buy two February 100 calls at $4 each, and sell one February 105 call at $2.

Strategy direction: Outside trading range.

Debit or credit: $100 credit.

Maximum profit: $100 (premium collected).

Maximum loss: $400 ($500 for five-point difference in strike prices less $100 credit).

Exercise and assignment: Can exercise long options if in-the-money; may be assigned on short options if in-the-money.

Break-even stock price: $96 and $104 (lowest strike price plus credit, highest strike price minus credit).

Maximum profit achieved: Stock at or below $95 or at or above $105.

Maximum loss achieved: Stock at middle strike price of 100.

Profit (loss) if stock unchanged: $400 loss (stock at middle strike price of 100).

The maximum loss is achieved when XYZ stock finishes at $100, and the trade loses value as the stock price moves from $100 in either direction. When the price reaches $95 or $105, the trade leads to the maximum gain of $100. The worst that can happen is that the trader loses $400. If XYZ stock is below $95 at expiration, the spread is worthless because all options are out-of-the-money. If the stock is at $100, the spread is worth $500 because the February 95 call is worth five points more than the February 100 calls. If the stock is above $105, the long 100 calls are offset dollar for dollar by the short calls.

Greeks: Table 15.9 contains sample Greeks converted to dollars at the time the position is established.

Position would reflect no gain or loss from stock rise (delta), time decay (theta), and volatility (vega) expansion. Gain or loss is zero from XYZ stock rising to $101; gain or loss is zero from one day of time decay.

Later expiration: The price and Greeks will differ at the purchase date if expiration is at a later date. For example, if the options expire in March, instead of February, the price of the March 95 call could be $9, the March 100 calls could be

TABLE 15.8 Short Call Butterfly

XYZ Stock Price ($)	Short Call (Lowest Strike)	Long Calls (Middle Strike)	Short Call (Highest Strike)	Spread	Spread Credit	Spread Profit (Loss)	Profit (Loss) Percentage
75	0	0	0	0	100	100	100
80	0	0	0	0	100	100	100
85	0	0	0	0	100	100	100
90	0	0	0	0	100	100	100
95	0	0	0	0	100	100	100
100	(500)	0	0	(500)	100	(400)	(400)
105	(1,000)	1,000	0	0	100	100	100
110	(1,500)	2,000	(500)	0	100	100	100
115	(2,000)	3,000	(1,000)	0	100	100	100
120	(2,500)	4,000	(1,500)	0	100	100	100
125	(3,000)	5,000	(2,000)	0	100	100	100

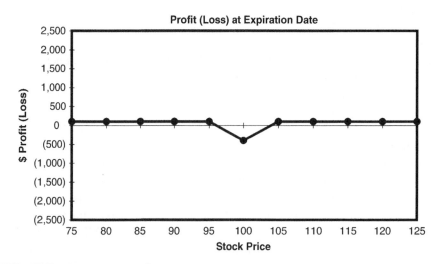

FIGURE 15.3 Short Call Butterfly

TABLE 15.9 Summary of Greeks: February Expiration

Option	Delta	Gamma	Theta	Vega
Short 1 February 95 call	−$64	−$2.00	$16	−$13
Long 2 February 100 calls	$106	$4.60	−$30	$24
Short 1 February 105 call	−$42	−$2.00	$14	−$11
Position	$0		$0	$0

TABLE 15.10 Summary of Greeks: March Expiration

Option	Delta	Gamma	Theta	Vega
Short 1 March 95 call	−$64	−$1.20	$14	−$19
Long 2 March 100 calls	$104	$2.60	−$24	−$34
Short 1 March 105 call	−$40	−$1.20	$10	−$15
Position	$0		$0	$0

$6 (instead of $5), and the March 105 call could be $4, for a credit of $1. Example Greeks are given in Table 15.10.

Gain or loss is zero from XYZ stock rising to $101; gain or loss is zero from one day of time decay.

Exercise and assignment: If XYZ stock closes above the highest strike price of 105 at expiration (each call expires in-the-money) and you allow the exercise and assignment process to run its course, to generate the maximum gain, you would (1) be assigned on the short 95 call and sell 100 shares at $95, (2) be assigned on the short 105 call and sell 100 shares at $105, and (3) exercise the two long 100 calls and buy 200 shares at $100. The net of all these transactions would be to gain the $1 credit ($100) you initially collected for the butterfly spread. You would, however, pay plenty of commissions along the way.

Short Put Butterfly

Before establishing a short put butterfly spread, you should first determine at what price you believe the underlying stock will most likely not be trading at the expiration date. That price is the strike price for two options that you will buy and is the middle strike price. At the same time, you will sell an option with a lower strike price and sell an option with a higher strike price, where the distance between strike prices is equal. A short butterfly (at expiration) will have a value somewhere between the amount between the exercise prices and zero. A short butterfly is a strategy that has limited profit potential and limited risk, and its maximum profit is achieved if the underlying stock trades outside the range of strike prices.

A short butterfly maximum gain occurs (at expiration) if the stock closes at or below the lowest strike price or at or about the highest strike price. Its maximum gain is the credit collected (less commissions). Its maximum loss occurs when the stock is at the middle strike price at expiration. At expiration, it is worth its maximum if the underlying stock is at the inside exercise price and is worth zero if the underlying stock is at or below the lowest exercise price or at or above the highest exercise price. A short butterfly is considered a limited-risk strategy because it cannot be worth more than the difference between the strikes. For example, a 95/100/105 short put butterfly cannot be worth (ignoring the premium collected) more than the strike price differential of $5 ($500). As a result, if you collected $1, your loss is a maximum of $4 ($400).

In a butterfly, there are two break-even points. The break-even point in a short butterfly occurs when the stock (at expiration) is at the lowest strike price plus the credit or at the highest strike price minus the credit.

In a short butterfly, the time decay of the short options typically approximates the time decay of the long options, and a volatility increase or decrease affects the value of short options by approximately the same amount as long options. In a short butterfly, margin (or buying power) is generally required for the short vertical portion of the spread. A short butterfly may be permitted in an IRA.

Example: Short Put Butterfly

Assumptions: XYZ stock is trading at $100 a share in January; sell a February 95/100/105 short put butterfly and collect a net credit of $1, as follows: Sell one February 105 put at $7, buy two February 100 puts at $4 each, and sell one February 95 put call at $2.

Strategy direction: Outside trading range.

Debit or credit: $100 credit.

Maximum profit: $100 (premium collected).

Maximum loss: $400 ($500 for five-point difference in strike prices less $100 credit).

TABLE 15.11   Short Put Butterfly

XYZ Stock Price ($)	Short Put (Highest Strike)	Long Puts (Middle Strike)	Short Put (Lowest Strike)	Spread	Spread Credit	Spread Profit (Loss)	Profit (Loss) Percentage
75	(3,000)	5,000	(2,000)	0	100	100	100
80	(2,500)	4,000	(1,500)	0	100	100	100
85	(2,000)	3,000	(1,000)	0	100	100	100
90	(1,500)	2,000	(500)	0	100	100	100
95	(1,000)	1,000	0	0	100	100	100
100	(500)	0	0	(500)	100	(400)	(400)
105	0	0	0	0	100	100	100
110	0	0	0	0	100	100	100
115	0	0	0	0	100	100	100
120	0	0	0	0	100	100	100
125	0	0	0	0	100	100	100

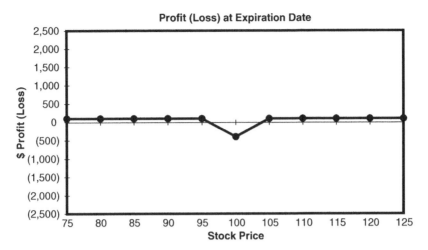

FIGURE 15.4 Short Put Butterfly

Exercise and assignment: Can exercise long options if in-the-money; may be assigned on short options if in-the-money.

Break-even stock price: $96 and $104 (lowest strike price plus credit, highest strike price minus credit).

Maximum profit achieved: Stock at or below $95 or at or above $105.

Maximum loss achieved: Stock at middle strike price of 100.

Profit (loss) if stock unchanged: $400 loss (stock at middle strike price of 100).

The maximum loss is achieved when XYZ stock finishes at $100, and the trade gains value as the stock price moves from $100 in either direction. When the price reaches $95 or $105, the trade leads to the maximum gain of $100. The worst that can happen is that the trader loses $400. If XYZ stock is above $105 at expiration, the spread is worthless because all options are out-of-the-money. If the stock is at $100, the spread is worth $500 because the February 105 put is worth five points more than the February 100 puts. If the stock is below $95, the long 100 puts are offset dollar for dollar by the short puts.

Greeks: Table 15.12 contains sample Greeks converted to dollars at the time the position is established.

TABLE 15.12 Summary of Greeks: February Expiration

Option	Delta	Gamma	Theta	Vega
Short 1 February 105 put	$64	−$2.00	$16	−$13
Long 2 February 100 puts	−$106	$4.60	−$30	$24
Short 1 February 95 put	$42	−$2.00	$14	−$11
Position	$0		$0	$0

TABLE 15.13 Summary of Greeks: March Expiration

Option	Delta	Gamma	Theta	Vega
Short 1 March 105 put	$64	−$1.20	$14	−$19
Long 2 March 100 puts	−$104	$2.60	−$24	$34
Short 1 March 95 put	$40	−$1.20	$10	−$15
Position	$0		$0	$0

Position would reflect no gain or loss from stock rise (delta), time decay (theta), and volatility (vega) expansion. Gain or loss is zero from XYZ stock rising to $101; gain or loss is zero from one day of time decay.

Later expiration: The price and Greeks will differ at the purchase date if expiration is at a later date; for example, if the options expire in March, instead of February, the price of the March 105 put could be $9, the March 100 puts could be $6 (instead of $5), and the March 95 put could be $4, for a credit of $1. Example Greeks are given in Table 15.13.

Gain or loss is zero from XYZ stock rising to $101; gain or loss is zero from one day of time decay.

Exercise and assignment: If XYZ stock closes below the lowest strike price of 95 at expiration (each put expires in-the-money) and you allow the exercise and assignment process to run its course, to generate the maximum gain, you would (1) be assigned on the short 105 put and buy 100 shares at $105, (2) be assigned on the short 95 put and buy 100 shares at $95, and (3) exercise the two long 100 puts and sell 200 shares at $100. The net of all these transactions would be to gain the $1 credit ($100) you initially collected for the butterfly spread. You would, however, pay plenty of commissions along the way.

BEYOND THE BASICS

Butterfly Analysis

You may want to use a long butterfly strategy when you forecast that a particular stock will remain within a trading range (neutral) and you want low volatility in your account, limited risk, low margin, and a reasonable trade-off between risk and reward. You may want to use a short butterfly strategy when you forecast that a particular stock will trade outside a trading range and you want low volatility, limited risk, and low margin.

In a butterfly, assuming that the price is $1 and the strike price differential is $5, a buyer is paying $1 for a chance to make up to a $4 profit, and a writer collects $1 with a chance of losing $4. A 95/100/105 butterfly will have some value at expiration if the underlying stock is within the 95 to 105 10-point range, with the middle strike representing the highest profit to a buyer and the highest loss to a writer. The range to make a profit, however, is not the full 10 points because a buyer needs to sell above the $1 paid and a writer needs to buy at a price below the $1 credit received. The true range for a profit, assuming a \$1 butterfly price, is therefore only eight points because the butterfly is worth \$1 at 96 and 104. If commissions are included, the range is less than eight points. Under this scenario, a 95/100/105 butterfly would have a break-even point at 96 and 104. There would be a profit to a buyer and a loss to a writer for a stock price above \$96 and below \$104 (ignoring commissions). There would be a loss to a buyer and a gain to a writer for a stock price below \$96 and above \$104 (ignoring commissions). In effect, a butterfly buyer is placing his \$1 (\$100) bet to make \$4 (\$400) based on where the stock will fall 30 to 60 days in advance.

The main decision you need to make is the middle strike price because that determines your maximum gain if you are long and your maximum loss if you are short. You should keep in mind that the middle strike price does not have to be at-the-money when it is established. For example, if XYZ stock is trading at \$100 a share, the middle strike price does not need to be at \$100 a share. Instead, if the stock is at \$100 a share, you can establish the middle strike price, for instance, at 90 or 105. You can use your trading platform to determine whether there is more favorable pricing using a call versus a put butterfly under your scenarios.

Keep in mind that you can close out an option position by offsetting it in the marketplace at any time prior to expiration, and you should use your trading platform software, option calculator, and option chain to estimate option values based on your own assumptions. If you are nearing expiration, you can offset your current position, because there are only a few days left in the option expiration cycle, and establish a similar position in a subsequent expiration month. It may be difficult, however, to roll a butterfly because there are four contracts involved.

Assignment Risk

There is assignment risk associated with a butterfly spread. Although it is generally accepted that spread trading reduces the risk of loss, spreads are subject to early exercise or assignment, which can remove the very protection that you wanted. This can lead to margin calls and/or greater losses than anticipated. As a general rule, it is best to avoid assignment on any leg in a butterfly, or any other short option position, for that matter. An alternative to being assigned is to offset a short option in the marketplace. You need to be careful not to be assigned in a butterfly spread because it can create margin problems and complexity. Being assigned could turn a well-constructed butterfly spread into a Three Stooges trade.

In a long call butterfly, for example, its maximum loss occurs (at expiration) if the stock closes at or below the lowest strike price or at or about the highest strike price. This may sound like equal results, but the close above the highest strike price has exercise/assignment risk. The close below the lowest strike price simply results in all options expiring worthless.

A Commission Extravaganza

The potentially high cost of commissions, including the bid/ask spread, should be taken into consideration before entering into a butterfly. Commissions are incurred to establish each butterfly leg, to offset the butterfly if you choose to do so, and to execute any exercise and assignment. As a result, commissions, including the bid/ask spread, may be incurred on the four contracts to establish the butterfly and possibly on an additional four contracts to offset those positions at a later date, for a total of eight commission transactions. Additional commissions would be incurred on exercise or assignment. Sometimes I believe they call it a "butterfly" because you pay so much in commissions that you will see your profits fly away.

Broken Wing Butterfly

Another butterfly strategy is called a "broken wing butterfly." In this strategy, assuming a long call butterfly, you move the highest-strike call to a higher strike to reduce the cost of the debit or even to convert the debit to a credit or zero cost. For example, if you predict that XYZ stock will be trading at $100 a share at a particular expiration date, you can buy a call butterfly centered on a 100 strike price, with strike-price increments of 5. You can buy one XYZ 95 call at $7, write two XYZ 100 calls at $4, and buy one XYZ 105 call at $2. In this position, you are long the 95/100/105 call butterfly, and you pay $1 ($100) for it. Instead of buying the 105 call at $2, you can buy a 110 call at $1 to make it an even cost spread. If you instead buy a 115 strike call, it converts the spread from even cost to a credit.

FINAL THOUGHTS

Excuse me, but I cannot help but notice the similarities between a butterfly spread and gambling. Maybe all trading, including option trading, in general, is like gambling in many respects, but the butterfly seems to exemplify gambling to a greater degree. In a long butterfly, you are, in effect, paying $1 for the chance to make $4. Maybe because you can place your bet (I mean trade) on a sophisticated trading platform in the privacy of your own home instead of in a Las Vegas casino makes it seem more like trading. Or, maybe it seems like trading because you can mathematically determine the chances of your success from your computer. In a short butterfly, you are, in effect, collecting $1 for the possibility of winning (I mean gaining) $4. Again, you can place your bet in the privacy of your own home using your sophisticated trading platform. The probabilities in trading butterflies are not determined by a Las Vegas casino but are instead determined by the Greek deltas.

If you ever wonder about the rationale of the butterfly, it goes something like this: Assume that XYZ stock is currently trading at $100. You decide to purchase one 95 call for $7 but you believe that it is too expensive, so you convert it into a vertical spread by selling one 100 call for $4. You then decide to sell a second 100 call to eliminate the debit. But then you notice that you have risk because of the naked call, so to reduce that exposure, you purchase one 105 call for $2. As a result, you have a 95/100/105 butterfly for a $1 debit ($100). The butterfly can have a lot of merit, but it could also serve as a fallback position for the indecisive trader.

In a butterfly strategy, your losses are limited, even if the stock moves appreciably in either direction. A trader may choose a long butterfly over a short straddle in a sideways market because of the limited risk of the butterfly. Unlike a short straddle or short strangle, in a long butterfly strategy, if the stock moves appreciably in one direction or the other, your losses are limited. In a long butterfly, the most you can lose is the amount paid to purchase the butterfly, but a short straddle has greater profit potential. If you recall from Chapter 14, a straddle or a strangle can be used to profit from a trading range or to profit from trading outside a range, but the problem with a straddle or a strangle is that there can be a lot of risk. A butterfly is designed to mitigate such risk. You can get an idea of your chances of success by examining the deltas of the various strike prices.

In general, you should use your trading platform and its simulated (paper) trading feature to enter hypothetical trades to determine the pricing of a call versus a put butterfly spread. If you are executing a long butterfly, you want to pay as little as possible (with as much upside as possible); if you are executing a short butterfly, you want to collect as much premium as possible (with as little downside as possible). Whether a butterfly should be executed with calls or puts depends on the relative prices of the options. In the next chapter, Chapter 16, "Condor Spread," we explore a similar spread to the butterfly. In a later chapter, we will explore spread strategies in which the options expire at different times.

Condor Spread

A long call *condor spread* consists of purchasing one call at a lower strike, selling two calls at middle strikes, and purchasing one call at a higher strike. In a condor, the outside strikes are referred to as the wings and the two short options located at the middle strikes are referred to as the body. A condor is a limited-risk/limited-reward strategy in which you can take advantage of a range-bound market (long condor) or an increase in volatility (short condor), with a relatively low margin requirement. Like a butterfly, a condor gets its name from the birdlike shape of its profit and loss graph at expiration. This chapter will cover a long condor and then a short condor. It will describe a condor from the perspective of a long call, long put, short call, and short put and then address how it is similar to a butterfly and its assignment risk.

OVERVIEW

A condor spread is a four-legged option spread consisting of all calls or all puts in which each leg has the same expiration date but different strike prices. All four options have equally spaced exercise prices and expire at the same time. A long condor spread is a strategy designed to profit from a trading range, with limited risk. A short condor spread is a strategy designed to profit from volatility, with limited risk. A condor is similar to a butterfly, covered in Chapter 15, except that a condor has two middle exercise prices instead of one. You can use the long condor strategy when you project that a particular stock will remain within a trading range (neutral) and you want low volatility, limited risk, and relatively low margin. A long condor achieves its maximum value at expiration when the underlying stock is at or between the inside exercise prices.

In a long condor, two outside exercise prices are purchased and two inside exercise prices are sold (four total contracts). A long condor spread might consist of one long call at a 95 strike price, one short call at a 100 strike price, one short call at a 105 strike price, and one long call at a 110 strike price. When you buy a condor, you typically pay a net debit, which is your maximum loss; for example, if you predict that XYZ stock will be trading between 100 and 105 a share at a particular expiration date, you can buy a call condor centered on 100/105 strikes. For example, you can go long a 95/100/105/110 call condor for a $2 debit ($200) by buying one XYZ 95 call at $7, writing one XYZ 100 call at $4, writing one XYZ 105 call at $2, and buying one XYZ 110 call at $1. A long call condor can be viewed as a combination of a bull call spread (the lower two strikes) and a bear call spread (the upper two strikes).

In a short condor, two outside exercise prices are sold and two inside exercise prices are purchased (also four total contracts). A short condor spread might consist of one short call at a 95 strike price, one long call at a 100 strike price, one long call at a 105 strike price, and one short call at a 110 strike price. When you sell a condor, you receive a net credit, which is your maximum gain. You can consider executing a short condor if you believe that a stock will trade outside a range (outside the middle strike prices). A short call condor can be viewed as a combination of a bear call spread (the lower two strikes) and a bull call spread (the upper two strikes). A short condor spread can be a way to profit from a volatile market.

A condor has many of the same risk–reward characteristics of a butterfly, but a condor usually has a higher debit (or credit) because the middle strike of a butterfly is split into two to create a condor. For instance, a long butterfly may incur a debit of $1, whereas a similar long condor may have a debit of $2. A short butterfly may have a credit of $1, whereas a similar short condor may have a credit of $2. The maximum value, minimum value, and break-even points for a butterfly and condor are determined in the same manner.

A long condor is considered a long position because the lowest strike price (assuming calls are used) is long. A short condor is considered a short position because the lowest strike price (assuming calls are used) is short. In other words, the lowest and highest strike prices in a long condor are long legs, whereas the lowest and highest strike prices in a short condor are short legs.

If you assume that a long condor is established for $2 with a five-point width in strike prices, you would have a maximum profit of $3 ($5 strike width less $2 debit) and a maximum risk of $2. If you were to collect $2 in a short condor with the same strikes, you would have a maximum risk of $3 ($5 strike width less $2 credit) and a maximum gain of $2.

In a condor, margin is generally required for the short vertical portion of the spread. A short condor spread, for example, might consist of one short call at a 95 strike price, one long call at a 100 strike price, one long call at a 105 strike price, and one short call at a 110 strike price. In this case, margin would be required on the 95/100 vertical credit spread portion of the position. Full payment is required if the spread is a long condor. You can execute a long or short condor with calls or puts, as shown in Table 16.1.

If a condor uses strike prices of 95/100/105/110, at expiration, it has a value of zero when the stock is at or below 95, achieves its maximum value when the stock is at or between the middle strike prices of 100 and 105, and declines to zero when the stock is

TABLE 16.1 Summary: Long and Short Condor

Spread Strategy	Strategy Description	Risk–Reward	Profitable	Debit or Credit	Two Breakevens	Maximum Profit at Expiration Date	Initial Margin
Long call condor	Buy one call at lower strike, sell one call at each middle strike, buy one call at higher strike	Limited profit, unlimited risk	Trade within range	Typically debit	Lowest strike plus debit; highest strike minus debit	At or between middle strikes	Full payment
Long put condor	Buy one put at higher strike, sell one put at each middle strike, buy one put at lower strike	Limited profit, limited risk	Trade within range	Typically debit	Lowest strike plus debit; highest strike minus debit	At or between middle strikes	Full payment
Short call condor	Sell one call at lower strike, buy one call at each middle strike, sell one call at higher strike	Limited profit, limited risk	Trade outside range	Typically credit	Lowest strike plus credit; highest strike minus credit	At or above highest strike or at or below lowest strike	On short vertical portion of the spread
Short put condor	Sell one put at higher strike, buy one put at each middle strike, sell one put at lower strike	Limited profit, limited risk	Trade outside range	Typically credit	Lowest strike plus credit; highest strike minus credit	At or above highest strike or at or below lowest strike	On short vertical portion of the spread

at or above a strike price of 110. A condor (at expiration) will have a value somewhere between zero and the amount between exercise prices (five points, in this example). A call condor, at expiration, has a value of zero when the stock is at or below the lowest strike price (e.g., 95), achieves its maximum value when the stock is at or between the middle strike prices (e.g., 100 and 105), and declines to zero when the stock is at or above the highest strike price (e.g., 110). As a result, the condor will have some value, provided it stays within the 15-point strike price range and will have values of 1, 2, 3, 4, 5, 5, 5, 5, 5, 5, 4, 3, 2, or 1 for each point interval above 95 and below 110, respectively. In this example, if you assume that a condor is established for $2, you would pay $2 in a long condor for a maximum profit of $3 and a maximum risk of $2. In this example, if you collect $2 in a short condor, you have a maximum risk of $3 with a maximum gain of $2. The break-even points in a condor occur when the stock (at expiration) is at the lowest strike price plus the debit or credit or at the highest strike price minus the debit or credit (ignoring commissions).

A condor is executed for a debit or a credit, and its amount depends on the width of strike prices, time remaining to expiration, the relative value of the options that are bought and sold, and the bid/ask spread. As a general rule, a wider strike price means a larger debit (if long) or credit (if short), whereas a wider bid/ask spread increases a debit (if long) and decreases a credit (if short). Keep in mind that although this chapter presents examples with a five-point strike spread, you can vary the width of the strike prices to fine-tune the risk profile.

An attraction of a condor is that it has low volatility because there are two long options and two short options that tend to offset one another. In a condor, time decay of short options typically approximates time decay of long options, and a volatility increase or decrease affects the value of short options by approximately the same amount as long options. In a condor, you combine the delta, gamma, theta, and vega of each option to establish your position.

STRATEGY EXAMPLES

Following are descriptions of a long and short condor from the perspective of calls and puts. As a reminder, you can close out an option position by offsetting it in the market-place any time prior to expiration, and the principles that are demonstrated for a stock can be applied to options on an ETF, index, and stock index futures. Appendixes A, B, and C illustrate many of the strategies covered throughout this book. The price of XYZ stock is assumed to be $105 for the put condors, instead of $100, to make the results comparable to the call condors. Option values and Greeks for these examples have been slightly changed by rounding to make it easier to focus on option principles.

Long Call Condor

A long condor is similar to a long butterfly, except that a long condor has two middle exercise prices. In a long call condor, you sell one option at each of the middle exercise prices and, at the same time, you buy an option at a lower strike price and buy an option at a higher strike price, where the distance between strike prices is equal. A long condor (at expiration) will have a value somewhere between the width of the exercise prices and zero. A long condor is a strategy that has limited profit potential and limited risk and is profitable if the underlying stock trades within the range of strike prices.

A long call condor maximum profit occurs when the stock is at or between the middle strike prices at expiration, and its maximum loss occurs (at expiration) if the stock closes at or below the lowest strike price or at or about the highest strike price. The maximum loss is the debit paid (plus commissions).

In a long condor, there are two break-even points. The break-even points in a long condor occur when the stock (at expiration) is at the lowest strike price plus the debit or at the highest strike price minus the debit.

In a long condor, the time decay of short options typically approximates the time decay of long options, and a volatility increase or decrease affects the value of short options by approximately the same amount as long options. For a long condor, a debit is charged to your account and must be paid in full. A long call condor may be permitted in an IRA.

Example: Long Call Condor

> **Assumptions**: XYZ stock is trading at $100 a share in January; buy a February 95/100/105/110 long call condor and pay a net debit of $2 ($200), as follows: Buy one February 95 call at $7, sell one February 100 call at $4, sell one February 105 call at $2, and buy one February 110 call at $1.
>
> **Strategy direction**: Neutral (trading range).

TABLE 16.2   Long Call Condor

XYZ Stock Price ($)	Long Call (Lowest Strike)	Short Call (Lower Strike)	Short Call (Higher Strike)	Long Call (Highest Strike)	Spread	Cost of Spread	Spread Profit (Loss)	Profit (Loss) Percentage
75	0	0	0	0	0	200	(200)	(100)
80	0	0	0	0	0	200	(200)	(100)
85	0	0	0	0	0	200	(200)	(100)
90	0	0	0	0	0	200	(200)	(100)
95	0	0	0	0	0	200	(200)	(100)
100	500	0	0	0	500	200	300	150
105	1,000	(500)	0	0	500	200	300	150
110	1,500	(1,000)	(500)	0	0	200	(200)	(100)
115	2,000	(1,500)	(1,000)	500	0	200	(200)	(100)
120	2,500	(2,000)	(1,500)	1,000	0	200	(200)	(100)
125	3,000	(2,500)	(2,000)	1,500	0	200	(200)	(100)

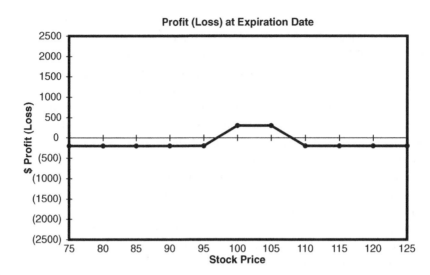

FIGURE 16.1 Long Call Condor

Debit or credit: $200 debit.

Maximum profit: $300 ($500 for five-point difference in strike prices less $200 debit).

Maximum loss: $200 (premium paid).

Exercise and assignment: Can exercise long option if in-the-money; may be assigned on short option if in-the-money.

Break-even stock price: $97 and $108 (lowest strike price plus debit, highest strike price minus debit).

Maximum profit achieved: Stock at or between middle strike prices of 100 and 105.

Maximum loss achieved: Stock at or below $95 or at or above $110.

Profit (loss) if stock unchanged: $300 profit (stock at or between inside strike price).

The maximum payoff is achieved when XYZ stock finishes at or between the middle exercise prices and loses value as the stock price moves above the higher middle strike price or below the lower middle strike price. When the stock price reaches $95 or $110, the trade leads to the maximum loss of $200. If XYZ stock is below 95 at expiration, the spread is worthless because all options are out-of-the-money. If the stock is between $100 and $105, the spread is worth $500 because the 95 call is worth five points more than the 100 call. If the stock is above $110, the short calls are offset dollar for dollar by the long calls.

Greeks: Table 16.3 contains sample Greeks converted to dollars at the time the position is established.

The Greeks, in this example, reflect an initial loss from stock rise (delta), a gain from time decay (theta), and a loss from volatility (vega) expansion. Loss is $7 from XYZ stock rising to $101; gain is $3 from one day of time decay.

TABLE 16.3 Summary of Greeks: February Expiration

Option	Delta	Gamma	Theta	Vega
Long 1 February 95 call	$65	$2.00	−$14	$11
Short 1 February 100 call	−$53	−$2.30	$15	−$12
Short 1 February 105 call	−$42	−$2.00	$14	−$11
Long 1 February 110 call	$23	$1.75	−$12	$8
Position	−$7		$3	−$4

TABLE 16.4 Summary of Greeks: March Expiration

Option	Delta	Gamma	Theta	Vega
Long 1 March 95 call	$63	$1.20	−$11	$16
Short 1 March 100 call	−$52	−$1.30	$12	−$17
Short 1 March 105 call	−$40	−$1.20	$10	−$15
Long 1 March 110 call	$20	$1.00	−$7	$10
Position	−$9		$4	−$6

Later expiration: The option price and Greeks will differ at the purchase date if expiration is at a later date. For example, if the options expire in March, instead of February, the price of the March 95 call could be $9, the March 100 call could be $6, the March 105 call could be $4, and the March 110 call could be $2, for a net debit of $1. Example Greeks are given in Table 16.4.

Loss is $9 from XYZ stock rising to $101; gain is $4 from one day of time decay.

Exercise and assignment: If XYZ stock closes above the highest strike price of 110 at expiration (each call expires in-the-money) and you allow the exercise and assignment process to run its course, you would (1) exercise the long 95 call and buy 100 shares at $95, (2) exercise the long 110 call and buy 100 shares at $110, (3) be assigned on the short 100 call and sell 100 shares at $100, and (4) be assigned on the short 105 call and sell 100 shares at $105. The net of all these transactions would be to lose the $2 debit ($200) you initially paid for the condor spread. You would, however, pay plenty of commissions along the way.

Long Put Condor

In a long put condor, you sell one option at each of the middle exercise prices and, at the same time, you buy an option at a lower strike price and buy an option at a higher strike price, where the distance between strike prices is equal. A long condor (at expiration) will have a value somewhere between the width of the exercise prices and zero. A long condor is a strategy that has limited profit potential and limited risk and is profitable if the underlying stock trades within the range of strike prices. A long condor is similar to a long butterfly, except that a long condor has two middle exercise prices.

A long call condor maximum profit occurs when the stock is at or between the middle strike prices at expiration, and its maximum loss occurs (at expiration) if the stock closes at or below the lowest strike price or at or about the highest strike price. The maximum loss is the debit paid (plus commissions).

In a long condor, there are two break-even points. The break-even points in a long condor occur when the stock (at expiration) is at the lowest strike price plus the debit or at the highest strike price minus the debit.

In a long condor, the time decay of short options typically approximates the time decay of long options, and a volatility increase or decrease affects the value of the short options by approximately the same amount as long options. For a long condor, a debit charged to your account must be paid in full. A long call condor may be permitted in an IRA. In the example that follows, the price of XYZ stock is assumed to be $105 for the put condor, instead of $100, to make the results comparable to the long call condor.

Example: Long Put Condor

Assumptions: In January, XYZ stock is trading at $105 a share (remember that the stock price is assumed to be $105, instead of $100); buy a February 95/100/105/110 long put condor and pay a net debit of $2 ($200), as follows: Buy one February 110 put at $7, sell one February 105 put at $4, sell one February 100 put at $2, and buy one February 95 put at $1.

Strategy direction: Neutral (trading range).

Debit or credit: $200 debit.

Maximum profit: $300 ($500 for five-point difference in strike prices less $200 debit).

Maximum loss: $200 (premium paid).

Exercise and assignment: Can exercise long option if in-the-money; may be assigned on short option if in-the-money.

Break-even stock price: $97 and $108 (lowest strike price plus debit, highest strike price minus debit).

Maximum profit achieved: Stock at or between middle strike prices of 100 and 105.

Maximum loss achieved: Stock at or below $95 or at or above $110.

Profit (loss) if stock unchanged: $300 profit (stock at or between inside strike price).

The maximum payoff is achieved when XYZ stock finishes at or between the middle exercise prices and loses value as the stock price moves above the higher middle strike price or below the lower middle strike price. When the price reaches 95 or 110, the trade leads to the maximum loss of $200. If XYZ stock is above $110 at expiration, the spread is worthless because all options are out-of-the-money. If the stock is between $100 and $105, the spread is worth $500 because the 110 put is worth five points more than the 105 put. If the stock is below $95, the short puts are offset dollar for dollar by the long puts.

Greeks: Table 16.6 contains sample Greeks converted to dollars at the time the position is established.

The Greeks, in this example, reflect an initial gain from stock rise (delta), a gain from time decay (theta), and a gain from volatility (vega) contraction. Gain is $7 from XYZ stock rising to $101; gain is $3 from one day of time decay.

TABLE 16.5 Long Put Condor

XYZ Stock Price ($)	Long Put (Highest Strike)	Short Put (Higher Strike)	Short Put (Lower Strike)	Long Put (Lowest Strike)	Spread	Cost of Spread	Spread Profit (Loss)	Profit (Loss) Percentage
75	3,500	(3,000)	(2,500)	2,000	0	200	(200)	(100)
80	3,000	(2,500)	(2,000)	1,500	0	200	(200)	(100)
85	2,500	(2,000)	(1,500)	1,000	0	200	(200)	(100)
90	2,000	(1,500)	(1,000)	500	0	200	(200)	(100)
95	1,500	(1,000)	(500)	0	0	200	(200)	(100)
100	1,000	(500)	0	0	500	200	300	150
105	500	0	0	0	500	200	300	150
110	0	0	0	0	0	200	(200)	(100)
115	0	0	0	0	0	200	(200)	(100)
120	0	0	0	0	0	200	(200)	(100)
125	0	0	0	0	0	200	(200)	(100)

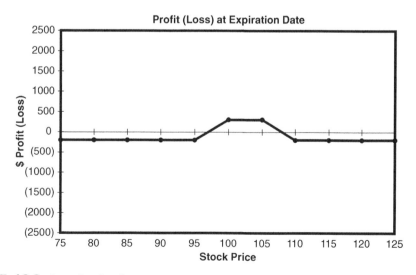

FIGURE 16.2 Long Put Condor

TABLE 16.6 Summary of Greeks: February Expiration

Option	Delta	Gamma	Theta	Vega
Long 1 February 110 put	−$65	$2.00	−$14	$11
Short 1 February 105 put	$53	−$2.30	$15	−$12
Short 1 February 100 put	$42	−$2.00	$14	−$11
Long 1 February 95 put	−$23	$1.75	−$12	$8
Position	$7		$3	−$4

TABLE 16.7 Summary of Greeks: March Expiration

Option	Delta	Gamma	Theta	Vega
Long 1 March 110 put	−$63	$1.20	−$11	$16
Short 1 March 105 put	$52	−$1.30	$12	−$17
Short 1 March 100 put	$40	−$1.20	$10	−$15
Long 1 March 95 put	−$20	$1.00	−$7	$10
Position	$9		$4	−$6

Later expiration: The option price and Greeks will differ at the purchase date if expiration is at a later date; for example, if the options expire in March, instead of February, the price of the March 110 put could be $9, the March 105 put could be $6, the March 100 put could be $4, and the March 95 put could be $2, for a net debit of $1. Example Greeks are given in Table 16.7.

Gain is $7 from XYZ stock rising to $101; gain is $3 from one day of time decay.

Exercise and assignment: If XYZ stock closes below the lowest strike price of 95 at expiration (each put expires in-the-money) and you allow the exercise and assignment process to run its course, you would (1) exercise the long 110 put and sell 100 shares at $110, (2) exercise the long 95 put and sell 100 shares at $95, (3) be assigned on the short 100 put and buy 100 shares at $100, and (4) be assigned on the short 105 put and buy 100 shares at $105. The net of all these transactions would be to lose the $2 debit ($200) you initially paid for the condor spread. You would, however, pay plenty of commissions along the way.

Short Call Condor

In a short call condor, you buy one option at each of the middle exercise prices and, at the same time, you sell an option at a lower strike price and sell an option at a higher strike price, where the distance between strike prices is equal. A short condor (at expiration) will have a value somewhere between the width of the exercise prices and zero. A short condor is a strategy that has limited profit potential and limited risk and is profitable if the underlying stock trades outside the range of strike prices. A short condor is similar to a short butterfly, except that a short condor has two middle exercise prices.

A short call condor maximum gain occurs (at expiration) if the stock closes at or below the lowest strike price or at or about the highest strike price. The maximum gain is the debit paid (plus commissions). Its maximum loss occurs when the stock is at or between the middle strike prices at expiration.

There are two break-even points. The break-even points in a short condor occur when the stock (at expiration) is at the lower strike price plus the credit or at the highest strike price minus the credit.

In a short condor, the time decay of short options typically approximates the time decay of long options, and a volatility increase or decrease affects the value of short options by approximately the same amount as long options. In a short condor, margin is generally required for the short vertical portion of the spread. A short call condor may be permitted in an IRA.

Example: Short Call Condor

Assumptions: XYZ stock is trading at $100 a share in January; sell a February 95/100/105/110 short call condor and collect a net credit of $2 ($200), as follows: Sell one February 95 call at $7, buy one February 100 call at $4, buy one February 105 call at $2, and sell one February 110 call at $1.

Strategy direction: Outside trading range.

Debit or credit: $200 credit.

Maximum profit: $200 (equal to credit).

Maximum loss: $300 ($500 for five-point difference in strike prices less $200 credit).

TABLE 16.8   Short Call Condor

XYZ Stock Price ($)	Long Call (Lowest Strike)	Short Call (Lower Strike)	Short Call (Higher Strike)	Long Call (Highest Strike)	Spread	Spread Credit	Spread Profit (Loss)	Profit (Loss) Percentage
75	0	0	0	0	0	200	200	100
80	0	0	0	0	0	200	200	100
85	0	0	0	0	0	200	200	100
90	0	0	0	0	0	200	200	100
95	0	0	0	0	0	200	200	100
100	(500)	0	0	0	(500)	200	(300)	(150)
105	(1,000)	500	0	0	(500)	200	(300)	(150)
110	(1,500)	1,000	500	0	0	200	200	100
115	(2,000)	1,500	1,000	(500)	0	200	200	100
120	(2,500)	2,000	1,500	(1,000)	0	200	200	100
125	(3,000)	2,500	2,000	(1,500)	0	200	200	100

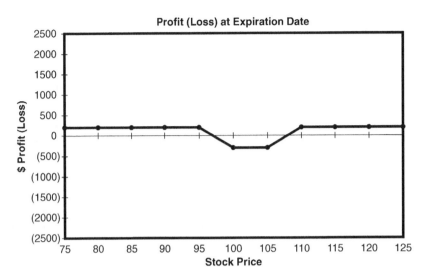

FIGURE 16.3 Short Call Condor

Exercise and assignment: Can exercise long option if in-the-money; may be assigned on short option if in-the-money.

Break-even stock price: $97 and $108 (lowest strike price plus credit, highest strike price minus credit).

Maximum profit achieved: Stock at or below $95 or at or above $110.

Maximum loss achieved: Stock at or between middle strike prices of 100 and 105.

Profit (loss) if stock unchanged: $300 loss (stock at or between inside strike prices).

The maximum loss occurs when XYZ stock finishes at or between the middle exercise prices and the trade gains value as the stock price moves above the higher middle strike price or below the lower middle strike price. When the stock price reaches $95 or $110, the trade leads to the maximum gain of $200. If XYZ stock is below $95 at expiration, the spread is worthless because all options are out-of-the-money. If the stock is between $100 and $105, the spread is worth $500 because the 95 call is worth five points more than the 100 call. If the stock is above $110, the short calls are offset dollar for dollar by the long calls.

Greeks: Table 16.9 contains sample Greeks converted to dollars at the time the position is established.

The Greeks, in this example, reflect an initial gain from stock rise (delta) and from volatility (vega) expansion. Position would reflect a loss from stock decline, time decay (theta), and volatility (vega) contraction. Gain is $7 from XYZ stock rising to $101; loss is $3 from one day of time decay.

Later expiration: The option price and Greeks will differ at the purchase date if expiration is at a later date. For example, if the options expire in March, instead of February, the price of the March 95 call could be $9, the March 100 call could

TABLE 16.9 Summary of Greeks: February Expiration

Option	Delta	Gamma	Theta	Vega
Short 1 February 95 call	−$65	−$2.00	$14	−$11
Long 1 February 100 call	$53	$2.30	−$15	$12
Long 1 February 105 call	$42	$2.00	−$14	$11
Short 1 February 110 call	−$23	−$1.75	$12	−$8
Position	$7		−$3	$4

TABLE 16.10 Summary of Greeks: March Expiration

Option	Delta	Gamma	Theta	Vega
Short 1 March 95 call	−$65	−$1.20	$11	−$16
Long 1 March 100 call	$52	$1.30	−$12	$17
Long 1 March 105 call	$40	$1.20	−$10	$15
Short 1 March 110 call	−$20	−$1.00	$7	−$10
Position	$9		−$4	$6

be $6, the March 105 call could be $4, and the March 110 call could be $2, for a net credit of $1. Example Greeks are given in Table 16.10.

Gain is $9 from XYZ stock rising to $101; loss is $4 from one day of time decay.

Exercise and assignment: If XYZ stock closes above the highest strike price of 110 at expiration (each call expires in-the-money) and you allow the exercise and assignment process to run its course, you would (1) exercise the long 100 call and buy 100 shares at $100, (2) exercise the long 105 call and buy 100 shares at $105, (3) be assigned on the short 95 call and sell 100 shares at $95, and (4) be assigned on the short 110 call and sell 100 shares at $110. The net of all these transactions would be to gain the $2 credit ($200) you initially collected for the condor spread. You would, however, pay plenty of commissions along the way.

Short Put Condor

In a short put condor, you buy one option at each of the middle exercise prices and, at the same time, you sell an option at a lower strike price and sell an option at a higher strike price, where the distance between strike prices is equal. A short condor (at expiration) will have a value somewhere between the width of the exercise prices and zero. A short condor is a strategy that has limited profit potential and limited risk and is profitable if the underlying stock trades outside the range of strike prices. A short condor is similar to a short butterfly, except that a short condor has two middle exercise prices.

A short call condor maximum gain occurs (at expiration) if the stock closes at or below the lowest strike price or at or about the highest strike price. The maximum gain is the debit paid (plus commissions). Its maximum loss occurs when the stock is at or between middle strike prices at expiration.

There are two break-even points. The break-even points in a short condor occur when the stock (at expiration) is at the lower strike price plus the credit or at the highest strike price minus the credit.

In a short condor, the time decay of short options typically approximates the time decay of long options, and a volatility increase or decrease affects the value of short options by approximately the same amount as long options. In a short condor, margin is generally required for the short vertical portion of the spread. A short call condor may be permitted in an IRA. In the example that follows, the price of XYZ stock is assumed to be $105 for the put condor, instead of $100, to make the results comparable to the short call condor.

Example: Short Put Condor

Assumptions: XYZ stock is trading at $105 a share in January (remember that the stock price is assumed to be $105, instead of $100); sell a February 95/100/105/110 short put condor and collect a net credit of $2 ($200), as follows: Sell one February 110 put at $7, buy one February 105 put at $4, and buy one February 100 put at $2, and sell one February 95 put at $1.

Strategy direction: Outside trading range.

Debit or credit: $200 credit.

Maximum profit: $200 (equal to credit).

Maximum loss: $300 ($500 for five-point difference in strike prices less $200 credit).

Exercise and assignment: Can exercise long option if in-the-money; may be assigned on short option if in-the-money.

TABLE 16.11 Short Put Condor

XYZ Stock Price ($)	Long Put (Highest Strike)	Short Put (Higher Strike)	Short Put (Lower Strike)	Long Put (Lowest Strike)	Spread	Spread Credit	Spread Profit (Loss)	Profit (Loss) Percentage
75	(3,500)	3,000	2,500	(2,000)	0	200	200	100
80	(3,000)	2,500	2,000	(1,500)	0	200	200	100
85	(2,500)	2,000	1,500	(1,000)	0	200	200	100
90	(2,000)	1,500	1,000	(500)	0	200	200	100
95	(1,500)	1,000	500	0	0	200	200	100
100	(1,000)	500	0	0	(500)	200	(300)	(150)
105	(500)	0	0	0	(500)	200	(300)	(150)
110	0	0	0	0	0	200	200	100
115	0	0	0	0	0	200	200	100
120	0	0	0	0	0	200	200	100
125	0	0	0	0	0	200	200	100

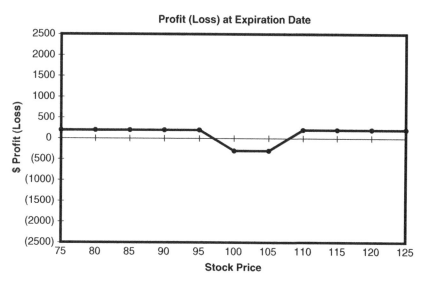

FIGURE 16.4 Short Put Condor

Break-even stock price: $97 and $108 (lowest strike price plus credit, highest strike price minus credit).

Maximum profit achieved: Stock at or below $95 or at or above $110.

Maximum loss achieved: Stock at or between middle strike prices of 100 and 105.

Profit (loss) if stock unchanged: $300 loss (stock at or between inside strike prices).

The maximum loss occurs when XYZ stock finishes at or between the middle exercise prices and the trade gains value as the stock price moves above the higher middle strike price or below the lower middle strike price. When the price reaches 95 or 110, the trade leads to the maximum gain of $200. If XYZ stock is above $110 at expiration, the spread is worthless because all options are out-of-the-money. If the stock is between $100 and $105, the spread is worth $500 because the 110 put is worth five points more than the 105 put. If the stock is below $95, the short puts are offset dollar for dollar by the long puts.

Greeks: Table 16.12 contains sample Greeks converted to dollars at the time the position is established.

The Greeks, in this example, reflect an initial loss from stock rise (delta), a loss from time decay (theta), and a loss from volatility (vega) contraction. Loss is $7 from XYZ stock rising to $101; loss is $3 from one day of time decay.

Later expiration: The option price and Greeks will differ at the purchase date if expiration is at a later date. For example, if the options expire in March, instead of February, the price of the March 110 put could be $9, the March 105 put could be $6, the March 100 put could be $4, and the March 95 put could be $2, for a net debit of $1. Example Greeks are given in Table 16.13.

TABLE 16.12 Summary of Greeks: February Expiration

Option	Delta	Gamma	Theta	Vega
Short 1 February 110 put	$65	−$2.00	$14	−$11
Long 1 February 105 put	−$53	$2.30	−$15	$12
Long 1 February 100 put	−$42	$2.00	−$14	$11
Short 1 February 95 put	$23	−$1.75	$12	−$8
Position	−$7		−$3	$4

TABLE 16.13 Summary of Greeks: March Expiration

Option	Delta	Gamma	Theta	Vega
Short 1 March 110 put	$63	−$1.20	$11	−$16
Long 1 March 105 put	−$52	$1.30	−$12	$17
Long 1 March 100 put	−$40	$1.20	−$10	$15
Short 1 March 95 put	$20	−$1.00	$7	−$10
Position	−$9		−$4	$6

Loss is $7 from XYZ stock rising to $101; loss is $3 from one day of time decay.

Exercise and assignment: If XYZ stock closes below the lowest strike price of 95 at expiration (each put expires in-the-money) and you allow the exercise and assignment process to run its course, you would (1) exercise the long 105 put and buy 100 shares at $105, (2) exercise the long 100 put and buy 100 shares at $100, (3) be assigned on the short 110 put and sell 100 shares at $110, and (4) be assigned on the short 95 put and sell 100 shares at $95. The net of all these transactions would be to gain the $2 credit ($200) you initially collected for the condor spread. You would, however, pay plenty of commissions along the way.

BEYOND THE BASICS

Condor Analysis

Like a long butterfly, you may want to use a long condor strategy when you forecast that a particular stock will remain within a trading range (neutral) and you want low volatility in your account and limited risk. You may want to use a short condor strategy when you project that a particular stock will trade outside a trading range and you want low volatility, limited risk, and low margin.

The most important decision is the selection of the middle strike prices because that determines where you incur your maximum gain if you are long and your maximum loss if you are short. You should keep in mind that the middle strike prices do not have to be near at-the-money when they are established; for example, if XYZ stock is trading at $100 a share, the middle strike prices do not need to be the strikes closest to 100. Instead, if the stock is at $100 a share, you can establish the middle strike prices, for instance, at 85 to 90. You can use your trading platform to determine whether there is more favorable pricing using a call versus a put condor under various scenarios.

If you are nearing expiration, you can offset your current position, because there are only a few days left in the option expiration cycle, and establish a similar position in the subsequent expiration month. It may be difficult, however, to roll a condor because there are four contracts involved.

Assignment Risk

There is assignment risk associated with a condor spread. Although it is generally accepted that spread trading reduces the risk of loss, spreads are subject to early exercise or assignment that can remove the very protection that you wanted. This can lead to margin calls and/or greater losses than anticipated. As a general rule, it is best to avoid assignment on any leg in a condor, or any other short option position, for that matter. An alternative to being assigned is to offset a short option in the marketplace. You need to be careful not to be assigned in a condor spread because it can create margin problems and unnecessary complexity.

In a long call condor spread, for example, its maximum loss occurs (at expiration) if the stock closes at or below the lowest strike price or at or about the highest strike price. This may sound like equal results, but the close above the highest strike price has exercise/assignment risk. The close below the lowest strike price simply results in all options expiring worthless.

A Commission Extravaganza

The potentially high cost of commissions and the bid/ask spread should be taken into consideration before entering into a condor. Commissions are incurred to establish each condor leg, to offset the condor if you choose to do so, and to execute any exercise and assignment. As a result, commissions, including the bid/ask spread, may be incurred on the four contracts to establish the condor and possibly on an additional four contracts to offset those positions at a later date, for a total of eight commission transactions. Additional commissions would be incurred on exercise or assignment. Like a butterfly, sometimes I believe that they call it a condor because you pay so much in commissions that you will see your profits fly away.

Ladder (Christmas Tree)

A *ladder* (also referred to as a Christmas tree) is a term that can describe a variety of spreads. A ladder usually consists of three different exercise prices, where all options are the same type and expire at the same time. In a long (bull) call ladder, one call is purchased at the lowest strike price, and one call is sold at each of the higher strike prices. It is similar to a long call condor, except that there is no purchase of a call at a higher strike price. In a long (bull) put ladder, one put is purchased at the highest exercise price, and one put is sold at each of the lower exercise prices. It is similar to a long put condor, except that there is no purchase of a put at a lower strike price.

A ladder can be considered a particular type of unbalanced (ratio) spread. A long ladder has unlimited risk and a short ladder has unlimited profit potential. For example, assume that in January, XYZ stock is trading at $100 a share, and you buy a February 95/100/105 long call ladder (buy one February 95 call at $7, sell one February 100 call at $5, and sell one February 105 call at $2, for an even cost spread—the amount paid equals the amount collected). In a condor, you would also buy one February 110 call; however, in a ladder, you omit that step.

Separately, you could buy a February 95/100/105 long put ladder (buy one February 105 put at $7, sell one February 100 put at $5, and sell one February 95 put at $2, for an even cost spread). In a condor, you would also buy one February 90 put; however, in a ladder, you omit that step.

In a short (bear) call ladder, one call is sold at the lowest strike price and one call is purchased at each of the higher exercise prices. It is similar to a short call condor except that there is no sale of a call at a higher strike price. In a short (bear) put ladder, one put is sold at the highest exercise price and one put is sold at each of the lower exercise prices. It is similar to a short put condor, except that there is no sale of a put at a lower strike price. For example, assume that in January, XYZ stock is trading at $100 a share and you can sell a February 95/100/105 short call ladder (sell one February 95 call at $7, buy one February 100 call at $5, and buy one February 105 call at $2, for an even cost spread).

Separately, you can sell a February 95/100/105 short put ladder (sell one February 105 put at $7, buy one February 100 put at $5, and buy one February 95 put at $2, for an even cost spread).

FINAL THOUGHTS

A trader may choose a long condor over a short straddle in a sideways market because of the limited risk of the condor. Unlike a short straddle or short strangle, in a long-condor strategy, if the stock moves appreciably in one direction or the other, your losses are limited. In a long condor, the most you can lose is the amount paid to purchase the condor, but a short straddle or strangle has greater profit potential. A straddle or strangle can be used to profit from a range or to profit from volatility, but the problem with a straddle or strangle is that there can be a lot of risk. A condor is designed to mitigate such risk.

A condor is similar to the butterfly spread that was discussed in Chapter 15. Many of the same comments that were made in Chapter 15 also apply here for a condor. For example, you may notice the similarities between a condor spread and gambling. In a long condor, you are, in effect, paying $2 for the chance to make $3. In a short condor, you are, in effect, collecting $2 with a possibility of losing $3.

You can get an idea of your chances of success by examining the deltas of the various strike prices. In general, you should use your trading platform and its simulated (paper) trading feature to enter hypothetical trades to determine the pricing of a call versus a put condor spread. In the next chapter, Chapter 17, "Calendar Spread," we explore spread strategies in which the options expire at different times.

Calendar Spread

A *calendar spread* attempts to exploit the difference in time decay between options that expire in different months. The typical calendar spread exploits the naturally inflated time decay of a near-term option relative to a longer-term option. A calendar spread, therefore, offers unique characteristics and can be a nice addition to your repertoire of option strategies. A calendar spread gets its name from the fact that all options in the strategy have the same terms, except for the expiration date. This chapter will cover long and short calendar spreads and move beyond the basics.

OVERVIEW

A calendar spread, also called a *time spread*, can be executed to take advantage of near-term time decay relative to longer-term time decay (long calendar spread) or to take advantage of longer-term time decay relative to near-term decay (short calendar spread). A calendar spread involves the purchase of a call (or put) option and the simultaneous sale of a call (or put) option with the same strike price but a different expiration date. You are long a calendar spread when the longer-term option (back month) is purchased and the near-term option (front month) is sold; for example, sell one XYZ February 100 call and buy one XYZ March 100 call. You are short a calendar spread when the longer-term option is sold and the near-term option is purchased; for example, buy one February 100 call and sell one March 100 call. A short calendar spread is also called a "reverse time spread." A summary follows:

- **Long calendar spread**: Longer-term option is purchased and shorter-term option is sold.
- **Short calendar spread**: Near-term option is purchased and longer-term option is sold.

TABLE 17.1 Calendar versus Vertical Spread

Spread Strategy	Strikes	Months
Calendar spread	Same	Different
Vertical spread	Different	Same

A calendar spread is a limited-risk/limited-reward strategy in which you can take advantage of a range-bound market (long calendar spread) or trading outside a range (short calendar spread). It has limited risk because the number of short and long options is equal, and all options have the same strike price.

A calendar spread is also called a "horizontal spread" or "time spread." As an aside, a calendar spread is the inverse of a vertical spread. A calendar spread involves the same strike price and a different expiration month, whereas a vertical spread involves different strike prices and the same expiration month (see Table 17.1).

How you profit in a calendar spread can be difficult to conceptualize at first. What you need to remember is that you profit in a debit spread (long calendar spread) when the value of the spread increases, and you profit in a credit spread (short calendar spread) when the value of the spread contracts. What can make a spread increase or contract depends on the interaction of the opposing long and short options that make up the spread.

The profit and loss of a calendar spread can be analyzed as of the expiration date of the near-term option. In a long calendar spread, the maximum profit cannot be determined in advance because it is impossible to determine the value of the longer-term option when the near-term option expires. A long call calendar spread offers limited risk, and the maximum loss is limited to the net debit paid. In a long calendar spread, you want the near-term (short) option to contract in value and the longer-term (long) option to rise as much in value. The calendar spread will show a profit as long as the gain from the near-term option exceeds the loss from the longer-term option. You can execute a long or short calendar spread with calls or puts, as shown in Table 17.2.

The gain or loss on a calendar spread cannot be determined in advance because the spread consists of options that expire at different times. As a reminder, the principles that are demonstrated in this chapter on a stock can be applied to options on an ETF, index, and stock index futures.

What Affects Calendar Spread Value

As a general rule, a calendar spread achieves its maximum value, on the near-term option expiration date, if the underlying stock closes at the calendar strike price. Assuming calls are used, if a stock plunges prior to the near-term option expiration date, near-term and longer-term call options will both simultaneously contract toward zero, thus contracting the spread. Likewise, if the stock surges prior to the near-term option expiration date, values of the near-month and longer-term call options will both simultaneously increase to near-parity, thus contracting the spread. As a result, volatility in either direction results

TABLE 17.2 Summary: Long and Short Calendar Spread

Spread Strategy	Strategy Description	Risk–Reward	Profitable	Debit or Credit	Breakeven	Initial Margin
Long call calendar spread	Sell near-month call option, buy far-month call option, same strike price	Limited risk, limited profit	Trade within range	Debit	Cannot determine in advance	Full payment
Long put calendar spread	Sell near-month put option, buy far-month put option, same strike price	Limited risk, limited profit	Trade within range	Debit	Cannot determine in advance	Full payment
Short call calendar spread	Buy near-month call option, sell far-month call option, same strike price	Limited risk, limited profit	Trade outside range	Credit	Cannot determine in advance	Short option leg
Short put calendar spread	Buy near-month put option, sell far-month put option, same strike price	Limited risk, limited profit	Trade outside range	Credit	Cannot determine in advance	Short option leg

in a contraction of the spread, whereas a trading range environment maximizes the value of the spread.

An analysis of a calendar spread should include a forecast of the value of the longer-term option at the time the near-term option expires. Unfortunately, you cannot know this value at the time a calendar spread is established, and it is simply a prediction. For example, assume that XYZ stock is currently trading at $100 a share, and you can purchase an at-the-money call calendar spread for a $5 debit (by selling one February 100 call for $5 and buying one April 100 call for $10). You can forecast that if XYZ stock is trading at $100 a share at the February expiration date, the February 100 call would be worthless, and the April 100 call may trade at approximately $8, but the April call value is only an estimate. In this forecast, the calendar spread is purchased at $5 and could be sold for $8. Keep in mind that if XYZ stock is trading below $100 a share at the February expiration date, the February call would be worthless, and the April call would be valued at less than $8. If XYZ is trading above $100 a share at the February expiration date, the February call would be valued at the in-the-money amount, and the April call would be valued at more than $8. As a result, the net debit (of $8) is highest when XYZ stock lands at the calendar strike price of 100 at the February expiration date.

In some option literature, it is stated that if the underlying stock is at the strike price at the expiration date of the near-term option, a long calendar spread will automatically produce a profit at that point in time. The theory behind this is that the time decay of the near-term option will exceed the time decay of the longer-term option, resulting in expansion of the calendar spread. However, implied volatility of the longer-term option is an important ingredient in determining the ultimate profitability of the spread. In a long calendar spread, if implied volatility of the longer-term option expands relative to the near-term option, then the debit of the calendar spread will expand, producing a greater gain. If implied volatility of a longer-term option contracts relative to the near-term option, then the debit of the calendar spread will contract, producing a lower gain, or even a loss. There are no guarantees because a severe collapse in implied volatility of the longer-term option can reduce the debit and even produce a loss, even though the underlying stock is at the strike price on the date the near-term option expires.

The profit and loss picture would be reversed for a short calendar spread so that an explosion in implied volatility of the longer-term short option works against the shorter calendar spread.

This also means that the break-even point cannot be determined in advance. An option chain and option calculator should be used to project values and determine the likely break-even point for a calendar spread to project possible outcomes.

STRATEGY EXAMPLES

Following are descriptions and a long and short calendar spread from the perspective of a call and put. As a reminder, you can close out an option position by offsetting it in the marketplace any time prior to expiration, and the principles that are demonstrated for a stock can be applied to options on an ETF, index, and stock index futures. Appendixes A, B, and C illustrate many of the strategies covered throughout this book.

As a general rule, a long calendar spread may be most effective using equity options, where the strike price is at-the-money. Conversely, a short calendar spread may be more appropriate for options on ETFs, indexes, and stock index futures (covered in Chapters 23 to 26). The following examples use equity options so that you can easily compare short calendar spreads to long calendar spreads.

Long Call Calendar Spread

In a long call calendar spread, you sell a near-term call option and buy a longer-term call option to take advantage of the accelerated time decay of the near-term option versus the longer-term option. If things go according to plan, the value of the near-term option will decline by more than the longer-term option.

A long calendar spread is profitable if the underlying stock trades within a range. The maximum profit of a long calendar spread is achieved when the stock closes at the calendar strike price at the near-term expiration date. However, you cannot precisely predict a calendar spread maximum profit dollar amount when you first establish the position because it is impossible to know in advance the value of an option at any point in time prior to its expiration. The maximum loss is limited to the net debit and occurs (at the near-term expiration date) if the underlying stock closes appreciably above or below the calendar spread strike price.

The break-even point at the expiration of the near-dated option cannot be determined because the value of the longer-term option cannot be determined in advance.

The time decay of the near-term option typically exceeds the time decay of the longer-term option, and a volatility increase or decrease typically affects the value of the longer-term option by a greater amount than the value of the near-term option as expiration approaches. For a long call calendar spread, a debit is charged to your account and must be paid in full. A long call calendar spread may be permitted in an IRA.

For example, assume that XYZ stock is currently trading at $100 a share, and you purchase an at-the-money call calendar spread for a $5 debit by selling one February 100 call for $5 and buying one April 100 call for $10. In this example, you are buying the February/April 100 call time spread for $500. In a best-case scenario, assuming that it is the last trading day for February expiration and the stock closes exactly at $100 a share, the February 100 call would expire worthless, and you would still own the April 100 call, which is assumed to be valued at $8 ($800). At that point, you would have a profit of $300, consisting of a $500 gain on the February option and a loss of $200 on the April option. When the February call expires, you can offset the April 100 call to close out the position entirely or you can keep the April 100 long call, depending on your view of the stock at that point in time. Alternatively, when the February call expires, you can again sell against the long April option by selling the next month (March) 100-strike call option at, for example, an additional $5. Remember that the example shows results at the expiration date of the near-term option.

Example: Long Call Calendar Spread

Assumptions: XYZ stock is trading at $100 a share in January; buy one February/April 100 call calendar spread and pay a net debit of $5 ($500), as follows: Sell one February 100 call at $5 and buy one April 100 call at $10.

Strategy direction: Neutral (trading range).

Debit or credit: $500 debit.

Maximum profit: Unknown.

Maximum loss: $500 (equal to net debit).

Exercise and assignment: Can exercise long option if in-the-money; may be assigned on short option if in-the-money.

Break-even stock price: Unknown.

Maximum profit achieved: Underlying stock at $100 (calendar strike price) at February expiration.

Maximum loss achieved: Stock appreciably above or below the strike price of 100 at February expiration.

Profit (loss) if stock unchanged: Unknown (value of April call not determinable in advance).

Stock unchanged: If XYZ stock is at $100 at February expiration, the February 100 call is worthless and the April call has value. You can estimate the value of the April option at the February expiration date (assuming that all factors remain the same) by using an option calculator or option chain. The April 100 call option, originally at $10, is estimated to be at $8 on the February expiration date.

Stock slightly below strike: If XYZ stock closes slightly below $100 on the February expiration date, the February call profit would be fully earned; however, there would be a loss on the April 100 call, the exact amount of which cannot be determined in advance.

TABLE 17.3 Long Call Calendar Spread Values at February Expiration

XYZ Stock Price	Short February 100 Call	Long April 100 Call (Estimated)	Spread	Cost of Spread	Spread Profit (Loss)	Profit (Loss) Percentage
75	0	50	50	500	(450)	(90)
80	0	100	100	500	(400)	(80)
85	0	200	200	500	(300)	(60)
90	0	400	400	500	(100)	(20)
95	0	600	600	500	100	20
100	0	800	800	500	300	60
105	500	1,100	600	500	100	20
110	1,000	1,400	400	500	(100)	(20)
115	1,500	1,700	200	500	(300)	(60)
120	2,000	2,100	100	500	(400)	(80)
125	2,500	2,550	50	500	(450)	(90)

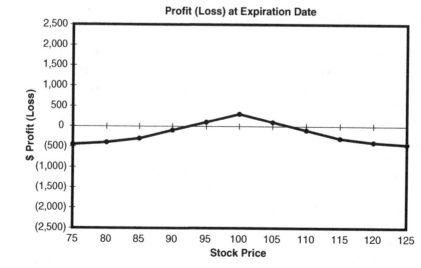

FIGURE 17.1 Long Call Calendar Spread

TABLE 17.4 Summary of Greeks: February Expiration

Option	Delta	Gamma	Theta	Vega
Short 1 February 100 call	−$53	−$2.30	$15	−$12
Long 1 April 100 call	$52	$1.30	−$12	$17
Position	−$1		$3	$5

Stock slightly above strike: If the XYZ stock closes slightly above $100 at the February expiration date, the calls will be in-the-money, resulting in some contraction in the spread (relative to at-the-money), the exact amount of which cannot be determined in advance.

Stock plunges: If XYZ stock plunges as of the February expiration date, the short February 100 call will be worthless, and the long April 100 call may be worth near zero. In this situation, you will have a loss for almost the entire $5 debit initially paid.

Stock surges: If XYZ stock surges as of the February expiration date, both the February and April 100 calls would be trading near their intrinsic values or parity (the long April 100 call may be worth slightly more than its intrinsic value). In this situation, you will have a loss for almost the entire debit initially paid because the time spread would be valued at near zero because both options would have approximately the same value.

Greeks: Table 17.4 contains sample Greeks converted to dollars at the time the position is established.

Position would reflect a loss from stock rise (delta), a gain from time decay (theta), and a gain from volatility (vega) expansion. Loss is $1 from XYZ stock rising to $101; gain is $3 from one day of time decay.

When the February 100 call expires, you can continue to hold the April 100 call and then sell the March 100 call. Alternatively, you can continue to hold the April 100 call, with the expectation that it will gain value if the stock rises after the February expiration date.

Later expiration: The option prices and Greeks will differ if the longer-term expiration is at a later date; for example, if the longer-term option expires in July, instead of April, the price of the July 100 call could be $15 (instead of $10).

Exercise and assignment: For the February/April 100 call calendar spread, if your short call is in-the-money, then you may be assigned and required to sell the XYZ stock at $100 per share, but you are protected by the long call.

Long Put Calendar Spread

In a long put calendar spread, you sell a near-term put option and buy a longer-term put option to take advantage of the accelerated time decay of the near-term option versus the longer-term option. If things go according to plan, the value of the near-term option will decline by more than the longer-term option.

A long calendar spread is profitable if the underlying instrument trades within a range. The maximum profit of a long calendar spread is achieved when the stock closes at the calendar strike price at the near-term expiration date. However, you cannot precisely predict a calendar spread maximum profit dollar amount when you first establish the position because it is impossible to know in advance the value of an option at any point in time prior to its expiration. The maximum loss is limited to the net debit and occurs (at the near-term expiration date) if the underlying stock closes appreciably above or below the calendar spread strike price.

The break-even point at the expiration of the near-dated option cannot be determined because the value of the longer-term option cannot be determined in advance.

The time decay of the near-term option typically exceeds the time decay of the longer-term option, and a volatility increase or decrease typically affects the value of the longer-term option by a greater amount than the value of the near-term option as expiration approaches. For a long put calendar spread, a debit is charged to your account and must be paid in full. A long put calendar spread may be permitted in an IRA.

For example, assume that XYZ stock is currently trading at $100 a share and you purchase an at-the-money put calendar spread for a $5 debit by selling one February 100 put for $5 and buying one April 100 put for $10: You are buying the February/April 100 put time spread for $500. In a best-case scenario, assuming that it is the last trading day for February expiration and the stock closes exactly at $100 a share, the February 100 put would expire worthless, and you would still own the April 100 put, which is assumed to be valued at $8 ($800). At that point, you would have a profit of $300, consisting of a $500 gain on the February option and a loss of $200 on the April option. When the February call expires, you can offset the April 100 put to close out the position entirely, or you can keep the April 100 put, depending on your view of the stock at that point in time. Alternatively, when the February put expires, you can again sell against the long April option by selling the next month (March) 100-strike put option at, for example, an additional $5. Furthermore, if you were long an option longer dated than April, you could continue to sell against it in later months as well. The idea is to continue selling a near-month option each month while continuing to hold the longer-term option. It should be kept in mind that this is a simplistic example because it assumes that there is no change in the underlying price of the stock or implied volatility. Remember that the example shows results at the expiration date of the near-term option.

Example: Long Put Calendar Spread

Assumptions: XYZ stock is trading at $100 a share in January; buy one February/April 100 put calendar spread and pay a net debit of $5, as follows: Sell one February 100 put at $5 and buy one April 100 put at $10.

Strategy direction: Neutral (trading range).

Debit or credit: $500 debit.

Maximum profit: Unknown.

Maximum loss: $500 (equal to net debit).

Exercise and assignment: Can exercise long option if in-the-money; may be assigned on short option if in-the-money.

Break-even stock price: Unknown.

Maximum profit achieved: Underlying stock at $100 (calendar strike price) at February expiration.

Maximum loss achieved: Stock appreciably above or below strike price of 100 at February expiration.

Profit (loss) if stock unchanged: Unknown (value of April call not determinable in advance).

Stock unchanged: If XYZ stock is at $100 at the February expiration, the February 100 put is worthless, but the April call has value. You can estimate the value

TABLE 17.5 Long Put Calendar Spread Values at February Expiration

XYZ Stock Price	Short February 100 Put	Long April 100 Put (Estimated)	Spread	Cost of Spread	Spread Profit (Loss)	Profit (Loss) Percentage
75	2,500	2,550	50	500	(450)	(90)
80	2,000	2,100	100	500	(400)	(80)
85	1,500	1,700	200	500	(300)	(60)
90	1,000	1,400	400	500	(100)	(20)
95	500	1,100	600	500	100	20
100	0	800	800	500	300	60
105	0	600	600	500	100	20
110	0	400	400	500	(100)	(20)
115	0	200	200	500	(300)	(60)
120	0	100	100	500	(400)	(80)
125	0	50	50	500	(450)	(90)

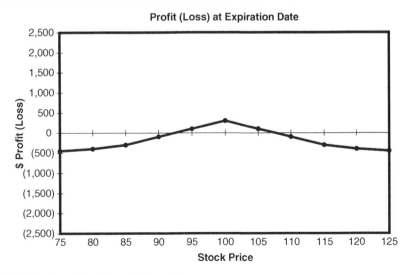

FIGURE 17.2 Long Put Calendar Spread

of the April option at the February expiration date (assuming that all factors remain the same) by using an option calculator or option chain. The April 100 option, originally at $10, is estimated to be at $8 on the February expiration date.

Stock slightly below strike: If XYZ stock closes slightly below $100 a share at the February expiration date, the puts will be in-the-money, resulting in some contraction in the spread (relative to at-the-money), the exact amount of which cannot be determined in advance.

Stock slightly above strike: If XYZ stock closes slightly above $100 on the February expiration date, the February put profit would be fully earned, but there would be a loss on the April 100 put, the exact amount of which cannot be determined in advance.

Stock plunges: If XYZ stock plunges as of the February expiration date, both the February and April 100 puts would be trading near their intrinsic values or parity (the long April 100 put may be worth slightly more than its intrinsic value). In this situation, you will have a loss for almost the entire debit initially paid.

Stock surges: If XYZ stock surges as of the February expiration date, the short February 100 put will be worthless, and the long April 100 put may be worth near zero. In this situation, you will have a loss for almost the entire $5 debit initially paid.

Greeks: Table 17.6 contains sample Greeks converted to dollars at the time the position is established.

Position would reflect a gain from stock rise (delta), a gain from time decay (theta), and a gain from volatility (vega) expansion. Gain is $1 from XYZ stock rising to $101; gain is $3 from one day of time decay.

When the February put expires, you can continue to hold the April 100 put, and then sell the March 100 put. Alternatively, you can continue to hold the April 100 put, with the expectation that it will gain value if the stock declines after the February expiration date.

Later expiration: The option prices and Greeks will differ if the longer-term expiration is at a later date. For example, if the longer-term option expires in July, instead of April, the price of the July 100 call could be $15 (instead of $10).

Exercise and assignment: For the February/April 100 put calendar spread, if your short put is in-the-money, then you may be assigned on your short put and will be required to buy the XYZ stock at $100 per share, but you are protected by the long put.

TABLE 17.6 Summary of Greeks: February Expiration

Option	Delta	Gamma	Theta	Vega
Short 1 February 100 put	$53	−$2.30	$15	−$12
Long 1 April 100 put	−$52	$1.30	−$12	$17
Position	$1		$3	$5

Short Call Calendar Spread

In a short call calendar spread, you sell a longer-term call option and buy a near-term call option to take advantage of the accelerated time decay of the longer-term option versus the near-term option. If things go according to plan, the value of the long-term option will decline by more than the near-term option.

The maximum gain is limited to the net credit and occurs (at the near-term expiration date) if the underlying stock closes appreciably above or below the calendar spread strike price. A short calendar spread is profitable if the underlying instrument trades outside a range. The maximum loss of a short calendar spread is achieved when the stock closes at the calendar strike price on the near-term expiration date. However, you cannot precisely predict a calendar spread maximum loss dollar amount when you first establish the position because it is impossible to know in advance the value of an option at any point in time prior to its expiration.

The break-even point at the expiration of the near-term option cannot be determined because the value of the longer-term option cannot be determined in advance.

The time decay of the near-term option typically exceeds the time decay of the longer-term option, and a volatility increase or decrease typically affects the value of the longer-term option by a greater amount than the value of the near-term option as expiration approaches. Margin is required for a short call calendar spread. A short call calendar spread may not be permitted in an IRA.

For example, assume that XYZ stock is currently trading at $100 a share, and you sell an at-the-money call calendar spread for a $5 credit by buying one February 100 call for $5 and selling one April 100 call for $10. You are selling the February/April 100 call time spread for $500. Assuming that it is the last trading day for February expiration and the stock closes at $75, the February 100 call would expire worthless and the April 100 call could be assumed to be valued at approximately $0.50 ($50). At that point, you would have a profit of $450, consisting of a $500 loss on the February option and a gain of $950 on the April option. If the stock is at $125 at the February expiration date, the February 100 call would be worth $25 ($2,500), and the April call could be assumed to be valued at approximately $25.50 ($2,550). At that point, you would have a profit of $450, consisting of a $2,000 gain on the February option and a loss of $1,550 on the April option. Remember that the example is presented showing results at the expiration date of the near-term option.

Example: Short Call Calendar Spread

> **Assumptions**: XYZ stock is trading at $100 a share in January; sell one February/
> April 100 call calendar spread and collect a net credit of $5, as follows: Buy one
> February 100 call at $5 and sell one April 100 call at $10.
> **Strategy direction**: Outside trading range.
> **Debit or credit**: $500 credit.
> **Maximum profit**: $500 (equal to net credit).

Maximum loss: Unknown.

Exercise and assignment: Can exercise long option if in-the-money; may be assigned on short option if in-the-money.

Break-even stock price: Unknown.

Maximum profit achieved: Stock appreciably above or below strike price of 100 at February expiration.

Maximum loss achieved: Underlying stock at $100 (calendar strike price) at February expiration.

TABLE 17.7 Short Call Calendar Spread Values at February Expiration

XYZ Stock Price	Long February 100 Call	Short April 100 Call (Estimated)	Spread	Spread Credit	Spread Profit (Loss)	Profit (Loss) Percentage
75	0	50	50	500	450	90
80	0	100	100	500	400	80
85	0	200	200	500	300	60
90	0	400	400	500	100	20
95	0	600	600	500	(100)	(20)
100	0	800	800	500	(300)	(60)
105	500	1,100	600	500	(100)	(20)
110	1,000	1,400	400	500	100	20
115	1,500	1,700	200	500	300	60
120	2,000	2,100	100	500	400	80
125	2,500	2,550	50	500	450	90

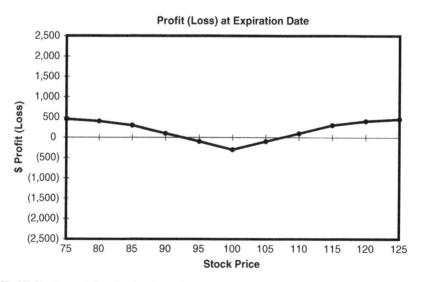

FIGURE 17.3 Short Call Calendar Spread

Profit (loss) if stock unchanged: Unknown (value of April call not determinable in advance).

Stock unchanged: If XYZ stock is at $100 at February expiration, the February 100 call is worthless, but the April call has value. You can estimate the value of the April option at the February expiration date (assuming that all factors remain the same) by using an option calculator or option chain. The April 100 call option, originally at $10, is estimated to be at $8 on the February expiration date.

Stock slightly below strike: If XYZ stock closes slightly below $100 on the February expiration date, the February call has a loss of $5, but there would be a gain on the April 100 call, the exact amount of which cannot be determined in advance.

Stock slightly above strike: If the XYZ stock closes slightly above $100 a share at the February expiration date, the calls will be in-the-money, resulting in some contraction in the spread (relative to at-the-money), the exact amount of which cannot be determined in advance.

Stock plunges: If XYZ stock plunges as of the February expiration date, the long February 100 call will be worthless, and the short April 100 call may be worth near zero. In this situation, you will have a gain for almost the entire $5 credit initially collected.

Stock surges: If XYZ stock surges as of the February expiration date, both the February and April 100 calls would be trading near their intrinsic values or parity (the short April 100 call may be worth slightly more than its intrinsic value). In this situation, you will have a gain for almost the entire credit initially collected because the time spread would be valued at near zero because both options would have approximately the same value.

Greeks: Table 17.8 contains sample Greeks converted to dollars at the time the position is established.

Position would reflect a gain from stock rise (delta), a loss from time decay (theta), and a loss from volatility (vega) expansion. Gain is $1 from XYZ stock rising to $101; loss is $3 from one day of time decay.

When the February call expires, you can continue to stay short the April 100 call and then buy the March 100 call. Alternatively, you can continue to stay short the April 100 call, with the expectation that it will decline in value if the stock declines after the February expiration date.

TABLE 17.8 Summary of Greeks: February Expiration

Option	Delta	Gamma	Theta	Vega
Long 1 February 100 call	$53	$2.30	−$15	$12
Short 1 April 100 call	−$52	−$1.30	$12	−$17
Position	$1		−$3	−$5

Later expiration: The option prices and Greeks will differ if the longer-term expiration is at a later date; for example, if the longer-term option expires in July, instead of April, the price of the July 100 call could be $15 (instead of $10).

Exercise and assignment: For the February/April 100 call calendar spread, if your short call is in-the-money, then you may be assigned on your short call and will be required to sell the XYZ stock at $100 per share, but you are protected by the long call before its expiration.

Short Put Calendar Spread

In a short put calendar spread, you sell a longer-term put option and buy a near-term put option to take advantage of the accelerated time decay of the longer-term option versus the near-term option. If things go according to plan, the value of the long-term option will decline by more than the near-term option.

The maximum gain is limited to the net credit and occurs (at the near-term expiration date) if the underlying stock closes appreciably above or below the calendar spread strike price. A short calendar spread is profitable if the underlying instrument trades outside a range. The maximum loss of a short calendar spread is achieved when the stock closes at the calendar strike price at the near-term expiration date. However, you cannot precisely predict a calendar spread maximum loss dollar amount when you first establish the position because it is impossible to know in advance the value of an option at any point in time prior to its expiration.

The break-even point at the expiration of the near-term option cannot be determined because the value of the longer-term option cannot be determined in advance.

The time decay of the near-term option typically exceeds the time decay of the longer-term option, and a volatility increase or decrease typically affects the value of the longer-term option by a greater amount than the value of the near-term option as expiration approaches. Margin is required for a short put calendar spread. Although margin is not permitted in an IRA, some brokerage firms allow the shorting of naked puts because the risk is mathematically limited to the difference between the strike price and zero.

For example, assume that XYZ stock is currently trading at $100 a share and you sell an at-the-money put calendar spread for a $5 credit by buying one February 100 put for $5 and selling one April 100 put for $10. You are selling the February/April 100 put time spread for $500. Assuming that it is the last trading day for February expiration and the stock closes at $125: The February 100 put would expire worthless, and the April 100 put could be assumed to be valued at approximately $0.50 ($50). At that point, you would have a profit of $450, consisting of a $500 loss on the February option and a gain of $950 on the April option. If the stock is at $75 at the February expiration, the February 100 put would be worth $25 ($2,500), and the April 100 put could be assumed to be valued at approximately $25.50 ($2,550). At that point, you would have a profit of $450, consisting of a $2,000 gain on the February option and a loss of $1,550 on the April option. Remember that the example shows results at the expiration date of the near-term option.

Example: Short Put Calendar Spread

Assumptions: XYZ stock is trading at $100 a share in January; sell one February/April 100 put calendar spread and collect a net credit of $5, as follows: Buy one February 100 put at $5 and sell one April 100 put at $10.

Strategy direction: Outside trading range.

Debit or credit: $500 credit.

Maximum profit: $500 (equal to net credit).

Maximum loss: Unknown.

Exercise and assignment: Can exercise long option if in-the-money; may be assigned on short option if in-the-money.

Break-even stock price: Unknown.

Maximum profit achieved: Stock appreciably above or below strike price of 100 at February expiration.

Maximum loss achieved: Underlying stock at $100 (calendar strike price) at February expiration.

Profit (loss) if stock unchanged: Unknown (value of April call not determinable in advance).

Stock unchanged: If XYZ stock is at $100 at February expiration, the February 100 put is worthless, but the April call has value. You can estimate the value of the April option at the February expiration date (assuming that all factors remain the same) by using an option calculator or option chain. The April 100 option, originally at $10, is estimated to be at $8 on the February expiration date.

Stock slightly below strike: If XYZ stock closes slightly below $100 a share at the February expiration date, the puts will be in-the-money, resulting in some contraction in the spread (relative to at-the-money), the exact amount of which cannot be determined in advance.

TABLE 17.9 Short Put Calendar Spread Values at February Expiration

XYZ Stock Price	Long February 100 Put	Short April 100 Put (Estimated)	Spread	Spread Credit	Spread Profit (Loss)	Profit (Loss) Percentage
75	2,500	2,550	50	500	450	90
80	2,000	2,100	100	500	400	80
85	1,500	1,700	200	500	300	60
90	1,000	1,400	400	500	100	20
95	500	1,100	600	500	(100)	(20)
100	0	800	800	500	(300)	(60)
105	0	600	600	500	(100)	(20)
110	0	400	400	500	100	20
115	0	200	200	500	300	60
120	0	100	100	500	400	80
125	0	50	50	500	450	90

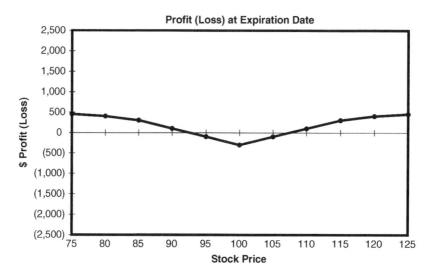

FIGURE 17.4 Short Put Calendar Spread

Stock slightly above strike: If XYZ stock closes slightly above $100 on the February expiration date, the February put has a loss of $5, but there would be a gain on the April 100 put, the exact amount of which cannot be determined in advance.

Stock surges: If XYZ stock surges as of the February expiration date, the long February 100 put will be worthless, and the short April 100 put may be worth near zero. In this situation, you will have a gain for almost the entire $5 credit initially collected.

Stock plunges: If XYZ stock plunges as of the February expiration date, both the February and April 100 puts would be trading near their intrinsic values or parity (the short April 100 put may be worth slightly more than its intrinsic value). In this situation, you will have a gain for almost the entire credit initially collected for the spread because the time spread would be valued at near zero because both options would have approximately the same value.

Greeks: Table 17.10 contains sample Greeks converted to dollars at the time the position is established.

TABLE 17.10 Summary of Greeks: February Expiration

Option	Delta	Gamma	Theta	Vega
Long 1 February 100 put	−$53	$2.30	−$15	$12
Short 1 April 100 put	$52	−$1.30	$12	−$17
Position	−$1		−$3	−$5

Position would reflect a loss from stock rise (delta), a loss from time decay (theta), and a loss from volatility (vega) expansion. Loss is $1 from XYZ stock rising to $101; loss is $3 from one day of time decay.

When the February put expires, you can continue to stay short the April 100 put and then buy the March 100 put. Alternatively, you can continue to stay short the April 100 put, with the expectation that it will lose value if the stock rises after the February expiration date.

Later expiration: The option prices and Greeks will differ if the longer-term expiration is at a later date. For example, if the longer-term option expires in July, instead of April, the price of the May 100 call could be $15 (instead of $10).

Exercise and assignment: For the February/April 100 put calendar spread, if your short put is in-the-money, then you may be assigned on your short put and will be required to buy the XYZ stock at $100 per share, but you are protected by the long put before its expiration.

BEYOND THE BASICS

Calendar Spread Basics

In a long calendar spread, you typically pay a debit and profit if the underlying stock trades within a range. It is interesting to note that this is contrary to the general rule that a debit in a vertical spread strategy typically attempts to profit as an underlying stock moves by a large amount in one direction. Likewise, a credit in a short calendar spread profits if the underlying stock trades outside a range and is contrary to the general rule that a credit in a vertical spread strategy typically profits as an underlying stock trades sideways or in one direction. An equity calendar spread typically involves options that are at-the-money, but it can be bullish (out-of-the-money call) or bearish (out-of-the-money put) as well. Let us take a look at how a profit or loss can occur.

Debit Spread Basics   In a long calendar spread, the longer-term option has a higher price than the shorter-term option and, in options lingo, this is consistent with referring to a spread that is executed as a debit as a long position (a credit is typically a short position). A debit spread can be viewed as an option position that profits when the spread difference (debit) increases; for example, a debit spread may consist of selling an option at $5 and buying a longer-term option at $10. A profit is made if the value difference between the two options increases, regardless of whether the increase is from one of the following:

- A decline in the value of the short option.
- A rise in the value of the long option.
- A greater decline in the short option value relative to the long option value.
- A greater rise in the long option value relative to the short option value.

The long calendar spread is attempting to exploit the higher rate of time decay typically associated with a near-term option relative to the decay of a longer-term option; for example, an option expiring in 30 days may be valued at $5, whereas an option expiring in 90 days may be valued at $10. If all options were subject to the same rate of time decay, the 90-day option would be valued at $15 because there is three times as long to expiration. A long calendar spread is a strategy that can be used to exploit this relative time decay discrepancy. As a result, a long calendar spread typically wants sideways movement of the underlying stock so that the time decay advantage associated with the near-term option can be exploited, whereas the longer-dated option, hopefully, retains its value.

Credit Spread Basics   A credit spread can be viewed as an option position that profits when the spread difference (credit) contracts; for example, a credit spread may consist of buying an option at $5 and selling a later-term option at $10. A profit is made if the value difference between the two options declines, regardless of whether the decline is from one of the following:

- A decline in the value of the short option.
- A rise in the value of the long option.
- A greater decline in the short option value relative to the long option value.
- A greater rise in the long option value relative to the short option value.

A short calendar spread may work best using out-of-the-money options on an index such as the S&P 500 (SPX) and S&P 500 futures. Contrary to equities, the near-term options, in general, in some cases can have a lower rate of time decay than longer-term options for out-of-the-money options on an index such as the SPX. For example, for SPX options, an out-of-the-money call option expiring in 30 days may be valued at $5, whereas a call option at the same exercise price expiring in 90 days may be valued at $20. If all options were subject to the same rate of time decay, the 90-day option would be valued at $15 because there is three times as long to expiration. A short calendar spread is a strategy that can be used to exploit this relative time decay discrepancy. A large movement in the underlying instrument in either direction can result in a contraction of the spread differential.

An analysis breaking down how much premium may be earned per day based on various option expiration scenarios can be helpful in deciding whether to enter into a calendar spread. For example, a stock option with 30 days to expiration may have a value of $5, whereas the 60-day option at the same strike price may have a value of $7. In this example, the rate of option time decay in the near-term option is $0.16 a day, on average, but is only $0.12 a day on the longer-term option. However, this relationship is typically reversed for out-of-the-money options on broad-based stock indexes such as the SPX (and S&P 500 futures). For example, for out-of-the-money SPX (and S&P 500 futures) options, a put option expiring in 30 days may be valued at $2, whereas a put option expiring in 60 days at the same strike price may be valued at $7. As a result, for SPX (and S&P 500 futures) options, the rate of time decay for the period from 60 to

30 days (in the longer-term option) exceeds the rate of decay from 30 days to expiration (in the near-month option) in dollar terms. If things go according to plan, the time decay for the near-term option is $2 (100 percent) over 30 days but is $5 for the longer-term month option as it moves from 60 days to expiration to 30 days to expiration. You can arrive at the anticipated time decay for the further-dated option in 30 days by subtracting the option value of the 30-day near-term option ($2) from the 60-day option ($7) and assuming that decay will occur over the next 30 days. As a result, long calendar spreads may be advisable on stocks, but short calendar spreads may be advisable on out-of-the-money SPX (and S&P 500 futures) options.

Repeating the Process

A unique feature of the long calendar spread is its flexibility to continue a new calendar spread each month. In a calendar spread, the near-term option expires and leaves the longer-term option with an effectively reduced cost basis. After expiration of the near-term option, in a perfect scenario, the next month option with the same strike price is sold to establish a new calendar spread, and so on. Converting the initial calendar spread into a new calendar spread should, in some cases, be accomplished before the actual expiration of the near-term option. In many cases, the rolling to the next month is accomplished by offsetting the near-term option before expiration and simultaneously selling the next month option, in a rollout. A rollout strategy should occur if the near-term option is in-the-money because expiration can trigger an assignment. In this case, the near-term option is rolled to avoid an assignment.

The overall objective of a long calendar spread is to sell the time value in the near-term option, with the objective that it will decay faster than the time value in the longer-term option. To exploit this difference, you can establish a longer-term option that expires at least two months after the expiration of the shorter-dated option. This will allow at least one new calendar spread to be established after the first expiration date.

Keep in mind that you can close out an option position by offsetting it in the market-place at any time prior to expiration, and you should use your trading platform software, option calculator, and option chain to estimate option values based on your own assumptions. It is best to examine your trading platform and option chain prior to buying or selling an option. If you are nearing expiration, you can offset your current position, because there are only a few days left in the option's expiration cycle, and establish a similar position in the subsequent expiration month. You can roll to minimize risk, cut losses, and/or take into account your new view of the market. To manage a calendar spread, you may consider rolling one leg at a time to fine-tune a position and mitigate risk.

Implied Volatility

A calendar spread is sensitive to changes in the underlying stock price but also to changes in implied volatility. A calendar spread tends to widen when implied volatility rises because a change in implied volatility has a greater dollar effect on a longer-term option as expiration approaches. Similarly, a calendar spread tends to contract when implied volatility declines. The contraction is that a long calendar spreader typically wants sideways movement in an underlying stock so the stock lands at or near the strike price, but sideways movement in a stock is typically accompanied by declining implied volatility, not rising implied volatility.

An increase in implied volatility will typically help a long calendar spread, whereas a decrease in implied volatility will hurt a long calendar spread. Likewise, an increase in implied volatility will hurt a short calendar spread, whereas a decrease in implied volatility will help a short calendar spread. In general, a longer-term option is more sensitive in total points (dollars) to a change in volatility than a near-term option with the same exercise price.

Selection of Strike Price

Like a butterfly spread, an important decision is the calendar spread strike price because that determines where you achieve your maximum gain if you are long and your maximum loss if you are short. You should keep in mind that the strike price does not have to be at-the-money when it is established; for example, if XYZ stock is trading at $100 a share, the strike price does not need to be at 100 a share. Instead, if the stock is at $100 a share, you can establish the strike price, for instance, at 105 (if bullish) or 90 (if bearish). You can use your trading platform to determine whether there is more favorable pricing using a call versus a put calendar spread under your scenarios.

Assignment Risk

There is assignment risk associated with a calendar spread. Although it is generally accepted that spread trading reduces the risk of loss, spreads are subject to early assignment, and that can remove the very protection that you wanted. This can lead to margin calls and/or greater losses than anticipated. As a general rule, it is best to avoid assignment on a calendar spread or any other short option position, for that matter. An alternative to being assigned is to offset a short option in the marketplace.

When the near-term month expires, a long calendar spread will continue to have limited risk because a long option will remain. However, in a short calendar spread, when the near-term option expires, you will be holding an uncovered short option, which means unlimited risk and a margin requirement. As a result, you need to make a decision regarding your position after the near-term option expires to make sure that your position continues to meet your risk–reward parameters.

Select an Appropriate Strategy

For a stock, a near-term option often has a higher value relative to a longer-term option, based on the number of days to expiration, and this pricing discrepancy can be inflated, for example, when a company is ready to release an earnings report (or approaches another significant event). At first glance, if you believe that volatility will increase after an earnings report, you may be tempted to buy a naked call or put (or establish a long straddle or strangle), but you need to be careful because option prices may already anticipate the volatility. Assume that XYZ stock at-the-money, near-term, implied volatility is typically in the range of 45 to 50 but it explodes to 70 ahead of earnings. In that case, you may want to avoid buying a February call or put (or establish a long straddle or strangle) ahead on the earnings because others have gotten in ahead of you and driven up the near-term option premium. In this circumstance, even if you are right about an increase in volatility of the stock, you can lose money because the implied volatility of the near-term option can decline after the earnings release.

If near-term implied volatility on an option is inflated relative to implied volatility on a longer-term option at the same strike price, you may want to consider exploiting this discrepancy using a long calendar spread because it can enable you to take advantage of disproportionate volatility contraction in the near-term option. If volatility contracts after the release of earnings, for example, the near-term option value will likely decline by a greater amount than the longer-term option, generating a profit in the calendar spread.

Margin

A short calendar spread typically has an initial margin requirement for the short option leg; for example, assume that XYZ stock is currently trading at $100 a share and you sell the February/April 100 call time spread, where you buy one February 100 call and sell one April 100 call. In this case, margin may be required on the April short-call portion of the position because the February call has an earlier expiration date. Full payment is required if the spread is a long calendar spread. Margin requirements are addressed in Chapter 30.

FINAL THOUGHTS

In a long calendar spread, like a long butterfly or condor, you are trying to predict where the underlying stock will land at a future point in time (the near-term expiration date). In a short calendar spread, like a short butterfly or condor, you are trying to predict where the underlying stock will not land at a future point in time.

Profiting in a long calendar spread can be counterintuitive. When executing a long calendar spread, you sell the near-term option and buy the later-term option at a greater price. If things go according to plan, the longer-term option will decline in value because time will lapse, which is counter to what you typically want when you purchase an option. However, the calendar spread is expected to be profitable because the short near-term option is expected to decline by more than the longer-term option. Therefore, you are attempting to profit from a decline in a long option simply because the short option will decline by even more. The net decline results in an expansion of the spread. A debit spread is initially created by purchasing one option at a price greater than an option that is sold. After an option position is established, the debit is the difference between the long option value and the short option value, and it does not matter if the differential is created by an increase in the long option value, a decrease in the short option value, or a decrease in both options at a different rate. For example, if the near-term option declines by \$4 and the longer-term option declines by \$3, the spread has increased by \$1.

Whether you are most likely to profit in a long calendar spread versus a short calendar spread depends on the facts and circumstances. As a general rule, you may want to execute a long calendar spread on stocks because the rate of time decay on a near-term option often exceeds the rate of time decay on a longer-term option. A near-term option may be abnormally inflated in value, for instance, because of the anticipation of an earnings release. Conversely, the rate of time decay on a near-term option on an index, such as the SPX (and S&P 500 futures), may be less than the rate of time decay on a longer-term option. This anomaly may be caused, in part, by the existence of the volatility skew, discussed in Chapter 27, and possibly can cause a short calendar spread to be a viable strategy.

You should understand various option strategies and how they can be tailored to your view of the market and used to exploit option pricing discrepancies. In many cases, simply buying a call or put is the best strategy if you anticipate volatility to increase; however, sometimes looks can be deceiving, and that is where a calendar spread can be useful. An implied volatility increase prior to the release of the earnings report (or other significant event) can create a near-term versus longer-term pricing discrepancy, and you can use a long calendar spread to exploit this discrepancy and take advantage of a volatility contraction in the near-term option. A calendar spreader should be aware of the effects of a change in volatility.

You can modify practically any spread strategy to a calendar-type spread; for example, you can establish a calendar condor by executing a condor spread utilizing different expiration months or establish an iron condor utilizing different expiration months. In the next chapter, Chapter 18, "Diagonal Spread," we explore spread strategies in which the options expire at different times and have a different strike price.

Diagonal Spread

A *diagonal spread* strategy consists of options with different strike prices and expiration dates. To illustrate basic principles, this chapter will address a diagonal spread in which one option is at-the-money and another option is out-of-the-money, where an equal number of options are bought as are sold. Examples are presented showing results at the expiration date of the near-term option. This chapter will cover long and short diagonal spreads.

OVERVIEW

A diagonal is a spread with different strike prices and different expiration dates, such as buy one XYZ February 100 call and sell one XYZ March 110 call. A diagonal consists of either all call or all put options. There can be a large number of variations of a diagonal spread, so each should be analyzed separately to determine the risks and rewards. It is difficult to generalize about the characteristics of a diagonal spread as you can with other spread strategies. However, for the purposes of this book, it is assumed that a diagonal spread behaves mostly like a calendar spread, which was analyzed in Chapter 17.

Like a calendar spread, a diagonal spread can take advantage of near-term time decay relative to longer-term time decay or longer-term time decay relative to near-term time decay. A diagonal spread can consist of the purchase of a call (or put) option and the simultaneous sale of a call (or put) option with different strike prices and expiration dates. Likewise, a diagonal spread can consist of the sale of a call (or put) option and the simultaneous purchase of a call (or put) option with different strike prices and expiration dates.

285

In general, a long diagonal call spread (diagonal call bull spread) consists of buying a lower-strike call while selling a higher-strike call, at a debit; for example, buy one XYZ February 100 call and sell one XYZ March 110 call. A long diagonal put spread (diagonal put bear spread) consists of buying a higher-strike put while selling a lower-strike put, at a debit; for example, buy one XYZ February 100 put and sell one XYZ March 90 put. A short diagonal call spread (diagonal call bear spread) consists of selling a lower-strike call while selling a higher-strike call, at a credit; for example, sell one XYZ February 100 call and buy one XYZ March 110 call. A short diagonal put spread (diagonal put bull spread) consists of selling a higher-strike put while buying a lower-strike put, at a credit; for example, sell one XYZ February 100 put and buy one XYZ March 90 put.

Comparison of Basic Spreads

Spreads can be broadly classified as vertical, horizontal (calendar), and diagonal. You can think of the terms *vertical*, *horizontal*, and *diagonal* in terms of how they may be presented in a newspaper, where you may read the same-month option prices vertically on the page, different calendar months horizontally on the page, and different months and striking prices diagonally on the page. Table 18.1 compares these basic spread strategies according to strike price and expiration date.

It might be a good idea, at this time, to compare the broad-spread strategy definitions, as follows:

- A vertical spread (see Chapter 11) is the purchase and sale of options at different strike prices, with the same expiration date, such as sell one XYZ February 100 call and buy one XYZ February 110 call.
- A calendar spread (see Chapter 17) is the purchase and sale of options at the same strike price with different expiration dates, such as sell one XYZ February 100 call and buy one XYZ March 100 call.
- A diagonal spread is a combination of vertical and calendar spreads, in which the trader buys and sells options with different strike prices and different expiration dates, such as buy one XYZ February 100 call and sell one XYZ March 110 call.

Each of these spread strategies assumes that the options are in the same class (all calls or all puts) on the same underlying stock.

TABLE 18.1 Broad Categories of Spreads

Spread Strategy	Strike Price	Expiration Month
Vertical	Different	Same
Calendar	Same	Different
Diagonal	Different	Different

TABLE 18.2 Comparison of Vertical, Calendar, and Diagonal Spreads

Vertical Spread	Calendar Spread	Diagonal Spread
Sell in, at, or out-of-the-money call; buy farther out-of-the-money call, same expiration date	Buy near-month call, sell later-month call, same strike price	Buy (or sell) near-month call, sell (or buy) later-month call, different strike prices and expiration months
Buy in, at, or out-of-the-money put; sell farther out-of-the-money put, same expiration date	Sell near-month put, buy later-month put, same strike price	Sell (or buy) near-month put, buy (or sell) later-month put, different strike prices and expiration months

Table 18.2 provides a side-by-side comparison of vertical, calendar, and diagonal spread strategies.

Like a calendar spread, you cannot precisely predict the maximum profit, maximum loss, and break-even point when you first establish a diagonal spread position because you cannot know in advance the value of the longer-term option at the time the near-term option expires. An important factor in the value of a diagonal spread is the implied volatility of the longer-term option at the time the near-term option expires. Unfortunately, you cannot know this at the time the spread is established, and it is simply a prediction; for example, assume that XYZ stock is currently trading at $100 a share and you can purchase a February 100/March 110 diagonal call spread. If XYZ stock is trading below $100 a share at the February expiration date, the February 100 call would be worthless but the March call value would be an estimate.

Diagonalizing a Spread

Assume that XYZ stock is currently trading at $100 a share and you purchase an at-the-money call calendar spread, in which you sell a February 100 call for $5 and buy an April 100 call for $10. You are, in effect, buying the February/April 100 call time spread for a net debit of $5, or a total of $500. However, you may want to modify the position if you are slightly bullish on the stock, so you buy the April 95 call instead of the April 100 call. This modification increases your position delta, and you have diagonalized your position from a calendar spread to a diagonal spread. In a calendar spread, the options share the same strike price but have different expiration dates; however, in a diagonal spread, the strike prices also differ.

Practically any spread strategy can be converted (diagonalized) to a diagonal spread because a diagonal spread can be executed with many combinations of strike prices and expiration months. For example, a long February 100/105 vertical call spread can be diagonalized by offsetting the short February 105 call leg and replacing it with a short March 105 call. A diagonal spread in this chapter consists of options for which the strike prices and expiration dates are slightly different, such as if you were to buy one XYZ February 100 call and sell one XYZ March 105 call.

STRATEGY EXAMPLES

Following are descriptions of long and short diagonal spreads from the perspective of calls and puts. As a reminder, you can close out an option position by offsetting it in the marketplace any time prior to expiration, and the principles that are demonstrated for a stock can be applied to options on an ETF, index, and stock index futures. Appendixes A, B, and C illustrate many of the strategies covered throughout this book.

For the purposes of this chapter, it is assumed that a diagonal spread is executed with one long-term option for each short-term option and that there is only one month's difference in expiration dates and a small difference in strike price. Keep in mind that a diagonal spread can be unbalanced (ratioed) where there is an unequal number of long and short options.

Long Diagonal Call Spread

In general, a long diagonal call spread (diagonal call bull spread) consists of buying a lower-strike call while selling a higher-strike call, at a debit; for example, buy one XYZ February 100 call and sell one XYZ March 110 call. This is consistent with referring to a spread that is executed as a debit as a long position.

In a long diagonal call spread, you typically buy an at-the-money or in-the-money option and sell an out-of-the-money option. The lower-strike call can be the near-term option or the longer-term option. In this example, it is assumed that the lower-strike call is the near-term option. The maximum profit, maximum loss, and break-even point depend on the strike prices and expiration dates chosen. The maximum profit cannot be determined in advance because the value of a call at a future point in time, when the near-term call expires, is not known. Remember that the example shows results at the expiration date of the near-term option.

Example: Long Diagonal Call Spread

Assumptions: XYZ stock is trading at $100 a share in January; execute one February 100/March 110 diagonal call spread and pay a net debit of $2.50 ($250), as follows: Buy one February 100 call at $5 and sell one March 110 call at $2.50.

Strategy direction: Bullish.

Debit or credit: $250 debit.

Maximum profit: Unknown.

Maximum loss: $250 (equal to net debit).

Exercise and assignment: Can exercise long option if in-the-money; may be assigned on short option if in-the-money.

Break-even stock price: Unknown.

Maximum profit achieved: Stock appreciably above strike price of 110 at February expiration.

Maximum loss achieved: Stock appreciably below strike price of 100 at February expiration.

Profit (loss) if stock unchanged: Unknown.

Stock unchanged: If XYZ stock is at $100 at February expiration, the February 100 call is worthless but the March call has value. You can estimate the value of the March option at the February expiration date (assuming that all factors remain the same) by using an option calculator or option chain. The March 110 option, originally at $2.50 ($250), is estimated to be at $1 ($100) on the February expiration date.

TABLE 18.3 Long Diagonal Call Spread Values at February Expiration

XYZ Stock Price ($)	Long February 100 Call	Short March 110 Call (Estimated)	Spread	Cost of Spread	Spread Profit (Loss)	Profit (Loss) Percentage
75	0	0	0	250	(250)	(100)
80	0	10	10	250	(240)	(96)
85	0	20	20	250	(230)	(92)
90	0	20	20	250	(230)	(92)
95	0	50	50	250	(200)	(80)
100	0	100	100	250	(150)	(60)
105	500	300	200	250	(50)	(20)
110	1,000	500	500	250	250	100
115	1,500	700	800	250	550	220
120	2,000	1,100	900	250	650	260
125	2,500	1,500	1,000	250	750	300

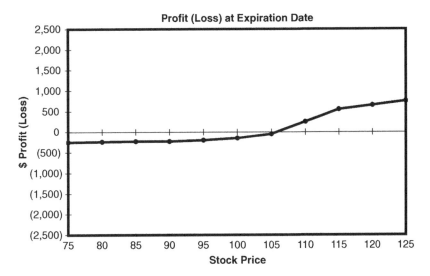

FIGURE 18.1 Long Diagonal Call Spread

TABLE 18.4   Summary of Greeks: February Expiration

Option	Delta	Gamma	Theta	Vega
Long 1 February 100 call	$53	$2.30	−$15	$12
Short 1 March 110 call	−$20	−$1.00	$7	−$10
Position	$33		−$8	$2

Stock slightly below strike: If XYZ stock closes slightly below $100 on the February expiration date, the February call is worthless, but there will be a gain on the March 110 call, the exact amount of which cannot be determined in advance.

Stock slightly above strike: If the XYZ stock closes slightly above $100 a share at the February expiration, the February call will be in-the-money, and the exact amount of the spread cannot be determined in advance.

Stock plunges: If XYZ stock plunges as of the February expiration date, the long February 100 call will be worthless, and the short March 110 call may be worth near zero. In this situation, you will have a loss for almost the entire $250 debit initially paid.

Stock surges: If XYZ stock surges as of the February expiration date, both the February and March 105 calls will be trading near their intrinsic values and parity (the short March call may be worth slightly more than its intrinsic value). In this situation, you will have a gain for the difference in strike prices (net of the premium) plus any extrinsic value of the March option.

Greeks: Table 18.4 contains sample Greeks converted to dollars at the time the position is established.

Position would reflect a gain from stock rise (delta) and volatility (vega) expansion. Position would reflect a loss from stock decline (delta), time decay (theta), and volatility (vega) contraction. Gain is $33 from XYZ stock rising to $101; loss is $8 from one day of time decay.

Later expiration: The option prices and Greeks will differ if the longer-term expiration is at a later date.

Exercise and assignment: For the February 100/March 110 diagonal call spread, if your short call is in-the-money, then you may be assigned on your short call and will be required to sell the XYZ stock at $110 per share. By exercising your long call, you can buy shares at $100 per share.

Long Diagonal Put Spread

A long diagonal put spread (diagonal put bear spread) consists of buying a higher-strike put while selling a lower-strike put, at a debit; for example, buy one XYZ February 100 put and sell one XYZ March 90 put. This is consistent with referring to a spread that is executed as a debit as a long position.

In a long diagonal put spread, you typically buy an at-the-money or in-the-money near-term option and sell an out-of-the-money option. The higher-strike put can be the near-term option or the longer-term option. In this example, it is assumed that the higher-strike put is the near-term option. The maximum profit, maximum loss, and break-even point depend on the strike prices and expiration dates chosen. The maximum profit cannot be determined in advance because the value of a put at a future point in time, when the near-term call expires, is not known. Remember that the example shows results at the expiration date of the near-term option.

Example: Long Diagonal Put Spread

Assumptions: XYZ stock is trading at $100 a share in January; execute one February 100/March 90 diagonal put spread and pay a net debit of $2.50 ($250), as follows: Buy one February 100 put at $5 and sell one March 90 put at $2.50.

Strategy direction: Bearish.

Debit or credit: $250 debit.

Maximum profit: Unknown.

Maximum loss: $250 (equal to net debit).

Exercise and assignment: Can exercise long option if in-the-money; may be assigned on short option if in-the-money.

Break-even stock price: Unknown.

Maximum profit achieved: Stock appreciably below strike price of 90 at February expiration.

Maximum loss achieved: Stock appreciably above strike price of 100 at February expiration.

Profit (loss) if stock unchanged: Unknown.

TABLE 18.5 Long Diagonal Put Spread Values at February Expiration

XYZ Stock Price ($)	Long February 100 Put	Short March 90 Put (Estimated)	Spread	Cost of Spread	Spread Profit (Loss)	Profit (Loss) Percentage
75	2,500	1,500	1,000	250	750	300
80	2,000	1,100	900	250	650	260
85	1,500	700	800	250	550	220
90	1,000	500	500	250	250	100
95	500	300	200	250	(50)	(20)
100	0	100	100	250	(150)	(60)
105	0	50	50	250	(200)	(80)
110	0	20	20	250	(230)	(92)
115	0	20	20	250	(230)	(92)
120	0	10	10	250	(240)	(96)
125	0	0	0	250	(250)	(100)

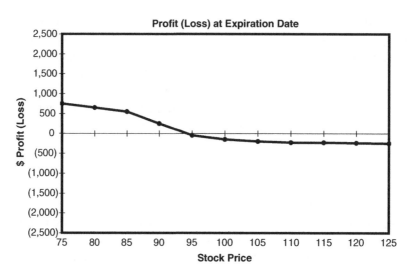

FIGURE 18.2 Long Diagonal Put Spread

Stock unchanged: If XYZ stock is at $100 at February expiration, the February 100 put is worthless but the March put has value. You can estimate the value of the March option at the February expiration date (assuming that all factors remain the same) by using an option calculator or option chain. The March 90 option, originally at $2.50 ($250), is estimated to be at $1 ($100) on the February expiration date.

Stock slightly above strike: If XYZ stock closes slightly above $100 on the February expiration date, the February put will be worthless, but there would be a gain on the March 90 put, the exact amount of which cannot be determined in advance.

Stock slightly below strike: If the XYZ stock closes slightly below $100 a share at the February expiration, the February put will be in-the-money, and the exact amount of the spread cannot be determined in advance.

Stock surges: If XYZ stock surges as of the February expiration date, the long February 100 put will be worthless, and the short March 90 put may be worth near zero. In this situation, you will have a loss for almost the entire $250 debit initially paid.

Stock plunges: If XYZ stock plunges as of the February expiration date, both the February and March puts would be trading near their intrinsic values and parity (the short March put may be worth slightly more than its intrinsic value). In this situation, you will have a gain for the difference in strike prices (net of the premium) plus any extrinsic value of the March option.

Greeks: Table 18.6 contains sample Greeks converted to dollars at the time the position is established.

Position would reflect a gain from stock decline (delta) and volatility (vega) expansion. Position would reflect a loss from stock rise (delta), time decay

TABLE 18.6 Summary of Greeks: February Expiration

Option	Delta	Gamma	Theta	Vega
Long 1 February 100 put	−$53	$2.30	−$15	$12
Short 1 March 90 put	$20	−$1.00	$7	−$10
Position	−$33		−$8	$2

(theta), and volatility (vega) contraction. Loss is $33 from XYZ stock rising to $101; loss is $8 from one day of time decay.

Later expiration: The option prices and Greeks will differ if the longer-term expiration is at a later date.

Exercise and assignment: For the February 100/March 90 diagonal put spread, if your short put is in-the-money, then you may be assigned on your short put and will be required to buy the XYZ stock at $90 per share. By exercising your long put, you can sell shares at $100 per share.

Short Diagonal Call Spread

A short diagonal call spread (diagonal call bear spread) consists of selling a lower-strike call while selling a higher-strike call, at a credit; for example, sell one XYZ February 100 call and buy one XYZ March 110 call. This is consistent with referring to a spread that is executed as a credit as a short position.

In a short diagonal call spread, you typically sell an at-the-money near-term option and buy an out-of-the-money option. The lower-strike call can be the near-term option or the longer-term option. In this example, it is assumed that the lower-strike call is the near-term option. The maximum profit, maximum loss, and break-even point depend on the strike prices and expiration dates chosen. The maximum profit cannot be determined in advance because the value of a call at a future point in time, when the near-term call expires, is not known. Remember that the example shows results at the expiration date of the near-term option.

Example: Short Diagonal Call Spread

Assumptions: XYZ stock is trading at $100 a share in January; execute one February 100/March 110 diagonal call spread and collect a net credit of $2.50 ($250), as follows: Sell one February 100 call at $5 and buy one March 110 call at $2.50.

Strategy direction: Bearish.

Debit or credit: $250 credit.

Maximum profit: $250 (equal to net credit).

Maximum loss: Unknown.

Exercise and assignment: Can exercise long option if in-the-money; may be assigned on short option if in-the-money.

Break-even stock price: Unknown.

Maximum profit achieved: Stock appreciably below strike price of 100 at February expiration.

Maximum loss achieved: Stock appreciably above strike price of 110 at February expiration.

Profit (loss) if stock unchanged: Unknown.

Stock unchanged: If XYZ stock is at $100 at February expiration, the February 100 call is worthless but the March call has value. You can estimate the value of the March option at the February expiration date (assuming that all factors remain the same) by using an option calculator or option chain. The March 110

TABLE 18.7 Short Diagonal Call Spread Values at February Expiration

XYZ Stock Price ($)	Short February 100 Call	Long March 110 Call (Estimated)	Spread	Spread Credit	Spread Profit (Loss)	Profit (Loss) Percentage
75	0	0	0	250	250	100
80	0	10	10	250	240	96
85	0	20	20	250	230	92
90	0	20	20	250	230	92
95	0	50	50	250	200	80
100	0	100	100	250	150	60
105	500	300	200	250	50	20
110	1,000	500	500	250	(250)	(100)
115	1,500	700	800	250	(550)	(220)
120	2,000	1,100	900	250	(650)	(260)
125	2,500	1,500	1,000	250	(750)	(300)

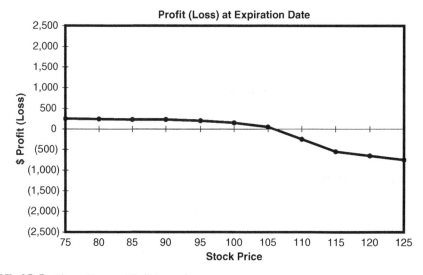

FIGURE 18.3 Short Diagonal Call Spread

TABLE 18.8 Summary of Greeks: February Expiration

Option	Delta	Gamma	Theta	Vega
Short 1 February 100 call	−$53	−$2.30	$15	−$12
Long 1 March 110 call	$20	$1.00	−$7	$10
Position	−$33		$8	−$2

option, originally at $2.50 ($250), is estimated to be at $1 ($100) on the February expiration date.

Stock slightly below strike: If XYZ stock closes slightly below $100 on the February expiration date, the February call will be worthless; however, there will be a loss on the March 110 call, the exact amount of which cannot be determined in advance.

Stock slightly above strike: If the XYZ stock closes slightly above $100 a share at the February expiration, the February call will be in-the-money, and the exact amount of the spread cannot be determined in advance.

Stock plunges: If XYZ stock plunges as of the February expiration date, the short February 100 call will be worthless, and the long March 110 call may be worth near zero. In this situation, you will have a gain for almost the entire $250 credit.

Stock surges: If XYZ stock surges as of the February expiration date, both the February and March 105 calls will be trading near their intrinsic values and parity (the long March call may be worth slightly more than its intrinsic value). In this situation, you will have a loss for the difference in strike prices (net of the premium) plus any extrinsic value of the March option.

Greeks: Table 18.8 contains sample Greeks converted to dollars at the time the position is established.

Position would reflect a gain from stock decline (delta), time decay (theta), and volatility (vega) contraction. Position would reflect a loss from stock rise (delta) and volatility (vega) expansion. Loss is $33 from XYZ stock rising to $101; gain is $8 from one day of time decay.

Later expiration: The option prices and Greeks will differ if the longer-term expiration is at a later date.

Exercise and assignment: For the February 100 /March 110 diagonal call spread, if your short call is in-the-money, then you may be assigned on your short call and will be required to sell the XYZ stock at $100 per share. By exercising your long call, you can buy shares at $110 per share.

Short Diagonal Put Spread

A short diagonal put spread (diagonal put bull spread) consists of selling a higher-strike put, while buying a lower-strike put, at a credit; for example, sell one XYZ February 100 put and buy one XYZ March 90 put. This is consistent with referring to a spread that is executed as a credit as a short position.

In a short diagonal put spread, you typically sell an at-the-money near-term option and buy an out-of-the-money option. The higher-strike put can be the near-term option or the longer-term option. In this example, it is assumed that the higher-strike put is the near-term option. The maximum profit, maximum loss, and break-even point depend on the strike prices and expiration dates chosen. The maximum profit cannot be determined in advance because the value of a call at a future point in time, when the near-term call expires, is not known. Remember that the example shows results at the expiration date of the near-term option.

Example: Short Diagonal Put Spread

Assumptions: XYZ stock is trading at $100 a share in January; execute one February 100/March 90 diagonal put spread and collect a net credit of $2.50 ($250), as follows: Sell one February 100 put at $5 and buy one March 90 put at $2.50.
Strategy direction: Bearish.
Debit or credit: $250 credit.
Maximum profit: $250 (equal to net credit).
Maximum loss: Unknown.
Exercise and assignment: Can exercise long option if in-the-money; may be assigned on short option if in-the-money.
Break-even stock price: Unknown.
Maximum profit achieved: Stock appreciably above strike price of 100 at February expiration.
Maximum loss achieved: Stock appreciably below strike price of 90 at February expiration.
Profit (loss) if stock unchanged: Unknown.

TABLE 18.9 Short Diagonal Put Spread Values at February Expiration

XYZ Stock Price ($)	Short February 100 Put	Long March 90 Put (Estimated)	Spread	Spread Credit	Spread Profit (Loss)	Profit (Loss) Percentage
75	2,500	1,500	1,000	250	(750)	(300)
80	2,000	1,100	900	250	(650)	(260)
85	1,500	700	800	250	(550)	(220)
90	1,000	500	500	250	(250)	(100)
95	500	300	200	250	50	20
100	0	100	100	250	150	60
105	0	50	50	250	200	80
110	0	20	20	250	230	92
115	0	20	20	250	230	92
120	0	10	10	250	240	96
125	0	0	0	250	250	100

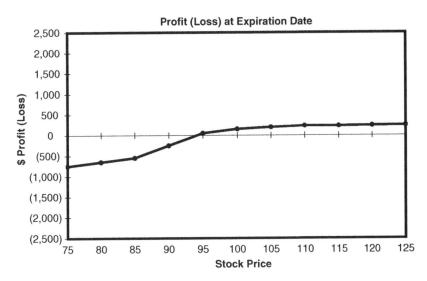

FIGURE 18.4 Short Diagonal Put Spread

Stock unchanged: If XYZ stock is at $100 at February expiration, the February 100 put is worthless but the March put has value. You can estimate the value of the March option at the February expiration date (assuming that all factors remain the same) by using an option calculator or option chain. The March 90 option, originally at $2.50 ($250), is estimated to be at $1 ($100) on the February expiration date.

Stock slightly above strike: If XYZ stock closes slightly above $100 on the February expiration date, the February put will be worthless; however, there will be a loss on the March 90 put, the exact amount of which cannot be determined in advance.

Stock slightly below strike: If the XYZ stock closes slightly below $100 a share at the February expiration, the February put will be in-the-money, and the exact amount of the spread cannot be determined in advance.

Stock surges: If XYZ stock surges as of the February expiration date, the short February 100 put will be worthless, and the long March 90 put may be worth near zero. In this situation, you will have a gain for almost the entire $250 credit.

Stock plunges: If XYZ stock plunges as of the February expiration date, both the February and March puts will be trading near their intrinsic values and parity (the short March put may be worth slightly more than its intrinsic value). In this situation, you will have a loss for the difference in strike prices (net of the premium) plus any extrinsic value of the March option.

Greeks: Table 18.10 contains sample Greeks converted to dollars at the time the position is established.

Position would reflect a gain from stock rise (delta), time decay (theta), and volatility (vega) contraction. Position would reflect a loss from stock decline

TABLE 18.10   Summary of Greeks: February Expiration

Option	Delta	Gamma	Theta	Vega
Short 1 February 100 put	$53	−$2.30	$15	−$12
Long 1 March 90 put	−$20	$1.00	−$7	$10
Position	$33		$8	−$2

(delta) and volatility (vega) expansion. Gain is $33 from XYZ stock rising to $101; gain is $8 from one day of time decay.

Later expiration: The option prices and Greeks will differ if the longer-term expiration is at a later date.

Exercise and assignment: For the February 100/March 90 diagonal put spread, if your short put is in-the-money, then you may be assigned on your short put and will be required to buy the XYZ stock at $100 per share.

BEYOND THE BASICS

Double Diagonal Spread

Some option software may refer to a double diagonal spread in addition to a diagonal spread. In such a case, a double diagonal spread may consist of a diagonal spread option in which there is a difference by at least two strike prices and two expiration dates, such as buy an XYZ February 100 call and sell an XYZ July 110 call. A double diagonal spread can offer additional unique option strategies and help create your own option strategies to match your risk profile. There are many double diagonal possibilities from which to choose to meet your risk profile and view of the market. A double diagonal spread can be executed where there is a one-to-one ratio of options sold versus purchased, or it can be ratioed (unbalanced) so that a different number of options are bought versus sold. There are many variations of a double diagonal spread, so it is difficult to provide general rules regarding how each spread will react to changing market conditions. For example, a double diagonal spread can be executed with many combinations of strike prices and expiration months.

Repeating the Process

Similar to a calendar spread, a potentially attractive feature of a short diagonal spread is its flexibility to continue a new diagonal spread each month. In a perfect scenario, the near-term option expires and leaves the longer-term option with effectively a reduced cost basis. After expiration of the near-term option, the next month option (with the same or different strike price) can be sold to establish a new diagonal spread, and so on. When the near-month option expires, you can continue to stay long the longer-term option and sell another near-term option, and the process can be repeated. Establishing the longer-term option at least two months after the expiration of the near-term option allows at least one new diagonal spread to be established after the first expiration date.

FINAL THOUGHTS

Learning diagonal spread strategies can enable you to fine-tune how you approach the markets to meet your risk–reward profile and forecast because each strategy can offer unique risks, rewards, margin, time frames, probabilities of success, and volatility characteristics. This can help you tailor your strategy to your situation. The diagonal spread can be a strong addition to your advanced option strategies. Do not forget that it is important to trade options on an underlying stock that you understand. If your trading platform defines an option strategy in one way, you should gain an understanding of how that trading platform intends to execute the trade.

You can modify practically any spread strategy into a diagonal-type spread; for example, you can establish a diagonal spread by executing a vertical spread but utilize different expiration months, or establish an iron condor but utilize a combination of strike prices and different expiration months. Keep in mind that a diagonal spread can be executed where there is a one-to-one ratio of options sold versus purchased, or it can be unbalanced, so that a different number of options are bought versus sold. The spread strategies covered thus far have assumed that the underlying stock was not owned, but that does not always have to be the case. In the next chapter, Chapter 19, "Covered Call," we explore selling a call while owning the underlying stock.

Covered Call

A *covered call* strategy consists of owning stock and selling at-the-money or out-of-the-money calls based on the shares owned. Selling a covered call means you can benefit from time decay and/or volatility contraction while you wait for the next move in the stock. To illustrate basic principles, this chapter assumes that a covered call is executed when there is a one-to-one ratio of options sold relative to the number of shares owned. This chapter provides an overview and comprehensive example and then describes how a covered call is equivalent to an uncovered put, how to choose the appropriate option to sell, how to repeat the process (rolling), and how to understand risks.

OVERVIEW

A covered call is a strategy in which you own stock and then sell at-the-money or out-of-the-money calls in proportion to the shares owned. For example, if you own 1,000 shares of XYZ stock, you can write up to 10 call options in a covered call transaction. A *buy-write* (also called a *covered call write*) strategy is a version of a covered-call strategy in which the stock purchase and option sale occur as part of the same transaction. Your trading platform may include the ability to execute a buy-right order; for example, if a stock is trading at $100 a share and a call is selling at $2 ($200), you can enter a single order to execute the transaction at $98 or better. As a result of entering a limit order in this manner, you will not be executed on only one side of the transaction unless the other side of the transaction is also executed. When you sell a covered call, you can potentially profit from three sources:

1. A rise in the underlying stock,
2. Dividends on the stock,
3. Option premium.

An option position is typically considered covered, for this purpose, if there is a fully offsetting opposite market position such as the long stock. Keep in mind that a disadvantage of a covered call or buy-write is the inability to earn interest on the proceeds used to purchase the stock. You are, however, entitled to receive dividends if you own the stock.

A covered option has unlimited risk (although the stock cannot go below zero). For example, if you are long 1,000 shares of a stock trading at $100 a share and you sell a call at $2 ($200), and the stock price plunges to $50 a share, you lose $50,000 on the long stock, and the premium collected would only be a small consolation. As explained later in the chapter, a covered call is the equivalent position to a short (uncovered) put.

To exit an option position, you can offset it in a closing transaction, wait for assignment (if it is in-the-money), or let it expire worthless (if it is out-of-the-money at expiration). Because a covered call is supported (covered) dollar for dollar by the underlying shares, many brokerage firms permit a covered call to be written in an IRA.

If you are short a call and are assigned, you are forced to sell the underlying stock at the exercise price, but you already own the shares. A covered call can be an effective strategy to automatically sell into strength. An American-style option can be exercised by the option holder (buyer) at any time up until the expiration date, whereas a European-style option can be exercised only at expiration. Equity options are American-style expirations.

An attraction of the covered-call strategy is that, ideally, calls can be sold every month, every couple of months, or every quarter so that you have an opportunity to collect additional premium. If the call option expires worthless, you may want to consider selling another call expiring in the next month or quarter to earn additional premium. In that case, you have already earned premium from the previous call sale, and you can earn additional premium on the second call sale, and so on. If the original call option has not yet expired, you can roll the call option by offsetting it in the marketplace and selling a call option expiring in the subsequent month. The idea is that this strategy can be used each month or quarter to earn premium. Keep in mind that a covered call as well as most options strategies can also be executed using LEAPS.

A *covered put* is the mirror image of the covered call. A covered put is a strategy in which you are short stock and then sell at-the-money or out-of-the-money puts in proportion to the shares shorted; for example, if you are short 1,000 shares of XYZ stock, you can write up to 10 put options in a covered put transaction. Table 19.1 provides a summary of a covered call and put.

Remember that an option position is considered covered if there is a fully offsetting opposite market position.

STRATEGY EXAMPLE

Following are descriptions and examples of a covered call. As a reminder, you can close out an option position by offsetting it in the marketplace any time prior to expiration, and the principles that are demonstrated for a stock can be applied to options on an ETF,

TABLE 19.1 Summary: Covered Call and Put

Spread Strategy	Strategy Description	Risk–Reward	Debit or Credit	Option Breakeven at Expiration	Position Breakeven at Expiration	Greatest Profit at Expiration
Covered call	Long stock, typically sell at-the-money or out-of-the-money call	Limited profit, unlimited risk	Credit from short call, debit from stock	Strike price plus credit	Original stock price minus credit	Stock at or above strike price
Covered put	Short stock, typically sell at-the-money or out-of-the-money put	Limited profit, unlimited risk	Credit from short put, credit from stock	Strike price minus credit	Original stock price plus credit	Stock at or below strike price

index, and stock index futures. Appendixes A, B, and C illustrate many of the strategies covered throughout this book.

To illustrate basic principles, this chapter discusses a covered call in which the call is slightly-out-of-the-money and is proportionate to the number of shares owned. You should review Chapter 9, "Short Call," if you need a refresher on the dynamics of selling a call.

Covered Call

Selling a covered call can enable you to profit in a sideways market, take advantage of an anticipated decline in volatility, and share in some stock appreciation. A covered call is primarily bullish but can profit in a neutral environment.

A covered call has limited profit potential and unlimited risk. The maximum profit of a covered call, at expiration, is equal to the out-of-the-money amount plus the premium and occurs when the underlying stock is at or above the exercise price. In this case, you profit from the option premium plus a rise in the underlying stock up to the strike price. The maximum loss is unlimited because of the potential decline in the stock price.

The break-even point of the call itself occurs when the stock, at expiration, is at the strike price plus the credit. The break-even point of the combined stock and call position is where the stock, at expiration, is at the original price of the stock minus the premium credit.

Time decay reduces the call value, benefiting the seller; an increase in volatility increases the call value; and a decrease in volatility reduces the call value. A credit is reflected in your account for the premium, but a covered call is, in total, a debit transaction because of the purchase of the stock. A covered call may be permitted in an IRA.

For example, if you own 100 shares of XYZ stock trading at $100 a share, you may be able to sell a call at a strike price of 105 and collect $2 ($200). Your maximum profit is achieved when the stock closes at or above the 105 strike price at expiration. If the stock closes at $105 at expiration, the short call expires worthless, and the long stock produces a profit of $500, the option is not assigned, and you can continue holding the stock. If the stock is above $105 at expiration and you choose not to offset the call, you will be assigned and required to sell the 100 shares at $105; however, because you already own shares, you can fulfill the terms of the assignment with the stock you already own. Your profit would be $500 from the rise in the price of the stock plus the $200 premium collected. If the price of XYZ stock is below the strike price of 105 at the expiration date, the call is worthless, you can retain the premium, and you can write another covered call and collect additional premium. If the stock rises to $103 a share, you can collect, for example, an additional $1.50 at the 110 strike price so that the total premium collected is $3.50. This process can be repeated every month, every couple of months, or every quarter.

Example: Covered Call

Assumptions: XYZ stock is trading at $100 a share in January, and you own 100 shares: Sell one February 105 call and collect $2 ($200).
Strategy direction: Neutral (trading range).
Debit or credit: $200 credit for call.
Maximum profit: $700 (out-of-the-money amount plus premium).
Maximum loss: Unlimited.
Exercise and assignment: May be assigned on short option if in-the-money.
Break-even stock price: $98 (stock price minus premium).
Maximum profit achieved: Stock at or above strike price of 105.
Maximum loss achieved: Loss increases as stock declines below break-even point.

TABLE 19.2 Covered Call

XYZ Stock Price ($)	Stock Gain (Loss)	Short Call	Premium Collected	Position Profit (Loss)
75	(2,500)	0	200	(2,300)
80	(2,000)	0	200	(1,800)
85	(1,500)	0	200	(1,300)
90	(1,000)	0	200	(800)
95	(500)	0	200	(300)
100	0	0	200	200
105	500	0	200	700
110	1,000	(500)	200	700
115	1,500	(1,000)	200	700
120	2,000	(1,500)	200	700
125	2,500	(2,000)	200	700

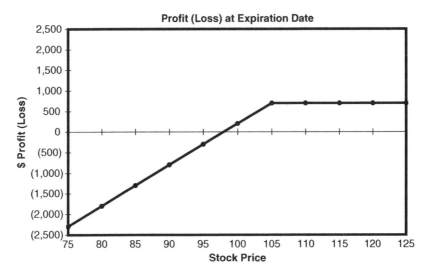

FIGURE 19.1 Covered Call

Profit (loss) if stock unchanged: $200 gain (premium).

Greeks: Table 19.3 contains sample Greeks converted to dollars at the time the position is established.

Position would reflect a gain from stock rise (delta), time decay (theta), and volatility (vega) contraction. Position would reflect a loss from stock decline (delta) and volatility (vega) expansion. Gain is $58 from XYZ stock rising to $101; gain is $14 from one day of time decay.

Later expiration: The option price and Greeks will differ if expiration is at a later date; for example, if the option expires in March, instead of February, the price of the March 105 call could be $5 (instead of $2). Example Greeks are given in Table 19.4.

Gain is $60 from XYZ stock rising to $101; gain is $10 from one day of time decay.

Exercise and assignment: If the strike price is in-the-money at the expiration date, then you may be assigned on your short call and will be required to sell the XYZ stock at $105 per share. However, if you are assigned, you are protected by the long stock.

TABLE 19.3 Summary of Greeks: February Expiration

Option	Delta	Gamma	Theta	Vega
XYZ stock	$100	$0	$0	$0
Short 1 February 105 call	−$42	−$2.00	$14	−$11
Position	$58		$14	−$11

TABLE 19.4 Summary of Greeks: March Expiration

Option	Delta	Gamma	Theta	Vega
XYZ stock	$100	$0	$0	$0
Short 1 March 105 call	−$40	−$1.20	$10	−$15
Position	$60		$10	−$15

The triple combination of stock appreciation, dividends, and premium income can make selling covered calls attractive. The stock dividend can be added to the premium income in calculating your potential return. If, for example, you sell an out-of-the-money call and collect $2 each month on a $100 stock, it will produce, assuming that all other factors remain constant, an annual return of 24 percent from the premium alone. If the underlying stock pays an annual dividend of 2 percent, you have a potential return of 26 percent, in addition to the underlying stock appreciation. As a result, selling covered calls can have a lot of upside potential. Of course, this example makes a lot of assumptions, such as the underlying stock fluctuating in an ideal fashion so that you can sell options each month and collect a reasonable premium while the stock moves sideways (scenarios that normally do not go hand in hand).

BEYOND THE BASICS

If you already own stock, and volatility in the marketplace rises dramatically, you may want to consider selling a covered call because the option premium may be attractive and you can profit from a decline in volatility (theta). If implied volatility declines after the call is sold, assuming that all other factors remain constant, a call option will decrease in value.

Selling a covered call can be an effective way to automatically sell into strength and trim a portfolio as stocks rise; for example, assume that you own XYZ stock that is trading at $100, and you sell a covered call at a strike price of 100 and collect $5 ($500) for the option. If the stock rises above $105 a share, you automatically sell the stock at a 105 strike price, plus you keep the premium.

Equivalent Position to Uncovered Put

The covered call is often described as popular, conservative, safe, simple, and a smart way to make money. However, referring to the typical covered call in this manner un-fortunately can be misleading, especially when you realize that a covered call has approximately the same amount of risk as a naked put. Selling an at-the-money covered call, in effect, is the equivalent position of selling a naked at-the-money put. When you sell a naked put, you benefit if the stock rises but can lose substantially if the stock declines substantially. For example, assume that in January, XYZ stock is trading at $100

TABLE 19.5 Covered Call versus Uncovered Put

XYZ Stock Price ($)	Stock Gain (Loss)	Call Premium Collected	Covered Call Position	Short Put Value	Put Premium Collected	Put Profit (Loss)
75	(2,500)	500	(2,000)	2,500	500	(2,000)
80	(2,000)	500	(1,500)	2,000	500	(1,500)
85	(1,500)	500	(1,000)	1,500	500	(1,000)
90	(1,000)	500	(500)	1,000	500	(500)
95	(500)	500	0	500	500	0
100	0	500	500	0	500	500
105	500	500	500	0	500	500
110	1,000	500	500	0	500	500
115	1,500	500	500	0	500	500
120	2,000	500	500	0	500	500
125	2,500	500	500	0	500	500

a share. Table 19.5 shows values at the expiration date under various scenarios for an at-the-money covered call for $5 in comparison to selling a February 100 put for $5. This example demonstrates that an at-the-money naked put is the equivalent position of an at-the-money covered call, and vice versa.

In this example, the gain or loss for the February 100 covered call (in the column labeled "Covered Call Position") is identical to the profit or loss of the February 100 naked put at expiration (in the column labeled "Put Profit (Loss)"). This example assumes that the call and put options are at-the-money. If the options, instead, were out-of-the-money, there would be a similar risk profile but the numbers would not be exactly the same. As a reminder, for simplicity throughout this book, examples are presented in which it is assumed that call premiums are symmetrical with put premiums so that the strike price is equidistant from the price of the underlying stock price. In reality, call prices on stocks are typically higher in comparison to put prices when the call and put are at an equal distance from the price of the underlying stock. As a result, a covered call and an out-of-the-money naked put should produce similar results but may not be exactly the same.

Choosing an Option to Sell

The strike price you choose is an important ingredient in determining the potential risk and reward. Selling an out-of-the-money covered call means that you can benefit from time decay. You should use your trading platform to determine the Greeks, including the probability of being assigned on the covered call position. The further the call is out-of-the-money, the lower the premium, the lower the delta, and the lower the probability of assignment. If you want to retain your stock, you should select a strike price that is far-out-of-the-money. If you are comfortable selling your stock near its current value, then you should consider selling an at-the-money option. Also, you also need to decide how far out in time the option will expire. In general, the near-term (front) month is often used to take advantage of time decay, but a longer-term option can be used. One of the advantages of using a longer-term option is that you collect greater premium and incur lower commission charges because you adjust the position less often.

The strike price and the time frame you choose should be determined based on your projection of the movement of the stock. For example, if you expect that the stock could easily rise 5 points over the next 30 days, then you may want to sell an option at least 5 or 10 points above the current price.

There are advantages and disadvantages to selling an at-the-money versus a slightly-out-of-the-money versus a far-out-of-the-money option in a covered call strategy. If you sell an at-the-money option, you will collect relatively more premium, but you will have a higher probability of being assigned; if you sell a slightly-out-of-the-money call option, you may collect a reasonable amount of premium, but there will still be reasonable assignment risk; and if you sell a far-out-of-the-money option, you will collect the least amount of premium, but you will have the least probability of being assigned.

Repeating the Process: Rolling

A covered-call strategy can be used every month, every couple of months, or every quarter so that you have an opportunity to collect additional premium. When transitioning from the original option to the new call option, you can wait until the initial call option expires and then sell a new call option. Alternatively, if the original call option is valued near zero and has not yet expired, you may want to roll the position by offsetting the option in the marketplace and establishing a call option in a subsequent month. A covered call can be viewed as a way to buy stock and to finance it, in part, by the sale of calls.

Rolling can be part of your overall strategy to earn income on a monthly or quarterly basis; for example, assume that it is January and you sell a February 105 call option for $2 while the stock is selling for $100. If the stock declines to $95 near the February expiration date, you can offset the February 105 call and replace it with a March 100 call, collecting another $2. If the stock remains at $100 near the February expiration date, you can offset the February 105 call and replace it with a March 105 call, collecting another $2 (of course, you will have to pay a small premium to exit the February call position). If the stock rises to $104 near the March expiration date, you can offset the March 105 call and replace it with an April 110 call, collecting a little less than $2.

Understanding Risks

The manner in which a covered call is described by the popular media, in many cases, is as a win-win proposition: If the stock rises, you profit from the gain in the stock as well as the call premium; if the stock declines, the option premium cushions the decline, and you are better off than if it had never been written. The flaw is that when the stock decline exceeds the premium collected, you lose money. In such a situation, you may feel good about your decision because you made money from the option, but when you look at your brokerage account, you will see that you have actually lost money in the process. The problem with the covered call strategy is that it assumes an oversimplification regarding how the underlying stock moves on a daily, weekly, and monthly basis. Rarely do stocks move in a predictable fashion so that we can simply collect premium every month on an option. If it were that simple, then everyone would be getting rich.

The Whipsaw   If the stock surges above the strike price, you should, in general, not offset the option without also selling the stock because if the stock subsequently plunges, you may have a loss on the option and on the stock. Likewise, if the stock initially plunges, you should not sell the stock without also offsetting the option because if the stock subsequently surges, you may have a loss on the option and on the stock.

The management of covered calls (and any option position, for that matter) at times is not always easy; for example, assume that in January, you purchase 1,000 shares of XYZ stock at $100 a share and sell 10 February 105 calls at $2 ($200) each. If the stock surges to $110 a share, the question becomes whether you should offset the short option at a loss and continue to hold the stock or allow the stock to be called away when the call is assigned, thus producing a profit of $7,000. If you decide to offset the option and continue to hold the stock, you may be able to sell a call for the next expiration month at a higher strike price (e.g., a March 115 call at $2). If the stock declines from $110 to $100 a share, you will need to decide whether you should offset the March 115 call at a profit or roll the March 110 call to a March 105 call, or roll, for example, to the April 110 call (to collect more premium). In such cases, it is usually best to not overtrade and to avoid chasing the market.

Match Strategy to Your Risk Profile   Some confusion may result because some strategies are more tailored toward protecting existing portfolios, whereas other strategies are designed to profit without regard to existing holdings. An outstanding strategy for a portfolio manager or hedge fund, such as selling a covered call, may be a risky strategy for the average investor. For example, a covered call can be an appropriate strategy for a portfolio manager because he may already own shares for the long run and, by selling a covered call, the manager can, in effect, automatically sell the stock as the stock rises and hits the manager's price target. The portfolio manager may not be as concerned with a market decline because he may have cash sitting on the sidelines waiting to invest, and his primary concern may be to beat various benchmarks and the performance of other managers. As an aside, portfolio managers have a tendency to sell covered calls against their existing positions and buy protective puts, thus driving down the price of calls and inflating the value of puts on broad-based indexes. The consequences of this tendency are discussed in Part Four, Chapters 23 to 26.

Conversely, the average investor is not operating under similar circumstances and is unlikely to have a broad-based portfolio of long-term stocks. As a result, the average investor selling a covered call may find himself with limited upside potential and a great deal of risk to the downside. If you own stocks that have been moving sideways or underperforming, and you do not have a lot of confidence that they will rise, you might be led to believe that you should write a covered call because the income that you will earn from the covered call option can earn money while you wait for your stock to rise. The faulty logic in this is that it implies you somehow own stocks for which you do not have confidence. If you own a stock that you do not think will rise, maybe you should consider selling that stock outright, instead of writing a covered call against it. Stock can decline in value, and you have risk by continuing to hold the stock.

Uncovered Put

Remember that a covered put is the mirror image of a covered call. A covered put is a strategy in which you are short stock and then sell at-the-money or out-of-the-money puts in proportion to the shares shorted. Selling a covered put can enable you to profit in a sideways market, take advantage of an anticipated decline in volatility, and share in some stock decline. A covered put is primarily bearish but can profit in a neutral environment. Like a covered call, a covered put has limited profit potential and unlimited risk.

FINAL THOUGHTS

At first glance, the amount of premium that you collect from selling a covered call may seem small, but the idea is to attempt to sell option premiums throughout the year so that the total premium collected is attractive. However, if you sell a call option against stock that you own and the stock surges, you have given up the upside potential; if you sell a call option against stock you own and the stock plunges, you have little downside protection. Very few advisers recommend the selling of naked put options because it is too risky, but many advisers recommend selling covered calls as a risk-reduction strategy. A flaw in the logic regarding covered calls is that most of the attention is focused on profiting from the decay of the call option, whereas in reality, it is the stock price that has a much greater effect on your overall gain or loss position. You should therefore set appropriate stop losses to protect your overall investment. The covered-call strategy is a popular strategy but seems to be overrated and misunderstood because it encourages individuals to take excessive risk, using the argument that such losses, should they occur, are intellectually appealing.

However, selling a covered call can be an effective strategy if you know what you are doing. The best candidates for covered calls are not necessarily the options with the highest implied volatility. Instead, in many cases, an underlying instrument that is more predictable may be the better choice. For example, high-yielding stocks tend to be more stable than high-volatility stocks and can serve as a cushion in the event of a sell-off. The covered-call strategy tends to be more appropriate for stocks that trade in a relatively narrow range. Selling calls on dividend-paying stocks provides an opportunity to profit from the dividend, option premium, and stock appreciation. Dividend-yielding ETFs may provide an opportunity for covered call opportunities. If you choose an underlying instrument that pays a high dividend, such as utilities, real estate investment trusts, selected bank stocks, and ETFs (e.g., high-yielding bond funds), you may be stacking the odds of success on your side. It is important that you select an underlying instrument that you understand and that fits your risk–reward profile. One of the keys to successful option trading is selecting an appropriate underlying stock, ETF, or stock index futures to match your strategy.

Remember that a covered call can be executed with many combinations of strike prices and expiration months, and it can be unbalanced with a different number of options relative to the number of shares. As an aside, if you purchase a deep-in-the-money call and sell a far-out-of-the-money call, you have created a position similar to a covered call position. Most spread strategies described in previous chapters assume that all options are all calls or all puts. In the next chapter, Chapter 20, "Combination," we explore option strategies utilizing calls and puts as part of the same spread.

Combination

A *combination* is any option strategy utilizing both call and put options. For the purposes of this chapter, a combination is typically long one side and short the other side, where both options work in the same direction. In contrast, in most spreads, the options are the same type (either all calls or all puts) and work in opposite directions (e.g., if you buy a call at a strike price and sell a call at a higher strike price).

A combination can be executed when there is a one-to-one ratio of options, it can be unbalanced (ratioed) when there is a different number of options on each side, and the options can expire in different months. To illustrate basic principles, this chapter assumes a combination in which there is one call for every put option, each option expires at the same time, both sides work in the same bullish or bearish direction, and you do not own the underlying stock. There can be many variations to a combination, so each should be analyzed separately to determine its own unique risks and rewards. A combination, such as a straddle or strangle, can consist of call and put options working in opposite directions, and you should refer to Chapter 14, "Straddle and Strangle," for a complete discussion of those strategies.

This chapter provides an overview and comprehensive examples of long and short combinations and then addresses debit versus credit positions, rolling, and combination strategies on ETFs, indexes, and stock index futures.

OVERVIEW

As mentioned previously, a combination is any option strategy utilizing both call and put options; however, a combination (sometimes called a *combo*), for the purposes of this chapter, is established by selling a put and buying a call (long combination) or by selling a call and buying a put (short combination). Of course, this assumes that each option is based on the same underlying stock.

In a long combination (short put/long call), if the underlying stock rises, the long call value should rise and the short put value should decline so that you have a gain from both sides. If the underlying stock declines, the long call value should decline and the short put value should rise so that you have a loss from both sides.

In a short combination (short call/long put), if the underlying stock rises, the short call value should rise and the long put value should decline so that you have a loss from both sides. If the underlying stock declines, the short call value should decline and the long put value should rise so that you have a gain from both sides. A straddle and a strangle can be considered types of combinations. A straddle and a strangle each consist of both a call and a put, where the options work in opposite directions. In this chapter, we will focus on combination strategies in which the long side and the short side both work in the same direction.

In a combination, for this chapter, the first strike price is the call and the second strike price is the price of the put. XYZ stock is assumed to initially trade at $100 a share. Therefore, a 105/95 long combination consists of a long 105 call and a short 95 put and a 105/95 short combination consists of a short 105 call and a long 95 put. A combination can share the same strike price, but it does not have to do so. For example, you might establish a 100/100 long combination, in which you buy a 100 strike price call and sell a 100 strike price put, or a 100/100 short combination, in which you sell a 100 strike price call and buy a 100 strike price put. The strike price chosen can be below, at, or above the current level of the underlying stock or can have a gap between the call and put strikes.

If the underlying stock, at the expiration date of the options, closes between the gap in strike prices of the call and put, then the gain or loss is equal to the credit or debit to establish the position. For example, if XYZ stock is trading at $100 a share, you might establish a long 105/95 combination, in which you buy one 105 call at $2.50 and sell one 95 put at $2, for a $0.50 net debit.

Your trading platform may permit you to enter a combination as one order; for example, if a stock is trading at $100 a share, a 105 call is trading at $2.50, and a 95 put is trading at $2, you may be able to enter a single order to enter into a 105/95 combination at a $0.50 debit or better. As a result of entering a limit order in this manner, you will not be executed on only one side of the transaction unless the entire transaction is executed.

If the underlying stock, at the expiration date, closes at or between 95 and 105, then the loss is equal to the $0.50 net debit. Such a long combination is a *synthetic equivalent* (discussed later in this chapter) of a long stock position (ignoring the gap in strike prices) because it profits in lockstep almost dollar for dollar when the stock price rises and loses in lockstep almost dollar for dollar when the stock price declines. However, if the stock lands between the 95 and 105 strike prices at expiration, there is no loss (or gain) except for the debit (or credit). You have unlimited upside profit potential from the call

TABLE 20.1 Summary: Long and Short Combination

Strategy Name	Strategy	Risk–Reward	Debit or Credit	Breakeven at Expiration	Greatest Profit at Expiration	Initial Margin	Maximum Profit at Expiration
Long combination	Long call, short put	Unlimited profit, unlimited risk	Credit, debit, or even cost	Call strike plus debit	Stock above call strike price	Short option side	Stock above call strike price
Short combination	Short call, long put	Unlimited profit, unlimited risk	Credit, debit, or even cost	Call strike plus credit	Stock below put strike price	Short option side	Stock below put strike price

(above the 105 strike price) and unlimited risk from the short put (below the 95 strike price).

Alternatively, you might establish a short 105/95 combination, in which you sell one 105 call at $2.50 and buy one 95 put at $2.50, for a $0.50 net credit. Such a long combination is a synthetic equivalent of a short stock position (ignoring the gap in strike prices) because it profits in lockstep almost dollar for dollar when the stock price declines and loses in lockstep almost dollar for dollar when the stock price rises. If the stock lands between the 95 and 105 strike prices at expiration, there is no gain (or loss) except for the $0.50 net credit. You have unlimited upside profit potential from the put (below the 95 strike price) and unlimited risk from the short call (above the 105 strike price).

A combination can be used to take advantage of a pricing discrepancy between calls and puts (e.g., where a call may be priced higher than a comparable put) or to reduce risk and fluctuations in an account to take advantage of the fact that the positions have no value at expiration if the underlying stock lands between the call/put strike prices. A combination would typically have an initial margin requirement equal to the short option side. See Table 20.1 for a summary.

A combination is established by selling a put and, in effect, using the proceeds to purchase a call (long combination) or by selling a call and, in effect, using the proceeds to purchase a put (short combination). There is no requirement that the strike prices of the call versus the put be equidistant from the price of the underlying stock. You can sell fewer calls relative to the number of puts, or you can sell more calls relative to the number of puts.

In a long combo, if you are short a put and are assigned, you are forced to buy the underlying stock at the exercise price. In a short combo, if you are short a call and are assigned, you are forced to sell the underlying stock at the exercise price. An American-style option can be exercised by the option holder (buyer) at any time up until the expiration date, whereas a European-style option can be exercised only at expiration. Equity options are American-style expirations.

Establishing a combination can be structured to vary the level of probability that an option will be in-the-money at the expiration date, depending on the strike prices and time frame selected. The further out-of-the-money the option, the lower the premium, the lower the delta, and the lower the probability of assignment. You should select strike prices and a time frame that meet your risk–reward parameters.

STRATEGY EXAMPLES

Following are descriptions and examples of a combination. As a reminder, you can close out an option position by offsetting it in the marketplace any time prior to expiration, and the principles that are demonstrated for a stock can be applied to options on an ETF, index, and stock index futures. Appendixes A, B, and C illustrate many of the strategies covered throughout this book.

To illustrate basic principles, examples assume that there is one call for every put option, each option expires at the same time, both sides work in the same bullish or bearish direction, and you do not own the underlying stock. To exit a position, you can offset it in a closing transaction, wait for assignment (if it is in-the-money), or let both options expire worthless (if they are out-of-the-money at expiration).

Long Combination

A long combination is a strategy that involves a short put and a long call on the same underlying stock. In a long combination, the call and put work together in the same direction, rather than as a hedge against one another, and the long combination performs like a long stock position. A long combination (short put/long call) is bullish, has unlimited profit potential based on the call strike price, and has unlimited risk based on the put strike price. If the underlying stock closes between the strike prices of the call and put at expiration, both options expire out-of-the-money. A long combination generates a gain if the underlying stock is above the call exercise price (ignoring the premium) and a loss if the underlying stock is below the put exercise price (ignoring the premium). The maximum loss of a long combination is considered unlimited because it consists of an uncovered put.

A long combination has one of two possible break-even points. The break-even point occurs where the stock, at expiration, is at the call strike price plus a debit or, alternatively, is at the put strike price minus a credit.

Time decay reduces call and put values. An increase in volatility increases call and put values, and a decrease in volatility reduces call and put values. A net credit or debit is reflected in your account; if it is a net debit, it must be paid at the time of purchase. There is margin requirement for the short option. Although margin is not permitted in an IRA, some brokerage firms may allow a long combination because the risk is mathematically limited to the difference between the put strike price and zero.

Example: Long Combination

Assumptions: XYZ stock is trading at $100 a share in January, and you do not own and are not short any shares; enter into a February 105/95 long combination for a $0.50 ($50) debit, as follows: Buy one February 105 call at $2.50 and sell one February 95 put at $2.

Strategy direction: Bullish.

Debit or credit: $50 debit.

Maximum profit: Unlimited.

TABLE 20.2 Long Combination

XYZ Stock Price ($)	Long Call Value	Short Put Value	Option Position Value	Premium Paid	Position Profit (Loss)
75	0	2,000	(2,000)	50	(2,050)
80	0	1,500	(1,500)	50	(1,550)
85	0	1,000	(1,000)	50	(1,050)
90	0	500	(500)	50	(550)
95	0	0	0	50	(50)
100	0	0	0	50	(50)
105	0	0	0	50	(50)
110	500	0	500	50	450
115	1,000	0	1,000	50	950
120	1,500	0	1,500	50	1,450
125	2,000	0	2,000	50	1,950

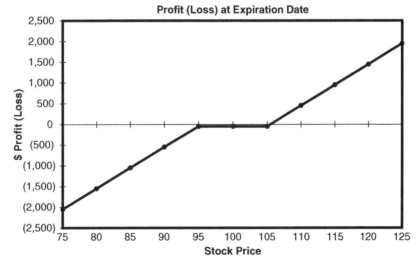

FIGURE 20.1 Long Combination

TABLE 20.3 Summary of Greeks: February Expiration

Option	Delta	Gamma	Theta	Vega
Long 1 February 105 call	$42	$2.00	−$14	$11
Short 1 February 95 put	$42	−$2.00	$14	−$11
Position	$84		$0	$0

TABLE 20.4 Summary of Greeks: March Expiration

Option	Delta	Gamma	Theta	Vega
Long 1 March 105 call	$40	$1.20	−$10	$15
Short 1 March 95 put	$40	−$1.20	$10	−$15
Position	$80		$0	$0

Maximum loss: Unlimited (technically, $9,550).

Exercise and assignment: Can exercise long option if in-the-money; may be assigned on short option if in-the-money.

Break-even stock price: $105.50 (call strike plus debit).

Maximum profit achieved: Stock above call strike price.

Maximum loss achieved: Stock below put strike price.

Profit (loss) if stock unchanged: $50 loss (net premium).

Greeks: Table 20.3 contains sample Greeks converted to dollars at the time the position is established.

Position would reflect a gain from stock rise (delta) but no gain or loss from time decay (theta) or volatility (vega) expansion. Position would reflect a loss from stock decline (delta) but no loss from time decay (theta) or volatility (vega) contraction. Gain is $84 from XYZ stock rising to $101; gain or loss is zero from one day of time decay.

Later expiration: The option price and Greeks will differ if expiration is at a later date; for example, if the option expires in March, instead of February, the price of the March 105 call could be $5 (instead of $2.50) and the price of the March 95 put could be $4.50 (instead of $2.00). Example Greeks are given in Table 20.4.

Gain is $80 from XYZ stock rising to $101; gain or loss is zero from one day of time decay.

Exercise and assignment: For the February 105/95 long combination, if the put is in-the-money, then you may be assigned on your short put and will be required to buy 100 shares of stock at $95 per share. If the call is in-the-money, you can exercise it and buy 100 shares of stock at $105 per share. If the stock price closes between the strike prices at expiration, your short put and long call will be out-of-the-money.

Short Combination

A short combination is a strategy that involves a short call and a long put on the same underlying stock. In a short combination, the call and put work together in the same direction, and the short combination performs like a short stock position. A short combination (short call/long put) is bearish, has unlimited profit potential based on the put strike price, and has unlimited risk based on the call strike price. If the underlying stock closes at or between the strike prices of the call and put at expiration, both options expire out-of-the-money. A short combination generates a gain if the underlying stock is below the put exercise price (ignoring the premium) and a loss if the underlying stock is above the call exercise price (ignoring the premium). The maximum loss of a long combination is unlimited because it consists of an uncovered call.

A short combination has one of two possible break-even points. The break-even point occurs where the stock, at expiration, is at the call strike price plus a credit or, alternatively, is at the put strike price minus a debit.

Time decay reduces call and put values. An increase in volatility increases call and put values, and a decrease in volatility reduces call and put values. A net credit or debit is reflected in your account; if it is a net debit, it must be paid at the time of purchase. There is margin requirement for the short option. An uncovered short call is not permitted in an IRA.

Example: Short Combination

> **Assumptions**: XYZ stock is trading at $100 a share in January, and you do not own and are not short any shares; enter into a February 105/95 short combination for a $0.50 ($50) credit, as follows: Sell one February 105 call at $2.50 and buy one February 95 put at $2.00.
> **Strategy direction**: Bearish.

TABLE 20.5 Short Combination

XYZ Stock Price ($)	Long Call Value	Short Put Value	Option Position Value	Premium Collected	Position Profit (Loss)
75	0	2,000	2,000	50	2,050
80	0	1,500	1,500	50	1,550
85	0	1,000	1,000	50	1,050
90	0	500	500	50	550
95	0	0	0	50	50
100	0	0	0	50	50
105	0	0	0	50	50
110	500	0	(500)	50	(450)
115	1,000	0	(1,000)	50	(950)
120	1,500	0	(1,500)	50	(1,450)
125	2,000	0	(2,000)	50	(1,950)

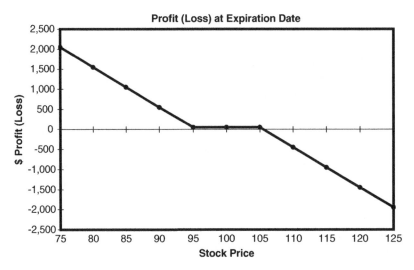

FIGURE 20.2 Short Combination

Debit or credit: $50 credit.

Maximum profit: Unlimited (technically, $9,550).

Maximum loss: Unlimited.

Exercise and assignment: Can exercise long option if in-the-money; may be assigned on short option if in-the-money.

Break-even stock price: $105.50 (call strike plus credit).

Maximum profit achieved: Stock below put strike price.

Maximum loss achieved: Stock above call strike price.

Profit (loss) if stock unchanged: $50 gain (net premium).

Greeks: Table 20.6 contains sample Greeks converted to dollars at the time the position is established.

Position would reflect a gain from stock decline (delta) but no gain or loss from time decay (theta) or volatility (vega) expansion. Position would reflect a loss from stock rise (delta) but no loss from time decay (theta) or volatility (vega) contraction. Loss is $84 from XYZ stock rising to $101; gain or loss is zero from one day of time decay.

Later expiration: The option price and Greeks will differ if expiration is at a later date. For example, if the option expires in March, instead of February, the price

TABLE 20.6 Summary of Greeks: February Expiration

Option	Delta	Gamma	Theta	Vega
Short 1 February 105 call	−$42	−$2.00	$14	−$11
Long 1 February 95 put	−$42	$2.00	−$14	$11
Position	−$84		$0	$0

TABLE 20.7 Summary of Greeks: March Expiration

Option	Delta	Gamma	Theta	Vega
Short 1 March 105 call	−$40	−$1.20	$10	−$15
Long 1 March 95 put	−$40	$1.20	−$10	$15
Position	−$80	$0	$0	$0

of the March 105 call could be $5 (instead of $2.50) and the price of the March 95 put could be $4.50 (instead of $2.00). Example Greeks are given in Table 20.7.

Loss is $80 from XYZ stock rising to $101; gain or loss is zero from one day of time decay.

Exercise and assignment: For the February 105/95 short combination, if the call is in-the-money, then you may be assigned on your short call and will be required to sell 100 shares of stock at $105 per share. If the long put is in-the-money, you can exercise it and sell 100 shares of stock at $95 per share. If the stock price closes between the strike prices at expiration, your short call and long put will be out-of-the-money.

BEYOND THE BASICS

Debit versus Credit

A combination can be established as a net credit, a net debit, or at *even cost* (*zero cost*), depending on the strike prices chosen and the current price of the options. Whether the combination is at a credit or debit depends on the relative price of the put and the call. For a long combination, assuming an equal number of options are bought as sold, if the price of the put is greater than the price of the call, it is established for a credit. If the price of the put is less than the price of the call, it is established for a debit. If the call and put prices are the same, then it is even cost. The term "zero cost" is used, at times, when the credit from the sale of an option equals the debit from the purchase price of another option.

Call versus Put Values   To establish a combination, you should compare call prices to put options on the same underlying stock. Initially, you may expect the price of a call to be equal to the price of a put if both have the same expiration date and the strike prices are equidistant from the underlying stock. For example, you may expect a February 105 call to be trading at the same price as a February 95 put if the underlying stock is trading at $100 a share. However, for many equity options, a close-to-the-money call will typically have a value greater than a comparable put. As a result, a February 105 call may be trading at $2.50 while the February 95 put may be trading at $2.

A call on an underlying stock almost always has a higher value relative to a put. As a result, a short combination may be priced more favorably than a long combination. There are a number of factors that can create this asymmetrical environment. In general, option pricing models have a tendency to value calls more than comparable puts because of interest rate assumptions and because of the fact that a stock can theoretically increase in value to infinity, but a stock can only decline in value to zero. If call values are greater than put values, you can execute a short combination for a credit more easily because a call is sold, and you can simultaneously use the proceeds to purchase a put.

Conversely, on broad-based indexes, the call/put pricing relationship is reversed. An out-of-the-money call on an underlying broad-based index typically has a lower value relative to a comparable put. Apparently, there is often a greater demand for buying puts relative to calls on broad-based indexes such as the S&P 500 index, creating higher put prices relative to calls for out-of-the-money options. As a result, a long combination may be priced more favorably than a short combination in that case. Options on broad-based indexes are discussed in Chapters 23 to 26.

Unbalanced Combinations

A combination is defined broadly to include any option strategy utilizing both call and put options. The umbrella of this definition is wide to cover option strategies not categorized elsewhere. As a result, you can become creative in initiating strategies that match your risk–reward profile.

A combination can be unbalanced so that the number of options bought differs from the number of options sold; for example, if XYZ stock is trading at $100 a share, you might establish an unbalanced 105/95 long combination, in which you buy one 105 strike price call and sell two 95 strike price puts. Also, a combination can have different expiration dates; for example, if XYZ stock is trading at $100 a share, you might establish a March 105/February 95 long combination, in which you buy one March 105 call and sell one February 95 put.

If you are bullish and want limited risk, you can sell a vertical put spread and buy a naked call; for example, if XYZ stock is trading at $100 a share, you can sell two of the 95/90 put spreads and use the proceeds to buy a 105 call. A combination can also be executed with a long or a short underlying stock, which is discussed in Chapters 21 and 22.

Rolling

When transitioning from an initial combination to a new combination, you can wait until the initial combination expires and then enter into the new combination. Alternatively, if the initial combination is near zero but has not yet expired, you may want to offset the options in the marketplace and simultaneously roll to a new combination. Reestablishing positions to take advantage of the various option cycles can be part of your overall strategy. When you roll, you can select different strike prices, based on the current level of the stock as well as on your view of the market and prospects for the stock. For example, you may have initially established a long February 105/95 long call combination when the underlying stock was trading at $100 a share. If it is near the February expiration date and the stock is trading at $104, you might offset the options and roll to a March 110/100 long call combination.

Synthetic Positions

In Chapter 19, it was demonstrated that, in effect, selling an at-the-money covered call is the equivalent position of selling a naked at-the-money put. In both a covered call and a short naked put, you benefit if the stock rises but lose substantially if the stock declines substantially. Both of these positions have the same risk–reward profile and profit and loss graph. This illustrates that a covered call is the equivalent position of a naked put, and vice versa.

One unique characteristic of options is that they can be combined with other options or underlying instruments to create positions with characteristics that are almost identical to some other strategy or combination of contracts. This leads to a new category of trading strategies that are unique to the option market; for example, if you buy a call and simultaneously sell a put without owning or shorting the underlying stock, it is considered a *synthetic long*. If you sell a call and simultaneously buy a put without owning or shorting the underlying stock, it is considered a *synthetic short*. A trader can use synthetics in a number of different ways, including in a directional strategy, a volatility strategy, or an arbitrage strategy.

A synthetic consists of two or more positions that, in combination with each other, act like a third position. A synthetic position can be composed of options and underlying instruments used in combination with other options and underlying instruments to create positions with characteristics that are almost identical to some other strategy or combination of contracts.

Combinations, sometimes in conjunction with the underlying stock, can be used to create synthetic positions and equivalent positions. A synthetic long can be created by combining a long call option and a short put option with the same expiration date and the same strike price. A synthetic short can be created by combining a long put and a short call with the same expiration date and the same strike price. You can create a synthetic long call, for example, by buying stock and buying a put and a synthetic short call by shorting stock and buying a call. Basic synthetic equivalents are shown in Table 20.8.

Accordingly, using synthetic equivalents, if you sell a call against a long stock, you have effectively sold a put; if you sell a put against a short stock, you have effectively sold a call; and so on.

Remember that the term *synthetic position* refers to the effect of using a combination of option strategies that, in essence, will give you more or less a similar result as another strategy. Two or more option strategies that are combined to achieve the same profit/loss potential as other strategies are synthetic equivalent positions. Equivalent positions have the same profit and loss graphs; for example, a covered call is the equivalent of selling a naked put.

TABLE 20.8 Basic Synthetic Equivalents

Synthetic	Positions
Synthetic long stock	Long call, short put
Synthetic short stock	Short call, long put
Synthetic long call	Long stock, long put
Synthetic short call	Short stock, short put
Synthetic long put	Short stock, long call
Synthetic short put	Long stock, short call

ETF, Index, and Futures Combinations

As is more fully described beginning in Part Four, Chapters 23 to 26, a representative ETF I like to use is the S&P 500 SPDR (SPY); as a representative index, I prefer the S&P 500 index (SPX); and as a representative stock index futures, I prefer the S&P 500 futures. The SPY is valued at only one tenth of the SPX and therefore can represent a good trading vehicle for relatively low dollar amounts.

You should not forget about using a combination with an ETF, stock index, or stock index futures. For example, if the SPX is at 1,500 and the SPY is at 150, and you are bullish, you can sell a 140 out-of-the-money put and purchase a 155 out-of-the-money call so that both sides of the trade profit from a rise in the SPY—not only that, but you can fine-tune your selection of strike prices to match your view of the market. Keep in mind that if you believe that the SPY has support at 140, it is usually best not to sell a put exactly at that level. Instead, it is advisable that you give yourself some wiggle room (cushion) so that the SPY put you sell is around a strike price of 130. Although you will receive less premium for the 130 strike price put in comparison to the 140 strike price put, it will probably be well worth it in the long run should the market move against you. By moving your put strike price away from the current level of the market, in the event that you are wrong, you will have a better opportunity to still make a profit.

Although such a combination is described as having unlimited risk, such risk may be mitigated by limiting the number of contracts you enter into on the short side and by trading options where the underlying instrument has a low dollar amount per point, such as on the SPY.

Alternatively, if the SPX is at 1,500 and you are bullish, you can sell an SPX 1,300 out-of-the-money put and purchase an SPX 1,550 out-of-the-money call so that both sides of the trade profit from a rise in the SPX.

FINAL THOUGHTS

A combination may be a viable strategy to trade long or short a stock and, at the same time, manage risk tailored to your particular view. Using out-of-the-money options in a combination trade can be a possible strategy for someone who does not want to incur the stress of small fluctuations in the marketplace and instead is more interested in a major move. In this way, a combination trade can enable you to stay with the trade longer. Utilizing out-of-the-money strike prices can give you room for error; for example, there is no loss for a long combination, at expiration, unless the underlying stock closes below the strike price of the put. As a result, the stock can decline without a loss to the extent that the put strike price is out-of-the-money.

By using a combination, you can utilize the market's money to execute all or a portion of the position. By using the market's money, you can lower your risk in comparison to going long or short in the underlying stock. Learning how to trade combination spreads can be a nice addition to your overall option-strategy portfolio. It seems that certain spread strategies, such as a vertical spread and butterfly, tend to get most of the attention. However, a combination seems underrated and worthy of serious consideration. In Chapter 21, we will explore a collar trade, in which you are short a call and long a put, while owning the underlying stock. In Chapter 22, we will analyze a covered combination strategy, in which you are short a call and short a put, while owning the underlying stock.

Collar

A *collar* consists of a covered call and a protective put. In a collar, the stock is essentially "collared" between two options. A collar can be executed where there is a one-to-one ratio of options sold versus stock owned, or it can be ratioed (unbalanced) where there is a different number of calls versus puts or a different number of options relative to shares owned. To illustrate basic principles, this chapter will assume that one call option is sold for every put purchased in proportion to the long stock and that all options have the same expiration date. In this chapter, we discuss call versus put values, rolling, and the volatility skew.

OVERVIEW

A collar can be viewed as a covered call and a protective put. A collar is established by owning stock, selling an out-of-the-money call, and, in effect, using the proceeds to purchase an out-of-the-money put. In a collar, you know the highest and lowest dollar amounts you can potentially lose or gain. A collar combines a protective put in return, in effect, for the limited upside profit potential of a covered call. A collar is the equivalent of a short combination with long stock.

If the stock rises, this strategy performs like a covered call. If the stock declines, this strategy limits the loss at the put strike price (ignoring the premium for a moment). If the underlying stock closes above the call strike price at expiration, the long put will expire out-of-the-money and is worthless, and the investor will most likely be assigned on the call. You would be obligated to sell the 100 shares at the call strike price if assigned, but you already own 100 shares of stock to cover it. If the underlying stock closes below the short put strike price at expiration, the short call will expire out-of-the-money and is worthless and the put will be in-the-money. In this case, you have the right to sell stock at the put strike price. If the underlying stock is between the strike prices of the call and put at expiration, both options expire out-of-the-money, resulting in a profit if established at a credit or a loss if at a debit for the option portion of the position.

There are numerous scenarios that can be used to illustrate a collar. In a collar, for this chapter, the first strike price is the call and the second strike price is the put. A collar can be established after stock is purchased to protect a gain; for example, assume that you purchased XYZ stock at $85 a share and that it is currently trading at $100 a share, so you have unrealized profit to protect. In this case, you might establish a 105/95 collar, in which you write a 105 call at $2.50 and purchase a 95 put at $2. The 95 put protects you from downside risk, thus guaranteeing a selling price at the 95 strike price if the stock price drops below that level. The 105 call establishes a selling price of the stock at $105 if the stock price rises to that level. Any potential loss from the 105 call is covered by potential gains on the underlying stock.

Your trading platform may permit you to enter a collar as one order; for example, if a stock is trading at $100 a share, a call is trading at $2.50, and a put is trading at $2, you may be able to enter a single order to enter into a collar at $99.50. As a result of entering a limit order in this manner, you will not be executed on only one leg of the transaction unless both legs are executed.

Depending on the strike prices chosen, an equity collar may be established at a net credit, with an investor being paid to protect underlying shares already owned. The credit or debit depends on the relative price of the put versus the call. If the price of the call is greater than the price of the put, the collar can be established for a credit (assuming all other factors are the same). When you establish a collar for a credit, you can profit potentially from a rise in the underlying stock, dividend on the stock, and net credit. If the price of the call is less than the price of the put, the collar would be established for a debit. If the call and put prices are approximately the same, it may be called a zero-cost collar (even-cost collar; see Table 21.1). A collar can be used to take advantage of a pricing discrepancy between calls and puts (e.g., where a call may be priced higher than a comparable put) or to reduce risk and fluctuations in an account.

TABLE 21.1 Summary: Collar

Strategy	Strategy Description	Risk–Reward	Debit or Credit	Breakeven at Expiration	Maximum Profit Achieved at Expiration	Initial Margin
Collar	Long stock, short call, long put	Limited profit, limited risk	Credit, debit, or even cost	Original stock price minus credit or plus debit	Stock at or above call strike price	None on options; stock purchase has margin requirement

Portfolio managers have a tendency to sell short-term calls to finance the purchase of puts (i.e., a collar). A collar is a limited-reward/limited-risk strategy. Profit is maximized when the underlying stock is at or above the call strike price at the expiration date. The long stock position protects you against assignment risk associated with the short call position because any assignment would be protected by the stock gain. A collar is considered limited risk because the put protects you from a loss below the put strike price (ignoring the premium). The break-even point, at expiration, is equal to the original stock price minus any net credit or plus any debit. There is no margin requirement for the call because it is covered by the stock, and the put is required to be paid in full at the time of purchase. The stock purchase has a stock margin requirement.

You should select strike prices and time frames that meet your risk–reward parameters. Establishing a collar can be structured to vary the levels of probability, depending on the strike prices selected. The strike prices and the time frame you choose should be determined based on your projection of the underlying movement of the stock. A disadvantage of a collar is the inability to earn interest on the proceeds used to purchase the stock. You are, however, entitled to receive dividends on the stock.

STRATEGY EXAMPLE

Following are a description and an example of a collar. As a reminder, you can close out an option position by offsetting it in the marketplace any time prior to expiration, and the principles that are demonstrated for a stock can be applied to options on an ETF, index, and stock index futures. Appendixes A, B, and C illustrate many of the strategies covered throughout this book.

To illustrate basic principles, examples assume that there is one call for every put option, and each option expires at the same time. To exit a position, you can offset it in a closing transaction, wait for assignment of the call (if it is in-the-money), or let both options expire worthless (if they are out-of-the-money at expiration).

Collar

A collar is a strategy that involves long stock, a short call, and a long put. In a collar, the call and put work together to define the maximum profit and loss. A collar is primarily bullish, has limited profit potential based on the call strike price, and has limited risk based on the put strike price. If the underlying stock closes between the strike prices of the call and put at expiration, both options expire out-of-the-money.

The break-even point, at expiration, is equal to the original stock price minus any net credit (or plus any debit).

Time decay reduces call and put values, an increase in volatility increases the call and put values, and a decrease in volatility reduces the call and put values. A collar may be executed for a credit or a net debit. Any net debit must be paid at the time of purchase. There is no margin requirement for the call because it is covered by the stock, the put is required to be paid in full at the time of purchase, and the stock purchase has a stock margin requirement. A collar may be permitted in an IRA.

If you assume that you own XYZ stock trading at $100 a share, you might establish a 105/95 collar, in which you buy 100 shares of stock, write a 105 call, and purchase a 95 put. For example, you might establish a collar at an initial net credit of $0.50 ($50), in which you sell one 105 call at $2.50 and buy one 95 put at $2. The collar is protection below the 95 strike price, but the upside participation is capped at $105 per share.

Example: Collar

Assumptions: XYZ stock is trading at $100 a share in January and you enter into one February 105/95 collar at a $99.50 ($9,950) debit, as follows: Buy 100 shares of stock at $100 a share, sell one February 105 call at $2.50, and buy one February 95 put at $2.

Strategy direction: Primarily bullish but can be neutral (trading range).

Debit or credit: $50 credit for option portion, $9,950 debit with stock.

Maximum profit: $550 (stock price at call strike price plus net credit from options).

Maximum loss: $450 (stock price at put strike price minus net credit from options).

Exercise and assignment: Can exercise long put option if in-the-money; may be assigned on short call option if in-the-money.

Break-even stock price: $99.50 (stock price minus net credit from options).

Maximum profit achieved: Stock at or above call strike price of 105.

Maximum loss achieved: Stock at or below put strike price of 95.

Profit (loss) if stock unchanged: $50 gain (net credit from options).

TABLE 21.2 Collar

XYZ Stock Price ($)	Stock Gain (Loss)	Short Call Value	Long Put Value	Option Position Value	Premium Collected	Option Profit (Loss)	Collar Profit (Loss)
75	(2,500)	0	2,000	2,000	50	2,050	(450)
80	(2,000)	0	1,500	1,500	50	1,550	(450)
85	(1,500)	0	1,000	1,000	50	1,050	(450)
90	(1,000)	0	500	500	50	550	(450)
95	(500)	0	0	0	50	50	(450)
100	0	0	0	0	50	50	50
105	500	0	0	0	50	50	550
110	1,000	(500)	0	(500)	50	(450)	550
115	1,500	(1,000)	0	(1,000)	50	(950)	550
120	2,000	(1,500)	0	(1,500)	50	(1,450)	550
125	2,500	(2,000)	0	(2,000)	50	(1,950)	550

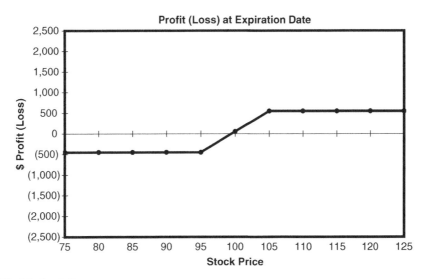

FIGURE 21.1 Collar

Greeks: Table 21.3 contains sample Greeks converted to dollars at the time the position is established.

Position would reflect a gain from stock rise (delta) and no gain or loss from time decay (theta) or volatility (vega) expansion. Position would reflect a loss from stock decline (delta) but no loss from time decay (theta) and volatility (vega) contraction. Gain is $16 from XYZ stock rising to $101; gain or loss is zero from one day of time decay.

Later expiration: The price and Greeks will differ if expiration is at a later date. For example, if the option expires in March, instead of February, the price of the March 105 call could be $5 (instead of $2.50) and the price of the March 95 put could be $4.50 (instead of $2.00). Example Greeks are given in Table 21.4.

Gain is $20 from XYZ stock rising to $101; gain or loss is zero from one day of time decay.

Exercise and assignment: If the short call expires in-the-money, it may be assigned, but you are protected by the long stock. If the put is in-the-money, you can exercise it and sell 100 shares of stock at 95 per share. If the stock price

TABLE 21.3 Summary of Greeks: February Expiration

Option	Delta	Gamma	Theta	Vega
XYZ stock	$100	$0	$0	$0
Short 1 February 105 call	−$42	−$2.00	$14	−$11
Long 1 February 95 put	−$42	$2.00	−$14	$11
Position	$16		$0	$0

TABLE 21.4 Summary of Greeks: March Expiration

Option	Delta	Gamma	Theta	Vega
XYZ stock	$100	$0	$0	$0
Short 1 March 105 call	−$40	−$1.20	$10	−$15
Long 1 March 95 put	−$40	$1.20	−$10	$15
Position	$20		$0	$0

closes between the strike prices at expiration, your long put and short call will be out-of-the-money.

BEYOND THE BASICS

A collar can be an effective way to automatically sell into strength and trim a portfolio as stocks rise. For example, assume that you own a stock that is trading at $100, and you sell, as part of a collar, a call at a strike price of 105 and collect $2.50 ($250) for the option. If the stock rises above $105 a share, you automatically sell the stock at the 105 strike price, plus you keep the net credit.

Short Collar

A collar can be executed in reverse (buy call and sell put) against a short stock position; for example, assume that you are short 100 shares of XYZ stock and that the stock is currently trading at $100 a share. It this case, you might establish a 105/95 reverse collar, in which you buy a 105 call and sell a 95 put. For example, assume that you establish a collar at an initial net debit of $0.50 ($50), in which you buy one 105 call at $2.50 ($250) and sell one 95 put at $2 ($200), thus paying a net debit of $100.50. The collar is protection above the 105 strike price, but the profit potential is capped at the 95 strike price. Any potential loss from the 95 put is covered by potential gain on the underlying short stock. A short collar is rare, so it will not be illustrated further.

Debit versus Credit

The analysis of a collar is similar to the analysis of a combination, discussed in Chapter 20, except a collar is also long stock. A collar can be established as a net credit, a net debit, or at even cost (zero cost), depending on the strike prices chosen and the current price of the options. Whether the collar is at a credit or a debit depends on the relative price of the put and the call. For a collar, assuming an equal number of options are bought as sold, if the price of the call is greater than the price of the put, it is established for a credit. If the price of the call is less than the price of the put, it is established for a debit.

If the call and put prices are the same, then it is even cost. The term "zero cost" is used, at times, when the credit from the call equals the debit from the put.

Even if you do not own the stock, your trading platform may permit you to enter a collar as one order. For example, if a stock is trading at $100 a share, a call is trading at $2.50, and a put is trading at $2, you may be able to enter a single (collar with stock) order to enter into a collar at $99.50 ($9,950) or better. As a result of entering a limit order in this manner, you will not be executed on only one leg of the transaction unless all three are executed.

Call versus Put Values   A call on an underlying stock almost always has a higher value relative to a put. If call values are greater than put values, you can execute a collar for a credit more easily. Conversely, on broad-based indexes, the call–put pricing relationship is reversed. An out-of-the-money call on an underlying broad-based index typically has a lower value relative to a comparable put. Apparently, there is a greater demand for buying puts relative to calls on broad-based indexes such as the S&P 500 index (SPX), creating higher put prices relative to calls for out-of-the-money options. Options on broad-based indexes are discussed in Chapters 23 to 26.

Unbalanced Collars

A collar can be unbalanced so that the number of options bought differs from the number of options sold. For example, if XYZ stock is trading at $100 a share, you might establish an unbalanced 105/95 collar, in which you sell one 105 strike price call and buy two 95 strike price puts. Also, a collar can have different expiration dates; for example, if XYZ stock is trading at $100 a share, you might establish a March 105/February 95 collar, in which you sell one March 105 call and buy one February 95 put.

Rolling

When transitioning from an initial collar to the new collar, you can wait until the initial collar expires and then enter into the new collar. Alternatively, if the initial collar is near zero but has not yet expired, you may want to offset the options in the marketplace and simultaneously roll to a new collar. If you roll, you can select different strike prices, based on the current level of the stock as well as on your view of the market and prospects for the stock. For example, you may have initially established a February 105/95 collar when the underlying stock was trading at $100 a share. If it is near the February expiration date and the stock is trading at $104, you might offset the options and roll them to a March 100/110 collar.

Index Skew

Portfolio managers have a tendency to sell short-term calls to finance the purchase of puts (i.e., a collar), having the effect of driving down the prices of short-term calls and driving up the prices of short-term puts in the SPX and S&P 500 futures. This creates a pricing environment in which the prices of puts are higher than the prices of comparable calls.

The tendency of the marketplace to sell SPX and S&P 500 futures out-of-the-money calls and buy such out-of-the-money puts creates a discrepancy in the relative pricing of SPX and S&P 500 futures calls versus puts. It should be noted, however, that the effects of such call suppression can be mitigated if you trade further out in time. By trading SPX and S&P 500 futures call options with a later expiration date, the downward pressure on call prices can be minimized. In other words, longer-term call options are more on par with longer-term put options. This issue is further described in Chapter 27.

FINAL THOUGHTS

A collar is a common strategy used by portfolio managers. In a collar, you can profit from the triple combination of stock appreciation, dividends, and a net credit. If you already own the underlying stock, a collar can be considered a low-risk and low-cost strategy. A collar may be used by a portfolio manager or corporate executive who wants to liquidate his stock holdings at some time or lock in a sale price within a certain range. Portfolio managers seem to like the collar trade on indexes because they have a tendency to sell covered calls against their existing positions and buy protective puts. Collar trades can be prudent whether the market is moving up, down, or sideways. In Chapter 22, we analyze a strategy called a covered combination, in which you are short a call and short a put, while owning the underlying stock.

Covered Combination

A *combination*, as discussed in Chapter 20, is any option strategy utilizing both call and put options. This chapter examines a combination that is established by selling a call and selling a put, in which the underlying stock is owned (*covered combination*). A covered combination is a combination in which the underlying stock is owned. There can be many variations to a covered combination, so each should be analyzed separately to determine its own unique risks and rewards. The word *covered* simply means that the underlying stock is owned and does not mean, for the purposes of this chapter, that all losses are offset by an opposing position.

This chapter will analyze a covered combination using a covered short strangle (a short strangle in which the stock is owned) as an example. A covered short strangle can be executed when there is a one-to-one ratio of calls written versus puts written, or it can be ratioed (unbalanced) with a different number of calls versus puts. To illustrate some basic principles, this chapter will assume that one call option is written for every put written, all options have the same expiration date, and the stock is owned in proportion to the number of options. This chapter provides an overview and comprehensive example and then addresses an unbalanced short covered strangle, rolling, covered long straddle, and other issues.

OVERVIEW

A covered (short) strangle consists of a long stock, a short call, and a short put. In such a covered combination, you receive two premiums: one for the written call and one for the written put. On the upside, this strategy performs like a covered call (ignoring the put for a moment); on the downside, it performs like an uncovered put (ignoring the stock for a moment). As mentioned in Chapter 20, a long stock and short call is the synthetic equivalent of a short put. As a result, overall, this position is like shorting two puts.

In a covered short strangle, you are positioned to sell your stock if you are assigned on the short call, but you will add to your stock position if assigned on the short put. You can use this strategy if you want to sell into strength but want to purchase additional shares if the stock price declines. For example, you can purchase half the shares when the position is established (and sell those shares if the stock rises above the call strike price) and purchase the other half at a lower price (if you are assigned on the short put). A covered short strangle can be viewed as a long stock and a short strangle if different exercise prices are used and as a long stock and a short straddle if the same exercise price is used. As mentioned previously, the word "covered" simply means that the underlying stock is owned and does not mean, for this strategy, that all losses are offset by an opposing position. A covered short strangle is a type of covered combination.

When you establish a covered short strangle, you can potentially profit from a rise in the underlying stock, the credit received, and any dividend on the stock. If the stock closes above the call strike price at expiration, you would be assigned on the call, and the long put would expire out-of-the-money. You would be obligated to sell the 100 shares at the call strike price if assigned, but you already own the stock to cover it. The strategy is called "covered," but it is not covered in the conventional sense if the underlying stock declines in value. Although the long stock protects against a loss from the short call, it does not protect against a loss from the short put and, instead, results in an additional loss if the stock price declines. If the stock closes below the short put strike price at expiration, the put would expire in-the-money, the short call would expire out-of-the-money, and the stock would show a loss. In this case, you can expect assignment on the put and an obligation to purchase additional shares at the put strike price. If the stock is between the strike prices of the call and put at expiration, both options expire out-of-the-money, resulting in a profit from the options to the extent of the credit. Remember, however, that the gain or loss from the stock would also need to be taken into account.

Assume that XYZ stock is trading at $100 a share. In this case, you might establish a 105/95 covered short strangle, in which you can sell a 105 call and a 95 put. If the stock price is above $105 a share at expiration, you would be assigned on the call and obligated to sell shares at $105. If the stock price is below $95 a share at expiration, you would be assigned on the put and obligated to buy shares at $95 (see Table 22.1).

TABLE 22.1 Summary: Covered Short Strangle

Spread Strategy	Strategy Description	Risk–Reward	Debit or Credit	Breakeven at Expiration	Maximum Profit at Expiration	Initial Margin
Covered short strangle	Long stock, short call, short put, different strike prices	Limited profit, unlimited risk	Credit	Original stock price minus credit	Stock at or above call strike price	Margin requirement for short put (and stock); no margin requirement for call

A covered short strangle can be an effective way to automatically sell into strength and add to your position at a lower price. For example, assume that you own a stock that is trading at $100, and you sell, as part of a covered short strangle, a 105 call at $2.50 and a 95 put at $2.50 for a total of $4.50 ($450). If the stock rises above $105 a share, you can offset the entire position as though you sold the stock at $109.50 (strike price plus premium). Likewise, a covered short strangle can be an effective way to add automatically more shares at a lower price. Assuming the same example, if the stock declines below $95 a share, you will be assigned and can buy the stock as though you paid $91.50 (strike price minus premium).

A covered short strangle is profitable if the stock rises or trades within a range and is designed to sell into strength if the stock price rises or add to the stock position if a stock decline occurs. You should select strike prices and a time frame that meet your risk–reward parameters. Establishing a covered short strangle can be structured to vary the levels of probability, depending on the strike prices selected. A disadvantage of a covered short strangle is the inability to earn interest on the proceeds used to purchase the stock. You are, however, entitled to receive dividends on the stock.

In the previous example, if your trading platform permits you to enter the covered combination as one order, you would place a single limit order at $96.50 (stock price minus credit). As a result of entering a limit order in this manner, you will not be executed on only one or two portions of the transaction unless the entire transaction is executed. Many trading platforms may not permit you to enter and exit a covered combination as one order and may require you to enter the orders separately. If you cannot enter a covered strangle as one order, you may be permitted to buy the stock and enter a separate strangle (or straddle) order. For example, if a stock is trading at $100 a share, a call is trading at $2.50, and a put is trading at $2, you can enter a limit order to buy the stock and a limit order to sell a strangle at $4.50 (or better).

Covered versus Uncovered

An option position is typically considered covered if there is a fully offsetting opposite market position; for example, a short call is considered covered if you are also long a call at the same or lower strike price on the same stock. However, the word "covered" is also used to indicate whether the underlying stock is owned; for example, a short call is considered covered if you also long the stock (covered-call strategy). An option strategy in which stock is owned can be called "covered" and an option strategy where stock is not owned can be called "uncovered." This can lead to confusion because, for example, the name "covered strangle" is a misnomer because the position is not fully covered in the usual sense as the call portion of the trade is covered by the long stock, but the put is uncovered.

Such terminology may have some traders shaking their heads, but please do not let the terminology get in the way of your trading. Any type of option sale can be covered (long or short stock) or uncovered (no underlying stock). The examples in Chapters 7 to 18 assume that the strategy is uncovered, whereas this chapter, as well as Chapters 19 and 21, assume that the strategy is covered. Practically any strategy can be modified to add a long or short stock position.

A covered strangle is a type of covered combination. In Chapter 19, "Covered Call," it was mentioned that an option position is typically considered covered if there is a fully offsetting opposite market position, such as the long stock. However, the names "covered strangle" and "covered combination" are misnomers because the position is not covered in the usual sense.

Strangle versus Straddle

A covered combination can include a covered strangle or a covered straddle. As described in Chapter 14, a strangle involves a call and a put with two different strike prices. A long strangle consists of a long call and a long put with different strike prices and the same expiration date; for example, buy one February 105 call and buy one February 95 put. A short strangle consists of a short call and a put with different strike prices and the same expiration date; for example, sell one February 105 call and sell one February 95 put. A covered short strangle is a short strangle while the stock is owned.

A covered strangle is similar to a covered straddle, except a straddle uses the same strike price. A long straddle consists of a long call and a long put with the same strike price and expiration date and is used to profit from volatility; for example, buy one February 100 call and buy one February 100 put. A short straddle consists of a short call and a put with the same strike price and expiration date and is used to profit from a trading range or volatility contraction; for example, sell one February 100 call and sell one February 100 put. A covered straddle is a short straddle while the stock is owned.

STRATEGY EXAMPLE

Following are a description and an example of a covered short strangle. As a reminder, you can close out an option position by offsetting it in the marketplace any time prior to expiration, and the principles that are demonstrated for a stock can be applied to options on an ETF, index, and stock index futures. Appendixes A, B, and C illustrate many of the strategies covered throughout this book. To illustrate basic principles, the example assumes that there is one call for every put option, that each option expires at the same time, and that stock is owned based on the number of options.

Covered Short Strangle

A covered short strangle consists of a long stock, a short call, and a short put. In such a strategy, you receive two premiums: one for the written call and one for the written put. Overall, this position is like shorting two puts. A covered short strangle is bullish, has limited profit potential based on the call strike price, and is worth its maximum value, at expiration, if the underlying stock is at or above the call exercise price. A covered short strangle has unlimited risk because it consists of a long stock and a short put. If the stock is between the strike prices of the call and put at expiration, both options expire out-of-the-money, resulting in a profit from the options to the extent of the credit.

The break-even point, at expiration, is equal to the original stock price minus the credit.

Time decay reduces call and put values. Prior to expiration, an increase in volatility increases call and put values, and a decrease in volatility reduces call and put values. A net credit is reflected in your account for the options. There is no margin requirement for the call because it is covered by the stock, but there is a margin requirement for the short put (and stock). Although margin is not permitted in an IRA, some brokerage firms may allow a short put because the risk is mathematically limited to the difference between the put strike price and zero.

If you assume that you own XYZ stock trading at $100 a share, you might establish a February 105/95 covered short strangle in which you buy 100 shares of stock, write a February 105 call, and write a February 95 put. For example, you might establish a covered short strangle at an initial net credit of $4.50 ($450), in which you sell one February 105 call at $2.50 ($250) and sell one February 95 put at $2 ($200). At expiration, if the stock price is above $105 a share, you would be assigned on the call and would be required to sell 100 shares at $105. Because you already own the shares, you can fulfill the terms of the assignment with the stock you already own. Your profit would be $500 from the rise in the price of the stock plus the $450 premium collected. If the stock price is below $95 a share, you would be assigned on the put and would be required to buy 100 shares at $95. If the stock price is between the strike prices at expiration, you can write another covered short strangle to collect additional premium. Assuming that the stock remains at $100 a share, you can collect another $4.50 ($450) on a March 95/105 covered combination so that the total premium collected is $9. This process can be repeated every month, every couple of months, or every quarter.

Example: Covered Short Strangle

Assumptions: XYZ stock is trading at $100 a share in January and you enter into a February 105/95 covered combination by buying 100 shares and collecting a $4.50 ($450) credit, as follows: Sell one February 105 call at $2.50 and sell one February 95 put at $2.

Strategy direction: Bullish.

Debit or credit: $4.50 credit.

Maximum profit: $950 (stock price at call strike price plus net credit).

Maximum loss: Unlimited (technically, $10,000 from stock plus $9,500 from short put, ignoring premium).

Exercise and assignment: May be assigned on short call or put if in-the-money.

Break-even stock price: $95.50 (stock price minus credit).

Maximum profit achieved: Stock at or above call strike price of 105.

Maximum loss achieved: Stock price below put strike price.

Profit (loss) if stock unchanged: $450 gain (credit).

In this example, the gain or loss (in the column labeled "Position Profit (Loss)") consists of the columns "Stock Gain (Loss)," "Option Position Gain (Loss)," and "Premium Collected."

Greeks: Table 22.3 contains sample Greeks converted to dollars at the time the position is established.

Position would reflect a gain from stock rise (delta), time decay (theta), and volatility (vega) contraction. Position would reflect a loss from stock decline

TABLE 22.2 Covered Short Strangle

XYZ Stock Price ($)	Stock Gain (Loss)	Short Call Value	Short Put Value	Option Position Gain (Loss)	Premium Collected	Position Profit (Loss)
75	(2,500)	0	(2,000)	(2,000)	450	(4,050)
80	(2,000)	0	(1,500)	(1,500)	450	(3,050)
85	(1,500)	0	(1,000)	(1,000)	450	(2,050)
90	(1,000)	0	(500)	(500)	450	(1,050)
95	(500)	0	0	0	450	(50)
100	0	0	0	0	450	450
105	500	0	0	0	450	950
110	1,000	(500)	0	(500)	450	950
115	1,500	(1,000)	0	(1,000)	450	950
120	2,000	(1,500)	0	(1,500)	450	950
125	2,500	(2,000)	0	(2,000)	450	950

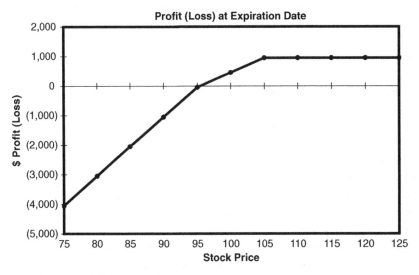

FIGURE 22.1 Covered Short Strangle

TABLE 22.3 Summary of Greeks: February Expiration

Option	Delta	Gamma	Theta	Vega
Stock	$100	$0	$0	$0
Short 1 February 105 call	−$42	−$2.00	$14	−$11
Short 1 February 95 put	$42	−$2.00	$14	−$11
Position	$100		$28	−$22

TABLE 22.4 Summary of Greeks: March Expiration

Option	Delta	Gamma	Theta	Vega
Stock	$100	$0	$0	$0
Short 1 March 105 call	−$40	−$1.20	$10	−$15
Short 1 March 95 put	$40	−$1.20	$10	−$15
Position	$100		$20	−$30

(delta) and volatility (vega) expansion. Gain is $100 from XYZ stock rising to $101; gain is $28 from one day of time decay.

Later expiration: The option price and Greeks will differ if expiration is at a later date. For example, if the option expires in March, instead of February, the price of the March 105 call could be $5 (instead of $2.50) and the price of the March 95 put could be $4.50 (instead of $2.00). Example Greeks are given in Table 22.4.

Gain is $100 from XYZ stock rising to $101; gain is $20 from one day of time decay.

Exercise and assignment: If the call strike price is in-the-money, you may be assigned on your short call and required to sell the XYZ stock at $105 per share, but you are protected by the long stock. If the put strike price is in-the-money, you may be assigned on your short put and required to buy XYZ stock at $95 per share.

BEYOND THE BASICS

Unbalanced Covered Short Strangle

A covered short strangle can be unbalanced so that the number of options bought differs from the number of options sold. For example, if XYZ stock is trading at $100 a share, you might establish an unbalanced 105/95 covered short strangle, in which you own 100 shares of stock, sell two 105 strike price calls, and sell one 95 strike price put. Also, a covered short strangle can have different expiration dates. For example, if XYZ stock is trading at $100 a share, you might establish a March 105/February 95 covered short strangle, in which you own 100 shares of stock, sell one March 105 call, and buy one February 95 put.

Rolling

When transitioning to the new covered short strangle, you can wait until the initial covered short strangle expires and then enter into the new covered short strangle. Alternatively, if the initial covered short strangle is near zero but has not yet expired, you may want to offset the options in the marketplace and simultaneously roll to a new covered short strangle. If you roll, you can select different strike prices, based on the current level of the stock as well as on your view of the market and prospects for the stock. For example, you may have initially established a February 105/95 covered short strangle when the underlying stock was trading at $100 a share. If it is near the February expiration date and the stock is trading at $104, you might offset the options and roll them to a March 100/110 covered short strangle.

Covered Long Strangle

A covered combination can be executed in reverse (buy call and buy put) against a short stock position; for example, assume that you are short 100 shares of XYZ stock and that the stock is currently trading at $100 a share. In this case, you might establish a 105/95 covered long strangle, in which you buy a 105 call and buy a 95 put. For example, assume that you establish a covered long strangle at an initial net debit of $4.50 ($450), in which you buy one 105 call at $2.50 ($250) and buy one 95 put at $2 ($200).

FINAL THOUGHTS

A covered combination is a combination in which the underlying stock is owned. There can be many variations to a covered combination, so each should be analyzed separately. This chapter analyzed a covered combination using a covered short strangle (a short strangle in which stock is owned) as an example. An attraction of the covered strangle strategy is collecting double premium. A covered short strangle can be an effective way to automatically sell into strength and/or add to your position at a lower price. If the stock rises, you will have a profit from the underlying shares and double premium. If the stock declines, you can purchase the shares at the put strike price and benefit from double premium. In Chapter 23, we begin Part Four and describe how the principles discussed throughout this book can be applied to an ETF, index, and stock index futures.

Comparing Underlying Instruments

It has been stated often in this book that the option principles that are demonstrated for a stock can be applied to options on an ETF, index, and stock index futures. Now it is time to move to the next level and see how the option principles described previously can be applied to other underlying instruments. Chapter 23 compares underlying instruments, Chapter 24 covers ETFs, Chapter 25 covers stock indexes, and Chapter 26 covers stock index futures.

By understanding how to trade options on a number of underlying instruments, you are able to pick the instrument that fits you best; for example, if you are interested in commodities, there are ETFs available, and if you are interested in index trading, there are indexes available. Understanding a number of underlying instruments can enable you to shift back and forth among U.S. markets, emerging markets, and commodities, depending on whether they are rising, moving sideways, or falling. In such a case, the U.S. stock market may be in a temporary downturn, there may be a bull market in emerging markets and/or commodities, or vice versa. Of course, you do not need a bull market to make money trading options; instead, you can trade a declining or sideways market. It is to your advantage to know how to trade multiple products so that you can execute a strategy at a moment's notice. Trading options on ETFs, indexes, and stock index futures can provide an opportunity to trade among a wide spectrum of markets, commodities, and sectors from around the world—not only that, but you can trade them from the long or short side, and the best thing of all is that you can trade them using options.

Part Four starts by examining important differences in trading options on different underlying instruments and then devotes an entire chapter to each of these. By analyzing option trading in this manner, you should develop a working knowledge of how options can be used to trade many underlying instruments.

CHAPTER 23

Comparing Stocks, ETFs, Indexes, and Stock Index Futures

T he hard part is learning the strategies, but the great thing is that once you have mastered them, you can apply them to other underlying instruments. For example, if you learn how to trade an iron condor on stocks, you can use that strategy to trade options on an ETF, index, and/or stock index futures. Being able to trade a number of underlying instruments should open up possibilities for you to trade in many market environments. This chapter provides a comparison of representative underlying instruments. The chapter will set the stage for Chapter 24, on ETF options; Chapter 25, on stock index options; and Chapter 26, on stock index futures options.

OVERVIEW

The principles that have been demonstrated for options on a stock can be applied to options on an ETF, index, and stock index futures. This is good news because all the option strategies that you have learned in previous chapters can be applied to these other instruments. For example, similar to an option on a stock, an ETF, index, and stock index futures option buyer has unlimited reward potential and limited risk, and the seller has limited reward potential equal to the option premium collected and unlimited risk. An ETF, index, or stock index futures call option provides the purchaser the right, but not the obligation, to buy (or settle) at the strike price. An ETF, index, or stock index futures put option provides the purchaser the right, but not the obligation, to sell (or settle) at the strike price. An ETF, index, or stock index futures call seller is obligated to sell (or settle) if assigned, and the put seller is obligated to buy (or settle) if assigned. The factors that affect the price of an ETF, index, or stock index futures option are the same as those affecting the price of an option on a stock, including the value of the underlying instrument, strike price, time to expiration, volatility, interest rate, and dividends.

To illustrate principles, we will use a representative ETF, stock index, and stock index futures that are derived from the same underlying index, the S&P 500 index: For a representative ETF, the S&P 500 SPDR (SPY) is illustrated; for an index, the SPX is illustrated; and for a stock index futures, S&P 500 futures is illustrated. By using instruments that are based on the same underlying index (S&P 500), you should be able to see a valid comparison. Following is a brief explanation of these representative instruments.

ETF

The SPY is an ETF valued at one tenth of the underlying SPX; for example, when the SPX is at 1,500, the SPY is valued at approximately $150. When the SPX moves 10 points, the SPY typically moves in lockstep by 1 point (although small differences may exist). You can trade the SPY as well as buy and sell put and call options on it. The SPY has strike prices at 1-point intervals instead of at the usual 5 or 10 points, as for stocks. The multiplier for ETF options is generally $100, which is the same as for options on stocks.

Stock Index

The SPX is an index with a multiplier of $100, which is the same as for options on stocks. An SPX option works essentially in the same manner as an equity option, except that there is *cash settlement* at expiration, and you cannot trade an index directly. It is assumed, for illustrative purposes, that the SPX is at 1,500.

Stock Index Futures

The S&P 500 futures contract derives its value from the underlying SPX. The S&P 500 futures contract works essentially in the same manner as an equity option, but the S&P 500 futures contract is $250 a point and has differences in how margin is calculated. Popular stock index futures are the S&P 500 futures, NASDAQ 100 futures, Dow futures, Russell 2000 futures, and S&P 100 futures. It is assumed, for illustrative purposes, that S&P 500 futures is at 1,500.

The SPY multiplier is $100, the SPX multiplier is $100, and the S&P 500 futures multiplier is $250.

SIZE OF INSTRUMENT

Each of these instruments is at a different price in the marketplace, with variations in its multiplier (dollars per point). The value of an instrument is equal to its level times the multiplier of the underlying instrument. Remember that the SPY multiplier is $100, the SPX multiplier is $100, and the S&P 500 futures multiplier is $250. Assume that the SPY is

TABLE 23.1 Comparison of Stocks, ETF, Stock Index, and Stock Index Futures

Underlying Instrument	Multiplier ($)	Value Assuming S&P 500 at 1,500 ($)	Option Value ($)	Exercise and Assignment	Margin	Subject to 60/40 Rule
Stock	N/A	N/A	100 per point	American	20% rule	No
SPY	100	15,000	100 per point	American	20% rule	No
SPX	100	150,000	100 per point	European, cash settled	15% rule	Yes
S&P 500 futures	250	375,000	250 per point	American	SPAN	Yes

at $150, the SPX is at 1,500, and the S&P 500 futures is at 1,500. The maximum exposure for these follows:

- $15,000 on the SPY (150 times $100),
- $150,000 on the SPX (1,500 times $100),
- $375,000 on the S&P 500 futures (1,500 times $250).

Therefore,

- One S&P 500 futures is 2.5 times the value of one SPX,
- One S&P 500 futures is 25 times the value of one SPY,
- One SPX is 10 times the value of one SPY.

Table 23.1 shows a comparison of a stock, ETF, stock index, and stock index futures. (The 60/40 rule is described later.)

The different values and multipliers among the SPY, SPX, and S&P 500 futures affect the maximum risk exposure associated with buying or selling options outright as well as spreads. For example, ignoring the premium, a vertical credit spread on the SPX with a 50-point width in strike prices has a maximum exposure of $5,000 (50 points times $100 per point); for S&P 500 futures, a 50-point width in strike prices has a maximum exposure of $12,500 (50 points times $250 per point).

EXERCISE AND ASSIGNMENT

The differences regarding exercise and assignment are summarized as follows:

- A stock is subject to American-style exercise.
- An SPY option is subject to American-style exercise, with exercise and assignment similar to a stock.

- An SPX option is subject to European-style exercise, with cash settlement at expiration.
- An S&P 500 futures option is subject to American-style exercise, with exercise and assignment similar to a stock. An S&P 500 futures option is cash settled if the option expires at the end of the same calendar quarter as the underlying S&P 500 futures.

Not all ETFs are American-style exercised; for example, the iShares S&P 500 (symbol IVV) tracks the S&P 500 like the SPY, except that it is subject to European-style exercise. Likewise, not all stock index futures are European-style exercised; for example, the S&P 100 (symbol OEX) tracks the S&P 100 index and is American-style exercised. Options are also available on S&P 500 futures that expire on the last day of the calendar month. These end-of-month (EOM) S&P 500 futures options are European-style exercised.

MARGIN

Chapter 30 is devoted to explaining margin on stocks, ETFs, indexes, and stock index futures, but some points are worth mentioning here. A margin requirement for options is the amount of cash (or other assets) an option seller is required to deposit and maintain to cover a position as collateral. It is the amount of cash (or other assets) that must be deposited by an option seller to ensure performance of the seller's obligations under an option contract. Initial margin is the amount of margin required when a position is opened. Maintenance margin is the amount that must be maintained on deposit after a position is opened. A margin call is a request from a brokerage firm to a customer to bring margin deposits up to initial levels.

Margin in a regular brokerage account is calculated using the traditional 20 percent margin requirement or, alternatively, if you qualify, the portfolio margining method. Margin in a futures account (called "SPAN," for standard portfolio analysis of risk) is typically calculated using a margining method that usually produces lower margin requirements in comparison to the traditional method.

Comparing Margin

It can be informative to compare margin requirements for an option on an uncovered stock, ETF, index, or stock index futures. That way, we can see a true apples-to-apples comparison of margin requirements.

The S&P 500 futures contract controls $375,000 of value, assuming that the S&P 500 futures is at 1,500 (1,500 times $250 a point). To make a valid comparison, assume that XYZ stock, SPY, SPX, and the S&P 500 futures all control the same $375,000. To simplify matters, we will assume that the option sold is at-the-money and that the premium collected is ignored. That way, we can focus solely on the difference in the margin

TABLE 23.2 Sample Comparison of Margin Requirements

Margin Type	XYZ Stock (Standard Method, $)	SPY (Standard Method, $)	SPX (Standard Method, $)	Futures (Estimated SPAN Margin, $)
Initial margin	75,000	75,000	56,250	15,000

requirements. Following are initial margin requirements for such an at-the-money short call or put option:

- **Stock**: XYZ initial margin is $75,000 ($375,000 times 20 percent),
- **ETF**: SPY initial margin is $75,000 ($375,000 times 20 percent),
- **Index**: SPX initial margin is $56,250 ($375,000 times 15 percent),
- **Stock index futures**: S&P 500 futures initial margin is approximately $15,000 using SPAN margin.

A sample comparison of initial margin requirements for an XYZ stock, ETF, index, and stock index futures is shown in Table 23.2.

Portfolio margining would likely produce a lower margin requirement than the traditional method. In some cases, the portfolio margining amount may more closely approximate the futures SPAN amount.

COMMISSION AND BID/ASK

As previously mentioned, one SPX is 10 times the value of one SPY. As a result, an advantage of trading an SPX stock index option versus an ETF is that an SPX index option may provide greater leverage relative to ETFs, resulting in lower commissions. If you were to pay commissions based on the number of option contracts you trade, you would be able to trade fewer index option contracts because you are trading the larger-size index product instead of the smaller-size ETF. As a result, you can use this leverage to your advantage when it comes to paying commissions because you can trade fewer contracts. You need to check with your futures and equity brokers to compare the commission structures of each instrument.

The index commission advantage, however, can be partially or totally offset by wide index option bid/ask spreads. For example, an SPX out-of-the-money put may have a bid/ask spread of approximately $1.50/$2.00, representing an onerous 33 percent spread cost ($0.50 divided by $1.50 if you buy at the ask price). An at-the-money SPX option usually has a lower percentage spread, with a bid/ask spread of something similar to $25/$27, reflecting an 8 percent cost.

Futures

As previously mentioned, one S&P 500 futures is 2.5 times the value of one SPX and is 25 times the value of one SPY. As a result, an advantage of trading a stock index futures option versus a stock option or ETF option is that its greater leverage allows for you to trade fewer contracts, resulting in an account that is easier to manage, with lower commissions.

In addition, the commission structure in the futures option market typically is different from the equity option market. In the equity option market, you typically pay a commission each time you buy or sell an option contract, with no commission if the option expires worthless. In the futures market, commissions are typically paid all up front (except for some fees) when a transaction is initiated (called a "round-turn commission"), with no additional commission if the option is offset or becomes worthless. For example, a stock option trader may pay $1 per option contract to trade 25 options on SPY and an additional commission of $1 per contract to offset at a later date, for a total commission of $50. A futures trader may pay, in contrast, $10 to $15 in round-turn commissions for one option contract (remember that each point change in S&P 500 futures options is 25 times the SPY). As a result, the SPY option trader would pay $50 in commissions and the S&P 500 futures option trader would pay $10 to $15. A futures account, based on your arrangements with your broker, can be paid based on each transaction instead of by round-turn.

In determining your costs, you should take into account differences in the bid/ask spreads by comparing spreads of the futures to a comparable index and ETF. Remember that a $0.05 spread in the SPY is the equivalent of 25 times that amount in the futures market, or $1.25. Regular S&P 500 futures options typically have a more narrow bid/ask spread than EOM S&P 500 futures options, probably because there is less liquidity in the EOM S&P 500 futures options. The bid/ask spread of an out-of-the-money S&P 500 futures option is typically wide, but it may be less than the SPX and SPY on a percentage basis.

Negotiating the Bid/Ask Spread   A wide index option bid/ask spread may make index options somewhat unattractive. To negotiate the best price, assuming that you are placing an order to sell an uncovered put, for example, you can place the order to sell at the midpoint between the bid/ask spread; if it does not fill in a minute or so, enter a cancel/replace order and move the sale price a fraction toward the bid. If it is not filled again, keep repeating the process. A wide bid/ask spread can be particularly onerous if there are multiple legs to an option strategy. Placing an option order is covered in Chapter 31.

Interestingly, a wide bid/ask spread may not hurt an option seller as much as an option buyer (if things go according to plan), provided he receives a favorable premium at the time of sale and the option expires worthless. If things go according to plan and an option expires worthless, an option seller is not required to offset the options, so he is not obligated to incur an additional commission. Conversely, an option buyer plans to sell those options at a later date at a higher price, thus intentionally subjecting himself to a potentially onerous wide bid/ask spread at a later date.

TAXES

Taxes are covered in Chapter 32 but are also worth mentioning here. There is a special federal income tax structure that applies to some options and futures called a *section 1256 contract*. A section 1256 contract consists of futures options (e.g., S&P 500 futures), options on broad-based indexes (e.g., SPX), and regulated futures contracts (e.g., trading the underlying S&P 500 futures contract). Under this treatment, a taxpayer can treat 60 percent (called the "60/40 rule") of any gains as a long-term capital gain (or loss). As a result, such a deemed long-term gain has a potentially lower tax rate structure and can be viewed as an advantage of trading options on stock index futures and options on broad-based indexes (like SPX) versus a stock or ETF. Apparently, options on the SPY are not subject to this special tax treatment.

FINAL THOUGHTS

Underlying instruments can differ in what underlies the instrument as well as size, exercise and assignment, margin, trading hours, tax consequences, and other factors. Selecting the most appropriate underlying instruments is one of the most important trading decisions you will make. For example, in general, I have found that a broad-based index, such as the SPX, can be a good candidate for option selling because an option sale is a bet against volatility and an index is typically less volatile than an individual stock. With an index, a decline in one stock can be offset by a rise in another stock, so it can have a smoothing out effect (in relative terms). However, I find that stocks can be a viable candidate for buying options. Buying and selling options on a broad-based index, such as the SPX, allows you to follow macroeconomic issues and avoid individual company risk. The other advantage of trading options on the SPX is that news about the SPX is widely disseminated, making it easier to follow. In addition, the underlying S&P 500 futures contract can be traded almost 24 hours a day. Chapters 24 to 26 cover options on ETFs, stock indexes, and stock index futures.

CHAPTER 24

ETF Options

An advantage of an ETF is that it can enable you to take advantage of your unique view of the market. This chapter will provide background information on ETFs, list some ETFs I like to follow that may help you in your trading, provide a sample ETF option chain, and describe double and inversely correlated ETFs. ETF strategies are presented Appendix A to help show you how ETF options can be used in numerous scenarios.

OVERVIEW

An ETF option works in essentially the same manner as an option on a stock. For example, like an option on a stock, the ETF option buyer has unlimited reward potential and limited risk, and the ETF option seller has limited reward potential and unlimited risk. An ETF call option provides the purchaser the right, but not the obligation, to buy 100 shares at the strike price on or before the (Friday) expiration date. An ETF put option provides the purchaser the right, but not the obligation, to sell 100 shares at the strike price on or before the (Friday) expiration date. The ETF call seller is obligated to sell if assigned and the ETF put seller is obligated to buy if assigned. The factors that affect the price of an ETF option are the same as those affecting the price of an equity option, including the value of the underlying instrument (an ETF, in this case), strike price, time to expiration, volatility, interest rate, and dividends.

WHAT IS AN ETF?

An ETF is typically an investment product that tracks a defined benchmark (usually an index) and trades like a stock. You can trade an ETF (and its options) throughout the trading day. ETFs, like conventional open-ended mutual funds, hold a basket of securities (stocks and/or bonds) and are usually passively managed. ETFs can focus on a single market sector or industry or can track single foreign countries or foreign indexes.

You may be wondering what the difference is between the traditional close-ended fund and an ETF. Traditional close-ended mutual fund shares can typically trade with a large premium or discount relative to the net asset value of the underlying assets. However, an ETF price attempts to track more closely the value of the underlying assets and eliminate a large portion of any premium or discount. For example, a traditional close-ended mutual fund may trade on an established exchange at $15 a share, whereas its underlying assets are valued at $14.50 (the fund is trading at a 3.4 percent premium) or $15.50 (the fund is trading at a 3.2 percent discount). The price paid for a close-ended fund is determined by the supply and demand for the shares trading in the marketplace, whereas the price of an ETF is primarily determined by its net asset value. Thus, an ETF attempts to eliminate the premium/discount uncertainty from the equation as much as possible. Many ETFs seem to do a respectable job of keeping the premium/discount to a minimum, but tracking and other errors do occur.

An advantage of buying and selling an ETF relative to stocks is that an ETF tends to be less volatile and is not subject to individual company risk. With an ETF, you can trade an industry segment, country, or commodity in a diversified basket of stocks; for example, if you want to trade the financial sector, there is an ETF (symbol XLF) that you can buy and sell (along with its options). An ETF (and its options) can be attractive to trade because it can offer a way to trade a diversified basket of stocks in a single trade in an efficient manner. You can trade an ETF using market and limit orders, short an ETF (except in an IRA), and buy on margin. Like a stock, you incur brokerage commission each time you buy or sell an ETF.

The S&P 500 SPDR (symbol SPY) is a popular ETF that tracks the S&P 500 stock index and is commonly heavily traded. The underlying ETF net asset value changes based on the value of an underlying index times a multiplier. For example, if the S&P 500 index is at 1,500, the SPY would be at approximately 150. How the benchmark index is converted to an ETF value can vary. For example, the divisor for the QQQ Trust PowerShares (symbol QQQQ) is 40 so that if the underlying NASDAQ 100 is at 2,000, the QQQQ would be at approximately 50.

ETF OPTIONS

An advantage to trading an ETF in comparison to a close-ended or open-ended mutual fund is that many ETFs offer the opportunity to trade options. Generally, the factors that affect the price of an ETF option are the same as those affecting the price of an equity option. For example, the price of an ETF call will generally increase as the level of its underlying benchmark index increases, and the price of an ETF put will generally increase as the level of its underlying benchmark index declines. The strategies for an

ETF option are the same as for an option on a stock; for example, a long ETF call is bullish and a long ETF put is bearish.

An ETF option is available on the broad market and in specific industry sectors such as technology, retail, pharmaceuticals, semiconductors, energy, foreign markets, bonds, and commodities. Following is a list of widely traded ETF options according to the Chicago Board Options Exchange (CBOE). A number of ETF options trade at the CBOE, and they are listed on the organization's web site (www.cboe.com). I have provided a list of the ones I like to follow:

U.S. stock market
SPY: S&P 500 SPDR
DIA: Dow Jones Industrial Average Diamonds Trust
IWM: Russell 2000 Index Fund iShares
QQQQ: NASDAQ 100 QQQ Trust PowerShares

Emerging-market ETFs
EEM: MSCI Emerging Markets Index iShares
EFA: MSCI EAFE Exchange Traded Fund iShares
EWH: MSCI Hong Kong Index iShares
FXI: FTSA/Xinhua China 25 iShares
ILF: S&P Latin America 40 Index iShares
VWO: Vanguard Emerging Markets ETF

U.S. sector ETFs
XLF: Financial Select Sector SPDR
BBH: Biotech HOLDRs Trust
OIH: Oil Services HOLDRs Trust
PPH: Pharmaceutical HOLDRs Trust
SMH: Semiconductor HOLDRs Trust
XLE: Energy Select Sector SPDR
USO: United States Oil Fund
DBA: Agriculture Fund PowerShares DB
UTH: Utilities HOLDRs Trust

U.S. bond market
SHY: Lehman 1–3 Year Treasury Bond Fund iShares
IEF: Lehman 7–10 Year Treasury Bond Fund iShares
TLT: Lehman 20+ Year Treasury Bond Fund iShares

You can purchase an ETF put to profit from a directional move or to hedge a position or portfolio. For example, to hedge (protect) a large-capitalization diversified portfolio, you may buy SPY puts, but to hedge a large-capitalization technology portfolio, you may buy QQQQ NASDAQ 100 puts.

ETF Option Specifications

The multiplier for an ETF option is generally 100. As a result, each point change in an ETF option represents $100. ETF option strike price intervals are usually set at a minimum of 1-point increments (instead of the 2.5-, 5-, or 10-point strike price intervals used for stocks). Options on an ETF typically have an American-style exercise feature.

Each ETF has unique product specifications, including its symbol, a description of its components, the dollar value of each point change, whether each quote is stated in decimals and the minimum tick for each option, how strike prices are determined, strike price intervals, expiration months, expiration dates, its exercise style (European vs. American), its last trading day, guidelines regarding the settlement of option exercises, position and exercise limits, its margin, and its trading hours. You should check with your broker (and visit CBOE's and other web sites) to determine current contract specifications.

An ETF can distribute fairly large capital gains. A capital-gain distribution from an ETF can result in a significant decline in the ETF value and can also affect option prices if it exceeds certain thresholds. Not all ETFs trade options, and some are illiquid with wide bid/ask spreads, so they should be avoided.

ETF Option Chain

Like options on a stock, a good place to find ETF option prices is an option chain. Table 24.1 shows a representative sample of SPY options that expire on the third Friday in October, assuming it is currently in late August, with SPY trading at $129. In this example, October is 50 days until expiration. Bid/ask prices for calls are shown on the left side, bid/ask prices for puts are shown on the right side, and strike prices are listed in the middle column.

TABLE 24.1   Sample SPY Option Chain (50 Days to Expiration)

Call Bid	Call Ask	Strike Price	Put Bid	Put Ask
7.05	7.20	124	1.99	2.00
6.35	6.40	125	2.26	2.28
5.65	5.75	126	2.57	2.59
5.00	5.05	127	2.91	2.93
4.35	4.45	128	3.25	3.35
3.75	3.85	129	3.70	3.75
3.25	3.30	130	4.15	4.20
2.75	2.78	131	4.65	4.75
2.30	2.32	132	5.20	5.30
1.89	1.91	133	5.80	5.90
1.54	1.55	134	6.45	6.55

You can see from Table 24.1 that SPY option strike price intervals are in one-point increments instead of the five-point strike price intervals used for comparable stocks.

ETF Quarterlys ETF Quarterlys are ETF options that have the same contract specifications as standard options, except that they expire on the last business day of each calendar quarter (March, June, September, and December). ETF Quarterlys options are included on, for example, the SPY options, iShares Russell 2000 Index Fund (symbol IWM), QQQQ, options on Dow Jones Diamonds (symbol DIA), and Energy Select Sector SPDR (symbol XLE). A Quarterly option is P.M. settled, like an option on a stock.

American- versus European-Style Exercising ETF options are typically American-style exercised, giving the buyer the right to exercise before expiration. A call buyer has the right to buy an underlying ETF, whereas a put buyer has the right to sell an underlying ETF. A call seller has the obligation to sell the underlying ETF if assigned, whereas a put seller has the obligation to buy an underlying ETF if assigned. An option on an ETF ordinarily expires on the third Friday of the expiration month, like an option on a stock (technically, it is on a Saturday, but the relevant date is Friday). Not all ETF options are American style; for example, iShares S&P 500 Index Fund (symbol IVV) is the European-style exercise version of SPY.

ETF Option Strategies

Strategies utilizing ETF options are the same as options on a stock. To emphasize this, following is a description of the four basic option strategies, consisting of a long call, a long put, a short call, and a short put.

Long ETF Call A long ETF call profits from a rise in the price of the underlying ETF with unlimited reward potential and limited risk. For example, assume that the S&P 500 index is at 1,500 and you buy one February SPY 155 call at $1.50 ($150). If the value of the call rises to $2, your profit is $50. You can exercise the option on or before the expiration date.

Long ETF Put A long ETF put profits from a decline in the price of the underlying ETF with unlimited reward potential and limited risk. For example, assume that the S&P 500 index is at 1,500 and you buy one February SPY 145 put at $1.50 ($150). If the value of the put rises to $2, your profit is $50. You can exercise the option on or before the expiration date.

Short ETF Call A short ETF call profits from a decline or sideways movement in the price of the underlying ETF with limited reward potential and unlimited risk. For example, assume that the S&P 500 index is at 1,500 and you sell one February SPY 155 call at $1.50 ($150). If the value of the call declines to $1, your profit is $50. You may be assigned on the option on or before the expiration date.

Short ETF Put   A short ETF put profits from a rise or sideways movement in the price of the underlying ETF with limited reward potential but unlimited risk. For example, assume that the S&P 500 index is at 1,500 and you sell one February SPY 145 put at $1.50 ($150). If the value of the put declines to $1, your profit is $50. You may be assigned on the option on or before the expiration date.

Overview of Spread Strategies   Appendix A illustrates many of the ETF strategies covered throughout this book. Prior to engaging in any option strategy, you should develop a view of the market or underlying instrument. After you have developed that forecast, you should select the best option strategy for your prediction; for example, you may be bullish on the broad U.S. stock market, bullish on an industry sector, bearish on the U.S. stock market, or bearish on an individual sector. You may be bullish on small caps or bearish on technology stocks, or bullish on emerging-market stocks. Conversely, you may simply believe that implied volatility is too high and that it will contract. Whatever your market prediction, there is likely an ETF option strategy that can be used to profit from that view. Following are sample ETF option strategies. Many of these strategies are illustrated in Appendix A; for example, you can utilize the following:

- Long or short call or put,
- Long or short vertical spread,
- Long or short iron condor,
- Ratio spread,
- Backspread,
- Long or short straddle,
- Long or short strangle,
- Long or short butterfly,
- Long or short condor,
- Long or short calendar spread,
- Long or short diagonal spread,
- Covered call or put,
- Long or short combination,
- Long or short covered combination.

After you have determined your view of the market, you can find a strategy that will profit if you are bullish or bearish or predict an increase in volatility, where an underlying instrument will trade outside a range, or a decrease in volatility, where an underlying instrument will trade within a range—not only that, but there are strategies that have a positive correlation to the market, other strategies with an inverse correlation to the market, and some that can be executed at the same rate as the underlying index or at double the daily index.

Inversely Correlated ETFs

The price of most ETFs closely tracks the value of the underlying benchmark assets so that a rise in the value of the underlying asset results in a proportionate rise in the net asset value and price of a corresponding ETF. However, some ETFs are inversely correlated to the benchmark index they track so that the price of the ETF rises when its underlying asset declines and declines when its underlying asset rises. An inversely correlated ETF can afford an opportunity to quickly short the market, industry, or commodity. Keep in mind that there is some risk associated with investing in these funds because the funds may have a tracking error and do not achieve their stated objective over a period of time greater than one day because mathematical compounding prevents the funds from achieving such results over a longer period of time. The ProShares group of funds sponsors a number of these ETFs. Sample ETFs negatively (inversely) correlated to the S&P 500 index are as follows:

- The ProShares Short S&P 500 (symbol SH) changes inversely (moves in the opposite direction) to the underlying S&P 500 index at the same percentage. As a result, if the S&P 500 index rises by 1 percent, SH attempts to decline 1 percent.
- The ProShares Short QQQ (symbol PSQ) changes inversely (moves in the opposite direction) to the underlying NASDAQ 100 index at the same percentage. As a result, if the NASDAQ 100 index rises by 1 percent, PSQ attempts to decline 1 percent.

Because you are not permitted to borrow on margin in an equity IRA account, you are not permitted to sell naked call options. As a result, you may only be permitted to buy call options, sell covered call options, sell defined-risk credit spreads, and sell cash-secured puts. However, an alternative for benefiting from a stock or market decline in an IRA is to buy an ETF, sell a put or buy a call option on an ETF, that moves inversely to the market.

Ultra (Double) ETFs

Some ETFs move at the same rate as the underlying index, whereas others move at double the rate of the underlying benchmark index (called "ultra"). Some ETFs move inversely at the same rate as the underlying index, whereas others move inversely at double the daily rate of the underlying index (called "double" or "ultrashort" funds).

Double Positive Correlation   Trading in an ultra (double) ETF allows you to take advantage of moves in the marketplace without having to buy or sell as many shares or option contracts. An ultra ETF can enable you to take advantage more quickly of moves in the marketplace in comparison to the traditional ETF. Sample ultra ETFs positively correlated to the underlying benchmark index are as follows:

- The ProShares Ultra S&P 500 (symbol SSO) corresponds to twice the percentage change of the S&P 500 index. As a result, if the S&P 500 index rises by 1 percent, SSO attempts to rise 2 percent.

- The ProShares Ultra QQQ (QLD) changes at twice the daily percentage rate of the NASDAQ 100 index. As a result, if the NASDAQ 100 index rises by 1 percent, QLD attempts to rise 2 percent.

Double Inverse Correlation   Sample ETFs that are double negatively (inversely) correlated to the underlying benchmark index are as follows:

- The ProShares UltraShort S&P 500 (symbol SDS) changes inversely at twice the daily percentage as the underlying S&P 500 index. As a result, if the S&P 500 index declines by 1 percent, SDS attempts to rise 2 percent.
- The ProShares UltraShort QQQ (symbol QID) changes inversely at twice the daily percentage rate of the NASDAQ 100 index. As a result, if the NASDAQ 100 index declines by 1 percent, QID attempts to rise 2 percent.

Tables 24.2 to 24.5 list ProShares ETFs that I like to follow, categorized as long, ultra-long, short, and ultrashort. Each of the ETFs listed in these tables has options available.

TABLE 24.2   Sample Long ETFs

ETF	Symbol	Benchmark Index
QQQ	QQQQ	NASDAQ 100 index
Dow 30	DIA	Dow Jones Industrial Average
S&P 500	SPY	S&P 500 index
Russell 2000	IWM	Russell 2000 index

TABLE 24.3   Sample Ultra Long ETFs

ETF	Symbol	Benchmark Index
Ultra QQQ	QLD	NASDAQ 100 index
Ultra Dow 30	DDM	Dow Jones Industrial Average
Ultra S&P 500	SSO	S&P 500 index
Ultra Russell 2000	UWM	Russell 2000 index
Ultra Oil and Gas	DIG	Dow Jones U.S. Oil and Gas index

TABLE 24.4   Sample Short ETFs

ETF	Symbol	Benchmark Index
Short QQQ	PSQ	NASDAQ 100 index
Short Dow 30	DOG	Dow Jones Industrial Average
Short S&P 500	SH	S&P 500 index

TABLE 24.5 Sample Ultra Short ETFs

ETF	Symbol	Benchmark Index
UltraShort QQQ	QID	NASDAQ 100 index
UltraShort Dow 30	DXD	Dow Jones Industrial Average
UltraShort S&P 500	SDS	S&P 500 index
UltraShort Russell 2000	TWM	Russell 2000 index
UltraShort Financials	SKF	Dow Jones U.S. Financials index
UltraShort Oil and Gas	DUG	Dow Jones U.S. Oil and Gas index
UltraShort MSCI EAFE	EFU	MSCI EAFE index
UltraShort MSCI Emerging Markets	EEV	MSCI Emerging Markets index
UltraShort FTSE/Xinhua China 25	FXP	FTSE/Xinhua China 25 index

Ultrashort Option Chain Like a regular ETF option, a good place to find ultra ETF option prices is an option chain. Table 24.6 shows a representative sample of ultrashort S&P 500 (symbol SDS) options that expire on the third Friday in October, assuming it is currently late August. The bid/ask prices are taken from SDS options, with SPY trading at 129 and SDS at $63.50. In this example, October is 50 days until expiration. Bid/ask prices for calls are shown on the left side, bid/ask prices for puts are shown on the right side, and strike prices are listed in the middle column.

Commission and Bid/Ask Spread When examining the bid/ask spread, you should compute the percentage difference between the bid price versus the ask price to determine its true potential cost; for example, there may be only a $0.10 difference between the bid and ask prices for an ETF. However, if the bid price is at $0.20 and the ask price is at $0.30, the ask price is 50 percent of the bid price. It is usually best to trade ETF options with high liquidity. For some ETF options, the bid/ask spread is so wide that trading an option on that ETF is impractical and ill advised.

TABLE 24.6 Sample SDS Option Chain (50 Days to Expiration)

Call Bid	Call Ask	Strike Price	Put Bid	Put Ask
6.10	6.30	59	1.30	1.45
5.50	5.70	60	1.65	1.75
4.90	5.10	61	2.10	2.25
4.40	4.60	62	2.60	2.75
3.90	4.10	63	3.10	3.30
3.60	3.70	64	3.70	3.90
3.20	3.30	65	4.30	4.50
2.80	3.00	66	5.00	5.20
2.50	2.65	67	5.70	5.90
2.25	2.40	68	6.40	6.60
2.00	2.15	69	7.20	7.40

Fixed-Income ETFs

Traders sometimes forget about the fixed-income ETFs because they have low volatility. However, dividends are paid on a monthly basis on many fixed-income ETFs and can represent a substantial benefit over time. With a bond ETF, you can get the dual benefit of both price appreciation and monthly dividend payouts, and a bond ETF can be a reasonable candidate with which to sell a covered call. Because bond prices are inversely correlated to interest rates, an interest-rate reduction has a positive effect on the prices of the fixed-income ETFs. The iShares 20+ Year T-bond (TLT) is one of numerous fixed-income ETFs that trade options.

Margin

The margin formula for an option on an ETF is typically the same as for an option on a stock. Chapter 30 describes margin requirements and provides a table (Table 30.1) that can be used as a guide for margin requirements.

FINAL THOUGHTS

An advantage of an ETF option is that it allows you to take advantage of your view across many markets, countries, and commodities. For example, if you are bullish on the broad market, you can buy a call option on the SPY or the SSO. If you are bearish on the broad market, you can buy a put on the SPY or a call on the SH or the SDS. To research ETFs, you may want to access the web site www.ETFconnect.com, which is a web site for index ETFs, close-ended funds, and exchange-traded notes. It provides daily pricing, fund data and fund search capability.

   If an ETF put is being used as a hedge, the index should be highly correlated to your portfolio. Otherwise, you may find yourself in a position in which your portfolio of stocks declines, and the ETF you chose does not move in lockstep with your stock portfolio, thus creating losses in your portfolio without the benefits of protection. In selecting the appropriate index, you should choose an index that is in the same sector as your stock, or you may select a broader-based index. When purchasing a protective put, you need to balance its degree of protection versus its cost.

   By learning about a number of ETFs, you can shift back and forth among U.S. markets, emerging markets, and commodities, depending on whether they are rising, moving sideways, or falling. For example, the U.S. stock market may be in a temporary downturn and there may be a bull market in emerging markets and/or commodities, or vice versa. Of course, you do not need a bull market to make money trading options; instead, you can trade a declining or sideways market. Chapter 25 will cover stock index options.

CHAPTER 25

Stock Index Options

T he equity option strategies you have learned throughout this book can be applied to index options. Like an equity option, an *index option* offers a trader an opportunity to capitalize on rising, declining, or sideways markets. Trading index options can be a nice addition to your option strategies, but there are some nuances, advantages, and disadvantages that you need to consider. This chapter provides background information, lists some indexes I like to follow, provides an example of an index option chain, provides examples of basic index strategies, describes differences in volatility at various strike prices, and discusses other issues. Index strategies are illustrated in Appendix B. This chapter will set the stage for Chapter 26, which covers stock index futures options.

OVERVIEW

An index option works in essentially the same manner as an option on a stock or ETF, except that on exercise or assignment it is cash settled and you cannot buy or sell an underlying cash index directly. Some index options are American-style exercised (e.g., the S&P 100 index, symbol OEX) or European-style exercised (e.g., the S&P 500 index, symbol SPX). The option strategies that you have learned throughout this book can be applied to an index. For example, like an option on a stock, the index option buyer has unlimited reward potential and limited risk, and the seller has limited reward potential and unlimited risk. An index call option provides the purchaser the right, but not the obligation, to buy (through cash settlement) at the strike price on or before the expiration date. An index put option provides the purchaser the right, but not the obligation, to sell (through cash settlement) at the strike price on or before the expiration date. An index call seller is obligated to sell (through cash settlement) if assigned, and an index put seller is obligated to buy (through cash settlement) if assigned. The factors that affect the price of an index option are the same as those affecting the price of an equity option, including the value of the underlying index, strike price, time to expiration, volatility, interest rate, and dividends. An index option can offer a way to trade a diversified basket of stocks in a single trade.

WHAT IS A STOCK INDEX?

A stock index is a collection of stock prices compiled into a single number. An index can be broadly based or narrowly based and constructed so that its weightings are biased toward the larger companies (*capitalization weighted*), based on an equal dollar weighting, based on earnings or dividends, or based on any other factor. Broad-based indexes cover a wide range of companies and industries, and narrow-based indexes consist of stocks in one industry, sector, or country. Indexes measure the ups and downs of stock, bond, and commodity markets. Among the best known indexes are the Dow Jones Industrial Average (DJX), SPX, NASDAQ 100 (NDX), and Russell 2000 (RUT). The SPX is probably the most followed broad-based, capitalization-weighted index, and the DJX is probably the most followed price-weighted index. The NDX represents the largest 100 companies in the NASDAQ, and the RUT represents 2,000 companies that are considered benchmarks of the U.S. small-capitalization market.

Unfortunately, you cannot buy or sell an underlying cash index directly, but there are various instruments you can trade that can act as a proxy and enable you to arrive in essentially the same place. For example, if you are short or long the cash market SPX option, you can buy or sell an ETF or futures contract, such as the S&P 500 SPDR (SPY) or S&P 500 futures, to serve as a proxy for the underlying index.

INDEX OPTIONS

Stock market indexes form the basis for trading in index options. You can buy or sell an option on an entire portfolio of stocks embedded in a single security in the same manner as you would trade an option on a stock. An index option can enable you to trade in a particular market or industry group without having to buy all the stocks individually; for instance, if you forecast that technology stocks are about to decline, you can buy a put on the NDX instead of buying puts on each technology company. You can trade an index option using market and limit orders. Like for a stock or ETF, you incur brokerage commissions each time you buy or sell an index option. An advantage of buying and selling options on an index, relative to a stock, is that an index tends to be less volatile and not subject to individual company risk. With an index, you can, in effect, trade a diversified basket of stocks. Indexes, and their corresponding options, are usually priced much higher in absolute terms than typical stock. As explained later, the size of an index can have a favorable effect on commissions. Following is a list of some actively traded index options I like to follow:

SPX: S&P 500 index.
RUT: Russell 2000 index.
NDX: NASDAQ 100 index.
MNX: CBOE Mini-NDX index (based on the NASDAQ 100).
DJX: Dow Jones Industrial Average.
VIX: CBOE Volatility index (options).
OEX: S&P 100 index (American-style exercised).
XEO: S&P 100 index (European-style exercised).
XSP: Mini-S&P 500 index.

An advantage of index options is that they allow you to quickly (that is another way of saying leverage) take advantage of your view of the market. For example, if you are bullish on the broad market, you can buy a call option on the SPX, and if you are bearish on the broad market, you can buy a put on the SPX. SPX options are European-style index option contracts settled in cash and are often one of the most heavily traded index option contracts.

Mini-index contracts are available on some indexes; for example, consider the following:

- Mini-SPX (XSP) options have one tenth the value of SPX index options; for example, if the SPX is at 1,500, the XSP would be at 150.
- Mini-NDX (MNX) options have one tenth the value of NDX index options; for example, if the NDX is at 1,500, the MNX would be at 150.
- Mini-RUT options (RMN) have one tenth the value of RUT index options; for example, if the RUT is at 2,000, the MNX would be at 200.

Index Contract Specifications

The multiplier for index options, similar to options on stocks and ETFs, is generally 100 but can vary from index to index. Each index has unique product specifications, including its symbol, a description of its components, the dollar value of each point change, whether each quote is stated in decimals, the minimum tick for each option, how strike prices are determined, strike price intervals, expiration months, expiration dates, its exercise style (European vs. American), its last trading day, guidelines regarding the settlement of option exercises, position and exercise limits, its margin, and its trading hours. You should understand index option product contract specifications for various index option classes before investing.

TABLE 25.1 Sample SPX Option Chain (50 Days to Expiration)

Call Bid	Call Ask	Strike Price	Put Bid	Put Ask
70.50	72.00	1,240	19.90	20.00
63.50	64.00	1,250	22.60	22.80
56.50	57.50	1,260	25.70	25.90
50.00	50.50	1,270	29.10	29.30
43.50	44.50	1,280	32.50	33.50
37.50	38.50	1,290	37.00	37.50
32.50	33.00	1,300	41.50	42.00
27.50	27.80	1,310	46.50	47.50
23.00	23.20	1,320	52.00	53.00
18.90	19.10	1,330	58.00	59.00
15.40	15.50	1,340	64.50	65.50

Index Option Chain

Like options on stocks and ETFs, a good place to find index option prices is an option chain. Table 25.1 shows a representative sample of SPX options that expire on the third Friday in October, assuming it is currently late August. The bid/ask prices assume that the SPX is at 1,295.

As a reminder from Chapters 24, the SPY is an ETF valued at one tenth of the underlying SPX. As a result, the SPX option prices in Table 25.1 are shown at 10 times the value of the SPY options shown in Table 24.1 (for SPY). This presentation is designed to reinforce the fact that SPY is one tenth the size of the SPX, as explained in Chapters 23 and 24. You should keep in mind that in the real world, the prices of SPX options will not be exactly 10 times the prices of SPY options. Strike prices for the SPX are typically in 5-point increments but are shown in Table 25.1 in 10-point strike price increments to make for an easy comparison to SPY. In this example, October is 50 days until expiration. Bid/ask prices for calls are shown on the left side, bid/ask prices for puts are shown on the right side, and strike prices are listed in the middle column.

My favorite trade in SPX options is selling far out-of-the-money put and call options. As a result, Table 25.2 shows an option chain with 50-point strike price increments for illustrative purposes, so you can see the lower strikes for puts and higher strikes for calls. The bid/ask prices assume that the SPX is at 1,300. SPX strike price intervals are usually in 5-point increments (instead of the 50-point strike price intervals in Table 25.2). The option prices differ slightly from the previous table because Table 25.2 assumes that the SPX is slightly higher.

I typically look for at least $2 ($200) when selling an option and will usually look up and down the option chain to find a put bid price at $2 ($200) or above. Likewise, I will usually look up and down on the option chain to find a call bid price at $2 ($200) or above. As a result, for example, a short put at approximately 1,125 (not shown here) and lower may be a reasonable position, and a short call at approximately 1,410 (not shown

TABLE 25.2 Sample SPX October Option Chain (48 Days to Expiration)

Call Bid	Call Ask	Strike Price	Put Bid	Put Ask
199.10	201.10	1,100	1.80	2.10
151.80	153.80	1,150	4.20	4.80
107.20	109.20	1,200	9.30	10.30
67.40	69.40	1,250	19.00	20.60
35.00	37.00	1,300	36.20	38.20
13.30	14.90	1,350	64.10	66.10
3.20	3.90	1,400	103.40	105.40
0.35	0.90	1,450	150.20	152.20
0	0.40	1,500	199.60	201.60

here) and above may be a reasonable position. Typically, I will sell a near-term put and a call with 30 to 90 days to expiration.

Index Weeklys and Quarterlys If you want to purchase a call (or put) option because you are bullish (or bearish) on an earnings report that will be released in one day, you only need an option covering that time period. However, the problem is that options are standardized contracts that expire on the third Friday of every calendar month, and that may not fit your time frame very well. For instance, you cannot purchase a listed option with only one day remaining, unless it is the last week of expiration. That is where Weeklys and Quarterlys can be useful.

Weeklys are index options that have a life of one week instead of the traditional life of months or years. The contract specifications for Weeklys are the same as for standard options, except for the time to expiration. Index Weeklys include, for example, SPX Weeklys, Mini-SPX (XSP) Weeklys, and S&P 100 index Weeklys (OEX, American-style exercised). In addition, there are S&P 100 index Weeklys with European-style exercise (XEO). Each new series of Weeklys is listed each Friday and they expire the following Friday, except that no new Weeklys are listed if it is the expiration week for standard options (the third Friday of each month).

SPX Weeklys are one-week, European-style options on the S&P 500 index with a Friday A.M. settlement (the last day of trading is a Thursday); OEX Weeklys are one-week, American-style options on the S&P 100 index with a Friday P.M. settlement (the last day of trading is a Friday).

Index Quarterlys are index options that have the contract specifications of standard options, except that they expire on the last business day of each calendar quarter (March, June, September, and December). Index Quarterlys include, for example, SPX Quarterlys, XSP Quarterlys, and XEO Quarterlys. Quarterlys S&P 500 index options are P.M. settled.

American versus European Style Exercise Index options ordinarily expire on the third Friday of the month, like stock options. Index options can be American style, such as the OEX, or European style, such as the SPX. As a reminder, American-style options can be exercised at any time on or before expiration, whereas European-style options can be exercised only at a specified time at expiration. An index option can be offset in the marketplace on or before its last trading day.

Index options are cash settled instead of being subject to the physical equity option exercise and assignment procedures. The *exercise settlement amount* is based on the difference between the strike price of the option and the *exercise settlement value* multiplied by 100 (assuming that the index has a multiplier of 100). The exercise (cash) settlement amount is based on the amount that the option is in-the-money (the difference between the strike price and the exercise settlement value of the underlying index). For example, assume that with the S&P 500 index at 1,500, you buy one February SPX 1,550 call and the index rises to 1,600. In this example, you can exercise the option and receive a cash settlement of $5,000.

Index option exercise settlement values can be classified as either A.M. or P.M. settlement. An *A.M. settlement*, such as for the SPX, is determined using the *opening* prices of an index's component stocks on the morning after the last trading day. An SPX-settled option settlement value is based on the opening print of all stocks that make up the SPX on the morning of the expiration Friday. The SPX settlement value is a special settlement value that is determined once all of the component stocks in the SPX open and is not the opening print of the SPX on Friday morning. A *P.M. settlement*, such as for the OEX, is determined by using the component stocks' closing values on the last day of exercise.

Option Strategies

Strategies for an index option are essentially the same as for an option on a stock or ETF except that on exercise or assignment it is cash settled and you cannot buy or sell an underlying cash index directly. To emphasize this, following is a description of the four basic option strategies, consisting of a long call, a long put, a short call, and a short put. As a reminder, you can close out an option position by offsetting it in the marketplace anytime prior to expiration.

Long Index Call   A long index call can enable a trader to profit from a rise in the price of the underlying index with unlimited reward potential and limited risk. For example, assume that the SPX is at 1,500 and you buy one February SPX 1,550 call at $15 ($1,500). If the underlying index settles at 1,600, for instance, on the expiration date, the cash received on exercise of the option is $5,000 (50 points times $100), for a net profit of $3,500.

Long Index Put   A long index put can enable a trader to profit from a decline in the price of the underlying index with unlimited reward potential and limited risk. For example, assume that the SPX is at 1,500 and you buy one February SPX 1,450 put at $15 ($1,500). If the underlying index settles at 1,400, for instance, on the expiration date, the cash received on exercise of the option is $5,000 (50 points times $100), for a net profit of $3,500.

Short Index Call A short index call can enable a trader to profit from a decline or sideways movement in the price of the underlying index with limited reward potential and unlimited risk. For example, assume that the SPX is at 1,500 and you sell one February SPX 1,550 call at $15 ($1,500). If the underlying index settles at 1,600, for instance, on the expiration date, the cash paid by you on assignment is $5,000 (50 points times $100), for a net loss of $3,500.

Short Index Put A short index put can enable a trader to profit from a rise or sideways movement in the price of the underlying index with limited reward potential and unlimited risk. For example, assume that the S&P 500 index is at 1,500 and you sell one February SPX 1,450 put at $15 ($1,500). If the underlying index settles at 1,400, for instance, on the expiration date, the cash paid by you on assignment is $5,000 (50 points times $100), for a net loss of $3,500.

Spread Strategies Appendix B illustrates many of the index strategies. The great feature about the strategies at a glance in Appendix B is that they, in effect, summarize many of the strategies covered throughout this book. Prior to engaging in any option strategy, you should develop a view of the market or underlying instrument. After you have developed that forecast, you should select the best option strategy for your prediction; for example, you may be bullish on the broad U.S. stock market, bullish on an industry sector, bearish on the U.S. stock market, or bearish on an individual sector. You may be bullish on small caps or bearish on technology stocks. Conversely, you may simply believe that implied volatility is too high and that it will contract. Following are sample index option strategies. Many of these strategies are illustrated in Appendix B. To summarize, you can utilize strategies such as the following:

- Long or short call or put,
- Long or short vertical spread,
- Long or short iron condor,
- Ratio spread,
- Backspread,
- Long or short straddle,
- Long or short strangle,
- Long or short butterfly,
- Long or short condor,
- Long or short calendar spread,
- Long or short diagonal spread,
- Long or short combination.

A covered strategy would need to use an instrument to act as a proxy because you cannot buy or sell an underlying cash index directly. After you have determined your view of the market, you can find a strategy that will profit if you are bullish or bearish or predict an increase in volatility, where an underlying instrument will trade outside a range, or a decrease in volatility, where an underlying instrument will trade within a range.

Taxes   As described in Chapter 32, there is modified tax treatment for trading options on a broad-based index (section 1256 contracts). Section 1256 contracts consist of futures options (e.g., S&P 500 futures), options on broad-based indexes (e.g., SPX), and regulated futures (e.g., trading the underlying S&P 500 futures). Under this modification, regardless of how long you have held the option, the gain or loss is deemed 60 percent long term and 40 percent short term (called the 60/40 rule); the option is marked to market at the end of each calendar year; net capital losses can be carried back; and to the extent the carryback is not utilized, losses can be carried forward. Once you understand these rules, you may conclude that you may be able to save taxes by trading options on one product instead of another. Fortunately, options on a broad-based index, such as the SPX, are subject to this special tax treatment and can represent an advantage of trading an index option versus a comparable ETF.

INDEX VOLATILITY SKEW

Portfolio managers have a tendency to sell short-term calls to finance the purchase of puts (i.e., a collar trade, as described in Chapter 21), having the effect of driving down the prices of short-term calls and driving up the prices of short-term puts in the SPX and S&P 500 futures. This creates a pricing environment in which the prices of puts are higher than the prices of comparable calls.

This pattern creates an environment in which at-the-money put and call options are approximately equal, but put options far exceed call options as you move out-of-the-money. This pattern is called a *volatility skew* and is described in Chapter 27. This can create attractive option-selling opportunities in puts and unattractive selling in calls. It should be noted, however, that the effects of the SPX call suppression can be mitigated by trading farther out in time. By trading call options with a later expiration date, the downward pressure on call prices can be minimized. Longer-term call options are typically more on par with longer-term put options.

INDEX TIME DECAY

Time decay can vary depending on whether an option is in-the-money, at-the-money, or out-of-the-money and can vary depending on whether it is a put or a call and on the type of instrument (stock, ETF, stock index, or stock index futures). Table 25.3 shows the projected time decay pattern of an at-the-money option at a particular point in time for a 10-week period on a representative stock (Research in Motion). For purposes of

TABLE 25.3 Sample Time Decay: SPX Out-of-the-Money Put

Weeks to Expiration (Beginning of Week)	Call Value ($)	Weekly Decay ($)	Percentage Decay	Average Weekly Decay to Expiration ($)
10	23.07	2.49	11	2.31
9	20.58	2.56	12	2.29
8	18.02	2.65	15	2.25
7	15.37	2.83	18	2.20
6	12.54	2.71	22	2.09
5	9.83	2.83	29	1.97
4	7.00	2.78	40	1.75
3	4.22	2.47	59	1.41
2	1.75	1.58	90	0.88
1	0.17	0.17	100	0.17

comparison, Table 25.3 shows time decay for a 10-week period on an SPX put, assuming that it is 100 points out-of-the-money.

Table 25.3 indicates that the dollar decay is fairly constant each week until the final two weeks, whereas the percentage increases each week. However, in Table 25.3, note that one month of time decay, beginning in week 10, of $10.53 ($23.07 minus $12.54) is greater than the one-month decay just prior to expiration of $7.00 ($7.00 minus zero). This type of information could be useful to an option seller because it indicates that selling an out-of-the-money put option within the last four weeks provides more rapid time decay but does not provide as much dollar profit.

Margin   The margin formulas for an index are similar to those for a stock or ETF, except that your broker may use 15 percent instead of 20 percent. Selling an uncovered stock equity index option can be difficult for investors because the margin requirements for index options can be high in an equity account. The margin rules for equity accounts treat an index as though the level of the index is equal to the price of the stock, and traditional margin rules use the price of the underlying stock as a starting point for calculating margin requirements. Remember that to lower your margin requirement, you can trade an option spread instead of an uncovered option. Chapter 30 describes margin requirements.

FINAL THOUGHTS

An index can be a valuable tool because it offers greater leverage than the typical ETF. This greater leverage can mean that fewer contracts may be traded at a lower commission. You can buy or sell an index option in your regular brokerage account. You can purchase an index put to profit from a directional move or to hedge a position or portfolio. For example, to protect a large-capitalization and diversified portfolio, you may buy an SPX put, but to protect a large-capitalization technology portfolio, you may buy a NDX put.

If an index put is being used as a hedge, the index should be highly correlated to your portfolio. Otherwise, you may find yourself in a position in which your portfolio of stocks declines, and the index you chose does not move in lockstep with your stock portfolio, thus creating losses in your portfolio, without the benefits of protection. In selecting the appropriate index, you may choose an index that is in the same sector as your stock or select a broader-based index. When purchasing a protective put, you need to balance its degree of protection versus its cost. Of course, an out-of-the-money put costs less than an at-the-money or in-the-money put but offers less protection.

Unfortunately, at this time, there are only a limited number of index options that have sufficient liquidity worth trading. For example, if you believe that the financial sector will be weak, there is an ETF (symbol XLF) that you can buy and sell, along with options, but there is no comparable liquid index option worth trading at this time.

Unlike an option on a stock, unfortunately, you cannot buy or sell the underlying index. Other potential problems in trading index options are wide bid/ask spreads, high margin because of the size of the index, and limited liquidity. Quite frankly, I prefer trading S&P 500 futures because you can buy or sell the underlying instrument and it generally has a more narrow bid/ask spread, lower margin, and greater liquidity.

It is usually best to trade index options with high liquidity so that you are not subject to an enormous bid/ask spread. For some index products, the bid/ask spread is so wide that trading options on that index is impractical and ill advised. You should compare the bid/ask spreads of equity index options relative to stock futures options. Keeping an eye on index option prices can be useful because, occasionally, the pricing of an index option can be more (or less) favorable in comparison to its sister ETF or futures contract. Futures contracts that are based on indexes, such as the S&P 500 and Russell 2000 futures, are discussed in Chapter 26.

Stock Index Futures Options

The option strategies you have learned throughout this book can be applied to *futures options*. This chapter describes futures basics; provides a list of popular stock index futures; describes stock index futures options; provides a sample option chain; provides examples of basic strategies; describes differences in volatility at various strike prices; addresses time decay, taxes, and margin; and provides a bonus section demonstrating a short strangle. This chapter addresses options on stock index futures, and the principles are primarily illustrated using S&P 500 futures. Stock index futures option strategies are illustrated in Appendix C. The first part of this chapter covers the basics of underlying futures and the second part covers options.

OVERVIEW

An attraction of futures trading is substantially lower margin requirements in comparison to margin on *cash market* stocks, ETFs, and indexes. This freedom to trade is viewed by many traders as a significant advantage of trading futures. Many traders also find futures options attractive because a futures offers unique products, a relatively favorable commission structure, extended hours of trading, and the ability to easily trade long or short.

Stock index futures are futures contracts that track the value of an underlying index; for example, the value of S&P 500 futures is derived from the value underlying the S&P 500 index (SPX). Futures exchanges offer options on such products as stock indexes, foreign exchange, interest rates, crude oil, heating oil, unleaded gasoline, natural gas, electricity, gold, silver, platinum, copper, aluminum, and other products. This chapter, however, will focus on stock index futures, such as S&P 500 futures.

A Futures Is Leverage

Futures are highly leveraged, and in a futures account both the buyer and seller of underlying futures are required to post margin. For example, if the S&P 500 futures is at 1,500, the contract has a nominal value of $375,000 (1,500 times $250 per point) and the initial margin requirement might only be approximately $25,000. If the S&P 500 futures rises by 10 points, the buyer of one such futures contract has a gain of $2,500 (10 points times $250), or a 25 percent return on margin. The opposite is true if such a futures declines by 10 points because this would create a $2,500 loss (25 percent of margin) to the buyer. Remember that leverage cuts both ways. In this example, the underlying futures only changed 10 points, which is 0.66 percent of the underlying index but 25 percent of margin. A buyer or seller of a stock index futures is considered to have unlimited potential gain or loss and can gain or lose more than the margin posted. Keep in mind that this discussion relates to trading the underlying futures contact and not to futures options; options are addressed later.

Advantages of Futures

There are various reasons the futures market may be attractive relative to the stock market:

- The futures market enables you to exit an underlying futures position overnight (options trade during regular trading hours). One of the unspoken disadvantages of the stock market is that if you hold a position overnight, you cannot exit that position, no matter how badly you want to get out. That is risk. At least the futures market provides an opportunity, in many cases, to get out of your position by trading the underlying stock index futures almost 24 hours a day during the workweek.
- The futures market has less stringent margin requirements. Futures margins typically use the standard portfolio analysis of risk (SPAN) margining system, which calculates margin based on the risk of your positions. Stock options typically calculate margin using a proxy method that is primarily based on the price of the underlying stock (unless you qualify for portfolio margining).
- The futures market can have contracts with a greater unit of measurement, enabling you to trade fewer contracts, resulting in lower commissions and less of an administrative burden. For example, the S&P 500 futures is 25 times the size of the S&P 500 SPDR (SPY) and, as a result, you can trade fewer futures contracts.
- You can more actively trade futures because futures trades are settled immediately, in comparison to stocks, which may have a three-day settlement.
- It can be easier to short a position in the futures market.
- In many cases, the bid/ask spread of stock index futures, such as S&P 500 futures, is more narrow on a percentage basis compared to the cash market SPX. The bid/ask spread on S&P 500 futures options may be less than on the SPY on a percentage basis, depending on the relative strike price.

- The futures market may offer different types of products to trade relative to the stock market such as commodities, including crude oil, foreign exchange, interest rates, gold, and silver. Although ETFs may offer opportunities in commodities, the futures market may offer a uniquely different product.
- The futures market may have fewer restrictions when trading in an IRA.

Stock Index Futures Option

A stock index futures option works essentially in the same manner as an option on a stock, ETF, or index. For example, like an option on a stock, the stock index futures option buyer has unlimited reward potential and limited risk. The stock index futures option seller has limited reward potential and unlimited risk. A stock index futures call option provides the purchaser the right, but not the obligation, to buy the underlying futures at the strike price on or before the expiration date. A stock index futures put option provides the purchaser the right, but not the obligation, to sell the underlying futures at the strike price on or before the expiration date. A call seller is obligated to sell if assigned, and a put seller is obligated to buy if assigned. The factors that affect the price of a stock index futures option are the same as those that affect the price of an equity option, including the value of the underlying instrument, strike price, time to expiration, volatility, interest rate, and dividends. You must open a futures brokerage account to trade futures. Next is a discussion of futures basics, followed by a discussion of futures options.

WHAT IS A FUTURES CONTRACT?

A *futures contract* is an agreement between two parties to purchase or sell a specific quantity of an index (or other commodity) at a certain price at a particular date in the future. The size and terms of a futures contract and its options are standardized by the regulated exchange on which the futures trades. Futures can be used for speculation, hedging, and risk management.

A stock index futures is a contract that tracks an index such as the S&P 500, Russell 2000, or NASDAQ 100. What makes futures unique is that each futures contract has a defined life at which time settlement occurs (in the future); for example, the underlying S&P 500 futures settles each calendar quarter (March, June, September, and December) on the third Friday of that month. Therefore, during a calendar year, you can trade the underlying S&P 500 futures contract that settles (matures/expires) in March, June, September, or December. Settlement dates vary depending on the futures contract so that the settlement dates of S&P 500 futures would be different than the settlement dates of commodities futures.

A stock index is a collection of stock prices compiled into a single number. An index option can enable you to trade in a particular market without having to buy all the stocks individually. You cannot buy or sell an underlying cash index directly, as explained in

Chapter 25, but you can trade a stock index futures. For example, you cannot buy or sell the SPX directly, but you can trade the S&P 500 futures. Popular stock index futures include the following:

- S&P 500 futures,
- Russell 2000 futures,
- NASDAQ 100 futures,
- Dow Jones Industrial Average futures,
- S&P 100 futures (American-style exercise),
- CBOE volatility futures,
- E-Mini S&P 500 futures,
- E-Mini NASDAQ 100 futures.

You can take a long or short position in a stock index futures. The buyer of futures is said to be long the contract; the seller of futures is said to be short the contract. An open position, either a long or short position, is closed by entering into an offsetting transaction (i.e., an equal and opposite transaction to the one that opened the position) prior to the contract expiration. For example, if you are long one S&P 500 futures, you can close the position by selling an identical S&P 500 futures; if you are short one Russell 2000 futures, you can close the position by buying an identical Russell 2000 futures.

When a futures is not liquidated (closed) prior to expiration, it is settled in accordance with the terms of the contract. Financial futures that are open at the end of the last trading day are settled through a final cash payment based on a final settlement price, which is determined by the exchange or clearing organization. Once this payment is made, neither party has any further obligations on the contract. You need to check such contract specifications prior to trading a futures option.

S&P 500 Futures

The S&P 500 futures, often the most actively traded stock index futures, is a derivative instrument that tracks the value of the S&P 500 index (SPX) (adjusted to fair value, explained later in the chapter) and trades on the Chicago Mercantile Exchange. An S&P 500 futures expires each calendar quarter (March, June, September, and December), but the near-term contract typically has the highest volume (liquidity) and most favorable bid/ask spreads. When you buy or sell an S&P 500 futures, you are controlling a highly leveraged position. Each point in an S&P 500 futures (and its options) is worth $250. As a result, if the S&P 500 futures is at 1,500, you are controlling $375,000 worth of stock (1,500 times $250). In comparison, a NASDAQ 100 futures (and its options) is $100 a point and a Russell 2000 futures (and its options) is $500 a point.

E-Mini Futures   An *E-Mini* S&P 500 futures (and its options) is $50 a point. An E-Mini NASDAQ 100 futures (and its options) is $20 a point. An E-Mini Russell 2000 futures (and its options) is $100 a point.

TABLE 26.1   Sizes of Futures Contracts

Underlying Instrument	Multiplier ($)
S&P 500 futures	250 times index
E-Mini S&P 500 futures	50 times index
NASDAQ 100 futures	100 times index
E-Mini NASDAQ 100 futures	20 times index
Russell 2000 futures	500 times index
E-Mini Russell 2000 futures	100 times index

It is interesting to point out that the manner in which minicontracts are priced in the cash market differs from the futures market. In the cash market, as mentioned in Chapter 24, the Mini-SPX (XSP) options have one tenth the value of the cash market SPX. In the futures market, however, the E-Mini contracts are at the same prices as the full-sized contracts, but each unit represents fewer dollars per point. For example, assuming that the SPX is at 1,500, the XSP would be at 150, whereas the E-Mini S&P 500 futures would be at 1,500, but each point would only be worth $50.

Size of Futures Contracts   Table 26.1 lists the sizes of futures contracts for popular stock index futures.

Extended Trading Hours   An advantage of trading stock index futures is that you can trade in the evening and nighttime hours. The S&P 500 futures is traded almost 24 hours a day, beginning Sunday evening (currently, at 6:00 P.M. EST) and ending at the close of business on Friday (currently, at 4:15 P.M. EST). S&P 500 futures options, however, are traded Monday through Friday during the regular business hours of 9:30 A.M. to 4:15 P.M. EST. Being able to trade in the overnight session can be viewed as an advantage of trading futures versus stocks.

Futures Margin

Margin for futures is required when you buy or sell an underlying futures contract or sell a futures option. Let us first address margin on underlying futures. Buying futures does not require a cash payment, and selling futures does not involve the receipt of money. Instead, a good faith deposit is required (margin) as a *performance bond* to enter and continue such a contract. As mentioned previously, in a futures account, both the buyer and seller of underlying futures are required to post margin. The fact that no payment is required to be made (other than a margin deposit) at the time of a futures purchase or sale represents a significant difference between the futures and stock markets. The good news is that you can earn interest on your futures margin deposit, such as from a Treasury bill, thus providing a potential advantage of trading futures relative to the cash market. Margin on futures options is addressed later in this chapter.

Futures Fair Value

The value of S&P 500 futures is derived from the underlying value of the S&P 500 cash index. However, the fair value of the S&P 500 futures is typically higher than the level of the cash market SPX because of carrying charges. The difference is called *basis*. Basis is the difference between the cash price of an underlying instrument and the price of the near-term futures for the same underlying instrument. The carrying charges represent an interest (and dividend) component that is added (or subtracted) to the cash index to determine the fair value of the futures.

Basis makes sense because if a futures was equal to a cash contract, an investor could buy the futures (which does not require a cash payment) and invest the proceeds in a Treasury bill to earn interest, thus providing a substantial advantage relative to investing in the cash market. As a general rule, with the S&P 500 cash index trading around 1,500 and short-term interest rates around 4 percent, fair value on the S&P 500 futures is approximately one point higher than the S&P 500 cash market index for every week remaining until the S&P 500 futures expires. For instance, if the June S&P 500 futures expires in 12 weeks, the fair value of that S&P 500 futures would be approximately 12 points above the cash index.

In this example, the S&P 500 futures exceeds the cash market index by approximately 12 points at the beginning of each calendar quarter, but that amount will, in effect, depreciate one point per week until the cash market and futures market converge on the third Friday of the month at the end of the quarter. Everything else being equal, assuming the same calendar year, June futures will typically be 12 points higher than March futures, September futures will typically be 12 points higher than June futures, and December futures will typically be 12 points higher than September futures, depending on interest rates and other factors. In this scenario, it should be noted that a buyer of an S&P 500 futures loses approximately one point per week, whereas a short seller automatically gains one point per week as a result of this built-in carrying charge.

Keep in mind that as the assumed interest rate declines, so does basis (fair value difference); for example, if the interest rate is 2 percent, the fair value of that S&P 500 futures may be only approximately 3 points (instead of 12) above the cash index with 12 weeks remaining. The cost of carry on the S&P 500 futures is essentially the risk-free rate of return that could be earned by investing in a T-bill minus expected dividends that you could earn by investing in each of the stocks included in the S&P 500 index (SPX). As a result, the cost of carry varies with changes in interest rates.

A stock index futures is trading at parity when the stock index futures equals the value of the underlying index plus basis, above parity when the stock index futures is above that level, and below parity when the stock index futures is below that level.

Effect of Basis   Basis affects call and put prices relative to the cash market. As result, call prices at a given strike price in the S&P 500 futures tend to be higher, and puts at a given strike price tend to be lower relative to the cash market if the S&P 500 futures is higher. A common technique is to compare the bid/ask prices of puts and calls in the cash market to their cousins in the S&P 500 futures market. An adjustment needs to be made in your pricing comparison analysis to take into account that the futures price is typically higher.

Basis should be a consideration when analyzing call and put prices. The strike price of a call for a S&P 500 futures may be 90 points out-of-the-money when the position is established, but that difference will increase, assuming that there is no fluctuation in the underlying S&P 500 futures index, if the basis (fair value vs. cash index differential) depreciates. Conversely, a put may initially be 100 points out-of-the-money when established but decline as basis depreciates, assuming that there is no fluctuation in the underlying S&P 500 futures.

STOCK INDEX FUTURES OPTION

As mentioned previously, generally, the factors that affect the price of a stock index futures option are the same as those that affect the price of an equity option, including the value of the underlying instrument relative to the strike price, volatility, time to expiration, interest rate, and dividends. For example, the price of a stock index futures call will generally increase as the level of its underlying index increases, and the price of a stock index futures put will generally increase as the level of its underlying index declines. The strategies for a stock index futures option are the same as for an option on a stock, ETF, or index. For example, a long stock index futures call is bullish where profit potential is unlimited and risk is limited to premium paid.

As previously mentioned, the principles of stock index futures options can be applied to S&P 500 futures, Russell 2000 futures, NASDAQ 100 futures, and Dow Jones Industrial Average futures and other stock indexes and futures. In this chapter, the principles of stock index futures options are primarily illustrated using S&P 500 futures.

Short puts and calls are subject to margin requirements. In general, futures options have a lower margin requirement than options on stocks, ETFs, and indexes. This freedom is viewed by many traders as an advantage of futures options versus options on stocks. Chapter 23 provides a sample comparison of margin on a stock, ETF, index, and stock index futures option. Margin is discussed in Chapter 30.

Leverage on a Futures Option

If the S&P 500 futures rises by 10 points, the buyer of one such futures contract has a gain of $2,500 and a seller has a loss of $2,500. If an option trader's delta is 0.50, for example, then he controls half of that amount. If you are long one at-the-money call option with a delta of 0.50, then each point rise in such an underlying futures produces a gain of $125 (delta of 0.50 times $250). If you are short one at-the-money call option with a delta of –0.50, then each point rise in such an underlying futures produces a loss of $125 (delta of 0.50 times $250). Assume that in January, you sell one February put contract at a strike price of 1,400, while the S&P 500 futures is at 1,500 and the margin (performance bond), according to SPAN, is $5,000. If the seller collects $500 for that option, his potential return is 10 percent, based on margin.

Expiration Cycles

As mentioned previously, the underlying S&P 500 futures expires each calendar quarter (March, June, September, and December) on the third Friday of those months. However, options are available with expiration dates for each month, similar to an option cycle on a stock. Therefore, during a calendar year, you can trade the S&P 500 March contract, S&P 500 June contract, S&P 500 September contract, or S&P 500 December contract, but you can trade options for each of the 12 calendar months. As a result, the underlying S&P 500 futures expires each calendar quarter, but options are available with expiration dates each month. An option expiring in one month may trade based on one S&P futures settlement date, and an option expiring in another month may trade based on a different S&P 500 futures settlement. For example, consider the following:

- January, February, and March options trade based on March S&P 500 futures,
- April, May, and June options trade based on June S&P 500 futures,
- July, August, and September options trade based on September S&P 500 futures,
- October, November, and December options trade based on December S&P 500 futures.

When buying or selling S&P 500 futures options, you need to make sure you know which underlying futures is used to determine the option price. For example, because S&P 500 futures settle each calendar quarter, if you sell a May call option, it is based on the June S&P 500 futures because that is the nearest calendar quarter; if you sell a July put option, it is based on the September S&P 500 futures because that is the nearest calendar quarter; and so on. If you sell, for example, a calendar spread, one leg of your position may be based on one futures settlement month and the other leg on another; for instance, if you sell a May/July call credit spread, the May put is based on the June S&P 500 futures and the July put is based on the September S&P 500 futures.

S&P 500 futures options typically expire on the third Friday of every month, similar to equity options. S&P 500 futures options are subject to A.M. settlement at the end of each calendar quarter and to P.M. settlement in other months.

Stock Index Contract Specifications

Each futures product has unique product specifications, including its symbol, a description of its components, the dollar value of each point change, whether each quote is stated in decimals and the minimum tick for each option, how strike prices are determined, strike price intervals, expiration months, expiration dates, its exercise style (European vs. American), its last trading day, guidelines regarding the settlement of option exercises, position and exercise limits, its margin, and its trading hours. You should check with your broker and applicable futures exchange web sites to determine current contract specifications.

S&P 500 futures options also have available options that expire at the end of each calendar quarter. Such option contracts have the same contract specifications as standard options, except that they expire on the last business day of each calendar quarter (March, June, September, and December) instead of on the third Friday of the month. Such options are P.M. settled; for example, regular March S&P 500 futures options may expire on Friday, March 21, and the quarterly options may expire on Monday, March 31. S&P 500 futures options that expire at the end of each month, instead of expiring on the third Friday of each month, are also available, but they may not be as liquid as standard options.

American- versus European-Style Exercise S&P 500 futures options are American-style exercised, giving the buyer the right to exercise on or before expiration. A call buyer has the right to buy an underlying S&P 500 futures, whereas a put buyer has the right to sell an underlying S&P 500 futures. If an S&P 500 futures option is held until expiration and it is the end of a calendar quarter, it is subject to cash settlement because there is no underlying futures to buy or sell at that time. S&P 500 futures options expire on the third Friday of a month and are P.M. settled. Options expiring at the end of each calendar quarter cease trading on the third Thursday of a month and are settled based on the next day's (Friday A.M.) settle price. Not all futures options are American-style exercised; for example, end-of-month S&P 500 futures options are European-style exercised and are P.M. settled.

Margin on a Futures Option A futures margin is typically determined by the SPAN margining system, which takes into account all positions in a customer's account and, in general, usually produces a lower margin requirement than traditional standard margin for stocks or ETFs. Chapter 30 is devoted to explaining margin on stocks, ETFs, indexes, and stock index futures. In some cases, the portfolio margining amount may more closely approximate the futures SPAN amount.

Stock Index Futures Option Chain

Like options on stocks, ETFs, and indexes, a good place to find stock index futures option prices is an option chain. Table 26.2 shows a representative sample of S&P 500 futures options that expire on the third Friday in October, assuming it is currently late August. The bid/ask prices assume that the S&P 500 futures is at 1,305 (while the SPX is at 1,295).

Table 26.2 assumes that the S&P 500 futures is 10 points higher than the SPX to reinforce that S&P 500 futures are typically higher than the SPX. As explained earlier in this chapter, the fair value of the S&P 500 futures is higher than the level of the cash SPX because of carrying charges (basis). Strike prices for the 500 futures options are typically in 5-point increments but are shown in Table 26.2 in 10-point strike price increments

TABLE 26.2 Sample S&P 500 Futures Option Chain (50 Days to Expiration)

Call Bid	Call Ask	Strike Price	Put Bid	Put Ask
70.50	72.00	1,250	19.90	20.00
63.50	64.00	1,260	22.60	22.80
56.50	57.50	1,270	25.70	25.90
50.00	50.50	1,280	29.10	29.30
43.50	44.50	1,290	32.50	33.50
37.50	38.50	1,300	37.00	37.50
32.50	33.00	1,310	41.50	42.00
27.50	27.80	1,320	46.50	47.50
23.00	23.20	1,330	52.00	53.00
18.90	19.10	1,340	58.00	59.00
15.40	15.50	1,350	64.50	65.50

to enable easy comparison to Table 25.1, which shows the SPX option chain. In this example, October is 50 days until expiration. Bid/ask prices for calls are shown on the left side, bid/ask prices for puts are shown on the right side, and strike prices are listed in the middle column.

Table 26.3 shows an option chain with 50-point strike price increments for illustrative purposes so you can see the lower strikes for puts and higher strikes for calls. The bid/ask prices assume that the S&P 500 futures is at 1,305. Strike-price intervals are usually in 5-point increments (instead of in the 50-point strike-price intervals in Table 26.3).

I typically look for at least $2 ($200) when selling an option and will usually look down the option chain to find put bid prices at $2 ($200) or above. Likewise, I will usually look up along the option chain to find call bid prices at $2 ($200) or above. As a result, for example, a short put at 1,135 (not shown here) and lower may be a reasonable position, and a short call at 1,420 (not shown here) and above may be a reasonable position. Typically, I will sell a near-month put (September expiration) and a call with 60 to 90 days to expiration (November or December).

TABLE 26.3 Sample S&P 500 Futures Option Chain (48 Days to Expiration)

Call Bid	Call Ask	Strike Price	Put Bid	Put Ask
199.10	201.10	1,110	1.80	2.10
151.80	153.80	1,160	4.20	4.80
107.20	109.20	1,210	9.30	10.30
67.40	69.40	1,260	19.00	20.60
35.00	37.00	1,310	36.20	38.20
13.30	14.90	1,360	64.10	66.10
3.20	3.90	1,410	103.40	105.40
0.35	0.90	1,460	150.20	152.20
0	0.40	1,510	199.60	201.60

Option Strategies

Strategies for a stock index futures option are the same as for an option on a stock, ETF, and index. To emphasize this, following is a description of the four basic option strategies, consisting of a long call, a long put, a short call, and a short put. As a reminder, you can close out an option position by offsetting it in the marketplace any time prior to expiration.

Long Call   A long stock index futures call can enable a trader to profit from a rise in the price of the underlying futures. For example, assume that the March S&P 500 futures is at 1,500 and you buy one March 1,550 call at $15, at a cost of $3,750 ($15 times $250 per contract). If the value of the call rises to $20, your gain is $1,250 ($5 gain times $250 per contract). If you hold the option until expiration, it is cash settled because the option and underlying futures both expire at the end of the same calendar quarter. For example, if the underlying March futures settles at 1,600, the cash settlement received is $12,500 (50 points times $250) and the gain is $8,750. Prior to expiration, you can exercise your right to buy one March S&P 500 futures if the option moves in-the-money.

Long Put   A long stock index futures put can enable a trader to profit from a decline in the price of the underlying futures. For example, assume that the March S&P 500 futures is at 1,500 and you buy one March 1,450 put at $15, at a cost of $3,750 ($15 times $250 per contract). If the value of the put rises to $20, your gain is $1,250 ($5 gain times $250 per contract). If you hold the option until expiration, it is cash settled because the option and underlying futures both expire at the end of the same calendar quarter. For example, if the underlying March futures settles at 1,400, the cash settlement received is $12,500 (50 points times $250) and the gain is $8,750. Prior to expiration, you can exercise your right to sell one March S&P 500 futures if the option moves in-the-money.

Short Call   A short stock index futures call can enable a trader to profit from a decline or sideways movement in the price of the underlying futures. For example, assume that the March S&P 500 futures is at 1,500 and you sell one March 1,550 call at $15, for $3,750 ($15 times $250 per contract). If the value of the call rises to $20, your loss is $1,250 ($5 gain times $250 per contract). If you are short until expiration, the option is cash settled because the option and underlying futures both expire at the end of the same calendar quarter. For example, if the underlying March futures settles at 1,600, the cash settlement paid is $12,500 (50 points times $250) and the loss is $8,750. Prior to expiration, you may be assigned and obligated to sell one March S&P 500 futures if the option moves in-the-money.

Short Put   A short stock index futures put can enable a trader to profit from a rise or sideways movement in the price of the underlying futures. For example, assume that the March S&P 500 futures is at 1,500 and you sell one March 1,450 put at $15, for $3,750 ($15 times $250 per contract). If the value of the put rises to $20, your loss is $1,250 ($5 gain times $250 per contract). If you are short until expiration, the option is cash settled because the option and underlying futures both expire at the end of the same calendar quarter. For example, if the underlying March futures settles at 1,400, the cash settlement paid is $12,500 (50 points times $250) and the loss is $8,750. Prior to expiration, you may be assigned and obligated to buy one March S&P 500 futures if the option moves in-the-money.

Spread Strategies   The great feature about the strategies at a glance in Appendix C is that they, in effect, summarize many of the strategies covered throughout this book. Prior to engaging in any option strategy, you should develop a view of the market or underlying instrument. After you have developed that forecast, you should select the best option strategy for your prediction; for example, you may be bullish on the broad U.S. stock market, bullish on an industry sector, bearish on the U.S. stock market, or bearish on an individual sector. You may be bullish on small caps or bearish on technology stocks. Conversely, you may simply believe that implied volatility is too high and that it will contract. The strategies described in this book can be executed with a stock index futures option. Following are sample stock index futures option strategies. Many of these strategies are illustrated in the strategies at a glance in Appendix C. To summarize, you can utilize strategies such as the following:

- Long or short call or put,
- Long or short vertical spread,
- Long or short iron condor,
- Ratio (front) spread,
- Backspread,
- Long or short straddle,
- Long or short strangle,
- Long or short butterfly,
- Long or short condor,
- Long or short calendar spread,
- Long or short diagonal spread,
- Covered call or put,
- Long or short combination,
- Long or short covered combination.

   An advantage of stock index futures is that they allow you to take advantage of your view of the market. For example, if you are bullish on the broad market, buy an S&P 500 futures call; if you expect an increase in volatility in the broad market, buy a Russell 2000 futures straddle or strangle; and if you expect a contraction in volatility, sell a NASDAQ 100 futures iron condor.

Hedging

You can purchase a stock index futures put to profit from a directional move or to hedge a position or portfolio; for example, to protect a large-capitalization and diversified portfolio, you may buy an S&P 500 futures put. To protect a large-capitalization technology portfolio, you may buy a NASDAQ 100 futures put. If a stock index futures put is being used as a hedge, the index should be highly correlated to your portfolio. Otherwise, you may find yourself in a position in which your portfolio of stocks declines, and the index you chose does not move in lockstep with your stock portfolio, thus creating losses in your portfolio, without the benefits of protection. In selecting the appropriate stock index futures, you should choose a stock index futures that is in the same sector as your stock or select a broader-based index.

Taxes

As described in Chapter 32, there is modified tax treatment for trading options on a broad-based index (section 1256 contracts). Section 1256 contracts consist of futures options (e.g., S&P 500 futures), options on broad-based indexes (e.g., SPX), and regulated futures (e.g., trading the underlying S&P 500 futures). Under this modification, regardless of how long you have held the option, the gain or loss is deemed 60 percent long term and 40 percent short term (called the 60/40 rule); the option is marked to market at the end of each calendar year; net capital losses can be carried back; and to the extent the carryback is not utilized, losses can be carried forward. Once you understand these rules, you may conclude that you may be able to save taxes by trading options on one product instead of another. Fortunately, options on S&P 500 futures are subject to this special tax treatment and can represent an advantage of trading futures and futures options.

BONUS SECTION

Short Strangle

Chapter 14 covers a short strangle. In some market environments, a short strangle on S&P 500 futures can be attractive using far-out-of-the-money calls and puts, so I will illustrate it here. The advantage of the strategy is that you can place the probabilities of success on your side by selling far-out-of-the-money options and use technical analysis to overweight (establish an unbalanced position) one side or the other. For example, if the S&P 500 futures is nearing overhead resistance and you are ready to establish a strangle, you may sell a greater number of calls than puts because your technical analysis indicators signal that the market is ready for a short-term pullback. Because this position involves uncovered options on both sides of the market, you need to be careful to make sure that you do not assume too much risk. Because such trades involve risk, it is important that the underlying S&P 500 futures trades almost 24 hours a day in the event that defensive protective action needs to be taken to cover positions. For example, if the S&P 500 futures is at 1,500 and you are short two calls at 1,500, you can purchase (or sell) one or more S&P 500 futures (or E-Mini contracts) to cover the naked calls (or puts) if the market moves against you. Risk management strategies are covered in Chapter 29.

In a short strangle, you sell out-of-the-money calls and puts so that the delta (or dollar amount) of the calls sold equals (or approximates) the delta (or dollar amount) of the puts sold. The idea is that as the call value increases, the puts decline by a similar amount; if the puts increase in value, the calls decline by a similar amount.

An advantage is that you collect double the premium and can benefit from double time decay and volatility contraction. In a short strangle, you want the underlying stock to fluctuate back and forth within a range, forcing both the call and the put sides to decay in value over time. The purpose of such a spread is to profit from time decay and/or volatility contraction, ideally on both sides. To execute a short strangle, you sell far-out-of-the-money call and put options.

In a typical short strangle, you simultaneously sell a call and put at different strike prices with the same expiration date. I prefer to sell calls 60 to 90 days prior to expiration at least 100 points above the S&P 500 level and sell puts 30 to 45 days prior to expiration at least 150 below the S&P 500 level.

The maximum profit, at expiration, occurs when the underlying stock is at or between the option strike prices (when all options are at or out-of-the-money). A profit is made in this strategy as the underlying stock fluctuates back and forth within a range (defined by the strike prices), allowing both the call and put sides to decay in value over time. This is a strategy that is used to try to double (or nearly double) the amount of premium collected in comparison to what could be obtained by only trading one side of the market. This strategy makes sense because it is based on the fact that the underlying stock cannot be in two places at one time.

The maximum loss potential is unlimited in both directions. The risk is that the underlying stock will advance or decline dramatically, substantially increasing the value of the put or call side, which would only be partially offset by the other side of the trade. The risk of writing a strangle is that the loss is unlimited because you have upside risk because of your uncovered short calls and downside risk because of your uncovered short puts. Keep in mind that if your short option rises in value above your risk level, you should consider offsetting the position and/or rolling. You should refer to risk management strategies covered in Chapter 29.

In a short strangle, there are two break-even points. The break-even points are the strike price of the short call plus the premium credit collected and the strike price of the short put minus the premium.

A short strangle benefits from the effects of time decay. Prior to expiration, an increase in volatility typically increases a strangle value and a decrease in volatility typically decreases a strangle value. For a short strangle, a credit is reflected in your account and margin is the greater of the call side margin or the put side margin, but not both.

Example: S&P 500 Futures Short Strangle

Assumptions: March S&P 500 futures is trading at 1,500 in January; sell one February 1,300/1,600 strangle at $4 ($1,000), as follows: Sell one March 1,600 call at $2 and sell one February 1,300 put at $2.

Debit or credit: $1,000 credit ($4 times $250).

Maximum profit: $1,000 credit ($500 call side and $500 put side).

Maximum loss: Unlimited in both directions.

Exercise and assignment: You may be assigned on your short call or put if it is in-the-money, but both options cannot be in-the-money at the same time.

TABLE 26.4 S&P 500 Futures Short Strangle

S&P 500 Futures	Short Call Value	Short Put Value	Spread	Spread Credit	Spread Profit (Loss)
1,200	0	25,000	(25,000)	1,000	(24,000)
1,250	0	12,500	(12,500)	1,000	(11,500)
1,300	0	0	0	1,000	1,000
1,350	0	0	0	1,000	1,000
1,400	0	0	0	1,000	1,000
1,450	0	0	0	1,000	1,000
1,500	0	0	0	1,000	1,000
1,550	0	0	0	1,000	1,000
1,600	0	0	0	1,000	1,000
1,650	12,500	0	(12,500)	1,000	(11,500)
1,700	25,000	0	(25,000)	1,000	(24,000)

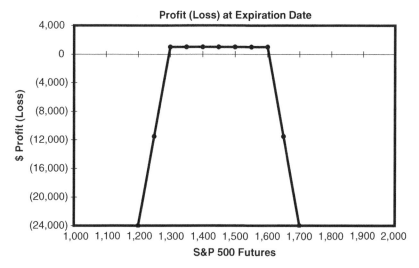

FIGURE 26.1 S&P 500 Futures Short Strangle

TABLE 26.5 Summary of Greeks: February Expiration

Option	Delta	Gamma	Theta	Vega
Short 1 February 1,600 call	−$23	−$1.75	$12	−$8
Short 1 February 1,300 put	$23	−$1.75	$12	−$8
Position	$0		$24	−$16

TABLE 26.6 Summary of Greeks: March Expiration

Option	Delta	Gamma	Theta	Vega
Short 1 March 1,600 call	−$20	−$1.00	$7	−$10
Short 1 March 1,300 put	$20	−$1.00	$7	−$10
Position	$0		$14	−$20

Break-even points: 1,604 or 1,296 (call strike price sold plus credit; put strike price minus credit).

Maximum profit achieved at expiration: Underlying S&P 500 futures at or between strike prices at expiration.

Maximum loss achieved at expiration: Underlying S&P 500 futures beyond the break-even point in either direction.

If stock unchanged at expiration: $1,000 gain (equal to credit).

Greeks: Table 26.5 contains sample Greeks converted to dollars at the time the position is established.

Position would reflect no gain from a small stock decline (delta), a gain from time decay (theta), and a gain from volatility (vega) contraction. Position would reflect no loss from a small stock rise (delta) and a loss from volatility (vega) expansion. Gain or loss is zero if the S&P 500 futures rises to 1,501; loss is $24 from one day of time decay.

Later expiration: The option price and Greeks will differ if expiration is at a later date; for example, if the options expire one month later, the strangle may be valued at $7 (instead of $4), with representative Greeks as given in Table 26.6.

Gain or loss is zero if the S&P 500 futures rises to 1,501; loss is $14 from one day of time decay.

Exercise and assignment: For the short strangle, you may be assigned on your short call or put, but both options cannot be in-the-money at the same time.

This is a strategy that is used to nearly double the amount of premium collected in comparison to what could be obtained by only trading one side of the market, based on the fact that the underlying instrument cannot be in two places at one time.

Keep in mind that if you believe that the S&P 500 futures has support at 1,400, it is usually best not to sell a put exactly at that level. Instead, it is advisable that you give yourself some wiggle room (cushion) so that the put you sell is around a strike price of

1,300. Although you will receive less premium for the 1,300 strike price put in comparison to the 1,400 strike price put, it will probably be well worth it in the long run should the market move against you.

Synthetic Futures

Chapter 20 covered equivalent and synthetic positions. The futures market can be used to create a position that mimics a cash market position. When a futures position mimics a cash position, it is considered a synthetic position. Like in the cash market, a *synthetic futures* is a position created by combining call and put futures options. A synthetic long futures position is created by combining a long call option and a short put option with the same expiration date and strike price. A synthetic short futures position is created by combining a long put and a short call with the same expiration date and strike price. Synthetic futures act like actual futures in terms of profits and losses. Synthetics can provide the ability to replicate futures and options and allow you to buy the cheapest option and sell the most expensive position.

FINAL THOUGHTS

Stock index futures options can be attractive because of leverage, margin, uniqueness of products, commission structure, hours of trading, and equal ability to go long or short quickly. Two of the main attractions of futures trading are leverage and margin—not only that, but you can earn interest on your deposit.

You can use stock index futures options to execute all of the strategies described in this book. In this chapter, an S&P 500 futures (and its options) was used to illustrate how stock index futures and futures options work, but keep in mind that these principles apply to other stock index futures and options as well. The futures market has become substantially more popular and has attracted a lot of attention from speculators, hedgers, risk managers, and even the media. Now it is time to move on to Part Five, which covers advanced topics.

PART FIVE

Advanced Topics

I love to coach basketball and have always been a big believer in the importance of fundamentals such as passing, dribbling, and playing defense, but you cannot always run the same play on offense and expect to win. It works the same way with options because you need a number of tools at your disposal to prosper under various market conditions. To have a solid foundation, you need to move past the fundamentals and learn advanced principles.

Confidence, discipline, and decisiveness are key components of developing your edge, and it is important to remember that always following the crowd can be hazardous to your wealth. It is important to trade with confidence, knowing that you hardly ever have access to all the facts. Instead, the nature of trading is that you trade with the best information that you can obtain, knowing that you cannot possibly know everything. But with options, you can trade with probabilities on your side.

If you want to treat the trading of options like a business and trade like a professional, you need to become more of an expert and rise to the next level. Part Five provides more details of option characteristics. Chapter 27 covers the important topic of volatility, Chapter 28 discusses the ramifications of exercise and assignment, Chapter 29 provides an overview of risk management strategies, Chapter 30 covers margin, Chapter 31 details placing an order, and Chapter 32 highlights key tax rules.

Assessing Volatility

I decided to devote an entire chapter to describing how to analyze volatility, including its role in determining an option's price and how to profit from changes in volatility. This chapter provides a general overview of volatility; defines implied volatility; differentiates between the different types of volatility; explains what it means for implied volatility to be expressed in terms of annual standard deviation; describes how to evaluate implied volatility prior to making a trade, how changes in circumstances can affect an option's price, how the volatility skew can present trading opportunities, how a change in conditions can affect volatility, how to trade volatility, and how to establish a delta-neutral position; and provides various trading tips. This chapter first covers volatility considerations prior to making a trade and then covers considerations after the position is established. This chapter is not intended to cover the complex mathematical aspects of volatility but, instead, is intended to cover the concepts that can help you as a trader.

This chapter is primarily concerned with addressing implied volatility and intends "implied volatility" to mean the measurement of volatility, stated as a percentage, reflected in an option's price. This chapter will not study the details of volatility in the context of an option pricing model or mathematical formulas.

OVERVIEW

When analyzing the price of an option, volatility is the most complex component and is probably the most misunderstood. As mentioned in Chapter 3, five variables affect an option's price, as follows:

1. Strike price versus stock price (the lower the strike price, the higher the price of a call and the lower the price of a put; the higher the strike price, the higher the price of a put and the lower the price of a call),

2. Time (the more time remaining until expiration, the higher the premium),

3. Volatility (the higher the implied volatility built into an option price, the higher the premium),

4. Interest rate (the higher the assumed interest rate, the higher the call premium but the lower the put premium),

5. Dividend (the higher the dividend on the underlying stock, the lower the call premium but the higher the put premium).

Four of these components are known, and the only missing link (input into an option pricing model) is the third variable, implied volatility. If all other variables remain constant, higher implied volatility results in a higher option price, and lower implied volatility results in a lower option price. Assume that in January, XYZ is trading at $100 a share. The February 100 call option may be at $5 with an implied volatility percentage of 50 percent. Assuming all other variables are the same, an increase in implied volatility would increase the price of the option and a decrease in implied volatility would decrease the price of the option. Another stock trading at the same $100 stock price would likely have an at-the-money option trading at an amount more or less than $5, depending on its own level of implied volatility. For example, assume that in January, XYZ and ABC are both trading at $100 a share. The February 100 call option may be $5 for XYZ and $9 for ABC. In this example, both options have the same strike price, time to expiration, dividend, and interest rate. The only difference is implied volatility, which in this case results in almost double the value for the ABC option versus the comparable XYZ option. This goes to show how important implied volatility can be in the determination of an option price.

Higher implied volatility means that there is a predicted greater price swing in the underlying stock price. A greater price swing in the underlying stock price translates into a greater probability that an option could have a higher value by the option expiration date. Likewise, lower implied volatility results in a lower option price. Lower implied volatility means that there is a predicted lower price swing in the underlying stock price. A lower price swing in the underlying stock price translates into a likely lower option value by the option expiration date.

There can be wide variation in the implied volatility percentage for different options. The implied volatility percentage differs for each individual option and can differ dramatically from stock to stock, from futures contract to futures contract, from strike price to strike price, and for puts versus calls. Later in this chapter, we compare implied volatility percentages. If you show the implied volatility percentage beside each strike price on an option chain, you will see that there is a different implied volatility percentage at each strike price, even though it is the same underlying stock. Your trading platform should provide the implied volatility percentage of an option.

What Is Volatility

In general, *volatility* is a statistical measurement of the rate of price change. Volatility is a statistical measurement of risk or uncertainty and can be defined as the degree to which a stock is likely to move up or down from its current price. The first thing you need to understand is whether the volatility being addressed is the volatility of the stock or the implied volatility reflected in the option price. The word "volatility" can be confusing because it can refer to the volatility of the underlying stock price (*historical* or *realized volatility*) or to the volatility component implicit in an option price (*implied volatility*). This distinction is often not clear because the word "volatility" is thrown around rather loosely. Commentators often say that volatility has risen or declined. What the pundits usually mean is that the rate of movement in the underlying stock or market has increased or decreased (historical volatility). However, whether the underlying stock price volatility has increased is a separate question, related to whether the volatility inherent in the option price (implied volatility) has risen or declined.

As previously mentioned, this chapter is primarily concerned with addressing implied volatility and intends *implied volatility* to mean the measurement of volatility, stated as a percentage, reflected in an option's price. This chapter will not study the details of volatility in the context of an option pricing model or mathematical formulas. There are other types of volatility, but they will not be covered here.

Implied volatility is built into an option's price by the marketplace and measures how expensive the option is after first taking into account the other option pricing factors. Implied volatility reflects the volatility component implicit in the option price at a particular moment in time. Implied volatility is a statistical measurement described in terms of one annual standard deviation (stated as a percentage). Implied volatility reflects the assumptions made regarding the degree to which an underlying stock is likely to move up or down from its current price (which can differ dramatically from the actual movement of the stock). It is built into the price of an option and is usually calculated using an option pricing model. Implied volatility can be viewed as a measurement that predicts the future price distribution of the underlying stock and translates that into an option's price.

In contrast, historical volatility measures the volatility (price distribution) of an underlying stock price over a past period of time, also stated as a percentage. When you look at a stock chart, in effect, you are looking at a graphic representation of historical volatility. In this definition, the volatility addressed is that of the underlying instrument and not volatility as reflected in the option.

If there is a change in the volatility of a stock, the option price can be affected by the change in the stock versus strike price relationship as well as by a change in implied volatility. The effect of volatility of the underlying stock price and the implied volatility of the option price can be easily confused. For example, assume that XYZ stock is trading at $100 a share and you sell one February 100 call at $5. If XYZ stock increases to $102 a share, the value of your option may increase from $5 to $6. You may be under the impression that an increase in implied volatility caused your option to increase in value. If you examine the implied volatility made available in your trading platform, you may notice that implied volatility did not increase and possibly declined. Therefore, the increase in your call option is entirely because of the change in the price of the stock relative to the strike price and is not technically a result of a volatility component built into the option price (implied volatility) as that term is used in the context of option pricing and option models.

Implied Volatility

The great feature about implied volatility is that it is calculated as an annual standard deviation, stated as a percentage. Therefore, you can compare the implied volatility of one option to any other option, including a stock, index, or futures. An option with a higher implied volatility percentage has a higher option price, assuming all other factors are the same. A higher percentage reflects a higher implied volatility and, accordingly, a higher option price. A lower percentage reflects a lower implied volatility and, accordingly, a lower option price.

Implied volatility is the number that must be imported into a theoretical option pricing model to produce the price of the option in the marketplace. You can think of implied volatility as the plug figure that is backed into an option pricing model to make it work because it is the only missing link. Implied volatility is available using a computer model, available at most brokerage firms or specialized software companies. The implied volatility percentages should be available in your trading platform.

Implied volatility can be defined as one standard deviation price change, in percentage terms, over one year. Standard deviation is the degree to which each return clusters about the mean. In a normal distribution, 68.3 percent of the returns will be within one standard deviation of the mean, 95.4 percent will be within two standard deviations of the mean, and 99.7 percent will be within three standard deviations of the mean.

As a result, a higher implied volatility percentage signals a likely (predicted) wider variation (distribution) in the stock price, at least according to how the option is priced at a particular point in time. Likewise, a lower implied volatility percentage signals a likely (predicted) narrower variation (distribution) in the stock price, according to how the option is priced at a particular point in time. A higher percentage implies greater volatility; a lower percentage implies lower volatility.

Implied Volatility Percentage Is a Fear Gauge   Implied volatility can be viewed as a gauge of fear and uncertainty. For example, when fear and uncertainty rise, the price of an option rises, and implied volatility is said to be high. When fear and uncertainty decline, the price of an option declines, and implied volatility is said to be low. As a general rule of thumb, when an underlying instrument declines quickly, the implied volatility percentage for an option increases because of the increase in uncertainty and fear. Likewise, as a general rule, if the market rises or moves sideways, the implied volatility percentage declines because of a reduction of fear and uncertainty.

The Chicago Board Option Exchange (CBOE) Volatility index (VIX) measures the implied volatility of options on the S&P 500 index (SPX) and is often referred to as the fear gauge of the overall market. Similarly, the implied volatility percentage can be viewed as the fear gauge of an individual option.

A basic principle of economics is that assets are priced according to the laws of supply and demand. Option pricing is no exception to this rule because implied volatility can be viewed as a gauge that isolates and quantifies the demand component for an option at a particular moment in time. If all other factors are held constant, when demand is high, an option price is high; when demand is low, an option price is low. In that respect, the price of an option is determined by the same economic forces as other assets. With an option price, you have a quantifiable mechanism to capture the demand component: the implied volatility percentage.

Implied Volatility Percentage Is a Measuring Stick

As previously mentioned, implied volatility is a statistical measurement of risk and is expressed in terms of annual standard deviation, as a percentage. A higher percentage means a likely greater variation in price, and a lower percentage means a likely lower variation in price. A higher percentage reflects greater implied volatility; a lower percentage reflects lower implied volatility.

Standard deviation is a statistic that tells you how tightly all the various prices are clustered around the mean in a set of data. When prices are tightly bunched together and the bell-shaped curve is steep, the standard deviation is low. When prices are spread apart and the bell curve is relatively flat, that tells you that you have a relatively high standard deviation.

Implied volatility (a measurement of relative expensiveness of an option price) is expressed as a percentage and represents one annual standard deviation of the underlying stocks. For example, if an underlying stock is currently trading at $100 a share and has an implied volatility percentage of 20 percent, this represents a price change of one standard deviation. As mentioned previously, one standard deviation encompasses 68.3 percent of all occurrences, two standard deviations include 95.4 percent of all occurrences, and three standard deviations encompass 99.7 percent of all occurrences. As a result, statistically speaking, within the next year, a $100 stock will trade in the range between $80 and $120 a share 68.3 percent of the time, between $60 and $140 a share 95.4 percent of the time, and between $40 and $160 a share 99.7 percent of the time. These results may differ slightly according to statistics and compounding, but this presents the information without complicating matters. Table 27.1 is a summary of standard deviations, assuming a stock price of $100 and implied volatility of 20 percent.

Standard deviation does not indicate direction of movement. Instead, standard deviation is a measure of the dispersion from its mean: the more spread apart the data, the

TABLE 27.1   Example: Implied Volatility Expressed as Standard Deviation

Standard Deviation	Statistical Price Range ($)	Statistical Probability (%)
One standard deviation	80–120	68.9
Two standard deviations	60–140	95.4
Three standard deviations	40–160	99.7

higher the deviation. When you enter the current price of an underlying instrument, you are, in effect, entering the mean of a normal distribution curve. The larger the difference between the anticipated closing prices and the average price, the higher the standard deviation and the higher the implied volatility percentage. In a normal distribution curve, the mean can be viewed as the location of the peak of the curve and a standard deviation as the measure of how far the curve spreads out.

Vega (Volatility)

As mentioned in Chapter 4, vega measures the change in the theoretical option value for a one-point increase in implied volatility. For example, assume that you are long one call (or put) with a vega of 0.12. In such a case, your position vega is $12 so that a one-point increase in volatility results in a gain of $12. To continue the example, assume that one XYZ long May 100 call is trading at $5 (position value is $500), the position vega is $12, and the implied volatility percentage is 25 percent. If implied volatility is increased to 26 percent, assuming no other changes, you would have a gain equal to the $12 vega and the option value would be revised to $512.

Likewise, assume that one XYZ short May 100 call is trading at $5 (position value is $500), the position vega is −$12 and implied volatility is at 25 percent. If implied volatility is increased to 26 percent, assuming no other changes, you would incur a loss equal to the $12 vega and the option value would be revised to $512 (remember that you have a loss on a short option when it increases in value). Vega reaches its peak when an option is close to at-the-money and declines gradually the further it moves out-of-the-money or in-the-money. This tells you that, in general, the effect of volatility change is greatest for an at-the-money option than for options in-the-money or out-of-the-money. Refer to Chapter 4 for additional analysis of the Greeks.

COMPARISON OF IMPLIED VOLATILITIES

Keep in mind that many options have expiration dates for periods of fewer than 100 days, but implied volatility is expressed as an annual (12-month) standard deviation percentage. The use of an annual standard deviation is practical because other measures, such as interest and dividends, are annual numbers and it creates a level playing field for comparison of all options. The mathematical number of implied volatility does not seem as important as the ability to use it as a gauge to make decisions. The good news is that standardization of implied volatility, expressed as an annual standard deviation, enables you to compare implied volatility percentages from one option to another.

Implied volatility can differ dramatically from stock to stock, from futures contract to futures contract, from strike price to strike price, and for puts versus calls. If you compare at-the-money options, it should help you make an apples-to-apples comparison to determine which options are priced higher in relative terms. For example, if a stock is selling at $100 a share with at-the-money implied volatility of 30 percent and another

TABLE 27.2 Sample Comparison of at-the-Money Implied Volatility

Underlying Instrument	At-the-Money Implied Volatility (%)
Research in Motion	61.52
Apple Computer	48.95
Intel	35.85
NASDAQ 100 index	32.32
ExxonMobil	29.55
Russell 2000 index	29.35
IBM	28.62
S&P 500 index	25.56

stock trades at $60 a share with at-the-money implied volatility of 80 percent, you can conclude that options on the $60 stock, everything else being equal, are relatively more expensive.

The implied volatility for at-the-money options on IBM, for example, is typically less than the implied volatility of an at-the-money option on Research in Motion. IBM may have an at-the-money implied volatility of 29 percent, whereas Research in Motion, in comparison, may have an implied volatility of 60 percent. Therefore, you can conclude that options on IBM are typically less expensive than options on Research in Motion, everything else being equal.

Table 27.2 illustrates representative implied volatility percentages of at-the-money call options on various stocks and indexes at a particular point in time (30 days prior to an option expiration date).

As can be seen from Table 27.2, there can be wide variation in implied volatility percentages. By comparing the implied volatilities of various options across a number of different stocks and indexes, you can begin to develop a feel for what is considered below average, average, or above average implied volatility.

HOW TO COMPARE VOLATILITY

Implied volatility is stated as a percentage (annual standard deviation percentage), so it is a great tool with which to compare the relative implied volatility of one option versus another, regardless of whether the stocks trade at dramatically different prices. To determine whether the implied volatility percentage of an option is high or low, you can take the following steps:

Compare at-the-money options: Examining the at-the-money implied volatility percentage of a particular option can be an effective way to quickly assess whether an option is considered high or low priced, relatively speaking. For example, if IBM has an at-the-money implied volatility percentage of 29 and

Research in Motion has an at-the-money implied volatility percentage of 60, you can conclude that options on IBM are typically less expensive than options on Research in Motion, everything else being equal. You can compare the at-the-money implied volatility percentages to get an apples-to-apples comparison.

Compare different strike prices: Each option has its own unique implied volatility percentage built into its option price. As a result, if you show implied volatility percentages beside each strike price on an option chain, you will be able to see how the implied volatility percentages vary. For example, if an at-the-money implied volatility percentage is 30 percent and a far-out-of-the-money put option percentage is 40 percent, you can conclude that options get more expensive the lower the strike price and/or the further that they are out-of-the-money.

Prior implied volatility: When comparing a current implied volatility percentage to implied volatility percentages of the past, you can compare implied volatility over a specified period of time such as the last 90 days. For instance, you may determine that the at-the-money implied volatility percentage of an option is 50 percent, whereas its recent implied volatility percentages were between 30 and 40 percent: This indicates a recent rise in the expensiveness of the option price.

Compare call to put prices: You can compare call prices to put prices (on the same stock) that are equidistant from the stock price (out-of-the-money). This can tell you which is more expensive in relative terms. For example, if it is January and XYZ stock is trading at $100, the February 105 call could be trading at $2.50, whereas the February 95 put could be trading at $2.00. Keep in mind that such differences in pricing, however, may be attributable to variables other than implied volatility

Compare to historic volatility: You can also compare the implied volatility percentage of an option to the historic volatility percentage of the underlying stock. When the implied volatility percentage exceeds the historic volatility percentage, this may be an indication that options are expensive. When the historic volatility percentage exceeds the implied volatility percentage, this may be an indication that options are cheap. For example, IBM may have an at-the-money implied volatility of 29, but the annual standard deviation percentage of its stock price may be only 25 percent, indicating that the option market is signaling an increase in the stock volatility.

Compare to VIX: The VIX can be used to determine whether the implied volatility percentage of a particular option is above or below the market volatility percentage as a whole. For example, if the VIX is at 25 percent and the implied volatility percentage of the option you want to buy is 50 percent, you can conclude that the option is much more expensive relative to the overall market. Conversely, if the implied volatility percentage of the option is 20 percent, then you can conclude that the option is less expensive.

Compare to industry index: Another method is to compare an implied volatility percentage to a volatility index in the same industry, if one exists. For example, Apple Computer is a component of the NASDAQ 100, so you could compare the implied volatility of the at-the-money Apple Computer option to the NAS-DAQ 100 volatility index (VXN), which represents, in effect, the weighted average composite implied volatility of the NASDAQ 100.

If you are interested in buying options on XYZ, for instance, you may determine that the at-the-money implied volatility percentage is 54 percent, its recent implied volatility percentages are between 40 and 55 percent, other stocks in its sector are typically trading at an implied volatility percentage of 60 to 80 percent, and the VIX is currently at 25 percent. By combining these comparisons, you may determine, for instance, that this option is trading at the higher end of its recent past implied volatility, the option has a relatively low price in comparison to other comparable stocks in the industry, and that it has a higher price relative to the overall market. By comparing implied volatility percentages in this manner, you can determine whether the implied volatility percentage on a particular option is cheap or expensive in relative terms to itself, other comparable stocks, and the market.

RESPONSE TO CHANGING CONDITIONS

Now we will examine how the implied volatility percentage is likely to respond based on changing conditions. Getting your hands around a likely change in an option price can be difficult because an option price is primarily affected by three factors (stock vs. strike price, time, and volatility), all of which are moving at the same time but not necessarily in the same direction. In effect, assessing an option's price is like a juggling act that has several balls in the air at the same time. This is illustrated using the S&P 500 futures, but it can apply to stocks, ETFs, and the SPX.

Call Implied Volatility

It is not uncommon for out-of-the-money call options to have one or more factors working in one direction, with other factors working in the opposite direction; for example, in some cases, the rise in a stock can be offset by time decay and contracting volatility, which can have the effect of the call price rising at a lower rate than anticipated, or even declining.

As a general rule, a rise in the S&P 500 futures is accompanied by a decline in S&P 500 futures call implied volatility percentages (and the VIX), and a decline in the S&P 500 futures is accompanied by a rise in S&P 500 futures call implied volatility percentages (and the VIX). The same correlation should hold true for many stocks but will depend on the facts and circumstances of each individual stock.

The effect on a call price from a rise in the S&P 500 futures comes down to how close the underlying futures level is to the strike price, how much time there is remaining, and the magnitude of the change in the call implied volatility percentage. It should be noted that this correlation between a rise in the S&P 500 futures and a decline in the call implied volatility percentage does not always occur. There have been years in which the S&P 500 futures rose in value and the implied volatility percentage did not decline because of continuing fears in the marketplace. I use the following rules of thumb for S&P 500 futures out-of-the-money calls. If the S&P 500 futures rises, the new call option value is equal to:

- The immediately previous option value, plus
- The effect of the new futures/strike price relationship, minus
- Time decay, minus
- Implied volatility contraction.

If the S&P 500 futures declines, the new call option value is equal to:

- The immediately previous option value, minus
- The effect of the new futures/strike price relationship, minus
- Time decay, plus
- Implied volatility expansion.

As the S&P 500 futures moves higher, the call price increases because the underlying instrument is closer to the strike price, but the call price increase can be mitigated by volatility contraction. For example, assume that the S&P 500 futures is at 1,500, you sell one February 1,600 call for $1 (for a credit of $250), and according to the option chain, the February 1,575 call is at $4. From this, you may assume that a quick rise by 25 points in the S&P 500 futures would increase the 1,600 call to around $4 (same as the 1,575 call) because the 1,600 call will be the same distance from the underlying instrument as the 1,575 was prior to the rise. However, when a rise in the S&P 500 futures occurs, it is typically accompanied by a contraction in implied volatility so that the call may only increase to something like $3.

Put Implied Volatility

As a general rule, a decline in the S&P 500 futures is accompanied by a rise in S&P 500 futures put implied volatility percentages, and a rise in the S&P 500 futures is accompanied by a decline in S&P 500 futures put implied volatility percentages. The same correlation should hold true for many stocks but will depend on the facts and circumstances of each individual stock.

As a general rule, a decline in the value of the S&P 500 futures is accompanied by an increase in S&P 500 futures put implied volatility percentages. As a result, both of these factors increase the value of a put option, and the effects of time decay are not typically great enough to offset the dual effects of the price decline and volatility increase. Conversely, a rise in the value of the S&P 500 futures is usually accompanied by a decline in S&P 500 futures put implied volatility percentages, both of which decrease the value of a put option. I use the following rules of thumb for S&P 500 futures out-of-the-money puts. If the S&P 500 futures declines, the new put option value is equal to:

- The immediately previous option value, plus
- The effect of the new futures/strike price relationship, minus
- Time decay, plus
- Implied volatility expansion.

If the S&P 500 futures rises, the new put option value is equal to:

- The immediately previous option value, minus
- The effect of the new futures/strike price relationship, minus
- Time decay, minus
- Implied volatility contraction.

Please bear in mind that there are exceptions.

As the S&P 500 futures moves lower, not only is the put price increasing because the underlying instrument is closer to the strike price but, typically, implied volatility increases as well. As a result, when the market moves lower and you are short a put, you may have the double whammy of being closer to the strike price and experiencing an increase in volatility. For example, assume that the S&P 500 futures is at 1,500, you sell one February 1,400 put for $1 (for a credit of $250), and according to the option chain, the February 1,425 call is at $4. From this, you may assume that a quick decline by 25 points in the S&P 500 futures would increase the 1,400 put to around $4 (same as the 1,425 put) because the 1,400 put will be the same distance from the underlying instrument as the 1,425 call was prior to the rise. However, when a decline in the S&P 500 futures occurs, it is typically accompanied by a rise in implied volatility so that the put may increase to something like $5 or $6.

Table 27.3 summarizes a typical call versus put response to a change in the underlying instrument.

TABLE 27.3 Call versus Put Response to a Change in the Underlying Instrument

Rise or Decline	Implied Volatility	Out-of-the-Money Call Option	Out-of-the-Money Put Option
Underlying instrument rises	Typically declines	Typically rises but can be partially mitigated by volatility decline	Declines
Underlying instrument declines	Typically rises	Declines but can be partially mitigated by volatility rise	Typically rises, accentuated by volatility rise

Implied Volatility and Delta

Assuming that all options are of the same type (all calls or all puts) and have the same amount of time to expiration, at-the-money options are more sensitive in total points to a change in the implied volatility percentage, and out-of-the-money options are more sensitive in percentage terms to a change in the implied volatility percentage. For example, assume that the implied volatility percentage is at 60 percent and at-the-money options and out-of-the-money options have values of $5 ($500) and $1 ($100), respectively. If you raise the implied volatility percentage to 61 percent, the options might increase to $5.12 ($512) and $1.08 ($108), respectively. In this example, the at-the-money option has the greater total point increase ($12 vs. $8), but the out-of-the-money option has the greatest percentage increase (8.0 vs. 2.4 percent).

As a general rule, a rise in the implied volatility percentage moves options toward a 0.50 delta. As a result, if there is a rise in the implied volatility percentage, an in-the-money option delta declines because it is above 0.50 and an out-of-the-money delta rises because it is below 0.50. For instance, assume that XYZ stock is trading at $100 a share, the February 95 call has a delta of 0.65, and the February 105 call has a delta of 0.42. A rise in volatility, assuming no other changes, will cause the delta of the February 95 call to decline and the delta of the February 105 call to rise. This movement in prices is why it can be to your advantage to sell a vertical credit spread instead of a naked option in a rising volatility environment. Likewise, as a general rule, options in a declining volatility environment move toward a 1.0 delta.

The effect of a decrease or increase in the implied volatility percentage on the delta of an option depends on whether the option is out-of-the-money, at-the-money, or in-the-money. At the same time that in-the-money options lose delta, out-of-the-money options gain delta, as discussed in the following sections.

Out-of-the-Money   As a general rule, an increase in the implied volatility percentage causes out-of-the-money options to gain delta, but a decrease in the percentage causes out-of-the-money options to lose delta. For example, if an XYZ February 105 out-of-the-money call has a delta of 0.42, an increase in the implied volatility percentage may increase the delta to some number above 0.42, such as 0.45. A decrease in the implied volatility percentage, assuming that all other factors remain constant, may reduce the delta to some number below 0.42, such as 0.39.

At-the-Money   As a general rule, an increase or decrease in the implied volatility percentage will not cause at-the-money options to gain or lose much in delta because such options have a delta of near 0.50, regardless of the volatility level. For example, if an XYZ February 100 at-the-money call has a delta of 0.50, a decrease or increase in the implied volatility percentage, assuming that all other factors remain constant, may not change the delta very much.

In-the-Money As a general rule, an increase in the implied volatility percentage causes in-the-money options to lose delta and a decrease in the percentage causes in-the-money options to gain delta. For example, if an XYZ February 95 in-the-money call has a delta of 0.65, an increase in the implied volatility percentage may reduce the delta to some number below 0.65, such as 0.60. A decrease in the implied volatility percentage, assuming that all other factors remain constant, may increase the delta to some number above 0.65, such as 0.70.

Implied Volatility and Time

Volatility and time to expiration are closely interconnected. More time to expiration means more time for volatility to take effect, whereas less time to expiration means that volatility will have less effect on an option's value. The effect that a change in the implied volatility percentage has on an option's price diminishes as expiration approaches. Therefore, everything else being equal, a longer-term option is more sensitive to a change in volatility and a near-term option is less sensitive to a change in volatility. For example, if XYZ is selling at $100 a share in January, the at-the-money March 100 call, in general, will be more sensitive to a change in volatility than the February 100 call.

This is one of the reasons why many option buyers prefer to purchase options with at least 60 to 90 days remaining until expiration, whereas option sellers prefer to write options with 45 days or less to expiration.

Implied Volatility and Volume

Another factor affecting implied volatility that is rarely discussed is its correlation to volume. As a general rule, I have observed anecdotally that as the volume of the underlying stock increases, implied volatility tends to increase. Likewise, as the volume of the underlying stock declines, implied volatility, everything else being equal, tends to decline. I imagine that the reason for this is that an increase in the volume of stocks tends to signal an increase in the level of uncertainty, whereas a decline in volume may be associated with complacency. For example, it has been my observation that if the SPX declines on high volume, the prices of SPX put options are more likely to rise by a greater amount than if the rise is on low volume. Likewise, if the SPX declines on low volume, the prices of SPX put options are more likely to rise by a lesser amount than if the rise is on high volume.

You should be alert to holidays and anticipated low-volume days. Holidays, weekends, and low-volume days are, in general, the friend of an option seller. On the basis of my trading experience, I have observed a correlation between lower volume and declining option prices, and I have also observed that option values tend to decline on days leading up to holidays, as volume declines. In the days near holidays, therefore, the seller has an advantage: As volume begins to decline, the markets are then closed during the holiday period and, in many cases, volume does not return to the market until two or three days after the holiday has ended. Of course, weekends are also the friend of an option seller because of time decay.

MARKET VOLATILITY GAUGES

As previously mentioned, implied volatility percentages fluctuate throughout the trading day and vary from stock to stock, strike price to strike price, and for puts versus calls. As a result, it is useful to have a gauge of market implied volatility to quickly measure whether option prices, in general, are relatively high or low. The CBOE VIX measures the implied volatility of options for the SPX based on the implied volatility of various strike prices and expiration dates. It is commonly used to measure the overall volatility of the U.S. equity markets. The VIX is often referred to as the fear gauge.

The VIX is a weighted-average composite of implied volatilities of relatively short-term options on the SPX that takes into account a number of exercise prices. Although implied volatility varies for each exercise price on the SPX, the variation is usually not that wide so that, in the end, the VIX, typically, is fairly close to the at-the-money implied volatility percentage. As a result, I view the VIX as a proxy of the at-the-money implied volatility of the SPX. Perhaps calling it an index makes it more understandable than simply calling it "average implied volatility." The CBOE also lists and trades options on the VXN and the Russell 2000 Volatility index (RVX), as shown in Table 27.4.

The implied volatilities of the S&P 500, NASDAQ 100, and Russell 2000 indexes are likely to be lower than the volatilities of the individual stocks that make up the indexes. This makes sense because the fluctuations in the stocks that comprise the indexes tend to offset one another to a certain degree because some stocks rise and others fall. The VIX can be a gauge of the overall market, the VXN a gauge of technology stocks, and the RVX a gauge of small-capitulation stocks.

Such indexes, in essence, measure the implied volatility of options. You can examine a chart of such indexes covering a number of years to determine whether the current level is high or low. With experience, you can acquire a feel for the index level and quickly assess overall volatility.

TABLE 27.4 Volatility Indexes

Underlying Index	Index Symbol	Volatility Index Symbol
S&P 500	SPX	VIX
NASDAQ 100	NDX	VXN
Russell 2000	RUT	RVX

VOLATILITY SKEW

Different implied volatility percentages at different strike prices can create trading opportunities. If you show the implied volatility percentage beside each strike price on an option chain, you will see that there is a different percentage at each strike price, even though it is the same underlying instrument. If you were to graph the different percentages as you move up and down the option chain, you would see that a pattern emerges, which is called a "skew." Your trading platform should allow you to show the implied volatility percentage next to each strike price.

A *forward skew* occurs when the implied volatility percentage increases as you move higher in strike price (i.e., at-the-money implied volatility is 25 percent and a higher strike price is at 32 percent). A *reverse skew* pattern occurs when the implied volatility percentage decreases as you move higher in strike price (i.e., at-the-money implied volatility is 25 percent and a higher strike price is at 22 percent). A *smiling skew* occurs when the implied volatility percentage increases as you move both higher and lower away from the at-the-money strike price (i.e., at-the-money implied volatility is 25 percent and equidistant higher and lower strike prices are at 32 percent). A *flat skew* occurs when the implied volatility percentage remains relatively constant whether you move lower or higher in strike price (i.e., at-the-money implied volatility is 25 percent and higher and lower strike prices are near 25 percent).

Can you guess which skew pattern graphically represents the typical stock? The correct answer is the reverse skew, so that is where you should focus your attention. A forward skew may be common for certain agricultural futures.

A reverse skew pattern occurs when the implied volatility percentage decreases as you move higher in strike price. This means that call implied volatility percentages decline as you move further out-of-the-money (to higher strike prices) and put implied volatility percentages rise as you move further out-of-the-money (to lower strike prices). The skew can help you determine which out-of-the-money options are best to buy and sell. For instance, assuming that all other factors are the same, you can sell an option with a higher implied volatility percentage and buy an option with a lower implied volatility percentage, thus providing a volatility theoretical edge.

An asymmetrical slant/bias in the value of calls versus puts can affect your trading strategy. For example, if call values are greater than puts, you can execute a collar trade more easily, in which a call is sold and the proceeds are used to purchase a put. The pattern of the implied volatility percentage may differ for calls versus puts, even if it is for the same underlying stock (or futures).

Understanding skew dynamics can be a helpful tool when deciding which underlying instrument and strike prices to exploit. The SPX and the S&P 500 futures, for example, typically trade with a fairly pronounced reverse skew. The implied volatility percentage for SPX puts, for example, typically increases as you move to lower prices on the option chain so that each subsequently lower strike price has a higher implied volatility percentage than its next higher strike price. This can create various opportunities and risks in trading SPX and S&P 500 futures options.

TABLE 27.5 Call Implied Volatility Pattern

Strike	Call Implied Volatility (%)
85	46.18
90	40.29
95	37.11
100	35.28
105	33.21
110	32.83
115	32.29

Table 27.5 shows call implied volatility percentages for XYZ stock starting deep-in-the-money and moving far-out-of-the-money. This example is taken from IBM when it was trading at $100 a share.

A volatility skew can be shown graphically to illustrate the pattern at various strike prices. Figure 27.1 shows the call option reverse skew pattern for the previous example and tells you that calls become relatively cheaper, assuming all other factors remain constant, as you move further out-of-the-money. Notice how each call has a different implied volatility percentage for each strike price and that this forms a pattern.

Table 27.6 shows put implied volatility percentages for XYZ stock starting deep-in-the-money and moving far-out-of-the-money. This example is taken from IBM when it was trading at $100 a share.

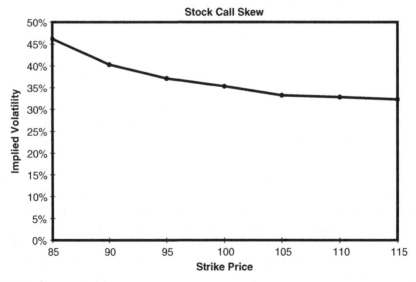

FIGURE 27.1 Stock Call Skew

TABLE 27.6 Put Implied Volatility Pattern

Strike	Put Implied Volatility (%)
115	28.90
110	29.80
100	33.17
105	31.23
95	34.75
90	37.46
85	40.24

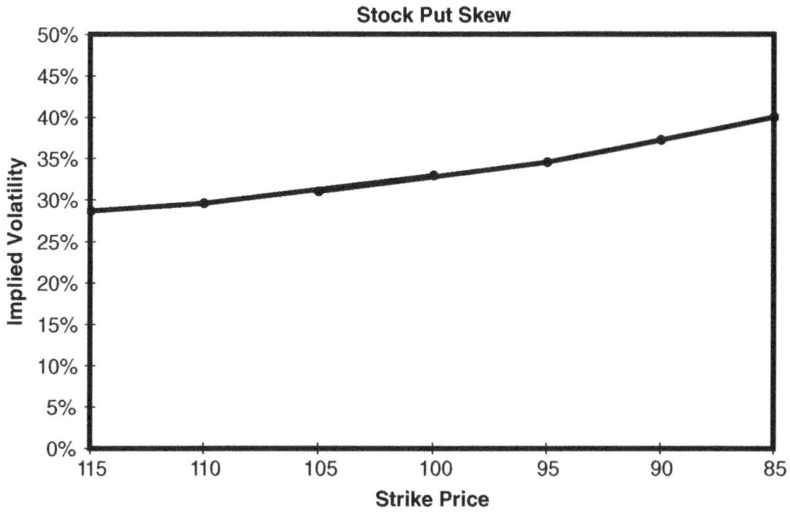

FIGURE 27.2 Stock Put Skew

Figure 27.2 shows a sample put option reverse skew pattern and illustrates that puts become relatively more expensive, assuming that all other factors remain constant, as you move further out-of-the-money.

The order of call and put strike prices has been reversed in Figures 27.1 and 27.2 to illustrate how implied volatility affects out-of-the-money option prices. The call options in Figure 27.1 start with the lower strike price on the left-hand side of the chart and show the higher strike price on the right-hand side. This is reversed for the put example in Figure 27.2 because moving to a lower strike price means moving further out-of-the-money.

Calendar Volatility Skew

A volatility skew can also exist as you move further out in time, even though the strike price is the same. For equity options, it is common for an at-the-money near-term (front month) option to have greater implied volatility than a longer-term option. For example, assume that in January, XYZ is trading at $100 a share. The February 100 call option may be $5 ($500) with an implied volatility percentage of 60 percent, and the March 100 call option may be $7 ($700) with an implied volatility percentage of 50 percent. The calendar spread strategy described in Chapter 17 can be used to exploit the differential in the implied volatility percentage between expiration months at the same strike price. Of course, you are always welcome to use different strike prices to exploit the differential in the implied volatility percentage (by using a diagonal spread, covered in Chapter 18).

Exploiting the S&P 500 Volatility Skew

Portfolio managers have a tendency to sell short-term calls to finance the purchase of short-term puts (i.e., a collar, covered in Chapter 21). This has the effect of driving down prices of short-term calls and driving up prices of short-term puts on broad-based indexes such as the SPX. This creates a pricing environment in which the prices of puts are higher than the prices of comparable calls. Table 27.7 shows call implied volatility for SPX starting slightly-in-the-money and moving far-out-of-the-money. This example was developed using SPX options as a guide when the SPX was at 1,378.

Table 27.7 demonstrates that the implied volatility percentage decreases as you move higher in strike price (i.e., 1,325 strike price is 23.26 percent and 1,660 strike price is 15.78 percent—a reverse skew pattern). Figure 27.3 shows this SPX reverse skew pattern.

Table 27.8 shows put implied volatility for the SPX starting slightly-in-the-money and moving far-out-of-the-money. This example was developed using SPX options as a guide when the SPX was at 1,378.

TABLE 27.7 SPX Call Implied Volatility Pattern

Strike	Implied Volatility (%)
1,325	23.26
1,350	22.62
1,375	21.83
1,400	20.99
1,425	20.10
1,450	19.14
1,475	18.26
1,500	17.41
1,525	16.56
1,550	16.17
1,575	15.73
1,600	15.65
1,625	15.38
1,650	15.26
1,660	15.78

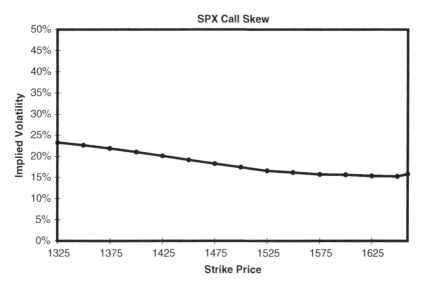

FIGURE 27.3 SPX Call Skew

Table 27.8 demonstrates that the implied volatility percentage increases as you move lower in strike price (i.e., 1,425 strike price is 24.32 percent and 1,100 strike price is 35.43 percent—a reverse skew pattern). Figure 27.4 shows the reverse skew pattern.

Asymmetrical Call and Put Prices   You may expect symmetry between the prices of the calls and puts if they are derived from the same underlying instrument, are an equal distance out-of-the-money, and expire in the same month. Under this expectation,

TABLE 27.8 SPX Put Implied Volatility Pattern

Strike	Implied Volatility (%)
1,425	24.32
1,400	25.05
1,375	25.92
1,350	26.85
1,325	27.79
1,300	28.78
1,275	29.72
1,250	30.62
1,225	31.45
1,200	32.31
1,175	33.08
1,150	33.87
1,125	34.70
1,100	35.43

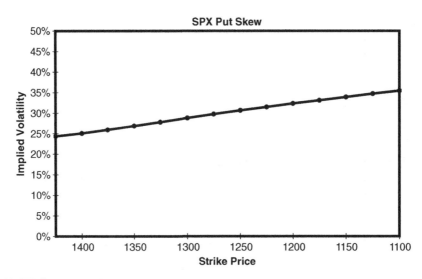

FIGURE 27.4 SPX Put Skew

the price of a call would be equal to the price of the put that has a strike price equidistant from the current underlying instrument value. For example, you may expect a February 105 call to be trading at the same price as a February 95 put if the underlying stock is trading at $100 a share. However, for a stock, a call usually has a higher value relative to a put. As a result, a February 105 call may be trading at $2.50, whereas the February 95 put may be trading at $2. Table 27.9 shows call versus put bid prices, assuming that the options are at an equal distance out-of-the-money. This example was developed using IBM options as a guide with the stock trading at $100.

Table 27.9 illustrates that a stock close-to-the-money call price is typically higher in comparison to a comparable put.

On the other hand, the opposite is true for S&P 500 futures and SPX options. Table 27.10 shows SPX call versus put prices assuming that they are at an equal distance out-of-the-money. This example was developed using SPX options as a guide, when the SPX was at 1,378.

TABLE 27.9 Comparison of Call and Put Prices

Distance Out-of-the-Money	Call ($)	Put ($)
At-the-money	4.90	4.00
5	2.60	2.20
10	1.25	1.15
15	0.55	0.55
20	0.25	0.25
25	0.10	0.10

TABLE 27.10 Comparison of SPX Call and Put Prices

Distance Out-of-the-Money	Call ($)	Put ($)
At-the-money	50.60	46.10
25	36.80	36.90
50	25.30	29.30
75	16.20	23.10
100	9.50	18.20
125	5.00	14.10
150	2.25	10.80
175	1.00	8.20
200	0.40	6.10
225	0.15	4.50
250	0.00	3.30
275	0.00	2.35

Table 27.10 shows that the tendency of the marketplace to sell SPX out-of-the-money calls and buy SPX out-of-the-money puts can create a discrepancy in the relative pricing of calls versus puts. The SPX reverse skew pattern creates an environment in which at-the-money put and call options are approximately equal, but put options far exceed call options as you move out-of-the-money. For example, a call option 100 points out-of-the-money is $9.50, whereas a put option is $18.20. Likewise, a call option 150 points out-of-the-money is $2.25, whereas a put option is $10.80.

It should be noted, however, that the effects of the SPX call suppression can be mitigated if you trade further out in time. By trading call options with a later expiration date, the downward pressure on call prices can be minimized because longer-term call options are more on par with longer-term put options.

Because short-term SPX and S&P 500 futures call premiums are deflated in price because of institutions executing collar-type trades, an opportunity may be present for a call buyer because a call can be acquired at a relative discount. However, an SPX and S&P 500 futures call option seller may be faced with accepting a lower premium. As a result, an option seller may, unwisely, be tempted to move closer to the level of the underlying SPX and S&P 500 futures to collect more call premium, but that means taking on more risk. One possible solution is to move further out in time so that the SPX skew effects are less pronounced.

However, because the SPX and S&P 500 futures put premiums are inflated, an opportunity may be present for the seller because a put can be sold at a higher premium relative to a call. I strongly prefer to take advantage of higher put premiums by selling at much lower strike prices (as far out-of-the-money as possible to achieve a desired return) to reduce risk. Selling a far-out-of-the-money put on the SPX can take advantage of a low-delta trade but also inflated put premiums created by portfolio managers. You are, in effect, taking the other side of the portfolio manager trade because he must purchase these puts as insurance for his portfolio, even though the portfolio manager may not believe that the options will make him money. A pronounced reverse skew can create attractive option-selling opportunities in puts and unattractive selling opportunities in calls. You should never, however, sell puts if you believe the market will decline substantially.

SPX and S&P 500 futures call options at higher strikes can be viewed as lower priced in relative terms because of lower implied volatility percentages. Thus, assuming that everything else is equal, a higher-strike call is more favorably priced for an option buyer and less favorably priced for an option seller. Put options at lower strikes can be viewed as higher priced in relative terms because of higher implied volatility percentages. Thus, assuming that everything else is equal, a lower-strike put is more favorably priced for an option seller and less favorably priced for an option buyer. As previously stated, you should never, however, sell puts if you believe the market will decline substantially.

SPX Skew: Spread Pricing and Risk   As mentioned previously, as you move along the option chain further out-of-the-money, SPX and S&P 500 futures call prices tend to decline fairly rapidly. This can make writing an SPX or S&P 500 futures call vertical credit spread attractive relative to a put vertical credit spread. For example, if you are attempting to establish an out-of-the-money credit spread at $1 (sell at $2 and buy further out-of-the-money at $1) on the sale of one S&P 500 futures call vertical spread, you may have a 25-point strike price differential between the call sold and call purchased. However, as you move to lower strike prices along the option chain, further out-of-the-money put prices tend to decline at a relatively low rate and can have wide bid/ask spreads, both of which can make writing a put vertical credit spread more difficult. As a result, to establish an out-of-the-money credit spread at $1 (sell at $2 and buy further out-of-the-money at $1) on the put side, you may have a 40 to 50 strike price differential between the put sold and the put purchased.

The skew and bid/ask spread can serve as a double-dose obstacle in establishing an attractive put strike price differential (remember that the differential determines maximum risk) for a vertical credit spread. The skew and wide bid/ask spread force you to continue down the option chain until you can find an ask price of a put you want to buy that is sufficiently lower than the bid price of the put you want to sell.

DELTA-NEUTRAL VOLATILITY TRADING

For the purposes of this book, an option strategy that attempts to profit from a trading range (nondirectional) is, in many cases, called *delta-neutral* because a loss on one leg (or side) of the position is approximately offset by another leg (or side), as long as the underlying stock stays within the trading range. Such a strategy attempts to take advantage of time decay and/or volatility contraction while attempting to minimize fluctuations in the account.

A market maker is someone who assists in the making of an orderly market by taking buy and sell orders from the public and by making bids and offers for his own account in the absence of orders. As a result, market maker–type trading can be concerned with what constitutes delta-neutral because maintaining an even flow and balance is important. However, that type of delta-neutral trading is not the focus of this book. Although much can be learned from such trading, you should instead direct your energies to how to profit from trades.

My definition of delta-neutral is defined broadly to include offsetting positions with a low net delta (perhaps 0.20 or less) that primarily relies on time decay and volatility contraction to create a profit. As a result, if you sell a far-out-of-the-money put and call option on the S&P 500 futures with a relatively low net delta, you are considered to be in a delta-neutral position because the underlying S&P 500 futures must move outside its normal trading range to create a large loss. For example, if you sell a credit spread, straddle, strangle, or short iron condor with a low net delta, you can, for this purpose, consider it delta-neutral because it is primarily nondirectional and attempt to take advantage of time decay and/or volatility contraction. Likewise, a long butterfly or long condor can also be considered delta-neutral. A delta-neutral position typically profits when there is a small movement in the underlying instrument and loses money when there is a large movement in either one or both directions.

Adjusting to Delta-Neutral

An increase in the underlying S&P 500 futures may result in a loss on the call side of a spread and a gain on the put side so that the value of your net position may not change much or may perhaps show a gain. To achieve a delta-neutral position, you may need to ratio the position, having more long positions than short positions, or more calls than puts, or vice versa.

A truly delta-neutral position rarely exists because option values change constantly. As a result, what may be delta-neutral when a position is established may not be delta-neutral a short time afterward or as market conditions change. As a result, any attempt to maintain a delta-neutral posture will require various adjustments. For example, if you began delta-neutral and an increase in the underlying S&P 500 futures results in short call positions increasing in delta and short put positions decreasing in delta, you can achieve a (temporary) delta-neutral posture by offsetting (or rolling) one or more calls or by adding (or rolling) puts. An adjustment to get back to delta-neutral can be accomplished by adding or offsetting option contracts or trading the underlying instrument.

CONSIDER TRADING VOLATILITY INDEX OPTIONS

As mentioned previously, the CBOE VIX is called the fear gauge because it is a barometer of stock market volatility and uncertainty. You can actually trade VIX options (and VIX futures) as a way to profit directly from changes in market implied volatility. VIX options can be traded in a standard stock brokerage account, but trading VIX futures contracts requires you to trade in a futures trading account. VIX options can be used, for example, to trade volatility and can be viewed as an alternative to buying puts for protection against a market decline.

Options on the volatility index have unique characteristics that make them different from most other options. You should contact your broker and read the product specifications on the CBOE web site (www.cboe.com).

FINAL THOUGHTS

At first glance, it may seem that options with the lowest level of relative premium, as measured by implied volatility, are the most attractive to buy and that options with the highest level of relative premium are the most attractive to sell. Although this sometimes can be true, it is not always the case. A relatively high implied volatility may seem attractive at first if you want to sell an option, but it may be inflated because that particular underlying instrument has more risk. Keep in mind that implied volatility changes constantly and can be high or low for long periods of time. You need to know what type of market you are trading in so that you can make educated decisions with respect to volatility.

There can be wide variation in implied volatility among underlying instruments. By comparing implied volatilities, you can develop some rules of thumb regarding what is considered an expensive option or an inexpensive option. As you develop your trading philosophy and experience in the area of trading options, you will begin to have a feel for which options are attractively priced.

Option strategies are available to take advantage of volatility expansion (e.g., a long strangle) and volatility contraction (e.g., a short straddle). You should understand how a volatility skew affects option pricing. After you understand skew, you will be in a better position to evaluate whether you should be buying or selling calls versus puts, whether a naked versus covered spread is a better strategy, and how far-out-of-the-money options should be bought or sold. In the next chapter, Chapter 28, we will explore exercise and assignment.

Exercise and Assignment

A full chapter is being devoted to explaining what you need to know about *exercise and assignment* so that you can trade with confidence and avoid pitfalls. This chapter compares physical versus cash settlement; compares exercise and assignment for different underlying instruments; and describes American- versus European-style exercise, *automatic exercise*, exercise and assignment for spread positions, likelihood of exercise, assignment risk, and procedures. Exercise and assignment are addressed throughout this book.

OVERVIEW

Before discussing exercise and assignment rules and procedures, let us set the stage by reviewing some basic definitions. As a general rule, an option buyer (holder/owner) has a right to exercise an option and an option seller (writer) has an obligation to satisfy it if assigned. A call owner has a right to exercise an option to buy an underlying instrument (or receive cash if an index). A put owner has a right to exercise an option to sell an underlying instrument (or receive cash if an index). A call writer has an obligation to sell the underlying instrument (or pay cash if an index) if assigned. A put seller has the obligation to buy an underlying instrument (or pay cash if an index) if assigned.

It can be a little confusing to try to remember the various rights and obligations for a long call, short call, long put, and short put. As a result, following are general guidelines to help you remember exercise and assignment:

> *A call is satisfied in the same direction as the option, and a put is satisfied in the opposite direction.*

417

TABLE 28.1 Long Option Exercise

Option	Exercise Stock Option	Exercise Index Option
Long call	Buy stock	Receive credit
Long put	Sell stock	Receive credit

TABLE 28.2 Short Option Assignment

Option	Assigned on Short Stock Option	Assigned on Short Index Option
Short call	Sell stock	Pay debit
Short put	Buy stock	Pay debit

As a result, a long call is exercised into long stock and a short call results in assignment of short stock. A put works in exactly the opposite direction because a long put is exercised into short stock and a short put is assigned into long stock. Just remember that a call is in the same direction (long vs. short) as the option and a put is in the opposite direction. However, if a long or short option relates to an index, the exercise/assignment is satisfied by settlement in cash (called *cash settlement*) rather than shares of stock. Tables 28.1 and 28.2 summarize what occurs when an option is exercised or is subject to assignment.

If an option is on a futures contract, then the long or short option is satisfied by buying or selling the underlying futures contract. However, if an S&P 500 futures option, for example, is held until expiration and it is the end of a calendar quarter (expiration date of the underlying futures), it is subject to cash settlement because there is no underlying futures to buy or sell at that time.

Assignment is the receipt of an exercise notice that obligates a writer to sell (in the case of a call) or buy (in the case of a put) the underlying stock. Keep in mind that a cash-settled index instead obligates the writer to pay (in the case of a call or put) the exercise settlement amount. *Early exercise* is exercise by a holder prior to when an option expires. Automatic exercise means an option is exercised on the expiration date if the option is in-the-money, absent instructions to the contrary.

The expiration date for equity options is the Saturday immediately after the third Friday of the expiration month. To a trader, however, the significant date is the third Friday of the expiration month. The third Friday is the day that equity options last trade and is the last day on which an option can be exercised by its owner. Saturday is reserved for brokerage firms to confirm their customer option positions and for related paperwork involved with expiration and exercise procedures. Throughout this book, the third Friday of the expiration month is referred to as the expiration date to simplify matters. The expiration date could be described in each instance as the last business day before the Saturday expiration date.

An American-style option can be exercised by an option owner at any time on or before the expiration date (technically, it can be exercised on or before the last business day before the Saturday expiration date). A European-style option can be exercised only at expiration of the option. Equity options, most ETFs, and stock index futures are American-style exercised. Index options are typically European-style exercised, but not in all cases.

Exercise: Physical versus Cash Settlement

Whether an option is American- or European-style exercised does not, by itself, address whether the option is exercisable into the underlying stock or is cash settled. American-versus European-style exercise simply addresses rights regarding timing of exercise. As a separate matter, the exercise of an option can provide the right to buy or sell the underlying stock, called *physical settlement* (as is the case with equity options and many ETFs), or be subject to cash settlement (where cash exchanges hands and the underlying instrument is neither bought nor sold). For example, if you own an option on a stock (American-style), you can exercise that option at any time on or before the Friday expiration date, and it will provide you the right to buy (in the case of a call) or sell (in the case of a put) the underlying stock. If you hold an American-style index option, you can exercise the option at any time on or before the expiration date, but you receive cash on that exercise.

Stocks, ETFs, Indexes, and Futures

An option on a stock is subject to American-style exercise, with settlement using the underlying stock. An option on an ETF is typically American-style exercised, with settlement using the underlying ETF. An option on an index is typically European-style exercised, with settlement using cash. An option on stock index futures is typically American-style exercised, with settlement using the underlying futures. However, as mentioned previously, S&P 500 futures options are cash settled at expiration if the option expires at the end of the same calendar quarter as the underlying S&P 500 futures.

An ETF, such as an S&P 500 SPDR (symbol SPY), option is typically American-style exercised, giving the owner the right to exercise on or before the Friday expiration date. An ETF call owner has the right to buy an underlying ETF, whereas a put owner has the right to sell an underlying ETF. An ETF call writer has an obligation to sell the underlying ETF if assigned, whereas a put writer has an obligation to buy an underlying ETF if assigned. An option on an ETF ordinarily expires on the third Friday of the expiration month, like an option on a stock. Not all ETF options are American-style exercised; for example, iShares S&P 500 Index Fund (symbol IVV) is the European-style version of SPY.

An index option ordinarily expires on the third Friday of the expiration month, like an option on a stock, and is typically European-style exercised. However, not all stock index options are European-style exercised. For example, the S&P 500 index (SPX) is European style exercised, but the S&P 100 index (OEX), which tracks the S&P 100 index, is American-style exercised. An index option is cash settled instead of being subject to the physical equity-type option exercise and assignment procedures. The cash settlement amount is based on the difference between the strike price of the option and the index settlement value multiplied by $100 (assuming that the index has a multiplier of 100). In other words, the cash settlement amount is based on the amount that the option is in-the-money (difference between the strike price and the exercise settlement value of the underlying index).

An S&P 500 futures option is subject to American-style exercise, giving the option buyer the right to exercise on or before the expiration date. A call buyer has the right to buy underlying S&P 500 futures, whereas a put buyer has the right to sell underlying S&P 500 futures. S&P 500 futures options expire on the third Friday of the expiration month and are P.M. settled. Options expiring at the end of each calendar quarter cease trading on the third Thursday of the expiration month and are settled based on the next day's (Friday A.M.) settlement price. Not all futures options are American-style exercised; for example, end-of-month (EOM) S&P 500 futures options are European-style exercised (and are P.M. settled).

AMERICAN-STYLE EXERCISE

As previously mentioned, options on stocks, ETFs, and S&P 500 futures are generally subject to American-style exercise. Following are examples of American-style exercise using XYZ stock:

Long stock call: By exercising a stock call option, you are choosing to purchase the underlying stock at the exercise price. For example, assume that XYZ stock is trading for $100 and you purchase an XYZ February 100 call expiring on February 20 (assume that it is the third Friday in February). You can exercise your right to purchase 100 shares at $100 per share on or before February 20, the expiration date. If the stock price climbs to $115 a share on February 15, for example, you can exercise the option and pay the exercise price of $100. If the stock price instead declines to $95, you should not exercise your option because you would be purchasing the shares at a price above the market.

Long stock put: By exercising a stock put option, you are choosing to sell the underlying stock at the exercise price. For example, assume that XYZ stock is trading for $100 and you purchase a XYZ February 100 put expiring on February 20 (the third Friday in February). You can exercise your right to sell 100 shares at $100 per share on or before February 20, the expiration date. If the stock price declines to $85 a share on February 15, for example, you can exercise the option and sell at the exercise price of $100. If the stock price instead climbs to $115, you should not exercise your option because you would be selling the shares at a price below the market.

Short stock call: Under an assignment, a call option writer is obligated to sell the underlying stock at the exercise price. For example, assume that XYZ stock is trading for $100 and you write an XYZ February 100 call expiring on February 20 (the third Friday in February). You may be assigned and required to sell 100 shares at $100 per share on or before February 20, the expiration date. If the stock price climbs to $115 a share on February 15, for example, you will likely be assigned (if you do not offset the position) and would be obligated to sell the underlying stock at the exercise price of $100. If the stock price instead declines to $85, you will likely not be assigned because the option owner would be purchasing the shares at a price above the market.

Short stock put: Under an assignment, a put option writer is obligated to buy the underlying stock at the exercise price. For example, assume that XYZ stock is trading for $100 and you write an XYZ February 100 put expiring on February 20 (the third Friday in February). You may be assigned and required to buy 100 shares at $100 per share on or before February 20, the expiration date. If the stock price declines to $85 a share on February 15, for example, you will likely be assigned (if you do not offset the position) and would be obligated to buy the underlying stock at the exercise price of $100. If the stock price instead climbs to $115, you will likely not be assigned because the option owner would be selling the shares at a price below the market.

Keep in mind that you can close out an option position by offsetting it in the marketplace prior to expiration to avoid the exercise/assignment process.

EUROPEAN-STYLE EXERCISE

As previously mentioned, options on stocks, ETFs, and S&P 500 futures are generally American-style exercised. There are exceptions, however; for example, the IVV is an ETF similar to SPY, except that it is European-style exercised. Likewise, EOM S&P 500 futures options are European-style exercised. Following are examples of European-style exercise using the IVV:

Long ETF call: If you buy a call option on a European-style ETF, such as IVV, you cannot exercise the option until the expiration date. For example, assume that IVV is trading for $100 and you purchase a February 100 call expiring on February 20 (the third Friday in February). You can exercise your right to purchase 100 shares at $100 per share on February 20, the expiration date. If the ETF price climbs to $115 a share on February 15, for example, you cannot exercise the option and pay the exercise price of $100 because you must wait until expiration.

Long ETF put: If you buy a put option on a European-style ETF, such as IVV, you cannot exercise the option until the expiration date. For example, assume that IVV is trading for $100 and you purchase a February 100 put expiring on February 20 (the third Friday in February). You can exercise your right to sell 100 shares at $100 per share on February 20, the expiration date. If the ETF price declines to $85 a share on February 15, for example, you cannot exercise the option and sell at the exercise price of $100 because you must wait until expiration.

Short ETF call: If you write a call option on a European-style ETF, such as IVV, you cannot be assigned on the option until the expiration date. For example, assume that IVV is trading for $100 and you sell a February 100 call expiring on February 20 (the third Friday in February). You may be assigned and therefore obligated to sell 100 shares at $100 per share on the expiration date. If the ETF price climbs to $115 a share on February 15, for example, you cannot be assigned (until expiration).

Short ETF put: If you write a put option on a European-style ETF, such as IVV, you cannot be assigned on the option until the expiration date. For example, assume that IVV is trading for $100 and you sell a February 100 put expiring on February 20 (the third Friday in February). You may be assigned and therefore obligated to buy 100 shares at $100 per share on the expiration date. If the ETF price declines to $85 a share on February 15, for example, you cannot be assigned (until expiration).

CASH SETTLEMENT

As previously mentioned, cash settlement is a process by which certain (primarily) index options require the payment or receipt of cash for the amount the option is in-the-money, as opposed to the physical delivery of the underlying instrument. As previously mentioned, an index option can be American-style exercised, such as the OEX, which tracks the S&P 100 index, or European-style exercised, such as the SPX. An index option cannot be exercised into an underlying index and, accordingly, is settled in cash. Following are examples of European-style exercise with cash settlement using the SPX:

Long index call: If you are long an SPX call with a strike price of 1,550 and the underlying index settles at 1,600 on an expiration date, the amount of cash received on exercise is $5,000 (50-point difference between the strike price and the settlement index value times $100). The net profit to you is $5,000 less the premium paid to purchase the call option to open the position.

Long index put: If you are long an SPX put with a strike price of 1,450 and the underlying index settles at 1,400 on an expiration date, the amount of cash received on exercise is $5,000 (50-point difference between the strike price and the settlement index value times $100). The net profit to you is $5,000 less the premium paid to purchase the put option to open the position.

Short index call: If you are short an SPX call with a strike price of 1,550 and the underlying index settles at 1,600 on an expiration date, the amount of cash you are required to pay on exercise is $5,000 (50-point difference between the strike price and the settlement index value times $100). The net loss to you is $5,000 less the premium collected to sell the call option to open the position.

Short index put: If you are short an SPX put with a strike price of 1,450 and the underlying index settles at 1,400 on an expiration date, the amount of cash you are required to pay on exercise is $5,000 (50-point difference between the strike price and the settlement index value times $100). The net loss to you is $5,000 less the premium collected to sell the put option to open the position.

The exercise settlement amount is the difference between the exercise price of an index option and the exercise settlement value of the index on the day an exercise notice is tendered multiplied by the index multiplier. The exercise settlement value is the price level of an underlying equity index used to calculate the exercise settlement amount.

A.M. versus P.M. Settlement

Index option exercise settlement values can be classified as either A.M. or P.M. settlement: A.M. settlement is a settlement style in which the exercise settlement value of an index option is determined based on the opening prices of the component securities; P.M. settlement is a settlement style in which the exercise settlement value of an index option is determined based on the closing prices of the component securities. For example, an SPX option settlement value is based on the opening prices of all stocks that comprise the S&P 500 index on the morning of expiration Friday. The SPX settlement value is a special settlement value that is determined once all of the component stocks in the S&P 500 open and is not the opening print of the SPX on Friday morning. OEX P.M. settlement is determined by using the component stocks' closing value on the last day of exercise.

AUTOMATIC EXERCISE

A brokerage firm (or the *Options Clearing Corporation*, called the *OCC*) can require automatic exercise of an option if it is in-the-money at the close of the expiration date by a certain threshold. For example, the threshold for automatic exercise is currently $0.01. As a result, a long equity option in-the-money by $0.01 or more will be automatically exercised unless you instruct your broker otherwise on a timely basis. Likewise, a long index option in-the-money by $0.01 or more may be automatically exercised unless you instruct your broker otherwise on a timely basis. You need to check with your brokerage firm regarding its policy.

Watch Out for Risks

Automatic exercise is an area that probably deserves more attention than it gets. When an option is automatically exercised, the owner of the option must purchase shares (if a call) or sell shares (if a put), and this occurs even if no action is taken on the part of the owner. As a result, an automatic exercise will result in gap risk because you cannot exit the long or short stock position until the following trading day. As a result, if you are long an in-the-money option at the expiration date, you should make a decision whether to exercise or else it will be subject to the automatic exercise provisions. Alternatively, you can offset the option prior to expiration.

Just think of the ramifications if you are subject to automatic exercise on a Friday and the stock gaps lower (if a call) or higher (if a put) at the opening on Monday. The Friday close to Monday morning time frame can be risky for anyone long an option as a result of automatic exercise. Of course, the stock can open flat on the following Monday or even at a profit. It is possible that on a Friday afternoon, your stock may be several points out-of-the-money and everything may look calm. If you leave your trading platform early to play golf that afternoon, you may be surprised to find that the stock moved in-the-money and that you have been subjected to automatic exercise by your broker. As a result, you have a gap risk associated with that exercise until the Monday morning opening. Keep in mind that you can avoid this scenario by simply offsetting the option in the marketplace prior to the close on the Friday expiration date or by instructing your broker not to exercise.

A similar risk exists for the option seller because he may not expect assignment only to learn too late that it occurred. This scenario can be avoided if you offset the option in the marketplace prior to close on Friday.

Automatic exercise illustrates that an option buyer has an obligation, in some respects, unless he takes proactive and timely action to avoid the exercise. The standard definition of a long option conferring rights may incorrectly lead some people to believe that nothing will happen if no action is taken. Following are examples regarding automatic exercise.

Call Examples

Assume that you are long one XYZ February 95 call with the stock trading at $95.50 at the close of the expiration date, so you are subject to automatic exercise (unless you timely notify your broker otherwise). When your call option is exercised, you own 100 shares of XYZ stock at $95 a share. If XYZ stock opens on Monday at $92 a share, you have an unrealized loss on the long stock of $300 ($95 minus $92, ignoring the premium). If XYZ stock opens on Monday at $98 a share, you have an unrealized gain on the long stock of $300 ($98 minus $95, ignoring the premium).

If you are short one XYZ February 95 call with the stock trading at $95.50 at the close of the expiration date, you may be assigned. If your call option is assigned, you will be short 100 shares of XYZ stock at $95 a share (assuming you did not already own shares).

If XYZ stock opens on Monday at $98 a share, you have an unrealized loss on the short stock of $300 ($98 minus $95, ignoring the premium). If XYZ stock opens on Monday at $92 a share, you have an unrealized gain on the short stock of $300 ($95 minus $92, ignoring the premium). You can avoid assignment by offsetting the position prior to the close of trading on Friday.

Put Examples

If you are long one XYZ February 95 put with the stock trading at $94.50 at the close of the expiration date, you are subject to automatic exercise (unless you timely notify your broker otherwise). When your put option is exercised, you are short 100 shares of XYZ stock at $95 a share (assuming you did not already own shares). If XYZ stock opens on Monday at $98 a share, you have an unrealized loss on the short stock of $300 ($98 minus $95, ignoring the premium). If XYZ stock opens on Monday at $92 a share, you have an unrealized gain on the short stock of $300 ($95 minus $92, ignoring the premium).

If you are short one XYZ February 95 put with the stock trading at $94.50 at the close of the expiration date, you may be assigned. If your put option is assigned, you are long 100 shares of XYZ stock at $95 a share. If XYZ stock opens on Monday at $92 a share, you have an unrealized loss on the long stock of $300 ($95 minus $92, ignoring the premium). If XYZ stock opens on Monday at $98 a share, you have an unrealized gain on the long stock of $400 ($98 minus $95, ignoring the premium). You can avoid assignment by offsetting the position prior to the close of trading on Friday.

SPREAD RISKS

There are special exercise and assignment risks associated with a spread. When you sell a vertical credit spread, for instance, the short option may move in-the-money, whereas the long option may remain out-of-the-money. For example, assume that XYZ stock is trading at $100 a share and you sell one February 100 call and buy one February 105 call. If XYZ stock is at $103 at the option expiration date, the short option will be assigned, and you will be required to sell XYZ stock at $100 a share, whereas the long option expires worthless. If both strike prices are in-the-money and you choose not to close out the spread position before expiration, then you will be assigned on your short call option and can exercise your long call.

If you establish a vertical debit spread, it is possible for the option that you bought to be in-the-money and the option that you sold to be out-of-the-money, giving you the right to exercise the long leg of the spread. For example, assume that XYZ stock is trading at $100 a share and you are long one February 100 call and short one February 105 call. If XYZ stock is at $103 at the option expiration date, you can exercise the long option, whereas the short option expires worthless. If both strike prices are in-the-money and you choose not to close out the spread position before expiration, then you will be assigned on your short call option but can exercise your long call.

Exercise and assignment can create havoc in a spread position, especially when the options expire at different times and there are multiple options at various strike prices. In most cases, it is advisable to avoid exercising an option and avoid assignment and instead focus on trading the options themselves. For example, if you establish a calendar spread, it is possible for the near-term option to be assigned while the longer-term option is also in-the-money. Assume that XYZ stock is trading at $100 a share and you sell one February 100 call and buy one April 100 call. If XYZ stock is at $103 at the February option expiration date, the near-term option will be assigned, and you will be required to sell XYZ stock at $100 a share. You can exercise the long April call, but if it has extrinsic value, you may want to offset the long call option and buy the shares in the marketplace to fulfill the assignment. To illustrate a spread exercise and assignment, following is a description of a butterfly spread (described in Chapter 15) from the perspective of a long call, long put, short call, and short put. Assume that XYZ stock is trading at $100 a share in January:

Long call butterfly exercise and assignment: Assume that you buy a February 95/100/105 long call butterfly. If XYZ stock closes above the highest strike of 105 at expiration (each call expires in-the-money) and you allow the exercise and assignment process to run its course, you would (1) exercise the long 95 call and buy 100 shares at $95, (2) exercise the long 105 call and buy 100 shares at $105, and (3) be assigned on the two short 100 calls and sell 200 shares at $100.

Long put butterfly exercise and assignment: Assume that you buy a February 95/100/105 long put butterfly. If XYZ stock closes below the lowest strike of 95 at expiration (each put expires in-the-money) and you allow the exercise and assignment process to run its course, you would (1) exercise the long 105 put and sell 100 shares at $95, (2) exercise the long 95 put and sell 100 shares at $95, and (3) be assigned on the two short 100 puts and buy 200 shares at $100.

Short call butterfly exercise and assignment: Assume that you sell a February 95/100/105 short call butterfly. If XYZ stock closes above the highest strike of 105 at expiration (each call expires in-the-money) and you allow the exercise and assignment process to run its course, you would (1) be assigned on the short 95 call and sell 100 shares at $95, (2) be assigned on the short 105 call and sell 100 shares at $105, and (3) exercise the two long 100 calls and buy 200 shares at $100.

Short put butterfly exercise and assignment: Assume that you sell a February 95/100/105 short put butterfly. If XYZ stock closes below the lowest strike of 95 at expiration (each put expires in-the-money) and you allow the exercise and assignment process to run its course, you would (1) be assigned on the short 105 put and buy 100 shares at $105, (2) be assigned on the short 95 put and buy 100 shares at $95, and (3) exercise the two long 100 puts and sell 200 shares at $100.

If you offset a long leg of the spread prior to expiration, keep in mind that you are then carrying a naked short position, so you would need to check with your brokerage firm to determine margin requirements.

LIKELIHOOD OF EXERCISE

Although anything is possible, it is relatively rare that an option with some extrinsic value is exercised because the holder is better off selling the option rather than exercising it. For instance, assume that XYZ stock is trading at $100 and you own a May 95 call valued at $7. If you exercise the call option, it gives you the right to purchase the stock at $95, which is a $5 ($500) benefit because that is the amount below the current value of the stock ($100 stock price minus 95 strike price). However, you can recognize a $7 ($700) benefit simply by selling the option. If an option buyer chooses to exercise his option even though extrinsic value exists, he is usually doing the option writer a favor because the option writer can pocket the extrinsic value ($200 in the previous example). Remember that you can close out an option position by offsetting it in the marketplace prior to expiration to avoid the exercise/assignment process.

Pay Attention to Parity

It is rare, but possible, that the price of an option may be at a level where it is at less than parity. As a result, it may be to your advantage not to offset the option in the marketplace but instead to exercise the option and immediately dispose of the underlying stock in an attempt to capture the entire difference between the exercise price and the stock price. For example, assume that XYZ stock is trading at $100 a share and you own a February 90 call with a bid price at $9 and an ask price at $10. If you sell the option in the marketplace, you may receive $9 (the option bid price); however, if you exercise the option and immediately sell the shares, you may be able to capture the entire $10 parity (less any commission) by exercising at $100 and then immediately selling the stock at the same price.

Deeper in-the-money options are more likely to trade at a discount to parity. For example, if XYZ stock is trading at $100 a share, the February 90 call is more likely to be trading at a parity discount in comparison to the February 95 call.

The same principle is true for puts; for instance, a put option with a strike price of 110 for a stock selling at $100 has an intrinsic value of $10, but if you want to sell the option, the bid may only be $9 (with the ask at $10 or greater). As a result, if you sell the option in the marketplace, you will be foregoing the difference between the full intrinsic value of $10 and your sale price of $9 (assuming that you sell at the option bid price). You should check with your broker to determine whether you can exercise the put option at $100 and simultaneously buy the stock at the market value of $100, capturing the full intrinsic value of the option.

Dividends and Interest

Dividends and interest typically have a minor effect on the decision to exercise but are worth covering here. Keep in mind that whoever owns a stock as of the ex-dividend date receives a cash dividend, but an owner of an option receives no dividend. A call owner, therefore, may be tempted to exercise an option if a dividend is large enough. You must exercise your call option prior to the ex-dividend date if you want to receive a dividend on the stock. At the opening of the ex-dividend date, the stock price is adjusted downward by the amount of the dividend by the stock exchange on which it trades. As a result, the stock price is expected to drop by the amount of the dividend (assuming that all other factors remain the same). For example, assume that XYZ stock closes at $100 and goes ex-dividend for $1 the next day. As a result, the stock will be adjusted to open at $99; a cash dividend payment may imply a lower call premium and a higher put premium. Remember that if you exercise early, you will forego extrinsic value, so the dividend should exceed the extrinsic value to make it worthwhile. Traders should monitor all expiring positions and be careful with large dividends that can be paid, especially from ETFs. Option prices and strike prices are usually not adjusted for ordinary cash dividends unless the dividend amount is above a prescribed threshold (e.g., 10 percent or more of the underlying value of the ETF or stock).

Interest rates may be a minor factor in determining whether to exercise a call or put option early. A call option more likely may be subject to early exercise if interest rates are low because the foregone interest to purchase the stock is low. A put option more likely may be subject to early exercise if interest rates are high because the proceeds from the exercise can be invested at a higher interest rate. Assuming that all other factors remain the same, a long call holder is less likely to exercise early in a high–interest rate environment because it will require a cash outlay.

In general, to a small degree, an in-the-money put is more likely to be exercised than an in-the-money call because a trader who exercises a put sells shares and receives cash, whereas a trader exercising a call option buys shares and pays cash.

Capital Constraints

In some cases, you may not have sufficient capital in your account to exercise all of your long call options and then hold the underlying stock position afterward. In this case, you should contact your broker to determine if you can exercise call options to buy the stock and immediately sell all or a portion of the stock in the marketplace (of course, you can always deposit additional funds if you are trading outside an IRA). The sale of stock after the exercise may be necessary to avoid a margin call.

A similar result could occur if you are short uncovered put options and you are assigned long stock. In this case, you may not have sufficient capital to buy and hold all the shares, and it may trigger a margin call. In this case, you may want to immediately sell all or a portion of the stock in the marketplace.

If you are short uncovered call options and you are assigned short stock, the assignment may trigger a margin call. In this case, you may want to immediately buy the stock in the marketplace. Likewise, if you are long uncovered put options and you are assigned short stock, the assignment may trigger a margin call, so you may want to buy the stock in the marketplace.

Keep in mind that an assignment results in gap risk, if you do exit the long or short stock position, until the following trading day. Also keep in mind that many option positions are spreads; one side of a spread position may be totally or partially offset by the other so that a margin call may not occur.

There are exceptions regarding exercise and assignment when an IRA is involved. For example, if you exercise a long in-the-money put, you will be short stock, which may not be permissible in an IRA. You should check with your broker to determine if you can, on assignment, immediately purchase the stock to avoid a short stock position. If you exercise long in-the-money calls, your purchase requirement may exceed your IRA balance, generating insufficient funds, and may not be permissible in an IRA. You should check with your broker to determine if you can, on exercise, immediately sell the stock.

It is interesting to note that a trader may be permitted to establish a long put position in an IRA account but may not hold short stock on exercise. Similarly, a trader may be permitted to go long numerous call positions in a regular account or IRA account but may not be permitted to exercise and hold the stock if there are insufficient funds.

ASSIGNMENT RISK

You can avoid assignment by closing (offsetting) a short option position prior to the close of trading. An exercise and/or assignment is effective at the close of business and is reflected in the accounts of both parties the following morning. As a result, the relevant price is the closing price on the effective date of the exercise. The bottom line is that you probably will not be assigned unless there is very little or no extrinsic value, and that does not typically occur until at or near the expiration date. Professional option traders typically do not exercise in-the-money options but instead roll them to another strike price and/or expiration date. Keep in mind that it is probably best to avoid assignment in any spread position and to exit positions prior to being assigned. Conversely, if you are short a put and want to buy the shares at the strike price, then letting the assignment run its course can be worthwhile. As explained later in this chapter, owing to random selection, if you are short more than one option, you may be assigned on some or on all options.

Option Writer: Advantage If European-Style Exercise

If you are an option writer and want to definitively avoid the risk of early assignment, you should sell European-style options. European-style options, relatively speaking, are more beneficial to the option writer because he does not have to worry about an assignment prior to the expiration date. Likewise, they are less beneficial to the buyer because he cannot exercise until expiration. Whether an option is American style or European style may affect an option's price because a buyer may be willing to pay more for an American-style option because it grants him more rights.

EXERCISE AND ASSIGNMENT PROCEDURES

Procedures for exercise and assignment are subject to change, but it may be worthwhile to provide some background information. You should check with your brokerage firm regarding its procedures and rules. The following can be used as a guide. To exercise an option on a stock, the owner notifies his broker by the prescribed cutoff time, such as around 5:30 P.M. EST. The stock brokerage firm of the exerciser submits an exercise notice to the OCC, and that firm randomly assigns exercise notices to brokerage firms with accounts having short positions of the same series. The assigned firm must then use an approved method, such as a random process or the so-called first-in, first-out method, to allocate to short options. A broker may use the method of random assignment on request. As a result, if you do not read the fine print, you may be subject to a method other than random assignment if you do not request it. Brokerage firms can submit exercise notices on a daily basis up to a cutoff time, such as 7:00 P.M. EST, and can establish an earlier deadline for customers. The writer of the option should be able to see the effect of the assignment in his account the following morning. If random selection applies, if you are short more than one option, you may be assigned on some or all of your short options.

There are different procedures for expiring options. For expirations, the OCC processes all exercises and assignments on Saturday. At the present time, at expiration, all equity options that are in-the-money by a penny or more are exercised, unless the option owner instructs his broker not to exercise. Notification to your broker that you intend to exercise may not be required until after the market actually closes—for instance, until around 5:30 P.M. EST. As a result, you can wait to see news after the closing bell to determine whether it benefits you to exercise. For example, assume that you are long one XYZ February 100 call, the stock closes at $98 a share during regular trading hours at 4:00 P.M., XYZ announces at 4:15 P.M. EST that its blockbuster drug has been approved by the U.S. Food and Drug Administration (FDA), and the stock surges to $115 a share in after-hours trading. You can notify your broker by his established cutoff time that you intend to exercise your long call option as of the 4:00 P.M. close. Likewise, assume that you are long one XYZ February 100 call, the stock closes at $103 a share during regular trading hours at 4:00 P.M., XYZ announces at 4:15 P.M. EST that its blockbuster drug has not been approved by the FDA, and the stock plunges to $90 a share in after-hours trading. In that case, you do not have to exercise your call option because exercise at the $100 strike price would result in an immediate loss.

The writer may prematurely celebrate for not being assigned during regular trading hours, not realizing that significant activity can occur in after-hours trading, and he may not find out about the assignment until the following business morning. If you offset your short option prior to the 4:00 P.M. close of business, you will not be assigned because assignments are determined based on net positions after the close of the market each day.

FINAL THOUGHTS

It is fairly well established that most options are not exercised. As a matter of fact, the OCC has reported that typically fewer than 20 percent of all options are exercised. Understanding exercise rules and the exercise and assignment process is important so that you not only understand your rights and obligations, but you can also take advantage of opportunities (e.g., providing notice to exercise after hours) and potential pitfalls (e.g., automatic exercise and gap risk). Keep in mind that in some cases, a spread subject to early exercise and assignment can remove the very protection that a spreader originally wanted. In Chapter 29, we will explore the all-important topic of risk management.

Risk Management

The old adage that an ounce of prevention is like a pound of cure applies to *risk management*. It is essential to keep your losses small, and it is important to protect your investment capital because it represents your freedom to invest. Warren Buffett has been quoted as saying, "Rule number one: Never lose money. Rule number two: Never forget rule number one." With this in mind, it is critical that you manage risk.

You cannot always play offense if you want to win. Playing defense is important if you want to trade successfully over the long run. This chapter will describe risk management strategies that should help you in your trading. Some of the strategies were covered in Chapter 1 but are repeated here for emphasis. The first part of the chapter emphasizes the importance of treating option trading like a business, and the second half describes risk management strategies.

RUN IT LIKE A BUSINESS

If you were running a business, you would put together a business plan encompassing trading strategies and detailed plans of how to operate the business and control expenses (prior to ever starting the business). You should develop the same mentality when trading options. Developing a plan and working hard are essential to your success. You should have targeted profit goals, risk management strategies, a philosophy of trading that fits your strengths and personality, and the best trading tools at your disposal. Remember the Wall Street adage that bulls make money, bears make money, and pigs get slaughtered.

Before engaging in any option transaction, you should determine your maximum profit, maximum loss, break-even point, and probabilities of success. You should develop a view of the direction, timing, and magnitude of the underlying stock and have strategies readily available at your fingertips to place yourself in a position to maximize your return and limit your losses. Before trading options, you should have an understanding of risks.

Create a Plan

Which option strategies are best for you depends, in part, on the amount of your capital, risk tolerance, and the confidence you have in determining the direction, timing, and magnitude of various moves in the marketplace. For example, if you are confident in your ability to predict direction, timing, and magnitude, then you may want to buy a call or put or utilize bull and bear debit spread strategies. If you are uncomfortable being so precise, you may want to sell options.

Discipline and decisiveness are important factors critical to your success. You should not allow your emotions to control your investment decisions. To trade successfully, it is important that you develop your own prescribed sets of guidelines on when to buy and when to sell. Buying and selling options, like other investments, can be an emotional roller coaster if you let it. You should trade when you are levelheaded and calm, using a systematic approach determined beforehand.

Establish Goals

A far-out-of-the-money option, in some cases, can be sold for what appears to be a small premium, but when you calculate your returns on an annualized basis, you may realize that the returns can be outstanding. The object is to repeat the selling cycle each month, every two months, or every quarter to enhance returns throughout the year. Because you have the short-term odds on your side, you may be tempted to sell a large number of options, but you should resist the urge because of the risks.

When selling an option, you cannot make more money than you collect, but there are various strategies that can be used to enhance your returns to more attractive levels. For example, assume that you have a $100,000 account and you sell five out-of-the-money S&P 500 futures put spreads at $1 each every month. In that case, you will collect $1,250 a month on those options, producing an annual return of $15,000. If you also write call spreads at the same time, you will collect an additional $1,250 per month. You will therefore increase your annual return to $30,000 a year, or 30 percent relative to the $100,000 beginning account balance. When you add interest of $2,000, your total return is $32,000, or 32 percent. Looked at another way, if you assume that you can earn $2,000 in interest a year, then you only have to earn $8,000 in options over the course of the year to have an outstanding $10,000 return (10 percent). Of course, you will not be able to generate a profit every month or quarter, but I think you get the idea.

You should exit a position with predetermined profit or loss objectives; for instance, a rule of thumb may be to exit a trade if a loss reaches 50 percent of the amount paid. Another rule may be to take a profit and close out a trade if you realize a profit of more than 75 percent of the premium paid or collected.

Develop an Edge

The average investor may find it difficult to compete with big funds that spend millions of dollars on research and that have access to knowledgeable sources. However, the small investor can have an edge over big funds in some respects because he can enter and exit the market as opportunities develop and not be hindered by requirements to be invested at all times.

Which option strategies are best for you depends in part on the amount of capital you have, your risk tolerance, and your confidence level. When trading, you should not trade to the point that you cannot sleep at night.

Most of the time you are trading options, you should be trading conservatively, but there are other times during which you need to know when to put on a full-court press. This does not mean that you should take excessive risk, but there are times when you should be more heavily invested than others. Of course, there are also times when you should be out of the market entirely. You should never feel compelled to be in the market.

Understand More Than One Strategy

One of the best ways to minimize your risk is to become as knowledgeable as possible so that you know what you are doing. There is no option strategy that works in all market conditions, so you need to learn a number of strategies. This does not mean that you have to become an expert in every option strategy, but it does mean that you need to understand more than one strategy so you can prosper under different market conditions. For example, in some cases, trading options on stocks is your best choice because you may see an individual company that you would like to trade; however, in other market conditions, trading an ETF, index, or S&P 500 futures option can be to your advantage. That way, you can trade moving from one market to the other, depending on which market presents the best opportunities at the time. Remember that there have been some outstanding ETF innovations, providing traders, for the first time, with practical ways to short markets and commodities.

The good news is that there are many different ways to make money trading options. You may be attracted to buying call or put options because you want large gains for a relatively small price, or you may be attracted to selling options because you want probabilities on your side or consistent returns. You should therefore try to match how you trade options with your risk tolerance and investing style. It is up to each individual to determine his own investment style and risk management profile. Unfortunately, there are just as many ways to lose money if you do not know what you are doing.

Open Appropriate Brokerage Accounts

You should open brokerage accounts to enable you to trade a host of different options and take advantage of margin. You should understand how option trading can be affected depending on whether an account is a taxable account, IRA, regular brokerage account, or futures account; you should also understand how to maximize interest income and minimize commissions and taxes.

Where to open accounts and which accounts to open can be confusing because brokers differ regarding what they offer in terms of software, trading options, futures, margin, and interest. Some brokers have specialized option software that permits you to enter, exit, and analyze complex option positions. You should find a broker that allows you to trade futures options. Firms like thinkorswim (www.thinkorswim.com) and OptionsXpress (www.optionsxpress.com) are online brokerage companies specializing in options. They have option trading platforms with single-click capabilities that execute trades, analyze options, and perform real-time position management. Some brokers only permit investors to trade traditional stock accounts, whereas other brokers only allow investors to trade futures. Some brokers provide a full range of stock and investing services but a limited range of futures trading. You should shop around and open at least one stock brokerage account and one futures account, making sure that both accounts permit you to trade options. You should contact various stock and futures brokers and open accounts that permit you to trade options as freely as possible. As a result, you will be in a position to have flexibility to trade stocks and options without unnecessary restrictions. By opening accounts in the stock and futures markets, including an IRA, you will be in a position to profit when opportunities arise. If you do not open up such accounts, you simply will not be able to seize the opportunities when they present themselves. The most restrictive type of account from a margin perspective is typically the equity IRA, and the least restrictive account is the regular futures account. Futures accounts, in general, provide a trader with greater flexibility in trading because of reduced margin requirements and the ability to short.

IRA Trading on margin is not permitted in an IRA, and some brokers do not allow trading of options in such accounts. However, some equity brokers allow certain defined-risk option transactions. There seems to be a wide discrepancy between what is allowed among brokers, so you need to contact your broker to determine what types of option trading, if any, you can execute. If you are unhappy with the answer from your broker, you should consider moving your account to another stock brokerage or opening up a futures account. Some stock brokerages may allow the trading of options in an IRA based on an investor's individual suitability, provided the trades are defined-risk trades such as call buying, put buying, cash-secured put writing, spreads, and covered calls. Unsecured (naked) call transactions are not permitted in an IRA, but a naked put transaction may be permitted if there are sufficient funds in the account. However, you may be permitted to trade a naked call or put option in a futures IRA account. If your capital is limited, you may consider buying options in your IRA (which does not require margin) and selling options outside your IRA (which requires margin).

Control Expenses

Commissions can be affected by the stock or other underlying instrument traded; for instance, S&P 500 futures is a more highly leveraged vehicle than the S&P 500 index

(SPX), and the SPX is a more highly leveraged vehicle than the S&P 500 SPDR (SPY). The number of contracts traded can affect the amount of commissions, as explained in Chapter 23. Some brokerage firms offer free use of their software if you open an account with them and/or maintain a minimum account balance.

The Importance of Interest Income

The manner in which interest is credited to your account may differ, depending on whether the account is a traditional brokerage account or a futures account. Traditional brokerage accounts typically credit a low rate of interest, whereas futures accounts may permit a higher rate because you are typically permitted to purchase Treasury bills in such an account. The magic of compounding should not be underestimated. I have often said that the best way to get a big raise is already to be making a lot of money, and earning interest on a bigger base means more income.

The Importance of Income Taxes

When discussing taxes, most investors have a tendency to roll their eyes. They are often either bored or intimidated by the subject, not wanting to learn the rules and planning to turn over their taxes to their accountant at the end of the year. But that can be a mistake when it comes to option and futures trading because your primary objective should be to achieve the highest after-tax returns. You do not need to know every tax rule, but there are a few tax rules in options and futures that make it worth your while to learn. Taxation of options and futures contracts is not like taxation of other investments. Once you understand these rules, you may conclude that you can save taxes by trading options on one option product versus another. Remember that it has often been said that it is not what you make, it is what you keep.

Tax rules may be different for options on broad-based indexes and options on futures contracts. They are called section 1256 contracts after an Internal Revenue Code section. Under this modification, regardless of how long you have held the option, the gain or loss is deemed 60 percent long term and 40 percent short term (called the 60/40 rule); the option is marked to market at the end of each calendar year; net capital losses can be carried back; and to the extent the carryback is not utilized, losses can be carried forward. Once you understand these rules, you may conclude that you may be able to save taxes by trading options on one product instead of another. Fortunately, options on the SPX and on S&P 500 futures are subject to this special tax treatment and can represent an advantage of trading such options. As a result, trading options on a broad-based index or futures may provide potential tax benefits relative to trading stocks. Taxes are covered in Chapter 32.

Practice Your Option Trading

To learn how to trade options efficiently, it may be useful to practice by using simulated trading (also called paper trading) prior to executing any real trades. Some brokerage firms have developed trading platforms that parallel their live trading platforms but with simulated (paper) trading, which does not use real money. Therefore, simulated trading enables you to practice using the trading platform of your broker as well as track gains and losses without the risk of loss. It can be an effective method through which to learn the unique features and capabilities of the trading platform so that you can efficiently enter and exit option trades. Simulated trading can help you become familiar with the types of option orders that can be entered. If simulated trading is not available, you can trade a small number of options, such as one option at a time (e.g., an option on SPY), making sure that the amount of money you are paying is small and that you have limited risk.

CONTROLLING RISK

Option pricing models do not take into account margin and other money management factors, including the number of positions that you have established. For example, an option pricing model may indicate that there is a 90 percent probability that a put option will expire above a certain strike price by a particular date. That may mean that if you sell one naked put, you have a 90 percent mathematical probability (according to market pricing) on earning that premium. But, if you sell several puts, for example, other factors come into play, such as margin requirements, which may not even permit you to hold the position once the underlying stock gets within a certain number of points of the strike price. In effect, the margin requirements have forced you out of your position before the underlying stock even had an opportunity to reach your strike price.

Therefore, if you sell an option with a 90 percent probability of success but add other options to it, you may need to exit your position before the strike price is reached and use that exit level to determine your true probability. In the world of options, each option you add affects the mathematical probabilities of the others you already own or are short. This occurs because adding options adds leverage (exponentially) to the position, thus potentially limiting your ability to hold your other contracts in the process.

Avoid Excessive Number of Contracts

What can make selling naked options more risky than buying or selling the underlying stock or futures is that naked option sellers typically do not sell just one; they tend to sell numerous options, thus increasing the leverage of their position and risk. It can be argued that, in effect, selling one out-of-the-money naked option is less risky than buying the underlying stock or futures because of the out-of-the-money strike price, in exchange for less upside potential. For example, if you are short one at-the-money naked put, your exposure is limited to the strike price times 100 shares. This is no more risky than owning 100 shares of stock. In fact, it is less risky because the market, in effect, is paying you to take the position.

Risk is increased, however, if an excessive number of option contracts is established, converting it to a position of greater risk. A big risk comes in where too many options are sold because leverage cuts both ways. The problem with continuing to add naked positions is that each position is leveraged so that if you double the number of options sold, you have more than doubled your risk exposure because option risk can increase exponentially.

Protect Your Capital

It is important to protect your investment capital. A popular risk and money management strategy is to let your profits run and keep your losses small. You simply cannot let your losses run too high. If you lose a certain level of capital, it becomes more difficult to ever get back to where you began. For example, if you have $100,000 in an account and lose $50,000, you must earn 100 percent to get back to even. Once you lose a substantial amount of your capital, it will limit how much you can invest going forward and may take you completely out of the investment picture. If you do not have the ability, emotionally or psychologically, to cut your losses, then you should not trade options. You should be prepared mentally and emotionally to take money off the table.

Have Exit Strategies

Probably one of the most difficult aspects of successful trading is deciding when to exit a position. A lot of the damage that resulted from the bursting of the 2000 stock market bubble and the 2008 stock market crash was done by investors who were frozen like a deer in headlights. When wrong (or just plain unlucky), know when to get out and act accordingly.

If you sell an out-of-the-money put on the S&P 500 futures, it is highly advisable not to allow the underlying futures to pierce the exercise price and move in-the-money. Instead, you should set stop losses and be prepared to offset positions to keep losses small and manageable. I do not recommend that an option seller allow an option that was out-of-the-money to go in-the-money. Instead, for risk management purposes, it is better to take proactive action prior to that occurring. In such times, capital preservation should be your main priority. The price of a put or call can inflate dramatically long before the underlying instrument reaches the strike price. It may seem, at first, that an option seller will simply wait out the volatility as the stock or futures moves toward the strike price; however, while he waits, the value of his option may be exploding. As a result, out-of-the-money option sellers are first concerned with the fluctuations of the underlying instrument prior to it reaching the strike price.

Use Margin as a Risk Gauge

Margin can be used as a gauge of risk, and you can have your own trading rule that you will offset a position if the initial margin exceeds certain preestablished thresholds. For example, if SPAN margining indicates that your margin is at 75 percent of the initial margin requirement, it may be telling you that you need to offset (or roll) positions to reduce risk. You may develop a guideline that positions will not exceed a predetermined threshold such as 25 percent of your account balance. Margining calculations can be used as an additional tool to gauge that risk.

Leverage, margin, and risk management go hand in hand. Leverage can help to produce large gains, but leverage is a two-way street and cuts both ways. Because options are leveraged positions, when you double the size of your position, you may have more than doubled your risk because you may not be able to withstand the greater volatility. Probably the best risk-control strategy is not to buy or sell any more options than you can afford to be long or short.

Understand Probabilities

When establishing a position, you should understand your probabilities of success. For example, the delta of an option can serve as a probability gauge: A delta of 0.50 can be interpreted to mean that there is approximately a 50 percent statistical probability (according to the market pricing) an option will expire in-the-money. Likewise, a delta of 0.25 means that there is a 25 percent probability that an option will expire in-the-money. Specialized option software can show a delta/probability analysis for each option and strike price. If you consistently purchase options with only a 10 percent probability/chance of success, with very little time remaining, you are not putting the odds on your side and you have a high probability of failure.

Conversely, in a credit spread, even though you have limited risk, it is suggested that you establish the short option sufficiently far enough away from the underlying stock so that the net delta remains relatively low. My own general rule is not to establish a short option position unless the probability of success is at least 75 percent. I like to use technical analysis to increase the chances of success.

Use Stop Losses

A risk-management strategy can be to exit the trade when the underlying instrument reaches a predetermined price level. For instance, the trader could offset all or a portion of his option positions if the S&P 500 futures contract closes below 1,300 on a particular day, regardless of the absolute value of the option.

Another risk-management technique is to exit any position in which the option reaches a prescribed price level; for example, if you sold an option at $2, you can have a plan to offset (or roll) any contract that reaches $5. As a result, your risk management not only takes into consideration how close the underlying instrument is to your strike price but also the price level of the option itself, which could be an early indicator that you need to get out of the way. Likewise, you can also use a prescribed price level on a long option. If you purchase an option at $5, you can have a plan to offset the contract if it declines to $2 to limit your loss. Keep in mind that a stop loss order is a market order triggered at a certain price level and that slippage can occur when buying options at the market, especially fast markets.

It is important to note that the underlying stock does not have to rise above (below) the strike price for a call (put) to increase in value, and you can offset it in a closing transaction at any time before expiration. The option buyer should have the mind-set that he may hold an option until expiration, but the more likely scenario is that the buyer will offset to that position prior to expiration, when the buyer determines that his price target is met, facts have changed, or that he is unwilling take further risk in the position.

Trade Limited-Risk Spreads

Various option strategy techniques can lessen the cost of options purchased and limit the exposure for options sold. Although the risk of selling naked options is unlimited, the risk of selling vertical spreads can be quantified as the difference between the strike prices times $100 (if a stock) times the number of contracts. However, in many cases, traders convert a lower-risk spread trade to a higher-risk trade. A trader may feel empowered because he has less risk by selling a spread, so the trader may sell more option contracts versus comparable uncovered options. Because more contracts are being sold, the main benefit of spreading can be diminished or eliminated. In this case, the risk profile of the spread is simply different than the risk profile of the uncovered options, but that does not mean you are taking on less real risk (even though your spread maximum risk is defined).

For example, assume that you want to sell an out-of-the-money put on S&P 500 futures, you are looking to collect at least $2 ($500), and you may be able to sell an uncovered put option 150 points below the current underlying S&P 500 futures level. If you instead sell a put spread, and you still want to collect $2, you may be forced to sell an option only 100 points below the current S&P 500 level. Even though the option you purchase provides some risk management protection, the fact that you are selling an option closer to the underlying S&P 500 futures means that you may have more risk in some respect.

It is important to determine the appropriate time frame. As a starting point, it is interesting to compare the amount of premium you would pay or receive per day based on the option expiration date that you choose.

Be Careful in Strike Price Selection

One of the biggest mistakes that a trader can make in selling an option is picking a strike price too close to the underlying stock price. Many traders are not aware that they do not need to trade so close to the underlying stock price to make a respectable profit.

You should be careful in the selection of the width in strike prices in any spread. The distance between the strike prices of the option sold and the option purchased defines the maximum amount of risk for a vertical credit spread. A smaller difference between strike prices means that there is less maximum risk, and a larger distance between strike prices means that there is greater maximum risk.

Learn How to Roll

You should learn how to roll options. When you roll an option position, you offset your current position and reestablish a new position. In some cases, you may offset your current position because there are only a few days left in the option expiration cycle and you are interested in reestablishing a new position in the subsequent expiration month. Many option professionals roll options with several days remaining to expiration and do not wait until the options expire. In other cases, you may roll options to minimize risk, cut losses, and/or take into account your new view of the market. For example, when you first established your option position, you may have been bearish, and now you have changed to bullish. When rolling, you can establish the new position with the same or different number of options, strike prices, and expiration dates. You are readjusting your option positions to take advantage of opportunities, play defense, or take into account new market conditions.

Because each call option has an expiration date, you can roll to a later expiration month if you want to continue a similar position. By rolling in this manner, you can convert a short-term option position into something that resembles a longer-term proxy of the stock. For example, assume that it is January and you purchase a February 90 call option for $11 while the stock is trading at $100. If the stock rises to $110 near the February expiration date, you can sell the February 90 call for $20 (at a profit) and replace it with a March 100 call, paying $11. That way, you have locked in your profit, and the roll enables you to participate in the movement of that stock as though you fully owned the shares.

Example: Roll-up-and-out Short Call   A rolling strategy can be used to play defense and manage risk if you are short calls and the underlying stock rises (by rolling to a higher strike price with a later expiration date). For example, assume that a trader wants to collect income from selling S&P 500 futures (or SPX) out-of-the-money calls and he does not want to be assigned. Assume that the trader is short three August 1,600 S&P 500 futures out-of-the-money calls at $1 a contract when the S&P 500 futures is at 1,500 and that the S&P 500 futures then rises to 1,550. As a result, the August 1,600 calls are worth $3 and the trader has an unrealized loss of $2. Even though the call options are not in-the-money, the trader understands that selling naked calls is risky, so he wants to take a proactive approach to managing risk. A trader can roll (up and out) by offsetting (buying) the three August 1,600 calls at $3 (a loss of $2) and selling the same number of calls at $3 at a higher strike price (with a later expiration date) such as at the 1,650 strike price (assume that the September 1,650 calls can be sold for $3).

A large number of variations of rolling strategies can be used. For example, the trader may offset the original three short calls and replace them with five short calls at a strike price of 1,650 at a later expiration date, thus attempting to profit should the market decline or move sideways. In this case, the trader has moved further away from the market but has assumed more risk with two additional naked calls.

Take Advantage of Delta-Neutral Positions

A delta-neutral position can be considered a risk-management strategy because it enables you to profit without determining the direction of the underlying stock. Delta-neutral refers to an option position that is designed to have an overall delta of zero or near-zero (I like to refer to an option position with a delta of less than 0.20 as delta-neutral). A delta-neutral position can be established using the same number of long versus short options, can be unbalanced, and can involve different expiration months.

You should understand how time decay can work for you if you are a seller and against you if you are a buyer. It is interesting to note that weekdays, holidays, and weekends all count in the cost-of-carry equation; as a result, days on which the stock market is not trading favor option sellers and are a disadvantage to option buyers.

Mind the Gap

Probably the biggest risk to an option seller is a major gap in the market in the wrong direction, accompanied by increased volatility (like the 2008 stock market crash). Should the underlying stock gap in the wrong direction, you may incur large losses. For example, a naked put would substantially increase in value if a stock closing at $100 on one day opens the next day at $80. The same holds true for naked calls, in which a stock closing at $100 on one day may open the next day at $120.

Although it may be your intention to exit an option position quickly should it reach a predetermined price, you may not be given that opportunity if the price of the underlying stock gaps. A gap in the underlying stock is a quick jump from one price to another. Gaps mostly occur at the opening of a session but can occur throughout the trading day, when there may be news affecting a particular stock or overall market such as in the overnight session. When an opening gap occurs, the opening price of a stock differs greatly from the close of the previous session. In such a case, you would not be able to offset your current option position until the market opens, and the price on those options may be extremely unfavorable. Likewise, if the gap is quick and severe, you may not be able to buy or sell the underlying stock in extended hours at a favorable price. The risk of a gap is that, in many cases, you may not have enough time to react. When dealing with an option, a gap in the stock price is often accompanied by a gap in implied volatility.

Buy and Sell Underlying Instrument to Hedge

You can also buy or sell an underlying instrument to hedge a position so that the loss on the options is negated by the gain in the underlying position, or vice versa. For example, you can hedge an out-of-the-money NASDAQ 100 futures short put by selling the underlying NASDAQ 100 futures. In this case, the loss on the put options (if a decline in the market occurs) is offset by the gain in the short underlying NASDAQ 100 futures. The key is to make sure that a proportionate number of options and underlying NASDAQ

100 index (NDX) instruments are sold so that the losses and gains offset each other. You may, for instance, only need to short one NDX contract for several short NDX put options because out-of-the-money options move at a fraction of the amount of the underlying instrument. Care should be exercised in determining the number of underlying instruments to use as a hedge.

Have the Capability to Trade outside Regular Hours

If you are short or long an option position, there is a risk of an opening gap each trading day. As a result, it is prudent to trade options on instruments that trade outside normal business hours. For example, if a sell-off begins overnight in the Asian stock markets, a trader who is short put spreads on S&P 500 futures can, at any time in the evening or morning hours, sell an underlying S&P 500 futures as a hedge.

Options on stocks can typically be traded during the regular trading hours of 9:30 A.M. to 4:00 P.M. EST. Options on some ETFs may trade during regular trading hours until 4:15 P.M. EST. You should check with your broker regarding timing because the rules can change. The underlying stock or ETF, however, may trade for two or three hours after regular trading hours and in the premarket session of the next day. S&P 500 futures options trade from 9:30 A.M. until 4:15 P.M. EST. The underlying S&P 500 futures, however, trades almost 24 hours a day, beginning Sunday evening and ending Friday at 4:15 P.M. EST.

If you are long a put on a stock and the stock plunges prior to the opening, you may have a profit that you want to capture. However, you will not be able to sell your put options until regular trading begins. Instead, you can purchase the underlying stock in the premarket to establish a position that offsets the change in the put value. As a result of this trade, if the stock rises, the trader will profit from owning the stock, which will offset the put value. Likewise, if you are long call options and the market surges before or after regular trading hours, you can short the stock, which has the effect of offsetting the call position in the premarket session.

Be Aware of Trading Halts

A trading halt can increase the risks associated with trading options because it can affect your ability to exit a position. For a naked option seller, a trading halt may mean that you cannot exit your position for several hours or days. In such a case, your losses can grow exponentially. Likewise, a buyer of options may not be able to exit his trade when it is profitable, and the buyer will need to wait until a later time, when the market may have reversed.

A trading halt can be a risk for anyone trading in the markets; for instance, if prices are limit down, there may be no bids to buy at the lower-down limit price. As result, a trader who is long the market and wishes to sell may not be able to do so. Moreover, occasionally, prices will reach limit down for several days in a row, so those wishing to trade may be unable to liquidate their losing positions. Such a situation, of course, can be disastrously expensive if you are on the wrong side of such a trade and is an illustration of the risks associated with short options (and stocks, in general), especially uncovered options.

Be Aware of the Bid/Ask Spread

Before trading any option, you should determine the size of the bid/ask spread. Bid/ask spreads tend to vary depending on volatility and fear in the marketplace. If there is a major stock market sell-off with an increase in volatility and fear, a put option with a typical bid/ask spread of 5.00/5.50 may explode to something like 12.00/16.00, or wider, adding insult to injury. Whenever a short option position moves against you, you can have a loss from both the increase in the overall price of the option and the bid/ask spread.

In a fast market, an option quote can change instantly without notice. In addition, bid/ask spreads tend to be less onerous when they are at-the-money because they tend to be the most liquid options. Trading options on large-capitalization stocks can mitigate the effects of wide bid/ask spreads because of greater liquidity (volume and open interest). Deep-in-the-money options tend to have wider bid/ask spreads than at-the-money options (on a percentage basis). At-the-money options tend to be the most highly liquid options with the greatest open interest and can have more narrow bid/ask spreads. Keep in mind that some options trade in nickel increments, whereas others trade in pennies.

Far-out-of-the-money options typically move by a relatively small amount relative to the movement in the underlying instrument. As a result, if the bid/ask spread is wide, the stock will have to move a large amount simply for you to recoup the cost of the spread. For example, assume that a stock is selling for $100 and the 115 strike price call has a bid of $0.25 and an ask of $0.75, the delta is 0.10, and you purchase a call at the ask price. In this example, the stock needs to rise by five points for the bid to increase by $0.50, increasing from $0.25 to $0.75. The relative sensitivity (fractional change) of an option price to a change in an underlying stock varies depending on how far the strike price is from the stock price, time to expiration, and other factors. It is interesting to note that the full cost of the bid/ask spread is avoided if a short option expires worthless. For example, if the option in the preceding example expired worthless, the gain from the option sale would be $25, and the bid/ask spread difference of $0.50 would not affect the profit (except that it may have affected the amount of option premium collected at the time of sale).

Avoid Selling Options near Parity

Selling an option near parity is usually not a wise choice; for example, as time approaches the expiration date, especially during the last week of expiration, some options may have low extrinsic value and can be bought or sold relatively cheaply. Selling such an option near parity can be a high-risk strategy, especially if volatility is expected to increase from an event such as the release of an earnings report. For example, assume that on Wednesday, XYZ stock is selling at $101 (during option expiration week) and the company will release earnings the following day (on Thursday morning). If a call option with a strike price of $100 is priced at $1.25, you could sell that option at $1.25 and collect $0.25 above parity (extrinsic value). If the stock should rise, you are liable for the full move minus the $0.25. If the stock should decline, you only gain $1.25. In effect, you get full exposure but limited gain potential if the stock drops below the strike price of $100 (above $1.25). As a result, selling a close-to-the-money call or put option with minimal extrinsic value is not a wise choice because it is a low-probability trade, with unlimited risk and limited profit potential. Conversely, buying such a close-to-the-money call or put option with minimal extrinsic value may be a wise choice relative to buying the stock outright because the option has limited risk and unlimited profit potential.

Trading Options on a Broad-Based Index

Trading options based on a broad-based index (e.g., the SPY, the SPX, the S&P 500 futures, and the Russell 2000 index) can be beneficial under certain market conditions. Trading such contracts can enable the trader to trade the market rather than individual stocks. If a trader is correct on the market direction, trading the SPX should be profitable, as opposed to individual stocks, which may not follow the market. Additionally, individual stocks present greater risk and are, in general, more volatile and less predictable than broad-based indexes. The collapse of companies such as Leman Brothers, Washington Mutual, Enron, and WorldCom illustrates how individual stocks can have greater risk and volatility than the broader market and may never recover. The 2008 stock market plunge and 2000 Internet bubble collapse illustrate how individual shares can be more volatile in both directions in comparison to the broad-based SPX. Trading the SPX avoids specific company risk inherent in owning individual company shares.

Use Technical Analysis

Before trading an option, you should have an opinion about the direction of the underlying stock, the magnitude of the move, and the time it will take to get there. Technical analysis can be a valuable tool to determine trends and can place you on a more level playing field with professional traders. Some brokers provide the service of sending an e-mail on a daily basis that analyzes the technical state of the market.

I primarily use technical analysis, and some fundamental analysis, to make decisions regarding which direction the market or underlying stock will likely move in the short and intermediate term. For example, if, based on technical analysis, the market has declined to a level of support, you can execute an option strategy to take advantage of a likely bounce (e.g., selling an out-of-the-money put spread). If the market has risen to resistance, you can execute an option strategy to take advantage of a likely pullback (e.g., selling an out-of-the-money call spread). If the market is trading sideways, you can execute an option strategy to take advantage of a range (e.g., a short strangle or short iron condor). If the market is prepared to break out of a trend or range, you can execute an option strategy to take advantage of that breakout (e.g., a long strangle).

You should keep in mind that option pricing models are agonistic with respect to the direction of the underlying stock and do not reflect technical analysis considerations. Therefore, you should use technical (and fundamental) analysis to select appropriate option strategies, timing, and strike prices. For instance, you would not want to sell an out-of-the-money put if the stock is in a downtrend and below key moving averages and support levels. Likewise, you would not want to sell an out-of-the-money call if the stock is in an uptrend and above key moving averages resistance levels.

You can use technical analysis and sell options to take advantage of the trend; for example, if the S&P 500 futures closes below support levels, it may serve as an early warning sign to avoid selling puts or to take defensive action by offsetting put positions. If the S&P 500 futures closes above resistance levels, it may serve as an early warning sign to avoid selling calls or to take defensive action by offsetting call positions.

Moving averages may be useful to determine a trend and whether support has been broken, such as the 21-day moving average (short-term trend), 50-day moving average (intermediate-term trend), and 200-day moving average (longer-term trend). It is usually best to remember the phrase "the trend is your friend." In general, if the market is trending upward, sell puts; if the market is trending downward, sell calls; if the market is moving sideways, sell puts and calls.

As an additional criterion, you should not sell options within a certain predetermined number of points from the underlying instrument, such as only selling a put option if it is at least 150 points below the current level of the SPX, assuming that there are four weeks to expiration, and only selling call options at least 100 points above the market, with 60 days remaining. You should also sell options with a delta of 0.25 or less. A delta of 0.25 or less means that there is a 75 percent or greater chance that the option will expire out-of-the-money and a 25 percent or less chance that it will expire in-the-money. All of these parameters, when taken together, can lay the groundwork for you to stack the odds on your side.

Be Aware of Opportunity Costs

There is an *opportunity cost* associated with choosing one trade or investment over another. For example, if you pay $10,000 for an option or for a stock, you forego the opportunity to earn interest on the money or to use that money elsewhere, such as to pay down a 7 percent mortgage (or other debt). It is reasonable to argue that an option or stock, or any other investment, should only be purchased if it is anticipated that the investment will produce a return greater than the risk-free rate of return or, in this case, the amount that would be credited in the brokerage account (or the cost of your mortgage). If we assume that the brokerage account credits interest at a rate of 3 percent (and the 30-day Treasury bill rate is 3 percent) and represents the risk-free rate of return, then a stock should, logically, only be purchased for the long run if you believe that the appreciation in that stock will exceed that 3 percent threshold by a sufficient amount to justify the risk, after taxes. For example, if you have a traditional brokerage account with $100,000 cash, you may be able to earn $3,000 of interest, assuming a 3 percent interest rate. If, instead, you decide to purchase stock for $100,000, you will forego the interest income. Should you decide instead to purchase stock for $150,000, not only would you forego the interest income on the $100,000 you could have earned, but you would be charged interest expense on the $50,000 borrowed on margin.

Each time you buy a stock in a brokerage account, you are foregoing the interest income that you otherwise would have been able to earn, and that interest income can be substantial over a period of time. You should trade only if it can reasonably be expected to produce a return attractively in excess of the anticipated interest rate to be credited to the account. It makes very little sense to engage in any investment strategy if your goal is to earn only 3 percent over the course of the year if you could accomplish that by maintaining the money in a brokerage account.

FINAL THOUGHTS

Risk increases dramatically if you do not have a game plan, establish goals, and understand how options move. Maybe the greatest risk to investors is not being knowledgeable. Traders should try to utilize their own personality strengths when trading options.

It is useful to back test and stress test options, like you would other strategies, but with options, you should also learn how to forward test by making assumptions about the future. If you do not understand how an option strategy will make or lose money and the risks associated with that position, you should not enter into that trade. Option strategies should only be initiated by individuals who fully understand options, and the risks should not be a secret. You should learn how to trade more than one product so that you can capitalize on opportunities under many market conditions and learn how to use technical analysis to identify opportunities and make high-probability trades.

Options can be used to add diversification to your portfolio, with the added benefit of having low correlation with your other investments. However, one of the main problems with many option buyers and sellers is that they trade too many contracts, so that when things go wrong, the leverage of options works against them. If you add the fact that they engage in low-probability trades, they are setting the stage for financial failure. Remember, leverage, margin, and risk management go hand in hand.

You should use discipline in adhering to protective stop losses. Your goal in some market conditions is simply to preserve capital. If you sell far-out-of-the-money options, in effect, you stack the odds in your favor that you will succeed, in exchange for the possibility that you may lose more money than you collected. Without such a focus on capital preservation, you may just run out of funds. It is best to have a well-diversified portfolio. Trading options in your brokerage account should be coordinated with your overall financial situation. We will learn about margin requirements in Chapter 30.

Margin

In the stock world, *margin* typically means a loan from a broker to a customer to purchase stock. But margin has a different meaning when it comes to option trading. In the options world, margin does not refer to a loan from a broker to a customer but instead is a calculation threshold that determines the amount of assets that must be held on deposit to originate and maintain a short option position. Margin on a stock is typically concerned with a long position; but, in contrast, margin on an option is concerned with a short option position. This chapter describes margin on stocks, ETFs, indexes, and stock index futures and addresses margin planning.

OVERVIEW

A margin requirement for options is the amount of cash (or other assets) an option seller is required to have on deposit to cover a position as collateral. It is the amount of money that must be deposited by an option writer to ensure performance of the writer's obligations under an option contract. Initial margin is the amount of margin required when a position is opened. Maintenance margin is the amount that must be maintained on deposit after a position is opened. Maintenance margin is set at a level below the initial margin requirement. The Federal Reserve Board and exchanges where an option trades establish minimum margin requirements for short options, but brokers can impose higher margin requirements.

After a short option position is established, every change in the value of the underlying instrument and option results in a change in the maintenance margin requirement. If the value of the assets in your margin account drops below the required maintenance margin level, your brokerage firm will issue a *margin call*. A margin call is a request (actually, it is more like a demand) from a brokerage firm to a customer to bring margin deposits up to the initial margin requirement level. A margin call can be communicated by your broker via e-mail, phone call, or other means. If you do not take appropriate action, your brokerage firm can liquidate assets in your account without your consent. Typically, a broker will allow several days to enable you to move the account out of a margin call position. Because options can change in value over a short period of time, it is important to monitor your account.

As previously mentioned, option margin rules are concerned with short option positions, not with long positions. In general, when a trader enters into a short option position, he is required to post (have on deposit by the date set by the broker) initial margin in an amount at least equal to an amount specified by the broker, exchange, or clearing organization. Thereafter, the position is monitored (usually) daily or more often than daily. If the amount of money in the margin account falls below the specified maintenance margin threshold, the trader is required to take appropriate action to bring the account up to the initial margin level. Alternatively, you can lower the initial margin requirement by closing a position or by establishing a long option that reduces the margin requirement. Thus, prior to establishing a short option position, you should determine the initial margin requirements to determine if you have enough room in your account to establish a new position. After your position is established, you should monitor the maintenance margin requirement to determine if you have to close (offset) that position or take other appropriate action. Your trading platform and broker should be helpful in determining margin requirements.

A long option position is not subject to a margin requirement and, instead, must be paid in full. As a result, for example, full payment is required for a long uncovered long call or put, long vertical, long butterfly or condor, long straddle or strangle, and long calendar spread.

STOCK, ETF, INDEX, AND FUTURES MARGIN

As described in previous chapters, option margin on stocks, ETFs, and indexes is typically determined based on a standard method or portfolio margining method. Margin for stock index futures is typically determined under the standard portfolio analysis of risk (SPAN; explained later in this chapter). The margin requirement can vary substantially, depending on the margining method used. For example, Chapter 23 compares the initial margin requirements for a hypothetical stock, ETF, index, and stock index futures.

Stock and ETF Margin

The standard (traditional) stock and ETF minimum initial margin requirement that most often comes into play for uncovered options is as follows:

- Option premium credited, plus
- 20 percent of the underlying stock or ETF price, minus
- Amount the option is out-of-the-money.

I refer to this margin requirement as *20 percent standard margin*, or simply standard margin. Some brokers raise the percentage to 25 percent. Stock and ETF initial margin may be based on two or three separate calculations, where the greatest number is the margin requirement. The 20 percent standard margin requirement is subject to a minimum; for example, the minimum for a call may be equal to the premium collected plus 10 percent of the underlying stock. The minimum for a put may be equal to the premium collected plus 10 percent of the strike price. A brokerage can impose its own minimum, such as the premium collected plus $50 per option. The margin formula for an ETF is typically the same as an option on a stock.

Sample Margin Schedule   Table 30.1 shows a sample stock margin schedule, with most items taken from thinkorswim. The thinkorswim margin schedule has been modified slightly to illustrate principles. You should examine the margin schedule to determine what types of positions require margin and to compare initial margin requirements to maintenance margin requirements. This schedule is presented only as an example because margin requirements vary from firm to firm and some traders are eligible for portfolio margining, which is not addressed in the schedule.

As mentioned previously, there is a subtraction for the amount the option is out-of-the-money. The out-of-the-money amount is the difference between the strike price and stock price times the number of contracts times the unit of measure ($100 for stocks). If XYZ stock is trading at $100 a share and you write a call with a strike price of 105, the out-of-the-money amount is considered to be $500 (five points times $100).

Assume that XYZ stock is trading at $100 and you write in three different accounts one February 105 call ($5 out-of-the-money) for $2, one February 100 call (at-the-money) for $5, and one February 95 call (in-the-money) for $7. The standard margin requirement calculation is shown in Table 30.2.

The starting point for the standard margining method is the price of the underlying stock and does not attempt to take into account the volatility associated with the position (except for the amount already built into the option price). For example, assume that Research in Motion and the SPDR S&P 500 index (symbol SPY) are trading at $150 a share and you sell one at-the-money call option. The standard margin method would compute the same margin requirements for both option transactions (other than the premium), even though the Research in Motion option is substantially more risky than the SPY option. For example, the Research in Motion at-the-money call option may have implied volatility of 70 percent, whereas SPY implied volatility may be around 25 percent. Because the standard margining methodology does not take into account implied volatility, it does not fully differentiate between a volatile stock and a less volatile stock and relies primarily, instead, on the stock value (and strike price). As explained later, portfolio margining is a method for computing margin on option (and stock) positions based on the risk profile of the account, rather than on fixed percentages, for qualified customers.

The option premium is added as part of the initial margin requirement, but at the same time, it is added to your account balance. As a result, the premium does not represent an additional requirement to initiate a short option position. When analyzing margin

TABLE 30.1 Sample Margin Schedule

Position	Initial Margin	Maintenance Margin
Long stock	50% of the purchase price, with a minimum account equity of $2,000	1. 30% of the current market value of the long securities positions in marginable securities 2. 100% of the current market value of the long securities positions in nonmarginable securities 3. $2,000 minimum account equity for all margin transactions
Short stock	The greater of (1) 50% of the sale price, or (2) the short sale maintenance margin requirement (see the following)	1. 30% for underlying stock priced $17.00 per share or more; or $5.00 per share for stock priced between $5.00 and $16 7/8 per share 2. The greater of 100% or $2.50 per share for stock priced less than $5.00 per share 3. $2,000 minimum account equity for all margin transactions
Long calls or puts	100% of the cost of the options	100% of the current market value of options
Short uncovered calls	The greater of (1) 100% of the option proceeds plus 20% of the underlying stock less any amount the option is out-of-the-money, or (2) 100% of the option proceeds plus 10% of the value of the stock price	The greatest of the current marked-to-market value of the option plus 10% of the underlying stock value
Short uncovered puts	The greater of (1) 100% of the option proceeds plus 20% of the underlying stock less any amount the option is out-of-the-money, or (2) 100% of the option proceeds plus 10% of the value of the strike price	The greatest of the current marked-to-market value of the option plus 10% of the value of the strike price
Short covered calls	1. None required on short call 2. Initial margin requirement on long stock is 50% of long stock position 3. Long underlying position must be valued at lower of current market value or call exercise price for margin equity purposes (this will be reflected in a higher margin requirement for the covered position) 4. $2,000 minimum account equity	1. None required on short call 2. Maintenance margin requirement on long stock is 30% of long stock position 3. Long underlying position must be valued at lower of current market value or call exercise price for margin equity purposes (this will be reflected in a higher margin requirement for the covered position) 4. $2,000 minimum account equity
Short covered puts	1. None required on short put	1. None required on short put

TABLE 30.1 (*Continued*)

Position	Initial Margin	Maintenance Margin
	2. Initial margin requirement on short stock is short sale proceeds plus 50% of short stock position	2. Maintenance margin requirement on short stock is 100% of stock market value plus the following: (1) for stock with market value of less than $5.00 per share, the greater of $2.50 per share or 100% of stock market value; (2) for stock with market value of $5.00 or more per share, the greater of $5.00 per share or 30% of stock market value
	3. Any amount (aggregate) by which the exercise price of the put exceeds the market price of the stock must be added to the stock initial requirement for purposes of determining if excess Reg. T equity exists	3. Any amount (aggregate) by which the exercise price of the put exceeds the market price of the stock must be added to the stock maintenance requirement for purposes of determining if excess Reg. T equity exists
	4. $2,000 minimum account equity In effect, the cash credit generated by the sale of the option will be applied to the margin requirement on the covered position. This cash credit is not available for financing other positions	4. $2,000 minimum account equity In effect, the cash credit generated by the sale of the option will be applied to the margin requirement on the covered position. This cash credit is not available for financing other positions
Long verticals	100% of the cost of vertical	100% of the current market value of vertical
Short verticals	The lesser of (1) value of the difference between the strike prices of the vertical, or (2) the initial margin requirement of the short call or put, or (3) $2,000 minimum account equity	The lesser of (1) value of the difference between the strike prices of the vertical, or (2) the maintenance margin requirement of the short call or put, or (3) $2,000 minimum account equity
Long butterflies/ condors	100% of cost of butterfly	100% of current market value of butterfly
Short butterflies/ condors	Initial margin requirement of the short vertical of the butterfly or condor	Maintenance margin requirement of the short vertical of the butterfly or condor
Long straddles/ strangles	100% of the cost of the straddle or strangle	100% of the current market value of the straddle or strangle
Short straddles/ strangles	1. The initial margin requirement for the short put or short call, whichever is greater, plus the premium of the other option	1. The maintenance margin requirement for the short put or short call, whichever is greater, plus the premium of the other option
	2. $2,000 minimum account equity	2. $2,000 minimum account equity

(*Continued*)

TABLE 30.1 (Continued)

Position	Initial Margin	Maintenance Margin
Long call or put calendar spreads	100% of the cost of the calendar spread	100% of the current market value of the calendar spread
Short call or put calendar spreads	1. Initial margin requirement of short call or put 2. $2,000 minimum account equity	1. Maintenance margin requirement of short call or put 2. $2,000 minimum account equity
Call or put backspreads	Initial margin requirement is for the short vertical component of the backspread	Maintenance margin requirement is for the short vertical component of the backspread
Call or put ratio spreads	Initial margin requirement is for the quantity of short options in excess of the quantity of long options	Maintenance margin requirement is for the quantity of short options in excess of the quantity of long options
Short box spreads	Initial margin requirement is the difference between the long and short strike prices	Maintenance margin requirement is the difference between the long and short strike prices
Short iron butterflies/condors	Initial margin requirement is on one of the short verticals of the iron wing spread	Maintenance margin requirement is on one of the short verticals of the iron wing spread

Source: thinkorswim. Reprinted with permission.

requirements, I usually exclude the premium from the margin calculation to simplify matters and to focus on the additional margin required as a result of the transaction. Typically, the option premium is relatively immaterial relative to an entire account balance.

Spread Margin As a general rule, the standard margin requirement (subject to a minimum), portfolio margin, or SPAN is used to determine the margin requirement for an uncovered option position—but what if the position is a spread? The formula used to determine a margin requirement depends on whether it is an uncovered option or spread. To lower your margin requirement, you can trade an option spread instead of an uncovered option. Margin on a vertical credit spread is calculated as the lesser of the short option margin or the difference between the strike prices less the premium collected. For

TABLE 30.2 Sample Initial Margin

Formula	105 Call ($)	100 Call ($)	95 Call ($)
Premium	200	500	700
Plus: 20% of stock price	2,000	2,000	2,000
Less: out-of-the-money	(500)	0	0
Initial margin	1,700	2,500	2,700
Minimum: premium plus 10% of stock value	1,200	1,500	1,700
Initial margin requirement	1,700	2,500	2,700

example, ignoring the premium, if XYZ is trading at $100 and you sell one XYZ February 100/110 vertical call spread, the initial margin requirement is $1,000 instead of the $2,000 required for an uncovered February 100 call option. Likewise, if you sell one XYZ February 90/100 vertical put spread, the initial margin requirement is $1,000 instead of the $2,000 required for an uncovered February 100 put option. Margin requirements can be reduced substantially if you qualify for portfolio margining, discussed later in this chapter.

A long butterfly or condor is considered a long position because the lowest strike price (assuming that calls are used) is long and is usually executed for a debit (but not always). The lowest and highest strike prices in a long butterfly or condor are long legs, whereas the lowest and highest strike prices in a short butterfly are short legs. In a short butterfly or condor, margin is generally required for the short vertical portion of the spread. A short butterfly spread might consist of one short call at a 95 strike price, two long calls at a 100 strike price, and one short call at a 105 strike price. In this case, margin would be required on the 95/100 strike price vertical credit spread portion of the position. Full payment is required if the spread is a long butterfly or condor.

Initial margin for a short straddle or strangle is the call or put margin, whichever is greater, plus the premium of the other side. Full payment is required if the straddle or strangle is a long position.

A short calendar spread has an initial margin requirement equal to the short option leg. For example, if you buy one S&P 500 index (SPX) February 1,200 put and sell one SPX April 1,200 put, your margin requirement is based on the short April 1,200 put because the long option expires prior to the short option. Full payment is required if the calendar spread is a long position.

In a call or put ratio (front) spread, margin is generally required on the short options in excess of the long options. For example, if you buy one February 100 call and sell two February 105 calls, margin is required on one short 105 call.

In a call or put backspread, margin is generally required for the short vertical portion of the spread. For example, if you sell one February 100 call and buy two February 105 calls, margin is required on one 100/105 vertical credit spread.

In a short iron condor, initial margin is the call or put side margin, whichever is greater. Full payment is required if it is a long position.

There is no margin requirement on a covered short call or put, but there is a margin requirement on the stock purchase.

Portfolio Margin   The standard margin methodology does not take into account the unique risk and volatility of the position and does not fully consider offsetting positions that may reduce risk in the account. As a result, a newer margin method for short options on equities is portfolio margining, which is an alternative method for certain qualified customers.

Portfolio margining is a method for computing margin based on the risk profile of the account rather than on fixed percentages. The portfolio margining uses theoretical pricing models to calculate the loss of a position at different price points above and below the current stock, ETF, or index price. For example, portfolio margining will essentially stress test a position, assuming that the underlying instrument rises and falls a certain percentage, such as up or down 8 percent. The largest loss identified is the margin of the position. Portfolio margining, like futures SPAN margining, discussed later, in effect, moves away from the mechanical standard margin to calculations based on the risk profile of your portfolio. The portfolio margining rules, in effect, simulate market moves up and down and account for offsets among positions held in the account that are highly correlated. Portfolio margining (and futures SPAN margining) use sophisticated mathematical calculations, so you will need help from your broker to determine such margin calculations in advance.

Traders can benefit from portfolio margining because it typically has a lower margin requirement in comparison to the standard methodology. Portfolio margining may bring stock margin rules more in line with futures SPAN margin requirements under various circumstances. You should check with your broker to determine whether your brokerage account is eligible for portfolio margining.

Index Margin

For index options, whether calls or puts, the standard margin requirement is typically calculated using the same formula as is used for options on stocks and ETFs. However, the initial and maintenance requirement is typically 15 percent for a broad-based index and 20 percent for a narrow-based index. For example, assume that the SPX, a broad-based index, is at 1,500, and you sell in separate accounts one 1,550 call for $10, one 1,500 call for $20, and one 1,450 call for $60. The initial margin requirement calculation is shown in Table 30.3.

Selling an uncovered index option can utilize a lot of margin (or buying power, if the transaction is in an IRA); for example, if you sell one SPX 1,500 put option, it takes $22,500 of margin (ignoring the premium and the out-of-the-money amount). To lower your margin requirement, you can trade an option spread instead of an uncovered option. For example, if you sell one SPX 1,400/1,500 vertical put spread, the margin is $10,000 (ignoring the premium) instead of the $22,500 required for the uncovered 1,500 put option. Please keep in mind that margin requirements can be reduced substantially if

TABLE 30.3　Sample Index Initial Margin

Formula	1,550 Call ($)	1,500 Call ($)	1,450 Call ($)
Premium	1,000	2,000	6,000
Plus: 15% of index	22,500	22,500	22,500
Less: out-of-the-money	(5,000)	0	0
Initial margin	18,500	24,500	28,500
Minimum: premium plus 10% of index value	16,000	17,000	21,000
Margin requirement	18,500	24,500	28,500

you qualify for portfolio margining. Also, margin requirements may be reduced if you trade in a futures account as opposed to a traditional stock equity account.

Futures Margin

As mentioned in Chapter 26, buying the underlying futures does not require a cash payment, and selling futures does not involve the receipt of money. Instead, a good-faith deposit is required (margin) as a performance bond to enter into and continue such a contract. In a futures account, both the buyer and seller of underlying futures are required to post margin. The fact that no payment is required to be made (other than a margin deposit) at the time of a futures purchase or sale represents a significant difference between the futures and stock markets. The good news is that you can earn interest on your futures margin deposit, such as from a Treasury bill, thus providing a potential advantage of trading underlying futures relative to the cash market. A discussion of margin on futures options follows.

Like an option on a stock, when a futures trader enters into a futures position, he is required to post *initial margin*. Thereafter, the position is marked to the market at least daily. However, if the futures position is profitable, the profits are added to the margin account. If the futures position loses value, the amount of money in the margin account will decline accordingly. If the amount of money in the margin account falls below the specified *maintenance margin*, the futures trader will be required to post an additional (*variation margin*) amount to bring the account up to the initial margin level. This can be accomplished by closing a position or adding to long options to create spreads.

A futures margin is typically determined by the SPAN margining system, which takes into account all positions in a customer's account and, in general, usually produces a lower margin requirement than traditional standard margin for stocks or ETFs.

SPAN can provide a trading advantage versus stocks. Assuming that the S&P 500 futures is at 1,500, the initial margin on that underlying futures contract is approximately $25,000, or 6.67 percent ($25,000 divided by $375,000, which is 1,500 times $250). However, for example, an at-the-money put or call option may have an initial margin requirement of approximately $15,000 (4.0 percent margin requirement), a call or put 5 percent out-of-the-money may have an initial margin requirement of approximately $10,000 (2.67 percent margin requirement), and a call or put 10 percent out-of-the-money may have an initial margin requirement of approximately $5,000 (1.33 percent margin requirement). Of course, these margin numbers are only approximations, for illustrative purposes, but they do represent how SPAN margin can be relatively low and declines the further an option is out-of-the-money.

After you have established a futures position, the maintenance margin requirements are calculated every day. As a result, you may enter into a trading day having plenty of margin room, but if the position moves against you, you may end up being close to a margin call by the end of the day. For example, if you have $100,000 in your account and you sell five uncovered S&P 500 futures options, you may have an initial margin requirement of $25,000 and a maintenance margin requirement of $15,000. If the underlying S&P 500 futures moves dramatically against you, the initial margin requirement may increase to $80,000 and the maintenance margin requirement may increase to $50,000.

Margin is telling you that there is much more risk in the account. As a result, SPAN margining can be used as an early warning system for excessive risk in your account; for example, you may develop a risk management rule that you will offset positions if margin in your account reaches 25 percent of your account balance. Therefore, for example, if you have a $100,000 account balance and your SPAN initial margin moves in excess of $25,000, you can voluntarily close (or roll) enough positions to reduce your margin requirement to below $25,000.

Your *futures commission merchant* (*FCM*) and futures brokerage should have calculators on their web sites that can determine margin requirements. Because SPAN is a one-day stress test calculation, it can be used as a gauge of overall short-term risk in your account.

A Closer Look at SPAN Margining   You should keep in mind that SPAN margining does not attempt to determine the probability of success of your option position at expiration. Instead, it is focused on a one-day calculation to determine whether you should be subject to a margin call—a big difference. SPAN stress tests option positions for a one-day period of time by assuming movements in the underlying instrument in both directions (higher and lower) based on standard deviations. In general, SPAN increases margin the more an option is in-the-money, the closer an out-of-the-money option becomes to being in-the-money, and the closer an option is to the expiration date. In general, an uncovered option has a greater margin requirement than a spread.

It is useful to understand that SPAN margining (and possibly portfolio margining) calculations are (mostly) primarily driven by the strike price versus futures price as well as time remaining to expiration. For example, assume that in January, the S&P 500 futures is at 1,500. You can sell a February 1,400 put option at $1, or you can sell a February 1,350 put option at $2. In this example, the February 1,400 put would have a higher margin requirement because it is closer to the underlying futures. A March 1,400 put would have a lower margin requirement in comparison to a February 1,400 put because it expires at a later date. If the February put creates a margin call, you may be able to eliminate the margin deficit by, for example, rolling the February 1,400 put to a March 1,400 put or March 1,350 put.

Assume that you are looking to collect $2 ($2 times $250 equals $500) in premium: You can, for example, sell two February 1,400 puts at $1 each or sell one March 1,350 put at $2. For margin purposes, the two February 1,400 puts will likely have at least twice the initial margin requirement of one March 1,350 put, even though both strategies collect the same amount of premium. Therefore, if you are an option writer, you want to use your margin wisely by comparing the amount of premium you can potentially earn to the initial margin requirement. It can be to your advantage to understand such nuances so that you can manage margin by establishing trades that efficiently utilize your account balances and so you can intelligently roll positions. Remember that to lower your margin requirement, you can typically trade an option spread instead of an uncovered option.

A margin requirement for options is the amount of cash (or other assets) an option seller is required to deposit and maintain to cover a position as collateral. It is the amount of cash (or other assets) that must be deposited by an option seller to ensure performance of the seller's obligations under an option contract. Initial margin is the amount of margin required when a position is opened. Maintenance margin is the amount that must be maintained on deposit after a position is opened. A margin call is a request from a brokerage firm to a customer to bring margin deposits up to initial levels.

COMPARING MARGIN

Chapter 23 presents a comparison of margin requirements that is worth repeating here because it can be informative to compare margin requirements for options on an uncovered stock, ETF, index, and stock index futures. The S&P 500 futures contract controls $375,000 of value, assuming that the S&P 500 futures is at 1,500 (1,500 times $250 a point). To make a valid comparison, assume that XYZ stock, SPY, SPX, and the S&P 500 futures all control the same $375,000. To simplify matters, we will assume that the option sold is at-the-money and that the premium collected is ignored. That way, we can focus solely on the difference in the margin requirements. Following are initial margin requirements for such an at-the-money short call or put option:

- **Stock**: XYZ initial margin is $75,000 ($375,000 times 20 percent),
- **ETF**: SPY initial margin is $75,000 ($375,000 times 20 percent),
- **Index**: SPX initial margin is $56,250 ($375,000 times 15 percent),
- **Stock index futures**: S&P 500 futures initial margin is approximately $15,000 using SPAN margining.

A sample comparison of initial margin requirements for XYZ stock, an ETF, an index, and a stock index futures is shown in Table 30.4.

Portfolio margining would likely produce a lower margin requirement than the traditional method. In some cases, the portfolio margining amount may more closely approximate the futures SPAN amount.

TABLE 30.4 Sample Comparison of Margin Requirements

Margin Type	XYZ Stock (Standard Method, $)	SPY (Standard Method, $)	SPX (Standard Method, $)	Futures (Estimated SPAN Margin, $)
Initial margin	75,000	75,000	56,250	15,000

MARGIN PLANNING

You need to understand how margining works because it defines the freedom you have to trade, and you need to make the right moves in avoiding a margin call. Understanding margin can help you determine how best to meet a margin call so that it does not cost you money in the process. To meet a margin call, it is sometimes best to deposit additional monies, but that is rare because you can instead offset a current position by adding certain long positions that reduce risk in a way that relieves the margin pressure, or you can roll.

Meeting a Margin Call

Literature distributed by brokerage firms typically indicates that if an account balance falls below the maintenance margin threshold, the trader must deposit money or the brokerage house has a right to liquidate positions. However, there are various ways to meet a margin call, including depositing additional money, liquidating a position, and establishing certain long positions. You should understand how margin is calculated so that you can take appropriate steps should you face a margin deficit or should you simply want to increase the amount of margin available. For example, instead of closing a short option, you can purchase a further out-of-the-money option to reduce the margin requirement for the uncovered option.

Exercise/Assignment Can Trigger Margin Call

In some cases, you may not have sufficient capital in your account to exercise all of your call options and hold the stock afterward. For example, assume that the balance in your account is $100,000, XYZ stock is trading at $100 a share, and you are long 50 in-the-money call options at a strike price of 95. In this case, you cannot exercise all 50 options and hold the stock because it would take $475,000 ($9,500 times 50). Instead, in this case, you should contact your broker to determine if you can exercise the options and sell the stock in the marketplace. Both parts of this twofold transaction could be executed at the same time or in the same day because the exercise of the 50 calls by itself would trigger a margin call. If you exercise all 50 call options, the brokerage firm margin department will contact you regarding a margin call. In this case, you should immediately sell all or a portion of the stock in the marketplace.

A similar result could occur if you are short 50 uncovered put options and you are assigned long stock. In this case, you may not have sufficient capital to buy all the shares, and it may trigger a margin call. In this case, you should determine if you can immediately sell the stock in the marketplace if assigned.

If you are short uncovered call options and you are assigned short stock, the assignment may trigger a margin call. In this case, you may want to immediately buy the stock in the marketplace to eliminate the margin requirement. Likewise, if you are long uncovered put options and exercise the options and are short stock, you may want to buy the stock in the marketplace to eliminate the margin requirement.

Keep in mind that a margin call may be avoided by using spreads.

Watch Out for Trading Halts

Exchanges generally place limits on the price range in which an underlying instrument can fluctuate during one day's trading session (daily price limits). In fact, the entire stock market stopped trading for days immediately after 9/11. Trading halts can serve as a risk for anyone trading in the options market; for instance, prices will reach limit down for several days in a row so that those wishing to trade may be unable to liquidate their losing positions. As a result, a trader who is long the market and wants to sell may not be able to do so. Such a situation can, of course, be disastrously expensive if you are on the wrong side of such a trade and is an illustration of the risks associated with options (and stocks), especially uncovered options.

A trading halt can increase the risks associated with trading options because it can affect your ability to exit a position. For a naked option seller, a trading halt may mean that you cannot exit your position for several hours or days. In such a case, your losses can grow exponentially. Likewise, a buyer of options may not be able to exit his trade when it is profitable, and the buyer would need to wait until a later date.

If a trading halt occurs, it could prevent you from offsetting a position in a futures contract. When the price of a commodity reaches its daily limit, trading usually stops altogether. For example, assume that the balance in your account is $100,000, the S&P 500 futures is at 1,500, and you are short out-of-the-money put options. If the S&P 500 futures declines by a certain amount prescribed by an exchange, it will have reached its daily limit and would temporarily stop trading because it is limit down. In this case, you could not exit your put contracts until the contracts began to trade. As an alternative, there may be other futures or cash market products open for trading that you could use as a proxy to trade your position. For example, if the futures is close, then maybe the cash market is open, and vice versa.

Watch Out for Fast Markets

You should be aware that fast market conditions can affect SPAN margin requirements. As a result, you may establish a short option position at one margin level and SPAN margining can subsequently increase substantially during volatile markets. In addition, a FCM or your futures broker may override the SPAN requirement and impose a higher margin requirement during difficult times. This can be critical because an increase in volatility may create a loss in your account, and an increase in the margin requirement may mean that you are forced to liquidate all or a portion of the position at the worst time.

To make matters worse, when markets become extremely volatile, the bid/ask spread can widen substantially; for example, you may establish an out-of-the-money option position on the S&P 500 futures for $3.00/$3.50. In an extremely volatile market, the bid/ask spread may explode to $15/$22. As a result, you have the perfect storm, where your short option position has substantially increased in value, the bid/ask spread has gapped wider, and you are being subject to a margin call.

Volatile and fast market conditions are not the only reasons why your broker may increase margin requirements; for example, a FCM may incur losses and, as a result, impose a higher margin requirement on you to protect itself. In a volatile or fast market, an FCM can, for example, increase margin requirements on S&P 500 stock index futures to the same level as a full underlying futures contract.

Reducing Futures Margin

After you have a basic understanding of how SPAN calculates margin, you are at a better position to plan and reduce futures margin when needed. For example, to decrease a margin requirement in your account, you can roll from out-of-the-money to further out-of-the-money, roll a near-term option to a later-term option, roll a near-term option to a later-term/further out-of-the-money option, purchase a further out-of-the-money option to reduce the margin requirement for a naked option, or buy or sell the underlying futures contract. You can take advantage of the way margin is calculated in a straddle or strangle because it only takes into account the margin requirement on one side of the position. As a result, if you are close to full margin on the call side and have a small margin requirement on the put side, you can add a put option without increasing your overall margin requirement. Likewise, if you have full margin on the call side and little margin on the put side, you can offset one or more call options and replace it with a put position to keep the same amount of short options on the table.

INTEREST

You may be under the impression that a margin requirement for a short option position requires foregoing interest income. However, that is not the case. In a regular brokerage account, a short call or put position requires margin, but interest can still be earned on your entire cash balance because no funds are expended. In a short option position, you actually collect cash rather than paying it. Likewise, in a futures account, a short call or put triggers a margin requirement, but interest can be earned from your broker or from a Treasury bill posted as a performance bond. You should check with your brokerage firm regarding its requirements. The ability to earn interest while trading options can be viewed as a distinct advantage of option trading over trading stocks.

CASH ACCOUNTS AND IRAs

A stock brokerage firm may permit option trading in an IRA provided that the positions are defined-risk trades such as call buying, put buying, cash-secured put writing, vertical

TABLE 30.5 Sample IRA Buying Power Requirements

Formula	Stock ($)	SPY ($)	SPX ($)	Futures (Estimated SPAN Margin, $)
Buying power	15,000	15,000	150,000	10,000

spreads, and covered calls. Unsecured call transactions are not permitted in an equity IRA because it requires margin, but naked put transactions may be permitted if there are sufficient funds in the account to fully cover the position if assigned. As explained subsequently, you may be permitted to trade naked options in a futures IRA account.

The terms *buying power* and *purchasing power* are used for an IRA instead of margin. For example, if you sell an at-the-money put in an IRA (or cash account not approved for margin), you do not have a margin requirement, but you need to determine your buying power. Assume that XYZ stock is trading at $150, the SPY is at 150, the SPX is at 1,500, and the S&P 500 futures is at 1,500. Also assume that you sell one at-the-money put option in separate IRA accounts. If the accounts are IRA, the buying power effect, ignoring the premium, is as follows:

- **Stock**: XYZ stock buying power effect is $15,000 ($150 times 100).
- **ETF**: SPY buying power effect is $15,000 ($150 times 100 shares).
- **Index**: SPX buying power effect is $150,000 ($1,500 times 100 shares).
- **Stock index future**: S&P 500 futures margin is approximately $10,000 using computer-generated SPAN margining.

Sample IRA buying power requirements are shown in Table 30.5.

A solution to the margin restriction in an IRA account is to write a credit spread instead of an uncovered option. Although an uncovered call option is not permitted in an IRA, a credit spread is permitted, provided that there are sufficient funds. For example, assume that XYZ is trading at $100. The sale of an uncovered February 100 call is not permitted in an IRA, but the sale of a February 100/115 call credit spread may be allowed. The sale of a February 100/115 call spread would require only $1,500 of buying power (ignoring the premium).

Likewise, if selling an uncovered put absorbs too much buying power, you can instead write a vertical put spread. For example, the sale of an uncovered February 100 put would take up $10,000 of buying power (ignoring the premium), but the sale of a February 80/100 credit spread would only absorb $2,000 of buying power (ignoring the premium).

Futures IRAs

Margin in a futures account is considered a performance bond and is not considered a loan. As a result, it may be possible to trade naked call and put options in an IRA using SPAN or some variation of it. Many FCMs may impose restrictions on trading in your futures IRA account by imposing requirements above the minimum required by exchanges or regulators. You should check with your FCM and futures broker to determine what is permitted.

FINAL THOUGHTS

As previously mentioned, if you are an option writer, you want to use your margin wisely by comparing the amount of premium you can potentially earn to the initial margin requirement. It can be to your advantage to understand such nuances so that you can manage margin by establishing trades that efficiently utilize your account balances, and so you can intelligently roll positions. Remember that to lower your margin requirement, you can typically trade an option spread instead of an uncovered option.

Margin rules can be complicated, so it is good to have resources at your disposal. The Chicago Board Options Exchange web site (www.cboe.com) has a margin calculator to assist in determining stock and index margin requirements. Other sources of option information are the Options Industry Council (www.optionseducation.org) and the Options Clearing Corporation (www.optionsclearing.com). For futures margin, you should check your futures brokerage web site and contact your FCM.

If you are going to trade options, it is important that you know how to effectively avoid and deal with margin calls. Option margin, in effect, represents the amount of leverage that a broker is willing to permit. It is safe to say that not all margin calculations are created equal. As you can see from this chapter, margin can vary drastically, depending on whether you have a traditional brokerage account trading on standard margin, whether you are eligible for portfolio margining, or whether you are trading futures using SPAN. Margin requirements can be reduced substantially if you qualify for portfolio or SPAN margining. To maximize use of your funds, you can consider, as a general rule, buying options (which does not require margin) or utilizing spreads in your IRA and selling higher margin option positions outside your IRA. In Chapter 31, we will address placing orders.

Placing an Order

Learning how to place orders for stocks is rather straightforward because you typically buy a stock and sell it later, and although you can sell stock short, many individuals never sell stock short because of the risk or the method's unfamiliarity. However, with options, you have many more decisions to make. Whereas a stock trade is usually concerned with the number of shares to buy, an option order is concerned with the number of contracts to buy or sell as well as what strategy is best, such as a long or short call or put, vertical spread, iron condor, ratio spread, backspread, straddle, strangle, butterfly, condor, time spread, diagonal spread, double diagonal spread, or covered call or put. A theme of this book is that you should learn how to trade options on different instruments; consistent with that theme is learning the different types of orders. This chapter will describe types of orders, strategies to use when placing orders, negotiation of the bid/ask spread, and commissions.

OVERVIEW

The mechanics of placing an equity option order are similar to the mechanics of entering an order for stocks. You execute a trade through your trading platform, online, or by calling your broker. You should have a trading platform supplied by your broker (or software provider) that automatically establishes simple and complex option orders to open or close positions. There are more than a dozen types of orders you can place for stocks. Similarly, you can generally enter the same types of orders for options; for example, you can enter option limit, market, good-until-canceled, and other types of orders like stock orders.

As mentioned in Chapter 1, some brokerage firms have developed practice accounts (also called paper trading or simulated trading) so you can buy and sell options without the fear of losing money. It may be useful to use a practice account prior to executing any real option trades so you can gain confidence. In their practice accounts, some brokerage firms have developed trading platforms that parallel their live trading platforms, but with simulated trading, which does not use real money. Therefore, simulated trading enables you to practice using the trading platform of your broker without the risk of loss and can be an effective method through which to learn the unique features and capabilities of your broker's software (trading platform) so that you can efficiently enter and exit option trades. Simulated trading can help you become familiar with the types of option orders that can be entered. If simulated trading is not available at your broker, you can trade one option at a time, making sure that the amount of money is small and that you have acceptable and limited risk.

It is an advantage to have access to a trading platform that can handle and quickly generate option orders. For example, rather than entering a collar as three separate orders (purchasing stock, selling a call, and buying a put), your trading platform may allow you to enter the entire collar transaction in a single order so that if a stock is trading at $100 a share, a call is trading at $2.50, and a put is trading at $2, you can enter a single order to enter into a collar transaction at $99.50 or better. As a result of entering an order in this manner, you will not be executed on only one or two portions of the transaction unless the entire transaction is executed. It can be more efficient to enter and exit positions all in the same order rather than leg in and out one position at a time.

TYPES OF OPTION ORDERS

An option order can be executed to open or close a position such as a long or short call or put, vertical spread, iron condor, ratio spread, backspread, straddle, strangle, butterfly, condor, calendar spread, diagonal spread, double diagonal spread, or covered call or put. In a spread order, however, you may be restricted from using certain types of orders such as a stop order, stop limit order, or trailing stop. Option order types are not the same for all brokers because some order types permitted at one broker may not be permitted at another broker. Following are summary descriptions of options.

Day Order   A *day order* is an order to buy or sell that expires at the end of the day on which it was entered if it is not executed; for example, you can place an order to buy one February 100 call at a limit of $5. If the order is not executed at the close of trading for that day, it is automatically canceled and does not carry over to any other trading day. All orders are automatically day orders, unless otherwise specified.

Good-until-Canceled Order   A *good-until-canceled order* (open order) is an order to buy or sell that remains in force until the order is filled or canceled or the option contract expires. All orders are either good-until-canceled or day orders. For example, assume that you place an order to buy one February 100 put at $5 in a good-until-canceled order. If the order is not executed at the close of trading for that day, it will stay in effect until it is executed on another trading day or when the contract expires.

Market Order   A *market order* is an order to buy or sell a stated number of option contracts that are to be executed at the best price obtainable. The risk of a market order is the execution price; for example, you can place an order to buy one February 100 call in a market order. In this case, you will purchase the call option at the market price at that time, which is typically the ask price. You should keep in mind that the bid/ask price that you see on your computer screen is not guaranteed. In addition, if you place a larger order, it is possible that some contracts will be filled at one price and other contracts will be filled at a different price. Many brokers recommend against placing market orders.

Limit Order   A *limit order* is an order to buy or sell a stated number of option contracts that can be executed only at a specified price or better. It is commonly the default order type for single-option, spread, and stock orders on a trading platform. For example, assume that you place an order to sell one February 100 put at a limit of $5. By placing a limit order, you are guaranteed to collect at least $5 if filled for the order. A risk is that the order may not be filled.

If you prefer to place a market order but are concerned about slippage in price, you may want to place a sell limit order below the current market price at a level that would be acceptable to you. For example, if a put option is currently at $5, you can place a limit order to sell at $4.75. In this type of order, you are likely to be filled at $5 because it is currently at that price, but you allow yourself some room in case the market moves slightly against you. If you place a limit order for more than one contract, you may be filled on a portion of your order; for example, if you place an order to sell 10 February 100 puts at a limit of $5, you may be filled on three contracts. The problem with placing a limit order at the bid or ask price is that it may not be filled, and you may find yourself chasing the order at a less favorable price. My general rule of thumb is that if the option is attractively priced and I am confident in the position, I will not haggle over a small difference in price. The most common types of orders are probably market orders and limit orders. A limit order is automatically considered a day order unless you change it to a good-until-canceled order.

Stop Order (Stop Loss)   A stop order (stop loss) becomes an active market order if and when the stop price is reached. A buy stop (stop order to buy) is triggered when the option trades (or is at the bid or ask price) on any exchange at or above the specified stop price. A buy stop is placed above the market. A sell stop is placed at a price below the market. A stop order can be based on the value of the underlying option trading price, the bid price, or the ask price. You should check with your broker regarding which types of orders are allowable. A stop order is an order used to open or close a position by buying if the market rises or selling if the market falls. For example, assume that you are long one February 100/105 call debit spread trading at $3 and you place a stop loss order at $2. The stop loss triggers a market order to sell when the spread trades at $2.

If you place a stop buy order at $6, it becomes a market order to buy when the spread trades at $6. I recommend stop loss and buy stop orders because they enable you to cut losses and manage risk.

If you are already long a position, a stop sell order can limit a loss. If you are already short a position, a stop buy order can limit a loss. Conversely, assuming that you do not have a current position, if you place a stop buy order above the market price, the market price will need to rise for you to be executed. If the option price declines before reaching your stop, you will not be executed and will not lose any money.

A stop loss order can be used to take profits in a short option position. For example, if you are short one February call at $5, and the price moves to $1, you can then enter a stop buy order at $2, triggering a market order if it trades at that price, thus exiting you from the short option position at a profit. A stop buy order can be used to manage a short option position. For example, if you are short one February call at $5, you can immediately enter a stop buy at $6, triggering a market order if it trades at that price, thus limiting your losses on your short option position. Using a buy stop order can be an outstanding technique to limit risk during regular trading hours in a short option position. Keep in mind, however, that you are subject to gap risk because markets can move dramatically against you in a short period of time. You are subject to gap risk that may occur during and outside normal trading hours. A stop order is automatically considered a day order unless you change it to a good-until-canceled order.

Stop Limit Order   A *stop limit order* is a stop order that turns into a limit order if and when the stop price is triggered. When the stop price is triggered, the limit order is activated. The stop price for a buy order is placed above the current market price. The stop price for a sell order is placed below the current market price. The stop price does not need to be the same as the limit price. Just as with a limit order, the stop limit order will be filled at the limit price or better or may not be filled at all. For example, assume that you are long one iron condor trading at $5 and you place a stop limit order with a sell stop at $4 and a limit of $3.80. A sell stop loss at $4 triggers a limit order to sell at $3.80. As a result, you are not guaranteed an execution on the sale, but if it is executed, it will be at a price of $3.80 or better. A stop limit order is automatically considered a day order unless you change it to a good-until-canceled order.

Trailing Stop   A *trailing stop order* is a stop order that continually adjusts the stop price based on changes in the market price. A trailing stop to sell raises the stop price as the option price increases but does not lower the stop price when the option price decreases. A trailing stop to buy lowers the stop price as the option price decreases but does not increase the stop price as the option price increases. When the stop price is reached, the order becomes a market order. For example, assume that you are long one February 100 call, trading at $5, and you place a trailing stop to sell $1 below the market price. If the option price rises immediately to $7, the trailing stop will automatically rise to $6. If the option price begins to decline, the $6 stop price will not change. This can be a good strategy to lock in profits as the value of your option rises. A trailing stop order is automatically considered a day order unless you change it to a good-until-canceled order.

Trailing Stop Limit A *trailing stop limit order* works the same way as the trailing stop, but instead of a market order, it becomes a limit order. With this order, you can specify the worst price you are willing to accept for a fill. There is no guarantee that you will be filled because the price may gap through your limit price. For example, assume that you are long one February 100 call, trading at $5, and you place a trailing stop limit to sell $1 below the market price, with a stop limit of $0.50 below the stop. If the option price rises immediately to $7, the trailing stop will automatically rise to $6 and the stop limit to $5.50. If the option price begins to decline, the $6 stop price and $5.50 stop limit will not change. A trailing stop limit order is automatically considered a day order unless you change it to a good-until-canceled order.

One-Cancels-Other Order A *one-cancels-other order* is an order involving the entry of two separate orders, where if one order is filled, the other is automatically canceled. For example, assume that you are expecting a lot of volatility but you are unsure of the direction. You could, for instance, place a one-cancels-other order for a long February 100 call at $5 and a long 100 February put at $4. If the call is executed, the put order is canceled. If the put is executed, the call is canceled. This type of order can enable you to take advantage of anticipated volatility in one direction, where you can see the next move in the market, without having to commit first to a position. A one-cancels-other order is automatically considered a day order unless you change it to a good-until-canceled order.

All-or-None Order An *all-or-none order* is a market or limit order that is to be executed in its entirety or not at all. Without instructions to the contrary, if you place a straight limit order for more than one contract, you may be filled on a portion of your order. To prevent this from occurring, you can place an all-or-none limit order, where you will not be filled unless you are executed on all options at your limit price or better. An all-or-none limit order is automatically considered a day order unless you change it to a good-until-canceled order.

Market-on-Close Order A *market-on-close order* is an order that executes at the market price at the close of trading. For example, assume that you place a market-on-close order to buy one February 95/100/105 call butterfly. By placing this order, you will be filled at the closing market price.

Limit-on-Close Order A *limit-on-close order* executes at a limit price at the close of trading. The order can be filled at the limit price or better, but you are not guaranteed a fill. For example, assume that you place a limit-on-close order to buy one February 95/100/105/110 long call condor at $1. By placing this order, you will be filled at the closing market price if it is $1 or better.

Fill-or-Kill Order A *fill-or-kill order*, in futures, is a limit order that is to be executed in its entirety when received; if not executed, it is canceled. A fill-or-kill order instructs the broker to make one attempt to fill and, if not filled immediately, to cancel the order. For example, assume that you place a fill-or-kill order to buy one February 100 call at a limit of $5. By placing this order, you will be filled at the first attempt or the order will be canceled. A fill-or-kill order is common in the bond market.

Order to Cancel   A *cancel order* is an order that attempts to cancel an existing order. This may also be called a straight cancel, which means the order being canceled is not being replaced with another order. After an order has been entered, you can attempt to cancel the order prior to its execution. You should check to make sure that the order you have attempted to cancel is verified as canceled.

Cancel/Replace   A *cancel/replace order* is an order that attempts to cancel an existing order and replace it with another order. After you have entered an order, you can attempt to cancel your existing order and replace it with another order. You should check to verify that your previous order has been canceled and that your new order has been executed.

Futures Option Orders

The types of orders for futures options are similar to orders for equity options. However, there can be a difference in the manner in which orders are placed. Some futures contracts and options, such as S&P 500 futures options, are pit-traded (*open outcry*) and not electronically traded. As a result, the full-sized S&P futures options are handled manually on the exchange floor. You can phone in your order to your broker, or you can call directly to the floor and place the order with a *floor broker*. If you call your broker to place the order, he will contact the floor broker to place the order and then get back to you regarding the execution fill. It is usually more efficient for you to call the floor of the exchange directly to place a pit-traded order if you decide not to use a trading platform. You should discuss with your futures broker or futures commission merchant whether you can bypass his trading desk. If you decide to place a pit-traded order by telephone, you are best served by having direct contact with a floor broker, even though you will be charged a floor brokerage fee. It can be worth the extra fee because you can communicate directly how you want the floor broker to negotiate the bid/ask spreads. In some cases, a futures broker will charge a floor brokerage fee whether you or he calls the floor.

If you transmit a pit-traded order electronically through a trading platform, it will be picked up on the floor for execution. In the futures market, online trading platforms with quick and advanced capabilities are not as readily available. I expect that this will change over time as the futures markets become more electronic.

Know Trading Hours

Listed equity options are only traded during regular trading hours, as opposed to stocks, which trade during regular trading hours and also during extended-hour sessions before the market opens and after the market closes. With an equity option, unfortunately, you are not able to take advantage of extended-hour trading (although this could be changed at some point). As a result, if you place an option trade outside regular trading hours, your order will be effective when the regular trading session begins. If you place an option order in the evening after the regular trading session has expired, your order will be effective the following day. If you place your option order in the morning prior to the beginning of the regular trading session, your order will be effective when the regular trading session begins to trade on that day. If you place an option order outside regular trading hours, you may not be able to place a market order. Instead, you will likely be required to place a limit order.

Limit orders are especially useful at the opening of trading. Placing a limit order prior to the market opening for regular trading hours means that it can be executed when the market opens. I find that the market opening can provide the greatest liquidity and the greatest chance of having an option order executed at the best price.

STRATEGY: THE MULTISTEP ORDER

An order to buy or sell an option should, in general, be placed at the midpoint between the bid/ask prices, but there is no guarantee that the order will be executed. As a matter of fact, your trading platform may default to automatically enter orders at the midpoint unless you modify the order. If you place an order at the bid/ask midpoint and it is not filled, a seller may want to subtract $0.05 or $0.10 from the midpoint in a cancel/replace order, whereas a buyer may want to add $0.05 or $0.10 to the midpoint in a cancel/replace order. If the order is not filled again, a seller of an option may want to subtract an additional $0.05 or $0.10, whereas a buyer may want to add an additional $0.05 or $0.10. This process can be repeated until the order is filled.

As an alternative, you can place limit sell orders $0.05, $0.10, or $0.20 above the bid and buy limit orders at $0.05, $0.10, or $0.20 below the ask price, depending on the width of the bid/ask spread, liquidity, if the market is moving rapidly, and so on. If your order is not filled, you can wait for about 30 seconds and change it to a market order by entering a cancel/replace order. That way, you have attempted to obtain a better price than what the market has offered and not allowed the option price to move away from you.

A spread position can be opened (and later closed) by placing separate orders for each leg of the spread or by placing one spread order. For instance, assume that you want to sell the 1,350/1,400 put spread to open on the S&P 500 index (SPX), where the 1,350 put you want to buy has a 0.90/1.00 bid/ask and the 1,400 put you want to sell has a 1.90/2.15 bid/ask. You can enter them as two separate orders or you can enter them as one spread order. As a result of entering a spread order, you will not be executed on only one leg of the transaction unless the entire transaction is executed. It can be more efficient to enter and exit positions all in the same order rather than leg in and out one position at a time. Placing an order as a spread can make a lot of sense, especially if there are multiple legs to the order.

However, an alternative to placing an order as a spread order is to leg into the spread by entering each leg separately. An advantage of this approach is that you can separately negotiate the bid/ask price of each leg. Whether the midpoint is filled depends on the liquidity of the option and other market factors, but it can be worth a try. The weakness of legging into or out of a position is that it requires more work, and the market may move against you while you are placing the orders.

BID/ASK SPREAD

If you place a market order to sell an option, you typically will be filled at the bid price, and if you place a market order to buy an option, you typically will be filled at the ask price. For example, if the bid/ask price is 3.00/3.50, a market order to sell can be expected to be filled at $3.00 and a market order to buy can be expected to be filled at $3.50. You can view the bid/ask price spread of an option as the markets first proposal to you for a specific number of options; however, that does not mean you need to pay what the market is proposing. The bid and ask prices are the market prices at a particular point in time for a specific number of options.

In a spread order, the bid is shown as one number and the ask is shown as one number, even though they are the difference between option prices. However, you can mechanically determine a bid/offer price so that it can be compared to what is being offered. Following is a summary calculation of a bid/ask spread for a call and put spread.

Call Spread

In a vertical call spread, the bid price is the difference between the bid price of the lower-strike call and the ask price of the higher-strike call. The ask price is the difference between the ask price of the lower-strike call and the bid price of the higher-strike call. For example, assume that you want to buy or sell a call spread when the February 100 bid/ask is 4.90/5.10 and the February 105 bid/ask is 1.90/2.10. Table 31.1 is a summary of the bid/ask calculation.

Therefore, the call spread bid/ask is 2.80/3.20, assuming that the spread is priced the same as the individual legs.

Put Spread

In a vertical put spread, the bid price is the difference between the bid price of the higher-strike put and the ask price of the lower-strike put. The ask price is the difference between the ask price of the higher-strike put and the bid price of the lower-strike put. For

TABLE 31.1 Call Spread Bid/Ask

Description	Spread Bid ($)	Spread Ask ($)
February 100 call	4.90	5.10
February 105 call	(2.10)	(1.90)
Call spread	2.80	3.20

TABLE 31.2 Put Spread Bid/Ask

Description	Spread Bid ($)	Spread Ask ($)
February 100 put	4.90	5.10
February 95 put	(2.10)	(1.90)
Put spread	2.80	3.20

example, assume that you want to buy or sell a put spread when the February 100 bid/ask is 4.90/5.10 and the February 95 bid/ask is 1.90/2.10. Table 31.2 summarizes the bid/ask calculation.

Therefore, the put spread bid/ask is 2.80/3.20, assuming that the spread is priced the same as the individual legs.

The Bid/Ask Hurdle

A wide bid/ask spread can be a hurdle to a trader. For example, assume that you want to sell a vertical put spread at $2 and you are trying to determine which far-out-of-the-money strike price can achieve that with the least amount of risk. Assume that you want to sell an out-of-the-money put at one strike price for $3 and buy an out-of-the-money put at a lower strike price for $1. You can determine the likely bid/ask spread by examining the option chain. After selecting a strike price where the $3 can be obtained, you continue to lower strike prices along the option chain to determine the strike price at which a put option can be bought for $1. The bid/ask spread of the lower versus higher strike can have a dramatic impact on how far down the option chain a trader must go to purchase the lower-strike put for $1. In some cases, depending on the underlying instrument, the ask price at the immediately next lower put strike price is actually higher, not lower, than the bid price of the immediately higher strike option that you want to sell.

The distance between the strike prices of the option sold and the option purchased defines the maximum amount of risk for a vertical credit spread. A smaller difference between strike prices means that there is less risk, and a larger difference between strike prices means that there is greater risk. A difference in the strike prices of 50 points would mean a maximum risk in an S&P 500 futures put position of $12,500 (50 points times $250 a point) less the premium received. If the bid/ask spread is wide, a trader can have difficulty buying an option at a strike price that is reasonably close to the option that he is selling to limit the maximum risk in the spread. The bid/ask spread is essentially the amount of money that the market gods charge you for the privilege of being able to trade.

Negotiating the Bid/Ask Spread If you purchase an at-the-money call option at $3.50 with a bid/ask spread of 3.00/3.50, the stock would have to move a full point (assuming a delta of 0.50) to increase the value of the bid price by $0.50 to the original ask price. Therefore, if you purchase the call option at $3.50 (the ask price), the stock will have to move one point before you can break even (assuming that you sold at the bid price). In this example, the stock would need to move less if the option were in-the-money because an in-the-money option has a delta greater than 0.50; however, the underlying stock would need to move by more than one point if the option were out-of-the-money because an out-of-the-money option has a delta of less than 0.50. Therefore, the first point move in this stock can be viewed as your contribution to the option bid/ask gods. If the stock moves against you, the wide bid/ask spread can add insult to injury. In this example, if the stock declines by $1, the bid would decline, for example, to $2.50, resulting in an unrealized loss on the option of $1 ($3.50 purchase price less $2.50 bid price).

Trading options on large-capitalization stocks can mitigate the effects of wide bid/ask spreads. Deep-in-the-money options may have wider bid/ask spreads than at-the-money options. At-the-money options tend to be the most liquid options with the greatest open interest and typically have more narrow bid/ask spreads. Some options only trade in nickel increments, whereas others trade in pennies, which can affect the spread size. The bid/ask spread can vary depending on volume and fear in the marketplace. If there is a major stock market sell-off with an increase in volatility, an SPX put option, for example, with a typical bid/ask of 4.00/4.50, may expand to something like 13.00/18.00 or wider, only adding insult to injury. In a fast market, an option bid/ask quote directly from the exchange floor can change instantly without notice.

The Pink Elephant in the Room If you calculate the percentage cost for the bid/ask, you may be shocked at the real cost of entering and exiting a trade. For instance, assume that you want to buy an option with a bid/ask of 1.50/2.50. Purchasing that option at $2.50, in some respects, is like purchasing the option at $2.50 and paying a commission equal to the other $1.00 (assuming that the option can be sold at $1.50), meaning that the commission percentage paid is 40 percent ($1.00 divided by $2.50). And that is not the worst-case scenario. If you were to purchase 10 calls, the bid/ask cost alone would be $1,000 ($1.00 times 10 contracts times 100 shares) plus commissions. Can you imagine the reaction that a homeowner would have if he were to pay a 40 percent commission on the purchase or sale of a home? But, that is what you are doing, occasionally, in the options market. In some respects, the bid/ask spread is the pink elephant in the room that very few people are willing to address directly.

A wide bid/ask spread may not hurt an option writer as much as an option buyer, provided that he receives a favorable premium at the time of sale and the option expires worthless or near worthless. As a result of the option expiring worthless, a writer is not required to offset the option at a later date by incurring the additional cost of paying at or near the ask price. Conversely, an option buyer intends to sell those options at a later date at a higher price, thus intending to subject himself to the detriments of a wide bid/ask spread at a later date.

Index Options A wide index option bid/ask spread, such as on the SPX, may make index options somewhat unattractive for many investors. To negotiate the best price, assuming that you are placing an order to sell an uncovered put, for example, you can place the order to sell at the midpoint between the bid/ask and, if it does not fill, enter a cancel/replace order and move the sale price a fraction toward the bid. If it is not filled again, keep repeating the process. A wide bid/ask spread can be particularly onerous if there are multiple legs to an index option strategy. You should compare the bid/ask spreads of equity index options relative to futures options. S&P 500 futures options tend to be more heavily traded, which can lower the bid/ask spread in relative terms.

COMMISSIONS

As mentioned in Chapter 23, one SPX is 10 times the value of one SPDR S&P 500 index (SPY). As a result, an advantage of trading an SPX stock index option versus an ETF is that an SPX index option may provide greater leverage relative to ETFs, resulting in lower commissions. If you pay commissions based on the number of option contracts you trade, you would be able to trade fewer index option contracts because you are trading the larger-sized index product instead of the smaller-sized ETF. As a result, you can use this leverage to your advantage when it comes to paying commissions because you can trade fewer contracts. You need to check with your futures and equity brokers to compare the commission structures of each.

The index commission advantage, however, can be partially or totally offset by wide index option bid/ask spreads. For example, an SPX out-of-the-money put may have a bid/ask spread of approximately 1.50/2.00, representing an onerous 25 percent spread cost ($0.50 divided by $2.00 if you buy at the ask price). An at-the-money SPX option usually has a lower percentage spread, with a bid/ask spread of something similar to 23/25, an 8 percent cost.

The commission structure in the futures market is different from the commission structure in the stock market. In the stock market, you typically pay a commission each time you sell an option contract, with no commission if the option expires worthless (and if it is not exercised). In the futures market, commissions are typically paid when the transactions are initiated (called a round-turn commission), without payment of a commission when the option is offset or becomes worthless. For example, a stock option trader may pay $1 per option contract to trade 25 options on the SPY and an additional commission of $1 per contract to offset them at a later date so that the total commission is $50. A futures trader may typically pay around $10 to $25 in round-turn commission for one contract. As a result, the SPY option trader paid $50 in commission, and the S&P 500 futures trader, in comparison, paid $10 to $25. You should take into account differences in the bid/ask spreads of instruments you are trading; for example, a $0.05 spread in the SPY is the equivalent of 25 times that amount in futures, or $1.25.

You should calculate your break-even point, taking into account commission costs to enter and exit the trade. For example, if you sell one put credit spread on the S&P 500 futures and incur commissions of $50, you need to collect $0.20 to break even ($50 divided by $250 a point). One way to look at it is that $0.20 of each vertical spread goes toward your costs, so that if you sell a vertical spread for $1, your potential profit is $0.80. You may also want to calculate a break-even point not only to cover the commissions but also to cover the bid/ask spread if you are a buyer.

An advantage of trading S&P 500 futures index options relative to the cash market SPX is that the future options trade in $250 increments and the cash market SPX options trade in $100 increments. As a result, you can use this leverage to your advantage when it comes to paying commissions because you can sell fewer contracts in the futures market, assuming that you have a similar commission structure in the futures versus cash market.

TRADING PLATFORM

Your trading platform should permit you, with the click of a mouse, to buy or sell complex option positions. It should enable you to click on any existing single or multileg position and quickly enter a closing order. Your trading platform can be a big help because you do not need to manually create each option strategy from scratch or exit a position one leg at a time. A trading platform is designed to aid decision making. Some platforms allow investors to perform technical analysis, including charting stock prices, volume, and other indicators, as well as fundamental analysis, such as screening stocks based on earnings, price/earning ratios, and dividend yields.

CLEARING OF TRADES

A potential source of confusion is that option sales are often described as being made to option buyers and option purchases as being made from option sellers. In reality, the buyers and sellers do not know the identity of each other, and the transactions take place through intermediaries. Although buying an option may be described as a buyer purchasing from a seller, in reality, the buyer never looks to the seller for fulfillment of that contract and, instead, looks to the clearinghouse. Orders are handled by option exchanges that clear the trades and establish fixed strike prices, expiration dates, and other terms.

For stocks, an option holder looks to the Options Clearing Corporation (OCC) rather than to any particular option writer because it is the common clearing entity for all exchange-traded option transactions. After the OCC matches orders from a buyer and a seller, it severs the link between the parties and, in effect, becomes the buyer to the seller and the seller to the buyer. As a result, the seller can buy back the same option he has written and a buyer can sell the same option, closing out his initial transactions. The OCC serves as the counterparty for stock option transactions and is the largest clearing organization in the world for financial derivative instruments. It issues, guarantees, and clears options on underlying financial assets, including common stocks, foreign exchange, stock indexes, U.S. Treasury securities, and interest rate composites.

FINAL THOUGHTS

If you are trading a stock, it is probably not necessary that you trade in a paper/practice account because such a trade is rather straightforward. However, when trading options, a practice account is recommended so that you can learn the trading platform and how your broker defines terms and strategies. If you do not have a trading platform that allows you to practice your trading, you should trade one contract for which risk is limited. For example, the SPY is one tenth of the SPX and may be a good starting point to learn how to trade options. It is recommended that you open accounts to trade options at a firm that specializes in option trading. If you do not, you will always be fighting against the wind or going uphill (or whatever analogy you want to use), and you will never realize your full potential as an option trader.

Understanding risk management and order execution is important to trade options effectively. The types of orders for stock transactions are similar to the kinds of orders for option transactions. However, when it comes to options, remember that many option positions are short positions, whereas most stock positions are long positions. Therefore, you need to keep in mind that an option order can be used to protect a short position. For example, in the stock market, a stop buy order is typically used to purchase a stock to add to your position if the market continues higher. However, in the option market, a stop buy order can be used to offset a short option position to manage risk. In many cases, especially if you are pleased with the bid or ask price, you should enter a market order and not let small amounts dictate your trades (assuming that you are trading a liquid instrument). In Chapter 32, we will cover taxes.

Taxation of Options

T his chapter summarizes some basic rules governing the *federal income taxation* of certain option transactions by individuals. It will not address most of the tax issues relating to investments, including state and local taxation; instead, it will focus on the unique nature of options for federal income tax purposes and tax issues that are important to maximize your after-tax returns. Remember that it is not what you make that matters; it is what you keep.

There are special tax rules for option transactions, including rules on uncovered long options, uncovered short options, exercise and assignment, and other transactions. There are rules for gains and losses considered short term (less than 12 months) and long term (12 months or more). What makes option taxation unique are special rules for what are called *section 1256 contracts*, which include options on broad-based indexes (e.g., the S&P 500 index, or SPX) and futures options (e.g., S&P 500 futures options).

GENERAL RULES

Outside an IRA, in general, a gain or loss from an option is not taxed until the option is offset or it expires. Thus, buying an option is not a taxable event but, instead, a tax is triggered at the time of sale or expiration of the option. A premium received for writing a call or put is not included in income at the time of receipt but is taxed at the time the option is offset or at expiration of the option. An exercise or assignment of an option can extend the timing of the taxable event. Gains from investments are typically taxed at your top marginal tax rate (currently up to 35 percent, ignoring the alternative minimum tax), unless you own the investment for at least 12 months. Option trading typically results in short-term capital gains, subject to your ordinary tax income rate. However, there is modified tax treatment for trading options on a broad-based index and futures options, and these rules are addressed in this chapter.

In general, if a transaction occurs in an IRA, there is no gain or loss at that time; instead, tax consequences are deferred and a tax is triggered at the time you receive a distribution from the account. Distributions from an IRA are treated as ordinary income at the time of distribution, even though the gain in the account would have been subject to a lower short-term capital gain rate if generated outside the IRA. In other words, the character and timing of a gain or loss in an IRA does not affect how and when taxation occurs. A distribution is taxed as ordinary income at the time of distribution to you.

OPTION TAXATION

Let us take a look at how taxes are determined outside an IRA. To determine the proper tax treatment of a transaction, you need to determine whether it is short-term versus long-term capital (because a long-term capital gain is taxed at a lower tax rate), when it should be reported, and how it should be reported.

When a Taxable Event Is Recognized

A basic principle of federal income taxation is that a taxpayer is not taxed until an investment is actually disposed of (i.e., on sale if initially bought and on purchase if initially sold). In general, without a sale or exchange of your investment, the fluctuations (unrealized gains and loses) of your investments are not reflected on your return, and the timing of your tax is under your control. For instance, if you buy a stock, there are no federal income tax consequences until you actually sell the stock; if you sell a stock short, there are no federal income tax consequences until you actually buy it back. Likewise, in general, gains or losses from options are typically not taxed until an option is offset or expires. Option transactions typically are short term in duration (less than one year) so that they usually are taxed at your top marginal tax bracket, but there are exceptions, as explained later.

Capital Gains and Losses

A gain or loss from an option transaction is reported as a capital gain or loss and is taxed when you offset the option or it expires worthless.

Short-term capital gains are taxed at your marginal tax rate, with the current top rate at 35 percent. (This discussion assumes that you are not subject to the alternative minimum tax. In general, the alternative minimum tax is imposed at a 26 or 28 percent rate, based on the amount of alternative minimum taxable income.) However, a maximum tax rate of 15 percent applies to a net capital gain (net long-term capital gains minus net short-term capital losses) with a holding period of more than 12 months. You need to contact your tax advisor regarding current rules. General rules for option transactions follow:

- Trading an option results in a short-term capital gain or loss taxed at your marginal tax bracket.
- Gain or loss is not recognized until an option is offset or expires.
- Net capital losses are limited to $3,000 per year.
- A net capital loss cannot be carried back but can be carried forward.

As explained later, these general rules do not apply to certain options (and futures) contracts.

Short Term versus Long Term   The treatment of gain or loss as long term (held at least 12 months) versus short term (held less than 12 months) can affect your after-tax return because the short-term capital gain tax rate (at the time this book is being written) differs substantially from the long-term capital gain rate. The general rule that option trading results in short-term capital gains is important because short-term capital gains are taxed at ordinary income rates.

As a general rule, if you sell an investment you have owned for less than 12 months, you pay based on your top marginal tax rate (currently up to 35 percent). For example, if you are in the 35 percent tax bracket and incur a short-term capital gain of $1,000, you incur $350 of tax (ignoring minor adjustments). However, a maximum tax rate of 15 percent applies to net capital gains (net long-term capital gains minus net short-term capital losses) with a holding period of more than 12 months. For example, if you generate a long-term capital gain of $1,000, you are required to pay $150 of tax.

With an up to a 20 percentage point spread between the 15 percent long-term and 35 percent short-term capital gain tax rates, individual investors have an incentive to generate long-term capital gains instead of short-term capital gains.

Capital Loss Limitation   Losses are subject to certain limitations. Capital losses (long term as well as short term) are allowed only to the extent of capital gains plus $3,000 in a single tax year. Capital losses, as a general rule, cannot be carried back to prior years. Gains and losses on investments are reported on Schedule D of Form 1040.

Long Call or Put   If a call or put is purchased and sold in one year or less, any resulting gain or loss is short term. Likewise, expiration of a purchased call or put results in a short-term capital loss if held for one year or less. The expiration of a purchased call or put results in a long-term capital loss if held for more than one year.

Short Call or Put   If a short call or put expires, the premium is a short-term capital gain at expiration, regardless of the length of time the call or put was outstanding. Similarly, gain or loss on the offset of a short option is short-term capital gain or loss, regardless of the length of time the option was outstanding. Closing an uncovered call or put before assignment results in short-term capital gain or loss; if an option expires, the writer realizes a short-term capital gain to the extent of the premium received, regardless of the length of time the option is outstanding. A premium received for writing a call or put is not included in income at the time of receipt but rather is held in suspense until the writer's obligation is terminated.

Exercise and Assignment   If a long call is exercised, there is no gain or loss at that time; instead, the premium paid (and commission) is added to the cost of the stock. The holding period of the stock begins on the day after the call is exercised and does not include the holding period of the call. If a long put is exercised, the cost of the put (and the commission on the sale of the stock) reduces the amount realized from the sale of the underlying stock delivered to satisfy the exercise.

   If a call is assigned, the strike price plus the premium that was received is treated as the sale price of the stock to determine gain or loss. If a put is assigned, the strike price minus the premium received is treated as the purchase price of the stock.

TAX REDUCTION FOR BROAD-BASED INDEX AND FUTURES OPTIONS

The general rules previously described are substantially changed for options on broad-based indexes, futures options, and futures contracts. Under this modification, regardless of how long you have held the option, the gain or loss is deemed 60 percent long term and 40 percent short term; the option is marked to market at the end of each calendar years; net capital losses can be carried back three years; and, to the extent the carryback is not utilized, losses can be carried forward. Such gains or losses are called section 1256 gains and losses after an Internal Revenue Code section and are reported on Form 6781, gains and losses from section 1256 contracts and straddles.

The 60/40 Rule

The modified tax treatment under section 1256 contracts is as follows:

- Gain or loss is deemed 60 percent long term and 40 percent short term.
- The option is marked to market at the end of each calendar year.
- Net capital losses can be carried back three years.
- To the extent the carryback is not utilized, it can be carried forward indefinitely to offset subsequent-year capital gains.

TABLE 32.1 60/40 Rule

Section 1256 Contract	Taxable Amount ($)	Tax Rate (%)	Tax ($)
60 percent of gain	600	15	90
40 percent of gain	400	35	140
Total tax	1,000		230

TABLE 32.2 Comparison of Taxes on $1,000 Gain

Gain	Stock Top Tax Bracket ($)	ETF Top Tax Bracket ($)	Stock or ETF Alternative Minimum Tax ($)	Futures ($)	Broad-Based Index ($)	IRA
Marginal tax rate	350	350	280	230	230	Deferred until withdrawn

Regardless of how long you have held a section 1256 option, the gain or loss is deemed 60 percent long term and 40 percent short term. For example, instead of the entire gain being taxed at 35 percent (if you are taxed in the highest tax bracket) under the usual federal income tax scheme, a section 1256 contract permits 60 percent of that gain to be taxed at the lower rate (currently 15 percent). As a result, a $1,000 gain, normally taxed at the 35 percent rate, would incur a tax of $350, whereas a section 1256 contract gain would incur a tax of $230 ($600 times 15 percent plus $400 times 35 percent). In effect, a taxpayer in the top tax bracket pays a blended rate of 23 percent instead of the usual 35 percent, as shown in Table 32.1.

This should be valuable information to an option trader because it describes how he can approach his trading in the most tax-efficient manner. For instance, in general, if you generate a $1,000 gain through options on a stock or ETF, you pay a $350 tax, but you only pay $230 tax if you generate the same gain from trading options on the SPX, or S&P 500 futures options. This is viewed by many traders as a distinct advantage of trading options on futures and broad-based indexes (like SPX) versus a stock or ETF. Table 32.2 is a comparison of taxes on different types of options assuming $1,000 of gain.

Section 1256 treatment can result in tax savings even if you are subject to the alternative minimum tax, but the calculations are a little more complicated. Following is more information regarding the section 1256 contract taxing structure.

Marked to Market

The offset of a section 1256 option contract, or its expiration, results in a capital gain or loss, computed in the usual way, as the difference between your cost and the proceeds received. However, if you still hold the section 1256 option on the last business day of the year, the tax code requires that it be revalued, or marked to market, at the settlement price determined by the exchange as of that day. You are charged with a capital gain or loss on that contract, measured by the difference between its value and your basis. Your basis is adjusted at the end of each year so you are not taxed twice. Regardless of how long you may have held a section 1256 option, the recognized capital gain or loss, whether as a result of its sale, expiration, or merely remaining in your portfolio at year's end, is deemed 60 percent long term and 40 percent short term and is treated as such for tax purposes. This is one of the very few occasions on which an asset achieves long-term status in less than a year and a day—not only that, but the wash-sale rules do not apply.

For example, assume that in November you purchase a February SPX option for $1,000 and it is valued at $1,500 on December 31. You would recognize a $500 capital gain, of which $300 (or 60 percent) is long term and $200 (40 percent) is short term. Under the section 1256 structure, your original $1,000 tax basis is increased to $1,500 to adjust for the $500 capital gain, even though no sale (offset) has occurred. Thus, if in year 2, you sell the option for $1,800, you would recognize an additional $300 capital gain ($180 long term and $120 short term). The same tax treatment would apply if you had purchased an S&P 500 futures option. For positions marked to market at year-end, the basis for determining gain or loss is the new mark-to-market value, thus preventing the gain or loss from being counted twice.

Loss Carryback and Carryforward

The general rule for most capital assets is that net capital losses can be deducted to the extent of capital gains plus $3,000 in a year, capital losses cannot be carried back to prior years, capital losses can be carried forward to future years, and gains and losses on investments are reported on Schedule D of Form 1040. However, a special feature of section 1256 is your ability to carry back section 1256 net capital losses three years. To the extent losses are not fully absorbed in the carryback period, you can carry section 1256 losses forward to future years.

Broad-Based Index

The section 1256 contract structure applies to broad-based U.S. stock index options such as the SPX, NASDAQ 100, and Russell 2000 index. Options on a stock index that is narrow based are subject to the rules governing the taxation of equity options and are not entitled to section 1256 contract treatment. Apparently, ETFs are not included in this special tax treatment.

Section 1256 Reporting

Gains and losses on 1256 contracts are reported on Form 6781, Gains and Losses from Section 1256 Contracts and Straddles, where they are separated into long- and short-term components, and the results are transferred from there to the appropriate parts of Schedule D. You should review Schedule D, Form 6781, and their instructions prior to trading. IRS Publication 550, "Investment Income and Expense," is also helpful. You would file Form 1045 or 1040X to collect your tax refund on a carryback.

You can obtain publications, forms, and instructions by going to the Internal Revenue Service web site (www.irs.gov). Tax preparation software, such as TurboTax, can also help.

You should carefully review your year-end brokerage statements to determine which trades are eligible for section 1256 treatment and contact your broker with questions. Your Form 1099 received from your broker should help you determine your reporting requirement.

INTERNAL REVENUE SERVICE CIRCULAR 230 NOTICE

The discussion in this book concerning taxes should not be considered as tax advice, and you should consult your own tax adviser. Tax rules change and can differ depending on facts and circumstances. The information in this book provides only a general discussion of the tax law affecting options and is not intended to be applicable to any individual investment and tax situation. Investors are strongly advised to contact their own tax consultants and legal advisers in considering the tax consequences of their own specific circumstances. Furthermore, material contained in this book may be affected by changes in law subsequent to publication. Any description of tax matters cannot be used by any taxpayer for the purpose of avoiding tax penalties that may be imposed under U.S. tax law. You should not refer to any such tax discussion in promotion or marketing. Each taxpayer should seek advice based on the taxpayer's particular circumstances from an independent tax adviser.

FINAL THOUGHTS

Taxes can have a significant effect on investment returns, and there are differences in tax treatment, depending on whether an option is on a stock, ETF, broad-based index, or futures contract and whether the gain or loss is in a taxable account or in an IRA. Once you understand these rules, you may be able to minimize taxes by trading options on one product instead of another and in one account versus another. You can place trades with your broker that seem similar because the outcome depends on fluctuations in the market, but the tax consequences can be very different. You may want to consider trading one type of instrument in your taxable account and another type of instrument in your IRA. For example, you may trade SPY options in your self-directed IRA because it is not tax advantaged and SPX options in your taxable brokerage account because it is subject to section 1256 treatment.

Strategies at a Glance—ETFs

A ppendixes A, B, and C cover option strategies on ETFs, indexes, and stock index futures, respectively, and illustrate many of the strategies covered throughout this book. Strategies are presented according to whether they are primarily bullish or bearish, and whether they profit inside a trading range or profit outside a trading range.

Whatever your market prediction, there is likely an ETF option strategy that can be used to profit from that view. For example, you can execute an option strategy that will profit if you are bullish, bearish, or want to profit from an increase in volatility (where an underlying instrument will trade outside a range) or a decrease in volatility (where an underlying instrument will trade within a range). Not only that, but an ETF can have a positive correlation to its benchmark or an inverse correlation to its benchmark and can be executed at the same rate as its underlying benchmark index or at double its benchmark index.

An advantage of trading an ETF is that it allows you to take advantage of almost any market view. For example, if you are bullish on the broad market, buy a SPDR S&P 500 (SPY) call or a ProShares Ultra S&P 500 (symbol SSO) call; if you expect an increase in volatility in the broad market, buy a SPDR S&P 500 or a ProShares Ultra S&P 500 straddle or strangle; and if you expect a contraction in volatility, sell a SPDR S&P 500 or a ProShares Ultra S&P 500 iron condor.

The following section presents strategies at a glance. The first line is intended to state a forecast and is immediately, on the same line, followed by a strategy that fits that view; the second line states an assumption regarding the level of an index or ETF; and the remaining line or lines describe the ETF option strategy. A similar approach is used in Appendix B on index strategies and in Appendix C on stock index futures. After you understand these strategy summaries, you should understand options at an advanced level so that you can use options wisely in almost any scenario.

The strategies shown in Appendixes A, B, and C are intended to provide a working knowledge of how options work and are not recommendations. Each strategy assumes that the option position is established in January of the current year.

BULLISH ETF STRATEGIES

Long Call (Chapter 7)

Bullish on market; deep-in-the-money long call.
SPY at 150.
Buy one SPY March 140 call.
Bullish on market; slightly-in-the-money long call.
SPY at 150.
Buy one SPY March 145 call.
Bullish on market; at-the-money long call.
SPY at 150.
Buy one SPY March 150 call.
Bullish on market; slightly-out-of-the-money long call.
SPY at 150.
Buy one SPY March 155 call.
Bullish on market; far-out-of-the-money long call.
SPY at 150.
Buy one SPY March 160 call.
Bullish on emerging markets; at-the-money long call.
iShares MSCI Emerging Markets Fund (EEM) at 40.
Buy one MSCI Hong Kong Index (EWH) March 40 call.
Bullish on Hong Kong market; at-the-money long call.
EWH at 20.
Buy one EWH March 20 call.
Bullish on Latin America; at-the-money long call.
iShares S&P Latin America 40 Index (ILF) at 50.
Buy one ILF March 50 call.
Bullish on pharmaceuticals; in-the-money long call.
HOLDRs Trust Pharmaceutical (PPH) at 75.
Buy one PPH March 70 call.
Bullish on agriculture; at-the-money long call.
PowerShares DB Agriculture Fund (DBA) at 40.
Buy one DBA March 40 call.
Bullish on energy; at-the-money long call.
Energy Select Sector (XLE) at 75.
Buy one XLE June 75 call.
Bullish in long run on Asia emerging markets; out-of-the-money long long-term equity antici-
pation securities (LEAPS) call (Chapter 7).
iShares MSCI EAFE Exchange Traded Fund (EFA) at 70.
Buy one EFA March (following year) 75 LEAPS call.

Short Put (Chapter 10)

Bullish on market; at-the-money short put.
SPY at 150.
Sell one SPY March 150 put.
Bullish on market; slightly-out-of-the-money short put.
SPY at 150.
Sell one SPY March 145 put.

Bullish on market; far-out-of-the-money short put.
   SPY at 150.
   Sell one SPY March 140 put.
Bullish on emerging markets; at-the-money short put.
   EEM at 40.
   Sell one EEM March 40 put.
Bullish on Hong Kong market; at-the-money short put.
   EWH at 20.
   Sell one EWH March 20 put.
Bullish on Latin America; at-the-money short put.
   ILF at 50.
   Sell one ILF March 50 put.
Bullish on pharmaceuticals; in-the-money short put.
   PPH at 75.
   Sell one PPH March 70 put.
Bullish on agriculture; at-the-money short put.
   DBA at 40.
   Sell one DBA March 40 put.
Bullish on energy; at-the-money short put.
   XLE at 75.
   Sell one XLE June 75 put.
Bullish in long run on Asia emerging markets; out-of-the-money short LEAPS put.
   EFA at 70.
   Sell one EFA March (following year) 65 LEAPS put.

Call Debit Spread (Chapter 11)

Bullish on market; call vertical debit spread.
   SPY at 150.
   Buy one SPY March 150 call.
   Sell one SPY March 155 call.
Bullish on small caps; call vertical debit spread.
   iShares Russell 2000 Index Fund (IWM) at 80.
   Buy one IWM February 80 call.
   Sell one IWM February 84 call.
Bullish on China; call vertical debit spread.
   iShares FTSA/Xinhua China 25 (FXI) at 150.
   Buy one FXI March 145 call.
   Sell one FXI March 155 call.
Bullish on financial sector; call vertical debit spread.
   Financial Select Sector (XLF) at 30.
   Buy one XLF March 30 call.
   Sell one XLF March 35 call.
Bullish on emerging markets; call vertical debit spread.
   Vanguard Emerging Markets ETF (VWO) at 100.
   Buy one VWO March 100 call.
   Sell one VWO March 110 call.
Bullish on biotech; call vertical debit spread.
   HOLDRs Trust Biotech (BBH) at 170.
   Buy one BBH March 170 call.
   Sell one BBH March 175 call.

Bullish on oil services; call vertical debit spread.
    HOLDRs Trust Oil Services (OIH) at 170.
    Buy one OIH March 165 call.
    Sell one OIH March 175 call.
Bullish on long-term Treasury bonds; call vertical debit spread.
    iShares Lehman 20+ Year Treasury Bond Fund (TLT) at 90.
    Buy one TLT March 90 call.
    Sell one TLT March 95 call.
Bullish on semiconductors; call vertical debit spread.
    HOLDRs Trust Semiconductor (SMH) at 30.
    Buy one SMH March 25 call.
    Sell one SMH March 33 call.
Bullish on oil; call vertical debit spread.
    United States Oil Fund (USO) at 75.
    Buy one USO March 75 call.
    Sell one USO March 80 call.

Put Credit Spread (Chapter 11)

Bullish on market; put vertical credit spread.
    SPY at 150.
    Sell one SPY March 145 put.
    Buy one SPY March 135 put.
Bullish on small caps; put vertical credit spread.
    IWM at 80.
    Sell one IWM February 80 put.
    Buy one IWM February 76 put.
Bullish on China; put vertical credit spread.
    FXI at 150.
    Sell one FXI March 145 put.
    Buy one FXI March 135 put.
Bullish on financial sector; put vertical credit spread.
    XLF at 30.
    Sell one XLF March 30 put.
    Buy one XLF March 25 put.
Bullish on emerging markets; put vertical credit spread.
    VWO at 100.
    Sell one VWO March 100 put.
    Buy one VWO March 90 put.
Bullish on biotech; put vertical credit spread.
    BBH at 170.
    Sell one BBH March 170 put.
    Buy one BBH March 165 put.
Bullish on oil services; put vertical credit spread.
    OIH at 170.
    Sell one OIH March 165 put.
    Buy one OIH March 155 put.
Bullish on long-term Treasury bonds; put vertical credit spread.
    TLT at 90.
    Sell one TLT March 90 put.
    Buy one TLT March 85 put.

Bullish on semiconductors; put vertical credit spread.
    SMH at 30.
    Sell one SMH March 25 put.
    Buy one SMH March 20 put.
Bullish on oil; put vertical credit spread.
    USO at 75.
    Sell one USO March 75 put.
    Buy one USO March 70 put.

Call Backspread (Chapter 13)

Bullish on market; call backspread.
    SPY at 150.
    Sell one SPY March 150 call.
    Buy five SPY March 155 calls.
Bullish on technology stocks; call backspread.
    PowerShares Trust QQQ (QQQQ) at 50.
    Sell one QQQQ March 50 call.
    Buy three QQQQ March 53 calls.

Put Ratio (Front) Spread (Chapter 13)

Bullish on market; put ratio (front) spread.
    SPY at 150.
    Buy one SPY March 150 put.
    Sell five SPY March 145 puts.

Diagonal Spread (Chapter 18)

Bullish on market; diagonal long call debit spread.
    SPY at 150.
    Buy one SPY March 150 call.
    Sell one SPY April 155 call.
Bullish on small caps; double diagonal long call debit spread (Chapter 18).
    IWM at 80.
    Buy one IWM February 80 call.
    Sell one IWM June 85 call.

Covered Call (Chapter 19)

Moderately bullish on market; covered call.
    SPY at 150.
    Buy 100 shares SPY at 150.
    Sell one SPY March 153 call.

Long Combination (Chapter 20)

Bullish on market; long combination.
    SPY at 150.
    Buy one SPY March 152 call.
    Sell one SPY March 147 put.

Bullish on utilities; long combination.
    HOLDRs Trust Utilities (UTH) at 130.
    Buy one UTH March 135 call.
    Sell one UTH March 130 put.

Covered Combination (Chapter 22)

Bullish on market; long covered combination.
    SPY at 150.
    Buy 100 shares SPY at 150.
    Sell one SPY March 153 call.
    Sell one SPY March 147 put.

Ultra Long ETF (Chapter 24)

Bullish on market; slightly-in-the-money long call (Ultra ETF).
    SSO at 50.
    Buy one ProShares Ultra long S&P 500 (SSO) March 47 call.
Bullish on market; at-the-money short put (Ultra ETF).
    SSO at 50.
    Sell one SSO March 50 put.
Bullish on market; call vertical debit spread (Ultra ETF).
    SSO at 50.
    Buy one SSO March 50 call.
    Sell one SSO March 54 call.
Bullish on market; put vertical credit spread (Ultra ETF).
    SSO at 50.
    Sell one SSO March 45 put.
    Buy one SSO March 40 put.
Bullish on market; call backspread (Ultra ETF).
    SSO at 50.
    Sell one SSO March 50 call.
    Buy five SSO March 52 calls.
Bullish on market; put ratio (front) spread (Ultra ETF).
    SSO at 50.
    Buy one SSO March 50 put.
    Sell five SSO March 48 puts.
Bullish on market; long combination (Ultra ETF).
    SSO at 50.
    Buy one SSO March 52 call.
    Sell one SSO March 48 put.

BEARISH ETF STRATEGIES

Long Put (Chapter 8)

Bearish on market; deep-in-the-money long put.
    SPY at 150.
    Buy one SPY March 160 put.

Bearish on market; slightly-in-the-money long put.
    SPY at 150.
    Buy one SPY March 155 put.
Bearish on market; at-the-money long put.
    SPY at 150.
    Buy one SPY March 150 put.
Bearish on market; slightly-out-of-the-money long put.
    SPY at 150.
    Buy one SPY March 145 put.
Bearish on market; far-out-of-the-money long put.
    SPY at 150.
    Buy one SPY March 140 put.
Bearish on emerging markets; at-the-money long put.
    EEM at 40.
    Buy one EWH March 40 put.
Bearish on Hong Kong market; at-the-money long put.
    EWH at 20.
    Buy one EWH March 20 put.
Bearish on Latin America; at-the-money long put.
    ILF at 50.
    Buy one ILF March 50 put.
Bearish on pharmaceuticals; in-the-money long put.
    PPH at 75.
    Buy one PPH March 80 put.
Bearish on agriculture; at-the-money long put.
    DBA at 40.
    Buy one DBA March 40 put.
Bearish on energy; at-the-money long put.
    XLE at 75.
    Buy one XLE June 75 put.
Bearish in long run on Asia emerging markets; out-of-the-money long LEAPS put.
    EFA at 70.
    Buy one EFA March (following year) 65 LEAPS put.

Short Call (Chapter 9)

Bearish on market; at-the-money short call.
    SPY at 150.
    Sell one SPY March 150 call.
Bearish on market; slightly-out-of-the-money short call.
    SPY at 150.
    Sell one SPY March 155 call.
Bearish on market; far-out-of-the-money short call.
    SPY at 150.
    Sell one SPY March 160 call.
Bearish on emerging markets; at-the-money short call.
    EEM at 40.
    Sell one EWH March 40 call.
Bearish on Hong Kong market; at-the-money short call.
    EWH at 20.
    Sell one EWH March 20 call.

Bearish on Latin America; at-the-money short call.
  ILF at 50.
  Sell one ILF March 50 call.
Bearish on pharmaceuticals; in-the-money short call.
  PPH at 75.
  Sell one PPH March 70 call.
Bearish on agriculture; at-the-money short call.
  DBA at 40.
  Sell one DBA March 40 call.
Bearish on energy; at-the-money short call.
  XLE at 75.
  Sell one XLE June 75 call.
Bearish in long run on Asia emerging markets; out-of-the-money short LEAPS call.
  EFA at 70.
  Sell one EFA March (following year) 75 LEAPS call.

Call Credit Spread (Chapter 11)

Bearish on market; call vertical credit spread.
  SPY at 150.
  Sell one SPY March 150 call.
  Buy one SPY March 155 call.
Bearish on small caps; call vertical credit spread.
  IWM at 80.
  Sell one IWM February 80 call.
  Buy one IWM February 84 call.
Bearish on China; call vertical credit spread.
  FXI at 150.
  Sell one FXI March 150 call.
  Buy one FXI March 155 call.
Bearish on financial sector; call vertical credit spread.
  XLF at 30.
  Sell one XLF March 30 call.
  Buy one XLF March 35 call.
Bearish on emerging markets; call vertical credit spread.
  VWO at 100.
  Sell one VWO March 100 call.
  Buy one VWO March 110 call.
Bearish on biotech; call vertical credit spread.
  BBH at 170.
  Sell one BBH March 170 call.
  Buy one BBH March 175 call.
Bearish on oil services; call vertical credit spread.
  OIH at 170.
  Sell one OIH March 170 call.
  Buy one OIH March 175 call.
Bearish on long-term Treasury bonds; call vertical credit spread.
  TLT at 90.
  Sell one TLT March 90 call.
  Buy one TLT March 95 call.

Bearish on semiconductors; call vertical credit spread.
    SMH at 30.
    Sell one SMH March 30 call.
    Buy one SMH March 33 call.
Bearish on oil; call vertical credit spread.
    USO at 75.
    Sell one USO March 75 call.
    Buy one USO March 80 call.

Put Debit Spread (Chapter 11)

Bearish on market; put vertical debit spread.
    SPY at 150.
    Buy one SPY March 145 put.
    Sell one SPY March 135 put.
Bearish on small caps; put vertical debit spread.
    IWM at 80.
    Buy one IWM February 80 put.
    Sell one IWM February 76 put.
Bearish on China; put vertical debit spread.
    FXI at 150.
    Buy one FXI March 145 put.
    Sell one FXI March 135 put.
Bearish on financial sector; put vertical debit spread.
    XLF at 30.
    Buy one XLF March 30 put.
    Sell one XLF March 25 put.
Bearish on emerging markets; put vertical debit spread.
    VWO at 100.
    Buy one VWO March 100 put.
    Sell one VWO March 90 put.
Bearish on biotech; put vertical debit spread.
    BBH at 170.
    Buy one BBH March 170 put.
    Sell one BBH March 165 put.
Bearish on oil services; put vertical debit spread.
    OIH at 170.
    Buy one OIH March 165 put.
    Sell one OIH March 155 put.
Bearish on long-term Treasury bonds; put vertical debit spread.
    TLT at 90.
    Buy one TLT March 90 put.
    Sell one TLT March 85 put.
Bearish on semiconductors; put vertical debit spread.
    SMH at 30.
    Buy one SMH March 25 put.
    Sell one SMH March 20 put.
Bearish on oil; put vertical debit spread.
    USO at 75.
    Buy one USO March 75 put.
    Sell one USO March 70 put.

Put Backspread (Chapter 13)

Bearish on market; put backspread.
   SPY at 150.
   Sell one SPY March 150 put.
   Buy five SPY March 145 puts.
Bearish on technology stocks; put backspread.
   QQQQ at 50.
   Sell one QQQQ March 50 put.
   Buy three QQQQ March 47 puts.

Call Ratio (Front) Spread (Chapter 13)

Bearish on market; call ratio (front) spread.
   SPY at 150.
   Buy one SPY March 150 call.
   Sell five SPY March 155 calls.

Diagonal Spread (Chapter 18)

Bearish on market; diagonal long put debit spread.
   SPY at 150.
   Buy one SPY March 150 put.
   Sell one SPY April 145 put.
Bearish on small caps; double diagonal long put debit spread.
   IWM at 80.
   Buy one IWM February 80 put.
   Sell one IWM June 75 put.

Covered Call (Chapter 19)

Moderately bearish on market; covered call.
   SPY at 150.
   Buy 100 shares SPY at $150.
   Sell one SPY March 153 call.

Short Combination (Chapter 20)

Bearish on market; short combination.
   SPY at 150.
   Sell one SPY March 152 call.
   Buy one SPY March 147 put.

Covered Combination (Chapter 22)

Bearish on utilities; short combination.
   UTH at 130.
   Sell one UTH March 135 call.
   Buy one UTH March 125 put.
Bearish on market; short covered combination.
   SPY at 150.
   Sell 100 shares SPY at $150.

Sell one SPY March 153 call.
Sell one SPY March 147 put.

Inverse (Ultra Short) ETF (Chapter 24)

Bearish on market; slightly-in-the-money long call (inverse ETF).
  SDS at 70.
  Buy one SDS March 65 call.
Bearish on market; at-the-money short put (inverse ETF).
  SDS at 70.
  Sell one SDS March 70 put.
Bearish on market; put vertical credit spread (inverse ETF).
  SDS at 70.
  Sell one SDS March 65 put.
  Buy one SDS March 60 put.
Bearish on market; call vertical debit spread (inverse ETF).
  SDS at 70.
  Buy one SDS March 70 call.
  Sell one SDS March 80 call.
Bearish on market; call backspread (inverse ETF).
  SDS at 70.
  Sell one SDS March 70 call.
  Buy five SDS March 75 calls.
Bearish on market; put ratio (front) spread (inverse ETF).
  SDS at 70.
  Buy one SDS March 70 put.
  Sell five SDS March 65 puts.
Bearish on market; long combination (inverse ETF).
  SDS at 70.
  Buy one SDS March 72 call.
  Sell one SDS March 68 put.

TRADING OUTSIDE A RANGE

Long Iron Condor (Chapter 12)

Bullish on volatility; long iron condor.
  SPY at 150.
  Buy one SPY March 155 call.
  Sell one SPY March 160 call.
  Buy one SPY March 145 put.
  Sell one SPY March 140 put.

Long Straddle and Strangle (Chapter 14)

Bullish on volatility; long straddle.
  SPY at 150.
  Buy one SPY March 150 call.
  Buy one SPY March 150 put.

Bullish on volatility; unbalanced long straddle (also Chapter 13).
>   SPY at 150.
>   Buy two SPY March 150 calls.
>   Buy one SPY March 150 put.

Bullish on volatility; long straddle.
>   SPY at 150.
>   Buy one SPY end of March Quarterlys 150 call.
>   Buy one SPY end of March Quarterlys 150 put.

Bullish on volatility; long strangle.
>   SPY at 150.
>   Buy one SPY March 155 call.
>   Buy one SPY March 145 put.

Bullish on volatility; unbalanced long strangle (also Chapter 13).
>   SPY at 150.
>   Buy one SPY March 155 call.
>   Buy three SPY March 145 puts.

Short Butterfly (Chapter 15)

Bullish on volatility; short call butterfly.
>   Diamonds Trust Dow Jones Industrial Average (DIA) at 140.
>   Sell one DIA March 138 call.
>   Buy two DIA March 140 calls.
>   Sell one DIA March 142 call.

Bullish on volatility; short put butterfly.
>   DIA at 140.
>   Sell one DIA March 142 put.
>   Buy two DIA March 140 puts.
>   Sell one DIA March 138 put.

Bullish on volatility; short broken-wing call butterfly.
>   DIA at 140.
>   Sell one DIA March 138 call.
>   Buy two DIA March 140 calls.
>   Sell one DIA March 144 call.

Bullish on volatility; iron butterfly.
>   SPY at 150.
>   Buy one SPY March 150 call.
>   Sell one SPY March 160 call.
>   Buy one SPY March 150 put.
>   Sell one SPY March 140 put.

Short Condor (Chapter 16)

Bullish on volatility; short call condor.
>   DIA at 140.
>   Sell one DIA March 138 call.
>   Buy one DIA March 140 call.
>   Buy one DIA March 142 call.
>   Sell one DIA March 144 call.

Bullish on volatility; short put condor.
    DIA at 140.
    Sell one DIA March 142 put.
    Buy one DIA March 140 put.
    Buy one DIA March 138 put.
    Sell one DIA March 136 put.

Ladder (Chapter 16)

Bullish on volatility; ladder.
    IWM at 80.
    Sell one IWM March 78 call.
    Buy one IWM March 80 call.
    Buy one IWM March 82 call.

Short Calendar Spread (Chapter 17)

Bullish on volatility; short call calendar spread.
    QQQQ at 50.
    Buy one QQQQ February 50 call.
    Sell one QQQQ March 50 call.
Bullish on volatility; short put calendar spread.
    QQQQ at 50.
    Buy one QQQQ February 50 put.
    Sell one QQQQ March 50 put.

TRADING INSIDE A RANGE

Short Iron Condor (Chapter 12)

Bearish on volatility; short iron condor.
    SPY at 150.
    Sell one SPY March 155 call.
    Buy one SPY March 160 call.
    Sell one SPY March 145 put.
    Buy one SPY March 140 put.

Short Straddle and Strangle (Chapter 14)

Bearish on volatility; short straddle.
    SPY at 150.
    Sell one SPY March 150 call.
    Sell one SPY March 150 put.
Bearish on volatility; unbalanced short straddle (also Chapter 13).
    SPY at 150.
    Sell three SPY March 150 calls.
    Sell one SPY March 150 put.

Bearish on volatility; short straddle.
  SPY at 150.
  Sell one SPY end of March Quarterlys 150 call.
  Sell one SPY end of March Quarterlys 150 put.
Bearish on volatility; short strangle.
  SPY at 150.
  Sell one SPY March 155 call.
  Sell one SPY March 145 put.
Bearish on volatility; unbalanced short strangle (also Chapter 13).
  SPY at 150.
  Sell one SPY March 155 call.
  Sell five SPY March 145 puts.

Long Butterfly (Chapter 15)

Bearish on volatility; long call butterfly.
  DIA at 140.
  Buy one DIA March 138 call.
  Sell two DIA March 140 calls.
  Buy one DIA March 142 call.
Bearish on volatility; long put butterfly.
  DIA at 140.
  Buy one DIA March 142 put.
  Sell two DIA March 140 puts.
  Buy one DIA March 138 put.
Bearish on volatility; long broken-wing call butterfly.
  DIA at 140.
  Buy one DIA March 138 call.
  Sell two DIA March 140 calls.
  Buy one DIA March 144 call.
Bearish on volatility; iron butterfly.
  SPY at 150.
  Sell one SPY March 150 call.
  Buy one SPY March 160 call.
  Sell one SPY March 150 put.
  Buy one SPY March 140 put.

Long Condor (Chapter 16)

Bearish on volatility; long call condor.
  DIA at 140.
  Buy one DIA March 138 call.
  Sell one DIA March 140 call.
  Sell one DIA March 142 call.
  Buy one DIA March 144 call.
Bearish on volatility; long put condor.
  DIA at 140.
  Buy one DIA March 144 put.
  Sell one DIA March 142 put.

Sell one DIA March 140 put.
Buy one DIA March 138 put.

Ladder (Chapter 16)

Bearish on volatility; ladder.
 IWM at 80.
 Buy one IWM March 78 call.
 Sell one IWM March 80 call.
 Sell one IWM March 82 call.

Long Calendar Spread (Chapter 17)

Bearish on volatility; long call calendar spread.
 QQQQ at 50.
 Sell one QQQQ February 50 call.
 Buy one QQQQ March 50 call.
Bearish on volatility; long put calendar spread.
 QQQQ at 50.
 Sell one QQQQ February 50 put.
 Buy one QQQQ March 50 put.

Diagonal Spread (Chapter 18)

Bearish on volatility; diagonal spread.
 QQQQ at 50.
 Sell one QQQQ February 50 call.
 Buy one QQQQ March 54 call.
Bearish on volatility; double diagonal spread.
 IWM at 80.
 Sell one IWM February 80 call.
 Buy one IWM June 85 call.

Covered Call (Chapter 19)

Bearish on volatility; covered call.
 SPY at 150.
 Buy 100 shares SPY at $150.
 Sell one SPY March 152 call.

Collar (Chapter 21)

Bearish on volatility; collar.
 SPY at 150.
 Buy 100 shares SPY at 150.
 Sell one SPY March 153 call.
 Buy one SPY March 147 put.

Strategies at a Glance—Indexes

ppendix B presents strategies at a glance for stock indexes. The first line is intended to state a forecast and is followed, on the same line, by a strategy that fits that view; the second line states an assumption regarding the level of an index; and the remaining line or lines describe the index-option strategy. A similar approach is used in Appendix A, regarding ETFs, and in Appendix C, regarding stock index futures. After you understand these strategies at a glance, you should have a working knowledge of the power of options so that you can use options wisely in almost any scenario. These strategies are intended to provide a working knowledge of how options work and are not recommendations. Each strategy assumes that the option position is established in January of the current year.

BULLISH INDEX STRATEGIES

Long Call (Chapter 7)

Bullish on market; deep-in-the-money long call.
    S&P 500 index (SPX) at 1,500.
    Buy one SPX March 1,400 call.
Bullish on market; slightly-in-the-money long call.
    SPX at 1,500.
    Buy one SPX March 1,450 call.
Bullish on market; at-the-money long call.
    SPX at 1,500.
    Buy one SPX March 1,500 call.
Bullish on market; slightly-out-of-the-money long call.
    SPX at 1,500.
    Buy one SPX March 1,550 call.
Bullish on market; far-out-of-the-money long call.
    SPX at 1,500.
    Buy one SPX March 1,600 call.

Bullish on blue chips; slightly-in-the-money long call.
Dow Jones Industrial Average (DJ) at 14,000, Mini-Dow index (DJX) at 140.
Buy one DJX March 135 call.
Bullish on market; far-out-of-the-money long call.
SPX at 1,500, Mini-SPX (XSP) at 150.
Buy one XSP March 160 call.
Bullish on small caps; slightly-in-the-money long call.
Mini-Russell 2000 index at 800, Mini-Russell (RMN) at 80.
Buy one RMN March 75 call.
Bullish in short run; at-the-money long call.
SPX at 1,500.
Buy one SPX Weeklys 1,500 call.
Bullish on technology; slightly-in-the-money long call.
NASDAQ 100 index (NDX) at 2,000.
Buy one NDX March 1,950 call.
Bullish on small caps; far-out-of-the-money long call.
Russell 2000 index (RUT) at 800.
Buy one RUT March 900 call.

Short Put (Chapter 10)

Bullish on market; at-the-money short put.
SPX at 1,500.
Sell one SPX March 1,500 put.
Bullish on market; slightly-out-of-the-money short put.
SPX at 1,500.
Sell one SPX March 1,450 put.
Bullish on market; far-out-of-the-money short put.
SPX at 1,500.
Sell one SPX March 1,300 put.
Bullish on blue chips; far-out-of-the-money short put.
DJX at 140.
Sell one DJX March 120 put.
Bullish in short run; far-out-of-the-money short put.
SPX at 1,500.
Sell one SPX Weeklys 1,400 put.
Bullish on technology; far-out-of-the-money short put.
NDX at 2,000.
Sell one NDX March 1,750 put.
Bullish on small caps; far-out-of-the-money short put.
RUT at 800.
Sell one RUT March 700 put.

Call Debit Spread (Chapter 11)

Bullish on market; call vertical debit spread.
SPX at 1,500.
Buy one SPX March 1,500 call.
Sell one SPX March 1,550 call.

Bullish on small caps; call vertical debit spread.
>   RUT at 800.
>   Buy one RUT February 800 call.
>   Sell one RUT February 850 call.

Put Credit Spread (Chapter 11)

Bullish on market; put vertical credit spread.
>   SPX at 1,500.
>   Sell one SPX March 1,400 put.
>   Buy one SPX March 1,350 put.
Bullish on small caps; put vertical credit spread.
>   RUT at 800.
>   Sell one RUT February 750 put.
>   Buy one RUT February 700 put.

Call Backspread (Chapter 13)

Bullish on market; call backspread.
>   SPX at 1,500.
>   Sell one SPX March 1,500 call.
>   Buy five SPX March 1,550 calls.
Bullish on technology stocks; call backspread.
>   NDX at 2,000.
>   Sell one NDX March 2,000 call.
>   Buy six NDX March 2,120 calls.

Put Ratio (Front) Spread (Chapter 13)

Bullish on market; put ratio (front) spread.
>   SPX at 1,500.
>   Buy one SPX March 1,500 put.
>   Sell five SPX March 1,450 puts.

Diagonal Spread (Chapter 18)

Bullish on market; diagonal long call debit spread.
>   SPX at 1,500.
>   Buy one SPX March 1,500 call.
>   Sell one SPX April 1,600 call.
Bullish on small caps; double diagonal long call debit spread (Chapter 18).
>   RUT at 800.
>   Buy one RUT February 780 call.
>   Sell one RUT April 850 call.

Covered Call (Chapter 19)

An underlying index cannot be purchased directly.

Long Combination (Chapter 20)

Bullish on market; long combination.
SPX at 1,500.
Buy one SPX March 1,550 call.
Sell one SPX March 1,450 put.

Covered Combination (Chapter 22)

An underlying index cannot be purchased directly.

BEARISH INDEX STRATEGIES

Long Put (Chapter 8)

Bearish on market; deep-in-the-money long put.
SPX at 1,500.
Buy one SPX March 1,600 put.
Bearish on market; slightly-in-the-money long put.
SPX at 1,500.
Buy one SPX March 1,550 put.
Bearish on market; at-the-money long put.
SPX at 1,500.
Buy one SPX March 1,500 put.
Bearish on market; slightly-out-of-the-money long put.
SPX at 1,500.
Buy one SPX March 1,450 put.
Bearish on market; far-out-of-the-money long put.
SPX at 1,500.
Buy one SPX March 1,400 put.
Bearish on blue chips; slightly-in-the-money long put.
DJ at 14,000, DJX at 140.
Buy one DJX March 145 put.
Bearish on market; far-out-of-the-money long put.
SPX at 1,500, XSP at 150.
Buy one XSP March 140 put.
Bearish on small caps; slightly-in-the-money long put.
Mini-Russell 2000 index at 800, RMN at 80.
Buy one RMN March 85 put.
Bearish in short run; at-the-money long put.
SPX at 1,500.
Buy one SPX Weeklys 1,500 put.
Bearish on technology; slightly-in-the-money long put.
NDX at 2,000.
Buy one NDX March 2,050 put.
Bearish on small caps; far-out-of-the-money long put.
RUT at 800.
Buy one RUT March 700 put.

Short Call (Chapter 9)

Bearish on market; at-the-money short call.
    SPX at 1,500.
    Sell one SPX March 1,500 call.
Bearish on market; slightly-out-of-the-money short call.
    SPX at 1,500.
    Sell one SPX March 1,550 call.
Bearish on market; far-out-of-the-money short call.
    SPX at 1,500.
    Sell one SPX March 1,600 call.
Bearish on blue chips; far-out-of-the-money short call.
    DJ at 14,000, DJX at 140.
    Sell one DJX March 160 call.
Bearish in short run; far-out-of-the-money short call.
    SPX at 1,500.
    Sell one SPX Weeklys 1,600 call.
Bearish on technology; far-out-of-the-money short call.
    NDX at 2,000.
    Sell one NDX March 2,200 call.
Bearish on small caps; far-out-of-the-money short call.
    RUT at 800.
    Sell one RUT March 900 call.

Call Credit Spread (Chapter 11)

Bearish on market; call vertical credit spread.
    SPX at 1,500.
    Sell one SPX March 1,500 call.
    Buy one SPX March 1,550 call.
Bearish on small caps; call vertical credit spread.
    RUT at 800.
    Sell one RUT February 800 call.
    Buy one RUT February 840 call.

Put Debit Spread (Chapter 11)

Bearish on market; put vertical debit spread.
    SPX at 1,500.
    Buy one SPX March 1,450 put.
    Sell one SPX March 1,350 put.
Bearish on small caps; put vertical debit spread.
    RUT at 800.
    Buy one RUT February 800 put.
    Sell one RUT February 760 put.

Put Backspread (Chapter 13)

Bearish on market; put backspread.
    SPX at 1,500.
    Sell one SPX March 1,500 put.
    Buy five SPX March 1,450 puts.

Bearish on technology stocks; put backspread.
NDX at 2,000.
Sell one NDX March 2,000 put.
Buy eight NDX March 1,880 puts.

Call Ratio (Front) Spread (Chapter 13)

Bearish on market; call ratio (front) spread.
SPX at 1,500.
Buy one SPX March 1,500 call.
Sell five SPX March 1,550 calls.

Diagonal Spread (Chapter 18)

Bearish on market; diagonal long put debit spread.
SPX at 1,500.
Buy one SPX March 1,500 put.
Sell one SPX April 1,450 put.
Bearish on small caps; double diagonal long put debit spread.
RUT at 800.
Buy one RUT February 800 put.
Sell one RUT April 750 put.

Covered Call (Chapter 19)

An underlying index cannot be purchased directly.

Short Combination (Chapter 20)

Bearish on market; short combination.
SPX at 1,500.
Sell one SPX March 1,520 call.
Buy one SPY March 1,470 put.

Covered Combination (Chapter 22)

An underlying index cannot be purchased directly.

TRADING OUTSIDE A RANGE

Long Iron Condor (Chapter 12)

Bullish on volatility; long iron condor.
SPX at 1,500.
Buy one SPX March 1,550 call.
Sell one SPX March 1,600 call.
Buy one SPX March 1,450 put.
Sell one SPX March 1,400 put.

Long Straddle and Strangle (Chapter 14)

Bullish on volatility; long straddle.
    SPX at 1,500.
    Buy one SPX March 1,500 call.
    Buy one SPX March 1,500 put.
Bullish on volatility; unbalanced long straddle (also Chapter 13).
    SPX at 1,500.
    Buy two SPX March 1,500 calls.
    Buy one SPX March 1,500 put.
Bullish on volatility; long straddle.
    SPX at 1,500.
    Buy one SPX end of March Quarterlys 1,500 call.
    Buy one SPX end of March Quarterlys 1,500 put.
Bullish on volatility; long straddle.
    SPX at 1,500.
    Buy one SPX Weeklys 1,500 call.
    Buy one SPX Weeklys 1,500 put.
Bullish on volatility; long strangle.
    SPX at 1,500.
    Buy one SPX March 1,525 call.
    Buy one SPX March 1,400 put.
Bullish on volatility; unbalanced long strangle (also Chapter 13).
    SPX at 1,500.
    Buy one SPX March 1,575 call.
    Buy three SPX March 1,450 puts.

Short Butterfly (Chapter 15)

Bullish on volatility; short call butterfly.
    DJ at 14,000, DJX at 140.
    Sell one DJX March 138 call.
    Buy two DJX March 140 calls.
    Sell one DJX March 142 call.
Bullish on volatility; short put butterfly.
    DJ at 14,000, DJX at 140.
    Sell one DJX March 142 put.
    Buy two DJX March 140 puts.
    Sell one DJX March 138 put.
Bullish on volatility; short broken-wing call butterfly.
    DJ at 14,000, DJX at 140.
    Sell one DJX March 138 call.
    Buy two DJX March 140 calls.
    Sell one DJX March 144 call.
Bullish on volatility; iron butterfly.
    SPX at 1,500.
    Buy one SPX March 1,500 call.
    Sell one SPX March 1,600 call.
    Buy one SPX March 1,500 put.
    Sell one SPX March 1,400 put.

Short Condor (Chapter 16)

Bullish on volatility; short call condor.
DJ at 14,000, DJX at 140.
Sell one DJX March 138 call.
Buy one DJX March 140 call.
Buy one DJX March 142 call.
Sell one DJX March 144 call.
Bullish on volatility; short put condor.
DJ at 14,000, DJX at 140.
Sell one DJX March 142 put.
Buy one DJX March 140 put.
Buy one DJX March 138 put.
Sell one DJX March 136 put.

Ladder (Chapter 16)

Bullish on volatility; ladder.
RUT at 800.
Sell one RUT March 780 call.
Buy one RUT March 800 call.
Buy one RUT March 820 call.

Short Calendar Spread (Chapter 17)

Bullish on volatility; short call calendar spread.
NDX at 2,000.
Buy one NDX February 2,000 call.
Sell one NDX March 2,000 call.
Bullish on volatility; short put calendar spread.
NDX at 2,000.
Buy one NDX February 2,000 put.
Sell one NDX March 2,000 put.

Volatility Index (Chapter 27)

Bullish on volatility; at-the-money long call.
CBOE Volatility index (VIX) at 20.
Buy one VIX March 20 call.
Bullish on volatility; at-the-money short put.
VIX at 20.
Sell one VIX March 20 put.

TRADING INSIDE A RANGE

Short Iron Condor (Chapter 12)

Bearish on volatility; short iron condor.
SPX at 1,500.
Sell one SPX March 1,550 call.

Buy one SPX March 1,600 call.
Sell one SPX March 1,450 put.
Buy one SPX March 1,400 put.

Short Straddle and Strangle (Chapter 14)

Bearish on volatility; short straddle.
SPX at 1,500.
Sell one SPX March 1,500 call.
Sell one SPX March 1,500 put.
Bearish on volatility; unbalanced short straddle (also Chapter 13).
SPX at 1,500.
Sell three SPX March 1,500 calls.
Sell one SPX March 1,500 put.
Bearish on volatility; short straddle.
SPX at 1,500.
Sell one SPX end of March Quarterlys 1,500 call.
Sell one SPX end of March Quarterlys 1,500 put.
Bearish on volatility; short straddle.
SPX at 1,500.
Sell one SPX Weeklys 1,500 call.
Sell one SPX Weeklys 1,500 put.
Bearish on volatility; short strangle.
SPX at 1,500.
Sell one SPX March 1,550 call.
Sell one SPX March 1,450 put.
Bearish on volatility; unbalanced short strangle (also Chapter 13).
SPX at 1,500.
Sell one SPX March 1,550 call.
Sell two SPX March 1,450 puts.

Long Butterfly (Chapter 15)

Bearish on volatility; long call butterfly.
DJ at 14,000, DJX at 140.
Buy one DJX March 138 call.
Sell two DJX March 140 calls.
Buy one DJX March 142 call.
Bearish on volatility; long put butterfly.
DJ at 14,000, DJX at 140.
Buy one DJX March 142 put.
Sell two DJX March 140 puts.
Buy one DJX March 138 put.
Bearish on volatility; long broken-wing call butterfly.
DJ at 14,000, DJX at 140.
Buy one DJX March 138 call.
Sell two DJX March 140 calls.
Buy one DJX March 144 call.

Bearish on volatility; iron butterfly.
    SPX at 1,500.
    Sell one SPX March 1,500 call.
    Buy one SPX March 1,600 call.
    Sell one SPX March 1,500 put.
    Buy one SPX March 1,400 put.

Long Condor (Chapter 16)

Bearish on volatility; long call condor.
    DJ at 14,000, DJX at 140.
    Buy one DJX March 138 call.
    Sell one DJX March 140 call.
    Sell one DJX March 142 call.
    Buy one DJX March 144 call.
Bearish on volatility; long put condor.
    DJ at 14,000, DJX at 140.
    Buy one DJX March 144 put.
    Sell one DJX March 142 put.
    Sell one DJX March 140 put.
    Buy one DJX March 138 put.

Ladder (Chapter 16)

Bearish on volatility; ladder.
    RUT at 800.
    Buy one RUT March 780 call.
    Sell one RUT March 800 call.
    Sell one RUT March 820 call.

Long Calendar Spread (Chapter 17)

Bearish on volatility; long call calendar spread.
    NDX at 2,000.
    Sell one NDX February 2,000 call.
    Buy one NDX March 2,000 call.
Bearish on volatility; long put calendar spread.
    NDX at 2,000.
    Sell one NDX February 2,000 put.
    Buy one NDX March 2,000 put.

Covered Call (Chapter 19)

An underlying index cannot be purchased directly.

Collar (Chapter 21)

An underlying index cannot be purchased directly.

Diagonal Spread (Chapter 18)

>   Bearish on volatility; diagonal spread.
>>   NDX at 2,000.
>>   Sell one NDX February 2,000 call.
>>   Buy one NDX March 2,100 call.
>   Bearish on volatility; double diagonal spread.
>>   RUT at 800.
>>   Sell one RUT February 800 call.
>>   Buy one RUT April 900 call.

Volatility Index (Chapter 27)

>   Bearish on volatility; at-the-money long put.
>>   VIX at 20.
>>   Buy one VIX March 20 put.
>   Bearish on volatility; at-the-money short call.
>>   VIX at 20.
>>   Sell one VIX March 20 call.

Strategies at a Glance—Stock Index Futures

Appendix C presents strategies at a glance for stock index futures. The first line is intended to state a forecast and is followed, on the same line, by a strategy that fits that view; the second line states an assumption regarding the level of a future index; and the remaining line or lines describe the option strategy. A similar approach is used in Appendix A, regarding ETFs, and in Appendix B, regarding indexes. These strategies are intended to provide a working knowledge of how options work and are not recommendations. Each strategy assumes that the option position is established in January of the current year.

BULLISH STOCK INDEX FUTURES STRATEGIES

Long Call (Chapter 7)

Bullish on market; deep-in-the-money long call.
    S&P 500 futures at 1,500.
    Buy one S&P 500 futures March 1,400 call.
Bullish on market; slightly-in-the-money long call.
    S&P 500 futures at 1,500.
    Buy one S&P 500 futures March 1,450 call.
Bullish on market; at-the-money long call.
    S&P 500 futures at 1,500.
    Buy one S&P 500 futures March 1,500 call.
Bullish on market; slightly-out-of-the-money long call.
    S&P 500 futures at 1,500.
    Buy one S&P 500 futures March 1,550 call.
Bullish on market; far-out-of-the-money long call.
    S&P 500 futures at 1,500.
    Buy one S&P 500 futures March 1,600 call.
Bullish on blue chips; slightly-in-the-money long call.
    Dow Jones Industrial Average futures (DJ) at 14,000.
    Buy one DJ March 13,500 call.

Bullish on market; far-out-of-the-money long call.
>S&P 500 futures at 1,500.
>Buy one E-Mini S&P 500 futures February 1,600 call.

Bullish on small caps; at-the-money long call.
>Russell 2000 futures at 800.
>Buy one Russell 2000 futures March 800 call.

Bullish in short run; at-the-money long call.
>S&P 500 futures at 1,500.
>Buy one S&P 500 futures February 1,500 call.

Bullish on technology; slightly-in-the-money long call.
>NASDAQ 100 March futures at 2,000.
>Buy one NASDAQ 100 futures March 1,950 call.

Bullish on small caps; far-out-of-the-money long call.
>Russell 2000 futures at 800.
>Buy one Russell 2000 futures March 900 call.

Bullish on market; slightly-in-the-money long call.
>S&P 500 futures at 1,500.
>Buy one E-Mini S&P 500 futures March 1,475 call.

Bullish on technology; at-the-money long call.
>NASDAQ 100 futures at 2,000.
>Buy one E-Mini NASDAQ 100 futures March 2,000 call.

Bullish on small caps; at-the-money long call.
>Russell 2000 futures at 800.
>Buy one E-Mini Russell 2000 futures March 800 call.

Bullish in long run; far-out-of-the-money long call.
>S&P 500 futures index at 1,500.
>Buy one S&P 500 futures January (following year) 1,600 LEAPS call.

Bullish to end of quarter; at-the-money long call.
>S&P 500 futures index at 1,500.
>Buy one S&P 500 futures end of March 1,500 call.

Short Put (Chapter 10)

Bullish on market; at-the-money short put.
>S&P 500 futures at 1,500.
>Sell one S&P 500 futures March 1,500 put.

Bullish on market; slightly-out-of-the-money short put.
>S&P 500 futures at 1,500.
>Sell one S&P 500 futures March 1,450 put.

Bullish on market; far-out-of-the-money short put.
>S&P 500 futures at 1,500.
>Sell one S&P 500 futures March 1,300 put.

Bullish on blue chips; slightly-in-the-money short put.
>DJ at 14,000.
>Sell one DJ March 14,500 put.

Bullish on blue chips; far-out-of-the-money short put.
>DJ at 14,000.
>Sell one DJ March 12,000 put.

Bullish on small caps; at-the-money short put.
>Russell 2000 futures at 800.
>Sell one Russell 2000 futures March 800 put.

Bullish in short run; far-out-of-the-money short put.
    S&P 500 futures at 1,500.
    Sell one S&P 500 futures Weeklys 1,400 put.
Bullish on technology; far-out-of-the-money short put.
    NASDAQ 100 futures at 2,000.
    Sell one NASDAQ 100 futures March 1,750 put.
Bullish on small caps; far-out-of-the-money short put.
    Russell 2000 futures at 800.
    Sell one Russell 2000 futures March 700 put.
Bullish on market; slightly-in-the-money short put.
    S&P 500 futures at 1,500.
    Sell one E-Mini S&P 500 futures February 1,550 put.
Bullish on technology; at-the-money short put.
    NASDAQ 100 futures at 2,000.
    Sell one E-Mini NASDAQ 100 futures March 2,000 put.
Bullish on small caps; at-the-money short put.
    Russell 2000 futures at 800.
    Sell one E-Mini Russell 2000 futures March 800 put.
Bullish in long run; far-out-of-the-money short put.
    S&P 500 futures index at 1,500.
    Sell one S&P 500 futures January (following year) 1,400 LEAPS put.
Bullish to end of quarter; at-the-money short put.
    S&P 500 futures index at 1,500.
    Sell one S&P 500 futures end of March Quarterlys 1,500 put.

Call Debit Spread (Chapter 11)

Bullish on market; call vertical debit spread.
    S&P 500 futures at 1,500.
    Buy one S&P 500 futures March 1,500 call.
    Sell one S&P 500 futures March 1,550 call.
Bullish on market; call vertical debit spread.
    S&P 500 March futures at 1,500.
    Buy one E-Mini S&P 500 futures March 1,500 call.
    Sell one E-Mini S&P 500 futures March 1,550 call.
Bullish on small caps; call vertical debit spread.
    Russell 2000 futures at 800.
    Buy one Russell 2000 futures March 780 call.
    Sell one Russell 2000 futures March 850 call.
Bullish on technology stocks; call vertical debit spread.
    NASDAQ 100 March futures at 2,000.
    Buy one NASDAQ 100 futures March 1,900 call.
    Sell one NASDAQ 100 futures March 2,150 call.

Put Credit Spread (Chapter 11)

Bullish on market; put vertical credit spread.
    S&P 500 futures at 1,500.
    Sell one S&P 500 futures March 1,400 put.
    Buy one S&P 500 futures March 1,325 put.

Bullish on market; put vertical credit spread.
    S&P 500 March futures at 1,500.
    Sell one E-Mini S&P 500 futures March 1,475 put.
    Buy one E-Mini S&P 500 futures March 1,375 put.
Bullish on small caps; put vertical credit spread.
    Russell 2000 futures at 800.
    Sell one Russell 2000 futures March 750 put.
    Buy one Russell 2000 futures March 700 put.
Bullish on technology stocks; put vertical credit spread.
    NASDAQ 100 March futures at 2,000.
    Sell one NASDAQ 100 futures March 2,000 put.
    Buy one NASDAQ 100 futures March 1,900 put.

Call Backspread (Chapter 13)

Bullish on market; call backspread.
    S&P 500 futures at 1,500.
    Sell one S&P 500 futures March 1,500 call.
    Buy five S&P 500 futures March 1,550 calls.
Bullish on technology stocks; call backspread.
    NASDAQ 100 March futures at 2,000.
    Sell one NASDAQ 100 futures March 2,050 call.
    Buy six NASDAQ 100 futures March 2,120 calls.

Put Ratio (Front) Spread (Chapter 13)

Bullish on market; put ratio (front) spread.
    S&P 500 futures at 1,500.
    Buy one S&P 500 futures March 1,500 put.
    Sell three S&P 500 futures March 1,450 puts.
Bullish on technology stocks; put ratio (front) spread.
    NASDAQ 100 March futures at 2,000.
    Buy one NASDAQ 100 futures March 2,000 put.
    Sell three NASDAQ 100 futures March 1,900 puts.

Diagonal Spread (Chapter 18)

Bullish on market; diagonal long call debit spread.
    S&P 500 futures at 1,500.
    Buy one S&P 500 futures March 1,500 call.
    Sell one S&P 500 futures April 1,600 call.
Bullish on small caps; double diagonal long call debit spread.
    Russell 2000 futures at 800.
    Buy one Russell 2000 futures February 780 call.
    Sell one Russell 2000 futures April 850 call.

Covered Call (Chapter 19)

Moderately bullish on market; covered call.
    S&P 500 futures at 1,500.
    Buy one S&P 500 futures at 1,500.
    Sell one S&P 500 futures March 1,550 call.

Long Combination (Chapter 20)

Bullish on market; long combination.
  S&P 500 futures at 1,500.
  Buy one S&P 500 futures March 1,550 call.
  Sell one S&P 500 futures March 1,450 put.

Covered Combination (Chapter 22)

Bullish on market; long covered combination.
  S&P 500 futures at 1,500.
  Buy one S&P 500 futures at 1,500.
  Sell one S&P 500 futures March 1,550 call.
  Sell one S&P 500 futures March 1,450 put.

BEARISH STOCK INDEX FUTURES STRATEGIES

Long Put (Chapter 8)

Bearish on market; deep-in-the-money long put.
  S&P 500 futures at 1,500.
  Buy one S&P 500 futures March 1,600 put.
Bearish on market; slightly-in-the-money long put.
  S&P 500 futures at 1,500.
  Buy one S&P 500 futures March 1,550 put.
Bearish on market; at-the-money long put.
  S&P 500 futures at 1,500.
  Buy one S&P 500 futures March 1,500 put.
Bearish on market; slightly-out-of-the-money long put.
  S&P 500 futures at 1,500.
  Buy one S&P 500 futures March 1,450 put.
Bearish on market; far-out-of-the-money long put.
  S&P 500 futures at 1,500.
  Buy one S&P 500 futures March 1,400 put.
Bearish on blue chips; slightly-in-the-money long put.
  DJ at 14,000.
  Buy one DJ March 14,500 put.
Bearish on market; far-out-of-the-money long put.
  S&P 500 futures at 1,500.
  Buy one E-Mini S&P 500 futures March 1,400 call.
Bearish on small caps; at-the-money long put.
  Russell 2000 futures at 800.
  Buy one Russell 2000 futures March 800 put.
Bearish in short run; at-the-money long put.
  S&P 500 futures at 1,500.
  Buy one S&P 500 futures February 1,500 put.
Bearish on technology; slightly-in-the-money long put.
  NASDAQ 100 March futures at 2,000.
  Buy one NASDAQ 100 futures March 2,050 put.

Bearish on small caps; far-out-of-the-money long put.
    Russell 2000 futures at 800.
    Buy one Russell 2000 futures March 700 put.
Bearish on market; slightly-in-the-money long put.
    S&P 500 futures at 1,500.
    Buy one E-Mini S&P 500 futures March 1,525 put.
Bearish on technology; at-the-money long put.
    NASDAQ 100 futures at 2,000.
    Buy one E-Mini NASDAQ 100 futures March 2,000 put.
Bearish on small caps; at-the-money long put.
    Russell 2000 futures at 800.
    Buy one E-Mini Russell 2000 futures March 800 put.
Bearish in long run; far-out-of-the-money long put.
    S&P 500 futures index at 1,500.
    Buy one S&P 500 futures January (following year) 1,400 LEAPS put.
Bearish to end of month; at-the-money long put.
    S&P 500 futures index at 1,500.
    Buy one S&P 500 futures end of February 1,500 put.

Short Call (Chapter 9)

Bearish on market; at-the-money short call.
    S&P 500 futures at 1,500.
    Sell one S&P 500 futures March 1,500 call.
Bearish on market; slightly-out-of-the-money short call.
    S&P 500 futures at 1,500.
    Sell one S&P 500 futures March 1,550 call.
Bearish on market; far-out-of-the-money short call.
    S&P 500 futures at 1,500.
    Sell one S&P 500 futures March 1,600 call.
Bearish on market; far-out-of-the-money short call.
    S&P 500 futures at 1,500.
    Sell one S&P 500 futures June 1,700 call.
Bearish on blue chips; slightly-in-the-money short call.
    DJ at 14,000.
    Sell one DJ March 13,500 call.
Bearish on blue chips; far-out-of-the-money short call.
    DJ at 14,000.
    Sell one DJ March 15,000 call.
Bearish on small caps; at-the-money short call.
    Russell 2000 futures at 800.
    Sell one Russell 2000 futures March 800 call.
Bearish in short run; far-out-of-the-money short call.
    S&P 500 futures at 1,500.
    Sell one S&P 500 futures February 1,550 call.
Bearish on technology; far-out-of-the-money short call.
    NASDAQ 100 March futures at 2,000.
    Sell one NASDAQ 100 futures March 2,200 call.
Bearish on small caps; far-out-of-the-money short call.
    Russell 2000 futures at 800.
    Sell one Russell 2000 futures March 900 call.

Bearish on market; slightly-in-the-money short call.
    S&P 500 futures at 1,500.
    Sell one E-Mini S&P 500 futures March 1,450 call.
Bearish on technology; at-the-money short call.
    NASDAQ 100 futures at 2,000.
    Sell one E-Mini NASDAQ 100 futures March 2,000 call.
Bearish on small caps; at-the-money short call.
    Russell 2000 futures at 800.
    Sell one E-Mini Russell 2000 futures March 800 call.
Bearish in long run; far-out-of-the-money short call.
    S&P 500 futures index at 1,500.
    Sell one S&P 500 futures January (following year) 1,600 LEAPS call.
Bearish to end of quarter; at-the-money short call.
    S&P 500 futures index at 1,500.
    Sell one S&P 500 futures end of March 1,500 call.

Call Credit Spread (Chapter 11)

Bearish on market; call vertical credit spread.
    S&P 500 futures at 1,500.
    Sell one S&P 500 futures March 1,500 call.
    Buy one S&P 500 futures March 1,550 call.
Bearish on market; call vertical credit spread.
    S&P 500 March futures at 1,500.
    Sell one E-Mini S&P 500 futures February 1,500 call.
    Buy one E-Mini S&P 500 futures February 1,550 call.
Bearish on small caps; call vertical credit spread.
    Russell 2000 futures at 800.
    Sell one Russell 2000 futures March 800 call.
    Buy one Russell 2000 futures March 840 call.
Bearish on technology stocks; call vertical credit spread.
    NASDAQ 100 March futures at 2,000.
    Sell one NASDAQ 100 futures March 2,000 call.
    Buy one NASDAQ 100 futures March 2,150 call.

Put Debit Spread (Chapter 11)

Bearish on market; put vertical debit spread.
    S&P 500 futures at 1,500.
    Buy one S&P 500 futures March 1,450 put.
    Sell one S&P 500 futures March 1,350 put.
Bearish on market; put vertical debit spread.
    S&P 500 March futures at 1,500.
    Buy one E-Mini S&P 500 futures February 1,475 put.
    Sell one E-Mini S&P 500 futures February 1,375 put.
Bearish on small caps; put vertical debit spread.
    Russell 2000 futures at 800.
    Buy one Russell 2000 futures March 800 put.
    Sell one Russell 2000 futures March 760 put.

Bearish on technology stocks; put vertical debit spread.
 NASDAQ 100 March futures at 2,000.
 Buy one NASDAQ 100 futures March 2,000 put.
 Sell one NASDAQ 100 futures March 1,900 put.

Put Backspread (Chapter 13)

Bearish on market; put backspread.
 S&P 500 futures at 1,500.
 Sell one S&P 500 futures March 1,500 put.
 Buy five S&P 500 futures March 1,450 puts.
Bearish on technology stocks; put backspread.
 NASDAQ 100 March futures at 2,000.
 Sell one NASDAQ 100 futures March 2,000 put.
 Buy eight NASDAQ 100 futures March 1,880 puts.

Call Ratio (Front) Spread (Chapter 13)

Bearish on market; call ratio (front) spread.
 S&P 500 futures at 1,500.
 Buy one S&P 500 index (SPX) March 1,500 call.
 Sell five SPX March 1,550 calls.
Bearish on technology stocks; call ratio (front) spread.
 NASDAQ 100 March futures at 2,000.
 Buy one NASDAQ 100 futures March 2,000 call.
 Sell eight NASDAQ 100 futures March 2,100 calls.

Diagonal Spread (Chapter 18)

Bearish on market; diagonal long put debit spread.
 S&P 500 futures at 1,500.
 Buy one S&P 500 futures March 1,500 put.
 Sell one S&P 500 futures April 1,450 put.
Bearish on small caps; double diagonal long put debit spread.
 Russell 2000 futures at 800.
 Buy one Russell 2000 futures February 800 put.
 Sell one Russell 2000 futures April 750 put.

Covered Call (Chapter 19)

Moderately bearish on market; covered call.
 S&P 500 futures at 1,500.
 Buy one S&P 500 futures at 1,500.
 Sell one S&P 500 futures March 1,525 call.

Short Combination (Chapter 20)

Bearish on market; short combination.
 S&P 500 futures at 1,500.
 Sell one S&P 500 futures March 1,525 call.
 Buy one S&P 500 futures March 1,475 put.

Covered Combination (Chapter 22)

Bearish on market; short covered combination.
   S&P 500 futures at 1,500.
   Sell one S&P 500 futures at 1,500.
   Buy one S&P 500 futures March 1,525 call.
   Buy one S&P 500 futures March 1,475 put.

TRADING OUTSIDE A RANGE

Long Iron Condor (Chapter 12)

Bullish on volatility; long iron condor.
   S&P 500 futures at 1,500.
   Buy one S&P 500 futures March 1,550 call.
   Sell one S&P 500 futures March 1,600 call.
   Buy one S&P 500 futures March 1,450 put.
   Sell one S&P 500 futures March 1,400 put.

Long Straddle and Strangle (Chapter 14)

Bullish on volatility; long straddle.
   S&P 500 futures at 1,500.
   Buy one S&P 500 futures March 1,500 call.
   Buy one S&P 500 futures March 1,500 put.
Bullish on volatility; unbalanced long straddle.
   S&P 500 futures at 1,500.
   Buy two S&P 500 futures March 1,500 calls.
   Buy one S&P 500 futures March 1,500 put.
Bullish on volatility; long straddle.
   S&P 500 futures at 1,500.
   Buy one S&P 500 futures end of March end of month 1,500 call.
   Buy one S&P 500 futures end of March end of month 1,500 put.
Bullish on volatility; long straddle.
   S&P 500 futures at 1,500.
   Buy one S&P 500 futures February end of month 1,500 call.
   Buy one S&P 500 futures February end of month 1,500 put.
Bullish on volatility; long strangle.
   S&P 500 futures at 1,500.
   Buy one S&P 500 futures March 1,525 call.
   Buy one S&P 500 futures March 1,400 put.
Bullish on volatility; unbalanced long strangle.
   S&P 500 futures at 1,500.
   Buy one S&P 500 futures March 1,575 call.
   Buy three S&P 500 futures March 1,450 puts.

Short Butterfly (Chapter 15)

Bullish on volatility; short call butterfly.
   DJ at 14,000.
   Sell one DJ March 13,800 call.

Buy two DJ March 14,000 calls.
Sell one DJ March 14,200 call.
Bullish on volatility; short put butterfly.
DJ at 14,000.
Sell one DJ March 14,200 put.
Buy two DJ March 14,000 puts.
Sell one DJ March 13,800 put.
Bullish on volatility; short broken wing call butterfly.
DJ at 14,000.
Sell one DJ March 13,800 call.
Buy two DJ March 14,000 calls.
Sell one DJ March 14,400 call.
Bullish on volatility; iron butterfly.
S&P 500 futures at 1,500.
Buy one S&P 500 futures March 1,500 call.
Sell one S&P 500 futures March 1,600 call.
Buy one S&P 500 futures March 1,500 put.
Sell one S&P 500 futures March 1,400 put.

Short Condor (Chapter 16)

Bullish on volatility; short call condor.
DJ at 14,000.
Sell one DJ March 13,800 call.
Buy one DJ March 14,000 call.
Buy one DJ March 14,200 call.
Sell one DJ March 14,400 call.
Bullish on volatility; short put condor.
DJ at 14,000.
Sell one DJ March 14,400 put.
Buy one DJ March 14,200 put.
Buy one DJ March 14,000 put.
Sell one DJ March 13,800 put.

Ladder (Chapter 16)

Bullish on volatility; ladder.
Russell 2000 futures at 800.
Sell one Russell 2000 futures March 780 call.
Buy one Russell 2000 futures March 800 call.
Buy one Russell 2000 futures March 820 call.

Short Calendar Spread (Chapter 17)

Bullish on volatility; short call calendar spread.
NASDAQ 100 March futures at 2,000.
Buy one NASDAQ 100 futures February 2,000 call.
Sell one NASDAQ 100 futures March 2,000 call.

Bullish on volatility; short put calendar spread.
 NASDAQ 100 March futures at 2,000.
 Buy one NASDAQ 100 futures February 2,000 put.
 Sell one NASDAQ 100 futures March 2,000 put.

Volatility Index (Chapter 27)

Bullish on volatility; at-the-money long call.
 CBOE Volatility index (VIX) at 20.
 Buy one VIX March 20 call.
Bullish on volatility; at-the-money short put.
 VIX at 20.
 Sell one VIX March 20 put.

TRADING INSIDE A RANGE

Short Iron Condor (Chapter 12)

Bearish on volatility; short iron condor.
 S&P 500 futures at 1,500.
 Sell one SPX March 1,550 call.
 Buy one SPX March 1,600 call.
 Sell one SPX March 1,450 put.
 Buy one SPX March 1,400 put.

Short Straddle and Strangle (Chapter 14)

Bearish on volatility; short straddle.
 SPX at 1,500.
 Sell one S&P 500 futures March 1,500 call.
 Sell one S&P 500 futures March 1,500 put.
Bearish on volatility; unbalanced short straddle.
 S&P 500 futures at 1,500.
 Sell three S&P 500 futures March 1,500 calls.
 Sell one S&P 500 futures March 1,500 put.
Bearish on volatility; short straddle.
 S&P 500 futures at 1,500.
 Sell one S&P 500 futures end of March 1,500 call.
 Sell one S&P 500 futures end of March 1,500 put.
Bearish on volatility; short straddle.
 S&P 500 futures at 1,500.
 Sell one S&P 500 futures February end of month 1,500 call.
 Sell one S&P 500 futures February end of month 1,500 put.
Bearish on volatility; short strangle.
 S&P 500 futures at 1,500.
 Sell one S&P 500 futures March 1,575 call.
 Sell one S&P 500 futures March 1,400 put.

Bearish on volatility; short strangle.
  S&P 500 futures at 1,500.
  Sell one S&P 500 futures March 1,600 call.
  Sell one S&P 500 futures March 1,350 put.
Bearish on volatility; unbalanced short strangle.
  S&P 500 futures at 1,500.
  Sell one S&P 500 futures March 1,550 call.
  Sell two S&P 500 futures March 1,400 puts.

Long Butterfly (Chapter 15)

Bearish on volatility; long call butterfly.
  DJ at 14,000.
  Buy one DJ March 13,800 call.
  Sell two DJ March 14,000 calls.
  Buy one DJ March 14,200 call.
Bearish on volatility; long put butterfly.
  DJ at 14,000.
  Buy one DJ March 14,200 put.
  Sell two DJ March 14,000 puts.
  Buy one DJ March 13,800 put.
Bearish on volatility; long broken-wing call butterfly.
  DJ at 14,000.
  Buy one DJ March 13,800 call.
  Sell two DJ March 14,000 calls.
  Buy one DJ March 14,400 call.
Bearish on volatility; iron butterfly.
  S&P 500 futures at 1,500.
  Sell one S&P 500 futures March 1,500 call.
  Buy one S&P 500 futures March 1,600 call.
  Sell one S&P 500 futures March 1,500 put.
  Buy one S&P 500 futures March 1,400 put.

Long Condor (Chapter 16)

Bearish on volatility; long call condor.
  DJ at 14,000.
  Buy one DJ March 13,800 call.
  Sell one DJ March 14,000 call.
  Sell one DJ March 14,200 call.
  Buy one DJ March 14,400 call.
Bearish on volatility; long put condor.
  DJ at 14,000.
  Buy one DJ March 14,400 put.
  Sell one DJ March 14,200 put.
  Sell one DJ March 14,000 put.
  Buy one DJ March 13,800 put.

Ladder (Chapter 16)

Bearish on volatility; ladder.
  Russell 2000 futures at 800.
  Buy one Russell 2000 futures March 780 call.
  Sell one Russell 2000 futures March 800 call.
  Sell one Russell 2000 futures March 820 call.

Long Calendar Spread (Chapter 17)

Bearish on volatility; long call calendar spread.
  NASDAQ 100 March futures at 2,000.
  Sell one NASDAQ 100 futures February 2,000 call.
  Buy one NASDAQ 100 futures March 2,000 call.
Bearish on volatility; long put calendar spread.
  NASDAQ 100 March futures at 2,000.
  Sell one NASDAQ 100 futures February 2,000 put.
  Buy one NASDAQ 100 futures March 2,000 put.

Covered Call (Chapter 19)

Moderately bearish on volatility; covered call.
  S&P 500 futures at 1,500.
  Buy one S&P 500 futures at 1,500.
  Sell one S&P 500 futures March 1,525 call.

Collar (Chapter 21)

Bearish on volatility; collar.
  S&P 500 futures at 1,500.
  Buy one S&P 500 futures at 1,500.
  Sell one S&P 500 futures March 1,525 call.
  Buy one S&P 500 futures March 1,475 put.

Volatility Index (Chapter 27)

Bearish on volatility; at-the-money long put.
  VIX at 20.
  Buy one VIX March 20 put.
Bearish on volatility; at-the-money short call.
  VIX at 20.
  Sell one VIX March 20 call.

Glossary

all-or-none order A market or limit order that is to be executed in its entirety or not at all. If you place a straight limit order for more than one contract, you may be filled on a portion of your order. To prevent this from occurring, you can place an all-or-none limit order, so that you will not be filled unless you are executed on all options at your limit price or better.

A.M. settlement A settlement style in which the exercise settlement value of an index option is determined based on the opening prices of the component securities.

American-style option An option that can be exercised on or before the expiration date.

ask See *bid/ask.*

assignment The receipt of an exercise notice by an option writer that obligates the writer to sell (in the case of a call) or buy (in the case of a put) the underlying instrument. For an index, an assignment obligates the writer to pay (in the case of a call or put) the exercise settlement amount.

at-the-money An option with a strike price that is the same as, or closest to, the current trading price of the underlying stock. For example, if XYZ stock is trading at $100 per share, the May 100 call and May 100 put are at-the-money. If XYZ stock is trading at $99 per share, the May 100 call and May 100 put options are still considered at-the-money.

automatic exercise An option that will be exercised automatically on the option expiration date if it is in-the-money by a specified amount, absent instructions to the contrary.

backspread A spread in which more options are bought than sold; for example, sell one XYZ April 100 call and buy two XYZ April 110 calls.

basis The difference between the cash price of an underlying instrument and the price of the near-term futures contract for the same underlying instrument. The carrying charges represent an interest (and dividend) component that is added (or subtracted) to the cash index to determine the fair value of the futures contract. For example, if the cash market S&P 500 index is at 1,500 and the S&P 500 futures fair value is at 1,505, the basis is 5.

bear An individual who expects a decline in prices. The opposite of a bull.

bear call spread A call spread with the intention of profiting from a decline in the underlying instrument. A call is sold at one strike price and a call is purchased at a higher strike price, generally with the same expiration date. All options are of the same class (calls or puts); for example, sell one February 100 call and buy one February 110 call.

bear put spread A put spread with the intention of profiting from a decline in the underlying instrument. A put is purchased at one strike price and a put is sold at a lower strike price, generally with the same expiration date. All options are of the same class (calls or puts); for example, buy one February 100 put and sell one February 90 put.

bear spread Any spread with the intention of profiting from a decline in the underlying instrument. Typically involves the simultaneous purchase and sale of options of the same class (calls or puts) and expiration date but different strike prices; for example, sell one February 100 call and buy one February 110 call.

bid See *bid/ask*.

bid/ask. When selling an option at the market, you will likely sell at the bid price. When buying an option at the market, you will likely pay at the ask price. A bid price is an offer from the market to buy from you a specific quantity of an option or other instrument at a stated price. It is the highest price the market is prepared to pay a seller at a particular time for a given option or other instrument. The ask price is an offer from the market to sell to you a specific quantity of an option or other instrument at a stated price. It is the lowest price the market is prepared to sell to a buyer at a particular time for a given option or other instrument. For example, if the bid/ask price is 3.00/3.50, a market order to sell can be expected to be filled at $3.00 and a market order to buy can be expected to be filled at $3.50.

bid/ask spread The difference between the bid and ask prices; for example, if the bid/ask price is 3.00/3.50, the spread is $0.50, the difference between the $3.00 bid price and $3.50 ask price.

Black-Scholes model An option pricing model initially developed by Fischer Black and Myron Scholes for options on securities. The Black-Scholes model determines the Greeks.

breakeven The point (or points) where the underlying stock must rise or fall for an option position to have no gain or loss, usually at expiration of the option. When buying a call, the break-even point is typically where the underlying stock, at the expiration date, equals the strike price plus the premium paid for the option contract. When buying a put, the break-even point is typically where the underlying stock, at the expiration date, equals the strike price minus the premium paid. For example, assume XYZ stock is trading at $100 and the price of the XYZ February 105 call is $2. The buyer, at the expiration date of the option, has a break-even point at a stock price of $107 (105 strike price plus $2 premium paid).

broad-based index An index that measures moves in a broad, diverse market; any index of securities that does not meet the legal definition of a narrow-based security index.

bull An individual who expects a rise in prices. The opposite of a bear.

bull call spread A call spread with the intention of profiting from a rise in the underlying instrument. A call is sold at one strike price and a call is purchased at a higher strike price, generally with the same expiration date. All options are of the same class (calls or puts); for example, buy one February 100 call and sell one February 110 call.

bull put spread A put spread with the intention of profiting from a rise in the underlying instrument. A put is sold at one strike price and a put is purchased at a lower strike price, generally with the same expiration date. All options are of the same class (calls or puts); for example, sell one February 100 put and buy one February 90 put.

bull spread Any spread with the intention of profiting from a rise in the underlying instrument. Typically involves the simultaneous purchase and sale of options of the same class (calls or puts) and expiration date but different strike prices; for example, buy one February 100 call and sell one February 110 call.

butterfly spread Consists of options at three equally spaced exercise prices, where all options expire at the same time. In a long butterfly, the same number of outside exercise prices are purchased, and twice the number of the inside exercise prices are sold; for example, buy one February 95 call, sell two February 100 calls, and buy one February 105 call. In a short butterfly, the same number of outside exercise prices are sold and twice the number of the inside exercise prices are purchased; for example, sell one February 95 call, buy two February 100 calls, and sell one February 105 call.

buy to close   A transaction to offset a short option position; for example, if you are short one February 100 call, you can enter an order as buy to close by buying one February 100 call.

buyer   The purchaser of an option or underlying instrument. A buyer takes on a long position. An option buyer is also called a holder or owner.

buy-write   A covered-call strategy where the stock purchase and option sale occur in the same transaction.

calendar spread   In a long calendar spread, the near-term option is sold and the longer-term option is purchased; for example, sell one XYZ February 100 call and buy one XYZ March 100 call. In a short calendar spread, the near-term option is purchased and the longer-term option is sold; for example, buy one February 100 call and sell one March 100 call. A calendar spread is also called a horizontal spread or a time spread. A short calendar spread is also called a *reverse time spread*.

call   An option contract giving the buyer the right, but not the obligation, to purchase an underlying instrument (e.g., a stock, ETF, or futures contract) on or before an expiration date at the strike price. If an index, it is an option contract providing the owner (holder) the right to receive, on exercise of the option, the exercise settlement amount.

called   Another term for exercised.

cancel order   An order that attempts to cancel an existing order. This also may be called a straight cancel, which means that the order being canceled is not being replaced with another order.

cancel/replace order   An order that attempts to cancel an existing order and replace it with another order.

capitalization-weighted index   An equity index in which more highly capitalized issues are proportionally weighted more heavily than the lesser-capitalized components.

cash market   The traditional stock and option markets where buying and selling is in the cash market, as contrasted to the futures market. Also called the *spot market*.

cash settlement   Process in which index options require the payment or receipt of cash for the amount the option is in-the-money, as opposed to the delivering or receipt of the underlying instrument.

CBOE   The Chicago Board Options Exchange.

class of option   Option contract of the same type (call or put) and style (American versus European) that covers the same underlying instrument.

close   The liquidation (offset) of an existing long or short option position with an equal and opposite transaction; for example, if you are long one February 100 call, you can close it out by selling one February 100 call. Also known as offset.

collar   A strategy in which you own underlying shares, write a call on those shares, and, at the same time, purchase a protective put to limit risk. The calls and puts have the same expiration date and are typically out-of-the-money compared to the current stock price. A collar strategy combines a covered call and a protective put; for example, if you own XYZ stock trading at $100 a share, you might establish a 105/95 collar in which you write a 105 call and purchase a 95 put. The collar is protection below the 95 strike price, but the upside participation is capped at 105 per share.

combination   A combination can be described as any option strategy using both puts and calls not defined elsewhere. A combination (sometimes called a combo) can be established by selling a put and buying a call (long combination) or by selling a call and buying a put (short combination). For example, a 105/95 long combination consists of a long 105 call and a short 95 put, and a 105/95 short combination consists of a short 105 call and a long 95 put.

condor A four-legged option spread in which options are at four equally spaced exercise prices, where all options expire at the same time. A long condor spread might consist of one long call at a 95 strike price, one short call at a 100 strike price, one short call at a 105 strike price, and one long call at a 110 strike price.

covered call A covered call is a strategy in which you own stock and then sell at-the-money or out-of-the-money calls in proportion to the shares owned. For example, if you own 1,000 shares of XYZ stock, you can write up to 10 call options in a covered call transaction.

covered call write A covered call write or a buy-write (also called covered stock) strategy is a version of a covered-call strategy where the stock purchase and option sale occur as part of the same transaction. Your trading platform may include the ability to execute a buy-right order; for example, if a stock is trading at $100 a share and a call is selling at $2, you can enter a single order to execute the transaction at $98 or better. As a result of entering a limit order in this manner, you will not be executed on only one side of the transaction unless the other side of the transaction is also executed.

covered combination A combination in which you are also long or short the underlying instrument; for example, you might establish a 105/95 covered short combination in which you buy 100 shares of stock, write a 105 call, and write a 95 put.

covered option An option position is typically considered covered if there is a fully offsetting opposite market position; for example, a short call is considered covered if you are also long a call at the same or lower strike price on the same stock. However, the word covered is also used to indicate whether underlying stock is owned; for example, a short call is considered covered if you also long the stock (covered-call strategy).

covered put A covered put is the mirror image of the covered call. A covered put is a strategy in which you are short stock and then sell at-the-money or out-of-the-money puts in proportion to the shorted shares. For example, if you are short 1,000 shares of XYZ stock, you can write up to 10 put options in a covered put transaction.

credit An addition to an account. A premium collected by a seller is reflected as a credit in his account.

credit spread Difference in the value of options, where the value of the sold option(s) exceeds the value of the purchased option(s); the opposite of a debit spread. For example, sell one February 100 call at $5 and buy one February 110 call at $1.

day order An order to buy or sell that expires at the end of the day on which it was entered if it is not executed. All orders are automatically day orders unless otherwise specified; for example, you can place an order to buy one February 100 call at a limit of $5. If the order is not executed at the close of trading for that day, it is automatically canceled and does not carry over to any other trading day.

debit A subtraction to an account. A premium paid by a buyer is reflected as a debit in his account.

debit spread Difference in the value of options, where the value of the purchased option(s) exceeds the value of the sold option(s). The opposite of a credit spread. For example, buy one February 100 call at $5 and sell one February 110 call at $1.

delta One of the Greeks. The fractional change in an option value in response to a one-point increase in the price of the underlying stock at any given moment, assuming all other variables are constant. For example, an option price with a delta of 0.50 would be expected to increase $0.50 when the underlying instrument rises $1.00.

delta-neutral An option strategy that attempts to profit from a trading range (nondirectional) is, in many cases, called delta-neutral because a loss on one leg (or side) of the position is approximately offset by another leg (or side), as long as the underlying stock stays within a trading range. Such a strategy attempts to take advantage of time decay and/or volatility contraction while attempting to minimize fluctuations in the account position. The option position has an overall position delta of zero (or close to zero). In contrast, directional trading speculates on the direction of the underlying instrument, in contrast to volatility or delta-neutral trading.

derivative   A financial instrument, the price of which is directly dependent on (i.e., derived from) the value of another. Derivatives involve the trading of rights or obligations but do not directly transfer property. Derivatives include futures and options.

diagonal spread   A diagonal is a spread with different strike prices and also different expiration dates; for example, buy one XYZ February 100 call and sell one XYZ March 110 call. A diagonal consists of either all call or all put options

directional trading   Trading strategies designed to speculate on the direction of the underlying instrument, in contrast to volatility or delta-neutral trading.

distant or deferred month   The later (longer-term) expiring option on a spread.

double diagonal spread   Defined broadly to include a diagonal spread where there is a difference by at least two strike prices and two expiration dates, such as buy one XYZ February 100 call and sell one XYZ July 110 call.

early exercise   Exercise of an option by an owner (holder) prior to when an option expires.

E-Mini   A contract electronically traded in which the futures contract has a smaller contract size than an otherwise identical futures contract; for example, the S&P 500 futures contract (and its options) is $250 a point, whereas its E-Mini contract is $50 a point. The NASDAQ 100 futures index (and its options) is $100 a point, whereas its E-Mini contract is $20 a point. The Russell 2000 futures index (and its options) is $500 a point, whereas its E-Mini contract is $100 a point.

equivalent position   Option positions that, when combined together, attain the same profit potential as other positions. Equivalent positions have profit and loss graphs with the same shape.

ETF   See *exchange-traded fund*.

European-style option   An option that may be exercised only on the expiration date.

exchange-traded fund (ETF)   An investment product that generally tracks an index and can be traded like a stock. An ETF that moves at a higher percentage rate than the underlying index is sometimes named "Ultra." Inversely correlated ETFs move in the opposite direction of the underlying index.

exercise   To invoke the right that has been granted under an option contract. A call owner exercises his right to buy an underlying instrument; a put owner exercises his right to sell an underlying instrument.

exercise notice   Notification by a broker of assignment.

exercise price   Same as *strike price*. The prices at which a call owner can exercise his right to buy an underlying instrument or the price at which a put holder can exercise his right to sell the underlying instrument. The strike price (or exercise price) of a cash-settled option is the base for determining the amount of cash, if any, that the option holder is entitled to receive on exercise.

exercise settlement amount   The difference between the exercise price of an index option and the exercise settlement value of the index on the day an exercise notice is tendered (multiplied by the index multiplier). The call (and put) owner for an index provides the owner the right to receive, on exercise of the option, the exercise settlement amount.

exercise settlement value   The price level of an underlying equity index used to calculate the exercise settlement amount.

expiration date   The date on which an option contract automatically expires; the last day an option may be exercised. Technically, the expiration date for equity options is the Saturday immediately after the third Friday of the expiration month. However, the significant date is the third Friday because that is the last day on which an equity option can trade. Saturday is reserved for brokerage firms for paperwork involved with expiration and exercise procedures.

extrinsic value   Also called *time value*. The amount of an option's value that is out-of-the-money. The intrinsic value of an option is the amount the current price for the underlying stock is above the strike price of a call option or below the strike price of a put option. The remainder of the option premium is extrinsic value. For example, assume that a stock is selling at $100 and that a call option with a strike price of 95 is selling for $6. The intrinsic value is $5 and the extrinsic value is $1.

fill-or-kill order   An order that demands immediate execution or it is canceled.

floor broker   A person with exchange trading privileges who executes for another person orders for the purchase or sale of any futures or futures option contracts.

front month   The nearest traded contract month in a spread.

front spread   Also called a *ratio spread*. A spread in which more options are sold than bought, for example, buy one XYZ February 100 call and sell two XYZ February 110 calls.

futures   An agreement (contract) to purchase or sell a commodity for delivery in the future at a price that is determined at initiation of the contract. It obligates each party to the contract to fulfill the contract at the specified price and may be satisfied by offset.

futures commission merchant (FCM)   Entity that solicits or accepts orders for the purchase or sale of any commodity for future delivery subject to the rules of any exchange and that accepts payment from or extends credit to those whose orders are accepted.

futures option   An option on a futures contract.

gamma   One of the Greeks. Gamma measures the change in the delta of an option as a result of a one-point increase in the stock.

good-until-canceled order   An order to buy or sell that remains in force until the order is filled, canceled, or the option contract expires. All orders are either day or good-until-canceled (open) orders.

grantor   The writer (seller) of an option contract obligated to sell the underlying instrument in the case of a call option or purchase the underlying instrument in the case of a put option.

Greeks   The Greeks measure the sensitivity of an option from a small change in price in the underlying stock, time, volatility, and interest rate. The main Greeks are delta (measures the change in the price of an option in response to a one-point increase in the underlying stock), gamma (measures the change in the delta of an option resulting from a one-point increase in the underlying stock), theta (measures the change in the price of an option from the passage of one day in time), and vega (measures the change in the price of an option from a one-point increase in implied volatility). Another Greek, rho, measures the sensitivity of an option value from a one-point increase in the assumed interest rate.

hedging   A position held to minimize the risk of financial loss from an adverse price change. One can hedge either a long position or a short position.

historical volatility   A statistical measure of the volatility of an underlying instrument over a specified period of time. The word volatility can refer to the volatility of the underlying stock price (historical or realized volatility) or to the volatility component implicit in an option price (implied volatility).

holder   The purchaser (owner) of an option.

horizontal spread A *calendar spread*.

implied volatility The volatility built into the price of an option measured in terms of annual standard deviation. Implied volatility of an option can be defined as one standard deviation price change, in percentage terms, over one year. The word volatility can refer to the volatility of the underlying stock price (historical) or to the volatility component implicit in an option price (implied volatility). Implied volatility is built into an option's price by the marketplace and measures how expensive the option is after first taking into account the other option pricing factors.

index A compilation of stock prices into a single number used as a benchmark against which financial or economic performance is measured.

index option An option contract that has an equity index as its underlying instrument.

instrument A stock, security, index, ETF, or futures that is used as a basis to derive an option's value.

in-the-money An option that has intrinsic value; for example, if XYZ stock is trading at $100, the May 95 call is $5 in-the-money and the May 105 put is $5 in-the-money.

intrinsic value The amount by which an option is in-the-money. The amount that an underlying instrument is below the strike price of a call or above the strike price of a put. The remainder of the option premium is extrinsic value; for example, assume that a stock is selling at $100 and that a call option with a strike price of 95 is selling for $6. The intrinsic value is $5 and the extrinsic value is $1.

iron condor Consists of four legs. In a long iron condor, you buy a vertical call spread and a vertical put spread; for example, buy one February 105/115 call spread and buy one February 85/95 put spread. In a short iron condor, you sell a vertical call spread and a vertical put spread; for example, sell one February 105/115 call spread and sell one February 85/95 put spread.

leg into a position Method to establish or offset a position one side at a time rather than all at once; for example, instead of selling a February 105/115 call spread in one transaction, you can leg into the position by selling the February 105 first and, in a separate order, buying the February 115 call. You can exit a February 105/115 call spread one leg at a time by offsetting the February 105 leg and, in a separate order, offsetting the February 115 leg.

limited and unlimited risk/reward The words limited and unlimited are used to describe the risks and rewards for options. A long option is a limited-risk strategy because an option buyer cannot lose more than the premium paid. An option buyer is commonly described as having unlimited reward potential based on the theory that there is no limit to how high numbers can go. A naked seller is often described as having limited reward because an option seller cannot gain more than the premium collected. A naked seller is considered to have unlimited risk even though a put seller's risk is mathematically limited to the underlying stock declining to zero.

limit-on-close order An order that executes at a limit price at the close of trading. The order can be filled at the limit price or better, but you are not guaranteed a fill.

limit order An order in which the customer specifies a minimum sale price or maximum purchase price.

liquid market A market in which selling and buying can be accomplished with minimal effect on price. *Liquidity* refers to the ability to buy and sell without having a major impact on price.

liquidate The closing (offsetting) of a long or short position.

long A position that profits when its value rises; the buying side of an option contract; a position in which the trader is a net holder (owner), where the number of contracts bought exceeds the number of contracts sold.

long-term equity anticipation securities (LEAPS)   Long-dated exchange-traded options. Options have option cycles that typically extend to nine months, but the option cycle may also include longer-term options, known as LEAPS. LEAPS are longer-dated options that typically have an expiration date of January of each year. LEAPS have all of the rights and obligations of a traditional option but are longer dated, typically up to three years, giving you an extended period of time in which to invest.

longer-term option   The longer-term option (back month, far month, distant month, or deferred month) is a month after the near-term month, and the near-term month (front month) is the expiration month closer to the present date. For example, for an option spread with expiration dates of February and March, the near-term month is February and the longer-term month is March.

maintenance margin   See *margin*.

margin   The amount an option writer is required to deposit and maintain to cover a position as collateral. Initial margin is the amount of margin required by the broker when a position is opened. Maintenance margin is an amount that must be maintained on deposit after a position is open.

margin call   A request from a brokerage firm to a customer to bring margin deposits up to initial levels.

market-on-close order   An order that executes at the market price at the close of trading.

market order   An order to buy or sell at the best price obtainable at the time an order is entered.

married put   The simultaneous purchase of stock and a protective put; for example, you can place one order to purchase 100 shares of stock and purchase one at-the-money put. If the stock is trading at $100 and the option is trading at $5, then you can place a single order to pay $105.

mini   Refers to an index or futures contract that has a smaller value than a full-size index or futures contract.

naked option   The sale of a call or put option without holding an opposite position to limit potential loss. Also called an uncovered option, naked call, or naked put.

near-term   The near-term (front month) is the expiration month closest to the present date, and the longer-term option (back month, far month, distant month, or deferred month) is a month after the near-term month. For example, for an option spread with expiration dates of February and March, the near-term month is February and the longer-term month is March.

net credit   A position that results in an addition to an account. Implies that the position is net short and benefits from the passage of time and declining volatility; for example, a credit spread, in general, attempts to take advantage of time decay.

net debit   A position that results in a subtraction to an account. Implies that the position is net long and benefits from an increase in volatility; for example, a debit spread, in general, attempts to profit by directional bets.

neutral   A position in which profit is generally achieved by a lack of movement in the underlying instrument (trading range) or from a decline in volatility.

offer price   The ask price. An indication of willingness to sell at a given price; opposite of bid.

offset   The liquidation of an existing long or short option position with an equal and opposite transaction; for example, if you are long one February 100 call, you can close it out (offset it) by selling one February 100 call. Also known as closing.

one-cancels-other order   An order involving two separate orders, where if one order is filled, the other is automatically canceled. You could, for instance, place a one-cancels-other order for a long February 100 call at $5 and a long 100 February put at $4. If the call is executed, the put order is canceled. If the put is executed, the call is canceled.

open interest   The total number of option contracts, long or short, that have not yet been liquidated by an offsetting transaction or fulfilled by delivery.

open order   An order that remains in force until it is canceled or the contract expires.

open outcry   A method of public auction, common to many U.S. commodity (futures) exchanges, where trading occurs on a trading floor. On many products, open outcry is being replaced by electronic trading platforms.

opening   The period at the beginning of the trading session officially designated by the exchange during which all transactions are considered made at the opening.

opportunity cost   The sacrifice made by choosing one alternative over another; for example, if you invest $1,000 in a stock, you forego the alternative opportunity to earn interest on that money.

option   A call or put. A call option is a contract giving the buyer the right, but not the obligation, to purchase an underlying instrument (e.g., a stock, ETF, or futures contract) on or before an expiration date at the strike price. A put option is a contract giving the buyer the right, but not the obligation, to sell an underlying instrument on or before an expiration date at the strike price. If an index, it is an option contract providing the owner (holder) the right to receive, on exercise of the option, the exercise settlement amount on or before an expiration date.

option chain   A list (i.e., chain) of all option prices on a particular underlying instrument, including bid/ask prices, for all strike prices and expiration dates. An option chain will typically show calls on the left side and puts on the right, with the lowest strike price at the top of a page and higher strike prices as you move down the page. You can access an option chain through your broker's trading platform or through the Internet. An option chain is typically a list of option prices at a specific point in time and is similar to a stock screen, except that it has information on option prices.

option cycle   Cycle of months in which option contracts expire on a particular underlying instrument. Options generally expire in the current month and subsequent month plus the months in its cycle. Common cycles are January, April, July, October (JAJO); February, May, August, November (FNAM); and March, June, September, December (MJSD).

option on stock   An option whose underlying instrument is common stock.

option pricing model   A mathematical model used to calculate the theoretical value of an option, including the Greeks. Inputs into option pricing models typically include the price of the underlying instrument, option strike price, time remaining until the expiration date, volatility, and risk-free interest rate. Examples of option pricing models include Black-Scholes and Cox-Ross-Rubinstein.

Options Clearing Corporation (OCC)   Clearing organization for financial derivative instruments. OCC issues, guarantees, and clears options on underlying financial assets. As the issuer and guarantor of option contracts, OCC serves as the counterparty for all such transactions.

out-of-the-money   An option that has no intrinsic value and, instead, consists entirely of extrinsic value. For example, if XYZ stock is trading at $100 per share, the May 105 call and May 95 put are out-of-the-money. If a call is in-the-money, a put with the same strike price must be out-of-the-money. Conversely, if the put is in-the-money, a call at the same strike price must be out-of-the-money.

outright option   An option that is purchased or sold by itself and is not hedged by another position. An outright option can include either a call or a put; for example, you can place an order to buy one February 100 call outright at a limit of $5.

parity   An option is at parity if the option price is equal to the intrinsic value (in-the-money amount). If the option is trading for more than intrinsic value, it is trading above parity; if it is trading at less than intrinsic value, it is trading below parity. The concept of parity applies if the option is selling in-the-money. For example, assume that XYZ stock is trading at $100 a share: If the XYZ February 95 call is more than $5, it is trading above parity; if it is at $5, it is trading at parity; and if it is less than $5, it is trading below parity. Most options trade above parity.

performance bond   A good faith deposit is required (margin) as a performance bond to trade futures and futures options.

portfolio margining   A method for computing margin for stock and option positions based on the risk of the position rather than on fixed percentages, often resulting in lower margin requirements than would be calculated under traditional margin calculations.

P.M. settlement   A settlement style in which the exercise settlement value of an index option is determined based on the closing prices of the component securities.

premium   The price of an option contract, which the buyer of the option pays and the option writer receives, for the rights and obligations conveyed by the option contract.

protective put   The buying of a put or puts to protect against a decline in a stock or other underlying instrument already owned. A protective put provides the holder with the right to sell the underlying stock at a strike price. If you own stock and you want to protect it against a decline, you can buy a put on the stock, allowing you, in effect, to lock in a selling price.

put   An option contract giving the buyer the right, but not the obligation, to sell an underlying instrument (e.g., a stock, ETF, or futures contract) on or before an expiration date at the strike price. If an index, an option contract providing the holder the right to receive, on exercise of the option, the exercise settlement amount in cash for a fixed period of time.

ratio spread   Also called a *front spread*. A spread in which more options are sold than bought; for example, buy one XYZ February 100 call and sell two XYZ February 110 calls.

rho   One of the Greeks. Measures the sensitivity of an option value from a one-point increase in the assumed interest rate.

roll back   Replacing a position by closing out one option with a new one having an earlier expiration date at the same strike price. This is sometimes referred to as a *roll backward* (e.g., offset one long March 100 call and buy one or more February 100 calls).

roll down   Replacing a position by closing out one option at one strike price and simultaneously opening another option at a lower strike price, with the same expiration date (e.g., offset one long February 100 put and buy one or more February 95 puts).

roll down and out   Replacing a position by closing out one option with a near-term expiration date and opening another position at a lower strike price with a later expiration (e.g., offset one long February 100 put and buy one or more March 95 puts).

roll forward (roll out)   Replacing a position by closing out one option with a near-term expiration date and opening another position at the same strike price but with a longer-term expiration date (e.g., offset one long February 100 call and buy one or more March 100 calls).

roll up   Replacing a position by closing out one option at one strike price and simultaneously opening another option at a higher strike price, with the same expiration date (e.g., offset one long February 100 call and buy one or more February 110 calls).

roll up and out   Replacing a position by closing out one option with a near-term expiration date and opening another position at a higher strike price with a later expiration (e.g., offset one long February 100 call and buy one or more March 105 calls).

rolling   Closing out one option position and simultaneously opening another option position.

section 1256 contract   Named after the Internal Revenue Code section providing special tax rules for futures options, options on broad-based indexes, and regulated futures contracts. Under this modification, gain or loss is deemed 60 percent long term and 40 percent short term; the option (or futures) is marked to market at the end of each calendar year; net capital losses can be carried back three years; and to the extent the carryback is not utilized, it can be carried forward indefinitely to offset subsequent-year capital gains.

security Generally, a transferable instrument representing an ownership interest in a corporation (equity security or stock) or the debt of a corporation. Certain derivatives on securities (e.g., options on equity securities) are considered securities for the purposes of the security laws.

sell Typically intended to mean to write an option contract.

sell to close A transaction to offset a long option position; for example, if you are long one February 100 call, you can enter an order as sell to close, by selling one February 100 call.

seller Typically intended to mean the writer of an option contract. An option seller is also called a *writer*.

selling short Selling an instrument with the idea of offsetting it at a lower price at a later date.

series (of options) Options of the same type (i.e., either puts or calls) covering the same underlying instrument.

settlement price The daily price at which the clearing organization clears all trades and settles all accounts between clearing members of each contract month.

short A trader (or entity) who has sold a position and profits when its value declines. A position in which a trader is a net seller, where the number of contracts sold exceeds the number of contracts bought.

speculate A speculator is an individual who trades with the objective of achieving profits through the successful anticipation of price movements.

spread A spread can have a variety of meanings but generally refers to the difference between two (or more) prices from different sides or legs of a trade. An option spread is the purchase (or sale) of one option contract against the sale (or purchase) of another option contract in the same underlying stock; for example, you can buy one XYZ February 100 call and sell one XYZ February 110 call. An option spread can be executed with calls or puts, or with a combination of calls and puts, and can be executed for a debit, credit, or zero cost.

SPY Ticker symbol for the S&P 500 SPDR. It is an ETF valued at one tenth of the underlying S&P 500 index; for example, if the S&P 500 index is at 1,500, the SPY is valued at approximately $150.

SPX Ticker symbol for the S&P 500 stock index options traded on the Chicago Board Options Exchange. It is a European-style index option contract and is settled in cash.

standard deviation The degree to which each return clusters about the mean. In a normal distribution, 68.3 percent of the returns will be within one standard deviation of the mean, 95.4 percent will be within two standard deviations of the mean, and 99.7 percent will be within three standard deviations of the mean. Implied volatility of an option, for instance, can be defined as one standard deviation price change, in percentage terms, over one year.

standard portfolio analysis of risk (SPAN) Futures margin is typically determined by the SPAN margining system, which takes into account all positions in a customer's account and, in general, usually produces a lower margin requirement than traditional standard margin for stocks or ETFs.

stock As used in this book, broadly defined to represent any underlying instrument, such as a stock, index, ETF, or futures, that is used as a basis to derive an option's value. See *underlying instrument*.

stock (equity) index option An option whose underlying instrument is an equity index.

stop limit order   An order that goes into force as soon as there is a trigger at a specified price. The order, however, can only be filled at the stop limit price or better. The stop price for a buy order is placed above the current market price. The stop price for a sell order is placed below the current market price.

stop order (stop loss)   An order that becomes a market order when a particular price level is reached. A sell stop is placed below the market; a buy stop is placed above the market.

straddle   A straddle consists of a call and a put with the same terms (strike price, expiration date, and underlying stock). A long straddle consists of a long call and put with the same strike price and expiration date and is used to profit from volatility; for example, buy one February 100 call and buy one February 100 put. A short straddle consists of a short call and put with the same strike price and expiration date and is used to profit from a trading range or volatility contraction; for example, sell one February 100 call and sell one February 100 put.

strangle   A strangle is similar to a straddle, except a strangle involves two different strike prices. A long strangle consists of a long call and put with different strike prices and the same expiration date; for example, buy one February 105 call and buy one February 95 put. A short straddle consists of a short call and put with different strike prices and the same expiration date; for example, sell one February 105 call and sell one February 95 put.

strike price   Same as *exercise price*. The price at which a call owner can exercise his right to buy an underlying instrument or the price at which a put holder can exercise his right to sell the underlying instrument. The strike price (or exercise price) of a cash-settled option is the base for determining the amount of cash, if any, that the option holder is entitled to receive on exercise.

synthetic equivalent   Options used in combination with other options and/or underlying contracts to create positions with characteristics that are almost identical to some other contract or combination of contracts.

synthetic futures   An equivalent position created by combining call and put futures options. A synthetic long position is created by combining a long call option and a short put option with the same expiration date and strike price. A synthetic short position is created by combining a long put and a short call with the same expiration date and strike price.

technical analysis   An approach to forecasting prices that examines patterns of price change, rates of change, and changes in volume of trading and open interest, without regard to underlying fundamental market factors.

theta   One of the Greeks. Theta measures the change in the price of an option from the passage of one day in time.

time decay   The tendency of an option price to decline in value as the expiration date approaches.

time spread   A *calendar spread*.

time value   Same as *extrinsic value*.

trailing stop limit order   This order type works in the same way as the trailing stop, but instead of a market order being sent to the exchange, a limit order is sent to the exchange.

trailing stop order   A stop order that continually adjusts the stop price based on changes in the market price. A trailing stop to sell raises the stop price as the market price rises but does not lower the stop price when the market price declines. A trailing stop to buy lowers the stop price as the market price declines but does not increase the stop price as the market price rises. When the stop price is reached, the order becomes a market order.

type   The classification of an option contract as either a call or a put.

unbalanced spread   A spread in which there is a difference between the number of options. When the number of options bought in a spread differs from the number of options sold, it is called a ratio spread. A ratio spread can be viewed as a variation of an existing option strategy, where additional options in one leg are bought or sold to create an unbalanced position.

uncovered option   See *naked option*.

underlying index   The equity index on which a class of index options is based.

underlying instrument   The stock, index, ETF, futures, or other instrument that is used as a basis to derive an option's value. As used in this book, the word *stock* is broadly intended to represent any underlying instrument, such as a stock, index, ETF, futures, or other instrument, on which an option contract is based.

unlimited risk/reward   See *limited* and *unlimited risk/reward*.

vega   One of the Greeks. Vega measures the change in the price of an option from a one-point increase in implied volatility.

vertical   A spread with different strike prices but the same expiration date.

vertical credit spread   A spread with different strike prices, the same expiration date, and established for a credit; for example, sell one XYZ February 100 call and buy one XYZ February 110 call.

vertical debit spread   A spread with different strike prices, the same expiration date, and established for a debit, for example; buy one XYZ February 100 call and sell one XYZ February 110 call.

vertical spread   Option spread involving the simultaneous purchase and sale of options of the same class and expiration date but different strike prices; for example, sell one XYZ February 100 call and buy one XYZ February 110 call.

VIX index   The Chicago Board Option Exchange Volatility index (VIX index) measures the implied volatility of options for the S&P 500 index based on the implied volatility of various strike prices and expiration dates. It is commonly used to measure the overall volatility of the U.S. equity markets. The VIX is sometimes called the market's "fear gauge" and is a barometer of stock market volatility. If the VIX is high, it can be said that volatility is high; if the VIX is low, it can be said that volatility is low.

volatility   The word volatility can refer to the volatility of the underlying stock price (historical or realized volatility) or to the volatility component implicit in an option price (implied volatility). See *historical volatility* and *implied volatility*.

volatility skew   A pattern in which individual options on the same underlying stock have different implied volatilities. If shown on a graph, the implied volatilities form a pattern.

volatility trading   Strategies designed to speculate on changes in volatility rather than direction.

write   To sell an option contract to open a position. An option seller is also called a *writer*. The word sell is commonly and loosely used to mean the writing (opening) of an option position.

writer (option writer)   The issuer, grantor, or seller of an option contract. A writer promises to perform certain obligations in return for the option premium.

About the Author

Mike Mullaney has traded equity and futures options utilizing a broad range of strategies and instruments, including options on stocks, stock and bond ETFs, indexes, and stock index futures. Mike executes option buying and selling strategies but concentrates most of his efforts on writing far-out-of-the-money options by using strategies that can profit in rising, declining, and sideways markets. Mike is a principal of a commodity trading advisor and a certified public accountant. He has been interviewed on national business radio, featured by national trading magazines, was formerly a partner at KPMG, vice president of a corporate tax department, instructor for a law school course, a contributor to a book on taxation, and author of six articles on merger and acquisition issues. He can be contacted at mmullaney@miminvestments.com.

Index

Printed and bound by CPI Group (UK) Ltd, Croydon, CR0 4YY

23/04/2025

14660909-0004